Ladbrokes

Pocket Comp

"If you do not find something of interest among its 400-odd pages, then you're certainly coming off *my* Christmas list . . . ."

Simon Stanley (Racing Post)

The 1992/3 N.H. Companion contains its usual mix of opinion, articles, information and statistics, including:-

- CHRIS HAWKINS *(Guardian)* View from the Press Box
- DEREK MITCHELL Races and Horses of 1991/2
- GEORGE RAE *(Times)* The Class of '92
- JACK MILLAN *(Daily Mail)* Winners for 1992/3
- MARCUS ARMYTAGE Hunter Chasers to Note
- RON FULLER What the Connections Have Said
- MARK COTON Cheltenham Antepost Betting
- DOMINIC GARDINER-HILL *(Racing Post)* Cheltenham Pointers
- IAN CARNABY Trainers & Jockeys
- ROBERT CARTER *(I.R.B.)* N.H. Sires

All this and Big Race Results, Favourites Records, Trainers to Follow Portfolio, Principal Records and Statistics, Betting Guide, Address Book, Directory of Winning Horses, Fixtures and Big Races. Also a FREE Horses to Follow Competition.

THE COMPANION HAS BEEN CONTINUALLY REVIEWED AS REALLY GOOD VALUE FOR MONEY FOR SERIOUS RACEGOERS AND NOVICES ALIKE.
IT IS!

Cover photograph by George Selwyn

© Aesculus Press 1992

First Published 1992
by Aesculus Press,
P.O.Box 10, Oswestry,
Shropshire SY10 7QR.

Typeset by Aesculus Press using MICROSOFT WORD
Output on a Hewlett Packard HP Laserjet III.

Printed and bound in Great Britain by
Richard Clay Ltd., Bungay, Suffolk, NR35 1ED.

1-871093-91-0

CONTENTS

4 . Contents

Illustrations

Ladbrokes

FOR A SPORTING BET

Ladbrokes are at the forefront of betting on a wide range of sports. With so many events covered on television, what better way to add to the excitement than a bet at Ladbrokes?

Soccer: Only at Ladbrokes can £$\frac{1}{2}$ million be won on midweek and weekend coupons. Correct score, double result forecasts and first player to score available on all live televised games. Ladbrokes now offer betting facilities at over 25 Football League grounds.

Golf: 1993 is a big year culminating in the Ryder Cup at The Belfry. Look out for the most extensive betting opportunities in the big tournaments - outright winner, exclusive forecast betting, match and group betting and daily 3-ball betting.

Tennis: Wimbledon in June and July is the highlight of the year. To accompany the action from The All England Club and the other majors, we are betting on the outright winner, set betting on featured matches and special odds exclusives.

Rugby: Can anyone stop England? For the Five Nations Championship a host of prices will be available - the championship winner, Grand Slam and Triple Crown, points margin, handicap match betting, first try-scorer and double result forecast.

Cricket: The battle for the Ashes between England and Australia will create real excitement over the summer. Prices available on the series, individual matches, top first-innings batsman, bowler taking most wickets in a particular match and batsman to total most runs in the series.

Snooker: We are betting on all of the top tournaments with the highlight the Embassy World Championships. As well as outright prices, frame score betting will be offered.

American Football: Touchdown at Ladbrokes for Divisional betting, points margin betting on the big games and handicap match betting leading up to the grand finale - the Superbowl.

Ladbrokes Fair Play Rules apply to all bets.

AESCULUS PRESS

P.O. Box 10
Oswestry
Shropshire
SY10 7QR

Tel: 0691 70 426
Fax: 0691 70 315

The following books are available in all good bookshops or direct
from the publishers. We endeavour to dispatch all orders within
24 hours by First Class Post.

Telephone orders are welcome.

ACCESS and VISA accepted.

<u>**Orders within the the UK and N.Ireland are post free.**</u>

For orders within Europe please add £1.00/book &
outside of Europe £1.50/book to enable Airmail Postage

AESCULUS PRESS

FORM *horses*

NATIONAL HUNT 1992/3

£ 3.25

by

Ian Carnaby & Derek Mitchell

FORM HORSES assesses the merits of 100 horses likely to win this season, including many that will be competing for the big prizes. It is designed to assist punters in drawing up their own list of horses to follow, and to indicate in what circumstances the horses featured are likely to strike form (and by the same token when they should be left alone). Every horse has its own *'Form Panel'* which also gives valuable information as to its strengths and weaknesses.

Last year's *Form Horses* contained the winners of 104 races, many paying their way handsomely, including:-

COOL GROUND - winner of the Gold Cup at 25-1 (also won at 9-4 & 12-1); PARTY POLITICS - winner of the Grand National at 14-1; THE FELLOW - winner of the King George at 10-1; plus Arctic Call (4-1, 7-2), Ardbrin (13-2, 5-4), Cab on Target (5-2, 5-4, 5-2), Cuddy Dale (9-4, 12-1), Current Express (7-2, 6-1), Docklands Express (6-1), Forest Sun (6-1), Fragrant Dawn (4-6, 5-1), King Credo (13-2, 9-2, 4-5), Laundryman (12-1, 3-1), Nomadic Way (15-2), Sir Crusty (10-1),

and many others!

" BACKING *trainers* "

£4.95

1992/3 N.H. Edition by Ian Carnaby & Derek Mitchell

By following a selected number of stables can you develop a feel for they way they operate, so that your money is down when the stable signals are right.

Ian Carnaby and Derek Mitchell both expert trainer watchers (Ian frequently talks to trainers for the QA trainer feature in ODDS ON magazine) scrutinise the records of last season's top 40 handlers, highlighting what to watch for and what to avoid.

Complementing their essays are extensive five-year statistics on each trainer that tell their own story and provide valuable pointers.

".... a useful reminder of trainers' preferences for serious and casual punters alike."

Melvyn Collier (Racing Post)

THE STABLE IN FORM

MORE RACING BOOKS

VALUE BETTING by Mark Coton

This best-selling title is now available in paperback. **£8.95**

What the Press has said:

"The best guide to bookie wrestling." *(The Independant)*

"Every aspect of the game is examined in asorbing detail." *(The Guardian)*

"Crammed with useful tips and caveats for the punter." *(The Sporting Life)*

"Value Betting goes a fair way to describing how to maximise your chances
of showing a season's profit." *(Daily Mail)*

"The book is fascinating . . . the concept of value in betting is relatively new
but has quickly become accepted as crucial." *(Racing Post)*

COUPS & CONS by Graham Sharpe

£4.95

"Its a fun read. . . . Buy it, you won't be disappointed." *(Racing Post)*

"Coups and Cons that made bookies weep" *(The Sun)*

"There are dozens of weird and wonderful stories that will provide many a
laugh, making it an essential buy for those who don't take betting too seriously."
(Raceform Update)

"You can simply dip in anywhere and find a jewel on any page covering the
ingenious coup attempts right the way along to the downright nefarious con bids.
All in all its a must." *(Odds On)*

FORTHCOMING TITLES (Pub. late November 1992)

EARNING A LIVING FROM BETTING
by Nick Mordin   (Hardback) **£18.00**

Nick Mordin, who writes the highly successful Systems Workshop feature in *Odds
On* magazine and the Systems column in the *Weekender,* reveals the methods that
underpin his profitable betting. Since catching 'racing fever', Nick has delved deep to
uncover systems and then tested them where it matters: in the market. Having made
a considerable amount of money, Nick now unveils his findings. They do not point
the way to instant riches, but show that punters can and should, with effort, make
the game pay.

Nick also recounts putting his systems into practice over a six month period in a
large diary section, showing the logic behind his bets, as well as the emotions on the
day!

An original and authoritative work that will prove invaluable for the betting man.

CONNECTWORD by Dave Thomas   **£1.95**

The ever popular Connectword puzzles as featured in *Odds On* magazine, now in a
book. All new puzzles, no repeats. Ideal stocking filler!

FROM AESCULUS PRESS

1 . VIEW FROM THE PRESS BOX

by

Chris Hawkins
(The Guardian)

After a break of just nine weeks, jump racing this season began at Bangor-on-Dee on July 31. There were 49 runners and the casualties began immediately: Castellani pulled up lame in the first race and Diana Clay broke a leg when her mount slipped up on the flat in the second. Whether these injuries had anything to do with the fast ground one cannot say with any certainty but there is a growing feeling within the game that in these days of arid summers the extent of jumping activity needs to be curtailed in August and May.

No-one is forced to run horses but the smaller operators know that this is the time to make hay before the big stables swing into action and economics dictate that risks (which are always prevalent) have to be taken. There are, of course, firm-ground animals who are in their element and have to be catered for, but the Jockey Club is to look at restructuring the programme, starting in the 1994/95 season, with less summer meetings.

Courses like Newton Abbot, with seven fixtures in August and September, and Exeter (five) have always relied upon the early meetings to balance their books by attracting crowds when the West Country is full of holiday makers. But Exeter in particular, which does not have watering facilities, may suffer under the new programming.

Conversely Worcester, Stratford and Bangor want to stage jump meetings throughout the summer, believing the ground at their tracks never gets too firm because of excellent watering systems. Whether there are enough runners to go round could be a problem and whether the trainers and jockeys want to keep going non-stop is another factor to be considered, but presumably they could take a holiday if and when they wanted.

These small jump meetings run in conjunction with a full

Racing at Newton Abbot

flat programme do little to boost betting turnover and one gets the impression the powers that be regard them as an irrelevance and, in cases where more horses than normal are injured, as an embarrassment.

A feature of racing over the last ten years or so has been the interest shown in it by outside welfare organisations expressing concern about the possible physical abuse of the thoroughbred. The exposure this has received in the media has made it a difficult period for public relations and the Jockey Club cannot afford any more bad publicity at a time when the recession is hitting hard and the owning of racehorses is being held-up as an act of unprecedented folly.

So although some of the smaller owners and trainers will be bound to suffer from a cutback in early and late season opportunities, the restructuring, taken on balance, looks a sound move. Compensating by instituting more fixtures at more suitable times should not be beyond the wit of the Jockey Club race planners who have already shown initiative in changing the make and shape of events on the flat.

Indeed, a body which was once ridiculed as being hopelessly reactionary is now making strenuous efforts - beyond what former members might have considered the call of duty - to take the industry into the 21st century.

On the flat racing front, the Jockey Club has unveiled plans, to be implemented at the turn of the year, to make racing more competitive and reduce the number of non-triers. The reason horses are not always asked to put their best feet forward is an attempt to hide their real ability from the handicapper so that when the day arrives for "the punt" the animal in question has a few pounds in hand.

With the law of libel and the difficulty of proving suspicion there has always been an unwritten conspiracy between officialdom and the media to perpetuate the myth that the game is straight, but one of the most refreshing aspects of this latest Jockey Club initiative has been their "come clean" attitude, as voiced by senior handicapper Geoffrey Gibbs.

"Some trainers' sole aim seems to be to achieve a

favourable handicap mark for their horses," said Gibbs. "The new programme will try to remove this emphasis by providing more opportunities for moderate horses to win."

To this end there will be an overall reduction in the number of standard handicaps from 46 per cent to 36 per cent. But to compensate, new ratings-related maiden races and maiden handicaps will be introduced so that the proportion of events for which the ratings list still has direct implications will rise to just over 50 per cent.

A horse will need to run three times to get a rating and will need five runs to qualify for the new maiden handicaps - thus enabling the handicapper to get a more accurate idea of an animal's ability.

This is an attempt to answer criticism so prevalent among many trainers that their horses have been overrated because they have finished within a few lengths of something from one of the powerful Newmarket yards.

The theory of the new scheme of things sounds fine but human nature being what it is, some trainers will no doubt simply stop horses for longer and the success or failure of the concept will very much depend on whether trainers are prepared to play ball.

Talking about the 21st century leads us on to Sunday racing and although virtually everyone seemed to agree that the Jockey Club's first experimental day at Doncaster at the end of July was a success, the signals at Westminster Junction are still at red - although there are signs they may be about to turn to amber.

Additional pressure will be put on the Government to amend the prohibitive legislation, through a second Sunday meeting at Cheltenham on November 15. This could not be better timed as it is in the autumn that the Sunday trading laws will be top of the parliamentary agenda, although an amendment to the Betting, Gaming and Lottery Act is just as vital.

Doncaster's meeting attracted a crowd of over 23,000 with the emphasis on family entertainment and this element must not be jettisoned when Sunday racing eventually comes with

The Pony Grand National - family entertainment at Doncaster

bookmakers and full betting facilities. The Doncaster experiment revealed the huge potential of racing on the week's principal leisure day and the young audience should not be allowed to drift away.

The big family attendance was an extra prod for the Government indicating that racing on the Sabbath will be more than just an opportunity for punters to pursue their evil habit on the Lord's Day.

There are two schools of thought about betting on a Sunday - one which says it will be perfectly adequate for wagering to take place only on the course, the other that betting shops throughout the land should be open to prevent illegal gambling.

Robin Cook, the Labour MP with a passion for racing, was

quoted in the Sporting Life as saying: "There is a better chance of getting Parliament to swallow racing on Sunday than opening betting shops on Sunday. No way will Parliament legislate for the opening of betting shops unless it has reached the point where it is prepared to legislate opening every other High Street shop. Betting shops would be the last to be approved."

Cook is no doubt right about the latter point but as racing depends for its livelihood on money from the Levy, can it afford to pass up the opportunity of staging Sunday racing without a return? This has been the principal reason why evening racing has been restricted, although the problem is not so serious as punters have plenty of opportunity for a bet beforehand.

The Jockey Club is of the view that it is an all or nothing situation and the big bookmakers are unlikely to discourage that opinion.

The problem of legislation will presumably be overcome one day. Then the number and frequency of fixtures will be the next major concern and related to that will be the remuneration and treatment of stable staff who for once in their lives will be in a strong bargaining position. Bill Adams, secretary of the Stable Lads' Association, has long complained that apathy has held back improvements in working conditions and wages of stable employees but this will be their chance to unite and help themselves.

Stable staff are not the only ones harbouring a grievance or two and flat jockeys still feel that the Irish jump jockeys let down all professional riders by their antics at Cheltenham in March 1988. There, following several instances of over-use of the whip, public outcry was such that new rules were brought into force, applying to both codes, restricting the use of the stick.

One could hardly argue with the general intent behind the regulations, but the specific instruction banning the hitting of a horse down the shoulder with the whip held in the forehand position for other than corrective purposes, was immediately held to be contentious.

Robin Cook, the MP with a passion for racing

It was argued that hitting down the shoulder was an excellent corrective measure against an animal hanging, but the problem with all rules governing the actual performing of a sporting activity is they inevitably bring in opinion, and, of course, opinion is very seldom unanimous.

Whether a horse is hanging or leaning is largely a matter of opinion and the jockey's view can be different from that of the official. The view that counts, however, is the one of the official and so the seeds of discontent are sown.

As we know, the particular issue came to a head at Goodwood in July when Steve Cauthen was twice found guilty in the same afternoon for misuse of the whip. Cauthen maintained that to correct Witness Box from leaning into the rail in the final stages of the Goodwood Cup he had to hit the horse down the shoulder and again when pulling Daru off a challenging rival in the Levy Handicap.

Because of his upbringing as a rider in America, he hit with the whip in the forehand position and as the stewards did not accept that he used it purely to keep his mounts straight, suspension was the inevitable outcome.

Following the second incident, which some saw as Cauthen putting up two fingers to the stewards, there was a stink of fairly formidable proportions and the jockey wound up before the disciplinary committee at Portman Square, fighting a corner for his profession. There was no way he would be let off for the shoulder whipping of Daru (although he hit the horse only four times) and he was duly suspended for a further six days, making ten in all. But he won a points decision and a promise that the rule would be looked at again.

The significance of this is that it provided incontrovertible evidence that the Jockey Club has come down off Mount Olympus and no longer sees itself ruling by divine right. Democracy is creeping in and the views of those at the sharp end are at last carrying some weight.

This brings us on to the British Horseracing Board which is due to draw its first breath on 1 January 1993 and will consist of 11 members - four from the Jockey Club (including the chairman Lord Hartington), three from the newly formed industry committee (replacing the old Horseracing Advisory Council), and two each from the Racehorse Owners' Association and the Racecourse Association.

The formation of such a body represents a watershed in the administration of racing in this country and it is to be hoped that the self-interest of the groups concerned will not make it an arena for argument rather than action. Once the Home Secretary is convinced of its viability, the Tote and ultimately the Levy should come under the Board's control and this is something racing has long lusted over.

The Jockey Club because of its unpopular authoritarian stance and its high proportion of retired military men out of touch with reality has always been held responsible for the inefficiency of the industry. The industry must now show that it can pull together to do a better job.

2 . RACES AND HORSES
OF 1991/92

by

Derek Mitchell

The 1991/92 National Hunt racing season was a touch surreal. The pinnacle of achievement in the jumping world is meant to be the winning of the Tote Cheltenham Gold Cup. Yet you could ask a dozen pub quiz teams: who won it? And perhaps two would come up with the right answer. Ask the same dirty dozen who came last and they would chorus to a man, "Carvill's Hill". It was that sort of a season.

It was in fact the winter of discontent in racing. There was a widespread feeling that Carvill's Hill had been placed gently on this earth as the supreme example of chasing excellence; a horse who would erase hoary memories of such second-class equine citizens as Golden Miller and Arkle.

Just to make sure his path to universal acceptance of this thesis was uncluttered by extraneous matter, he was assigned to the tender loving care of one Martin Pipe, a proven expert in the art of thoroughbred husbandry. And the big gelding prospered under this stewardship, arriving at Cheltenham not only unbeaten but totally untested and unextended. En route he collected bloodless victories in the Rehearsal Chase at Chepstow, the Coral Welsh National on the same course, and in the Irish version of the Hennessy Cognac Gold Cup at Leopardstown.

He merely had to jump round at the Festival to insinuate himself smoothly into the top slot of the N.H. Hall of Fame. Unfortunately when he set off on his exercise round, he found himself accompanied by a talentless oik called Golden Freeze. This beast not only continuously outjumped him but provoked him into mistakes and denied him the freedom of his customary front-running isolation.

As a result Carvill's Hill eventually knackered himself and, totally disillusioned, all but pulled up, a couple of distances behind the winner (remember who he was yet?).

An outcry ensued. It was deemed disgraceful by the press that Golden Freeze, a stablemate of Toby Tobias, another contestant, had acted as "a spoiling horse", solely in the line-up to undermine the claims of the new N.H. Messiah. The hue and cry gathered volume and, after a discreet interval, the Jockey Club held an inquiry, demanding to know whether under various sub-sections of Rule 151, Golden Freeze had actually run on his merits. Or, indeed, whether he was there purely as "a spoiling horse".

Enter the defendant: Mrs Jenny Pitman, trainer of both Golden Freeze and Toby Tobias. Mrs Pitman is relatively surreal herself. It is not known precisely what occurred behind the impenetrable doors of Portman Square but it is safe to assume that the plumptious Jenny administered a verbal spanking all round. Anyway, she emerged with career untarnished and chequered disciplinary record unenhanced.

And quite right too. As David Elsworth pointed out at Cheltenham: "Everybody took on Desert Orchid but you never saw him jack it in." Or words to that effect.

I couldn't quite perceive at the time what all the fuss was about. Day in and day out in novice chases, jockeys attempt to discompose rivals by taking off at a fence half a length to the good. Indeed, if a rider on a more experienced horse did not employ such tactics over a freshman, questions would be asked long before the following breakfast time.

Fences are there to be jumped and if a hot favourite in the Cheltenham Gold Cup cannot cope with a little outside attention, no matter whether it is orchestrated or not, he does not deserve the title of "champion". And, to be sure, Carvill's Hill does not merit that accolade, much as most of us were yearning to plonk the crown on his bonny head.

Okay, let's put 80 per cent of you out of your misery: the Gold Cup was won by Cool Ground, who finished a short head in front of The Fellow, who ended up a length in front of Docklands Express. The lame Toby Tobias was a distance away fourth and the only other finisher was Carvill's Hill, another distance away.

The resultant furore masked a truly memorable climax to an exciting heat. It is manifestly clear that the first and third are little more than very good staying handicappers. Yet The Fellow, beaten an agonising short head in the race for the second successive year, is rather more than that. He did, after all, lift the King George VI Rank Chase at Kempton's Boxing Day fixture, ironically walloping Docklands Express by a length and a half and inflicting the only chasing defeat upon Remittance Man.

I was rather rude in this space 12 months ago about the on-going potency of French-trained The Fellow. I observed that although he is still only seven, that is Methuselahville in Gallic terms and that his prospects of immortality probably lay ahead in some elaborate gastronomic concoction by Anton Mosiman. I must now concede he is an extremely tough, thoroughly reliable and - yes - classy individual. It is to be deplored he is quartered on the distaff side of what is after all the English Channel. But a few weeks under the supervision of Mrs Pitman would soon put a hair or two on his chest.

Remittance Man, his Kempton defeat apart, was the major act of the season. He won everything, including the Queen Mother Champion Chase, and he stirred a rousing debate as to whether he actually stayed the three miles of the King George, succumbing between the last two fences after giving

Bet that Remittance Man will stay three miles this Christmas

the impression he was travelling first class while the rest of the field were picking their way through empty Coke cans in the tourist section.

The consensus was he didn't stay and, as per usual, I maintain a different view. I think he was simply run ragged by the suicidal pace of Sabin du Loir (the race lopped more than three seconds off the record) and that the out-and-out stayers picked up the pieces in the dying stages when the proper combatants had cried enough. Remittance Man comfortably stayed beyond three miles over hurdles and in my book that is evidence enough. Don't take my word for it though, watch him this Christmas when he hopefully tries again.

The 1991 King George marked the final businesslike appearance of Desert Orchid, although he is still to be witnessed at garden fetes, school galas and the occasional opening of an up-market bordello. Regular readers will recognise my chagrin at the extra-curricular activities of a modern legend of the N.H. scene. I, too, was a member of the unofficial Desert Orchid Fan Club but the official version - or at least some of its adherents - do not figure prominently on my regular list of house guests. I quail at the thought of being importuned into parting with cash for an official Desert Orchid Snowstorm Paperweight.

But full marks to trainer David Elsworth, who never once attempted to bask in the reflected glory of his equine hero. He always (to me, at least) gave a realistic appraisal of the gallant grey's chances and was sufficiently honest to harbour serious doubts last December. As it turned out, even the fearless front-running Desert Orchid could not live with a demonic pace. He tired and tipped over at the third last fence. Yet, such was his character, he picked himself up and cantered riderless past the grandstand to rapturous applause.

Desert Orchid, starting as a no-hoper and ending as a hardy annual, won that particular race a record four times. It might have been even more. His overall CV stands comparison with most of the very best. He won only one Gold Cup but that was achieved in truly appallingly heavy conditions and I shall never forget the emotional greeting that momentous, heart-stopping success induced.

He was - and hopefully still is - a spur to every single N.H. aspirant, be he owner, trainer, jockey or lad. And if that sentence sounds sexist, I apologise to the inestimable Janice Coyle, who was not only the great horse's lass but his undying friend. I wish Desert Orchid the happiest retirement possible and one hopefully free of the tacky betting shop-opening circuit, an after-life that surely cannot be suitable for proper champions, much as they pretend to grin and bear it. Desert Orchid, we salute you.

The Cheltenham Festival provided its usual cracking entertainment with the first day dominated by the Champion Hurdle. The Smurfit-sponsored contest was won by Royal Gait, the horse, you may remember, who smashed the track record when ambling home in the Ascot Gold Cup of 1988, only to be stripped of the prize shortly afterwards. Britain -

The modern legend of the N.H. scene

or perhaps I should say England - has a proud record when it comes to mugging innocent foreigners and it was good to see the Ascot stewards were not found wanting in our hour of needs-must.

Since then, however, the formerly French-trained Royal Gait had been relocated to Newmarket under the watchful eye of the owlish James Fanshawe, an engaging young man who perpetually looks as if he is auditioning for the part of Mr Chipps. Fanshawe may be predominantly a flat-race trainer but he had a thorough grounding in the point-to-point field (he broke his neck and you don't get groundings more thorough than that). When asked by Sheikh Mohammed, of Kribensis fame, to prepare the moke for the Champion Hurdle, he leaped at the chance.

Come Cheltenham, the nine-year-old Royal Gait arrived as the oldest horse in the race yet the one with the least hurdling experience - just three outings, a second and two victories. But he jumped gracefully and economically and he battled on tenaciously to seize the £80,000 prize by half a length from Oh So Risky, with the fastest-finishing Ruling a short head away. Considering he needed about five and a half miles to prove effective on the Flat, Royal Gait did remarkably well to win over the minimum trip in a Champion that wasn't run at a particularly hectic pace.

Being essentially a Flat animal, he quickly showed symptoms of over-exertion. The medics were called in and he was prescribed the whole summer off. There is the belief he will return this winter. I hope so. Despite my jocularity, I am a fan of the horse and he deserves to gobble up every morsel Britain can offer following that disgraceful Ascot disqualification all those years ago.

Nomadic Way, second in 1990 and 1991, gave the race a miss this year and won instead the Bonusprint Stayers' Hurdle. The victory halted a victory famine that lasted 25 months. Now I'm as big a fan of Barry Hills as the next guy but I really can't fathom why he couldn't have placed this tough, genuine and highly-talented horse to winning effect over the space of two years. Okay, I know the entire was picking up valuable place-money (he found it impossible to finish out of the first three) but surely the occasional win is a concrete confidence-builder and a launching pad for greater enthusiasm and efficiency.

I will make the same point about Ruling, who has now placed third in each of the two latest Champions, finishing best of all each time and going down over the two years by an aggregate of two and a half lengths. Yet he hasn't won a race since January 1991. It's crazy. It would seem almost more difficult to go through a season and a half without winning with a horse of that calibre than it would be actually to lift a prize or two.

The second day of Cheltenham was dominated largely by Remittance Man, who emerged triumphant by a length from a thrilling battle with deposed champ Katabatic in the Queen Mum. Waterloo Boy was placed for the third successive year. He will probably never win it now but there are no Festival alternatives for him and he can still earn good money elsewhere, judged on his four victories during the season.

Thetford Forest and Miinnehoma were other Wednesday winners who would have been automatic inclusions in your horses to follow for this winter. Happily, Sun Alliance Chase hero Miinnehoma still is and despite his comparative longevity, he has been sparingly used and must have at least two or three good seasons in him. Unhappily, Thetford Forest, a horse of immense promise, fell fatally at Liverpool subsequently. It's a fine line between greatness and oblivion.

The Martell Grand National itself inspires fewer calamities these days and while that is obviously a plus I'm wondering whether it has lost something as a spectacle. I found it an exciting contest this year but my judgment may have been clouded by accepting the morning price of 16-1 about Party Politics, who led four out and never looked in the slightest danger of being overhauled. Less fortunate chums reported finding the race not boring by any stretch of the imagination but slightly pallid when measured against some of the heroics of yesteryear. When next spring I revert to my normal form and back a loser I shall be in a better position to judge.

Nick Gaselee's gargantuan Party Politics

Party Politics, a giant of a gelding, found the fences all too easy and so did most of the others. Eighteen failed to finish the marathon but only three of those instances came as a result of falls. My immediate reaction after collecting my winnings was to seek a price about Nick Gaselee's gargantuan staging a repeat in 1993, my reasoning being that his size will limit the impact of any strictures meted out by the handicapper. I was offered 20-1. I may not be the most astute of punters but the thought of accepting such indifferent odds about a contest a year away, given the in-built hazards of long-distance chasing, struck me as the sort of financial short-cut that leads to the canal.

The punitive exertions of the Gold Cup first and third resulted in desperately tired horses at Aintree. Docklands Express was backed down to 15-2 favourite but faded from three out and finished a remote fourth; Cool Ground, actually receiving a pound from the horse he vanquished at Cheltenham, was never really at the races and trailed home in 10th. Sterner critics than I might point to the folly of running that brace of battlers in the National at all. I would not. It was, after all, the ultimate goal for which they had been trained all season. And neither could expect a comparable weight again following their unexpected Festival form up-turn.

Precisely a week after the Martell marathon came the William Hill Scottish National over an extended four miles and 27 fences at Ayr. And blow me if I didn't back the winner again. Captain Dibble, a mere seven-year-old, took it up before half-way and galloped more experienced handicappers senseless. This time, however, I did not nick the odds.

By a series of misadventures, which I won't bore you with, instead of having a half-hundred on at 12-1, I ended up with a tenner on at 9-1 SP in a Victoria betting shop, which on the afternoon in question was obviously aiming at a Guinness Book of Records entry for cramming the largest number of lager louts into the smallest possible space. I have never felt less enthusiastic at picking up a oner in my life. Had I plonked down the whole fifty quid, I would have asked them to post the winnings on.

On a different tack, I must make mention of another horse who captured my rapt attention during 1991/92: Bright Barley. What do you mean, you have never heard of him? Here was a winning novice hurdler who had show-jumped for fun and was raring to get his hooves on the top three-mile novice chasing prizes. A horse, moreover, sound in wind and limb and one who was available for leasing virtually free of charge. What sporting gent could possibly refuse? Well, a quartet of us couldn't at any rate. We shall henceforth be known as the Four Bust Men.

Anyone who has shared the cost of a thoroughbred will know that racehorses, no matter how modest, dine almost exclusively on £20 notes. And when they are not scoffing, they are out shopping for expensive new shoes or seeking costly medical advice. Their twice-weekly aerobics class needs to be paid for and that's before you begin funding their entry to a racecourse. While, last winter, Lord Carnarvon was taking £12,000 out of petty cash to buy a runty, untried yearling that turned out to be Lyric Fantasy, the Four Bust Men were digging deep to underwrite the chasing aspirations of a proven winner.

No contest. While Bright Barley clearly had ability, the part of his brain reserved for racing enthusiasm (probably the quarter I owned) steadfastly refused to trigger. Timeform summed him up rather neatly: "Plain gelding, quite modest hurdler at best, no promise of late." In his five races for us, he fell and pulled up once apiece, was twice unplaced and he finished last of four (beaten more than 40 lengths) at Taunton. Gosh it was fun.

The most exquisite story of the whole season, to my mind, was that of Koracle Bay in a listed novice hurdle at Punchestown in April. She finished stone last in a 10-horse field. Nothing too surprising about that; something must finish last and a 100-1 debutante is as likely a candidate as any. By some quirk of fate, however, her jockey managed to weigh in no fewer than 13lb light and this blatant piece of chicanery was swiftly pounced upon by the ever-vigilant clerk of the scales. There was only one course of action to be taken.

Disqualified from last place! Even Bright Barley never plumbed those depths.

3 . BIG RACE RESULTS

The race times show the deviations from the standard time for the race. Faster than standard is shown by a '-', slower than standard by a '+'. 'R' signifies a record race time, 'CR' a course record.

In position column or before the horses name amongst the also-rans

B	=	Brought Down
C	=	Carried Out
F	=	Faller
P	=	Pulled Up
R	=	Refused or Ran Out
S	=	Slipped Up
U	=	Unseated Rider

* after jockeys name denotes Conditional Jockey

'F' after the odds denotes Favourite.

1 CHARLIE HALL CHASE   3m 100y   (Good)   Wetherby
2 Nov   1st: £ 16,204, 2nd: £ 6,088, 3rd: £ 2,944, 4th: £ 1,303

1-	CELTIC SHOT	9-11-10	G Bradley	C E P Brooks	4/5 F
2-	DOCKLANDS EXPRESS	9-11-02	A Tory	K C Bailey	11/4
3-	KILLBANON	9-11-02	B Powell	C C Trietline	8/1
4-	OLD APPLEJACK	11-11-02	B Storey	J H Johnson	20/1
5-	TARTAN TAILOR	10-11-02	N Doughty	G Richards	33/1
6-	BISHOPDALE	10-11-02	C Grant	W A Stephenson	11/1

ALSO: ---

6 Ran DISTANCES: 2½, 8, 1, 6, 12   **TIME:** 6m 25.7s (+18.7s)

90	CELTIC SHOT	8-11-02	P Scudamore	C P E Brooks	7/4 F
89	DURHAM EDITION	11-11-02	A Merrigan	W A Stephenson	33/1
88	HIGH EDGE GREY	7-11-02	T Reed	J K M Oliver	13/2
87	CYBRANDIAN	10-11-02	C Grant	M H Easterby	7/4
86	FORGIVE'N'FORGET	9-11-10	M Dwyer	J FitzGerald	5/2
85	WAYWARD LAD	10-11-06	G Bradley	Mrs M Dickinson	Evs F
84	BURROUGH HILL LAD	8-11-09	P Tuck	Mrs J Pitman	10/11F
83	WAYWARD LAD	8-11-10	R Earnshaw	M Dickinson	1/3 F
82	RIGHTHAND MAN	5-11-07	G Bradley	M Dickinson	11/10
81	GAY RETURN	6-11-10	T Ryan	E O'Grady Ire	12/1

2 TOTE SILVER TROPHY H'CAP HURDLE   2m 4f   (Soft)   Chepstow
02 Nov   1st: £ 15,931, 2nd: £ 4,798, 3rd: £ 2,324, 4th: £ 1,087

1-	DANNY HARROLD	7-11-10	M Pitman	Mrs J Pitman	16/1
2-	THE DEMON BARBER	9-10-03	M Moloney	G Richards	16/1
3-	AMBUSCADE	5-09-07	R Hodge	Mrs G R Reveley	16/1
4-	CATCH THE CROSS	5-10-09	M Foster	M C Pipe	15/2
5-	SWEET GLOW	4-09-07	D Richmond	M C Pipe	12/1
6-	MUDAHIM	5-10-08	D Tegg	C D Broad	16/1
7-	COE	5-10-05	L Harvey	R Akehurst	7/1
8-	PEANUTS PET	6-10-13	T Wall	B A McMahon	7/1
9-	ROYAL SQUARE	5-10-12	M Perrett	G Harwood	10/3 F
0-	FIGHTING WORDS	5-10-00	E Murphy	J T Gifford	14/1

ALSO: Midfielder, Propero, **P:** Shannon Glen, Southover Lad

14 Ran DISTANCES: 2½, hd, ¾, ¾, 4, hd, 3½, 5   **TIME:** 5m 8.1s (+30.1s)

90	BRADBURY STAR	5-10-11	R Rowe	J T Gifford	6/1
89	PIPERS COPSE	7-10-04	M Perrett	G Harwood	7/2
88	BUCKSKIN'S BEST	6-10-03	R Dunwoody	R Dickin	16/1

First run in 1988

32 . Big Race Results

3 MACKESON GOLD CUP H'CAP CHASE   **2m 4f**   **(Good)**   **Cheltenham**
9 Nov   **1st: £ 33,100, 2nd: £ 12,400, 3rd: £ 6,075, 4th: £ 2,625**

1-	ANOTHER CORAL	8-10-01	R Dunwoody	D Nicholson	15/2
2-	TORANFIELD	7-9 -09	A Maguire	F Lennon (Ire)	16/1
3-	SWORD BEACH	7-10-00	R Fahey	M H Easterby	16/1
4-	CASHEW KING	8-10-00	T Wall	B A McMahon	20/1
5-	IDA'S DELIGHT	12-10-06	B Storey	J I A Charlton	20/1
6-	ANTI MATTER	6-10-00	P Scudamore	M C Pipe	6/1
7-	PEGWELL BAY	10-11-10	J Railton	Capt T A Forster	9/1
8-	SHANNAGARY	10-10-00	A Tory	R J Hodges	50/1
9-	SOUTHERN MINSTREL	8-10-11	C Grant	W A Stephenson	16/1
0-	MAJOR MATCH	9-10-02	H Davies	Capt T A Forster	5/1

ALSO: New Halen, **F:** Espy, Guiburn's Nephew; **P:** Cuddy Dale, Hogmanay

15 Ran DISTANCES: ½,15,1½,sh,1½,3,10,12,30,30   **TIME:** 5m 8.1s (+30.1s)

90	MULTUM IN PARVO	7-10-02	N Williamson	J A C Edwards	12/1
89	JOINT SOVEREIGNTY	9-10-04	G McCourt	P J Hobbs	10/1
88	PEGWELL BAY	7-11-02	P Scudamore	Capt T A Forster	6/1
87	BEAU RANGER	10-10-02	M Perrett	M C Pipe	13/2
86	VERY PROMISING	8-11-13	R Dunwoody	D Nicholson	7/1
85	HALF FREE	9-11-10	R Linley	F T Winter	9/2
84	HALF FREE	8-11-10	R Linley	F T Winter	5/2 F
83	POUNENTES	6-10-06	N Doughty	W McGhie	7/1
82	FIFTY DOLLARS MORE	7-11-00	R Linley	F T Winter	11/1
81	HENRY KISSINGER	7-10-13	P Barton	D Gandolfo	5/1

4 RACECALL ASCOT HURDLE   **2m 4f**   **(Good)**   **Ascot**
15 Nov   **1st: £ 15,566, 2nd: £ 5,825, 3rd: £ 2,797, 4th: £ 1,218**

1-	MORLEY STREET	7-11-10	J Frost	G B Balding	4/9 F
2-	KING'S CURATE	7-11-10	M Perrett	S Mellor	16/1
3-	DANNY HARROLD	7-11-00	M Pitman	Mrs J Pitman	7/2
4-	UPTON PARK	6-11-00	C Llewellyn	J Fanshawe	9/1
5-	CALAPAEZ	7-11-00	B Powell	Miss B Sanders	33/1
P-	RAKES LANE	6-11-00	D J Murphy	J R Jenkins	66/1

ALSO: ---

6 Ran DISTANCES: nk, 7, 7, 7   **TIME:** 4m 52.8s (+12.8s)

90	MORLEY STREET	6-11-10	J Frost	G B Balding	4/5 F
89	NODFORMS DILEMMA	5-10-11	R Rowe	J T Gifford	12/1
88	SABIN DU LOIR	9-10-11	P Scudamore	M C Pipe	1/2 F
87	SABIN DU LOIR	9-10-11	P Scudamore	M C Pipe	5/2
86	IBN MAJED	4-10-11	J McLaughlin	C Spares	9/2
85	GAYE BRIEF	8-10-11	R Linley	Mrs M Rimell	13/8 F
84	GAYE BRIEF	7-10-11	R Linley	Mrs M Rimell	4/6 F
83	DAWN RUN	5-10-13	J J O'Neill	P Mullins Ire	1/3 F
82	AL KUWAIT	6-10-13	J Francome	F Winter	Evs F
81	LUMEN	6-10-13	R Rowe	J Gifford	14/1

5 HURST PARK NOVICES' CHASE   2m   (Good)   Ascot
15 Nov   1st: £   9,920, 2nd: £   3,704, 3rd: £   1,772, 4th: £   764

1-	POETIC GEM	6-11-00	Richard Guest	Mrs S J Smith	4/1
2-	BOOK OF GOLD	6-11-00	D J Murphy	J T Gifford	4/9 F
3-	SAINT SUPREME	8-11-00	C Llewellyn	N Twiston-Davies	8/1
4-	NO DAW	7-11-00	B Powell	F Sheridan	12/1

ALSO: ---

4 Ran DISTANCES: 15, 25, 4   **TIME:** 4m 3.4s (+15.4s)

90	AFRICAN SAFARI	6-11-00	R Stronge	Mrs S J Smith	7/2
89	YOUNG SNUGFIT	5-11-08	J Osborne	O Sherwood	11/8 F
88	FRED THE TREAD	6-11-04	R Dunwoody	T Casey	8/1
87	BARNBROOK AGAIN	7-11-08	S Sherwood	D R C Elsworth	5/6 F
86	TEN OF SPADES	6-11-04	G Charles Jnes	S Mellor	8/1
85	DESERT ORCHID	6-11-04	C Brown	D Elsworth	4/9 F
84	TOWNLEY STONE	5-11-08	G McCourt	J Webber	9/4 F
83	MONZA	5-10-10	R Rowe	P Cundell	6/4 F
82	JUBILEE MEDAL	5-11-01	J Francome	N Henderson	7/1
81	RUN WITH PRIDE	6-11-07	N Madden	M O'Toole	10/3

6 H & T WALKER GOLD CUP HANDICAP CHASE   2m 4f   (Good)   Ascot
16 Nov   1st: £ 27,344, 2nd: £ 10,235, 3rd: £   4,917, 4th: £   2,143

1-	KINGS FOUNTAIN	8-11-01	A Tory	K C Bailey	7/2
2-	FAR SENIOR	5-10-07	Mr M Armytage	K C Bailey	14/1
3-	TIPPING TIM	6-10-07	C Llewellyn	N Twiston-Davies	10/1
4-	ANTI MATTER	6-11-04	P Scudamore	M C Pipe	6/1
5-	FIRIONS LAW	6-12-00	M Flynn	V Bowens (Ire)	10/1
6-	BUCK WILLOW	7-10-09	D J Murphy	J T Gifford	3/1 F
P-	ARDBRIN	8-10-12	G Bradley	T P Tate	14/1
U-	BRADBURY STAR	6-10-12	E Murphy	J T Gifford	5/1

ALSO: ---

8 Ran DISTANCES: 15, 8, 12, 25, 12,   **TIME:** 4m 54.3s (+11.3s)

90	BLAZING WALKER	6-11-06	C Grant	W A Stephenson	7/2
89	MAN O'MAGIC	8-11-05	M Perrett	K C Bailey	9/1
88	SAFFRON LORD	6-11-03	R Rowe	J T Gifford	8/11F
87	WEATHER THE STORM	8-11-00	T Taaffe	A L T Moore Ire	6/1
86	CHURCH WARDEN	7-10-07	R Dunwoody	D Murray Smith	12/1
85	VERY PROMISING	7-11-07	P Scudamore	D Nicholson	6/1
84	CYBRANDIAN	6-10-09	A Brown	M H Easterby	6/4 F
83	THE TSAREVICH	7-11-06	Mr J White	N Henderson	9/2
82	PAY RELATED	8-11-02	J J O'Neill	M H Easterby	7/1

First Run in 1981

34 . Big Race Results

7 GERRY FEILDEN HURDLE   2m 100y   (Good)   **Newbury**
23 Nov   1st: £ 9,285, 2nd: £ 3,513, 3rd: £ 1,719, 4th: £ 783

1-	GRAN ALBA	5-11-00	G McCourt	R Hannon	5/4 F
2-	OH SO RISKY	4-11-06	P Holley	D R C Elsworth	5/2
3-	SONG OF SIXPENCE	7-11-00	J Frost	I A Balding	6/1
4-	BELSTONE FOX	6-11-00	R Dunwoody	D Nicholson	20/1
5-	REVE DE VALSE	4-11-03	G Moore	Denys Smith	16/1
6-	KAHER	4-11-00	D J Murphy	N A Callaghan	6/1

ALSO: ---

6 Ran DISTANCES: 10, 3, 1, 2½, 15   **TIME:** 4m 4.7s (+14.7s)

90	FIDWAY	5-11-06	S Smith Eccles	T Thomson Jones	7/2
89	CRUISING ALTITUDE	6-11-03	J Osborne	O Sherwood	6/5 F
88	KRIBENSIS	4-11-06	R Dunwoody	M R Stoute	8/11F
87	CELTIC CHIEF	5-11-00	P Scudamore	Mrs M Rimell	8/11F
86	BARNBROOK AGAIN	5-11-00	R Arnott	D Elsworth	7/2
85	GALA'S IMAGE	5-11-00	R Linley	Mrs M Rimell	9/2
84	RA NOVA	5-11-03	M Perrett	Mrs N Kennedy	11/8 F
83	BUCK HOUSE	5-11-08	T Carmody	M Morris Ire	4/1
82	ROYAL VULCAN	4-11-00	J J O'Neill	N Callagham	4/6 F
81	HEIGHLIN	5-11-08	S Jobar	D Elsworth	4/1

---

8 HENNESSY COGNAC GOLD CUP   3m 2f   (Good)   **Newbury**
23 Nov   1st: £ 37,462, 2nd: £ 14,144, 3rd: £ 6,897, 4th: £ 3,116

1-	CHATAM	7-10-00	P Scudamore	M C Pipe	10/1
2-	PARTY POLITICS	7-10-05	A Adams	N A Gaselee	7/1
3-	DOCKLANDS EXPRESS	9-11-00	A Tory	K C Bailey	13/2
4-	WHATS THE CRACK	8-10-00	B Dowling	Miss H C Knight	14/1
5-	ESPY	8-10-03	G Bradley	C P E Brooks	20/1
6-	CUDDY DALE	8-09-11	A Maguire	F Murphy	25/1
7-	BORACEVA	8-10-03	J Frost	G B Balding	11/1
8-	KIRSTY'S BOY	8-10-00	M Bowlby	Miss L A Perratt	100/1
P-	GOLD OPTIONS	9-10-06	M Dwyer	J G FitzGerald	6/1JF
P-	GARRISON SAVANNAH	8-12-00	M Pitman	Mrs J Pitman	6/1JF

ALSO: P: Arctic Call, Master Bob, Rawhide, Rowlandsons Jewels, Buckshee Boy

15 Ran DISTANCES: 4, 7, 3½, ¾, 2½, 6, dist   **TIME:** 6m 34.5s (+3.5s)

90	ARCTIC CALL	7-11-00	J Osborne	O Sherwood	5/1
89	GHOFAR	6-10-02	H Davies	D R C Elsworth	5/1
88	STRANDS OF GOLD	9-10-00	P Scudamore	M C Pipe	10/1
87	PLAYSCHOOL	10-10-08	P Nicholls	D H Barons	6/1
86	BROADHEATH	9-10-05	P Nicholls	D Barons	6/1
85	GALWAY BLAZE	9-10-00	M Dwyer	J G FitzGerald	11/2
84	BURROUGH HILL LAD	8-12-00	J Francome	Mrs J Pitman	100/30
83	BROWN CHAMBERLAIN	8-11-08	J Francome	F T Winter	7/2
82	BREGAWN	8-11-10	G Bradley	M Dickinson	9/4 F
81	DIAMOND EDGE	10-11-10	W Smith	F Walwyn	9/2

9 BELLWAY HOMES FIGHTING FIFTH HURDLE   **2m**   **(Good)**   **Newcastle**
23 Nov   1st: £ 9,840, 2nd: £ 3,679, 3rd: £ 1,764, 4th: £   765

1-	ROYAL DERBI	6-11-04	C Grant	N A Callaghan	7/2
2-	NOMADIC WAY	6-11-00	B Powell	B W Hills	6/4JF
3-	SYBILLIN	5-11-00	D Byrne	J G FitzGerald	6/4JF
4-	FIDWAY	6-11-08	S Smith Eccles	T Thomson Jones	8/1

ALSO: ---

4 Ran DISTANCES: nk, 3½, 12   **TIME:** 3m 56.3s (+4.3s)

90	BEECH ROAD	8-11-04	R Guest	G B Balding	4/6 F
89	KRIBENSIS	5-11-09	M Dwyer	M R Stoute	4/7 F
88	FLOYD	8-11-06	S Sherwood	D R C Elsworth	9/4
87	FLOYD	8-11-06	C Brown	D R C Elsworth	5/6 F
86	TOM SHARPE	6-11-00	S J O'Neill	W Wharton	7/2
85	OUT OF THE GLOOM	4-11-06	J J O'Neill	R Hollinshead	9/1
84	BROWNE'S GAZETTE	6-11-09	D Browne	Mrs M Dickinson	1/2 F
83	GAYE BRIEF	6-12-00	S Morshead	Mrs M Rimell	4/9 F
82	DONEGAL PRINCE	6-11-05	P Tuck	P Kelleway	10/1
81	EKBALCO	5-11-05	D Goulding	R Fisher	7/2

10 WILLIAM HILL HANDICAP HURDLE   **2m**   **(Good)**   **Sandown**
30 Nov   1st: £ 21,251, 2nd: £ 7,992, 3rd: £ 3,871, 4th: £ 1,720

1-	BALASANI	5-10-00	M Perrett	M C Pipe	7/1
2-	NATIVE MISSION	4-10-01	A Maguire	J G FitzGerald	9/1
3-	SHU FLY	7-10-08	S Smith Eccles	Mrs S Oliver	5/1 F
4-	LIADETT	6-10-12	M Richards	M C Pipe	12/1
5-	EGYPT MILL PRINCE	5-10-00	D Gallagher	Mrs J Pitman	7/1
6-	BADRAKHANI	5-10-04	R Dunwoody	N J Henderson	14/1
7-	RIVERHEAD	7-11-10	P Holley	D R C Elsworth	33/1
8-	IMPERIAL BRUSH	7-10-05	A McCabe	D R C Elsworth	33/1
9-	COE	5-10-04	L Harvey	R Akehurst	14/1
0-	MIAMI IN SPRING	8-10-00	Lorna Vincent	Miss B Sanders	50/1

ALSO: Elegant Stranger, Wahiba, Star Season, Trimlough, Winnie the
Witch, Mudahim, Spanish Servant, Cheerful Times, Propero, Rakes Lane

20 Ran DISTANCES: 2, 1, hd, ¾, 2½, 1, 2½, ¾   **TIME:** 3m 55.7s (+8.7s)

90	WONDER MAN	5-10-12	M Pitman	Mrs J Pitman	11/4 F
89	LIADETT	4-10-00	J Lower	M C Pipe	12/1
88	CORPORAL CLINGER	9-10-07	M Perrett	M C Pipe	9/2
87	CELTIC SHOT	5-10-06	P Scudamore	F T Winter	6/4 F
86	AONOCH	7-11-07	Jacqui Oliver	Mrs S Oliver	16/1
85	CHRYSAOR	7-10-08	R Beggan	S Christian	16/1
84	PRIDEAU BOY	6-10-03	R Dunwoody	G Roach	6/1
83	Abandoned - frost				
82	ALLTEN GLAZED	5-10-02	Mr D Browne	M Naughton	5/1
81	CELTIC RYDE	6-11-13	J Francome	P Cundell	9/2

36 . Big Race Results

```
11 BULA HURDLE                        2m    (Gd-Fm)    Cheltenham
7 Dec   1st: £ 15,475, 2nd: £  5,855, 3rd: £  2,865, 4th: £ 1,305

1-   ROYAL DERBI          6-11-08  D J Murphy    N A Callaghan      9/2
2-   NOMADIC WAY          6-11-08  R Dunwoody    B W Hills        7/4 F
3-   RULING               5-11-02  H Davies      R F J Houghton     9/2
4-   FIDWAY               6-11-08  S Smith Eccles T Thompson Jones 17/2
5-   OH SO RISKY          4-11-04  P Holley      D R C Elsworth    11/4
```

ALSO: ---

```
5 Ran  DISTANCES: nk, nk, hd, 1½              TIME: 3m 59s (+2s)

90   Abandoned - snow
89   CRUISING ALTITUDE    6-11-04  J Osborne     O Sherwood       8/11F
88   CONDOR PAN           5-11-02  C F Swan      J S Bolger (Ire)  12/1
87   PAT'S JESTER         5-11-02  P Niven       R Allan           11/2
86   FLOYD                6-11-02  C Brown       D Elsworth         7/2
85   CORPORAL CLINGER     6-11-02  P Leach       M Pipe            20/1
84   BROWNE'S GAZETTE      6-11-04  Mr R Beggan   Mrs M Dickinson    7/2
83   AMARACH              5-11-06  J Duggan      R Fisher           7/2
82   EKBALCO              6-11-10  J J O'Neill   R Fisher         2/1 F
81   Abandoned - snow
```

```
12 A F BUDGE GOLD CUP HANDICAP CHASE    2m 4f  (Gd-Fm)    Cheltenham
7 Dec   1st: £ 15,475, 2nd: £  5,855, 3rd: £  2,865, 4th: £ 1,305

1-   KINGS FOUNTAIN       8-11-10  A Tory        K C Bailey       7/4 F
2-   ANOTHER CORAL        8-11-09  R Dunwoody    D Nicholson        4/1
3-   IDA'S DELIGHT       12-11-07  B Storey      J I A Charlton    16/1
4-   TORANFIELD           7-11-04  A Maguire     F Lennon (Ire)     6/1
5-   TIPPING TIM          6-10-03  P Scudamore   N A Twiston Davies 8/1
P-   NOS NA GAOITHE       8-11-07  R Garritty    M H Easterby      16/1
P-   LUMBERJACK           7-10-02  M Dwyer       J G FitzGerald     6/1
F-   CASHEW KING          8-11-03  T Wall        B A McMahon       25/1
```

ALSO: ---

```
8 Ran  DISTANCES: 8, 6, ½, 15                 TIME: 5m 7.6s (+1.6s)

90   Abandoned - snow
89   CLEVER FOLLY         9-10-04  N Doughty     G Richards         4/1
88   PEGWELL BAY          7-10-13  B Powell      Capt T A Forster   7/2
87   BISHOPS YARN         9-10-07  Richard Guest G B Balding     100/30
86   OREGON TRAIL         6-10-07  R Beggan      S Christian        3/1
85   COMBS DITCH          9-11-09  C Brown       D Elsworth        13/2
84   BEAU RANGER          6-09-10  J Hurst       J Thorpe           8/1
83   FIFTY DOLLARS MORE   8-11-10  R Linley      F T Winter         3/1
82   OBSERVE              6-10-11  J Francome    F T Winter        11/2
81   Abandoned - snow
```

13 MERCURY COMMS. PRINCE'S TRUST HURDLE   2m 4f   (Gd-Fm)   Cheltenham
7 Dec   1st: £ 16,968, 2nd: £ 5,538, 3rd: £ 2,744

1-	GRANVILLE AGAIN	5-11-06	P Scudamore	M C Pipe	4/9 F
2-	TYRONE BRIDGE	5-11-06	R Dunwoody	M C Pipe	10/1
3-	CRYSTAL SPIRIT	4-11-01	J Frost	I A Balding	11/4
F-	TALAMERO	5-11-06	S Smith Eccles	Miss J Elliot	16/1

ALSO: ---

4 Ran DISTANCES: ¾, 20   **TIME:** 5m 5.3s (+10.3s)

90	Abandoned - snow				
89	MORLEY STREET	5-11-06	J Frost	G B Balding	4/7 F
88	ABBREVIATION	5-11-00	Peter Hobbs	J T Gifford	16/1
First run in 1988					

14 CORAL WELSH NATIONAL HANDICAP CHASE   3m 6f   (Good)   Chepstow
21 Dec   1st: £ 23,654, 2nd: £ 8,786, 3rd: £ 4,243, 4th: £ 1,765

1-	CARVILL'S HILL	9-11-12	P Scudamore	M C Pipe	9/4 F
2-	PARTY POLITICS	7-10-07	A Adams	N A Gaselee	7/2
3-	AQUILIFER	11-10-09	R Dunwoody	M C Pipe	8/1
4-	BONANZA BOY	10-11-05	S Smith Eccles	M C Pipe	14/1
5-	ZETA'S LAD	8-10-00	R Supple	John R Upson	66/1
6-	BORACEVA	8-09-11	A Maguire	G B Balding	20/1
P-	ESHA NESS	8-10-00	M Bowlby	Mrs J Pitman	14/1
P-	WHATS THE CRACK	8-10-00	B Dowling	Miss H C Knight	20/1
F-	KILLBANON	9-10-00	B Powell	C C Trietline	18/1
P-	COOL GROUND	9-11-06	J Frost	G B Balding	14/1

ALSO: P: On The Twist, The West Awake, Twin Oaks, Kildimo, Mweenish, Mister Ed, Chief Ironside

17 Ran DISTANCES: 20, sh, 20, dist, 8,   **TIME:** 8m 10.1s (+46.1s)

90	COOL GROUND	8-10-00	L Harvey	R Akehurst	9/2
89	BONANZA BOY	8-11-11	P Scudamore	M C Pipe	15/8 F
88	BONANZA BOY	7-10-01	P Scudamore	M C Pipe	9/4 F
87	PLAYSCHOOL	10-10-11	P Nicholls	D H Barons	5/1
86	STEARSBY	7-11-05	G Bradley	Mrs J Pitman	8/1
85	RUN AND SKIP	7-10-08	P Scudamore	J Spearing	13/1
84	RIGHTHAND MAN	7-11-05	G Bradley	Mrs M Dickinson	6/1
83	BURROUGH HILL LAD	7-10-09	J Francome	Mrs J Pitman	10/3
82	CORBIERE	7-10-10	B de Haan	Mrs J Pitman	12/1
81	PEATY SANDY	7-10-03	Mr T G Dun	Miss H Hamilton	3/1

38 . Big Race Results

15 KING GEORGE VI RANK CHASE   3m   (Good)   Kempton
26 Dec   1st: £ 44,170, 2nd: £ 16,716, 3rd: £ 8,183, 4th: £ 3,731

1-	THE FELLOW	6-11-10	A Kondrat	F Doumen (Fra)	10/1
2-	DOCKLANDS EXPRESS	9-11-10	M Perrett	K C Bailey	25/1
3-	REMITTANCE MAN	7-11-10	J Osborne	N J Henderson	3/1 F
4-	TOBY TOBIAS	9-11-10	M Pitman	Mrs J Pitman	4/1
5-	NORTON'S COIN	10-11-10	G McCourt	S G Griffiths	10/1
F-	DESERT ORCHID	12-11-10	R Dunwoody	D R C Elsworth	4/1
F-	SABIN DU LOIR	12-11-10	P Scudamore	M C Pipe	10/3
F-	FOYLE FISHERMAN	12-11-10	D J Murphy	J T Gifford	66/1

ALSO: ---

8 Ran DISTANCES: 1½, 2, 8, 25,   **TIME:** 5m 46.4s(-1.2s)

90	DESERT ORCHID	11-11-10	R Dunwoody	D R C Elsworth	9/4 F
89	DESERT ORCHID	10-11-10	R Dunwoody	D R C Elsworth	4/6 F
88	DESERT ORCHID	9-11-10	S Sherwood	D R C Elsworth	1/2 F
87	NUPSALA	9-11-10	A Pommier	F Doumen Fr	25/1
86	DESERT ORCHID	7-11-10	S Sherwood	D Elsworth	16/1
85	WAYWARD LAD	8-11-10	G Bradley	Mrs M Dickinson	12/1
84	BURROUGH HILL LAD	8-11-10	J Francome	Mrs J Pitman	1/2
83	WAYWARD LAD	8-11-10	R Earnshaw	M Dickinson	11/8
82	WAYWARD LAD	7-11-10	J Francome	M Dickinson	7/2
81	Abandoned due to Frost				

---

16 BUTLIN'S FELTHAM NOVICES' CHASE   3m   (Good)   Kempton
26 Dec   1st: £ 24,260, 2nd: £ 9,145, 3rd: £ 4,447, 4th: £ 1,996

1-	MUTARE	6-11-07	R Dunwoody	N J Henderson	11/8 F
2-	CAPTAIN DIBBLE	6-11-07	P Scudamore	N A Twiston Davies	7/1
3-	GRANVILLEWATERFORD	6-11-07	J Osborne	S E Sherwood	11/2
4-	FAR SENIOR	5-11-07	M Armytage	K C Bailey	9/2
5-	JUNIOR PARKER	7-11-07	M Perrett	J A C Edwards	33/1
6-	BUCK WILLOW	7-11-07	D J Murphy	J T Gifford	5/1
P-	MAN ON THE LINE	8-11-07	G McCourt	R Akehurst	12/1
P-	MOZE TIDY	6-11-07	T Grantham	R Rowe	50/1
P-	PORCHESTER RUN	9-11-02	C Gordon	L J Bowman	200/1

ALSO: ---

9 Ran DISTANCES: 8, 6, 2, 30, 6   **TIME:** 5m 48.2s (-1.8s)

90	SPARKLING FLAME	6-11-07	R Dunwoody	N J Henderson	7/2
89	FRENCH GOBLIN	6-10-11	P Hobbs	J T Gifford	15/8 F
88	SIR BLAKE	7-11-04	B Poweel	D R C Elsworth	8/11F
87	TWIN OAKS	7-11-04	P Croucher	D Murray-Smith	9/4
86	AHERLOW	6-11-00	R J Beggan	S Cristian	13/8 F
85	VON TRAPPE	8-11-04	R Dunwoody	M Oliver	13/8 F
84	CATCH PHRASE	6-11-00	R Rowe	J T Gifford	9/2
83	DUKE OF MILAN	6-11-04	P Scudamore	N A Gaselee	9/4
82	GALLAHER	6-11-04	W Smith	F Walwyn	10/11F
81	Abandoned due to Frost				

17 ROWLAND MEYRICK HANDICAP CHASE   **3m 100y**   **(Good)**   **Wetherby**
26 Dec   1st: £ 17,815, 2nd: £ 4,990, 3rd: £ 2,395

1-	STAY ON TRACKS	9-10-00	C Grant	W A Stephenson	6/1
2-	KINGS FOUNTAIN	8-11-04	A Tory	K C Bailey	8/13F
3-	KILDIMO	11-11-03	L Wyer	Mrs S J Smith	16/1
P-	PHOENIX GOLD	11-10-13	M Dwyer	J G FitzGerald	7/2
U-	RINUS	10-10-13	M Moloney	G Richards	9/1

ALSO: ---

5 Ran DISTANCES: ¾, 25,   **TIME:** 6m 28.5s (+21.5s)

90	BLUFF KNOLL	7-10-00	G Harker	R Brewis	2/1 F
89	DURHAM EDITION	11-10-06	A Merrigan	W A Stephenson	5/1
88	WHATS WHAT	9-10-01	B Bousfield	B Bousfield	3/1
87	YAHOO	7-10-04	T Morgan	J A C Edwards	11/8 F
86	THE THINKER	8-11-06	R Dunwoody	W A Stephenson	12/1
85	FORTINA'S EXPRESS	8-11-01	R Hawkins	W A Stephenson	14/1
84	FORGIVE'N'FORGET	7-11-07	M Dwyer	J FitzGerald	4/6 F
83	PHIL THE FLUTER	8-10-00	S Keightley	H Wharton	12/1
82	RICHDEE	6-10-06	C Hawkins	N Crump	5/1
81	Abandoned	- snow and frost			

18 TOP RANK CHRISTMAS HURDLE   **2m**   **(Good)**   **Kempton**
27 Dec   1st: £ 31,520, 2nd: £ 11,928, 3rd: £ 5,839, 4th: £ 2,662

1-	GRAN ALBA	5-11-07	G McCourt	R Hannon	3/1
2-	ROYAL DERBI	6-11-07	D J Murphy	N A Callaghan	5/2 F
3-	RULING	5-11-07	P Niven	R F J Houghton	7/2
4-	FIDWAY	6-11-07	S Smith Eccles	T Thomson Jones	4/1
5-	RIVERHEAD	7-11-07	P Holley	D R C Elsworth	25/1
6-	FOREST SUN	6-11-07	J Frost	G B Balding	8/1
7-	ARMY OF STARS	6-11-07	S Keightley	C E Brittain	100/1

ALSO: ---

7 Ran DISTANCES: 2½, 7, 2½, 2, ½, dist   **TIME:** 3m 41s (+1s)

90	FIDWAY	5-11-07	S Smith Eccles	T Thomson Jones	10/3
89	KRIBENSIS	5-11-07	R Dunwoody	M R Stoute	4/6 F
88	KRIBENSIS	4-11-03	R Dunwoody	M R Stoute	4/9 F
87	OSRIC	5-11-03	G McCourt	M J Ryan	12/1
86	NOHALMDUM	5-11-03	P Scudamore	M H Easterby	15/8 F
85	AONOCH	6-11-03	J Duggan	Mrs S Oliver	14/1
84	BROWNE'S GAZETTE	6-11-03	D Browne	Mrs M Dickinson	11/8 F
83	DAWN RUN	5-10-12	J J O'Neill	P Mullins Ire	9/4 F
82	EKBALCO	6-11-13	J J O'Neill	R Fisher	1/2 F
81	Abandoned	- frost			

19 CASTLEFORD CHASE   2m 50y   (Good)   **Wetherby**
27 Dec   1st: £ 31,730, 2nd: £ 12,009, 3rd: £ 5,879, 4th: £ 2,681

1-	WATERLOO BOY	8-11-10	R Dunwoody	D Nicholson	4/11F
2-	LAST 'O' THE BUNCH	7-11-10	N Doughty	G W Richards	4/1
3-	CASHEW KING	8-11-10	T Wall	B A McMahon	16/1
4-	GREENHEART	8-11-10	C Grant	W A Stephenson	10/1

ALSO: ---

4 Ran DISTANCES: 7, 5, 7   **TIME:** 4m 2.6s (+8.6s)

90	WATERLOO BOY	7-11-10	R Dunwoody	D Nicholson	6/4
89	IDA'S DELIGHT	10-10-07	B Storey	J I A Charlton	17/2
88	MIDNIGHT COUNT	8-12-02	Peter Hobbs	J T Gifford	15/8
87	PEARLYMAN	8-12-07	T Morgan	J A C Edwards	Evs F
86	LITTLE BAY	11-11-07	P Tuck	G Richards	9/1
85	OUR FUN	8-10-11	R Rowe	J T Gifford	9/4
84	RYEMAN	7-11-10	G Bradley	Mrs A E Dickinson	5/2
83	BADSWORTH BOY	8-12-00	G Bradley	M W Dickinson	10/11F
82	LITTLE BAY	7-10-08	R Barry	G Richards	9/2
81	Abandoned - snow and frost				

20 MANDARIN HANDICAP CHASE   3m 2f   (Good)   **Newbury**
28 Dec   1st: £ 7,984, 2nd: £ 2,224, 3rd: £ 1,072

1-	CHATAM	7-11-10	P Scudamore	M C Pipe	1/2 F
2-	MASTER BOB	11-10-06	R Dunwoody	N J Henderson	4/1
3-	MAN O'MAGIC	10-11-06	J Osborne	K C Bailey	5/1

ALSO: ---

3 Ran DISTANCES: 6, 12   **TIME:** 6m 44s (+13s)

90	PARTY POLITICS	6-11-02	A Adams	N A Gaselee	4/5 F
89	POLYFEMUS	7-10-05	J White	M H B Robinson	3/1
88	TEN PLUS	8-11-10	K Mooney	F Walwyn	11/10F
88	CAVVIES CLOWN	8-11-03	R Arnott	D R C Elsworth	7/2
87	MAORI VENTURE	11-11-03	S C Knight	A Turnell	4/1
85	Abandoned - frost				
84	MAORI VENTURE	8-11-05	S C Knight	A Turnell	4/1
83	OBSERVE	7-11-07	J Francome	F Winter	8/13F
83	EARTHSTOPPEER	9-11-01	Mr G Sloan	J Gifford	9/2
82	NIGHT NURSE	11-11-12	J J O'Neill	M H Easterby	11/2

21* A MILDMAY P CAZALET MEM. HCP CHASE   3m 5f 18y   (Good)   Sandown
4 Jan   1st: £ 13,875, 2nd: £ 4,200, 3rd: £ 2,050, 4th: £   975

1-	ARCTIC CALL	9-11-06	J Osborne	O Sherwood	4/1
2-	GIVUS A BUCK	9-10-00	P Holley	D R C Elsworth	20/1
3-	ROWLANDSONS JEWELS	11-10-04	G Bradley	D Murray Smith	7/2
4-	MR FRISK	13-11-07	Mr M Armytage	K C Bailey	8/1
5-	PARTY POLITICS	8-10-12	R Dunwoody	N A Gaselee	5/4 F
D-	ON THE TWIST	10-09-11	A Maguire	F Murphy	11/1

ALSO: ---

6 Ran DISTANCES: -, 10, 1½, 1½, 2, 3½   **TIME:** 7m 24.3s (+12.3s)

91	COOL GROUND	9-10-11	L Harvey	R Akehurst	6/4 F
90	COOL GROUND	8-10-05	A Tory	N R Mitchell	6/1
89	MR FRISK	10-10-13	R Dunwoody	K C Bailey	3/1
88	RHYME 'N' REASON	9-10-07	C Brown	D R C Elsworth	11/8 F
87	STEARSBY	8-11-05	G McCourt	Mrs J Pitman	11/8 F
86	RUN AND SKIP	8-11-01	P Scudamore	J Spearing	7/2
85	WEST TIP	8-10-01	R Dunwoody	M Oliver	11/4
84	BURROUGH HILL LAD	8-10-09	J Francome	Mrs J Pitman	11/8 F
83	FIFTY DOLLARS MORE	8-11-05	R Linley	F Winter	4/6 F
82	Abandoned - frost and snow				

---

22 NEWTON CHASE   2m 4f   (Good)   Haydock
4 Jan   1st: £ 27,310, 2nd: £ 10,219, 3rd: £ 4,997, 4th: £ 2,148

1-	PAT'S JESTER	9-11-10	N Doughty	G Richards	7/1
2-	KATABATIC	9-11-10	L Harvey	A Turnell	9/4 F
3	GOLD OPTIONS	10-11-10	M Dwyer	J G FitzGerald	20/1
4-	GOLDEN FREEZE	10-11-10	M Pitman	Mrs J Pitman	17/2
5-	DOCKLANDS EXPRESS	10-11-10	A Tory	K C Bailey	3/1
6-	SABIN DU LOIR	13-11-10	P Scudamore	M C Pipe	5/2

ALSO: ---

6 Ran DISTANCES: 7, 4, 1½, 1½, 5   **TIME:** 5m 14.4s (+17.4s)

91	SABIN DU LOIR	12-11-10	M Perrett	M C Pipe	1/2 F

First run in 1991

42 . Big Race Results

23 VICTOR CHANDLER HANDICAP CHASE 2m (Good) Ascot
11 Jan 1st: £ 30,438, 2nd: £ 11,390, 3rd: £ 5,470, 4th: £ 2,381

1-	WATERLOO BOY	9-11-10	R Dunwoody	D Nicholson	6/4 F
2-	YOUNG SNUGFIT	8-11-02	J Osborne	O Sherwood	3/1
3-	SURE METAL	9-10-05	B Storey	D McCain	6/1
4-	CASHEW KING	9-10-04	T Wall	B A McMahon	20/1
5-	GOOD FOR A LAUGH	8-10-04	B Sheridan	A L T Moore (Ire)	3/1

ALSO: ---

5 Ran DISTANCES: 2, dist, 7, dist   **TIME:** 3m 51.9s (+3.9s)

91	BLITZKREIG	8-10-04	T Carmody	E J O'Grady	11/4
90	MEIKLEOUR	11-10-00	D Byrne	J G FitzGerald	10/1
89	DESERT ORCHID	10-12-00	S Sherwood	D R C Elsworth	6/4 F
88	Abandoned - Fog				
87	Abandoned - snow and frost				
First run in 1989					

---

24 BIC RAZOR LANZAROTE HANDICAP HURDLE 2m (Good) Kempton
18 Jan 1st: £ 14,300, 2nd: £ 4,331, 3rd: £ 2,115, 4th: £ 1,007

1-	EGYPT MILL PRINCE	6-10-13	M Pitman	Mrs J Pitman	11/2
2-	JUNGLE KNIFE	6-11-10	A Maguire	M H Tompkins	7/2 F
3-	SARTORIUS	6-10-09	D J Murphy	T Thomson Jones	11/2
4-	PEACE KING	6-11-09	M Perrett	G Harwood	13/2
5-	MARLINGFORD	5-10-11	D Morris	Mrs J Jordan	6/1
6-	SHIMSHEK	8-10-00	P Holley	D R C Elsworth	13/2
R-	VALIANT BOY	6-10-06	Mr S Lyons	S E Kettlewell	5/1

ALSO: ---

7 Ran DISTANCES: 3, 30, ¾, 7, 7   **TIME:** 3m 43.9s (+3.9s)

91	STAR SEASON	7-10-03	N Mann	R J Holder	9/2
90	ATLAAL	5-10-03	R Dunwoody	J R Jenkins	10/1
89	GREY SALUTE	6-10-07	R Dunwoody	J R Jenkins	9/4 F
88	FREDCOTERI	12-11-04	M Hammond	G M Moore	15/2
87	STRAY SHORT	9-09-10	Ms G Armytage	G Hubbard	16/1
86	PRIDEAUX BOY	8-11-00	M Bowlby	G Roach	11/1
85	Abandoned - snow and frost				
84	JANUS	6-11-01	C Brown	Mrs N Smith	5/1
83	BRAVE HUSSAR	5-10-07	R Rowe	J Gifford	16/1
82	KNIGHTHOOD	7-10-00	S C Knight	R Turnell	10/1

25 PETER MARSH HANDICAP CHASE   3m   (Good)   Haddock
18 Jan   1st: £ 16,200, 2nd: £ 6,117, 3rd: £ 2,983, 4th: £ 1,348

1-	TWIN OAKS	12-11-10	N Doughty	G Richards	5/4 F
2-	GOLD OPTIONS	10-10-10	M Dwyer	J G FitzGerald	8/1
3-	ROMANY KING	8-10-10	R Guest	G B Balding	4/1
4-	AUNTIE DOT	11-10-10	M M Lynch	J Webber	8/1
5-	AQUILIFER	12-10-13	P Scudamore	M C Pipe	4/1
6-	YAHOO	11-10-10	N Williamson	J A C Edwards	25/1
7-	SOUTHERN MINSTREL	9-10-10	C Grant	W A Stephenson	25/1
8-	BUCKSHEE BOY	10-10-10	D Tegg	J Pilkington	200/1

ALSO: ---

8 Ran DISTANCES: 5, sh, 7, 2, 15, 3½, 25   **TIME:** 6m 16.9s (+7.9s)

91	Abandoned - frost				
90	NICK THE BRIEF	8-10-09	M M Lynch	John R Upson	15/8 F
89	BISHOPS YARN	10-10-12	R Guest	G B Balding	13/2
88	Abandoned - snow				
87	THE THINKER	09-11-10	R Lamb	W A Stephenson	9/2
86	COMBS DITCH	10-11-08	C Brown	D Elsworth	3/1
85	Abandoned - frost				
84	Abandoned - frost				
83	ASHLEY HOUSE	09-10-07	R Earnshaw	M Dickinson	11/8
82	BREGAWN	08-10-07	R Earnshaw	M Dickinson	11/2

---

26 TOTE JACKPOT H'CAP HURDLE   2m 5f 75y   (Good)   Sandown
1 Feb   1st: £ 15,514, 2nd: £ 5,860, 3rd: £ 2,860, 4th: £ 1,294

1-	BLACK SAPPHIRE	5-10-00	B Powell	M H Tompkins	33/1
2-	HOLY JOE	10-10-04	D Bridgwater	A J Wilson	33/1
3-	BALASANI	6-11-00	M Perrett	M C Pipe	5/1
4-	DWADME	7-10-11	J Osborne	O Sherwood	11/2
5-	MIAMI IN SPRING	9-10-12	Lorna Vincent	Miss B Sanders	25/1
6-	AMBUSCADE	6-11-04	P Niven	Mrs G R Reveley	7/1
7-	SIR PETER LELY	5-09-10	Mr S Lyons	M D Hammond	12/1
8-	SWEET GLOW	5-11-08	P Scudamore	M C Pipe	3/1 F
9-	SECRET FOUR	6-11-07	L Harvey	R Akehurst	6/1
0-	GO SOUTH	8-10-06	R Dunwoody	J R Jenkins	16/1

ALSO: F: Champagne Lad, **B:** Wahiba

12 Ran DISTANCES: nk, 1½, 2½, 3, 3½, 3, ½, 1½ **TIME:** 5m 17.6s (+11.6s)

91	ROUYAN	5-10-00	W Morris	R Simpson	8/1
90	Abandoned - waterlogged course				
89	SPECIAL VINTAGE	9-10-12	M Dwyer	J G FitzGerald	20/1
88	HILL STREET BLUES	10-10-02	S Moore	J C Fox	25/1
87	TABERNA LORD	06-09-10	L Harvey	A J Wilson	8/1
86	HOORAY HENRY	06-10-05	H Davies	J B Sayers	8/1

First run in 1986

44 . Big Race Results

```
27 AGFA DIAMOND HANDICAP CHASE              3m 118y    (Good)     Sandown
1 Feb    1st: £ 19,020, 2nd: £  7,198, 3rd: £  3,524, 4th: £ 1,607
```

1-	ESPY	9-10-07	G Bradley	C P E Brooks	11/1
2-	DALKEY SOUND	9-10-07	P Niven	Mrs G R Reveley	2/1 F
3-	GHOFAR	9-10-07	B Powell	D R C Elsworth	5/1
4-	KARAKTER REFERENCE	10-10-04	D O'Sullivan	R J O'Sullivan	8/1
5-	NORTON'S COIN	11-11-12	G McCourt	S G Griffiths	7/1
6-	ROWLANDSONS JEWELS	11-10-07	D J Murphy	D Murray Smith	7/1
7-	LACIDAR	12-10-07	A Orkney	J H Johnson	100/1
8-	BROWN WINDSOR	10-10-11	R Dunwoody	N J Henderson	7/1
P-	OKLAOMA II	12-10-07	Miss C Troquet	R Kleparski (Fra)	25/1

ALSO: ---

```
9 Ran  DISTANCES: ½, hd, 5, 2, 20, 7, 15        TIME: 6m 11.3s (+9.3s)
```

91	DESERT ORCHID	12-12-00	R Dunwoody	D R C Elsworth	4/6 F
90	Abandoned - course waterlogged				
89	DESERT ORCHID	10-12-00	S Sherwood	D R C Elsworth	6/5 F
88	CHARTER PARTY	10-10-11	R Dunwoody	D Nicholson	10/3 F
87	DESERT ORCHID	8-11-10	C Brown	D Elsworth	11/4
86	BURROUGH HILL LAD	10-12-00	P Scudamore	Mrs J Pitman	10/3
85	BURROUGH HILL LAD	9-12-00	J Francome	Mrs J Pitman	W/O
84	BURROUGH HILL LAD	8-11-10	J Francome	Mrs J Pitman	11/8 F
83	OBSERVE	7-11-03	J Francome	F Winter	11/8 F
82	BREGAWN	8-10-07	R Earnshaw	M Dickinson	3/1

```
28 CHARTERHOUSE MERCANTILE HANDICAP CHASE    3m    (Gd-Fm)      Ascot
5 Feb    1st: £ 25,146, 2nd: £  7,488, 3rd: £  3,564, 4th: £ 1,602
```

1-	COMBERMERE	8-10-10	P Scudamore	R G Frost	11/4
2-	ROWLANDSONS JEWELS	11-11-08	G Bradley	D J Murray Smith	10/1
3-	GOLD HAVEN	8-10-00	A Tory	K C Bailey	9/4 F
4-	FOYLE FISHERMAN	13-11-10	D J Murphy	J T Gifford	9/1
5-	BIGSUN	11-11-10	R Dunwoody	D Nicholson	12/1
F-	PENDENNIS	9-10-07	J R Kavanagh	N J Henderson	11/4

ALSO: ---

```
6 Ran  DISTANCES: sh, 2, dist, 25        TIME: 6m 9.7s (+6.7s)
```

91	Abandoned - frost				
90	TEN OF SPADES	10-10-00	K Mooney	F Walwyn	11/2
89	PROUD PILGRIM	10-10-09	M Dwyer	J G FitzGerald	6/1
88	AQUILIFER	8-10-01	P Croucher	D Murray-Smith	5/2 F
87	CASTLE WARDEN	10-09-12	Mr M Richards	J Edwards	10/1
86	BRUNTON PARK	8-10-04	G Bradley	Mrs M Dickinson	14/1
85	GREENWOOD LAD	8-10-06	R Rowe	J Gifford	10/1
84	TRACY'S SPECIAL	7-10-05	S C Knight	A Turnell	10/3
83	Abandoned - frost				
82	CAVITY HUNTER	9-10-03	R Earnshaw	M Dickinson	5/1

29 REYNOLDSTOWN NOVICES CHASE   **3m**   **(Gd-Fm)**   **Ascot**
5 Feb   1st: £ 16,627, 2nd: £ 5,689, 3rd: £ 2,729

1-	DANNY HARROLD	8-11-05	M Pitman	Mrs J Pitman	2/1
2-	JODAMI	7-11-09	P A Farrell	P Beaumont	8/13F
3-	MAJOR INQUIRY	6-11-05	G Bradley	D R C Elsworth	8/1

ALSO: **---**

3 Ran DISTANCES: 15, dist   **TIME: 6m 5.7s (+2.7s)**

91	Abandoned - frost				
90	ROYAL ATHLETE	7-11-08	M Pitman	Mrs J Pitman	11/4
89	VULGAN WARRIOR	7-11-08	J Osborne	S Christian	8/1
88	KISSANE	7-11-08	T Morgan	J A C Edwards	4/1
87	TAWBRIDGE	7-11-12	S C Knight	Andrew Turnell	2/1
86	BOLANDS CROSS	7-11-08	P Scudamore	N Gaslee	2/1 F
85	DRUMADOWNEY	7-11-12	H Davies	Capt T A Forster	3/1
84	DUKE OF MILAN	7-11-12	S S Eccles	N A Gaslee	11/4
83	Abandoned - Frost				
82	RICHDEE	6-11-10	C Hawkins	N Crump	3/1

30 ARLINGTON PREMIER SERIES CHASE (Final) 2m 4f   (Gd-Fm)   Newbury
8 Feb   1st: £ 19,920, 2nd: £ 6,060, 3rd: £ 2,980, 4th: £ 1,440

1-	REMITTANCE MAN	8-11-07	R Dunwoody	N J Henderson	2/7 F
2-	CAPTAIN DIBBLE	7-11-07	P Scudamore	N A Twiston Davies	6/1
3-	ARMAGRET	7-11-07	L O'Hara	B E Wilkinson	8/1
4-	MIGHTY FALCON	7-11-07	G Bradley	D R C Elsworth	16/1
P-	HEIGHT OF FUN	8-11-07	P Hobbs	C L Popham	100/1

ALSO: **---**

5 Ran DISTANCES: 20, 5, 1½   **TIME: 5m 5.9s (+9.9s)**

91	Abandoned - Frost				
90	SABIN DU LOIR	11-11-07	G McCourt	M C Pipe	9/4
89	BARNBROOK AGAIN	08-11-07	S Sherwood	D R C Elsworth	5/2
88	No Race				
87	No Race				
86	VERY PROMISING	08-11-10	P Scudamore	D R C Elsworth	5/2
	Abandoned- Snow and frost				
84	BALLINACCURRA LAD	09-11-07	P Leech	J Crowley (Ire)	10/11
83	COMBS DITCH	07-11-07	C Brown	D R C Elsworth	11/2
82	WAYWARD LAD	07-11-07	R Earnshaw	M Dickinson	13/8

46 . Big Race Results

31 TOTE GOLD TROPHY HANDICAP HURDLE   2m 100y   (Good)   **Newbury**
8 Feb   1st: £ 30,405, 2nd: £ 11,470, 3rd: £ 5,585, 4th: £ 2,514

1-	RODEO STAR	6-10-10	G McCourt	N Tinkler	15/2
2-	NATIVE MISSION	5-10-13	M Dwyer	J G FitzGerald	13/2 F
3-	EGYPT MILL PRINCE	6-11-02	M Pitman	Mrs J Pitman	15/2
4-	BOOKCASE	5-10-00	A Procter	D R C Elsworth	16/1
5-	BOARDING SCHOOL	5-11-01	B Storey	C Parker	14/1
6-	MARLINGFORD	5-10-07	D Morris	Mrs J Jordan	14/1
7-	JUNGLE KNIFE	6-11-10	A Maguire	M H Tompkins	12/1
8-	ONE FOR THE POT	7-10-10	G Bradley	Mrs J R Ramsden	14/1
9-	OLD VIRGINIA	6-10-06	J Leech	R Akehurst	16/1
0-	VIKING FLAGSHIP	5-10-05	R Dunwoody	D Nicholson	7/1

ALSO: Kibreet, Shannon Glen, Imperial Brush, Galway Star, **F:** Spanish
Servant

15 Ran DISTANCES: 5, 2½, 3, 10, 1½, 2½, 2½, 2½ **TIME:** 3m 55.9s (+5.9s)

91	Abandoned - frost				
90	DEEP SENSATION	5-11-03	R Rowe	J T Gifford	7/1
89	GREY SALUTE	6-11-05	R Dunwoody	J R Jenkins	8/1
88	JAMESMEAD	7-10-00	B Powell	D R C Elsworth	11/1
87	NEBLIN	8-10-00	S Moore	G B Balding	10/1
86	Abandoned - snow				
85	Abandoned - snow and frost				
84	RA NOVA	5-10-06	P Farrell	Mrs N Kennedy	16/1
83	Abandoned - snow and frost				
82	DONEGAL PRINCE	6-10-08	J Francome	P Kelleway	13/1

32 KINGWELL HURDLE   2m   (Good)   **Wincanton**
20 Feb   1st: £ 10,880, 2nd: £ 4,109, 3rd: £ 2,004, 4th: £ 906

1-	FIDWAY	7-11-10	P Scudamore	T Thomson Jones	11/4
2-	GRAN ALBA	6-11-10	G Bradley	R Hannon	10/11F
3-	OH SO RISKY	5-11-10	P Holley	D R C Elsworth	3/1
4-	LANDYAP	8-11-02	J Frost	R G Frost	150/1
5-	VESTRIS ABU	6-11-02	Mr E Kearns	M C Pipe	20/1
6-	KADAN	8-11-02	S Burrough	W G Turner	100/1

ALSO: ---

6 Ran DISTANCES: ½, 12, 10, 2, dist   **TIME:** 3m 43.1s (+9.1s)

91	WELSH BARD	7-11-02	P Scudamore	C P E Brooks	11/1
90	KRIBENSIS	6-11-12	R Dunwoody	M R Stoute	4/6 F
89	FLOYD	9-11-08	R Dunwoody	D R C Elsworth	10/11F
88	FLOYD	8-11-08	C Brown	D R C Elsworth	9/2
87	HYPNOSIS	8-11-02	P Scudamore	D R C Elsworth	25/1
86	Abandoned - Frost				
85	Abandoned - Snow & Frost				
84	DESERT ORCHID	5-11-02	C Brown	D R C Elsworth	2/1 F
83	MIGRATOR	7-11-07	R Linley	L Kennard	8/1
82	WALNUT WONDER	7-11-07	C Brown	D R C Elsworth	4/1

33 RACING POST HANDICAP CHASE   **3m**   (Good)   **Kempton**
22 Feb   **1st:** £ 31,875, **2nd:** £ 12,033, **3rd:** £ 5,866, **4th:** £ 2,649

1-	DOCKLANDS EXPRESS	10-11-10	A Tory	K C Bailey	6/1
2-	PEGWELL BAY	11-11-03	J Osborne	Capt T A Forster	20/1
3-	ROMANY KING	8-10-10	Richard Guest	G B Balding	8/1
4-	ON THE TWIST	10-10-04	A Maguire	F Murphy	14/1
5-	BROWN WINDSOR	10-11-01	R Dunwoody	N J Henderson	25/1
6-	GHOFAR	9-10-04	G Bradley	D R C Elsworth	10/1
7-	KARAKTER REFERENCE	10-10-00	D O'Sullivan	R J O'Sullivan	10/1
8-	COMBERMERE	8-10-00	P Scudamore	R G Frost	15/2
F-	MR ENTERTAINER	9-10-07	B Powell	N A Gaselee	5/1
P-	DALKEY SOUND	9-10-06	P Niven	Mrs G R Reveley	4/1 F

ALSO: P: Nodform

11 Ran   **DISTANCES:** 1, ½,1, 20, 4, 20, dist   **TIME:** 5m 51.5s (+1.5s)

91	DOCKLANDS EXPRESS	9-10-07	A Tory	K C Bailey	7/2
90	DESERT ORCHID	11-12-03	R Dunwoody	D R C Elsworth	8/11F
89	BONANZA BOY	8-11-01	P Scudamore	M C Pipe	5/1
88	RHYME'N'REASON	09-10-11	B Powell	D R C Elsworth	7/2 F

First run in 1988

34 TIMEFORM CHASE   **2m 4f**   (Good)   **Haydock**
29 Feb   **1st:** £ 8,169, **2nd:** £ 2,472, **3rd:** £ 1,206, **4th:** £ 573

1-	LAST 'O' THE BUNCH	8-11-04	N Doughty	G W Richards	5/1
2-	HENRY MANN	9-11-00	G McCourt	S Christian	6/4
3-	UNCLE ERNIE	7-11-07	M Dwyer	J G FitzGerald	11/8 F
4-	POETIC GEM	7-11-00	Richard Guest	Mrs S J Smith	14/1
5-	JESTERS PROSPECT	8-11-04	B Storey	Mrs J Goodfellow	33/1

ALSO: ---

5 Ran   **DISTANCES:** 4, 6, 3½, 15   **TIME:** 5m 13.7s (+16.7s)

91	CARRICK HILL LAD	8-11-06	N Doughty	G Richards	4/6 F
90	TARTAN TAKEOVER	8-11-00	M Dwyer	G Richards	2/1
89	SOUTHERN MINSTREL	6-11-00	A Merrigan	W A Stephenson	Evs F
88	RAISE AN ARGUMENT	9-11-04	J Osborne	Mrs M Dickinson	7/2
87	Abandoned - snow				
86	Abandoned - frost				
85	FORGIVE'N'FORGET	8-11-08	M Dwyer	J FitzGerald	4/7 F
84	FORGIVE'N'FORGET	7-11-00	M Dwyer	J FitzGerald	5/2
83	FIFTY DOLLARS MORE	8-11-08	R Linley	F Winter	13/8 F
82	WAYWARD LAD	7-11-12	R Earnshaw	M Dickinson	2/5 F

35 GREENALLS GOLD CUP HANDICAP CHASE   3m 4f   (Good)   Haydock
29 Feb   1st: £ 24,086, 2nd: £ 9,074, 3rd: £ 4,487, 4th: £ 1,985

1-	COOL GROUND	10-11-03	A Maguire	G B Balding	12/1
2-	KILDIMO	12-10-02	Richard Guest	Mrs S J Smith	10/1
3-	TWIN OAKS	12-11-10	N Doughty	G W Richards	11/8 F
4-	WILLSFORD	9-10-00	M Bowlby	Mrs J Pitman	6/1
5-	PARTY POLITICS	8-10-09	R Dunwoody	N A Gaselee	11/2
6-	SOLIDASAROCK	10-10-00	P Scudamore	R Akehurst	12/1
F-	WITHY BANK	10-10-02	R Stronge	Mrs S J Smith	100/1
P-	ON THE TWIST	10-10-02	R J Beggan	F Murphy	14/1
P-	BOREEN OWEN	8-10-10	C Grant	J J O'Neill	100/1
U-	DAVID'S DUKY	10-09-07	K Hartnett	A S Reid	11/1

ALSO: U: Seagram

11 Ran DISTANCES: 1½, 7, 1½, hd, 20,   **TIME:** 7m 27.8s (+9.8s)

91	TWIN OAKS	11-11-00	N Doughty	G Richards	7/4 F
90	RINUS	9-10-04	R Dunwoody	G Richards	11/2
89	ETON ROUGE	10-10-01	J Bryan	Mrs M Rimell	11/2
88	YAHOO	7-10-10	T Morgan	J A C Edwards	11/4 F
87	Abandoned - snow				
86	Abandoned - frost				
85	EARLS BRIG	10-10-06	P Tuck	W Hamilton	3/1
84	MIDNIGHT LOVE	9-10-03	C Grant	D Smith	14/1
83	RIGHTHAND MAN	6-10-09	R Earnshaw	M Dickinson	9/4
82	SCOT LANE	9-10-00	C Smith	M Tate	14/1

---

36 SUNDERLANDS IMPERIAL CUP H'CAP HURDLE   2m   (Good)   Sandown
7 Mar   1st: £ 16,648, 2nd: £ 4,984, 3rd: £ 2,392, 4th: £ 1,096

1-	KING CREDO	7-10-04	A Maguire	S Woodman	9/2
2-	RODEO STAR	6-11-10	J Osborne	N Tinkler	9/2
3-	SPINNING	5-10-09	J Frost	I A Balding	7/4 F
4-	VIKING FLAGSHIP	5-11-02	R Dunwoody	D Nicholson	14/1
5-	EGYPT MILL PRINCE	6-11-10	M Pitman	Mrs J Pitman	15/2
6-	SARTORIUS	6-10-08	H Davies	T Thomson Jones	8/1
7-	ALREEF	6-10-09	G Rowe	T Thomson Jones	33/1
8-	MARLIN DANCER	7-10-09	Dale McKeown	Miss B Sanders	20/1
9-	BRIERY FILLE	7-10-01	S Woods	A Hide	100/1
U-	ONEUPMANSHIP	7-10-12	S Woods	D R C Elsworth	15/2

ALSO: ---

10 Ran DISTANCES: 2½, 3, 2, 1½, 2, 8, 2½, nk,   **TIME:** 3m 52.9s (+6.5s)

91	PRECIOUS BOY	5-10-06	L Wyer	M O'Neill	16/1
90	MOODY MAN	5-10-13	P Hobbs	P J Hobbs	20/1
89	TRAVEL MYSTERY	6-10-00	P Scudamore	M C Pipe	3/1 F
88	SPROWSTON BOY	5-10-11	S McCrystal	P A Kelleway	10/1
87	INLANDER	6-10-03	S S Eccles	R Akehurst	10/1
86	INSULAR	6-09-10	E Murphy	I Balding	14/1
85	FLOYD	5-10-03	C Brown	D Elsworth	13/8 F
84	DALBURY	6-09-12	P Corrigan	P Haynes	9/2
83	DESERT HERO	9-09-08	R Chapman	F Walwyn	20/1
82	HOLEMOOR STAR	5-11-07	M O'Halloran	Miss S Morris	2/1

37 TRAFALGAR HOUSE SUPREME NOVICES' HURDLE   2m   (Good)   Cheltenham
10 Mar   1st: £ 32,096, 2nd: £ 11,957, 3rd: £ 5,803, 4th: £ 2,447

1-	FLOWN	5-11-08	J Osborne	N J Henderson	13/2
2-	HALKOPOUS	6-11-08	A Maguire	M H Tompkins	11/2
3-	FORTUNE AND FAME	5-11-08	B Sheridan	D K Weld (Ire)	6/1
4-	NEW YORK RAINBOW	7-11-08	R Dunwoody	N J Henderson	4/1 F
5-	CURRENT EXPRESS	5-11-08	J White	N J Henderson	20/1
6-	MISS BOBBY BENNETT	5-11-03	M Foster	M C Pipe	100/1
7-	STEVEADON	6-11-08	D J Murphy	N A Callaghan	40/1
8-	SOFT DAY	7-11-08	T J Taaffe	A L T Moore (Ire)	8/1
9-	BAYDON STAR	5-11-08	M Pitman	Mrs J Pitman	16/1
0-	BUCKBOARD BOUNCE	6-11-08	K F O'Brien	J E Mulhern (Ire)	20/1

ALSO: Chafold Copse, Barry Window, Polishing, Aston Again, Song Of Sixpence, French Ivy, Talbot

17 Ran DISTANCES: 10, 3, hd, 1½, 10, 2½, 8, 5, 2 **TIME:** 3m 54.6s (+1.6s)

91	DESTRIERO	5-11-08	P McWilliams	A Geraghty	6/1
90	FOREST SUN	5-11-08	J Frost	G B Balding	7/4 F
89	SONDRIO	8-11-08	J Lower	M C Pipe	25/1
88	VAGADOR	5-11-08	M Perrett	G Harwood	4/1 F
87	TARTAN TAILOR	6-11-08	P Tuck	G Richards	14/1
86	RIVER CEIRIOG	5-11-08	S S Eccles	N Henderson	40/1
85	HARRY HASTINGS	6-11-08	C Grant	J S Wilson	14/1
84	BROWNE'S GAZETTE	6-11-08	Mr D Browne	M Dickinson	11/2
83	BUCK HOUSE	5-11-08	T Carmody	M Morris Ire	8/1
82	MILLER HILL	6-11-08	T Morgan	D Hughes Ire	20/1

38 WATERFORD CASTLE ARKLE CHAL. TROPHY CHASE   2m   (Good)   Cheltenham
10 Mar   1st: £ 37,345, 2nd: £ 13,855, 3rd: £ 6,677, 4th: £ 2,762

1-	YOUNG POKEY	7-11-08	J Osborne	O Sherwood	4/1
2-	TINRYLAND	8-11-08	P Scudamore	N J Henderson	5/1
3-	SPACE FAIR	9-11-08	A Maguire	R Lee	11/1
4-	DEEP SENSATION	7-11-08	D J Murphy	J T Gifford	3/1 F
5-	FRAGRANT DAWN	8-11-08	G Bradley	D R C Elsworth	20/1
6-	BOUNDEN DUTY	6-11-08	M Perrett	G Harwood	50/1
7-	MASS APPEAL	7-11-03	C F Swan	V Bowens (Ire)	21/1
8-	VALRODIAN	9-11-08	I Lawrence	M H B Robinson	16/1
F-	SHAMANA	6-11-03	R Dunwoody	D Nicholson	10/1
U-	FLASHY BUCK	8-11-08	T J Taaffe	A L T Moore (Ire)	20/1

ALSO: P: Alkinor Rex

11 Ran DISTANCES: 3½, 2, 2½, ½, 10, 4   **TIME:** 4m (+7s)

91	REMITTANCE MAN	7-11-08	R Dunwoody	N J Henderson	85/40F
90	COMANDANTE	8-11-08	P Hobbs	J T Gifford	9/2
89	WATERLOO BOY	6-11-08	R Dunwoody	D Nicholson	20/1
88	DANISH FLIGHT	9-11-08	M Dwyer	J G FitzGerald	11/27
87	GALA'S IMAGE	7-11-08	R Linley	Mrs M Rimell	25/1
86	OREGON TRAIL	6-11-08	R Beggan	S Christian	14/1
85	BOREEN PRINCE	8-11-08	N Madden	A McNamara Ire	15/2
84	BOBSLINE	8-11-08	F Berry	F Flood Ire	5/4 F
83	RYEMAN	6-11-08	A Brown	M H Easterby	16/1
82	THE BROCKSHEE	7-11-08	T Carberry	A Moore Ire	12/1

50 . Big Race Results

39 SMURFIT CHAMPION HURDLE CHALLENGE TROPHY   2m   (Good)   Cheltenham
10 Mar   1st: £ 80,065, 2nd: £ 29,935, 3rd: £ 14,617, 4th: £ 6,262

1-	ROYAL GAIT	9-12-00	G McCourt	J Fanshawe	6/1
2-	OH SO RISKY	5-12-00	P Holley	D R C Elsworth	20/1
3-	RULING	6-12-00	P Niven	R F J Houghton	20/1
4-	FIDWAY	7-12-00	H Davies	T Thomson Jones	7/1
5-	BANK VIEW	7-12-00	M Duffy	N Tinkler	50/1
6-	MORLEY STREET	8-12-00	J Frost	G B Balding	2/1 F
7-	CHIRKPAR	5-12-00	L Cusack	J S Bolger (Ire)	20/1
8-	PROPERO	7-12-00	D J Murphy	J T Gifford	150/1
9-	MINORETTES GIRL	7-11-09	A Maguire	P Mullins (Ire)	16/1
0-	WINNIE THE WITCH	8-11-09	D Bridgwater	K S Bridgwater	22/1

ALSO: Royal Derbi, Mardood, Shu Fly, Kribensis, **U:** Valiant Boy; **F:**
Granville Again

16 Ran DISTANCES: ½, sh, 6, 1, sh, ¾, 1½, 3½, 2 **TIME:** 3m 57.2s (+4.2s)

91	MORLEY STREET	7-12-00	J Frost	G B Balding	4/1 F
90	KRIBENSIS	6-12-00	R Dunwoody	M R Stoute	95/40
89	BEECH ROAD	7-12-00	R Guest	G B Balding	50/1
88	CELTIC SHOT	6-12-00	P Scudamore	F T Winter	7/1
87	SEE YOU THEN	7-12-00	S S Eccles	N Henderson	11/10F
86	SEE YOU THEN	6-12-00	S S Eccles	N Henderson	5/6 F
85	SEE YOU THEN	5-12-00	S S Eccles	N Henderson	16/1
84	DAWN RUN	6-11-09	J J O'Neill	P Mullins	4/5 F
83	GAYE BRIEF	6-12-00	R Linley	Mrs M Rimell	7/1
82	FOR AUCTION	6-12-00	Mr C Magnier	M Cunningham	40/1

40* BONUSPRINT STAYERS' HURDLE   3m 1f   (Good)   Cheltenham
10 Mar   1st: £ 40,535, 2nd: £ 15,065, 3rd: £ 7,282, 4th: £ 3,037

1-	NOMADIC WAY	7-11-10	J Osborne	B W Hills	15/2
2-	UBU III	6-11-10	A Kondrat	F Doumen (Fra)	10/1
3-	CRYSTAL SPIRIT	5-11-10	P Scudamore	I A Balding	7/2
4-	BURGOYNE	6-11-10	L Wyer	M H Easterby	12/1
5-	RANDOLPH PLACE	11-11-10	N Doughty	G W Richards	16/1
7-	FOREST SUN	7-11-10	J Frost	G B Balding	11/2
8-	TYRONE BRIDGE	6-11-10	G Bradley	M C Pipe	16/1
9-	JEASSU	9-11-10	A Maguire	A J Wilson	66/1
0-	SECRET FOUR	6-11-10	L Harvey	R Akehurst	50/1
0-	NANCY MYLES	7-11-05	F J Flood	F Flood (Ire)	16/1

ALSO: Shannon Glen, Upton Park, Rustle, Orbis; **P:** Derring Valley, Father
Time; **D:** Trapper John,

17 Ran DISTANCES: 5, 2½, 6, 1½, 7, 2, 4,   **TIME:** 6m 34s (+14s)

91	KING'S CURATE	7-11-10	M Perrett	S Mellor	5/2 F
90	TRAPPER JOHN	6-11-10	C F Swan	M F Morris Ire	15/2
89	RUSTLE	7-11-10	M Bowlby	N J Henderson	4/1
88	GALMOY	9-11-10	T Carmody	J E Mulhern Ire	2/1 F
87	GALMOY	8-11-10	T Carmody	J Mulhern	9/2
86	CRIMSON EMBERS	11-11-10	S Shilston	F Walwyn	12/1
85	ROSE RAVINE	6-11-05	R Pusey	F Walwyn	5/1
84	GAVE CHANCE	9-11-10	S Morshead	Mrs M Rimell	5/1
83	A KINSMAN	7-11-12	T G Dun	J Brockbank	50/1
82	CRIMSON EMBERS	7-11-12	S Shilston	F Walwyn	2/1 F

41 F WALWYN KIM MUIR CHAL. CUP H'CAP CHASE   3m   (Good)   Cheltenham
10 Mar   1st: £ 17,883, 2nd: £ 5,364, 3rd: £ 2,582, 4th: £ 1,191

1-	TUG OF GOLD	7-10-02	Mr M Armytage	D Nicholson	11/1	
2-	PACO'S BOY	7-09-11	Mr N Moore	M C Pipe	9/1	
3-	LATENT TALENT	8-10-09	Mr J Durkan	S E Sherwood	7/1	
4-	STRONG GOLD	9-09-12	Mr G Lewis	Mrs J Pitman	20/1	
5-	GOLDEN MINSTREL	13-09-09	Mr G Cosgrove	J T Gifford	25/1	
6-	RONANS BIRTHDAY	10-09-09	Mr S Lyons	P J Hobbs	11/1	
7-	STATELY LOVER	9-09-12	Mr M Phillips	D M Grissell	20/1	
8-	AUCTION LAW	8-10-00	Mr G Oxley	D H Barons	7/1	
9-	THIRD IN LINE	9-10-00	Mr R Farrant	J A C Edwards	13/2 F
0-	TRUSTY FRIEND	10-09-10	Mr R Davies	J A C Edwards	16/1	

ALSO: Lacidar, Team Challenge, Moze Tidy; **P:** Huntworth, Secret Rite, Laura's Beau, Border Archer, Pharoah's Laen; **U:** Damers Cavalry

19 Ran DISTANCES: 1½, 5, 5, nk, sh, 6, 6, nk, 5   **TIME:** 6m 19.9s (+9.9s)

91	OMERTA	11-09-13	A Maguire*	M C Pipe	11/1	
90	MASTER BOB	10-10-01	Mr J Berry	N J Henderson	20/1	
89	COOL GROUND	7-10-00	Mr A Tory	N R Mitchell	7/2 F
88	GOLDEN MINSTREL	9-11-01	Mr T Grantham	J T Gifford	7/1
87	THE ELLIER	11-10-05	Ms G Armytage	N Tinkler	16/1	
86	GLYDE COURT	9-11-00	Mr J Queally	F Winter	13/2	
85	GLYDE COURT	8-10-05	Mr S Sherwood	F Winter	11/1	
84	BROOMY BANK	9-11-04	Cpt A J Wilson	J Edwards	16/1	
83	GREASEPAINT	8-11-05	Mr C Magnier	M Cunningham Ire	8/1	
82	POLITICAL POP	8-12-00	Mr D Browne	M Dickinson	15/2	

42 CHELT. GR. ANNUAL CHAL. CUP H'CAP CHASE   2m   (Good)   Cheltenham
10 Mar   1st: £ 20,647, 2nd: £ 61,800, 3rd: £ 2,965, 4th: £ 1,357

1-	MY YOUNG MAN	7-11-10	G Bradley	C P E Brooks	7/1	
2-	WHATEVER YOU LIKE	8-10-00	J Kavanagh	N J Henderson	14/1	
3-	WIDE BOY	10-10-00	M Perrett	P J Hobbs	16/1	
4-	NOS NA GAOITHE	9-10-09	R Garrity	M H Easterby	33/1	
5-	EDBERG	8-10-07	A Orkney	J H Johnson	6/1 F
6-	SHANNAGARY	11-10-00	A Tory	R J Hodges	25/1	
7-	AL HASHIMI	8-10-12	R Dunwoody	D Nicholson	13/2	
8-	MACARTHUR	7-10-01	J Osborne	M W Easterby	7/1	
9-	TRESIDDER	10-10-00	C F Swan	M W Easterby	9/1	
0-	ACRE HILL	8-10-04	H Davies	N J Henderson	10/1	

ALSO: Evening Rain, Emsee-H, Antinous; **P:** Pick Roundstone, Good For A Laugh, Tildebo; **F:** Freeline Finishing

17 Ran DISTANCES: 12, 1½, nk, 1½, 3, 1½, sh, nk **TIME:** 3m 57.3s (+4.3s)

91	ALDINO	8-10-00	J Osborne	O Sherwood	15/2	
90	KATABATIC	7-10-08	H Davies	Andrew Turnell	11/4 F
89	PUKKA MAJOR	8-10-02	P Scudamore	T Thomson Jones	4/1	
88	VODKATINI	9-10-13	R Rowe	J T Gifford	4/1 F
87	FRENCH UNION	9-11-03	R Dunwoody	D Nicholson	13/2	
86	PEARLYMAN	7-11-05	G Bradley	J Edwards	14/1	
85	KATHIES LAD	8-11-10	S S Eccles	A Jarvis	7/1	
84	MOSSY MOORE	8-10-00	J J O'Neill	B Chinn	11/12	
83	CHURCHFIELD BOY	7-10-00	J P Byrne	M Cunningham Ire	8/1	
82	RELDIS	8-10-00	P Barton	D Gandolfo	11/2	

52 . Big Race Results

43 `SUN ALLIANCE' NOVICES' HURDLE   2m 4f   (Good)   Cheltenham
11 Mar   1st: £ 34,152, 2nd: £ 12,768, 3rd: £ 6,234, 4th: £ 2,670

1-	THETFORD FOREST	5-11-07	R Dunwoody	D Nicholson	7/1
2-	MUSE	5-11-07	P Holley	D R C Elsworth	13/2
3-	ASHFOLD COPSE	6-11-07	M Perrett	G Harwood	25/1
4-	TRIPLE WITCHING	6-11-07	M Pitman	Mrs J Pitman	20/1
5-	YOUNG HUSTLER	5-11-07	C Llewellyn	N Twiston-Davies	50/1
6-	NATIVE PRIDE	5-11-07	A Tory	K C Bailey	14/1
7-	TRAVADO	6-11-07	J Kavanagh	N J Henderson	15/2
8-	COMMERCIAL ARTIST	6-11-07	T J Taaffe	V Bowens (Ire)	40/1
9-	SUKAAB	6-11-07	M Fitzgerald	B J M Ryall	100/1
0-	FLASHING STEEL	7-11-07	K F O'Brien	J E Mulhern (Ire)	8/1

ALSO: Tallywagger, Charterforhardware, Sweet Duke, Man Of Mystery,
Hawthorn Blaze, Barton Bank, Finely Balanced, Windsor Park, Apsimore,
Gnomes Tycoon, Fight To Win, Future King; **B:** Bollin Patrick; **F:** Dury
Lane, Muir Station; **P:** Tipp Mariner, My Key Silca

27 Ran DISTANCES: 6, 2½, 6, 5, 1, 5, 3, ½, 1, 1½ **TIME:** 5m 2.7s (+4.7s)

91	CRYSTAL SPIRIT	4-10-12	J Frost	I A Balding	2/1 F
90	REGAL AMBITION	6-11-07	P Scudamore	M C Pipe	3/1 F
89	SAYFAR'S LAD	5-11-07	M Perrett	M C Pipe	12/1
88	REBEL SONG	6-11-07	S Sherwood	O Sherwood	14/1
87	THE WEST AWAKE	6-11-07	S Sherwood	O Sherwood	16/1
86	TEN PLUS	6-11-07	K Mooney	F Walwyn	5/2
85	ASIR	5-11-07	Mr R Beggan	P Kelleway	9/1
84	FEALTY	4-10-12	S O'Neill	P Brookshaw	33/1
83	SABIN DU LOIR	4-10-08	G Bradley	M Dickinson	16/1
82	MISTER DONOVAN	6-11-08	T Ryan	E O'Grady Ire	9/2

44 QUEEN MOTHER CHAMPION CHASE   2m   (Good)   Cheltenham
11 Mar   1st: £ 63,390, 2nd: £ 23,610, 3rd: £ 11,455, 4th: £ 4,825

1-	REMITTANCE MAN	8-12-00	J Osborne	N J Henderson	1/1 F
2-	KATABATIC	9-12-00	S McNeill	Andrew Turnell	6/1
3-	WATERLOO BOY	9-12-00	R Dunwoody	D Nicholson	5/2
4-	REDUNDANT PAL	9-12-00	C O'Dwyer	P Mullins (Ire)	66/1
5-	MASTER RAJH	8-12-00	M M Lynch	J Chugg	14/1
6-	STAR'S DELIGHT	10-12-00	P Scudamore	M C Pipe	20/1

ALSO: ---

6 Ran DISTANCES: 3½, 2½, 5, 10   **TIME:** 3m 56.5s (+3.5s)

91	KATABATIC	8-12-00	S McNeill	A Turnell	9/1
90	BARNBROOK AGAIN	9-12-00	H Davies	D R C Elsworth	11/10F
89	BARNBROOK AGAIN	8-12-00	S Sherwood	D R C Elsworth	7/4 F
88	PEARLYMAN	9-12-00	T Morgan	J A C Edwards	15/8 F
87	PEARLYMAN	8-12-00	P Scudamore	J Edwards	13/8 F
86	BUCK HOUSE	8-12-00	T Carmody	M F Morris Ire	5/2
85	BADSWORTH BOY	10-12-00	R Earnshaw	Mrs M Dickinson	11/8 F
84	BADSWORTH BOY	9-12-00	R Earnshaw	M Dickinson	8/13F
83	BADSWORTH BOY	8-12-00	R Earnshaw	M Dickinson	2/1 F
82	RATHGORMAN	10-12-00	K Whyte	M Dickinson	10/3

45 CORAL GOLDEN HANDICAP HURDLE (FINAL)   3m 1f   (Good)   Cheltenham
11 Mar   1st: £ 28,840, 2nd: £ 8,683, 3rd: £ 4,204, 4th: £ 1,964

1-	MY VIEW	8-10-04	J F Titley	M Purcell (Ire)	33/1
2-	PRAGADA	9-10-10	J Frost	M C Pipe	33/1
3-	THE WIDGET MAN	6-10-07	E Murphy	J T Gifford	12/1
4-	MR GOSSIP	10-10-02	R Dunwoody	N J Henderson	20/1
5-	TAMARPOUR	5-10-00	M Richards	M C Pipe	33/1
6-	SHUIL AR AGHAIDH	6-10-00	K F O'Brien	P Kiely (Ire)	25/1
7-	SPROWSTON BOY	9-10-00	G Crant	Miss L A Perratt	12/1
8-	CAPABILITY BROWN	5-10-00	P Scudamore	M C Pipe	8/1 F
9-	PETTY BRIDGE	8-10-00	R Bellamy	A P James	100/1
0-	TRAPPER JOHN	8-12-00	C F Swan	M F Morris (Ire)	16/1

ALSO: Lake Teereen, Sayyure, Sweet Glow, Pactolus, Bart Owen, Cosmic Dancer, Dwadme, Better Times Ahead, Royal Square, Holy Joe, Super Sense, Urizen, Crystal Heights; **P:** Battalion, Black Sapphire, Mushtaaq, Rostreamer, Enborne Lad, Torkabar, Kings Rank, Just as Hopeful

31 Ran DISTANCES: 1, 1, 2, 1½, ½, 2, sh, 1½, 1½ **TIME:** 6m 27.9s (+7.9s)

91	DANNY CONNORS	7-10-12	M Swyer	J J O'Neill	9/1
90	HENRY MANN	7-11-09	A Mulholland	S Christian	20/1
89	ROGERS PRINCESS	7-10-00	S Keightley	M Tate	8/1
88	PRAGADA	5-11-00	R Rowe	J T Gifford	16/1
87	TABERNA LORD	6-11-05	L Harvey	A J Wilson	10/1
86	MOTIVATOR	6-10-07	G McCourt	M Ryan	15/2
85	VON TRAPPE	8-10-06	R Dunwoody	M Oliver	12/1
84	CANIO	7-10-09	J Francome	R Hodges	20/1
83	FORGIVE'N'FORGET	6-11-06	M Dwyer	J FitzGerald	5/2
82	TALL ORDER	8-10-02	A Stringer	L Foster	15/1

46 'SUN ALLIANCE' NOVICES' CHASE   3m   (Good)   Cheltenham
11 Mar   1st: £ 43,507, 2nd: £ 16,192, 3rd: £ 7,846, 4th: £ 3,293

1-	MIINNEHOMA	9-11-14	P Scudamore	M C Pipe	7/2 F
2-	BRADBURY STAR	7-11-04	D J Murphy	J T Gifford	11/2
3-	RUN FOR FREE	8-11-04	J Frost	M C Pipe	11/1
4-	ROUGH QUEST	6-11-04	G McCourt	T J Etherington	12/1
5-	CAPTAIN DIBBLE	7-11-04	C Llewellyn	N Twiston-Davies	33/1
6-	SPRINGALEAK	7-10-13	J Osborne	O Sherwood	8/1
7-	MISTER TICKLE	7-11-04	S Cowley	N Twiston-Davies	100/1
F-	GENERAL IDEA	7-11-04	B Sheridan	D K Weld (Ire)	6/1
U-	GRAND HABIT	8-11-04	J F Titley	Hde Bromhead (Ire)	66/1
F-	MUTARE	7-11-04	R Dunwoody	N J Henderson	11/2

ALSO: **P:** Parson's Thorns, Norman Conqueror, Pacific Sound, Welsh Commander, Forever Aston, Poetic Gem; **F:** Call Me Later, Truely Royal

18 Ran DISTANCES: ½, 10, 4, 12, ½, 4,   **TIME:** 6m 6.6s (-3.4sRec)

91	ROLLING BALL	8-11-04	P Scudamore	M C Pipe	7/2 F
90	GARRISON SAVANNAH	7-11-04	B de Haan	Mrs J Pitman	12/1
89	ENVOPAK TOKEN	8-11-04	P Hobbs	J T Gifford	16/1
88	THE WEST AWAKE	7-11-04	S Sherwood	O Sherwood	11/4 F
87	KILDIMO	7-11-04	G Bradley	G Balding	13/2
86	CROSS MASTER	9-11-04	R Crank	T Bill	16/1
85	ANTARTIC BAY	8-11-04	F Berry	P Hughes Ire	6/4 F
84	A KINSMAN	8-11-04	T G Dun	J Brockbank	10/1
83	CANNY DANNY	7-11-04	N Mdden	J FitzGerald	33/1
82	BROWN CHAMBERLIN	7-11-04	J Francome	F Winter	7/1

54 . Big Race Results

47 NATIONAL HUNT CHASE (AM.)   **4m**   (Good)   Cheltenham
11 Mar   1st: £ 16,310, 2nd: £ 4,880, 3rd: £ 2,340, 4th: £ 1,070

1-	KEEP TALKING	7-12-07	Mr M Armytage	T Thomson Jones	5/2 F
2-	HIGH PEAK	8-12-07	Mr P Fenton	E J O'Grady (Ire)	13/2
3-	BELMOUNT CAPTAIN	7-12-07	Mr R Alner	G B Balding	8/1
4-	EXTRA MILE	5-11-00	Mr P Graffin	A Mullins (Ire)	25/1
5-	THE FORTIES	7-12-07	Mr A Martin	T T Bill	9/1
6-	MASTER CORNET	7-12-04	Mr A Sansome	B S Rothwell	33/1
7-	LARKSMORE	7-11-13	Mr S Baker	Miss D J Baker	100/1
8-	PROGRESSIVE	13-12-00	Ms L Blackford	Mrs S D Williams	100/1
9-	OFF THE BRU	7-12-04	Mr J Bradburne	Mrs S C Bradbunre	25/1
P-	CLOSUTTON EXPRESS	6-12-04	Mr W Mullins	W P Mullins (Ire)	50/1

ALSO: **F:** Here Comes Charter, Captain Frisk, Pry's-Joy, Tagmoun Chaufour, Boom Time, Just Moss; **P:** Mr Vergette, Juranstan, Mr Pantomime;
R: Carousel Crossett; **U:** Woodlands Genhire, Deep Bramble, Bishop's Staff, Yukon Quest

24 Ran DISTANCES: 4, 7, 15, 7, 2½, 8, dist, dist **TIME:** 8m 22.2s (+8.2s)

91	SMOOTH ESCORT	7-12-00	Mr A Martin	Mrs D Haine	7/1
90	TOPSHAM BAY	7-12-00	Mr P Hacking	D H Barons	40/1
89	BORACEVA	6-12-00	Mr S Mullins	G B Balding	4/1 F
88	OVER THE ROAD	7-12-04	Mr T Costello	T Casey	10/1
87	MIGHTY MARK	8-12-07	Mr J Walton	F Walton	8/1
86	OMERTA	6-12-07	Mr L Wyer	H Scott Ire	9/4 F
85	NORTHERN BAY	9-12-04	Mr A Fowler	T Bill	12/1
84	MACKS FRIENDLY	7-12-07	Mr W Mullins	P Mullins Ire	11/4
83	BIT OF A SKITE	7-12-00	Mr F Codd	E O'Grady Ire	5/1
82	HAZY DAWN	7-12-07	Mr W Mullins	P Mullins Ire	8/1

---

48 MILDMAY OF FLETE CHAL. CUP H'CAP CHASE   **2m 4f**   (Good)   Cheltenham
11 Mar   1st: £ 21,785, 2nd: £ 6,530, 3rd: £ 3,140, 4th: £ 1,445

1-	ELFAST	9-11-00	M M Lynch	Webber J	10/1
2-	SEA ISLAND	8-10-00	P Scudamore	M C Pipe	13/2 F
3-	KING OF THE LOT	9-10-06	G McCourt	D Nicholson	11/1
4-	HOWE STREET	9-10-02	A Orkney	J H Johnson	16/1
5-	SIBTON ABBEY	7-10-00	Gee Armytage	F Murphy	33/1
6-	MONUMENTAL LAD	9-09-07	D Leahy	Mrs H Parrott	25/1
7-	ANOTHER CORAL	9-11-07	R Dunwoody	D Nicholson	13/2 F
8-	WESTERN COUNTIES	13-09-11	B M Clifford	R J Holder	16/1
9-	IDA'S DELIGHT	13-10-13	B Storey	J I A Charlton	16/1
0-	SWORD BEACH	8-10-09	L Wyer	M H Easterby	7/1

ALSO: Kittinger, Maple Dancer, Ardbrin, Catch The Cross, New Halen, Sirrah Jay, Derrymore Boy, Rust Never Sleeps; **P:** Farmlea Boy

19 Ran DISTANCES: 3½, 2½, ½, 7, ½, 8, 2, 3, 2½ **TIME:** 5m 3.5s (+3.5s)

91	FOYLE FISHERMAN	12-11-00	E Murphy	J T Gifford	33/1
90	NEW HALEN	9-09-07	E Tierney	A P James	66/1
89	PADDYBORO	11-10-07	R Rowe	J T Gifford	9/2
88	SMART TAR	7-10-02	C Llewellyn	M J Wilkinson	11/1
87	GEE-A	8-09-10	Ms G Armytage	G Hubbard	33/1
86	THE TSAREVICH	10-11-05	J White	N Henderson	8/1
85	THE TSAREVICH	9-11-07	J White	N Henderson	5/1
84	HALF FREE	8-11-06	R Linley	F Winter	16/1
83	MR PEAPOCK	7-09-07	L Bloomfield	T Hallett	20/1
82	DOUBLEUAGAIN	8-10-00	F Berry	A Geraghty (Ire)	11/1

49 DAILY EXPRESS TRIUMPH HURDLE   2m   (Good)   Cheltenham
12 Mar   1st: £ 31,991, 2nd: £ 11,917, 3rd: £ 5,783, 4th: £ 2,438

1-	DUKE OF MONMOUTH	11-00-00	M Richards	S E Sherwood	33/1
2-	CROWDED HOUSE	11-00-00	R Dunwoody	B V Kelly (Ire)	12/1
3-	AL MUTAHM	11-00-00	C Llewellyn	J A B Old	16/1
4-	CANNY CHRONICLE	11-00-00	P Campbell	M H Tompkins	25/1
5-	SALWAN	11-00-00	R Stronge	P J Bevan	20/1
6-	HEAD OF CHAMBERS	11-00-00	P McWilliams	M O'Toole (Ire)	25/1
7-	ABSALOM'S LADY	10-09-00	J Frost	G B Balding	33/1
8-	GAMARA	10-09-00	J Banahan	M O'Toole (Ire)	14/1
9-	MUBIN	11-00-00	H Davies	C C Elsey	100/1
0-	SNOWY LANE	11-00-00	P Scudamore	M C Pipe	16/1

ALSO: Beebob, Novello Allegro, Ballaat, Kashan, Aiybak, Roman Forum, Radar Knight, Green's Van Goyen, Dancing Paddy, Valiant Warrior, Qualitair Sound, Master Foodbroker, Irish Peace, Pharly Story, Duharra, Kayfaat, Hashar; **P:** Nijmegen, Staunch Friend, The Blue Boy

30 Ran DISTANCES: 6, 2½, 2, nk, sh, nk, ¾, 6, ½ **TIME:** 4m 3.8s (+6.8s)

91	OH SO RISKY	4-11-00	P Holley	D C R Elseworth	33/1
90	RARE HOLIDAY	4-11-00	B Sheridan	D K Weld Ire	25/1
89	IKDAM	4-11-00	N Coleman	R J Holder	66/1
88	KRIBENSIS	4-11-00	R Dunwoody	M R Stoute	6/1
87	ALONE SUCCESS	4-11-00	S S Eccles	N Henderson	11/1
86	SOLAR CLOUD	4-11-00	P Scudamore	D Nicholson	40/1
85	FIRST BOUT	4-11-00	S S Eccles	N Henderson	5/1
84	NORTHERN GAME	4-11-00	T J Ryan	E O'Grady	20/1
83	SAXON FARM	4-11-00	M Perrett	S Mellor	12/1
82	SHINY COPPER	4-11-00	A Webb	Mrs N Smith	66/1

---

50 RITZ CLUB NATIONAL HUNT H'CAP CHASE   3m 1f   (Good)   Cheltenham
12 Mar   1st: £ 26,805, 2nd: £ 8,040, 3rd: £ 3,870, 4th: £ 1,785

1-	TIPPING TIM	7-10-00	C Llewellyn	N Twiston-Davies	20/1
2-	HENRY MANN	9-10-09	G McCourt	S Christian	3/1 F
3-	GAMBLING ROYAL	9-10-08	R Dunwoody	D Nicholson	13/2
4-	ROMANY KING	8-11-06	Richard Guest	G B Balding	15/2
5-	WHATS THE CRACK	9-10-13	A Maguire	Miss H C Knight	20/1
6-	AQUILIFER	12-11-06	P Scudamore	M C Pipe	15/2
7-	FOREST RANGER	10-10-00	D Tegg	J A C Edwards	40/1
8-	ROWLANDSONS JEWELS	11-10-11	G Bradley	D Murray Smith	20/1
9-	AUNTIE DOT	11-11-03	M M Lynch	J Webber	14/1
0-	IN THE FASHION	10-10-00	A Orkney	R Tate	66/1

ALSO: Birling Jack; **P:** Seagram, Knight Oil, Topsham Bay, Sooner Still, Withy Bank; **U:** Esha Ness,

17 Ran DISTANCES: 2, 4, 2½, 1½, 2½, 3½, 5, 15, 2 **TIME:** 6m 30.3s (+8.3s)

91	SEAGRAM	11-10-11	N Hawke	D H Barons	6/1
90	BIGSUN	9-11-01	R Dunwoody	D Nicholson	15/2
89	DIXTON HOUSE	10-11-00	T Morgan	J A C Edwards	13/2
88	AQUILIFER	8-10-12	P Croucher	D Murray-Smith	9/2
87	GAINSAY	8-10-05	B de Haan	Mrs J Pitman	10/1
86	CHARTER PARTY	8-10-10	P Scudamore	D Nicholson	12/1
85	WEST TIP	8-10-13	R Dunwoody	M Oliver	6/1
84	TRACY'S SPECIAL	7-11-01	S C Knight	A Turnell	5/1
83	SCOT LANE	10-11-07	C Smith	M Tate	20/1
82	SCOT LANE	9-10-12	C Smith	M Tate	15/2

51 TOTE CHELTENHAM GOLD CUP   3m 2f   (Good)   Cheltenham
12 Mar   1st: £ 98,028, 2nd: £ 35,647, 3rd: £ 17,348, 4th: £ 7,367

1-	COOL GROUND	10-12-00	A Maguire	G B Balding	25/1
2-	THE FELLOW	7-12-00	A Kondrat	F Doumen (Fra)	7/2
3-	DOCKLANDS EXPRESS	10-12-00	M Perrett	K C Bailey	16/1
4-	TOBY TOBIAS	10-12-00	M Pitman	Mrs J Pitman	15/2
5-	CARVILL'S HILL	10-12-00	P Scudamore	M C Pipe	1/1 F
P-	NORTON'S COIN	11-12-00	G McCourt	S G Griffiths	33/1
P-	GOLDEN FREEZE	10-12-00	M Bowlby	Mrs J Pitman	150/1
U-	KINGS FOUNTAIN	9-12-00	A Tory	K C Bailey	8/1

ALSO: ---

8 Ran DISTANCES: sh, 1, dist, dist   **TIME:** 6m 47.5s (+9.5s)

91	GARRISON SAVANNAH	8-12-00	M Pitman	Mrs J Pitman	16/1
90	NORTON'S COIN	9-12-00	G McCourt	S G Griffiths	100/1
89	DESERT ORCHID	10-12-00	S Sherwood	D R C Elsworth	5/2 F
88	CHARTER PARTY	10-12-00	R Dunwoody	D Nicholson	10/1
87	THE THINKER	9-12-00	R Lamb	W A Stephenson	13/2
86	DAWN RUN	8-11-09	J J O'Neill	P Mullins Ire	15/8
85	NORGIVE 'M' FORGET	8-12-00	M Dwyer	J FitzGerald	7/1
84	BURROUGH HILL LAD	8-12-00	P Tuck	Mrs J Pitman	7/2
83	BREGAWN	9-12-00	G Bradley	M Dickinson	10/3
82	SILVER BUCK	10-12-00	R Earnshaw	M Dickinson	8/1

---

52 CHRISTIES FOXHUNTER CHALLENGE CUP   3m 2f   (Good)   Cheltenham
12 Mar   1st: £ 16,310, 2nd: £ 4,880, 3rd: £ 2,340, 4th: £ 1,070

1-	RUSHING WILD	7-12-00	Mr J Farthing	R Barber	9/1
2-	ARDESEE	12-12-00	Mr J Wintle	D J Wintle	100/1
3-	FEDERAL TROOPER	11-12-00	Mr T McCarthy	Denis McCarthy	12/1
4-	THE RED ONE	8-12-00	Mr S Swiers	P R Haley	33/1
5-	WALL GAME	7-12-00	Mr A Hill	J S Delahooke	9/2
6-	LOVELY CITIZEN	9-12-00	Mr O'Sullivan	Eugen O'Sullivan	10/1
7-	QUEENSWAY BOY	13-12-00	Mr N Bradley	Miss R Knight	66/1
8-	RAISE AN ARGUMENT	13-12-00	Mr A Sansome	Mrs J Docker	8/1
9-	SPORTING MARINER	10-12-00	Mr D Bloor	D R Bloor	100/1
0-	FIBREGUIDE TECH	9-12-00	Mr G Hanmer	Mrs T R Kinsey	100/1

ALSO: Dun Gay Lass, Curaheen Boy, Katesville, Dromin Joker; **F:** Busted Spring; **P:** Double Turn, Final Chant, Matsix, Mount Argus, Starember Lad, Ballyeden, Turn Mill, **U:** Celtic Leisure, Knox's Corner

24 Ran DISTANCES: 25, 2, 1½, sh, 12, 6, 3, 3½   **TIME:** 6m 55.8s (+17.8s)

91	LOVELY CITIZEN	8-12-00	MrW O'Sullivan	E M O'Sullivan	14/1
90	CALL COLLECT	9-12-00	Mr R Martin	J Parkes	7/4 F
89	THREE COUNTIES	12-12-00	Ms K Rimell	Mrs M Rimell	6/1
88	CERTAIN LIGHT	10-12-00	Mr P Hacking	Angus Campbell	9/1
87	OBSERVE	11-12-00	Mr C Brooks	F T Winter	14/1
86	ATTITUDE ADJUSTER	6-12-00	Mr T Walsh	M F Morris Ire	10/1
85	ELMBOY	7-12-00	Mr A Hill	W Mawle	10/1
84	VENTURE TO COGNAC	11-12-00	Mr O Sherwood	F Winter	7/1
83	ELIOGARTY	8-12-00	Ms C Beasley	B Kelly Ire	3/1
82	THE DRUNKEN DUCK	9-12-00	Mr B M-Wilson	B Munro-Wilson	21/1

53 COUNTY HANDICAP HURDLE   **2m**   (Good)   **Cheltenham**
12 Mar   1st: £ 18,964, 2nd: £ 7,146, 3rd: £ 3,473, 4th: £ 1,556

1-	DUSTY MILLER	6-10-06	J Osborne	S E Sherwood	9/1
2-	BANK VIEW	7-11-03	G McCourt	N Tinkler	9/1
3-	VIKING FLAGSHIP	5-10-03	R Dunwoody	D Nicholson	11/1
4-	ALTEREZZA	5-10-03	M Flynn	M J Grassick (Ire)	25/1
5-	KEPPOLS PRINCE	5-10-00	D Byrne	J Houghton (Ire)	50/1
6-	RARE HOLIDAY	6-11-01	B Sheridan	D K Weld (Ire)	20/1
7-	OLYMPIAN	5-10-00	N Mann	T P McGovern	50/1
8-	LOGAMIMO	6-10-10	A Orkney	J A Hellens	33/1
9-	VAYRUA	7-10-09	C Grant	J A Hellens	20/1
0-	BOARDING SCHOOL	5-10-10	B Storey	C Parker	20/1

ALSO: Bookcase, Miss Daisy Dee, Native Mission, Five Lamps, How's The
Boss, L'Uomo Piu, Wake Up, Rosgill, Kanndabil, Cheerful Times, Carbonate,
Trimlough, Honest Word, Kadan; **F:** Larnaca, Galway Star; **P:** Don Valentino

27 Ran DISTANCES: 1½, nk, nk, 3, 4, ½, 1½, 1½, hd**TIME:** 4m 2.8s (+5.8s)

91	WINNIE THE WITCH	7-09-08	D Bridgwater	K S Bridgwater	33/1
90	MOODY MAN	5-11-02	P Hobbs	P J Hobbs	9/1
89	WILLSFORD	6-10-08	M Bowlby	Mrs J Pitman	11/1
88	CASHEW KING	5-10-04	T Wall	B A McMahon	9/1
87	NEBLIN	8-11-00	R Guest	G Balding	14/1
86	JOBROKE	6-10-03	J J O'Neill	M H Easterby	6/1
85	FLOYD	5-10-05	C Brown	D Elsworth	5/2
84	HILL'S GUARD	5-10-11	A Stringer	A Scott	6/1
83	ROBIN WONDER	5-10-03	J Davies	D Elsworth	10/1
82	PATH OF PEACE	6-10-06	J J O'Neill	C Thornton	4/1

---

54 CATHCART CHALLENGE CUP (CHASE)   **2m 4f**   (Good)   **Cheltenham**
12 Mar   1st: £ 24,075, 2nd: £ 7,200, 3rd: £ 3,450, 4th: £ 1,575

1-	REPEAT THE DOSE	7-11-00	M Richards	T J Etherington	14/1
2-	TORANFIELD	8-11-07	A Maguire	F Lennon (Ire)	5/1
3-	MY YOUNG MAN	7-11-03	G Bradley	C P E Brooks	15/8 F
4-	FAR SENIOR	6-11-00	A Tory	K C Bailey	8/1
P-	GOOD FOR A LAUGH	8-11-03	T J Taaffe	A L T Moore (Ire)	14/1
P-	CLIFFALDA	9-11-00	N Doughty	G Richards	9/1
P-	THE ILLYWHACKER	7-11-00	M Pitman	Mrs J Pitman	11/4

ALSO: ---

7 Ran DISTANCES: 1½, 2½, 10,   **TIME:** 5m 19.1s (+13.1s)

91	CHATAM	7-11-00	P Scudamore	M C Pipe	3/1
90	BROWN WINDSOR	8-11-03	J White	N J Henderson	13/8 F
89	OBSERVER CORPS	8-11-00	T Morgan	J A C Edwards	66/1
88	PRIVATE VIEWS	7-11-00	B Powell	N A Gaselee	7/1
87	HALF FREE	11-11-12	P Scudamore	F Winter	5/4 F
86	HALF FREE	10-11-08	S Sherwood	F Winter	11/8 F
85	STRAIGHT ACCORD	10-11-08	S Shilston	F Walwyn	15/2
84	THE MIGHTY MAC	9-11-08	Mr D Browne	M Dickinson	4/7 F
83	OBSERVE	7-11-08	J Francome	F Winter	1/2 F
82	DRAMATIST	11-11-08	W Smith	F Walwyn	15/8 F

58 . Big Race Results

55 LETHEBY & CHRISTOPHER LONG DISTANCE HURDLE   3m   (Good)   Ascot
28 Mar   1st: £ 13,720, 2nd: £ 5,136, 3rd: £ 2,468, 4th: £ 1,076

1-	PRAGADA	9-11-03	P Scudamore	M C Pipe	5/1
2-	TRAPPER JOHN	8-11-10	C F Swan	M F Morris (Ire)	9/4 F
3-	SWEET GLOW	5-11-03	G McCourt	M C Pipe	16/1
4-	MUDAHIM	6-11-10	D Tegg	C D Broad	33/1
5-	BURGOYNE	6-11-03	L Wyer	M H Easterby	4/1
6-	SECRET FOUR	6-11-03	H Davies	R Akehurst	16/1
7-	CHIRKPAR	5-11-10	L Cusack	J S Bolger (Ire)	4/1
8-	RUSTLE	10-11-10	R Dunwoody	N J Henderson	20/1
9-	HOLY JOE	10-11-03	J Osborne	A J Wilson	20/1
0-	BATTALION	8-11-10	G Bradley	C P E Brooks	33/1

ALSO: P: Don Keydrop, Theo's Fella

12 Ran DISTANCES: ½, nk, nk, 6, 6, 15, 25, 10   **TIME:** 5m 43.3s (+12.3s)

91	MOLE BOARD	9-11-03	J Osborne	J A B Old	6/1
90	BATTALION	6-11-07	B de Haan	C P E Brooks	10/3
89	Abandoned - snow				
88	GAYE BRIEF	11-12-02	D Browne	Mrs M Rimell	14/1
87	MRS MUCK	6-11-02	P Scudamore	N Twiston Davies	9/4
86	GAYE BRIEF	9-12-02	P Scudamore	Mrs M Rimell	4/1
85	BAJAN SUNSHINE	6-12-02	P Scudamore	M Tate	4/1
84	ALASTOR O MAVROS	5-11-03	H Davies	J Gifford	9/1
83	SANDALAY	5-11-03	P Charlton	P Cundell	8/1
82	GAYE CHANCE	7-11-12	P Scudamore	Mrs M Rimell	7/4

---

56 MARTELL CUP CHASE   3m 1f   (Good)   Liverpool
2 Apr   1st: £ 23,065, 2nd: £ 8,625, 3rd: £ 4,137, 4th: £ 1,796

1-	KINGS FOUNTAIN	9-11-09	A Tory	K C Bailey	11/4 F
2-	TIPPING TIM	7-11-05	C Llewellyn	N Twiston-Davies	14/1
3-	SPARKLING FLAME	8-11-05	R Dunwoody	N J Henderson	11/2
4-	MR ENTERTAINER	9-11-05	G Bradley	N A Gaselee	9/1
5-	AQUILIFER	12-11-05	P Scudamore	M C Pipe	13/2
U-	ARCTIC CALL	9-11-05	M Richards	O Sherwood	5/1
U-	HENRY MANN	9-11-05	G McCourt	S Christian	6/1
U-	NORTON'S COIN	11-11-05	A Maguire	S G Griffiths	14/1

ALSO: ---

8 Ran DISTANCES: 10, sh, 15, 12   **TIME:** 6m 26.6s (+15.6s)

91	AQUILIFER	11-11-05	R Dunwoody	M C Pipe	11/2
90	TOBY TOBIAS	8-11-09	M Pitman	Mrs J Pitman	1/1 F
89	YAHOO	8-11-05	T Morgan	J A C Edwards	5/1
88	DESERT ORCHID	9-11-05	S Sherwood	D R C Elsworth	3/1
87	WAYWARD LAD	12-11-05	G McCourt	Mrs M Dickinson	7/1
86	BEAU RANGER	8-11-05	H Davies	J Thorne	40/1
85	WAYWARD LAD	10-11-05	J Francome	Mrs M Dickinson	6/1
84	ROYAL BOND	11-11-05	T Taaffe	A Moore Ire	11/2

First run in 1984

57 JOHN HUGHES MEMORIAL H'CAP CHASE   2m 6f   (Soft)   Liverpool
2 Apr   1st: £ 17,725, 2nd: £ 5,336, 3rd: £ 2,583, 4th: £ 1,206

1-	THE ANTARTEX	9-10-02	R Dunwoody	G W Richards	33/1
2-	CAPTAIN MOR	10-10-06	C Grant	W A Stephenson	16/1
3-	STRONG GOLD	9-10-04	M Bowlby	Mrs J Pitman	14/1
4-	INTERIM LIB	9-10-04	Mr Bradburne	Mrs S Bradburne	25/1
5-	WREKIN HILL	10-10-00	K Johnson	W A Stephenson	20/1
6-	EIGHT SPRINGS	11-10-00	P Scudamore	M C Pipe	12/1
7-	SIRRAH JAY	12-11-09	A Maguire	G B Balding	12/1
8-	RONANS BIRTHDAY	10-10-00	C Maude	P J Hobbs	12/1
9-	BISHOPS HALL	6-10-04	C F Swan	H De Bromhead (I)	12/1
0-	SKINNHILL	8-10-00	M Fitzgerald	T Thompson Jones	50/1

ALSO: Another Schedule, Blue Dart, Red Columbia, Artic Teal, Technics;
B: Elfast, Golden Freeze; **F:** J-J-Henry, Shannagary, Folk Dance,
R: Butlers Pet; **U:** Latent Talent, Tom Bir, Solidasarock, Ainsty Fox,
Willowson

26 Ran DISTANCES: nk, 5, 2½, nk, 1, 5, 1½, 8, 5 **TIME:** 5m 39.3s (+7.3s)

91	J-J-HENRY	12-10-10	Ms A Farrell	P Beaumont	11/1
90	WONT BE GONE LONG	8-10-02	R Dunwoody	N J Henderson	25/1
89	VILLIERSTOWN	10-11-10	S Sherwood	W A Stephenson	5/2 F
88	WIGGBURN	9-10-02	M Williams	Mrs A R Hewitt	12/1
87	STRATH LEADER	9-11-10	T Morgan	J A C Edwards	12/1
86	GLENRUE	9-10-02	R Dunwoody	T Casey	20/1
85	SMITHS MAN	7-10-02	M Perrett	Mrs J Pitman	10/1
84	FABULOUS	11-10-00	A Stringer	J S Wilson	33/1
83	TIEPOLINO	11-10-04	H Davies	K Bishop	16/1
82	BEACON TIME	8-10-09	K Mooney	F Walwyn	13/2

58 GLENLIVET ANNIVERSARY HURDLE   2m   (Good)   Liverpool
2 Apr   1st: £ 21,580, 2nd: £ 8,112, 3rd: £ 2,926, 4th: £ 1,742

1-	SALWAN	11-00-00	Stronge R	P J Bevan	5/1 F
2-	STAUNCH FRIEND	11-00-00	S Smith Eccles	M H Tompkins	5/1 F
3-	ABSALOM'S LADY	10-09-00	A Maguire	G B Balding	8/1
4-	QUALITAIR SOUND	11-00-00	J J Quinn	J F Bottomley	10/1
5-	GOOD PROFILE	11-04-00	L Wyer	G Moore	5/1 F
6-	NOVELLO ALLEGRO	11-00-00	C F Swan	N Meade (Ire)	5/1 F
7-	PARIS OF TROY	11-00-00	C Llewellyn	N Twiston-Davies	18/1
8-	DIAMOND CUT	11-00-00	P Scudamore	M C Pipe	10/1
9-	GALLATEEN	11-00-00	N Doughty	G W Richards	20/1
0-	KASHAN	11-00-00	R Dunwoody	N J Henderson	20/1

ALSO: Mizyan; **P:** Namaste, Iwan

13 Ran DISTANCES: 3½, 2, 2, 8, 10, 6, 1, 12, 12   **TIME:** 3m 54.2s (+5.2s)

91	MONTPELIER LAD	4-11-00	N Doughty	G Richards	9/1
90	SYBILLIN	4-11-00	D Byrne	J G FitzGerald	25/1
89	VAYRUA	4-11-00	M Perrett	G Harwood	12/1
88	ROYAL ILLUSION	4-11-00	M Hammond	G M Moore	9/1
87	ALDINO	4-11-00	S Sherwood	O Sherwood	11/1
86	DARK RAVEN	4-11-00	T Carmody	D Weld Ire	7/1
85	HUMBERSIDE LADY	4-10-09	M Dwyer	G Huffer	15/2
84	AFZAL	4-11-00	M CcCourt	R Hollinshead	9/1
83	BENFEN	4-11-00	A Brown	M H Easterby	16/1
82	PRINCE BLESS	4-11-00	M O'Halloran	Mrs N Smith	12/1

```
59 MUMM MELLING CHASE                    2m 4f    (Good)    Liverpool
3 Apr     1st: £ 42,341, 2nd: £ 14,575, 3rd: £ 7,062
```

1-	REMITTANCE MAN	8-11-10	R Dunwoody	N J Henderson	4/9 F
2-	EDBERG	8-11-10	A Orkney	J H Johnson	25/1
3-	PAT'S JESTER	9-11-10	N Doughty	G Richards	9/2
F-	UNCLE ERNIE	7-11-10	M Dwyer	J G FitzGerald	11/2

ALSO: ---

```
4 Ran  DISTANCES: 8, 20                  TIME: 5m 10.9s (+17.9s)
```

91	Blazing Walker	07-11-10	C Grant	W A Stephenson	5-1

First run in 1991

```
60 MUMM MILDMAY NOVICES' CHASE           3m 1f    (Good)    Liverpool
3 Apr     1st: £ 21,948, 2nd: £ 8,228, 3rd: £ 3,964, 4th: £ 1,739
```

1-	BRADBURY STAR	7-11-09	E Murphy	J T Gifford	6/4 F
2-	JODAMI	7-11-06	P A Farrell	P Beaumont	11/2
3-	RUN FOR FREE	8-11-06	P Scudamore	M C Pipe	9/4
4-	REAL CLASS	9-11-03	N Doughty	G W Richards	20/1
5-	VIRIDIAN	7-11-03	M M Lynch	Mrs A L M King	33/1
F-	SHELTON ABBEY	6-11-03	C Grant	W A Stephenson	50/1
F-	CALABRESE	7-11-03	R Dunwoody	N J Henderson	7/1

ALSO: ---

```
7 Ran  DISTANCES: ¾, 7, dist, 12         TIME: 6m 22.3s (+11.3s)
```

91	SPARKLING FLAME	7-11-09	R Dunwoody	N J Henderson	4/1 F
90	ROYAL ATHLETE	7-11-09	M Pitman	Mrs J Pitman	5/2 F
89	SWARDEAN	7-11-03	B Dowling	R Lee	16/1
88	DELIUS	10-11-03	B Dowling	R Lee	9/1
87	AGAINST THE GRAIN	6-11-03	R Dunwoody	D Nicholson	8/1
86	STEARSBY	7-11-06	G Bradley	Mrs J Pitman	11/4
85	RHYME'N'REASON	6-11-03	G Bradley	D Murray-Smith	11/8 F
84	BARON BLAKNEY	7-11-06	Mr O Sherwood	M C Pipe	14/1
83	EVERETT	8-11-09	S Shilston	F Walwyn	7/2
82	BURROUGH HILL LAD	6-11-05	P Tuck	Mrs J Pitman	9/1

61 MARTELL FOXHUNTERS' CHASE 2m 6f (Good) Liverpool
3 Apr 1st: £ 9,359, 2nd: £ 2,823, 3rd: £ 1,370, 4th: £ 644

1-	GEE-A	13-12-00	Mr P Murphy	G A Hubbard	66/1
2-	RAISE AN ARGUMENT	13-12-00	Mr A Sansome	Mrs J Docker	11/1
3-	GLENAVEY	11-12-00	Mr P Hacking	Michael Roberts	20/1
4-	LISLARY LAD	12-12-00	Mr T Jones	Lee Bowles	16/1
5-	HARLEY	12-12-00	Mr McCain Jr	Miss J Eaton	12/1
6-	BARTRES	13-12-00	Mr J Durkan	D Murray Smith	22/1
7-	DOUBLE TURN	11-12-00	Mr H-Jones	J R Jenkins	50/1
8-	PROVERBIAL LUCK	8-12-00	Mr J Greenall	Miss C Saunders	66/1
9-	AHERLOW	12-12-00	Mr Hollowell	Kerry Hollowell	100/1
0-	ANDREW	9-12-00	Mr J Bradburne	G McGuinness	100/1

ALSO: Risk A Bet, Katesville, Krystle Saint, Ardesse, Lodato, Corked,
B: Rig Steel, Polygonum; **F:** Couture Color, Dromore Castle, Rushing Wild,
Strands Of Gold, Broad Beam, Paddy Hayton, Pastoral Pride; **P:** No Escort;
R: Queensway Boy; **U:** Bob Tisdall, Lordy Boy.

29 Ran DISTANCES: 1, 1, nk, 10, 6, 6, 7, 2½, 1½, **TIME:** 5m 43s (+11s)

91	DOUBLE TURN	10-12-00	Mr P H Jones	J R Jenkins	100/1
90	LEAN AR AGHAIDH	13-12-00	Mr D Gray	S Mellor	5/1 F
89	CALL COLLECT	8-12-00	Mr R Martin	J Parkes	5/1
88	NEWNHAM	11-12-00	Mr S Andrews	Michael A Johns	50/1
87	BORDER BURG	10-12-00	Mr A Hill	J Delahooke	7/2
86	ELIOGARTY	11-12-00	Ms C Beasley	D Murray Smith	11/1
85	CITY BOY	10-12-00	Mr T T Jones	Mrs J Mann	4/1
84	GAYLE WARNING	10-12-00	Mr A Dudgeon	J Dudgeon	85/40
83	ATHA CLIATH	8-12-00	Mr W Mullins	P Mullins Ire	5/1
82	LONE SOLDIER	10-12-00	Mr P Greenall	J Docker	25/1

62 MARTELL AINTREE HANDICAP CHASE 2m (Good) Liverpool
4 Apr 1st: £ 18,368, 2nd: £ 6,868, 3rd: £ 3,294, 4th: £ 1,429

1-	KATABATIC	9-12-00	S McNeill	Andrew Turnell	6/5 F
2-	MASTER RAJH	8-11-02	M M Lynch	J Chugg	7/2
3	REDUNDANT PAL	9-11-02	C O'Dwyer	P Mullins (Ire)	3/1
4-	MOMENT OF TRUTH	8-10-07	B Storey	P Monteith	6/1

ALSO: ---

4 Ran DISTANCES: 3½, 1½, 1 **TIME:** 4m 2.1s (+12.1s)

91	BLITZKREIG	8-10-13	T Carmody	E J O'Grady	4/1 F
90	NOHALMDUN	9-10-07	L Wyer	M H Easterby	11/1
89	FERODA	8-10-07	T J Taaffe	A L T Moore Ire	9/1
88	PRIDEAUX BOY	10-10-07	A Webb	C G Roach	25/1
87	SEA MERCHANT	10-10-07	R Lamb	W A Stephenson	9/1
86	KATHIES LAD	9-10-13	S S Eccles	A Jarvis	11/8 F
85	KATHIES LAD	8-11-07	S S Eccles	A Jarvis	6/5 F
84	LITTLE BAY	9-11-07	J Francome	G Richards	11/4
83	ARTIFICE	12-11-00	P Scudamore	J Thorne	9/1
82	LITTLE BAY	7-10-07	J J O'Neill	G Richards	14/1

62 . Big Race Results

63 MARTELL AINTREE HURDLE 2m 4f (Good) Liverpool
4 Apr 1st: £ 26,948, 2nd: £ 10,083, 3rd: £ 4,841, 4th: £ 2,106

1-	MORLEY STREET	8-11-07	R Dunwoody	G B Balding	4/5 F
2-	MINORETTES GIRL	7-11-02	A Mullins	P Mullins (Ire)	11/2
3-	FOREST SUN	7-11-07	Richard Guest	G B Balding	8/1
4-	BANK VIEW	7-11-07	G McCourt	N Tinkler	11/2
5-	PROPERO	7-11-07	E Murphy	J T Gifford	11/1
6-	VALIANT BOY	6-11-07	Mr S Lyons	S E Kettlewell	50/1

ALSO: ---

6 Ran DISTANCES: ½, 10, 10, 15, 12   **TIME:** 4m 46.4s (+6.4s)

91	MORLEY STREET	7-11-07	J Frost	G B Balding	11/8 F
90	MORLEY STREET	6-11-06	J Frost	G B Balding	4/5 F
89	BEECH ROAD	7-11-09	R Guest	G B Balding	10/1
88	CELTIC CHIEF	5-11-06	R Dunwoody	Mrs M Rimell	4/5 F
87	AONOCH	8-11-09	Jacqui Oliver	Mrs S Oliver	5/2
86	AONOCH	7-11-09	J Duggan	Mrs S Oliver	16/1
85	BAJAN SUNSHINE	6-11-06	P Scudamore	M Tate	11/1
84	DAWN RUN	6-11-06	A Mullins	P Mullins Ire	4/6 F
83	GAYE BRIEF	6-11-11	R Linley	Mrs M Rimell	11/8 F
82	DARING RUN	7-11-09	Mr T Walsh	P McCreery Ire	2/1 F

64 MARTELL GRAND NATIONAL HANDICAP CHASE 4m 4f (Good) Liverpool
4 Apr 1st: £ 99,943, 2nd: £ 37,468, 3rd: £ 18,379, 4th: £ 7,967

1-	PARTY POLITICS	8-10-07	C Llewellyn	N A Gaselee	14/1
2-	ROMANY KING	8-10-03	Richard Guest	G B Balding	16/1
3-	LAURA'S BEAU	8-10-00	C O'Dwyer	F Berry (Ire)	12/1
4-	DOCKLANDS EXPRESS	10-11-02	P Scudamore	K C Bailey	15/2 F
5-	TWIN OAKS	12-11-07	N Doughty	G W Richards	9/1
6-	JUST SO	9-10-02	S Burrough	P F Nicholls	50/1
7-	OLD APPLEJACK	12-10-00	A Orkney	J H Johnson	35/1
8-	OVER THE ROAD	11-10-00	R Supple	John R Upson	22/1
9-	STAY ON TRACKS	10-10-00	C Grant	W A Stephenson	16/1

ALSO: Cool Ground, Ghofar, Forest Ranger, Whats The Crack, Rubika, Golden Minstrel, Auntie Dot, Roc De Prince, Mighty Falcon, Radical Lady, Willsford, Team Challenge, Sirrah Jay; **F:** Cloney Grange, Mister Ed, Brown Windsor; **P:** Seagram, Huntworth, Karakter Reference, Hotplate, Royal Battery, Why So Hasty, Omerta; **R:** Bonanza Boy, New Halen, Golden Fox, Stearsby, Kittinger; **U:** Rowlandsons Jewels, Honeybeer Mead, Rawhide

40 Ran DISTANCES: 2½, 15, 8, 2, hd, 3, 4, 2½, 4 **TIME:** 9m 6.3s (+10.3s)

91	SEAGRAM	11-10-06	N Hawke	D H Barons	12/1
90	MR FRISK	11-10-06	Mr M Armytage	K C Bailey	16/1
89	LITTLE POLVEIR	12-10-03	J Frost	G B Balding	28/1
88	RHYME 'N' REASON	9-11-00	B Powell	D R C Elsworth	10/1
87	MAORI VENTURE	11-10-13	S Knight	A Turnell	28/1
86	WEST TIP	9-10-11	R Dunwoody	M Oliver	15/2 F
85	LAST SUSPECT	11-10-05	H Davies	T Forster	50/1
84	HALLO DANDY	10-10-02	N Doughty	G W Richards	13/1
83	CORBIERE	8-11-04	B de Haan	Mrs J Pitman	13/1
82	GRITTAR	9-11 05	C Saunders	F Gilman	10/1

65 SCOTTISH CHAMPION HURDLE   2m   (Good)   Ayr
10 Apr   1st: £ 7,644, 2nd: £ 2,893, 3rd: £ 1,416, 4th: £   646

1-	GRANVILLE AGAIN	6-11-10	P Scudamore	M C Pipe	4/7 F
2-	JINXY JACK	8-11-06	G McCourt	G W Richards	12/1
3-	FIDWAY	7-11-10	S Smith Eccles	T Thomson Jones	5/2
4-	WINNIE THE WITCH	8-10-11	D Bridgwater	K S Bridgwater	15/2
5-	MARLINGFORD	5-11-06	D Morris	Mrs J Jordan	66/1

ALSO: ---

5 Ran DISTANCES: 5, 2, 4, 20   **TIME:** 3m 35.2s (-3.8s)

91	PRECIOUS BOY	5-11-02	L Wyer	M O'Neill	9/2
90	SAYPAREE	5-10-07	J Lower	M C Pipe	11/2
89	ALDINO	6-12-00	S Sherwood	O Sherwood	13/2
88	PAT'S JESTER	5-11-01	B Storey	R Allan	5/1
87	POSITIVE	5-10-08	P Croucher	K Bailey	11/2
86	RIVER CEIRIOG	5-10-09	S S Eccles	N Henderson	4/1
85	SAILER'S DANCE	5-11-01	J Duggan	F Winter	5/2
84	RUSHMOOR	6-10-13	P Scudamore	R Peacock	3/1
83	ROYAL VULCAN	5-11-13	P Scudamore	N Callaghan	7/2
82	GAY GEORGE	6-11-07	W Smith	F Walwyn	4/6 F

---

66 WILLIAM HILL SCOTTISH NATIONAL H'CAP CHASE   4m 120y   (Good)   Ayr
11 Apr   1st: £ 36,950, 2nd: £ 13,917, 3rd: £ 6,758, 4th: £ 3,023

1-	CAPTAIN DIBBLE	7-11-00	P Scudamore	N Twiston-Davies	9/1
2-	DALKEY SOUND	9-11-07	P Niven	Mrs G R Reveley	12/1
3-	OFF THE BRU	7-10-02	Mr Bradburne	Mrs S Bradburne	200/1
4-	MERRY MASTER	8-10-00	Gee Armytage	R C Armytage	12/1
5-	BORACEVA	9-11-01	Richard Guest	G B Balding	11/1
6-	ALL JEFF	8-11-01	G Bradley	C P E Brooks	20/1
7-	RUBIKA	9-10-08	S Earle	S Mellor	22/1
8-	VIKING ROCKET	8-10-00	B Storey	C Parker	33/1
9-	BOW HANDY MAN	10-09-07	P Waggott	Denys Smith	100/1
0-	BLUE DART	12-10-02	H Davies	Capt T A Forster	100/1

ALSO: Jelupe, Smooth Escort, Carousel Rocket; **P:** Combermere, Fifth
Amendment, Shoon Wind, Sire Nantais, Plenty Crack, Tom Troubadour;
U: Third In Line, Sheer Steel

21 Ran DISTANCES: 8, 6, 4, nk, sh, hd, 4, 1½, 25 **TIME:** 8m 21.9s (+20.9s)

91	KILLONE ABBEY	8-10-00	C Grant	W A Stephenson	40/1
90	FOUR TRIX	9-10-00	D Byrne	G Richards	25/1
89	ROLL-A-JOINT	11-10-00	B Powell	C L Popham	4/1
88	MIGHTY MARK	9-10-04	B Storey	F T Walton	9/1
87	LITTLE POLVEIR	10-10-01	P Scudamore	J Edwards	12/1
86	HARDY LAD	9-10-00	M Hammond	B Wilkinson	28/1
85	ANDROMA	8-10-00	M Dwyer	J FitzGerald	11/1
84	ANDROMA	7-10-00	M Dwyer	J FitzGerald	7/1
83	CANTON	9-10-02	K Whyte	N Crump	16/6
82	COCKLE STRAND	9-09-11	D Dutton	K Oliver	9/1

67 S. WALES SHOWERS SILVER TROPHY (CHASE)   2m 4f   (Good)   Cheltenham
15 Apr   1st: £ 15,325, 2nd: £ 5,797, 3rd: £ 2,836, 4th: £ 1,291

1-	KATABATIC	9-11-04	L Harvey	Andrew Turnell	8/13F
2-	WATERLOO BOY	9-11-07	R Dunwoody	D Nicholson	5/2
3-	GOLDEN FREEZE	10-11-00	M Pitman	Mrs J Pitman	16/1
4-	NORTON'S COIN	11-11-04	G McCourt	S G Griffiths	7/1

ALSO: ---

4 Ran DISTANCES: 8, 8, 25   **TIME:** 5m 25.5s (+19.5s)

91	NORTON'S COIN	10-11-04	G McCourt	S G Griffiths	9/4
90	BARNBROOK AGAIN	9-11-10	H Davies	D R C Elsworth	6/4 F
89	NORTON'S COIN	8-11-00	R Dunwoody	S G Griffiths	20/1
88	BEAU RANGER	10-11-00	P Scudamore	M C Pipe	11/10 F
87	DUKE OF MILAN	10-10-02	S Sherwood	N A Gaslee	11/2
86	MR MOORAKER	9-11-02	B Powell	L G Kennard	7/2 JF

First run in 1986

---

68 WELSH CHAMPION HURDLE   2m   (Good)   Chepstow
20 Apr   1st: £ 8,358, 2nd: £ 2,520, 3rd: £ 1,222, 4th: £ 573

1-	DON VALENTINO	7-11-10	M Pitman	Mrs J Pitman	10/1
2-	GAY RUFFIAN	6-11-10	D J Burchell	D Burchell	9/1
3-	DIS TRAIN	8-11-06	G Bradley	Mrs J Pitman	25/1
4-	WINNIE THE WITCH	8-11-01	D Bridgwater	K S Bridgwater	7/2
5-	BANK VIEW	7-11-06	G McCourt	N Tinkler	7/4 F
6-	ANNICOMBE RUN	8-11-01	W McFarland	R Lee	14/1
P-	SAYPAREE	7-11-06	J Lower	M C Pipe	2/1

ALSO: ---

7 Ran DISTANCES: 3, 1, 12, 1, 12   **TIME:** 4m 0.3s (+13.3s)

91	WONDER MAN	6-11-10	M Pitman	Mrs J Pitman	4/1
90	BEECH ROAD	8-12-01	R Guest	G B Balding	1/3 F
89	CELTIC SHOT	6-11-06	P Scudamore	C P E Brooks	1/7 F
88	PAST GLORIES	5-11-06	P A Farrell	C W C Elsey	8/1
87	HIGH KNOWL	4-11-00	J Lower	M Pipe	6/1
86	Abandoned - waterlogged course				
85	BROWNE'S GAZETTE	7-11-13	Mr D Browne	Mrs M Dickinson	8/13F
84	RA NOVA	5-11-08	M Perrett	Mrs N Kennedy	11/10F
83	ROYAL VULCAN	5-11-13	D Goulding	N Callaghan	9/4 F
82	EKBALCO	6-11-09	J J O'Neill	R Fisher	2/1 F

69 WHITBREAD GOLD CUP HANDICAP CHAS E   **3m 5f**   **(Good)**   **Sandown**
25 Apr   **1st: £ 57,400, 2nd: £ 21,400, 3rd: £ 10,400, 4th: £ 4,400**

1-	TOPSHAM BAY	9-10-01	H Davies	D H Barons	9/2
2-	ARCTIC CALL	9-11-07	J Osborne	O Sherwood	9/2
3-	THE LEGGETT	9-10-00	R Bellamy	M C Pipe	20/1
4-	ROWLANDSONS JEWELS	11-10-00	A Maguire	D Murray Smith	14/1
5-	PACO'S BOY	7-09-11	J F Titley	M C Pipe	25/1
6-	STAY ON TRACKS	10-10-00	C Grant	W A Stephenson	14/1
7-	MR FRISK	13-10-06	Mr M Armytage	K C Bailey	25/1
8-	MIRAGE DAY	9-10-00	N Williamson	J A C Edwards	100/1
9-	TIPPING TIM	7-10-00	C Llewellyn	N Twiston-Davies	6/1
0-	BROWN WINDSOR	10-11-00	R Dunwoody	N A Twiston-Davies	3/1 F

ALSO: Espy

11 Ran DISTANCES: 2½, 2, 8, 8, 2, 3, 8, 2   **TIME:** 7m 19.8s (+7.8s)

91	DOCKLANDS EXPRESS	9-10-03	A Tory	K C Bailey	4/1JF
90	MR FRISK	11-10-05	Mr M Armytage	K C Bailey	9/2 F
89	BROWN WINDSOR	7-10-00	M Bowlby	N J Henderson	12/1
88	DESERT ORCHID	9-11-11	S Sherwood	D Elsworth	6/1
87	LEAN AR AGHAIDH	10-09-10	G Landau	S Mellor	6/1
86	PLUNDERING	9-10-06	S Sherwood	F T Winter	14/1
85	BY THE WAY	7-10-00	R Earnshaw	Mrs M Dickinson	11/2
84	SPECIAL CARGO	11-11-02	K Mooney	F Walwyn	8/1
83	DRUMLARGAN	9-10-10	Mr F Codd	E O'Grady	11/1
82	SHADY DEAL	9-10-00	R Rowe	J T Gifford	4/1

70 SWINTON HANDICAP HURDLE   **2m**   **(Good)**   **Haydock**
4 May   **1st: £ 17,425, 2nd: £ 6,602, 3rd: £ 3,238, 4th: £ 1,483**

1-	BITOFABANTER	5-11-01	T J Taaffe	A L T Moore (Ire)	14/1
2-	CASTLE SECRET	6-11-05	D J Burchell	D Burchell	25/1
3-	FLAKEY DOVE	6-11-03	D Tegg	R J Price	6/1 F
4-	MISS BOBBY BENNETT	5-09-13	M Foster	M C Pipe	7/1
5-	NINEPINS	5-11-05	R Dunwoody	A L T Moore (Ire)	13/1
6-	BELAFONTE	5-10-05	S Mackey	R J Holder	14/1
7-	PARIS OF TROY	4-09-11	D Bridgwater	N Twiston-Davies	33/1
8-	PERSIAN HOUSE	5-09-09	B Dalton	J M Jefferson	33/1
9-	EGYPT MILL PRINCE	6-11-04	M Pitman	Mrs J Pitman	16/1
0-	CHAMPAGNE LAD	6-11-02	P Hide	J T Gifford	33/1

ALSO: Fox Chapel, The Slater, Bottles, Qualitair Sound, Ketti, Derab, Love Anew, Liadett; **F:** Cheerful Times; **U:** Sagaman, Kaher, Shu Fly

22 Ran DISTANCES: 1, 4, 1, 2½, 5, 2½, 5, nk, 1½   **TIME:** 3m 45.2s (+2.2s)

91	WINNIE THE WITCH	7-10-02	D Bridgwater	K S Bridgwater	8/1
90	SYBILLIN	4-10-01	D Byrne	J G FitzGerald	8/1
89	STATE JESTER	6-10-00	J J Quinn	C W C Elsey	14/1
88	PAST GLORIES	5-11-09	P A Farrell	C W C Elsey	16/1
87	INLANDER	6-10-08	S S Eccles	R Akehurst	4/1
86	PRIDEAUX BOY	8-11-02	M Bowlby	G Roach	15/2
85	CORPORAL CLINGER	6-10-03	P Leach	M Pipe	11/2
84	BAJAN SUNSHINE	5-10-13	P Scudamore	M Tate	6/1
83	Abandoned - waterlogged course				
82	SECRET BALLOT	8-10-03	A Turnell	R Turnell	10/1

AMENDED RESULTS

21* A MILDMAY P CAZALET MEM. HCP CHASE 3m 5f 18y 4 January Sandown
On The Twist was disqualified from 1st place for carrying the incorrect
weight. Arctic Call, Givus a Buck, Rowlandsons Jewels and Mr Frisk were
promoted to 1st, 2nd, 3rd and 4th places respectively.

40* BONUSPRINT STAYERS' HURDLE 3m 1f 10 March Cheltenham
Trapper John was disqualified from 2nd place for carrying the incorrect
weight. Ubu II, Crystal Spirit, Burgoyne and Randolph Place were promoted
to 2nd, 3rd, 4th and 5th places respectively.

INDEX TO RUNNERS

Bold Race Numbers denote a win.

68 . Big Race Results Index

70 . Big Race Results Index

4 . THE CLASS OF '92

by

George Rae
(The Times)

STAYING CHASERS

The king is dead, or at least retired, but where is his successor?

Desert Orchid, for so long the cornerstone of the staying chasers, was retired after his attempt to win a fifth King George VI Chase at Kempton ended in a fall. Brave though his challenge had been, age was the opponent he could not defeat.

In those days around Christmas, the succession had looked crystal clear. Carvill's Hill, having joined Martin Pipe from Jim Dreaper in Ireland, had looked every inch the champion in waiting when he destroyed his field in the Welsh National at Chepstow.

"That performance made him the leading chaser of the season," Christopher Mordaunt, the Jockey Club's senior National Hunt handicapper, said. "It put him on a mark of 175, which turned out to be 8lb clear of the next best, Remittance Man.

"To put Carvill's Hill's rating in context, the highest mark I gave Desert Orchid during his career was 182."

But no sooner had Carvill's Hill announced his

undisputed arrival in the top flight than he had gone again. Although he won the Hennessy Cognac Gold Cup at Leopardstown in February, his challenge for the Cheltenham Gold Cup was left in tatters in a race which will always be remembered for the "stalking horse" tactics of Golden Freeze.

Golden Freeze kept pace with Carvill's Hill to force him into jumping errors, and Carvill's Hill's flawed fencing did indeed become evident once more.

The sad postscript was not just that Carvill's Hill was beaten a very long way but that he injured himself so severely during the race that his career must be considered in jeopardy.

As Carvill's Hill slipped further behind at Cheltenham, the race developed into a relentless struggle between The Fellow, Cool Ground and Docklands Express, in which Cool Ground prevailed by a short head from The Fellow under an aggressive ride from Adrian Maguire. Docklands Express was another length away third.

Cool Ground ended the season rated 167, one pound ahead of The Fellow for whom this must have seemed like a bad case of deja vu.

A year earlier he had again lost out in a photo-finish, that time to Garrison Savannah, and for the second season running he ended the season rated 166, one pound ahead of Docklands Express.

He did, however have a victory in the King George VI Chase to his name, beating Docklands Express by a length and a half, with Remittance Man, probably a victim of stamina failure, another two lengths away third.

Garrison Savannah proved disappointing but still ended the season rated at 166. "Garrison Savannah was difficult to rate because he was so clearly out of sorts during the season," Mordaunt said. "I might well take another look at his handicap mark but the fact remains he is still a Gold Cup winner."

With Garrison Savannah needing to show a return to his best and Remittance Man not guaranteed to stay three miles and beyond, where is the new wearer of the staying chase crown to be found?

"Miinnehoma, the Sun Alliance Chase winner, was the best novice," Mordaunt said. "I have him on 147, not quite as high as Remittance Man (151) the previous year, but one would like to see him develop to take his place in the front rank."

In a wide-open year, there will be plenty to play for in the coming months.

TWO-MILE CHASERS

The scene for the two-mile division was set at Kempton Park on Boxing Day. After Remittance Man's defeat in the King George, Nicky Henderson decided to bring him back in distance. The decision was absolutely right, and the result spectacular.

He won a relatively minor race at Newbury before taking on Waterloo Boy and Katabatic in the Queen Mother Champion Chase over two miles at Cheltenham. Although Henderson feared a slow pace - Remittance Man is perhaps ideally suited by two and a half miles - his charge was to make no mistake.

Produced to lead at the last, he stayed on well up the hill to beat Katabatic, the winner the previous year, by a length with Waterloo Boy another three and a half lengths away third.

Remittance Man completed the season with a bloodless victory in the Mumm Melling Chase at Aintree over two and a half miles.

What now then for Remittance Man? Henderson has not ruled out further challenges for steeplechasing's great prizes at three miles and beyond, yet Remittance Man is clearly well suited by shorter distance.

"I am always a little saddened when connections are so keen to step horses up in distance," says Christopher Mordaunt. "Horses always seem to be being stretched to stay that bit farther.

"But I suppose that with the Cheltenham Gold Cup being the acknowledged highlight of the jumping season that becomes inevitable."

Katabatic was a case in point. He began the campaign with an impressive win over two miles, but on his next run, over three, he was comprehensively outpointed by Carvill's Hill and Aquilifer.

When returned to two miles at Cheltenham he was a different proposition, going down by only a length to Remittance Man. He added further emphatic wins at Aintree (two miles) and Cheltenham (two and a half miles).

Waterloo Boy was the archetypal two-miler. The sort of horse everyone would love to own, he ran with great consistency at the minimum trip, collecting four good races in mid-season, including the Castleford Chase at Wetherby and the Victor Chandler Chase at Ascot.

Although Remittance Man and Katabatic were a little too good for him, he was shrewdly campaigned by David Nicholson to make the very best of him.

Remittance Man was the best of the two-milers, with a rating of 167 (the second highest chaser overall behind Carvill's Hill). Just behind was Katabatic on 166, while Waterloo Boy, as if to underline his consistency, was on 163, the third year in succession he had been awarded that mark.

The disappointment of the season was Uncle Ernie (153), who failed to progress significantly from his second to Remittance Man in the Arkle Trophy of the previous year. It should be remembered, however, that his stable was short of its best form for much of the year and he may yet fulfil his promise.

On the rise, though, was My Young Man (156), six times a winner during the season. If he can continue to progress and Remittance Man and Katabatic seek their fortunes elsewhere he could be a force in the top races in the coming months.

And remember Blazing Walker? He missed the 1991/92 season but if he can be coaxed back to his top-class form of the previous term he will have a major say in the top prizes of 1992/93.

THE GRAND NATIONAL

When the weights for the Grand National were announced in February there was just one talking point: Carvill's Hill.

He was allotted 12st, a mark which some trainers felt gave him an unfair advantage. David Barons, trainer of the previous year's winner, Seagram, was one who believed his charge was far too close to Carvill's Hill in the weights.

But for Christopher Mordaunt, who compiles the National weights "by hand", rather than simply applying the runners' existing handicap ratings to the race, the issue was not so clear cut.

"Certainly on park-course ratings Carvill's Hill would have been long way clear of the rest," Mordaunt said, "but I didn't feel justified in giving Carvill's Hill 12st 7lb. My view was that he had not achieved as much as either Burrough Hill Lad or Desert Orchid when they were entered in the race, and I had given them 12st 5lb and 12st 2lb respectively. On that line of reasoning, he could not be allotted as much weight."

Sadly, the argument proved academic, as Carvill's Hill's season, and perhaps his career, lay in ruins after his Gold Cup defeat.

But as the Gold Cup effectively laid to rest Carvill's Hill Grand National participation, it produced the next subject for discussion. Cool Ground, the Gold Cup winner, was announced a runner at Aintree, following in the footsteps of Garrison Savannah the previous year.

And, like Garrison Savannah, he was, on paper at least, a handicap "snip". Had Mordaunt been able to employ the Cheltenham form in framing the National weights Cool Ground would have had more than 11st 11lb to carry.

But there the comparison with Garrison Savannah ended. Where Garrison Savannah had looked the likely winner jumping the last, only to be run out of it by Seagram on the dash to the line, Cool Ground gave his supporters only the faintest hope. With Martin Lynch replacing the Gold Cup-winning Maguire, who was injured, Cool Ground could manage only tenth.

Victory went to the impossibly appropriate Party Politics, landing a memorable success in the shadow of a General Election.

There was, however, rather more to recommend him than simply his name. Seconds in the Hennessy Gold Cup at Newbury and the Welsh National at Chepstow had shown him to be a good-class staying chaser, and the extreme distance of the National brought out the best in him.

Carl Llewellyn did everything right on the Nick Gaselee-trained chaser but it is impossible not to feel some sympathy for Andy Adams, Party Politics' regular rider, who was sidelined with a broken leg received in a fall at Doncaster some six weeks earlier.

Adams, although not one of the sport's leading lights, is a model of loyalty to the stable and it was the cruellest twist of fate that he should be deprived of his big moment.

Romany King, who was going so well he found himself in front rather earlier than ideal for him, could not regain the lead once Party Politics had surged to the front four fences from home and had to be content with a two and a half length second.

Laura's Beau and Docklands Express, the 15-2 favourite and, like Cool Ground, apparently well treated on his Gold Cup running, were third and fourth respectively.

Party Politics confirmed once more the trend of the National becoming the domain of the better handicappers. There would be little to choose between him and Seagram, the previous year's winner, although Mr Frisk, successful in 1990, would have a few pounds in hand of both of them.

But the critical point, and I make no apology for repeating it, is that the National has become a good race for punters despite its popular image as a lottery.

Horses running off 10st have a poor record and those backers who concentrate on the quality horses higher up the handicap have every chance of finding a winner at a decent price.

HURDLERS

On only his fourth run over hurdles, Royal Gait became the first novice since Doorknocker in 1956 to land the Champion Hurdle. It was a deserved, if belated, reward for his suffering a controversial disqualification after winning the Ascot Gold Cup in 1988, a decision which, even years later, is guaranteed to start an argument.

Royal Gait came to Cheltenham with wins in a novices' hurdle and a limited handicap, both at Nottingham, behind him. On paper he had plenty to find, but with questions asked about several of his rivals and undeniable quality on his side, he was sent off third favourite.

Approaching the last he delivered his challenge but had to dig deep to hold off Oh So Risky by half a length with Ruling a short head away third. Incredibly, the spectre of another disqualification loomed as Royal Gait had wandered on the run-in, but this time the stewards found in his favour. Justice, at last, had taken his side.

As Royal Gait's star rose, so Morley Street's fell. The defending champion, sent off as favourite, was never the force of a year earlier and had to make do with sixth place. He went on to win a third consecutive Martell Aintree Hurdle, but only after a sustained duel with Minorettes Girl. He looked some way short of the imposing champion he had once been.

The official ratings tell the same story. "I had Morley Street on 158, against 175 in his heyday," said Bill Paton-Smith, one of the Jockey Club handicappers responsible for the hurdlers.

"Royal Gait was the best of the season on 162 although that probably does not do him full justice," he added. "If he sustained the injury that kept him out for the rest of the season jumping the last at Cheltenham, then it was clearly a better performance than it looked.

"He is difficult to assess. He was a high-class Flat horse, has kept improving over hurdles and I hope he goes on again next season.

"Oh So Risky was next on 161 with Ruling and Granville Again jointly on 160."

If there was a hard luck story during the year it was Granville Again's fall at the second-last in the Champion when right in the firing line. Jockey Peter Scudamore was adamant Granville Again would have had a big say in the outcome, but he was at least recompensed by victory in the Scottish Champion Hurdle at Ayr the following month.

Kribensis, the 1990 Champion Hurdler, was a bitter disappointment. Michael Stoute had fought a race against time all season with the eight-year-old, who made his seasonal debut less than a month before finishing a distant last of the 14 finishers.

He is, in fact, a year younger than Royal Gait but will have to show a lot more if he is to regain his crown in 1993.

Nomadic Way came out best of the stayers, and a close second overall, on 161, on the strength of his win in the Stayers' Hurdle at Cheltenham.

Apart from the reappearance of Royal Gait, the hurdlers this coming season will have Carobee among them as a distinguished talking point.

Beaten only once in six starts, the David Nicholson-trained five-year-old ended the season with an emphatic four-length defeat of Halkopous, who was receiving 8lb, in the Seagram Top Novices' Hurdle at Aintree.

National Hunt bred, he has more scope to progress than most novices nowadays and looks the type to shake up the old guard. An interesting prospect indeed.

5 . WINNERS FOR 1992/93

by

Jack Millan
(Robin Goodfellow, Daily Mail)

INDEX TO HORSES

AL MUTAHM 4 b c   Form: 2123
Green Dancer(USA) - Musical Medicine (FR) (Margouillat (FR))

Al Mutahm's departure from Newmarket coincided with his
new trainer Jim Old's from Somerset to Barbury Castle, near
Swindon, in the Autumn of 1991, and neither has looked back
since.

No more than useful on the flat that year, this rangy, long-
striding gelding has shown big improvement to win a Group
Three contest over two miles as well as a twelve-furlong
handicap since joining Old.

And, between his latest two campaigns on the level, he
showed himself one of last season's best juvenile hurdlers,
winning only one of his four races over obstacles but
reaching places in the other three, including the Triumph
Hurdle.

Al Mutahm's best on the flat has been shown with plenty
of give in the ground, and he has not yet encountered really
testing conditions over jumps. When he does, he is liable to
be even more formidable than he was last winter. *(J. Old)*

BEACHY HEAD 4 gr g   Form: 111
Damister (USA) - No More Rosies (Warpath)

When Beachy Head was racing on the flat, there were times
when he looked less than enthusiastic, but his attitude since
his switch to hurdling could not have been more positive.

The occasional horse likes jumping so much that, as soon
as he has cleared one obstacle, he is looking for the next. Last
season, this agile grey was one of those, and he had all three
of his races in safe keeping long before the finish, recording
winning margins of 25, 20 and six lengths.

His best performance was produced on heavy going at
Ayr on his second appearance, when the demoralised runner-
up was a useful juvenile in Gallateen. But give in the ground
is important to Beachy Head only because of the greater
emphasis it places on stamina.

When he wound up his first N.H. campaign on the same

course, he tackled half a mile more than the minimum trip and finished full of running. (*C. Thornton*)

BETTER TIMES AHEAD 6 ro g   Form: 305402P
Scallywag - City's Sister (Maystreak)

A lot was expected of this attractive roan last season, but he failed in seven attempts to add to his three successes of the previous winter and got into the first three only twice.

Last season was one in which most of Gordon Richards' horses were never quite right, however, and Better Times Ahead had a blood disorder more than once.

So, as Greystoke's early results have suggested that the yard is now problem-free, it would be no surprise to see him live up to the great promise of his first season.

On an attractive handicap mark as a consequence of last term's disappointments, Better Times Ahead is probably capable of winning stayers' handicap hurdles, especially when the ground is taking at least a good cut, and he may be seen in that sort of contest in the near future.

It has always been as a chaser that he has been regarded, however, and he may well develop into one of this season's better staying novices. (*G.W. Richards*)

BRADBURY STAR 7 b g   Form: 11U111121
Torus - WARE Princess (Crash Course)

The only race over fences in which Bradbury Star has got round and been beaten has been the Sun Alliance Novices' Chase, and even in that ultimate test of staying newcomers his losing margin was only half-a-length.

So he is one of several relatively inexperienced performers likely to be challenging for this season's major awards over the big jumps.

With uncertainty clouding the future for Carvill's Hill and Blazing Walker, and doubts about the stamina of Remittance Man and Katabatic, the biggest barriers between the rising generation and success in events like the King George VI Chase and the Gold Cup seem to be the first two home in last

December's running of the Kempton feature, The Fellow and Docklands Express, and the rival who only just held them off at Cheltenham, Cool Ground.

And, although those three are officially rated about a stone and a half in front of the likes of Bradbury Star and his Sun Alliance Chase conqueror Miinnehoma, even the Jockey Club Handicapper would surely be tempted by an offer of even-money Josh Gifford's gelding in a match on those terms with any of the principals in last March's title decider.

With 25 races over hurdles as well as nine chases behind him, Bradbury Star is much more experienced than Miinnehoma. But the Findon gelding is also the younger by two years, and for that reason he is the one likely to make the greater improvement.

Effective on all going except the most testing, he stays beyond three miles but also has another gear, and must be a major contender for any target he is aimed at in the coming months. *(J. Gifford)*

BURGOYNE 6 b g   Form: 122245
Ardross -Love Match (USA) (Affiliate(USA))

In the season before last, doubts about Burgoyne's enthusiasm were widespread following several second placings in races he had seemed to have at his mercy.

But his real problem was an inability to accelerate, and, once he settled down to long-distance racing last winter, he quickly silenced his detractors.

Admittedly, he failed to add to gains made impressively in a Cheltenham handicap on his return to action, and he followed that performance by running-up in three consecutive races. But he was invariably taking on the best and never failed to perform with distinction.

Unfortunately, that consistent record at high level guarantees Burgoyne crippling weights in handicaps. So, as it looks as though he is not quite up to matching the best at levels in races like the Stayers' Hurdle, an early graduation to fences is expected, and that could be the making of him.

A rangy gelding with a big stride, he is a quick, clean jumper of hurdles and ought to adapt well to the bigger fences.

Any going apart from firm seems to suit him. (*M.H. Easterby*)

CAB ON TARGET 6 br g   Form: 1112
Strong Gale -Smart Fashion (Carlburg)

Far from well after being beaten at odds-on at Kempton in February, Cab On Target did not appear again last season. Otherwise, there might have been a different result to the Stayers' Hurdle, or even to the Champion Hurdle, at the Cheltenham Festival.

In winning on his other three outings last term, Mary Reveley's imposing gelding included among his victims the first two to finish in the Cheltenham stamina-test.

Yet until his trainer found it impossible to get him ready for a return to action in March she still had not decided against a tilt at the shorter title event.

Cab On Target has never raced over less than two and a half miles over hurdles. But he does have a two-mile N.H. Flat race to his credit, and flashing finishing speed has characterised most of his efforts. So, with that final climb to help him, he could have been a Champion Hurdle contender.

In all probability, however, that will never be more than conjecture. This lengthy individual has always looked a chaser in the making, and the strong likelihood is that he will be racing over the big jumps before the season is far advanced. If so, he is likely to have few peers, over any distance, among the novice ranks.

He acts on just about any going. (*Mrs G.R. Reveley*)

CAROBEE 5 b g   Form: 131111
Kings Ride -No Honey (Dual)

David Nicholson's stable was full of good horses last season, but it was only when he mentioned Carobee that there was the suspicion of a tremor in his voice.

No wonder. This full brother to a useful hurdler in Alekhine followed a winning debut in a N.H. Flat race by finishing only third when he tackled timber at Towcester in December. But he showed huge improvement after that.

And, although his cantering wins at Leicester and Worcester were scored over third-raters, he dealt just as contemptuously with useful opposition at Chepstow before confirming himself the pick of the two-mile novices with an emphatic victory at Aintree.

Carobee's flat race success was gained on good going. But, although it was on a similar surface that he routed Cheltenham's Supreme Novices' Hurdle principals Flown and Halkopous at Liverpool, it is probable that he will always be at his best when there is give in the ground.

He flowed through the mire in his Chepstow race, and his

Carobee (nearest) is likely to threaten the very best over hurdles

victims (all previous winners) were running on the spot from a long way out.

Carobee is from a good jumping family and should make a high class chaser one day. But in the meantime he is liable to threaten the very best over the lower jumps. *(D. Nicholson)*

CASTIGLIERO 4 br c   Form: 02050111
Cadoudal (FR) -Castigliera (FR) (Dapper Dan (USA))

A winner of a two-mile juveniles' hurdle in France in May, Castigliero re-crossed the Channel to tackle mini-fences against animals of his own age around the turn of the year. But he made little show, and it was when his stamina was tested over the lower jumps that he shone.

Second over two and a half miles at Haydock on his second outing in this country, this half-brother to four winners on the flat went one better over that distance at Chepstow in March, and he was at least as effective when battling to success over three miles at Worcester immediately before and immediately after.

On all three of those spring ventures, Castigliero overcame seasoned campaigners, showing remarkable endurance for his years, and, with a lot of improvement to come, he could one day trouble the best in marathons - at least when there is give underfoot.

All his winning form has been shown on ground taking at least a good cut, and clinging mud did not bother him in the first of his Worcester races. *(C. Brooks)*

CHATAM 8 b g   Form: 11
Big Spruce (USA) - Cristalina (FR) (Green Dancer(USA))

Not an easy training subject, Chatam has been able to race only 18 times in five seasons, his latest problem preventing him from taking his chance in the Cheltenham Gold Cup last March.

And, in view of what happened to stablemate Carvill's Hill, that would surely have been a big chance.

Successful in Newbury's Hennessy Cup and Mandarin

Chase over the full Gold Cup trip on his only two appearances last term, the ex-French gelding was in receipt of only eight pounds from Docklands Express when beating him 11 lengths into third place in the first-named contest, and Docklands Express wound up only a length down when similarly placed in Cheltenham's title event.

So, provided Chatam can be kept sound in the coming months, he could be a more than adequate stand-in for Carvill's Hill next March.

He seems to need give in the ground, the more the better, but the Cheltenham course is ideal for him. An animal with a tendency to jump markedly to his left, he races in a special bit which enables his jockey to keep him straight at most of his fences. *(M. Pipe)*

COOL GROUND 10 ch g   Form: 5P210110
Over The River (FR) - Merry Spring (Merrymount)

If the Jockey Club were serious about stamping out excessive use of the whip, they would disqualify the horse as well as zthe rider concerned.

The horse wouldn't care, but the owner and the trainer, as well as the jockey, certainly would, and the inevitable outcome would be the disappearance of stomach-turning performances of the sort put on by Adrian Maguire when he forced Cool Ground to the front in the last few strides of last season's Cheltenham Gold Cup.

It was by no means the worst case of its kind. But the race which ought to be the highlight of the season was ruined for many by that crunching climax . . . . if it had not been ruined already by the antics of Michael Bowlby on Golden Freeze.

In the course of giving his mount every possible chance of winning, in the later expressed view of the Jockey Club, Bowlby harrassed and unsettled the favourite Carvill's Hill, and the injuries inflicted by a series of shattering blunders have resulted in the disappearance from the racecourse, possibly for ever, of the best steeplechaser seen in years.

Worse horses than Cool Ground have won the race

regarded as chasing's championship, but not very many. It should not be forgotten that, less than three months before his Cheltenham victory, a telescope would have been required to see him walking home after pulling-up in the Welsh National in which Carvill's Hill, conceding six pounds to him, led all the way to win by twenty lengths.

Yet Cool Ground, in the more than likely continued absence of Carvill's Hill, could again be a contender for all the major stamina tests this term.

How much was taken out of him by his punishing race in the Gold Cup? He certainly looked a spent force when, outstandingly leniently weighted on Cheltenham form, he trailed in tenth in the Grand National just over three weeks later, and it may not have been in his best interests that he completed that greatly modified but still exhausting course.

But toughness and resilience, along with the unflinching courage he showed up the final cruel hill at Cheltenham last March, have always been among his characteristics, and it could be expensive to assume that his best days are behind him.

Essentially a stayer, Cool Ground is effective on any going other than firm. But mud favours him because it slows so many others in addition to placing a premium on stamina. (G.Balding)

CYPHRATE 6 b or br g   Form: 12142F11
Crystal Glitters (USA) - Sihame (Crystal Palace(FR))

The third and the fifth in Young Pokey's Arkle Trophy were beaten much more emphatically when they reappeared in the similar contest at the Grand National meeting won by Cyphrate. So it is hardly surprising that Martin Pipe regards this ex-French gelding as a potential two-mile champion.

His rating at Liverpool was higher than any he had attained previously, and there is a possibility that the animals providing the form lines were less effective on the softened going there than they had been on the sound surface at the Cheltenham Festival.

But there had been only a trace of give underfoot when, immediately before the Aintree triumph, Cyphrate fell when alongside Shamana at the last fence at Haydock, and Shamana went on from there to look a danger to all until a similar fate befell her at the second-last in the Arkle Trophy.

Still young enough to be improving, Cyphrate has the physique to shrug off heavy burdens, and, although he begins this season high in the weights, the handicapper may take time to catch up with him. (*M. Pipe*)

DUKE OF MONMOUTH 4 b g   Form: 13313
Secreto (USA) -Queen For The Day (USA) (King Emperor (USA))

The opposition was modest when Duke Of Monmouth made a winning hurdling debut on soft going, and this big strong gelding, whose flat race successes had been scored on top of the ground, floundered in the mud when he wound up his first N.H. campaign at Punchestown.

He was certainly a better horse when crushing 29 opponents in the intensely competitive Triumph Hurdle at the Cheltenham Festival immediately before. So it is probable that he will always be best on ground as good as he found on that occasion.

Also important, evidently, are the blinkers he wore for the first time in the Triumph, and when they are on he ought to be capable of defying the handicapper.

Whether he is capable of a serious Champion Hurdle challenge is open to question, though. Four-year-olds did not perform with great distinction against their elders in handicaps last winter, and, although Duke Of Monmouth looked the best of them when conditions were right for him, there is a yawning gap between him and the likes of Royal Gait and Granville Again. (*S. Sherwood*)

FLOWN 5 b g   Form: 1145
Hotfoot - My Own II (El Relicario)

Never raced on soft going on the flat, Flown showed why when he tackled it at Aintree and in Ireland on the last two of

Flown's brilliant finishing speed will demoralise oppostition on good ground or better

his four ventures in his first hurdling campaign, performing far below the form which had enabled him to run away with Cheltenham's Supreme Novices' Hurdle.

In that contest run on good going, this half-brother to two winning jumpers raced home ten lengths clear of the runner-up Halkopous. But when they filled second and fourth places to Carobee at Liverpool, Halkopous, on only 8lb more favourable terms, was 12 lengths the better.

It should pay to be interested in Flown when he races on a sound surface, however, for his brilliant finishing speed will demoralise most hurdlers. *(N. Henderson)*

GRAN ALBA 6 gr h   Form: 2112
El Gran Senor (USA) - Morning Games (USA) (Grey Dawn II)

A foot injury prevented Gran Alba from taking part in last season's Champion Hurdle, but he is sound again and seems bound to be a serious contender for top honours this time around.

This grey, who finished sixth to Nashwan in the 1989 Derby, overcame strong opposition on the second and third of his four outings last season, and when he ran-up in Wincanton's Kingwell Hurdle on his only subsequent appearance he was only half a length behind Fidway, who went on to look a danger to all until tangling with the winner, Royal Gait, on landing over the final flight in the Champion Hurdle.

Gran Alba's pace makes him particularly effective on good or fast going, but a certain amount of give underfoot makes little difference to him. *(R. Hannon)*

GRANVILLE AGAIN 6 ch g   Form: 1111F1
Deep Run - High Board (High Line)

Until falling at the second-last flight in last season's Champion Hurdle, Granville Again looked sure to go close to emulating his full brother Morley Street's triumph in the previous year, and he will surely be a major contender again next March.

It is unlikely, however, that the next race for the hurdles crown will be run as slowly as Royal Gait's was, and the usual searing gallop might not be ideal for this ex-Irish gelding.

That sort of pace could take the edge off the brilliant acceleration which has hallmarked all his best efforts, and it may be recalled that when he was drawn into a protracted battle over half a mile more than the minimum journey he was a let-down.

That defeat at the beginning of the season before last was sustained on Granville Again's first outing in this country and when he was little more than a baby, however, and it could be expensive to assume that he will never be at his best when the accent is switched from speed to staying power. After all, however good a champion hurdler Morley Street was, he was and is a better horse over about half a mile more, while the best of the other members of their notable jumping family have been stayers.

Granville Again, who has the make and shape of a future chaser, acts on any going. *(M. Pipe)*

JODAMI 7 b g   Form: 111223
Crash Course - Masterstown Lucy (Bargello)

When all the top trainers of jumpers were asked at the beginning of last season to name the horse they would like to take from another yard, the most popular choice was Jodami.

Winner of five out of six races over hurdles in the previous campaign, this raw-boned young giant then had scope for further improvement and looked sure to be at least as good over fences. So he was.

Following jumping exhibitions at Kelso on his first two ventures over the big jumps, mistakes began to creep in when he moved up in class. And, although they did not prevent him from completing the hat-trick at Ayr, they had a lot to do with his failure to add to those gains on three further appearances.

But the last two were in the best of novice company, and his performance against Bradbury Star at the Grand National meeting placed him among the best half-dozen staying recruits to the big game. An early blunder steadied him, but he had command before the penultimate fence, and it was only on the run-in that the winner, who had been a very close second in the Sun Alliance Novices' Chase, got on top.

Jodami, then beaten three-quarters of a length, was in receipt of three pounds. But improvement in his jumping would account for more than that, and, provided that is made, he could bother the very best this season.

The state of the ground does not seem to matter much to him. *(P. Beaumont)*

KATABATIC 9 br g   Form: 132211
Strong Gale - Garravogue (Giolla Mear)

What would have happened had Katabatic avoided his out-of-character error at the last fence in last season's Queen Mother Champion Chase?

A personal view is that, instead of going under by a length to Remittance Man, he would have repeated his triumph of 1991.

He pulled back more on the run-in than the mistake cost him. And, on two subsequent outings against the third, fourth and fifth in the Cheltenham contest, he gave them more decisive beatings than Remittance Man had done.

This lightning finisher has not won over more than two and a half miles, and when he attempted three in the early part of last term he was beaten long before the finish. But he was a sick horse after that outing, and Andy Turnell is still of the opinion that the trip is within his capabilities, at least on an undemanding course.

So a tilt at the King George VI Chase this Christmas is by no means out of the question, and if Katabatic were to reach the final fence on terms he would not easily be held off.

The likelihood is, however, that most of his racing will again be over the minimum to half a mile more, and he jumps and finishes so well that another profitable season must be expected. He acts on any going. *(A. Turnell)*

KINGS FOUNTAIN 9 br g   Form: 31121U1
Royal Fountain - K-King (Fury Royal)

Kings Fountain is yet another with serious Cheltenham Gold Cup ambitions because of the uncertainty about Carvill's Hill's future.

It was long before the finish that a blunder fired his rider out of the saddle when he was going well in last season's race. But when he went on to take advantage of Arctic Call's freak accident at the last fence in Liverpool's Martell Cup he confirmed a handicap mark 25lb higher than the one on which he had begun the campaign.

And, although that apparently still leaves him with the best part of a stone to find to match, for instance, his stablemate Docklands Express, their trainer certainly does not rate the Gold Cup third and National fourth that much the better.

Indeed, Kim Bailey spent a good deal of time last season telling us that Kings Fountain had more potential than any horse he had ever trained.

An aggressive front runner, Kings Fountain has Gold Cup ambitions

An aggressive front runner with a great spring in him, this long-striding gelding has winning form on most shades of going. But a personal view is that he is at his happiest on a sound surface. He has yet to prove he stays much more than three miles (the Martell Cup, over a furlong more, is run on one of the least demanding circuits in the country) but the farther he has gone the better he has performed, and his stamina is highly unlikely ever to let him down. *(K. Bailey)*

MAGIC SECRET 4 b g   Form: 3
Local Suitor (USA) - Meissarah (USA) (Silver Hawk(USA))

Magic Secret made a lot of mistakes on the way to finishing third in fairly useful juvenile company at Newcastle last November on his first outing over hurdles, and he was not asked to face them in public again.

Now stronger, following another flat campaign in which he has been twice on target, he has re-schooled encouragingly and should not find it difficult to win in novice company.

Some give underfoot suits him, and so do the all-weather surfaces at Lingfield (where he has winning form) and Southwell. *(P. Haslam)*

MASAI MARA (USA) 4 ch g   Form: 11
Mogambo (USA) -Forever Command (USA) [Top Command(USA)]

Masai Mara's wins in novices' hurdles at Kelso and Ayr came immediately after a busy 1991 flat campaign in which he appeared 14 times (for four successes over ten to 14 furlongs) so the lengthy rest which followed was well earned.

His 1992 season on the level has been much less strenuous, and when he returns to jumping he should be in shape to realise the considerable promise held out by last winter's efforts. Certainly, we have not yet seen the best of him, and he could pose problems for the handicapper.

All his winning, on the flat and over jumps, has been done on sound surfaces. *(P. Haslam)*

MIGHTY FALCON 7 br g — Form: UP1443010
Comedy Star (USA) - Lettuce (So Blessed)

A full brother to Mighty Fly, winner of a Lincoln Handicap as well as a Royal Hunt Cup, Mighty Falcon attempted last season to complete a unique Spring Double for their sire and dam, Comedy Star and Lettuce.

And, from 22lbs out of the handicap in the Grand National, he showed up remarkably well until the pace was increased and he was forced into a serious mistake at the fourth-last fence.

A virtual novice in a race which, in spite of many modifications, remains the most rigorous on the Calendar, this tall, long-striding individual surely has his best years in front of him, and the chances are that he will be back at Aintree next spring with a realistic chance.

Meanwhile, he should not find it difficult, over three miles and upwards, to add to the four fencing successes already to his credit. He acts on any going. *(D. Elsworth)*

MIINNEHOMA 9 b or br g — Form: 111
Kambalda - Mrs Cairns (Choral Society)

There are more communicative individuals than Martin Pipe. When asked after Miinnehoma's return to action at Newton Abbot last January what had prevented the gelding from racing in the previous season, the leading trainer said: "He had some minor problems."

Whatever they were, Miinnehoma had clearly made a complete recovery. One of the top staying novice hurdlers of the 1989/90 campaign, he was attempting fences in public for the first time at Newton Abbot, and he outpointed relatively experienced opposition there before going on to stamp himself our top staying recruit to the big jumps by overcoming Mutare at Chepstow and Bradbury Star, in record time, in the Sun Alliance Novices' Chase.

Whether he can stay in front of those two, who are both two years younger, must be in some doubt. But, in spite of his age, he has had only 13 races, including two between flags in Ireland when he was a five-year-old, and he will surely last long enough to add considerably to the nine successes already on his score-sheet.

Miinnehoma's performance at Cheltenham showed that he does not have to have give in the ground. But Peter Scudamore was so convinced about the horse's preference for such conditions that he would have switched to stablemate Run For Free had he been allowed to. *(M. Pipe)*

MILFORD QUAY 9 ch h   Form: 101D1
Milford - Miss Quay (Quayside)

Milford Quay, who was found to have a blood disorder after failure at Leicester between novice chase successes on that course and at Market Rasen, did not prove himself an exceptional recruit until running away from useful Irish opposition at Punchestown in April.

And, having carried the wrong weight, he later had that prize taken away from him.

But any doubts about his ability were removed on his only subsequent appearance last season. That was at Warwick, where he gave Beech Road 4lb and a six-length beating following a great duel from the third-last fence.

There is not a lot of Milford Quay, and, although he has three times defied 12st over hurdles, he has yet to carry that much in a chase. So, especially as he is at his best on testing going, it remains to be seen how well he will cope with the welter burdens he is bound to be alloted in some handicaps.

He is effective over two miles but at his best over about half a mile more. *(M. Pipe)*

MUTARE 7 b g   Form: 112F
Boreen (FR) - Slave Trade (African Sky)

Having run freely in front until shortly before falling at the second-last fence in last spring's Sun Alliance Novices' Chase, Mutare probably would have had to settle for third place to Miinnehoma and Bradbury Star had he stood up.

But a more settled attitude would surely lead to

improvement, and it should be recalled that he had been conceding three pounds to Miinnehoma when taking a three-and-a-half-length beating from that two-year older rival on soft going at Chepstow immediately before.

So, especially as he is still a comparatively young horse, the odds are that this ex-Irish gelding has a good deal more to show us, and he is yet another obvious threat to the established long-distance chasing stars.

He is effective on fast ground, but is almost certainly at his best after a lot of rain. *(N. Henderson)*

MY YOUNG MAN 7 b g   Form: 211111413
Young Man (FR) - Hampsruth (Sea Hawk II)

Those who doubted My Young Man's ability to deal with the difficult Cheltenham fences were made to look foolish when he jumped brilliantly to run away with the Grand Annual Cup, and his failure in the Cathcart Cup two days later may be overlooked. He is a two-mile specialist, and that race was over half a mile more.

Admittedly, jumpers who take as flat a trajectory over their fences as My Young Man does invariably pay greater penalties when they make mistakes. But he made only the occasional one last term, improving throughout, and he could be a serious candidate for the Queen Mother Champion Chase next March.

Immediately before last season's Cheltenham Festival ventures, this aggressive front-runner had been 7lbs and eight lengths behind Waterloo Boy when they were first and fourth at Newbury, and Waterloo Boy was only third when he went on to contest the two-mile title decider.

But the Newbury contest was one of the few last season in which My Young Man made a serious jumping misjudgement, while he was not given a hard time once it was clear, after the penultimate fence, that he could not win.

He acts on mud, but he is at his best on surfaces which allow him to stride out freely, and in those conditions he is always going to be difficult to catch at any level. *(C. Brooks)*

NEW YORK RAINBOW 7 br g   Form: 1114
Good Thyne (USA) - Alice Starr (Windjammer(USA))

Wind problems resulted in New York Rainbow failing to
come up to expectations in the season before last, but they
were dealt with in time to enable him to win his first three
races in the 1991/92 campaign, and he might have run
unbeaten through it had he found slower going in the
Cheltenham Festival's Supreme Novices' Hurdle, or waited
24 hours to run in the Sun Alliance Novices' Hurdle instead.

This big, lengthy individual, whose successes have all
been gained on good or fast going over the minimum journey
at Sandown, has always left the impression that longer trips
will help him, while Nicky Henderson is in no doubt that
eased underfoot conditions also will be a help.

Anyway, he was a creditable fourth in the race he did
contest at Cheltenham, while his closest victims in the second
of his Sandown races took the first two places in the half-mile
longer event on the following day.

So even his form as it stands makes him one the best
prospects around. And, likely as it is that he will be even
better as a chaser, he is an animal with an exciting future.
Rising eight, he may be expected to graduate to the big jumps
in the near future, and it is unlikely that there will be many
novices in his class. *(N. Henderson)*

NOMADIC WAY 7 b h   Form: 2231
Assert - Kittyhawk (Bustino)

The 1988 Cesarewitch winner had enough speed to get into
photo-finishes in two-mile Champion Hurdle trials on his
first two outings last season.

But there was never much likelihood that he would
attempt to step up on his second placings in the 1990 and
1991 runnings of that event, and, after setting a funereal pace
which led to defeat in a two-and-a-half-mile terms' event at
Cheltenham's New Year meeting, he returned in March to
win the race which has looked made for him since his

Nomadic Way must be favourite for a second win in the Stayers'
Hurdle at Cheltenham in 1993

attentions were turned to jumping, the Stayers' Hurdle over three miles and a furlong.

In command before the turn for home, he was from that point always travelling too strongly for all the other long-distance hurdlers in training, and, all being well, must be favourite to repeat the performance next March.

This brave little horse acts on any going. *(B. Hills)*

REMITTANCE MAN 8 b g   Form: 13111
Prince Regent (FR) - Mittens (Run The Gantlet(USA))

When Remittance Man ran-up to Miinnehoma in the 1990 Saddle Of Gold Final over three miles and a furlong, he did not fail for want of stamina. He was beaten 12 lengths, but the third in a truly run race finished 15 lengths farther behind. So was it really because he found even undemanding Kempton's three miles beyond him that he sustained his only defeat in ten races over fences to date in last Christmas's King George VI Chase?

It is difficult to believe, even though the time was a course record, and a more likely explanation is that he simply was not good enough.

Beautifully polished though Remittance Man's fencing technique is, that alone is not enough to win at the highest level, and it is a fact that he has raced at that level only twice since he graduated from hurdles. The first time was in the King George VI Chase. The second was in the Queen Mother Champion Chase, which he might have lost instead of winning by a length had the runner-up Katabatic not made a telling mistake at the final fence.

Remittance Man is clearly one of the best chasers around, however, on any going with the possible exception of heavy and over any distance from the minimum (at any rate on a demanding track) up to at least three miles, and he is likely to be the one they all have to beat in the Cheltenham Gold Cup as well as Kempton's Boxing Day feature this season.

In both, we may expect him to wait until a late stage before making his effort, because another possible explanation for his Kempton failure is that he was in front too long, having taken up the running on leaving the back straight. *(N. Henderson)*

ROYAL GAIT 9 b g   Form: 2111
Gunner B - High Gait (High Top)

The novice who beat Royal Gait when he bowed in over timber at Kempton last Boxing Day was beaten on both his subsequent ventures. But the moral winner of the 1988 Ascot Gold Cup made great strides, running away with a novices' event and a handicap (under 10st 7lb) at Nottingham before completing the hat-trick in the Champion Hurdle.

Was he a fortunate winner? Perhaps. An unusually slow pace meant that his jumping technique was not examined as rigorously as it normally would have been, while Granville Again was moving at least as strongly when falling at the second-last flight.

By the time he lines up to defend his crown, however, Royal Gait will surely be a much more experienced hurdler. So the headlong gallop at which the Champion Hurdle is usually run ought to be in favour of such a thorough stayer.

And some give in the ground would probably help him. Deep mud would put too much strain on the legs which let him down when he was at the height of his flat-racing career. But he did not look entirely at ease, hanging during the run-in, on the sound surfaces at Nottingham and Cheltenham.

Whatever the underfoot conditions in his preliminary races, however, he should continue to prosper. Valuable non-handicaps over hurdles rarely attract many runners, and the accent is almost invariably on finishing speed. *(J. Fanshawe)*

RYDE AGAIN 9 ch g   Form: 1121
Celtic Cone - Ryde Well (Blast)

Ryde Again was almost nine years old when he graduated to fences, but he had none of the bad habits of the experienced hurdler, and his good first-season record was due in no small measure to a sound jumping technique.

A back problem - which he has had for years and which affects him from time to time - prevented his appearance in the Sun Alliance Novices' Chase. But the odds are that he would have shown up prominently in that contest involving most of the best staying recruits.

Having won two of his first three races over the major obstacles - all over two and a half miles - he tackled the Sun Alliance trip, three miles, at Leicester in February, and, after moving easily throughout, had to be ridden on the run-in only because he knocked himself out of his stride with a mistake on his final jump.

A high class performer over timber in previous seasons, this thorough stayer begins this campaign on an unexceptional chaser's handicap mark, and the likelihood is that he will win worthwhile prizes over three miles and more before his measure is taken. He acts on any going. *(Mrs J. Pitman)*

STAUNCH FRIEND 4 b g   Form: 21P21
Secreto (USA) - Staunch Lady (USA) (Staunchness)

The going was not the reason for the favourite Staunch Friend pulling up, when out of contention, between the last two flights of the Triumph Hurdle, but it was because he had earlier been so impressive on a similar surface at Newbury that he was so strongly fancied for the Cheltenham showdown with all the other top juveniles.

But give underfoot, and the more the better, certainly suits him. The going was on the easy side when, at Aintree three weeks after the Triumph flop, he ran-up less than four lengths behind the Cheltenham fifth Salwan. Then he turned the tables on the Triumph winner Duke Of Monmouth when hacking up at Punchestown.

So, when Staunch Friend is in handicaps or opposed at levels by animals with official ratings close to his, he will almost certainly need plenty of give underfoot to give him a chance of beating them. Clearly, his prospects in the coming month depend on the weather. *(M. Tompkins)*

SUNSET AND VINE 5 gr g   Form: 51311
Norwick (USA) - Starky's Pet (Mummy's Pet)

Sunset And Vine won three of his five races last season. But there was no comparison between the form he produced to win at Ascot on his final appearance and anything he had shown before.

Opposition included three rivals who would have met him on terms 7lb to 23lb less favourable in a handicap. Yet he did not have to be seriously ridden to come home six lengths clear after taking over at the penultimate jump.

The distance was two and a half miles, while the going was soft, but neither was new to Sunset And Vine, and the conclusion has to be that he was improving fast at the end of last season.

So the odds are that he will continue on the upgrade, creating problems for the handicapper for some time to come. *(S. Dow)*

SWEET GLOW 5 b g   Form: 43122531110030
Crystal Glitters (USA) - Very Sweet (Bellypha)

There was not a great deal of Sweet Glow last season, and at the beginning of it no-one could have seen the scope for the improvement which, in the course of 14 races, resulted in his rising in the handicap by 34lbs.

Is he capable of the continued progress required to beat the handicapper? His trainer, with whom only an idiot would argue, thinks so, basing his optimism on marked physical development during the close season - not entirely surprising, as this ex -French gelding will not be six years old until January 1.

Even so, the likelihood is that Sweet Glow's best chances will come when he is carrying less than 12st against high class stayers rather than when he is under welter burdens in handicaps.

His best performance, for instance, was produced when, under 11st 3lb, he came back from being hampered at the second-last flight to be beaten only a neck by Trapper John

(11st 10lb) for second place to another Pipe-trained marathon star in Pragada, over three miles at Ascot last March.

The ground then was taking a print, but Sweet Glow, most of whose racing has been done on sound surfaces, is probably unsuited by really testing conditions. *(M. Pipe)*

TOOGOOD TO BE TRUE 4 br g   Form: 1
Sonnen Gold - Lady Relka (Relko)

Last April 25, minutes before Wellwotdouthink won the most competitive N.H. flat race of the season at Sandown, a similar event took place at Market Rasen, and a form line between the two suggests that the winner of the contest on the Lincolnshire course, Toogood to Be True, is not greatly inferior.

So, as this gelding won with a good deal to spare, he is probably out of the ordinary, and reports of early schools over obstacles suggest that he will pay to follow in novice hurdles in the north at least. *(M.H. Easterby)*

TURNING TRIX 5 b g   Form: 1
Bucksin (FR) - Merry Run (Deep Run)

Another whose only outing so far has been in an N.H. flat race, Turning Trix had 12 lengths to spare at Cheltenham in April, in spite of coming from a long way behind, then losing concentration and leaving a true line on the final hill.

Big things are expected of this stoutly bred gelding, and, whether or not he ever approaches the standard of past winners of the Cheltenham contest like Remittance Man, Young Pokey and Mrs Muck, novice hurdles should be his for the taking in the coming months. *(S. Sherwood)*

VERY VERY ORDINARY 6 b g   Form: 4F3114
Furry Glen - Very Very (Vulgan)

Following wins over two and a half miles at Southwell and Ascot, Very Very Ordinary failed to maintain his improvement when he wound up his first chasing campaign

From a family of stayers, Very Very Ordinary is likely to progress for some time to come

over three miles on the latter course.

But, although he faded into fourth place after moving up to have every chance between the last two obstacles, it could be dangerous to assume that he does not stay the distance.

He was still at an early stage in his development, racing against animals two and three years older, and the likelihood is that he will last longer as he strengthens. Certainly, he comes from a family of stayers, his dam having produced three winners over three miles and more.

Likely to progress for some time to come, this tall, angular individual seems to act on just about any going and should be worth following in handicaps. (*J. Upson*)

WELLWOTDOUTHINK 6 b m   Form: 111
Rymer - Doubly Royal (Royal Buck)

It was with ease that this mare won N.H. flat races at Doncaster and Edinburgh in December and January, and, although she had to work harder to remain unbeaten in a similar event at Sandown in April, it was the most strongly contested of its type all season.

An exceptionally well-put-together individual, she is out of a mare who had more than a little ability over hurdles, and all the signs are that the family reputation will be at least upheld.

All three of Wellwotdouthink's races have been on sound surfaces, but her action suggests that she will not be troubled by some give. (*Mrs G.R. Reveley*)

WINTER SQUALL 4 gr g   Form: 13
Celio Rufo - No Honey (Dual)

Third in Wellwotdouthink's N.H. flat race at Sandown, this previously impressive winner of a similar event at Ascot is a half-brother to high-class hurdlers in Alekhine and Carobee, and it is quite likely that their dam has produced another of that calibre.

There is no doubt that his trainer views him as a star hurdler in the making, and, particularly on ground with give in it, he is liable to be difficult to beat in forthcoming novices' races.

The going was yielding when he scored so impressively on his debut, and, after inexplicably losing a lot of ground at the end of the back straight at Sandown, he hung on the faster surface when he was at the height of a strong rally in the last quarter-mile. (*Mrs J. Pitman*)

WONDER MAN 7 ch g   Form: 1
The Wonder (FR) - Juvenilia (FR) (Kashmir II)

When David Nicholson took charge of Wonder Man shortly before this season began he said the horse was so high in the hurdles' handicap that an early switch to chasing seemed inevitable.

In fact, this ideal type for the big game schooled encouragingly over fences before leaving Jenny Pitman's yard, and he seems bound to be one of the leading novice chasers in the coming months.

Sound again after being able to race only once last term, he had reached a high level over hurdles in the previous campaign, and the speed he produced to wind it up with a decisive success in the Welsh Champion Hurdle will demoralise most animals he meets over fences.

He seems to be able to quicken as readily on softened ground as he does in fast conditions. *(D. Nicholson)*

YOUNG POKEY 7 b g   Form: 212112
Uncle Pokey - Young Romance (King's Troop)

A certain amount of yield in the ground does not prevent Young Pokey from producing his best, but, even over the minimum journey, his attacking style over-taxes him on testing going, which is why he was hammered by Classical Charm at Punchestown at the end of last season.

It had been a different story in the Arkle Trophy on good going at the Festival Meeting. First or second, jumping as fast and as accurately as usual, this son of a mare who has produced three flat winners took command before the turn for home and was always holding a strong field from that point.

Built to carry big weights, he also has the right attitude, and, on good or fast going, his speed between and over the obstacles will win him handicaps as well as terms' events over two miles. *(O. Sherwood)*

Ladbrokes

HORSES TO FOLLOW COMPETITION

A **FREE** Competition open to all **Companion** buyers

1st PRIZE	**£ 100**	**Ladbrokes** Free Bet Vouchers
2nd PRIZE	**£ 50**	**Ladbrokes** Free Bet Vouchers
3rd PRIZE	**£ 30**	**Ladbrokes** Free Bet Vouchers
4th PRIZE	**£ 20**	**Ladbrokes** Free Bet Vouchers

In the preceding pages Jack Millan has chosen 40 horses likely to win this season. Most are the sort we can expect to see running on TV for the better prizes. **THE LADBROKES COMPETITION** *is for you to choose which will be most profitable to follow to level-stakes.*

THE *Ladbrokes* COMPETITION

THE COMPETITION IS SIMPLE, BUT PLEASE READ THE DIRECTIONS AND THE RULES CAREFULLY.

The first step is to short-list **SIX** horses from the forty Jack has selected. Next put them in order of preference.

Selection A will carry   10   pts investment every run
Selection B   6   pts
Selection C   4   pts
Selection D   2   pts
Selection E   1   pt
Selection F   1   pt

Thus whatever level-stake returns are made by your selection over the period of the competition, it will be multiplied by the above figures. If your selection A ends up showing a £10 (or "point") profit to a pound level-stake, your profit will be ten times that, or 100 pts. Likewise if selection B shows a £5 loss to a pound level-stake, your loss will be 30 pts as you have elected to back it for six points a run.

Next write your name, address and selections (clearly marked A-F) in BLOCK CAPITALS. Then turn to the very back page of the Companion and cut out the special triangle in the top left corner - this is your ticket to play.

Finally, send your entry to:

Ladbrokes Competition
Aesculus Press
P.O. Box 10
Oswestry
Shropshire
SY10 7QR

THE *Ladbrokes* COMPETITION

RULES:-

1. All entries must be postmarked no later than the 31st December 1992. Entries received after that date will be automatically disqualified.

2. The competition will run from the 1st January 1993 to the 30th April 1993 inclusive).

3. Only U.K. races to count.

4. Results are taken as they appear in the Raceform Annual.

5. The six selections must come exclusively from the 40 *"Winners for 1992/93"* by Jack Millan.

6. No entry will be accepted without the special triangle to be found on the back page.

7. Wrongly or illegibly written entries will be disqualified.

8. Winners names will be printed in next year's *N.H. Pocket Companion*.

9. In the event of a tie(s), a special tie-breaker will be devised.

10. The editor's decision is final in all matters. No correspondence will be entered into.

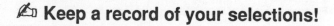 **Keep a record of your selections!**

GOOD LUCK!

1991/92 LANSON COMPETITION

Yet again the number of non-runners in last year's selection of horses was disappointing. This seems to affect the National Hunt list far more than the Flat. Over the jumps it is not unusual for horses to miss a season when they are not quite right, or to take extra time to recover from injury, whereas on the Flat if a season is missed it generally means retirement which is flagged more clearly in advance.

This does make it more difficult to draw up a list of Horses To Follow for the N.H. Last year Jack had 13 non-runners within the period of the competition - eight of those did not appear at all in the 91/92 season. However he did have 14 winners, who between them won 23 races. The overall strike-rate was 25.5%, a little lower than in 90/91.

Quite a few of the winners were at short odds so the very best possible entry was not as high as it has been, but it did beat last year's total of £130.37.

The perfect entry this time would have been:-

		Wins	/	Races	L/Stake		Unit		Profit
1	Nomadic Way	1	/	1	7.50	x	10	=	75.00
2	Captain Dibble	1	/	3	7.00	x	6	=	42.00
3	Spinning	2	/	3	2.83	x	4	=	11.32
4	Remittance Man	3	/	3	1.73	x	2	=	3.46
5	Run For Free	4	/	6	1.08	x	1	=	1.08
6	Book of Gold	1	/	5	1.00	x	1	=	1.00
		12	/	**21**					**133.86**

The two top horses, Nomadic Way and Captain Dibble, were not in many people's lists. Only three people put either one of them at the top of their list, and not many others had them in at all.

There was a dead-heat for the most popular horse to be the ten-point choice between Remittance Man, who ended the season in profit, and Blazing Walker, a non-runner. Close runners-up were Mr Woodcock, who ended the competition period on minus three points and Carvill's Hill. He only ran once within the prescribed dates, and that was in the Gold Cup - so he did no-one any favours!

Mr A J SMITH of Bolton was one of two to have Nomadic Way in pole position, he also had Remittance Man in second place, the profit from that combination along with the non-runner Blazing Walker more than offset the losses his other choices made. His total profit was £79.58 and this was enough for him to win the jeroboam.

The first magnum went to the only entry with Captain Dibble as the 'A' selection. ALAN HEATHWAITE of Darlington also put Remittance Man in as his second choice, but Mr Woodcock let the side down in third place. The total profit ended up being £66,52.

Mr K BRIDDON of Hitchin was the only other person with Nomadic Way in top spot. He backed up with Granville Again in second place and Remittance Man lower down the order. However he had a bad loser in Super Sense which curbed his profits to £63.15, but this was enough to come third in the competition and win the other magnum.

There was quite a gap between the scores of the first three and the rest. In fourth was Mr L COURT of Stratford-on-Avon with a total of £44.58. He had put Remittance Man top of his list, with Captain Dibble as his six-point selection. Like Mr Briddon his profits were also damaged by Super Sense.

The other bottles were won by Mr J HOCKING of Poole with £37.45 (Granville Again topped his list followed by Nomadic Way); Mr F NEALE of Leicester with £36.67, (Remittance Man top and Nomadic Way in fourth place) and Mr P CHRISTOU of Hornsey with £31.18 (Carvill's Hill was his ten-point selection, but he had Remittance Man & Nomadic Way in second and third places).

Congratulations to all winners.

6 . HUNTER CHASERS TO NOTE

by

Marcus Armytage
(Freelance)

INDEX TO HORSES

BEAU ROSE 9 b g   Form: 1
Beau Charmer - Rosantus

Beau Rose, like a number of hunter-chasers, has been plagued by leg problems without which he would surely have made a name for himself as a decent handicap chaser.

Last year was his first as a hunter and it was short-lived. First time out, he won impressively at Ludlow, showing a useful turn of foot to beat Baluchi by ten lengths.

A good jumper, he was going to be aimed at Cheltenham and Liverpool. Unfortunately he subsequently knocked himself in the box, then was beset by virus problems and was not seen out again.

He gets three miles without any difficulty, but must have decent ground, the faster the better. Clearly, if Stratford trainer Chris Trietline can keep him sound this year, he will be a serious candidate for both the big races, although he is more my idea of an Aintree foxhunter. There he would be more likely to get his ground and, I think, he would take to the fences well. *(C. C. Trietline)*

DOUBLE SILK 8 b g   Form: 2211
Dubassoff - Yellow Silk

Double Silk began the season as a point-to-pointer, but soon showed he was easily capable of holding his own in hunter-chases.

First time out at Wincanton he was a good second to Wellington Brown, who was in good form at the time, and followed it up with a second to Gunner's Flight at Wolverhampton when he was unlucky to peck at two of the last three fences. He soon began to put things right with a narrow, hard fought victory over Busy Mittens at Ascot.

On his last appearance he looked very impressive against mainly point-to-pointers in a final at Cheltenham. His win, by 30 lengths, proved he was a class above them. Ground doesn't seem to worry him and it seems the farther he goes the better he goes. *(R. C. Wilkins)*

DUNCAN 7 b g
Form: 121
Cut Above - Tristan du Cunha

Duncan is a little horse built like a tank. It took a couple of
races last season to establish that his optimum trip is two and
a half miles on fastish ground. His win first time out, beating
The Red One over three miles at Nottingham, misled us all
about his best distance, especially as he appeared to being
staying on that day. However, on softer ground at Hereford
over the same trip he was well beaten by Busy Mittens and
was never really happy from two and a half miles onwards.

Next time out, he was pretty impressive at Doncaster.
Sharper on the fast ground and with the benefit of more
experience, he came to the lead approaching the twelfth fence
and flew home over the last four very smartly, before pulling
up slightly lame. He had suffered a shin injury which,
although not very serious, was enough to rule him out for the
rest of the season.

A good jumper, with speed that belies his shape, Duncan
is a very sporting little horse and sure to give his connections
a lot of fun again this year. *(Miss C. Sanders)*

NORTHUMBRIAN KING 6 b g
Form: 211
Indian King - Tuna

This horse is owned and trained by Middleham farmer's wife
Kate Walton. He was given to her by local trainer Chris
Thornton, after he had developed leg problems whilst in
training, although he had shown useful form running up a
sequence of five hurdle races early on in the 90/91 season.

Last year was his first as a hunter-chaser and, after
winning a couple of northern point-to-points, he upgraded to
it well.

First time out he was two lengths second to Mary
Reveley's useful novice Bertie Boy over three miles at
Southwell. He then went to Huntingdon, where he drew
clear of the favourite, Sheer Jest, from the second last, to win

impressively by 20 lengths (on good ground). His third and last outing was at Market Rasen where, despite a bad blunder at the sixth fence and some none too fluent jumping on what had become greasy ground after a heavy shower, he again put 25 lengths between himself and the second over the last couple of fences.

For a staying chaser he has a very good turn of foot at the end of a race. He will probably always be lightly raced because of his history of leg problems, which is not helped by his preference for firm ground, but he is certainly one to keep an eye on when the ground is good. He has more class than most hunter-chasers and clearly enjoys life on a farm. *(Mrs K. Walton)*

PASTORAL PRIDE 8 b g   Form: 110F1
Exceller - Pastoral Miss

Pastoral Pride looked like being one of the best hunter-chasers of the season last year, beginning with two very impressive victories at Warwick and Windsor. He was then well beaten by Loch Blue at Leicester and fell at Liverpool before finishing with a confidence-boosting success at the Cheltenham hunter-chase meeting at the end of April.

A bold, charging, front-runner, his style of racing is not conducive to his getting much beyond two and a half miles on good ground. Certainly the soft ground took its toll on him at Leicester when he finished very tired. You can ignore his fall at Aintree; it was typical of a horse racing too keenly in the early stages. His win at Cheltenham was on softer ground but over only two miles.

His front-running tactics must be disheartening for other horses, as he can keep up a relentless gallop for just over two miles - two-and-a-half on an easy track and on good ground. He may be best when fresh, and West Country-based Polly Curling is one of the most experienced lady riders around. Her assistance in the saddle should not be overlooked. *(Miss Polly Curling)*

POLYGONUM 10 b g
Form: 12B413
Kemal - Wacoty

Last February the point-to-point graduate The Red One was the talk of the hunter-chase world, so much so that he was entered for the Sun Alliance Novices' Chase, as well as the Christies Foxhunter Challenge Cup. Regular rider, Wayne Burnell, was taken off the horse at Cheltenham, when he ran in the latter race. So there must have been something very sweet about victory at Wetherby in April, when Burnell partnered his family's horse, Polygonum, to victory over The Red One.

Polygonum is a strong gelding and looks the type to pick up a couple more hunter-chases in the forthcoming season, especially when campaigned around the north. He acts on most going and stays two and three-quarter miles plus. *(W. M. Burnell)*

RELEKTO 10 b g
Form: 10112
Relko - Heaven Knows

Relekto was a very useful hurdler in his youth. Then trained by Michael Jarvis in Newmarket, he won a couple of decent novice hurdles before finishing third in the Waterford Crystal Supreme Novices' Hurdle at Cheltenham and second in the Kestral Hurdle at Ascot. That was in 1988. Ever since he has been beset by problems. However, under the guidance of champion point-to-point rider Mike Felton, he proved he has lost little of his enthusiasm or ability when hacking up in a hunter-chase at Leicester on his debut over fences.

There then followed a defeat in a muddling race at Sandown and two more very comfortable wins within four days, at Uttoxeter and Ascot. His jumping was fluent and he clearly appreciated the heavy ground. Being best between two and two and a half miles opportunities are slightly limited hunter-chasing. Nevertheless, one to follow - soft ground being the key. *(M. J. Felton)*

RUSHING WILD 7 b g   Form: 1F1
Rushmere - Lady Emm II

Rushing Wild made the most spectacular of debuts last
season. Having shown considerable form between the flags,
he was thrown in at the deep end with a large field of
experienced chasers - although there was nothing
outstanding among them - in the Christies Foxhunter
Challenge Cup at Cheltenham. Rushing Wild, a powerful
gelding, coped more than admirably with the fences and the
opposition coming, home 25 lengths clear of the runner-up,
Ardesse. With Justin Farthing on board, he led from the
second-last ditch and, baring mistakes, never looked likely to
get beaten.

Rushing Wild jumping the last at Cheltenham to win by 25 lengths

Next time out, trying to complete the double at Aintree, he fell at Valentines, when travelling smoothly. His third outing at Chepstow, some three weeks later, was disappointing despite his success. In beating Fiddlers Pike by a length and a half he was clearly not right.

Several large offers were made for the horse at the end of last season to move to a big yard. However, at the time of writing, he remains with top point-to-point trainer Richard Barber for another season. He again looks destined for another spell at the top. *(R. Barber)*

SHEER JEST 7 b g   Form: 2211
Mummy's Game - Tabasheer

Sheer Jest was one of the most improved hunter-chasers of the season. Having won an early point-to-point, he was struggling to win an average maiden hunter chase at Doncaster, when a mistake five fences from home put him out of contention and he finished second. He regained his confidence in another point-to-point, but he still needed the race when second to Northumbrian King at Huntingdon. That put him right for two end-of-season wins at Stratford, the first by 30 lengths in an average novice hunter-chase, and then in the prestigious John Corbet Cup, the novices' championship. Continued improvement along those lines could see Bill Warner's tall gelding, ridden by Alan Hill, go all the way to the top in the coming season. *(W. J. Warner)*

TEAPLANTER 9 b g   Form: 11
National Trust - Miss India

It was anticipated that Teaplanter and his owner Richard Russell would make amends for their spill when favourites for the 1991 Christies' Foxhunters at the Festival by winning it in 1992. That was not to be the case. Early in the season Richard Russell injured his back in a fall at Ludlow. Then Teaplanter returned home from winning at Newbury, shortly before the Festival, with heat in one of his legs. It was decided not to risk running him again that season.

He had nevertheless shown that he had lost none of his old sparkle. Up Towcester's long hill, first time out in the mud, he had won as easily as any, and I mean any, horse I have ever seen or ridden at that course. He had a slightly harder race at Newbury but it was thought at the time ideal to put him straight for Cheltenham.

His jumping is not always foot perfect, often because he's going so easily and not always concentrating. Although he has never fallen he sometimes takes a bit of sitting on. A clash between Teaplanter and Rushing Wild, both at the top of their form, would be one of the most mouth-watering contests of the coming season were it to occur. (*Miss C. Saunders*)

7 . WHAT THE CONNECTIONS HAVE SAID

by

Ron Fuller

*In this chapter trainers, owners, jockeys and head lads reveal their
professional opinion about horses, immediately after a race.
Ron Fuller has gathered quotes from the 1991/92 National Hunt
season from all branches of the media. These have been put together
with a view to providing useful information for the punter.*

Trainer Howard Johnson remarked:

> *"ABNEGATION is progressing very well."*

ABSALOM'S LADY ran on well to be third in the Glenlivet
Hurdle at Liverpool. Trainer Toby Balding informed:

> *"Anything she's doing now is a bonus because she'll be
> better next year - she's got so much scope."*

Trainer Jeremy Glover remarked of his Windsor N.H. flat
race winner:

> *"ARCOT has a lot of speed and at home can pass the
> seven-furlong horses. He is a promising sort and jumps
> well at home."*

One that looks to be progressing along the right lines is **AVRO ANSON**, who quickened up from two flights out to put the issue beyond doubt in the Northern Champion (4-Y-O) Handicap Hurdle at Newcastle. Trainer Maurice Camacho said:

> "He's a nice horse and this proves it. He was well handicapped and is still weak and will improve, so we won't run him much more this season."

BALAAT, an 11,000gns. buy out of Peter Walwyn's stable, stayed on well despite a blunder at the last in the Flamborough Head Novices' Hurdle at Doncaster. Trainer Michael Chapman revealed his secret:

> "I am feeding Royal Jelly to four of my horses at the moment and they all seem to be thriving on it. Mrs Thatcher and Princess Diana take the stuff and it certainly seems to help."

Owner Alan Mann added:

> "This horse had some good form as a two-year-old and he was second to Selkirk in a decent race on the flat."

Trainer Phillip Hobbs said of **BANKROLL**, a son of Chief Singer:

> "This horse loves fast ground, the firmer the better."

BAYDON STAR never looked in danger when landing the E.B.F. N.H. Novices' Hurdle at Windsor and looks to have a bright future. Jenny Pitman's assistant, David Stait, said:

> "It's nice to see a horse that's bred to get three miles have the pace to win over two - and he's still green."

Relishing the testing conditions **BEACHY HEAD** was never

headed in the Harcross Scottish Novices' Hurdle at Ayr and galloped his opponents into the ground. Trainer Chris Thornton revealed:

> *"This horse is the best jumper I've had for a long time. His future is as a long-distance hurdler. I think he'll be top class. The only problem is he does want some cut in the ground."*

◆

A blunder at the last did not stop **BIBENDUM** winning comfortably at 25-1 from the heavily backed French Charmer in the E.B.F. Novices' Hurdle at Warwick. Trainer Bob Waley-Cohen explained:

> *"He's bred to win a 2,000 Guineas but has the looks of a chaser. I bought him as an unbroken three-year-old and he was relatively cheap compared with some of the chasing types at the sale. He is still very green and weak and should have plenty of improvement in him."*

◆

Bought in Ireland after winning his fifth point-to-point, **BISHOPS ISLAND** looks to have a future. Leading two out, the result was quickly put beyond doubt, when winning unextended in the Watergall Maiden Hurdle at Warwick. David Nicholson observed:

> *"Although he is bigger, he reminds me of Very Promising both in the way he travels and jumps - let's hope he proves as good."*

◆

Chiropractor Tony Gilmour put back a dislocated vertebra at the base of **BLACK HUMOUR**'s neck. This has certainly helped the Buckskin gelding to jump more fluently, as witnessed when landing the Northern Trust Opal Novices' Chase at Lingfield, in a gruelling tussle with Man On The Line. Trainer Charlie Brooks said:

"I think that he must have done as much schooling as the rest of the horses put together; I've got tractor tyres in the Fibresand School, set a stride and a half apart, so if they hit them they don't hurt themselves but they do learn. He is getting the hang of it and is a very good horse."

Do not forget smart chaser **BLAZING WALKER**, who missed all of last season due to a number of niggling injuries. Owner Peter Piller announced:

"He is too good a horse to take a risk with and we have finally decided to give him a break and come back for next season."

Josh Gifford commented on **BOOK OF GOLD**:

"I keep rattling on about what a good horse this is, but he needs soft ground to show it."

Having his first run over three miles, **BOOM TIME** ran on strongly from the last to land the Butts Novices' Handicap Chase at Ludlow and looks to have a future. Nicky Henderson's assistant, Charlie Morlock, said:

"He will be a stronger, better horse next year and would be suited by a more-galloping track on better ground."

BOUNDEN DUTY, making virtually all, pulverised the opposition to win as he pleased in the Eastgate Novices' Chase at Warwick. Trainer Guy Harwood's daughter Amanda, in charge of the stable's jumpers said:

"This year we'll keep the horse to tracks like this, but next year he could be good enough to take to Cheltenham."

"BUCK OWENS is still a baby but he's a nice horse in the making,"

remarked Howard Johnson.

◆

One to keep an eye on when fresh is **BURNT FINGERS** who was always in command and landed the Alfred McAlpine Homes Novices' Handicap Chase at Bangor with a fair bit in hand. John White, a trainer with a bright future, said:

"This was the first time the horse had jumped fences in public. He must have jumped at least 800 obstacles in our loose school in the evenings. All mine know their job, even if they fall, you'll still see them jumping round on their own. He's a three-stone better horse first time out."

◆

Jimmy Black, representing Mark Tompkins, said of **CADENCY**, a son of Derby winner Teenoso:

"He has always jumped well and loves a sharp track."

◆

"I think CANDY TUFF will make a nice staying chaser,"

advised trainer Mary Reveley.

◆

The well-built **CAROBEE** pulverised some smart opposition and ran away with the Seagram Top Novices' Hurdle at Liverpool in impressive fashion. A delighted David Nicholson said:

"Carobee is the most exciting horse I have handled - he could prove to be a superstar. Next term he'll start off in races like the Gerry Fielden at Newbury and the Bula at Cheltenham, but the Champion Hurdle is on hold until

December. If he misses the top grade we could always go chasing after the New Year."

Jockey Richard Dunwoody reported:

"Carobee has shown he is a bit special. He has what it takes to go right to the top."

◆

CHANGE THE ACT, given a favourable mention in last season's *Companion*, duly lived up to expectations with wins at Lingfield and the Jack O'Newbury Novices' Chase, where he forged his way to the front from the last to win comfortably. Trainer Oliver Sherwood commented:

"He is still novicey and next year will be his year - he's a very, very nice horse and you won't see him at his best until he gets soft ground."

◆

Useful novice chaser **CLAY COUNTRY** progressed throughout last season until injuring himself when second to Deep Sensation at Nottingham. Trainer Dick Allen explained:

"We decided to rough him off for the season. He will be even better with another summer on his back and, fingers crossed, will be up to tackling all next season's top two-mile events."

◆

Having only his second race following a two-year absence, **CLIFFALDA** landed some hefty wagers with a sustained run to the line in the Ship Hotel Novices' Chase at Kelso. Trainer Gordon Richards, who was asked if the gelding was Cheltenham bound, recounted:

"He could be anything one day and I don't know if we should rush him."

◆

One very much to keep on the right side this coming season

is the strapping grey gelding **COOL DODGER**, who jumped like the proverbial buck when landing the Corton Denham Novices' Chase at Wincanton. Trainer Gerald Ham emphasised:

> "Cool Dodger loves jumping. He's still a big baby and he'll be a tremendous prospect in a year's time."

COPPER MINE was never in any danger throughout the two-mile H.M.S. Sandown N.H. Novices' Hurdle, and looks to have a bright future. Oliver Sherwood said:

> "He is still a big baby and he has now twice had to make his own running here. He has still got a bit to learn about jumping and is better when going for a long one. When he goes in short, it takes a lomg time to get from his brain to his legs!"

In characteristically buoyant mood, Mick Easterby stressed:

> "**COULTON** is a lovely horse and I think he is the best hurdler I've trained - better even than my Triumph winner, Peterhof. He has the speed for two miles but should also stay three miles next season."

COUNTERBID, on his debut over hurdles, ran away with the Marshbrook Novices' Hurdle at Ludlow, winning by twenty lengths, and looks one to keep an eye on. Trainer John Edwards explained:

> "He's done quite well in his bumpers, winning first time and then running well under his penalty. He's still very green, which is why I kept him to bumpers up to now, but he jumped really well despite that."

COUNTORUS asserted himself three from home and outshone his rivals to seal the Askham Bryan Novices' Handicap Hurdle at Wetherby. Howard Johnson commented:

> *"I bought him for 30,000gns. as an unbroken three-year-old at Doncaster Sales. He is still only a baby and will be a lovely horse next season."*

◆

One that seems to be going the right way is **COUNTRY MEMBER,** who ran on well from three out to capture the Fairmile Novices' Handicap Chase at Sandown. Trainer Andy Turnell observed:

> *"That was quite pleasing but he's still a big, lean, weak horse with a bit to learn and another summer will do him a lot of good."*

◆

One that looks to have a bright future is **CURRENT EXPRESS,** who readily went clear from the last under top weight to outclass his field in the Novices' Final Handicap at the Cheltenham April meeting. Nicky Henderson said:

> *"This is a serious horse who can only get better. In an ideal world we'd be looking at fences next season but I think we'll have to start off with conditions' hurdles."*

◆

Trainer Reg Akehurst was pleased with a change in the weather for his Lingfield Gold Cup Handicap Hurdle winner, **DARA DOONE:**

> *"The rain came at just the right time. He will make a nice chaser next year."*

◆

A son of Vaguely Great, **DAYS OF THUNDER** opened his account over timber when stepping up a gear over two out, finding little difficulty in winning the Chailey Juvenile Novices' Hurdle at Plumpton by ten lengths. John White said:

Current Express looks to have a bright future

> *"He looks like being a really nice horse, his dam won twice round here, and he was not fully fit today."*

Trainer Thomas Tait, observing his Hamilton Memorial Chase winner **DEEP COLONIST**, remarked:

> *"He likes soft ground and perhaps he will go for the National next year."*

Jenny Pitman, commenting on **DO BE BRIEF**, comfortable winner of the Betterton Chase at Newbury said:

> *"When Errol Brown (lead singer of the group Hot Chocolate) and partners asked me to buy them a horse, the only instruction was that it would win the Grand National and that's what Do Be Brief will do. I look after my novice chasers and we are in no hurry with him. He could run in next year's National, or we may wait until 1994."*

A strong recommendation in last year's *Companion*, **DUSTY MILLER** fully justified the confidence when he forged clear on the run-in to win the County Hurdle at the Cheltenham Festival and land a nice touch at 9-1. Trainer Simon Sherwood confessed:

> *"I adore this horse. I ride him out every morning and he is the apple of my eye. He is going to make up into a very nice horse over fences."*

Quickening up coming to the last in the Elmbridge Handicap Chase at Sandown, **EDBERG** went on to land some hefty wagers. Jockey Andy Orkney enthused:

> *"Edberg is the most thrilling jumper I have sat on. He's got so many gears."*

"FAIR CROSSING should come into his own in novice chases next season,"

said trainer Charlie Brooks.

"FIDDLE A LITTLE is a useful horse,"

informed Ferdie Murphy.

Jenny Pitman's assistant, David Stait, said of Worcester hurdle winner **FINO**:

"He has been a bit immature, but he has been schooled over the small fences, jumps them beautifully and will go chasing next season."

FIVELEIGH BUILDS, a son of Deep Run, had too many guns for his rivals and ran out a comfortable winner of the Alfred McAlpine Novices' Hurdle at Bangor-on-Dee. Trainer John Upson said:

"Fiveleigh Builds is still learning - he came off a hillside in Connemara only ten months ago. He'll stay three miles all right and is another chaser in the making."

"FLAKEY DOVE has got that bit of class and give her another twelve months and she won't be far off top class,"

predicted trainer Richard Price.

FLOWN quickened up well from two out to take command of the Trafalgar House Supreme Novices' Hurdle at the Cheltenham Festival, winning decisively in the style of a very useful horse. Jockey Jamie Osborne reported:

"I was always in second gear. I can't believe how easily

> he's won it. I only saw one other horse all the way. He
> had plenty left."

◆

FORTUNE AND FAME ran on strongly, winning decisively
the B.M.W. Champion Novice Hurdle at Punchestown. In
ebullient mood, trainer Dermot Weld said:

> "He is a better and more experienced horse than he was
> at Cheltenham. But he is growing up now and he is a
> horse to look forward to. He goes on any ground and is
> going to make a smashing two-mile chaser. That is what
> he will be doing next winter. He will not be aimed at the
> Champion Hurdle."

◆

FRAGRANT DAWN won decisively on his introduction to
fences in the Bic Razor Chase at Kempton and is an
interesting prospect. David Elsworth revealed:

> "I don't like comparing horses with Desert Orchid but
> at this stage he's the best novice I've had since him.
> He's got such enthusiasm for the job, when he's
> schooled he wants to jump two at a time."

◆

Having been runner-up to the smart Carobee at Chepstow,
GALAXY HIGH had a much easier task in the Webb Travel
Novices' Hurdle at Devon & Exeter and duly obliged with an
effortless victory. Jockey Lorcan Wyer reported:

> "I've always felt he was going the right way. I don't
> think he'd be disgraced wherever he went because the
> farther he goes, the better he feels. He's a lovely little
> horse and I like him a lot."

◆

Gordon Richards commented:

> "**GALLATEEN** is still green and will make a chaser.
> Neale (Doughty) is dying to sit on him over a fence."

A young chaser that looks to have a future is **GLEN CHERRY**, who got up close to home in a gruelling tussle to the line in the Welshpool Novices' Handicap Chase at Ludlow. Trainer Tim Forster commented:

> "Glen Cherry got a bit outpaced two out but kept on again in the style of a real stayer. This was only the fifth race of his life and I'm delighted with him."

◆

Trainer Nicky Henderson, observing his **GOLDEN ARCTIC**, winner of the Wantage Novice Hurdle at Newbury, predicted:

> "He's a horse for next year and I think he can make a lovely novice chaser."

◆

GOOD PROFILE had little difficulty in winning the Harcross Scottish Juvenile hurdle at Ayr and looks very useful. Trainer George Moore stressed:

> "I don't want to overdo it this season and he'll have a maximum of two more races."

◆

GREY MINSTREL, who won a couple of point-to-points in Ireland, landed the Anick Handicap Chase at Hexham in the style of a useful sort. Trainer Denys Smith explained:

> "I knew he was a horse who would need a bit of time, but I liked him as soon as I saw him."

◆

A half-brother to that fine chaser Badsworth Boy, the six-year-old **HANGOVER** got off the mark in the Bridgnorth Novices' Hurdle at Wolverhampton. Trainer Richard Lee bought the gelding as a three-year-old to eventually go over fences and that's where he should make his mark. Wife Carol Lee commented:

> *"We don't normally buy store horses but we liked this one so much when we saw him at Doncaster that we decided to step in."*

◆

> *"I think **HASHAR** is a good horse,"*

said David Elsworth.

◆

A good-looking sort, **HAWTHORN BLAZE** never quite reached the heights expected of him this season. He finished the campaign with a fourth in the B.M.W. Champion Novice Hurdle at Punchestown. Trainer David Elsworth emphasised:

> *"Hawthorn Blaze is not the complete horse yet, but he has the potential to be good. He will make a nice chaser next season."*

◆

Trainer George Moore predicted:

> *"When **HIGH ALLTITUDE** becomes stronger he will be a nice horse."*

◆

A sturdy sort, **HOUXTY LAD** surprised many when winning at 20-1 on his introduction to fences in the Stayers' Novices' Chase at Catterick, but he had previously proved his worth at home, as his trainer Alister Charlton explained:

> *"I galloped Houxty Lad the other day with Truely Royal over two miles six furlongs. There was nothing between them and, as Truely Royal had run King's Curate to half a length at Ayr, I thought we must have a chance as there wasn't a King's Curate among the rivals today. He can't go a yard in the soft - he's got such big feet they act like suction pads and he can't get them out of the ground."*

INTERPRETATION ran his field ragged when coming home twenty lengths clear of Mountain Kingdom in the F.T.C. Corporate Recovery Novices' Hurdle at Kempton. Nicky Henderson commented:

> *"I know he has bumped into a few good ones but I've always thought he was decent."*

Simon Christian said of his twenty-length Ludlow Novice Hurdle winner **JIMMY THE GILLIE**:

> *"He's still big, lanky and loose-limbed, and still has not got his strength yet, but he'll make a chaser."*

Never looking in danger from three out, **KALOGY** ran on to record a decisive eight-length victory over Billy Bathgate in the Final Novices' Hurdle at Newbury. Trainer Jackie Retter emphasised:

> *"Everything she does over hurdles is a bonus. She hasn't filled into her frame yet - she's very tall and is a good three-mile chaser in the making."*

Trainer John Jenkins commented on his Folkestone winner **KAYTAK**:

> *"I bought him in France and think he could be a decent horse, but he's probably better going left-handed."*

Trainer Len Lungo said of his five-year-old Sedgefield Novice Hurdle winner **LOTHIAN PILOT**:

> *"This family are late developers and don't usually do anything until they are six, so this is a bonus. He will make up into a nice novice chaser next season."*

Trainer Terry Casey remarked on his Towcester winner **MACEDONAS**:

> *"He is still a baby but he is a late foal and I think he has a big future."*

> *"MAN OF MYSTERY could be a decent horse when he gets his act together. He wants a test of stamina,"*
>
> informed trainer Chris Trietline.

Bought out of Guy Harwood's stable for 4,000gns., **MARA ASKARI** landed a nice touch in the two-mile Rock Novices' Hurdle on the all-weather at Southwell. Trainer Jimmy Harris admitted:

> *"He is a nice little buy, being a strong, tough sort of horse and a winner on the flat. I fancied him a bit today but would have done so even more over an extra half-mile. This course is a great benefit to us. We bring horses to work here every Sunday morning and we have had much more success since it has opened as we are able to work the horses properly."*

MARTELL SPIRIT impressed on his debut, with an emphatic victory in the Look Before You Leap N.H. Flat Race at Haydock. This is yet another promising recruit from New Zealand and trained by David Barons, who revealed:

> *"This is a very, very good horse and it will take a good one to stop him."*

> *"MASTER RAJH just can't go on soft ground,"*
>
> stressed trainer John Chugg.

MERRY MASTER, who needs it soft, was a good third in the Ship Hotel Novices' Chase at Kelso. Jockey Gee Armytage reported on her father's horse:

> *"The two miles, six furlongs on good ground was too fast for him. He is a real staying horse and perhaps will be a Scottish National horse one day."*

> *"**MIGHTY MOGUL** is an improving horse with bags of scope,"*

said Jenny Pitman's assistant Gordon Johnson-Houghton.

A 35,000gns. buy at Doncaster Sales by comedian Freddie Star, **MIINNEHOMA** fully justified the price tag when he ran on bravely for a hard-fought victory from Bradbury Star to take the Sun Alliance Chase at Cheltenham. Jockey Peter Scudamore reported:

> *"I haven't ridden in a better novice chase. They are two very good horses. I think Miinnehoma could be up to coming back for the Gold Cup next year."*

A good effort by **MONTEBEL** to capture the Ripley Four-Year-Old Hurdle at Sandown from Swift Sword and Master Foodbroker augers well for the future. Owner Michael Arnold said:

> *"This hurdling is all a bonus for Montebel. He'll make a three-mile chaser in due course."*

Trainer Chris Thornton declared:

> *"I think **NANDA MOON** is a nice horse and should go on."*

OK CORRAL battled on well from the last to take first prize in the Steel Plate & Sections Young Chasers' Novices Chase at Chepstow from Hey Cottage. Trainer John White said:

> *"Brian (Clifford) said the horse was hating the soft ground and he's much better suited by fast, which is why he could run well in the final of this series at Cheltenham next autumn."*

◆

Trainer David Murray-Smith commented on his impressive Doncaster N.H. Flat race winner **OSMOSIS**:

> *"He'll go over fences straight away next season."*

◆

> *"OUNAVARRA MILL is a real soft ground horse,"*
>> stressed David Murray Smith.

◆

PEANUTS PET, a half-brother to Cashew King, has joined Thomas Tate and won the Potterton Myson Novices' Chase at Kelso on his first run for his new stable. The Tadcaster handler said:

> *"He's a handy horse, a little professional, who comes from a great jumping family. I think he wants farther than two miles and should make a nice handicap chaser."*

◆

QUALITAIR SOUND caught the eye with a sustained run from two out to gain an eight-length success from some well-thought of rivals in the Tote Placepot Hurdle at Kempton. Trainer John Bottomley admitted:

> *"I've always thought he was a good horse. I have nothing to work him with at home and I had to give him a run on the flat at Southwell two weeks ago, before he won there over hurdles five days ago."*

A strong run from the last landed the spoils for **REPEAT THE DOSE** from Toranfield and My Young Man in the Cathcart Challenge Cup Chase at the Cheltenham Festival. Trainer Tim Etherington explained:

> *"This horse has always been our best galloper at home but his first two races this season were disappointing and he had not been jumping properly. He wants some cut in the ground, but I think more important is that he wants a galloping track. He's such a long-striding horse that he's always been having to check to put himself right on the less galloping tracks."*

David Barons informed:

> *"I think **ROCKTOR** has got plenty of improvement in him for the next season and he does like fast ground."*

Tim Etherington remarked on another fine young chaser in the making:

> *"**ROUGH QUEST** will be better over three miles and ideally he needs good to soft ground."*

ROYAL SAXON fought back bravely on the flat to open his account in the Longwood Fen Novices' Hurdle at Huntingdon. Trainer Henrietta Knight emphasised:

> *"He was bought as a future chaser and anything he won over hurdles was always going to be a bonus. He may have one more run before we put him away for the season."*

SALWAN, a 12,000gns. buy out of William Jarvis' yard, led three out to capture the Glenlivet Four-Year-Old Hurdle at Liverpool in clear-cut fashion. Trainer Peter Bevan emphasised:

Salwan can go all the way

"*Salwan loves his work and has the right temperament to go all the way. I just hope I can persuade owner Peter Douglas to let me have him gelded.*"

"SENDAI is a very tough filly and will go chasing next season,"

said Josh Gifford.

Mick Easterby's grey gelding **SILVER STICK** quickened up well from the last to land the South West Durham Hospice Appeal Novices' Hurdle at Sedgefield. The Sheriff Hutton trainer declared:

"This horse is a full-brother to Combermere, who was killed in the Scottish National. I've schooled him over fences and he jumps brilliantly."

Head lad Mark Elliott said:

"SNITTON LANE will stay three miles with no trouble and will go chasing next season straight away."

Andy Turnell said of his Stratford-on-Avon Novices' Hurdle winner **SOVEREIGN SOUND**:

"He ran very green at Warwick the last time. I bought him unbroken at Doncaster Sales and he'll go chasing next season."

"SPRUCER really needs three miles and soft ground,"
said trainer Tockie McKie.

Neville Callaghan made the following comment on his huge Don gelding, **STEVEADON**:

"He's nearly 17 hands and will go over fences next season. I think he will be a good horse one day and a summer on his back will do him the world of good."

Two young chasers in the making, **STORM ALERT** and Cool Dodger, fought out the finish of the Georgie Newell Novices' Chase at Wincanton with the former prevailing by a neck. Trainer Andy Turnell said:

> *"He has a go and he's still learning."*

Assistant trainer Colin Platts said of N. H. Flat race winner **STORMHEAD**:

> *"He's still a big baby and will go on to better things."*

> *"SUNSET AND VINE will be a nice novice chaser next season,"*

said Simon Dow.

All concerned thought **SUPER SENSE** had prevailed in a very tight finish with Mr Gossip in the Clive Graham Handicap Hurdle at Chepstow. The judge consulted the photo and to the amazement of jockey Declan Murphy, the Findon gelding was placed second. Josh Gifford announced:

> *"We'll keep him over hurdles for the rest of the season and save his maiden chases for next."*

Trainer Peter Easterby's son Tim explained why **SWORD BEACH** was not running in the Grand National:

> *"Maybe that will be a race for him next year. He loves it firm and is a grand jumper."*

SYDMONTON, a son of Deep Run, has distinct possibilities for the future. He followed up a promising debut at Lingfield to record a decisive six-length win from Fair Brother in the Slough Novices' Hurdle at Windsor. Nicky Henderson said:

"He didn't jump a twig at Lingfield, but still ran very well. He was very green there. Today, though, he was fantastic bar the last. I've never bullied the horse and I just liked the way he pricked his ears and galloped to the line."

◆

"THE ILLYWHACKER is a very good horse but we think he is better going right-handed,"

said Jenny Pitman.

◆

Following a disappointing run at Ayr, **TOPSAWYER** seemed more at home on firm ground when landing the spoils in the E.B.F. N.H. Flat Race at Doncaster from the odds-on Dunraven Bay. Trainer Sally Hall explained:

"I bought him as a two-year-old out of my nephew William Jarvis' Newmarket stable for 1,800gns. Topsawyer must be the best-bred horse ever to win a bumper. He is by Kris out of Catalpa, who won the Ribblesdale Stakes at Royal Ascot and was third best filly of her year."

◆

The lightly raced **TOUCHING STAR**, a winner on the flat, had little difficulty in landing the Sheaf & Sickle Novices' Handicap Chase at Devon & Exeter. Trainer Philip Hobbs advised:

"He's looked good ever since we schooled him and can be expected to improve as this was only his third chase. I think he's got quite a bit of ability."

◆

TRUBLION made an extremely favourable impression, having little difficulty landing the Sorn Novices' Handicap Chase at Ayr. Stan Mellor commented:

> *"I was delighted with that and he really is the most lovely horse. He's got the ability and it's quite exciting to see him quickening into his fences. He's going to get better."*

◆

URON V, a French-bred gelding, showed a deal of promise for the future when running on to some purpose to land the Milton N.H. Novices' Hurdle in soft ground at Carlisle. Trainer Micky Hammond informed:

> *"Peter (Niven) said he'll make a fine chaser. The horse has schooled well and will probably go straight over fences next season. He is still very much of a baby and we'll go carefully with him for the rest of the term."*

◆

Although beaten when unseated at the last in the Champion Hurdle, Shane Lyons, rider of **VALIANT BOY**, reported:

> *"I had a great ride to the top of the hill. He'll be a Cheltenham horse over fences."*

◆

Trainer John Upson predicted of his Southwell Maiden Chase winner **VERY VERY ORDINARY**:

> *"You will see him in a lot higher grade in two years' time. He is big and backward at the moment, but is a very nice horse."*

◆

VIRIDIAN landed a nice touch from 10-1 to 13-2 in the Feversham Novice Chase at Doncaster. Trainer Annabel King stressed:

> *"Contrary to what some say, Veridian is a most genuine horse and he likes quick ground."*

◆

WELL WRAPPED, a lightly-raced gelding, is expected to progress to greater heights this coming season, following a twelve-length success in the Peter Duncanson Memorial Trophy Novices' Chase at Fontwell. Trainer Henrietta Knight commented:

> *"I adore this horse, he's the apple of my eye. He is a most beautiful jumper and is still very green. He got a leg after his first race under rules and was fired, so there is plenty to look forward to."*

WELSH BARD had little trouble in landing the Ikley Moore Novices' Chase at Doncaster when he spread-eagled his field from four fences out. Charlie Brooks commented:

> *"He is a very talented horse and jumps well. He had some smart form over hurdles and will be a good two-mile chaser in time, but I think patience is the key."*

Soft going and a stiff uphill finish at Carlisle held no fears for **WHISPERING STEEL**, a son of Furry Glen out of a Deep Run mare, who ran on in good style to take the Nawort Novices' Hurdle. Trainer's son Nicky Richards said:

> *"He jumped super but Neil (Doughty) said the two miles and a bit was a little sharp for him. He'll be a lovely horse when he goes over fences."*

Having his first run over hurdles, **WHY RUN** looks the type to improve with maturing when collecting the Carlsberg Pilsner Novices Hurdle at Newton Abbot. David Murray Smith said:

> *"He's a hell of a nice horse and a good three-mile chaser in the making - he must have soft ground."*

8 . ANTE-POST BETTING

1993 CHELTENHAM
ANTE-POST BOOKS
by Mark Coton
(Freelance)

SMURFIT CHAMPION HURDLE
CHALLENGE TROPHY
[16th March 1993, 2m, Cheltenham]

7-2	Granville Again	20-1	Flown
6-1	Royal Gait	25-1	Coulton
10-1	Oh So Risky	25-1	Staunch Friend
12-1	Carobee	25-1	Halkopous
12-1	Vintage Crop	33-1	Duke Of Monmouth
16-1	Gran Alba	33-1	Al Mutahm
20-1	Destriero	33-1	Spinning
20-1	Fidway	40-1	*Bar*

Prices correct at time of going to press

7-2 GRANVILLE AGAIN

Highly productive season spoiled only when falling two out in Champion. Going well then and speed shown when landing five other races would probably have landed him the spoils. A worthy favourite but just too short to tempt ante-post backers at this stage.

6-1 ROYAL GAIT

Superbly produced by James Fanshawe to land Champion on only fourth start over hurdles, surviving stewards' inquiry into interference during rough race. Former top-class stayer on the flat, but injured again after Cheltenham so hold a watching brief.

10-1 OH SO RISKY

Cheltenham specialist who followed 1991 Triumph success with bold showing in Champion, failing by just a half length having looked sure to collect at the last. Failed to win otherwise and backers must wait until closer to the day before stepping in.

12-1 CAROBEE

Made particularly favourable impression with five successes in first campaign, including fluent Liverpool win over Halkopous and Flown. Entitled to take on the best, but future probably as much over fences and price short enough.

12-1 VINTAGE CROP

Dark horse from always to be respected Dermot Weld yard. Has form on the flat and made useful start to hurdling career when winning at Leopardstown. Cannot be fancied on that evidence but certainly one to keep an eye on.

16-1 GRAN ALBA

Fancied in some circles but forced to miss Champion after useful early season campaign. Found Fidway just too good at Wincanton in February and would have a little to find on that evidence, but is in the right hands and cannot be discounted.

20-1 DESTRIERO

Gambled-on winner of novice event at '91 Festival but failed to cut much ice in three runs last term. Cannot be fancied at this stage.

20-1 FIDWAY

Reformed character who landed two good wins before decent Champion fourth which may have come a touch too soon. Entitled to respect but has miles on the clock and others make more appeal.

20-1 FLOWN

Deeply impressive when slamming Halkopous 10 lengths in Trafalgar House Supreme Novice Hurdle, but disappointing by comparison when beaten at Liverpool and Punchestown subsequently. Past Cheltenham form always counts double at Festival, so maybe worth forgiving those failures at an attractive price.

25-1 COULTON

Improving fast towards end of last season, signing off with narrow success in valuable Uttoxeter contest. Entitled to come on again but Champion flying high on current evidence.

25-1 STAUNCH FRIEND

Disappointing favourite in Triumph but made amends with impressive 12-length success in the mud at Punchestown next time. Looks to lack something in class and the older horses make more appeal.

25-1 HALKOPOUS

Useful on flat and over hurdles but has plenty to find on last season's novice form when behind both Flown and Carobee in races at Cheltenham and Liverpool.

33-1 DUKE OF MONMOUTH

First time blinkers did the trick in Triumph hurdle and probably unsuited by heavy ground when beaten in Staunch Friend's race at Punchestown next time. Makes only limited appeal given poor record of five-year-olds.

33-1 AL MUTAHM

Useful third in Triumph Hurdle but biggest moment came with Pattern race success on flat at Ascot in April. Has plenty to find.

33-1 SPINNING

Smart if often frustrating character on the flat who took well to hurdles, winning three small races before Imperial Cup failure. Well below Champion class on that effort.

CONCLUSION:

GRANVILLE AGAIN was probably unlucky not to collect last season and is the one to beat, though odds fail to tempt. **CAROBEE** and **FLOWN** are two novices with a future and the latter, so impressive at last year's Festival, is well worth a second glance around 20-1.

TOTE CHELTENHAM GOLD CUP CHASE

[18th March 1993, 3m 2f, Cheltenham]

8-1	The Fellow	20-1	Cahervillahow
12-1	Docklands Express	20-1	Carrick Hill Lad
12-1	Miinnehoma	20-1	Chatam
14-1	Blazing Walker	20-1	Garrison Savannah
14-1	Cool Ground	20-1	Jodami
14-1	Kings Fountain	25-1	Morley Street
14-1	Remittance Man	25-1	Mutare
16-1	Carvill's Hill	33-1	Run For Free
20-1	Bradbury Star	40-1	*Bar*

Prices correct at time of going to press

8-1 THE FELLOW

Again denied Gold Cup triumph he deserves when caught on the line by Cool Ground last season. Earlier King George success proved he was top class and young enough to claim the biggest prize. Odds no more than reflect chance, however.

12-1 DOCKLANDS EXPRESS

Superbly tough and genuine chaser who ran above himself to claim close third in 1992 renewal. Brave National fourth indicated remarkable toughness, but preference for sound surface limits ante-post appeal.

12-1 MIINNEHOMA

Came again to beat Bradbury Star in superb Sun Alliance finish last season, breaking course record. Unbeaten over fences and open to yet more improvement, so with Pipe in charge must be one for the short-list.

14-1 BLAZING WALKER

Never right last season and did not race, but much to like about 90/91 campaign with six wins including top class effort in valuable chase at Liverpool. Stays well and still plenty young enough, though yet to prove himself around Cheltenham.

14-1 COOL GROUND

Gold Cup success something of a surprise and hard race there led to National failure. Previously thought a mud-lark, so Cheltenham win all the more creditable and lacks nothing in toughness, though probably lacks class needed to land elusive back-to-back triumphs.

14-1 KINGS FOUNTAIN

Still very much in touch when dislodging rider last year, but had luck on his side when gaining Liverpool compensation after Arctic Call came down. Bags of scope and well worth another crack. Yet to fully prove himself on soft ground.

14-1 REMITTANCE MAN

Only defeat over fences when disappointing third to The Fellow in King George, giving impression he failed to get home. Dramatic success in Queen Mother Champion Chase underlined toughness and class and well worth another chance over longer trips, though too risky for ante-post support just now.

16-1 CARVILL'S HILL

Invincible in many eyes before chink in armour ruthlessly

exposed by Golden Freeze last year. Brilliant earlier successes suggested jumping flaws had been ironed out but doubtful through injury and cannot be considered at this stage.

20-1 BRADBURY STAR

Took to fences in no uncertain style and brilliant jumping nearly enough to claim Sun Alliance prize. Good Liverpool win followed and sure to win more races, but slight stamina doubts give reason for caution.

20-1 CAHERVILLAHOW

Tough old-fashioned chaser denied 1991 Whitbread Triumph by Sandown stewards. Plenty of other good form, but had to miss last season and probably best watched before support is considered.

20-1 CARRICK HILL LAD

Multiple winner in fine 1990/91 campaign but off last season and not really a Cheltenham type on all known form.

20-1 CHATAM

Interesting outsider who is not easy to train but near top-class on his day as first time out Hennessy success showed. Inclined to take liberties with his fences so a risky proposition, but still young enough to make a big impression if all goes well.

20-1 GARRISON SAVANNAH

Out of luck last season after excellent 1990/91 campaign with Gold Cup win and National second. Watch for a return to form before considering support.

20-1 JODAMI

Most consistent and genuine young chaser who enjoyed fine novice campaign over fences winning three races. Blunders did not help cause when good second to Bradbury Star at Liverpool and needs to improve jumping to trouble the best.

25-1 MORLEY STREET

Interesting name creeping in at bottom of list, but previous chasing experience does not incline one to confidence. Stamina also not guaranteed.

25-1 MUTARE

Much fancied but probably held when falling two out in Sun Alliance. Found Miinnehoma too good at Chepstow previously and has work cut out to make an impression at highest level.

33-1 RUN FOR FREE

Ten lengths third to stable-mate Miinnehoma in Sun Alliance ended winning streak of four. Took to fences well, but has it to do on the book and possibly better over shorter distances.

CONCLUSION:

THE FELLOW has done all but win in the last two seasons and remains the class act, though last season's novices impressed. Sun Alliance winner MIINNEHOMA would look the pick at this stage and has decent ante-post claims. CHATAM is the interesting outsider.

1992 ANTE-POST ACTION

by Dave Thomas

THE GOLD CUP & GRAND NATIONAL

When Carvill's Hill spread-eagled a high class field in the Coral Welsh Grand National at Chepstow last December, it seemed the decision to send the horse from Ireland over to Martin Pipe's Wellington yard had been well and truly vindicated.

If anyone could iron out the jumping flaws in the then nine-year-old Carvill's Hill, it was reckoned Pipe was the man to do it. Much-touted as a 'wonder' horse in his novice days, cynics had begun to dub him 'blunder' horse, not least because his own distinctive style of jumping, although effective if not pretty most times, would occasionally lead to mistakes.

His only two appearances on a racecourse during 1990/91, for example, resulted firstly in a facile win over some admittedly moderate opposition at Punchestown (even though he contrived to make life difficult for himself by making mistakes throughout), and then in him coming a cropper at Gowran Park's first fence on his next outing.

"Enough," cried his owner and duly dispatched him to England, to the west country, in the hope that the Pond Farm House team could work the oracle. His first race for his new trainer was the three-mile Rehearsal Handicap Chase at Chepstow. There, despite some minor mistakes, Carvill's Hill ran out the 20-length winner of a small but select field, consisting of Aquilifer, Katabatic, Bonanza Boy, Gold Cup winner-elect Cool Ground and the disappointing 1991 Gold Cup favourite Celtic Shot.

Three weeks later he was back at Chepstow and proving

that, like humans, horses are never too old to learn. His jumping hadn't changed in style all that much, but he was jumping bigger and bolder, as well as with a new-found confidence and he landed the Welsh National in hugely impressive style, leading home Party Politics and stable-mate Aquilifier by 20 lengths and a short head, the rest of the field strung out hopelessly behind. Pipe, ably assisted by Peter Scudamore in the saddle, had, not for the first time, done the trick and at last the 'wonder' horse was looking what he had always promised to be: a likely Gold Cup winner.

The betting public thought so too: from being available at 16-1 in October, Carvill's Hill went into the New Year as low as 9-4 favourite for the Gold Cup. The manner of his Chepstow wins led to a good deal of uncertainty over who would and who wouldn't be prepared to take him on at Cheltenham and the number of horses quoted at this time was the lowest for many years.

Of those that were, only Kings Fountain (16-1), King George winner and the previous year's Gold Cup runner-up The Fellow (6-1), and Toby Tobias (12-1) were to go to post. Others advertised over the winter included Blazing Walker (12-1), who was sidelined at the time and was to remain so to the end of the season, and the 1991 winner Garrison Savannah (14-1), who was pulled up in the Hennessy Cognac Gold Cup at Newbury and not seen out at all thereafter.

As always the picture was a little clearer in the month leading up to the Festival. A virtually flawless round had seen Carvill's Hill return home to land the Irish version of the Hennessy Gold Cup at Leopardstown, and afterwards he hardened to 7-4 for the Gold Cup . By this stage the eventual winner, Cool Ground, and third, Docklands Express, were being generally quoted, at 40-1 and 33-1 respectively. There had been small support for The Fellow (down to 9-2), but the only horse punters were interested in was Carvill's Hill.

Despite fears from some quarters that the stiff Cheltenham fences would catch him out, backers remained undaunted and Carvill's Hill was down to 5-4 a full two weeks before the race. Elsewhere, Docklands Express won the Racing Post

Handicap Chase at Kempton, a victory which saw his Cheltenham price reduced to 20-1, while confident noises from Weathercock House concerning Toby Tobias led to Jenny Pitman's more fancied of her two intended runners (the outsider Golden Freeze being the other) being backed down to 8-1.

Cool Ground, meanwhile, having been steady at around 40-1 and 50-1, saw his odds tumble down to 25-1 after his success in the Greenall's Gold Cup at Haydock on the last day of of February

Just eight runners made it to post, including the 1990 winner Norton's Coin. However, the pro-money wasn't on a repeat of glories past, but on potential soon to be fulfilled, and Carvill's Hill was sent off the warm even-money favourite. With the favourite having such cramped odds on the day, the bookmakers offered generous early-morning prices on some of the other runners. Cool Ground was available at 40-1, which was cracking each-way value in a field of eight, given he had some decent form and could definitely stay the trip. Some shrewder punters must have got on because his odds contracted and he started at 25-1.

The machinations of the race itself are well-documented elsewhere in the *Companion*, so don't need repeating here. In many ways it was an untypical ante-post book. Rarely does a horse talk so much as Carvill's Hill did for the 1992 Cheltenham Gold Cup and it would be unwise to draw conclusions from the book.

The difference between success and failure is all relative of course, and it's a sad fact that the failings of one horse will probably be remembered long after the triumph of another has been forgotten. And that is a fate which will befall both Carvill's Hill and Cool Ground, not matter how unfair that may be.

Carvill's Hill was also winter favourite in the Grand National ante-post book, being as low as 10-1 at the turn of the year

and down to 7-1 before the back injury sustained in the controversial Gold Cup race finally ended any hopes that he might carry top weight round Aintree's demanding four and a half miles.

His defection, and Cool Ground's confirmed participation saw the ante-post book change dramatically. Originally available at 20-1 for the National, Cool Ground was slashed to 14-1 following his Haydock win, and 6-1 favouritism after his hard-fought Gold Cup success. There was support too for Docklands Express, who trainer Kim Bailey had always rated the equal of his previous National winner Mr Frisk, despite a first fence fall in the 1991 race. Docklands Express, available at 25-1 before his Racing Post Kempton success, was heavily backed down to 8-1.

Elsewhere the only other support of significance in the two weeks leading up to the race was for Brown Windsor (25-1 to 12-1) and the prolific Haydock winner Twin Oaks (16-1 to 12-1). Haydock is considered by many to be a good test for Aintree-bound animals and the run of success enjoyed by Twin Oaks at that course led many to consider him the best each-way value in the race. Frustratingly for backers, Twin Oaks was to finish fifth, after further support hardened him to 9-1 third-favourite.

Carvill's Hill apart, there were few defectors from those quoted in ante-post lists. Nearly all stood their ground, again underlining the National as being a race offering less of a risk for ante-post backers.

Sitting steady in the book was the Coral Welsh National second and eventual Grand National winner Party Politics. This huge stamp of a horse, who looked capable of stepping over Aintree's modified fences, was available at 25-1 following his Chepstow run, a price which stayed steady up until the two weeks prior to the Aintree meeting when, following less than conclusive runs in the Greenall's Gold Cup behind Cool Ground and a fifth of sixth when sent off 5-4 favourite for the Anthony Mildmay Peter Cazalet Memorial Handicap Chase at Sandown, he drifted out to 33-1.

But with a General Election looming, the appropriately named Party Politics attracted support in the ante-post 'opinion polls' and was backed down through 20-1 to 14-1 on the day. Unlike the polls which predicted a change of Government, however, money spoke louder than hot air and supporters of Party Politics were rewarded with a two-and-a-half length success.

Two other horses backed on the day were Romany King (22-1 to 16-1), who was to finish second, and Midlands' National winner Laura's Beau (16-1 to 12-1), who was to finish third. Surprisingly, Cool Ground drifted out to 10-1, while Docklands Express hardened to 15-2 favourtism, just ahead of Brown Windsor, at 8-1.

Close scrutiny of the ante-post book reveals that the optimum time for punters to strike Grand National bets is around two weeks before the race. Nearly all quoted runners will stand their ground, and as most of the form is in place by then fancies can be backed at prices which are likely to be substantially reduced thereafter.

With 22 runners completing the race, and the first five home being well up the betting, the belief that the Grand National is no more than a good handicap for out-and-out stayers these days gains further converts. For all that, it is still a race which captures the public imagination like no other in the racing calendar and it takes a very good horse to succeed. Perhaps the race did come too soon after Cheltenham for Cool Ground, but he was fairly handicapped on his Gold Cup win and on the day was beaten by better horses.

Cool Ground's detractors, who labelled him no better than a handicapper - albeit a very good one - who would not have lived with the likes of Dawn Run or Burrough Hill Lad, are probably being most unfair on him. He was most unfortunate to come up against Carvill's Hill and the subsequent brouhaha over the race detracted from his win. And only the benefit of hindsight could determine the wisdom of running him at Aintree so soon after.

Poor old Cool Ground: life's unfair, but it's more unfair for some than others.

GOLD CUP ANTE-POST BOOK 1992

	Winter	1 Mnth	2 weeks	1 week	Same Day	S.P.	Pos
Aquilifer	-	-	66-1	100-1	-	-	-
Blazing Walker	12-1	-	-	-	-	-	-
Bonanza Boy	-	-	100-1	100-1	-	-	-
Carvill's Hill	*9-4*	*7-4*	*5-4*	*5-4*	*Evens*	*Evens*	*5*
Chatham	-	25-1	25-1	20-1	-	-	-
COOL GROUND	-	40-1	50-1	25-1	40-1	25-1	1
Docklands Express	-	33-1	20-1	20-1	16-1	16-1	3
Firions Law	-	-	66-1	100-1	-	-	-
Garrison Savannah	14-1	16-1	-	-	-	-	-
Golden Freeze	-	-	66-1	100-1	200-1	150-1	P
Kildimo	-	-	-	40-1	-	-	-
Kings Fountain	16-1	16-1	10-1	8-1	8-1	8-1	U
Nortons Coin	-	-	40-1	40-1	40-1	33-1	P
Pats Jester	16-1	12-1	12-1	25-1	-	-	-
Rolling Ball	-	20-1	-	-	-	-	-
Sparkling Flame	-	40-1	50-1	-	-	-	-
The Fellow	**6-1**	**9-2**	**4-1**	**7-2**	**10-3**	**7-2**	**2**
Toby Tobias	**12-1**	**12-1**	**12-1**	**8-1**	**10-1**	**15-2**	**4**
Twin Oaks	-	-	40-1	-	-	-	-

8 Ran

GRAND NATIONAL ANTE-POST BOOK 1992

	Winter	1 Mnth	2 weeks	1 week	Same Day	S.P.	Pos
Ace Of Spies	-	-	-	50-1	-	-	-
Auntie Dot	25-1	25-1	25-1	25-1	18-1	12-1	16
Big Sun	33-1	33-1	40-1	-	-	-	-
Bonanza Boy	-	33-1	40-1	50-1	40-1	25-1	R
Brown Windsor	-	25-1	12-1	11-1	11-1	8-1	F
Carvill's Hill	10-1	7-1	-	-	-	-	-
Cloney Grange	-	-	-	-	200-1	100-1	F
Cool Ground	20-1	14-1	6-1	11-2	15-2	10-1	10
Docklands Express	*25-1*	*16-1*	*8-1*	*10-1*	*9-1*	*15-2*	*4*
Esha Ness	-	33-1	40-1	-	-	-	-
Firions Law	-	33-1	-	50-1	-	-	-
Forest Ranger	-	-	-	-	200-1	200-1	12
Garrison Savannah	33-1	-	33-1	-	-	-	-
Ghofar	-	33-1	-	40-1	33-1	25-1	11
Gold Options	-	33-1	33-1	-	-	-	-
Golden Fox	-	-	-	-	200-1	200-1	R
Golden Freeze	-	-	-	50-1	-	-	-
Golden Minstrel	-	-	-	-	150-1	150-1	15
Have A Barney	-	-	-	40-1	-	-	-
High Peak	-	-	-	50-1	-	-	-
Honeybear Mead	-	-	-	-	250-1	100-1	U
Hotplate	-	-	-	50-1	50-1	50-1	P
Huntworth	-	-	-	-	100-1	66-1	P
Just So	-	-	-	-	66-1	50-1	6
Karakter Referance	-	-	-	50-1	66-1	50-1	P
Kildimo	-	25-1	-	-	-	-	-
Kittinger	-	-	-	-	250-1	200-1	R
Lanigans Wine	-	-	-	50-1	-	-	-
Laura's Beau	-	-	-	25-1	16-1	12-1	3
Mighty Falcon	-	-	-	-	100-1	80-1	18
Mister Ed	-	-	-	-	100-1	100-1	F
New Halen	-	-	-	-	66-1	66-1	R
Old Apple Jack	-	-	-	-	100-1	35-1	7
Omerta	-	28-1	25-1	25-1	50-1	33-1	P
Our Nobby	-	-	-	50-1	-	-	-
Over The Road	-	-	33-1	33-1	22-1	22-1	8

GRAND NATIONAL ANTE-POST BOOK 1992 (cont.)

	Winter	1 Mnth	2 weeks	1 week	Same Day	S.P.	Pos
PARTY POLITICS	25-1	25-1	33-1	20-1	18-1	14-1	1
Radical Lady	-	-	-	-	100-1	80-1	19
Rawhide	-	-	-	50-1	66-1	50-1	U
Rinus	25-1	25-1	25-1	-	-	-	-
Roc De Prince	-	-	-	-	66-1	40-1	17
Romany King	-	-	33-1	33-1	22-1	16-1	2
Rowlandson Jewels	-	-	-	-	100-1	60-1	U
Royal Battery	-	-	-	50-1	100-1	80-1	P
Rubika	-	-	-	40-1	28-1	28-1	14
Seagram	-	28-1	33-1	40-1	40-1	33-1	P
Sirrah Jay	-	-	-	50-1	100-1	100-1	22
Solidasarock	-	-	40-1	-	-	-	-
Stay On Tracks	-	-	33-1	40-1	25-1	16-1	9
Stearsby	-	-	-	-	300-1	250-1	R
Team Challenge	-	-	-	-	100-1	100-1	21
Tipping Tim	-	-	40-1	-	-	-	-
Toby Tobias	-	28-1	-	-	-	-	-
Twin Oaks	12-1	16-1	12-1	10-1	10-1	9-1	5
Whats The Crack	-	-	-	40-1	33-1	20-1	13
Why So Hasty	-	-	-	-	500-1	250-1	P
Willsford	25-1	25-1	25-1	25-1	20-1	16-1	20

40 Ran

ANTE-POST BETTING EXPLAINED

Traditionally ante-post betting is racing's 'future market', though nowadays this aspect plays only a small part of the overall service to backers. Literally, to bet ante-post is to bet before the contenders have reached the starting post - in other words in advance of a race. Technically it means betting at least a day before the event.

There are effectively three forms of ante-post betting: long-range, mid-range and on the day. The first is the traditional form and has a life of six months and more, concerning the summer Classics and the Cheltenham showpieces. All, but especially the Flat events, are extremely risky but offer the possibility of high financial rewards and the tremendous satisfaction of securing sometimes dramatically better odds than SP.

The mid-range ante-post books are generally more predictable and less prone to the often wild movements of the long-range. Many of the biggest handicaps and top stakes races have books lasting a few weeks, and while there is seldom the opportunity for big gains, there is every chance to detect good value bets.

In each of the above markets the regular backer will experience a switch-back of highs and lows. For most people it is do or die, win or lose, but serious players make their own books and take 'positions'. This involves paying a great deal of attention to the market, snapping up good prices when they are on offer, hedging bets by backing rivals to recoup stakes or better - or even selling their bets back to their bookmakers. Great fun, potentially very profitable, but quite demanding.

The third way of ante-post betting is on-the-day. This is actually classified as 'Early Prices' and, unlike true ante-post, stakes are returned if the selection is a non-runner. On many days, and always when there is televised racing, one or two races are priced-up and here the challenge is a simple one. With the race just a few hours away, the backer is being asked not to show prophetic powers, but merely to beat SP. By comparing bookmaker's prices, seeing the run of tips and reading reports, this is made the easiest, if least exciting, form of ante-post betting.

Unless something untoward happens, even a novice backer should be able to get consistently better than SP odds about their selections. The 'Pricewise' feature in the *Racing Post* highlights where the best value is to be obtained for all selections in the day's ante-post races, and whether the individual is swayed by the accompanying editorial or not, the tables give all the basic information. As it happens, the editorial has proved to be very worthy of attention, with nearly all suggestions being tipped at better value than SP.

Bookmakers claim that ante-post betting is a "shop window" - good for profile, but unprofitable. In view of the above, and most ante-post activity now is on the day, it is quite understandable that bookmakers are unable to make their usual profits. Take the hint and bet ante-post - but be quick reaching a decision because prices can change rapidly.

9 . CHELTENHAM POINTERS

by

Dominic Gardiner-Hill
(The Racing Post)

[In the tables Fav. = where the favourite finished]

INTRODUCTION

Despite the claims of Aintree's Grand National meeting, the Cheltenham Festival is still the only true Festival as far as the die-hard National Hunt fan is concerned. These are the races that are targeted by trainers for their stable stars from early in the season; for most a run at Aintree is only considered once Cheltenham is over.

This is the meeting where the best of the English try to repel the challenge from the stars of Ireland and, in more recent years, a number of French raiders who have proved worthy of their place in the season's premier races.

Competition is naturally fierce and nowhere throughout the whole of the jumps season is it more difficult to back winners. The biggest aid to the punter is, of course, an intimate knowledge of the form, the horses and the ability of their trainers to get them onto the track in tip-top form.

There is also benefit to be gained from the study of previous results: which contests traditionally throw up surprises and are to be avoided, which contests have proved kindest to punters, which age-groups do best in which races and how important is pre-Cheltenham form? Hopefuly, the following information will help provide the answers to some of these questions.

TRAFALGAR HOUSE SUPREME NOVICES' HURDLE (2m)

Winners	92	91	90	89	88	87	86	85	84	83
S. P.	13-2	6-1	7-4	25-1	4-1	14-1	40-1	14-1	11-2	8-1
Pos Mkt	4	3J	1	0	1	5	0	4J	3	4
Last out	1	1	1	7	1	2	3	1	1	2
Runners	17	21	18	21	26	20	29	30	18	22
Fav.	4	2	1	3	1	8/0	2	8	3	4

The traditional opening to the Festival - and a contest on which the Irish had a remarkable stranglehold during the late seventies and early eighties, providing eight out of nine winners between 1975 and 1983. Since then the English have had much the better of the opening exchanges, with only the gambled-on Destriero (1991) breaking their run of success.

Those who use race trends as a guide would definitely have short-listed last season's winner Flown. As a five-year-old he was the perfect age, with eighteen of the last nineteen winners having been either five or six, and his victory also meant that eight of the last ten winners have come from the top five in the betting market.

The importance of a successful pre-Cheltenham outing was also highlighted and he became the sixth of the last ten winners to have gone into the race with a victory under their belt.

In a race that since 1983 has seen a smallest field of 18, there is always the chance of a shock result and in that period River Ceiriog (40-1 in 1986) and Sondrio (25-1 in 1989) have been winners on the side of the bookmakers. The latter, in fact, defies all the trends of the race as he was an eight-year-old when winning and is the only victor in the last ten years to have failed to at least have made the frame in his pre-Cheltenham outing.

WATERFORD CASTLE ARKLE CHALLENGE TROPHY CHASE (2m)

Winners	92	91	90	89	88	87	86	85	84	83
S.P.	4-1	85-40	9-2	20-1	11-2	25-1	14-1	15-2	5-4	16-1
Pos Mkt	2	1	2J	7J	4	12J	7	4J	1	5J
Last out	1	1	1	2	1	3	2	U	1	2
Runners	11	14	14	14	12	19	14	16	8	16
Fav.	4	1	6	3	2	3	5	2	1	9

Only two favourites have managed to justify their position in the market during the last ten years and they were the brilliant duo of Bobsline (1984) and Remittance Man (1991). This proves what a competitive contest the Arkle usually is, and a glance along the winning S.P. line in the table gives ample evidence that the race has the potential to throw up a shock.

That said, the last three years have gone slightly more in the punter's favour, with Remittance Man splitting successful second-favourites Comandante and Young Pokey, with the latter showing many of the attributes that the recent history of the race demands of its winners.

Because of the fast pace of the race, a fluent jumper with plenty of pace is essential and Oliver Sherwood's charge had both. He also possessed good recent form and became the fifth winner in the last ten years who had scored in their previous outing. Of the other five, four had finished in the frame whilst Boreen Prince (1985) had unseated his jockey.

As a seven-year-old Young Pokey was also in the correct age bracket, with six, seven and eight-year-olds having taken nine of the last ten runnings. Jimmy FitzGerald's Danish Flight (nine) being the exception in 1988.

The Irish enjoyed a fine run in the race with five successes between 1979 and 1985, but have failed to add to that subsequently, despite several placed efforts.

SMURFIT CHAMPION HURDLE (2m)

Winners	92	91	90	89	88	87	86	85	84	83
S. P.	6-1	4-1	95-40	50-1	7-1	11-10	5-6	16-1	4-5	7-1
Pos Mkt	3	1	2	12	4	1	1	J3	1	4
Last out	1	1	1	1	2	1	1	1	1	1
Runners	16	24	19	15	21	18	23	14	14	17
Fav.	6	1	4	7	3	1	1	6	1	3/5

Whilst it would be pure folly to suggest that the Champion Hurdle is an easy race in which to find the winner, if the heavy ground success of Beech Road in 1989 is ignored then recent results have a certain predictability about them.

For instance, of the last ten winners only Beech Road came from outside the top four in the betting and four outright favourites have been successful. In addition, recent winning form has proved vital with nine of the last ten winners having been successful in their previous outing, the exception being Celtic Shot who had finished second.

Last season's winner Royal Gait was somewhat unusual in as much that he was a novice and was having only his fourth ever outing over hurdles. A top class stayer on the flat, he did however figure prominently in the market (third-favourite) and had been successful on his previous start. Another novice, Ruling, had run well to finish third the year before so it is not impossible for first-season hurdlers to make their presence felt in the race.

With a big ante-post market existing for the race, speculation about future contenders is always rife but few come through to genuinely make the grade. In fact, many consider the best pointer to the race to be the previous year's running as horses often perform well in the race more than once, with four horses having completed a hat-trick and another six having won it twice

As a nine-year-old Royal Gait was the oldest winner of the race since Sea Pigeon in 1981. Six-year-olds are the most prolific age group in recent times, winning five of the last ten runnings.

THE STAYERS' HURDLE (3m 1f)

Winners	92	91	90	89	88	87	86	85	84	83
S. P.	15-2	5-2	15-2	4-1	2-1	9-2	12-1	5-1	5-1	50-1
Pos Mkt	4	1	4	2	1	2	6J	1	2J	19J
Last out	3	4	1	2	1	2	0	1	1	4
Runners	17	15	22	21	16	14	19	22	14	21
Fav.	2D	1	F	2	1	2	2/F	1	9	4/0

If the 50-1 success of A Kinsman in 1983 is ignored this is another event that has been a relatively successful source of revenue to punters over the last ten years, with the last nine winners all coming from the top six in the betting.

As with all of the long distance races at the Festival, the ability to see out the trip is vital and the majority of recent winners had earlier proved themselves over three miles plus. And, as with the Champion Hurdle and Queen Mother Champion Chase, several horses have run well in this event more than once.

One exception to both those rules is last year's winner Nomadic Way, who was having his first crack at the trip when winning the race. He was a classy stayer on the flat, however, and had already proved himself a top-notch hurdler by finishing runner-up in the two previous Champion Hurdles.

Where he did fit the pattern was that he had figured prominently in his pre-Cheltenham race and nine of the last ten winners have finished in the frame in their previous outing. He also figured prominently in the betting, going off 15-2 fourth-favourite.

His victory also preserved the four successes in the last ten runnings record of seven-year-olds, with six and nine-year-olds having recorded two each in the same period.

The recent record of the Irish in this race is better than in most of the contests under review, with Galmoy and Trapper John winning the race three times in four years between 1987 and 1990, as well as both making the frame.

SUN ALLIANCE NOVICES' HURDLE (2m 4f)

Winners	92	91	90	89	88	87	86	85	84	83
S. P.	7-1	2-1	3-1	12-1	14-1	16-1	5-2	9-1	33-1	16-1
Pos Mkt	3	1	1	6	6J	5J	1	3J	10	8J
Last out	1	1	1	1	2	2	1	1	1	1
Runners	27	29	22	22	25	28	28	27	29	27
Fav.	0	1	1	5	8	6/9	1	2	2	0

The opening event of the second day is always very well contested, with an average field of 26 runners over the last ten years. Despite the sheer numbers, however, the field can normally be whittled down to half-a-dozen with a real chance, and this is borne out by the fact that since 1983 only Fealty (33-1 in 1984) was outside the top six in the market.

Study of the recent winners' table will also point out the extreme importance of recent winning form. No less than eight of the last ten winners scored on their previous outing, whilst the other two finished second.

Proven ability at the two-and-a-half mile trip has also proved important of late. Last season's ill-fated winner Thetford Forest, had indicated that the distance would hold no fears for him when scoring over 2m 5f at Warwick on his previous outing, whilst seven of the previous nine winners had come into the contest with winning form at the trip behind them.

Four, five and six-year-olds have taken every running of this event, apart from Brown Lad in 1984. Thetford Forest is another who would have been short-listed by trend followers. He was the right age, occupied the correct position in the market, had recent winning form and was proven at the trip.

Those looking for Champion Hurdle pointers from this race can look elsewhere as this contest throws up far more top-class chasers than hurdlers, whilst the Irish have not been successful since Mister Donovan in 1982.

THE QUEEN MOTHER CHAMPION CHASE (2m)

Winners	92	91	90	89	88	87	86	85	84	83
S. P.	Evs	9-1	11-10	7-4	15-8	13-8	5-2	11-8	8-13	2-1
Pos Mkt	1	4	1	1	1	1	2	2	1	2
Last out	1	1	1	1	2	1	2	2	1	1
Runners	6	7	9	8	8	8	11	5	10	6
Fav.	1	2	1	1	1	1	5	F	1	5

The race of the Festival for the professional punter with the most predictable results of the last ten years. The average small-money punter is unlikely to get rich, however, with eight winners since 1983 going off at 2-1 or shorter.

Six winning favourites and three winning second-favourites in the period under review highlight the fine record of fancied horses in the race, with Katabatic's 9-1 victory in 1991 being by far the longest winning price in recent history. He lost nothing except his crown when defeated by Remittance Man in last season's renewal, the latter being another to fit in well with recent trends for the race.

He had won his previous outing, as had a further six of the last ten winners whilst the other three all finished second. He continued the fine record of favourites in the race and, as an eight-year-old, was the sixth member of that age group to take the race since 1983. Nine-year-olds have taken three of the other four runnings, so his chances of a repeat must be high this term.

So why the relative ease in finding the winner of this contest? A major reason is the fact that there is a real dearth of top two-mile chasers around and those that do exist usually have to undertake their Cheltenham preparation in handicaps, so their form is exposed and known to everyone.

The lack of top class performers leads to small fields and also means that some horses come back and perform well year after year. Badsworth Boy recorded a hat-trick in the race, whilst another six horses have won it twice.

SUN ALLIANCE NOVICES' CHASE (3m)

Winners	92	91	90	89	88	87	86	85	84	83
S. P.	7-2	7-2	12-1	16-1	11-4	13-2	16-1	6-4	10-1	33-1
Pos Mkt	1	1	5	8	1	4	9J	1	5J	10
Last out	1	1	2	2	1	4	1	1	1	2
Runners	18	20	9	15	14	18	30	11	18	14
Fav.		1	1	F	2/P	1	F	F	1	2	F

Martin Pipe has come to the rescue of punters in this race over the last couple of years, with his Miinnehoma and Rolling Ball improving the recent record of favourites which now stands at four from the last ten. With another four winners in that period going off at 12-1, 16-1 twice and 33-1, however, it is clear to see what a minefield this contest can be for punters.

The need for a proven safe jumper is paramount and punters have suffered with four of the last ten favourites hitting the deck. The abilty to see out the trip is also vital and several recent winners had proved themselves at three miles or more over hurdles, including Miinnehoma who had won the 3m 1f Philip Cornes' Saddle of Gold Final at Newbury as a novice; many consider that he owed his victory over Bradbury Star to his superior stamina.

Only the second nine-year-old in the last ten years to win the event, Miinnehoma is older than the average victor with seven and eight-year-olds having each won four of the last ten. He did, however, possess the prerequisite good recent form, being the sixth winner since 1983 to have won his previous race whilst three others finished second.

The Irish record in the contest is far from impressive with just six victories in 28 years. Antartic Bay (1985) is their only winner since 1976 and unless they have an outstanding candidate who has the necessary credentials their challengers can usually be discounted.

THE DAILY EXPRESS TRIUMPH HURDLE (2m)

Winners	92	91	90	89	88	87	86	85	84	83
S. P.	33-1	14-1	25-1	66-1	6-1	11-1	40-1	5-1	20-1	12-1
Pos Mkt	16J	6	11	17J	3	4	13	2	5J	5J
Last out	3	5	2	4	1	1	1	1	3	1
Runners	30	27	30	27	26	29	28	27	30	30
Fav.		P	9	0	8/15	7/11	4	P	0	2	0

Going off at 33-1 and occupying joint-sixteenth place in the betting market having been a disappointing third in a Towcester juvenile the time before, Duke of Monmouth's success in last year's Triumph Hurdle just about sums up the lottery that this race is.

A number of factors combine to make this race one that the serious punter should avoid at all costs. The break-neck pace it is run at is unfamilier to the majority of the inexperienced four-year-olds, that, combined with the tough Cheltenham course, places an emphasis on stamina that the pre-Cheltenham trials do not and the large field (smallest 26 in the last ten years) often means a rough race.

The gallant Attivo, way back in 1974, was the last to justify favouritism in the race, whilst the only successful second-favourite within the last ten years was First Bout in 1985. During the same period Alone Success (1987) and Kribensis (1988) are the only other victors to have occupied the top four in the market.

Add to that appalling record the 66-1 victories of Ikdam (1989), Shiny Copper (1982) and Baron Blakeney (1981), 40-1 shots Solar Cloud (1986) and Heighlin (1980), and numerous other long-priced winners, it becomes obvious why this is a contest that must be left well alone.

THE TOTE CHELTENHAM GOLD CUP CHASE (3m 2f)

Winners	92	91	90	89	88	87	86	85	84	83
S. P.	25-1	16-1	100-1	5-2	10-1	13-2	15-8	7-1	7-2	10-3
Pos Mkt	6	8J	11	1	6	2	1	3	2	1
Last out	1	2	3	1	1	1	4	1	1	1
Runners	8	14	12	13	15	12	11	15	12	11
Fav	5	7	3	1	P	7	1	7	P	1

The last three years have rather knocked a hole in the theory that this a good race for the punter. Following a seven-year period during which the longest-priced winner was Charter Party (10-1) in 1988, the victories of Norton's Coin (100-1) in 1990 Garrison Savannah (16-1) in 1991, and Cool Ground (25-1) last season have seen the bookmakers get the better of recent exchanges.

Like the top two-milers in preparation for the Queen Mother Champion Chase, the Gold Cup horses have to build up to the race in handicaps and, as such, their form is fairly exposed and this led to a number of well-supported winners. The last three years, however, have seen the well backed Desert Orchid beaten twice and last year the 'unbeatable' Carvill's Hill humbled, which may go some way to explaining the generous SP's of the winners.

Cool Ground continued the revival in fortunes of ten-year-olds in the race, his victory being the third in the last six years for the age group. Younger horses had dominated the contest in the five previous seasons with eight-year-olds (three wins) and nine-year-olds (two) sharing the spoils between them.

Seven-year-olds did particularly well during the seventies with five successes to their credit; but only Little Owl (1981) has added to the total since.

The importance of good pre-Cheltenham form was once again underlined by Cool Ground's victory. He came into the race having returned to winning form at Haydock previously and became the seventh of the last ten winners to have gone to the Festival with a victory behind them. Of the other three, two finished in the frame and Dawn Run (1986) was remounted after falling.

The latter's popular sucess is the one bright spot in a very poor recent record for the Irish whose previous success in the race came via Davy Lad way back in 1977.

CONCLUSION

So which are the races that the serious punter should concentrate on in an effort to make the three greatest days racing of the season profitable?

Without doubt the Queen Mother Champion Chase is the place to start, whilst the other level-weights Championship contests such as the Champion Hurdle, the Stayers' Hurdle and, to a lesser extent in recent seasons, the Gold Cup should also be given serious consideration.

In the ten years under review, 16 favourites have obliged at a strike rate of 40% in these races, whilst 33 of the winners (82.5%) have gone off in the top four in the betting. Indeed, a level-pound stake on all the favourites in these races since 1983 would have resulted in a small individual profit in each contest and an overall profit of £7.92, nearly 20% on turnover.

In contrast, the Triumph Hurdle must be avoided like the plague whilst the novice chases must be treated with caution.

Another major factor that must be taken into account is the state of the ground. Soft or heavy ground traditionally produces shock results and punters are warned to curtail activities if the rains come.

The 1989 Festival was the last hit by rain when the likes of Ikdam (66-1), Observer Corps (66-1), Beech Road (50-1), Sondrio (25-1), Waterloo Boy (20-1) and Envopak Token (16-1) all found their way into the winner's enclosure, whilst the wet 1982 Festival also threw up more than its fair share of surprises including Shiny Copper (66-1) and For Auction (40-1).

But what of the races, mostly handicaps, that are not covered in detail here? As far as the chases are concerned the best method is the traditional in-depth knowledge of the form-book and the horses concerned. With the big handicap hurdles this is also a valuable weapon, but look out also for the horses that appear to have been 'laid-out' for these races, especially those from renowned gambling yards.

The Irish have been an integral part of Cheltenham over the years and long may it continue. Their fortunes have taken something of a nosedive in recent years, however, which may have something to do with their keenness to sell many of their best young prospects to the English at vastly inflated prices. Their top performers, however, are worth a second glance in their chosen engagements as the likes of Dawn Run, Galmoy and Trapper John have proved.

Francois Doumen's The Fellow has also proved that the French are to be respected with two close misses in the Gold Cup. His stable companion Ubu III also ran a fine race in the Stayers' Hurdle last year and when it is remembered that these two are in no way dominant in their homeland, then further challengers from across the channel must be given due respect.

10 . FAVOURITES RECORDS

These records have a twofold purpose. The first is to supply information to backers using favourites as the basis of various betting strategies; the second is to test conventional theories by demonstrating the state of play between the punter and bookmaker at the sharp end of the market.

Market leaders are basically created by punters' and book-makers' interpretation of form. The betting market can be swayed by a great many factors, but for the majority and on the majority of occasions, a favourite is the horse whose form suggests greatest likelihood of success given the race circumstances. As such, the more often a favourite obliges the more the form book is seen to work, making the record of favourites a "Form Index" whose performance is significant to all enthusiasts.

The main attraction about this survey is that it proves punters have a real chance providing a little thought and care is put into selecting - and that sort of involvement is the fun of the game.

Certainly backing all favourites blind is never going to make a profit, but that is to be expected. The point is that with the slightest of discipline - tax considerations apart - margins can be narrowed at a stroke. As a system in itself, careful following of favourites could result in small profits. But taken along with other statistical pointers and sound judgement of form, either worked out personally or from one of the many professional experts, making racing pay is not just a pipe dream. Margins in the region of 5% are surmountable - possibly by the simple expedient of excluding lower class contests at smaller courses, for example - but discipline is the key. Finally, remember a punter worth his or her salt should be able to get better than S.P. more often than not, so all the returns given below should be seen as the minimum.

We have been monitoring the records of favourites for some years now and commentary is following similar lines year after year, which is all to the good as it shows punters can trust the trends. Every season has its trend-bucking categories but by and large there is a clearly discernible flow.

As usual, favourites in Chases come out distinctly better than Hurdles, both in terms of strike-rate and return on investment. Many professional punters claim Chases are the best races to bet in, and on the basis of the 'form-index' they are right.

FAVOURITES BY MONTH

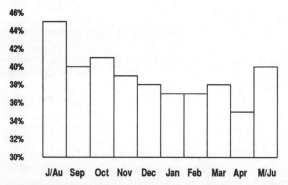

STRIKE-RATE BY MONTH 1987-92 (ALL RACES)

At no time is it easier to back winners than in Chases in July and August. Just stick your cash on the favourite and you'll collect ten times in every 21 attempts.

On the Flat you'll be hard pressed to get above a 30% strike-rate at any time. But while the mugs are at Glorious Goodwood and York, just nip along to Bangor, Worcester, Hereford or Plumpton and on an average day you'll cheer home half the winners on the card. Easy. You won't win any money - of course - but 4p in every quid invested is not a lot to pay for the fun of being right so often!

The strike-rate is remarkable in Chases all the way through to November, and then again at the other end in May and June. Hurdles are not bad either up until September, though you'll lose more.

Not surprisingly, mid-winter is the trickiest time to punt the jolly if numbers of winners are what you need (if you're tempted by multiple bets).

In terms of the best return for every pound you hand over the counter, save your big bets for November, December and March.

FAVOURITES BY GOING

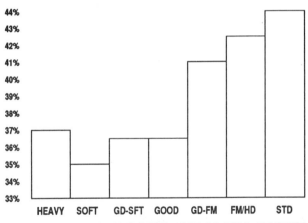

STRIKE-RATE BY GOING 1987-92 (ALL RACES)

As we noted last year, although there is a general conformity to the golden rule with Flat racing that the faster the ground the better form works out, it is noteworthy how in both

Chases and Hurdles, favourites on heavy going tend to perform better than on soft, and then the strike-rate rises as the going firms.

It is probably just a statistical quirk, but with one exception, over the past five years the return to the pound is best from favourites in Chases on good-to-soft.

The one exception is that favourites in Chases on Standard going offer a whacking profit followed blind. But of course the statistical pool is still very light so this might turn out to be nonsense. However, the fact that favourites in Hurdles also post their best gains on Standard offers some confirmation that this could be a trend.

FAVOURITES BY DISTANCE

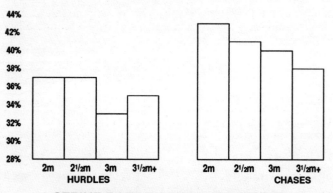

STRIKE-RATE BY DISTANCE 1987-92

Regular readers will be aware that we have reached the conclusion that, although it didn't make very much difference, the rule of thumb was the shorter the distance, the better the strike-rate. With one small exception, the latest five-year spread confirms this.

It has to be said, though, that while the strike-rate by

month and going are significant, by distance they are not. Indeed in terms of return on investment they are probably irrelevent.

FAVOURITES BY COURSE

Last year we signed off this chapter by asking: What odds about Ascot again collecting the wooden spoon for favourites' strike-rates? With 46 racecourses (counting All Weather as separate courses) we reckoned about 10-1 would be about right given Ascot's pathetic record.

Well, the wooden spoon went to Wolverhampton where hapless favourite-backers received a mere 66p back for every pound they invested. But, even though Ascot was not the worst of the lot in 91/92, favourite-backers once again lost money at the Berkshire course, and the average return over the last five years has been just 77p, and that is far and away the worst five-year record.

Back an outsider at Ascot. Back the second favourite. Back anything but the favourite and you may have a chance of making a profit. And the same applies to Wolverhampton, Market Rasen, Liverpool and Nottingham.

The course where market interpretation seems to have a reasonable bearing on results remains Haydock. Regular readers will know Haydock has long been prominent, although last year a 6p in the £ loss didn't help.

Lingfield All-Weather deserves a mention because although returns are still decidedly light, it is shaping as a very promising venue for favourite backers.

Fontwell has been a reliable venue for the 'form-index', as has Doncaster, Edinburgh, Ludlow and Perth. The form-index at Taunton and Worcester, meanwhile, inflict minimal damage. All the rest and . . . beware.

And whatever you do, if your fancy is favourite at Ascot, think about halving your stakes, or better still betting your fancy will be beaten (it's perverse, but it works!).

1991/92 FAVOURITES RECORDS SUMMARIES

FAVOURITES RECORDS BY MONTH

ALL RACES	Races	Winners	%	+/-Level£		Av. Ret
JULY/AUGUST	174	89.5	51.4	+	11.65	£ 1.07
SEPTEMBER	173	69.8	40.3	-	32.35	£ 0.81
OCTOBER	292	132.8	45.4	+	5.40	£ 1.02
NOVEMBER	450	160.3	35.6	-	62.78	£ 0.86
DECEMBER	344	148.9	43.3	+	50.44	£ 1.15
JANUARY	380	153.0	40.2	-	13.74	£ 0.96
FEBRUARY	458	171.4	37.4	-	18.86	£ 0.96
MARCH	361	143.0	39.6	-	0.89	£ 1.00
APRIL	343	117.0	34.1	-	26.92	£ 0.92
MAY/JUNE	305	113.5	37.2	-	18.59	£ 0.94
TOTAL	**3280**	**1299.6**	**39.6**	**-**	**106.64**	**£ 0.97**

FAVOURITES RECORDS BY GOING

ALL RACES	Races	Winners	%	+/-Level£		Av. Ret
HEAVY	29	11.5	39.6	+	1.74	£ 1.06
SOFT	210	77.1	36.7	+	1.72	£ 1.01
GOOD - SOFT	367	141.4	38.5	+	4.95	£ 1.01
GOOD	1361	502.8	36.9	-	94.84	£ 0.93
GOOD - FIRM	787	336.4	42.7	+	2.69	£ 1.00
FIRM / HARD	325	145.5	44.7	-	22.97	£ 0.93
STANDARD	201	84.8	42.2	+	0.07	£ 1.00
TOTAL	**3280**	**1299.6**	**39.6**	**-**	**106.64**	**£ 0.97**

FAVOURITES RECORDS BY DISTANCE

ALL RACES	Races	Winners	%	+/-Level£		Av. Ret
2 MILES	1436	570.1	39.7	-	71.23	£ 0.95
2.5 MILES	973	413.4	42.5	+	17.64	£ 1.02
3 MILES	711	257.4	36.2	-	43.19	£ 0.94
3.5 MILES	160	58.5	36.5	-	9.86	£ 0.94
TOTAL	**3280**	**1299.6**	**39.6**	**-**	**106.64**	**£ 0.97**

1987-92 FAVOURITES RECORDS BY MONTH

HURDLES	Races	Winners	%	+/-Level£		Av. Ret
JULY/AUGUST	592	255.8	43.2	- 54.06	£	0.91
SEPTEMBER	538	199.8	37.1	- 85.75	£	0.84
OCTOBER	786	311.4	39.6	- 33.29	£	0.96
NOVEMBER	1097	398.4	36.3	- 111.86	£	0.90
DECEMBER	1054	383.3	36.3	- 9.08	£	0.99
JANUARY	1097	404.4	36.8	- 130.67	£	0.88
FEBRUARY	936	326.1	34.8	- 126.04	£	0.87
MARCH	1027	362.9	35.3	- 98.41	£	0.90
APRIL	892	290.3	32.5	- 103.39	£	0.88
MAY/JUNE	927	349.6	37.7	- 83.62	£	0.91
TOTAL	**8946**	**3282.4**	**36.7**	**- 836.17**	**£**	**0.91**

CHASES	Races	Winners	%	+/-Level£		Av. Ret
JULY/AUGUST	331	158.3	47.8	- 17.89	£	0.95
SEPTEMBER	336	149.1	44.3	- 24.05	£	0.93
OCTOBER	574	241.4	42.0	- 30.07	£	0.95
NOVEMBER	897	383.4	42.7	- 46.98	£	0.95
DECEMBER	871	343.9	39.4	- 67.30	£	0.92
JANUARY	724	269.6	37.2	- 92.38	£	0.87
FEBRUARY	687	277.5	40.3	- 18.21	£	0.97
MARCH	861	358.6	41.6	+ 40.75	£	1.05
APRIL	754	281.9	37.4	- 32.38	£	0.96
MAY/JUNE	802	335.9	41.8	- 41.96	£	0.95
TOTAL	**6837**	**2800.1**	**41.0**	**- 330.47**	**£**	**0.95**

ALL RACES	Races	Winners	%	+/-Level£		Av. Ret
JULY/AUGUST	923	414.1	44.8	- 71.95	£	0.92
SEPTEMBER	874	348.9	39.9	- 109.80	£	0.87
OCTOBER	1360	552.9	40.6	- 63.36	£	0.95
NOVEMBER	1994	781.8	39.2	- 158.84	£	0.92
DECEMBER	1925	727.3	37.7	- 76.38	£	0.96
JANUARY	1821	674.0	37.0	- 223.05	£	0.88
FEBRUARY	1623	603.6	37.1	- 144.25	£	0.91
MARCH	1888	721.6	38.2	- 57.66	£	0.97
APRIL	1646	572.3	34.7	- 135.77	£	0.92
MAY/JUNE	1729	685.6	39.6	- 125.58	£	0.93
TOTAL	**15783**	**6082.5**	**38.5**	**-1166.64**	**£**	**0.93**

1987-92 FAVOURITES RECORDS BY GOING

HURDLES	Races	Winners	%	+/-Level£	Av. Ret
HEAVY	433	146.3	33.7	- 70.82	£ 0.84
SOFT	1030	329.1	31.9	- 153.19	£ 0.85
GOOD - SOFT	1237	422.0	34.1	- 113.85	£ 0.91
GOOD	2397	825.7	34.4	- 225.91	£ 0.91
GOOD - FIRM	1774	682.5	38.4	- 114.56	£ 0.94
FIRM / HARD	1491	621.1	41.6	- 130.65	£ 0.91
STANDARD	584	255.4	43.7	- 27.19	£ 0.95
TOTAL	**8946**	**3282.4**	**36.7**	**- 836.17**	**£ 0.91**

CHASES	Races	Winners	%	+/-Level£	Av. Ret
HEAVY	318	130.8	41.1	- 15.90	£ 0.95
SOFT	844	328.4	38.9	- 37.48	£ 0.96
GOOD - SOFT	1044	407.5	39.0	- 27.73	£ 0.97
GOOD	2078	813.3	39.1	- 132.05	£ 0.94
GOOD - FIRM	1477	644.9	43.6	- 31.78	£ 0.98
FIRM / HARD	1062	468.1	44.0	- 88.27	£ 0.92
STANDARD	14	7.0	50.0	+ 2.74	£ 1.20
TOTAL	**6837**	**2800.1**	**41.0**	**- 330.47**	**£ 0.95**

ALL RACES	Races	Winners	%	+/-Level£	Av. Ret
HEAVY	751	277.1	36.9	- 86.72	£ 0.88
SOFT	1874	657.5	35.0	- 190.67	£ 0.90
GOOD - SOFT	2281	829.6	36.3	- 141.58	£ 0.94
GOOD	4475	1639.0	36.6	- 357.96	£ 0.92
GOOD - FIRM	3251	1327.4	40.8	- 146.34	£ 0.95
FIRM / HARD	2553	1089.2	42.6	- 218.92	£ 0.91
STANDARD	598	262.4	43.8	- 24.45	£ 0.96
TOTAL	**15783**	**6082.5**	**38.5**	**-1166.64**	**£ 0.93**

1987-92 FAVOURITES RECORDS BY DISTANCE

HURDLES	Races	Winners	%	+/-Level£	Av. Ret
2 MILES	5496	2052.8	37.3	- 520.13	£ 0.91
2.5 MILES	2258	830.6	36.7	- 233.28	£ 0.90
3 MILES	1091	363.9	33.3	- 71.33	£ 0.93
3.5 MILES	101	35.0	34.6	- 11.43	£ 0.89
TOTAL	**8946**	**3282.4**	**36.7**	**- 836.17**	**£ 0.91**

CHASES	Races	Winners	%	+/-Level£	Av. Ret
2 MILES	1,854	790.7	42.6	- 54.75	£ 0.97
2.5 MILES	2,070	849.1	41.0	- 147.56	£ 0.93
3 MILES	2,212	893.4	40.3	- 86.38	£ 0.96
3.5 MILES	701	266.8	38.0	- 41.78	£ 0.94
TOTAL	**6837**	**2800.1**	**41.0**	**- 330.47**	**£ 0.95**

ALL RACES	Races	Winners	%	+/-Level£	Av. Ret
2 MILES	7350	2843.5	38.6	- 574.88	£ 0.92
2.5 MILES	4328	1679.7	38.8	- 380.84	£ 0.91
3 MILES	3303	1257.4	38.0	- 157.71	£ 0.95
3.5 MILES	802	301.8	37.6	- 53.21	£ 0.93
TOTAL	**15783**	**6082.5**	**38.5**	**-1166.64**	**£ 0.93**

1991/92 FAVOURITES RECORDS BY COURSE

COURSE	RACES	WINNERS	%	+/-LEVEL£		AV. RET	
ASCOT	55	19.5	35.4	-	2.79	£	0.95
AYR	59	25.5	43.2	-	1.27	£	0.98
BANGOR	90	29.0	32.2	-	18.18	£	0.80
CARLISLE	71	28.3	39.9	-	4.73	£	0.93
CARTMEL	30	12.5	41.6	-	3.83	£	0.87
CATTERICK	64	19.2	30.0	-	13.82	£	0.78
CHELTENHAM	97	37.0	38.1	+	0.53	£	1.01
CHEPSTOW	82	31.0	37.8	-	7.20	£	0.91
DONCASTER	34	17.5	51.4	+	3.96	£	1.12
EDINBURGH	46	22.3	48.5	+	2.90	£	1.06
EXETER	87	42.0	48.2	-	5.81	£	0.93
FAKENHAM	30	14.0	46.6	+	5.97	£	1.20
FOLKESTONE	44	16.0	36.3	+	1.84	£	1.04
FONTWELL	91	47.0	51.6	+	16.46	£	1.18
HAYDOCK PARK	44	17.0	38.6	-	2.54	£	0.94
HEREFORD	93	39.5	42.4	+	11.65	£	1.13
HEXHAM	76	27.5	36.1	+	1.33	£	1.02
HUNTINGDON	80	27.0	33.7	-	21.45	£	0.73
KELSO	71	35.3	49.7	+	0.81	£	1.01
KEMPTON PARK	55	17.5	31.8	-	9.81	£	0.82
LEICESTER	61	24.5	40.1	+	1.34	£	1.02
LINGFIELD	44	19.8	45.0	+	9.33	£	1.21
LINGFIELD-AW	91	44.3	48.7	+	9.33	£	1.10
LIVERPOOL	20	5.5	27.9	-	4.63	£	0.77
LUDLOW	71	25.0	35.2	-	7.82	£	0.89
MARKET RASEN	105	46.0	43.8	-	5.03	£	0.95
NEWBURY	84	37.3	44.4	+	4.80	£	1.06
NEWCASTLE	71	27.0	38.0	-	12.54	£	0.82
NEWTON ABBOT	126	42.5	33.7	-	33.48	£	0.73
NOTTINGHAM	51	18.0	35.2	-	3.87	£	0.92
PERTH	67	30.5	45.5	+	1.17	£	1.02
PLUMPTON	85	32.0	37.6	-	7.79	£	0.91
SANDOWN PARK	65	25.0	38.4	-	11.50	£	0.82
SEDGEFIELD	95	38.3	40.3	+	11.07	£	1.12
SOUTHWELL	49	18.5	37.7	-	2.08	£	0.96
SOUTHWELL-AW	108	38.5	35.6	-	11.42	£	0.89
STRATFORD	81	28.0	34.5	-	14.13	£	0.83
TAUNTON	77	35.8	46.5	+	22.62	£	1.29
TOWCESTER	82	28.0	34.1	+	9.83	£	1.12
UTTOXETER	103	39.3	38.1	-	3.30	£	0.97
WARWICK	69	30.0	43.4	+	5.90	£	1.09
WETHERBY	81	28.0	34.5	-	12.55	£	0.85
WINCANTON	76	31.5	41.4	+	2.01	£	1.03
WINDSOR	51	23.5	46.0	+	6.63	£	1.13
WOLVERHAMPTON	60	16.0	26.6	-	20.47	£	0.66
WORCESTER	108	41.8	38.7	-	5.92	£	1.05

1987-92 FAVOURITES RECORDS BY COURSE

COURSE	RACES	WINNERS	%	+/-LEVEL£		AV. RET
ASCOT	272	83.7	30.7	- 63.27	£	0.77
AYR	378	148.6	39.3	- 26.78	£	0.93
BANGOR	379	137.0	36.1	- 38.09	£	0.90
CARLISLE	277	104.6	37.7	- 24.04	£	0.91
CARTMEL	150	74.0	49.3	- 2.44	£	0.98
CATTERICK	307	108.5	35.3	- 41.01	£	0.87
CHELTENHAM	486	170.8	35.1	- 38.82	£	0.92
CHEPSTOW	334	124.8	37.3	- 6.43	£	0.98
DONCASTER	207	90.5	43.7	+ 4.64	£	1.02
EDINBURGH	217	95.8	44.1	+ 6.66	£	1.03
EXETER	441	190.6	43.2	- 52.78	£	0.88
FAKENHAM	176	65.5	37.2	- 22.52	£	0.87
FOLKESTONE	209	69.3	33.1	- 23.36	£	0.89
FONTWELL	447	194.5	43.5	+ 26.96	£	1.06
HAYDOCK PARK	245	117.5	47.9	+ 21.65	£	1.09
HEREFORD	450	178.3	39.6	- 35.38	£	0.92
HEXHAM	383	146.4	38.2	- 38.36	£	0.90
HUNTINGDON	421	156.3	37.1	- 54.91	£	0.87
KELSO	344	134.8	39.1	- 23.73	£	0.93
KEMPTON PARK	279	108.3	38.8	- 7.54	£	0.97
LEICESTER	289	111.5	38.5	- 32.21	£	0.89
LINGFIELD	283	105.9	37.4	- 35.28	£	0.88
LINGFIELD-AW	174	86.8	49.9	+ 13.00	£	1.07
LIVERPOOL	96	24.4	25.4	- 13.87	£	0.86
LUDLOW	346	137.9	39.8	+ 6.29	£	1.02
MARKET RASEN	531	206.5	38.8	- 88.05	£	0.83
NEWBURY	397	153.4	38.6	- 20.48	£	0.95
NEWCASTLE	323	135.4	41.9	- 15.20	£	0.95
NEWTON ABBOT	599	239.4	39.9	- 73.50	£	0.88
NOTTINGHAM	271	95.0	35.0	- 38.20	£	0.86
PERTH	308	133.4	43.3	+ 8.53	£	1.03
PLUMPTON	456	180.9	39.6	- 13.87	£	0.97
SANDOWN PARK	297	113.5	38.2	- 17.36	£	0.94
SEDGEFIELD	539	222.9	41.3	- 8.43	£	0.98
SOUTHWELL	486	194.3	39.9	- 38.03	£	0.92
SOUTHWELL-AW	215	83.0	38.6	- 12.21	£	0.94
STRATFORD	405	142.0	35.0	- 42.57	£	0.89
TAUNTON	329	127.3	38.7	- 0.13	£	1.00
TOWCESTER	383	129.5	33.8	- 46.32	£	0.88
UTTOXETER	460	168.1	36.5	- 48.12	£	0.90
WARWICK	361	125.8	34.8	- 39.12	£	0.89
WETHERBY	404	145.5	36.0	- 57.60	£	0.86
WINCANTON	378	137.8	36.4	- 38.69	£	0.90
WINDSOR	210	73.2	34.8	- 20.53	£	0.90
WOLVERHAMPTON	291	92.0	31.6	- 56.29	£	0.81
WORCESTER	550	215.9	39.2	+ 1.15	£	1.00

11 . TRAINERS AND JOCKEYS

by

Ian Carnaby

Every now and then MARTIN PIPE indicates that he would like to concentrate on quality rather than quantity. He even hints that the richer arena of flat racing is more than passing interest to him.

However, the army of supporters which follows his every move from Monday to Saturday throughout a long and demanding N.H. season has no need to worry yet. Last winter Pipe sent out 224 winners, of which four were on the all-weather. Although he failed by six to reach his 1990/91 record, he was responsible for more than twice as many winners as anyone else. If Cheltenham and Aintree were a little disappointing for the yard, a prize-money return of over £900,000 was more than satisfactory. In addition, Pipe's strike-rate was bettered only by Mary Reveley (a mighty impressive 30.7%).

In all, the champion trainer contested 839 races. His firm ground specialists were on the go in August and reappeared in May. No selling hurdle escaped his attention, but a top-class performer like Sabin Du Loir was also in action by late October and had won over £45,000 before November was out.

Pipe is interested in records, and it will not be long before he goes through the card at a West Country meeting. He sent his strongest team yet to the Cheltenham Festival but won only the Sun Alliance Chase, with Miinnehoma. His bitter, or rather silent, reaction to the defeat of Carvill's Hill in the Gold Cup showed him to be an obsessive perfectionist, and one who quite possibly believes there is still much to prove. Few members of the public would agree. He has won the Irish Grand National with Omerta, the Coral Welsh equivalent twice with Bonanza Boy, and the Midlands version at Uttoxeter with the same horse. But for coming to grief at the penultimate flight, Granville Again might well have taken last season's Champion Hurdle.

It is simply untrue that Pipe presses horses into action before they are ready. He was extremely patient with Chatam, who won the Hennessy at Newbury on his seasonal debut, and with Aquilifer, who finally rewarded him at Punchestown. Chatam could still develop into a Gold Cup horse, and Cyphrate will be very difficult to beat at shorter distances.

PETER SCUDAMORE rode 175 winners, his best score since the phenomenal campaign of 1988/89, when he obliged on 221 occasions. He remains the consummate professional, with a driving passion for detail and a welcome readiness to help the media, where this does not encroach upon his loyalty to Pipe. If there is justice in the sport he will ride a Grand National and Gold Cup winner for the trainer. His achievement in passing the 1500-winner mark - nearly half as many again as John Francome, remember - was well-documented in the racing press but treated very lightly elsewhere.

In terms of prize-money, DAVID NICHOLSON leapt from ninth place to second during the last campaign. Nicholson has silenced those who doubted his ability at the highest level, and it is by no means impossible that he will be champion trainer this time around. (Financially rather than numerically, that is.)

Much will depend upon the exploits of Carobee, who is

already being spoken of as a Gold Cup horse and who won five of his six races last season. Nicholson took the tragic loss of Thetford Forest at Liverpool with great dignity; he won the Heidsieck Dry Monopole Novices' Hurdle there with Barton Bank, and the Kim Muir at Cheltenham with Tug of Gold.

This winter, Nicholson will be operating from Ford in Gloucestershire, having moved from nearby Condicote. 63 winners last term represented his best total and this is very much a yard to watch. Although the supremely stylish RICHARD DUNWOODY will still be riding many of the horses, he will now have his pick of Nicholson's and Nicky Henderson's runners. Most crucially, perhaps, he will be free to partner the very gifted Remittance Man for Henderson. Nicholson, meanwhile, has taken on Grand National-winning jockey CARL LLEWELLYN on a second retainer basis.

HENDERSON was another to crack the half-century last season. His 52 winners took him to third place in the prize-money table and, like Nicholson, he will be trying to improve upon that tally from different surroundings, having taken over Seven Barrows in Lambourn in a straight swap with Peter Walwyn.

Henderson has many strengths, among them the ability to prepare ex-Flat racers for top hurdling prizes with only limited experience in public. Flown was a perfect example, appearing only once at Kempton before running away with the Supreme Novices' at Cheltenham. Flown was below his best on softer ground afterwards, but remains a top-class prospect.

Remittance Man may never stay the Gold Cup distance, but will attempt three miles again this season. He put up one of the best performances of the whole campaign when holding Katabatic and Waterloo Boy in the Queen Mother Champion Chase, and is still only eight. Henderson will also be looking to Everaldo to compete at the highest level in long-distance hurdles, and the Stayers' Hurdle at the Festival may not be beyond him.

The only other trainer to break through the £300,000 mark was TOBY BALDING. His £318,308 put him in fourth place,

Nicky Henderson's Everaldo will be entered in the top long-distance hurdle events

the same as the previous year, although the number of winners rose from 48 to 53.

The move to Whitcombe Manor has undoubtedly been successful, and Balding vindicated owner Peter Bolton's faith in the best possible way by winning the Gold Cup for him with Cool Ground. It was an extraordinary race, and all the subsequent brouhaha over Carvill's Hill's disappointing display and Mrs Pitman's tactics with Golden Freeze tended to obscure the fact that Cool Ground found some 18 lengths with The Fellow compared with their running in the Gold Cup 12 months earlier.

Balding is a big-race specialist, of that there can be no

doubt. He produced Beech Road and Morley Street to win the Champion Hurdle (both after fairly unorthodox preparations) and sent out Little Polveir to win the 1989 Grand National only weeks after taking the horse over from John Edwards.

The key to his success may be a readiness to adapt to changed circumstances. Both Beech Road and Morley Street were all set for chasing careers, but failed to impress in that sphere. Morley Street will be given another chance to show that British fences hold no terrors for him, but not every trainer would have realised that the Breeders' Cup Chase (or two of them, in fact) would make a handy consolation in the meantime.

ADRIAN MAGUIRE rode 17 winners, including the Gold Cup of course, in his first full season as a professional. He is not officially retained by Balding but lives at Whitcombe and will ride many more big-race winners for the establishment. There is a touch of 'iron in the soul' about him - a fierce determination to succeed which will take him to Sedgefield for six ordinary rides early in the new season. There is no stronger man riding, and he will probably be champion one day. He has already committed himself to riding here for another ten to 15 years.

Balding is the first to admit that he is lucky to have access to several gifted jockeys. However, with Maguire around, both JIMMY FROST and RICHARD GUEST will do well to match the scores in the forties they achieved last time.

It delighted everyone in the jumping fraternity that ARTHUR STEPHENSON reached the century again. His 101 winners made him runner-up to Pipe numerically, and some £262,000 in prize-money left him in fifth place overall. It should not be forgotten that he managed this without stable star Blazing Walker, who was sidelined all season, whilst Southern Minstrel achieved only a single success, at Cartmel in May.

Stephenson won a host of lesser contests in the north, often with horses defying unlikely burdens. He has the very tough Gale Again at his disposal in the months to come, whilst Captain Mor will no doubt be aimed at the John Hughes Memorial Chase at Aintree once again.

The indestructible CHRIS GRANT finished fifth in the jockeys table with 78 winners, but Stephenson has plenty of people to call on when the iron man is injured. Kenny Johnson and Andrew Larnach can both do 9st 7lbs and will be riding their share of winners once again.

Stephenson sent out 34 more winners than GORDON RICHARDS (67) but was only marginally ahead in terms of prize-money. After his magnificent 90/91 season, when he struck 118 times, Richards was understandably disappointed and resolved to make an early start this autumn, which he proved by saddling two winners on the opening day at Bangor.

The horses were not quite right at various stages of last winter, and it hardly helped that NEALE DOUGHTY endured a long lay-off through injury. His final tally of 44 was a good effort under the circumstances.

There is still time for Carrick Hill Lad to win a Gold Cup if Richards can bring him back fit and refreshed. His stable star missed the whole of last season after pulling up lame in the race in 1991, but will still be only ten when March comes round again. There are also more prizes in the tough and versatile The Antartex, who reverted successfully to two miles after winning over two and three-quarter miles at Aintree. After a summer of vigorous exercise and physiotherapy, Doughty pronounced himself fit. Both men should have a much better season.

If the same remark applies to MARY REVELEY, she will notch her first century. One of the great success stories of the past few years, Mrs Reveley is pressing forward on all fronts but remained, agonisingly, on 99 when last season came to an end. Not overly concerned with statistics, she must nevertheless be proud of winning tallies over the last five years which read: 25: 23: 41: 58: 99.

The really good horses have been slow in coming, which makes the trainer's rise even more creditable. However, the likes of Dalkey Sound and Cab on Target have won valuable

Mary Reveley has a phenomenal strike-rate

prizes, and Mrs Reveley also won the 1991 Cambridgeshire with Mellottie. Her strike-rate is quite phenomenal: 30.7% in a sport as unpredictable and hazardous as this is hugely impressive, and even out-distances Martin Pipe by four clear percentage points.

Sheer hard work lifted PETER NIVEN to third place in the jockeys' list with 105 winners, the great majority of them for Mrs Reveley. This is a yard to follow closely, and of those which have a fair chance of reaching three figures again it is easily the most likely to show a level-stakes profit.

PHILIP HOBBS is a good example of a trainer making the most of fairly modest resources. 51 winners last season was a splendid achievement and meant that he finished just above Jenny Pitman, Josh Gifford and Oliver Sherwood, even if he could not match them for prize-money.

Hobbs always has his team ready early, and everything partnered by his brother in the opening weeks is worth watching. PETER HOBBS completed his remarkable recovery from a serious neck injury and a final score of 31 was a creditable effort.

JENNY PITMAN reached her half-century (just) but things did not run smoothly at Weathercock House. Over a relatively short period of time the Hitchins, the Robins and Mr Oberstein have seen fit to remove horses from the yard, and the overall strength has been seriously affected.

Mrs Pitman is a born competitor and will, no doubt, fight back. For sure she is a handler of the very highest class as her training Garrison Savannah in 1990/91 demonstrated. However, the Gold Cup of '92 provided a stark contrast in fortune. Leaving aside the tactics adopted in the race, the fact is that the two Hitchins runners - Toby Tobias and Golden Freeze - finished lame and pulled up respectively in a field of eight. Nor were there any successes to report at Liverpool, a venue which has been so kind to the trainer in the past.

The most serious losses to the yard may turn out to be Mighty Mogul and Wonder Man. They have both joined David Nicholson, who already looks after the long-term Gold Cup prospect Carobee. The talented hurdler Wonder Man was not seen out again after a bloodless victory at Warwick in November.

Mrs Pitman's prize-money in 91/92 amounted to just over £300,000, a long way behind the figures for the previous two seasons. Even so, she still has an enormous reservoir of talent in the stable, with any number of ex-Irish horses waiting in the wings. This trainer would not hurry one of her inmates, even if it meant falling out with everyone. Such strength of character must not go unmentioned. In any case, a fully fit

Garrison Savannah or Toby Tobias could well put a different complexion on things in a few months' time.

MARK PITMAN's fortunes are inextricably bound up with his mother's, and his winning tally last season was down to 35, after scores of 27 and an outstanding 57 two years ago. He has been criticised most unfairly in some quarters, but it does not seem likely at this fairly advanced stage that other big yards will suddenly start offering him attractive rides.

Even JOSH GIFFORD's most loyal supporters probably feel that the glory days are a thing of the past. 49 was his lowest total for many years, and the passing of Jim Joel means an inevitable reduction in stable strength.

Yet Gifford clearly remains a trainer of the very highest calibre. Patience is the name of the game, and many of his most beautifully-bred animals merely gain experience over hurdles before tackling the job for which they were born. Certain types of contest do not interest Gifford (or his patrons) and it is surely wrong to think of him as being left behind by the 'century' merchants.

Much will be expected of Bradbury Star this season. He was just edged out by Miinnehoma at Cheltenham but gained compensation at Liverpool, where the tough mare Brief Gale won a hotly-contested bumper on her racecourse debut. There are also possibilities about the Bulldozer gelding San Fernando, whose win over hurdles was a bonus.

DECLAN MURPHY eased to his best total so far, 48, as his retainer with Gifford started to bear fruit. In terms of style he may be ranked with Richard Dunwoody, and there is no praise higher than that. Barring accidents, Murphy is likely to pass the half-century quite comfortably this time.

Another jockey to claim his share of the limelight was JAMIE OSBORNE, whose hat-trick on the opening day at Cheltenham virtually assured him of the Ritz Club Trophy for leading rider at the Festival. Osbourne goes on improving his score every year, and recorded 76 successes in all. Very stylish, and with the support of not only Oliver Sherwood but his brother Simon as well, he will never be short of

Jamie Osborne goes on improving his score every year

winning opportunities in the most important races. It is easy enough to discern what the top trainers think of him: on that opening day at Cheltenham he rode winners for Nicky Henderson and Barry Hills as well as Oliver Sherwood. With Richard Dunwoody claimed for Waterloo Boy, he also won the Champion Chase for Henderson on Remittance Man.

OLIVER SHERWOOD may have been slightly disappointed by a final score of 48 after reaching 50-plus in each of the previous three years. However, this remains a powerful yard, with the emphasis very much on quality, and the Irish link with Arthur Moore is of considerable significance.

SIMON SHERWOOD was responsible for 12 winners in his first season and moved on to 17 last time. More significantly, he saddled two Festival winners in the shape of Duke of Monmouth in the Triumph Hurdle and Dusty Miller in the County Hurdle. There seems no reason why Desert Orchid's former pilot should not match his brother eventually. As noted previously, their joint strength is very good news for Osborne.

Four big-name trainers did rather less well than of late, but for contrasting reasons. DAVID BARONS, on a high after the 1991 Seagram Grand National triumph, sent out only 25 winners. Sickness in the yard meant a very slow start, and, but for the exploits of Topsham Bay whose Whitbread gold Cup victory alone was worth nearly £60,000, the returns would have been grim reading. Barons is certain to pick up again with his New Zealand-breds, and is always a man to watch in bumpers. Both Martell Boy and Martell Spirit showed promise last season.

Whether DAVID ELSWORTH will be a major force in the post-Desert Orchid era is rather more doubtful. He has expressed a desire to concentrate more on flat racing (where his record is already outstanding) and it would be rash to expect a winning tally much in excess of 20 this winter. On the other hand, he still trains Oh So Risky, who was beaten only half-a-length in the Champion Hurdle.

JIMMY FITZGERALD and JONJO O'NEILL endured miserable campaigns, and in FitzGerald's case the horses were below par for months on end. As MARK DWYER relies on both men for a steady flow of winners he is to be complimented on a final total of 73, only eight fewer than in the previous year.

Captain TIM FORSTER has become used to scores in the mid-thirties, so 44 will have pleased him. It is an excellent total for someone whose passion for the game does not extend far beyond steeplechases, and who regards novice and handicap hurdles as little more than a necessary evil. He had his string well forward quite early on last season, and in company with long-serving jockey HYWEL DAVIES - who also finished on 44 - ensured that the stable made a good start. Davies set the seal on a highly satisfactory few months when winning the Whitbread on Topsham Bay for David Barons and Michael Marsh.

One of the best performances from the training ranks came from Cheltenham-based NIGEL TWISTON-DAVIES. After an encouraging 19 in 1990/91, he moved on to 31. Not only that, but he saddled a four-timer at Uttoxeter last October - Tipping Tim, Gulsha, Captain Dibble and Grange Brake. Twiston-Davies is in business with Peter Scudamore, who rides for him when available, but on this occasion all four winners were partnered by Carl Llewellyn. Twiston-Davies has the ability and the ammunition to go to the top.

Mr Frisk's Grand National victory a couple of years ago was just the springboard KIM BAILEY's career needed. Docklands Express and Kings Fountain both did him proud, and the latter (who unseated Anthony Tory in the Gold Cup) will be only ten when the race is run again. Bailey's total of 38 was his best so far, whereas CHARLIE BROOKS' 29 compared with 56 only two years ago.

In his case this is probably not too worrying, because everything he does marks Brooks out as a shrewd trainer. He won the Grand Annual at the Festival with My Young Man, and then watched the same horse run an honourable third in the Cathcart only 48 hours later. He also did well with the long-distance hurdler Castigliero, who returned from France after unsuccessfully contesting steeplechases at Cagnes-sur-Mer.

The way GRAHAM BRADLEY nursed Castigliero through one of his races on very soft ground encouraged the belief that this extremely talented jockey can put all his problems of the past behind him and enjoy a successful autumn of his career. He will always be more readily associated with talented horses than run-of-the-mill ones, and that is not a bad reputation to have. Certainly the top trainers (David Elsworth, in particular) continue to look for him when some special finesse is required.

NICK GASELEE's Aintree triumph with Party Politics did

not obscure the fact that it was, in all other respects, a routine year for him. Indeed, his total of 15 winners was four down on each of the last two winters. ANDY ADAMS would have been on the National winner but for breaking his leg six weeks previously, and earned the sympathy of everyone inside the weighing-room and outside it as well. The luckless BRENDAN POWELL also faces another lengthy spell on the sidelines, but LORCAN WYER came back from a bad fall to end with 35 victories, only nine short of his 1991 total.

Top freelance GRAHAM McCOURT showed for the second time that riding a hundred winners without a powerful retainer can be done through sheer hard graft. Regularly travelling from Lambourn to Scotland, McCourt ended on 102, his best-ever score. Not only that, but he did it in a year when NIGEL TINKLER's yard, a principal source of winners, struck only 38 times. When McCourt rode exactly 100 winners in 1989/90, Tinkler's tally was 49.

Lower down the table, a young man with a glowing future is MICK FITZGERALD, who rode out his claim and ended on the 38 mark. Competing on level terms with senior jockeys will not worry him as he seeks to build on the experience gained whilst riding for canny west country handler JACKIE RETTER. She goes from strength to strength and moved into the twenties after scoring 11 the previous year. Still in the west country, Michael Hourian was leading amateur and has now turned professional.

RICHARD HOLDER had a good season from his Bristol base, but his talented claimer NICK MANN struggled to get close to his tally of 27 for the previous campaign. Holder also unveiled another gifted youngster in DAVID MATTHEWS, who clearly lost track of what had happened to the opposition in a selling handicap hurdle at Chepstow in January and came home 30 lengths clear on Ballyanto. Holder's expression afterwards was an intriguing mixture of bafflement and despair, but he got Ballyanto back for 3,200 guineas at the auction and Matthews has already won a non-seller on him this season.

Two more of Holder's youngsters, the amateur riders

RODNEY and ASHLEY FARRANT (sons of the Chepstow clerk of the course) furthered their education with Tim Forster and John Edwards respectively. Rodney Farrant, a very stylish rider, has joined the ranks of the professionals and will be seen to advantage if given sufficient opportunities.

Finally, the racing world mourned the loss of PHILIP BARNARD, who never recovered consciousness after a fall from Sayyure at Wincanton on Boxing Day. A hard-working, reliable and much respected member of his profession, Philip was conditional jockey to Tim Thomson-Jones and had also worked for Mick Ryan, Richard Whitaker and Lester Piggott.

12 . A - Z of WINNING JOCKEYS

Showing the record of wins, win% and level-stake over the past five years for every jockey to have had a winner in the 1991/92 season. Lowest riding weights are given where known.
'*' after name signifies conditional jockey

	1991/92 Wns Mts(%)	:	1990/91 Wns(%)	1989/90 Wns(%)	1988/89 Wns(%)	1987/88 Wns(%)
ADAMS A 10st 0lbs	1/ 45 2% - 35.00	:	11 12% - 10.09	8 12% + 65.00	3 8% - 24.00	14 11% + 35.11
AHERN M 10st 0lbs	10/ 88 11% - 9.50	:	10 13% + 11.71	10 10% - 20.17	3 7% - 18.59	1 2% - 41.00
ALNER Mr R 10st 12lbs	8/ 25 32% + 15.43	:	4 27% - 1.63	2 100% + 3.04	1 50% + 2.50	1 33% + 5.50
ANDERSON Mr K 10st 13lbs	2/ 7 29% - 2.77	:	4 40% - 4.45	4 57% + 4.17	6 55% + 2.94	2 11% - 13.97
ARMYTAGE Gee 10st 0lbs	11/ 75 15% - 22.37	:	2 3% - 54.87	6 10% - 25.75	4 3% - 55.00	10 7% - 68.04
ARMYTAGE Mr M 10st 0lbs	21/ 79 27% + 20.03	:	6 14% - 32.57	6 14% - 7.79	7 9% - 49.40	12 12% - 24.47
ASTAIRE Mr S	1/ 6 17% - 3.25	:	0 0% - 6.00	0 0% - 2.00	0 0% - 3.00	0 0% - 3.00
AYLES W*	1/ 2 50% + 24.00	:	0 0% - 4.00	0 0% - 4.00	0 0% 0.00	0 0% 0.00
BAILEY Mr E 10st 5lbs	2/ 15 13% + 9.00	:	2 6% - 26.00	1 3% - 4.00	4 13% - 3.75	0 0% - 9.00
BAILEY Mrs T	1/ 7 14% - 3.00	:	0 0% 0.00	1 100% + 2.25	0 0% - 1.00	0 0% - 7.00
BARRY D* 9st 8lbs	2/ 31 6% - 10.00	:	0 0% - 5.00	1 7% - 10.50	0 0% - 1.00	0 0% 0.00
BATES A* 9st 10lbs	4/ 12 33% + 2.90	:	0 0% 0.00	0 0% 0.00	0 0% 0.00	0 0% 0.00
BATTERS Mr M 11st 7lbs	2/ 6 33% + 1.50	:	0 0% - 4.00	0 0% - 1.00	1 33% + 2.00	0 0% 0.00
BAXTER Miss S	1/ 3 33% + 12.00	:	0 0% - 3.00	0 0% - 1.00	1 5% - 13.50	5 19% + 65.00
BEALBY Mr C 11st 9lbs	2/ 5 40% + 4.33	:	2 29% + 15.50	0 0% 0.00	0 0% 0.00	0 0% 0.00
BEGGAN R J 10st 0lbs	22/138 16% - 22.49	:	13 9% - 0.62	22 10% - 121.60	24 11% - 119.67	28 11% - 37.64

	1991/92 Wns Mts (%)	1990/91 Wns (%)	1989/90 Wns (%)	1988/89 Wns (%)	1987/88 Wns (%)
BELLAMY R* 9st 11lbs	12/179 7% - 110.18	13 9% - 58.59	16 8% - 89.94	4 7% - 29.00	6 6% - 43.25
BENTLEY D* 9st 7lbs	12/157 8% - 91.71	2 8% - 18.75	0 0% - 5.00	0 0% 0.00	0 0% 0.00
BENTLEY N* 9st 7lbs	16/ 82 20% + 41.30	3 12% - 7.50	0 0% 0.00	0 0% 0.00	0 0% 0.00
BILLOTT Miss S 10st 0lbs	3/ 14 21% - 1.62	9 26% + 79.21	0 0% 0.00	0 0% 0.00	0 0% 0.00
BLOOM Mr N	1/ 9 11% - 5.00	0 0% - 3.00	1 14% - 3.00	1 20% + 8.00	0 0% - 4.00
BLOOR Mr D 11st 3lbs	2/ 11 18% + 17.25	0 0% - 20.00	0 0% - 4.00	0 0% - 15.00	1 7% + 11.00
BOSLEY M 10st 2lbs	5/129 4% - 83.82	8 6% - 47.62	5 5% - 80.00	4 3% - 85.00	10 7% - 70.92
BOWLBY M 10st 0lbs	4/108 4% - 97.13	13 8% - 74.48	25 14% - 54.97	28 18% + 56.22	14 8% - 80.09
BRADBURNE Mr J 10st 2lbs	3/ 53 6% - 3.00	8 11% - 29.17	5 13% - 10.50	0 0% - 20.00	0 0% - 5.00
BRADLEY G 10st 3lbs	29/294 10% - 150.41	26 12% - 104.05	30 14% - 50.46	34 16% - 40.43	38 16% - 78.00
BRENNAN Helen* 10st 4lbs	2/ 21 10% - 5.00	0 0% - 9.00	0 0% - 6.00	0 0% - 8.00	0 0% 0.00
BRENNAN M 10st 0lbs	10/122 8% - 37.87	17 10% - 24.96	22 14% + 92.37	17 12% + 24.13	16 7% - 58.40
BRIDGWATER D* 9st 9lbs	22/285 8% - 134.54	20 12% + 33.25	3 6% - 32.62	0 0% - 20.00	0 0% 0.00
BRISBY Mr S	1/ 21 5% + 5.00	0 0% - 1.00	0 0% 0.00	0 0% 0.00	0 0% 0.00
BROOKSHAW Mr S 11st 5lbs	4/ 10 40% - 1.62	3 20% - 2.06	4 21% - 8.18	0 0% - 4.00	0 0% - 2.00
BROWN J	1/ 3 33% + 0.50	3 13% - 2.50	4 10% + 20.50	5 12% + 22.51	1 3% - 24.00
BROWN M*	1/ 6 17% - 1.00	0 0% 0.00	1 14% - 2.50	1 13% - 3.00	1 6% - 8.50
BROWN Mr H 11st 0lbs	3/ 11 27% + 5.25	2 17% - 5.14	1 6% - 11.00	0 0% - 18.00	0 0% - 33.00
BROWNLESS C*	1/ 12 8% - 4.00	0 0% 0.00	0 0% 0.00	0 0% 0.00	0 0% 0.00
BUCKLEY Mr M 9st 7lbs	4/ 25 16% - 9.25	4 16% + 2.50	0 0% - 4.00	0 0% - 1.00	0 0% 0.00
BURCHELL D J 10st 0lbs	15/109 14% - 20.07	13 14% - 32.27	12 11% - 55.82	13 11% - 36.29	14 12% - 30.14
BURNELL Mr W 11st 2lbs	2/ 9 22% + 27.00	0 0% 0.00	0 0% - 1.00	0 0% 0.00	0 0% 0.00
BURNETT-WELLS Mr C 9st 13lbs	2/ 12 17% + 7.38	2 7% - 6.50	2 8% - 10.00	2 6% - 20.50	3 33% + 13.38

204 . A - Z of Winning Jockeys

	1991/92 Wns Mts(%)	:	1990/91 Wns(%)	1989/90 Wns(%)	1988/89 Wns(%)	1987/88 Wns(%)
BURROUGH S 10st 0lbs	6/134 4% - 106.87	: :	16 9% - 22.07	5 9% + 14.75	4 17% - 4.75	0 0% - 3.00
BUSH Mr S	1/ 9 11% - 2.00	: :	1 20% + 12.00	0 0% - 3.00	1 10% - 1.00	0 0% - 12.00
BUTLER Miss J 11st 0lbs	2/ 12 17% - 4.79	: :	0 0% - 4.00	0 0% 0.00	0 0% 0.00	0 0% 0.00
BYRNE D 10st 0lbs	14/143 10% - 6.73	: :	21 11% - 104.00	44 18% + 12.96	29 15% - 21.93	9 19% - 10.52
BYRNE E 10st 0lbs	3/ 85 4% - 72.25	: :	2 4% - 26.50	0 0% - 11.00	0 0% 0.00	0 0% 0.00
BYRNE Mr T 10st 2lbs	2/ 20 10% - 8.00	: :	0 0% - 1.00	0 0% - 1.00	0 0% - 1.00	0 0% - 3.00
CALDWELL Peter 10st 11lbs	2/ 41 5% + 10.00	: :	1 3% - 34.33	1 2% - 41.00	6 9% - 12.56	2 3% - 25.00
CALLAGHAN J 9st 11lbs	28/224 13% - 92.85	: :	15 9% - 76.15	24 11% - 74.90	11 13% + 7.98	0 0% - 12.00
CAMBIDGE Mr J	1/ 14 7% - 4.00	: :	0 0% - 6.00	1 6% - 11.50	0 0% - 26.00	0 0% - 17.00
CAMPBELL R 10st 11lbs	8/ 54 15% - 21.21	: :	3 11% - 12.50	2 6% - 27.50	5 10% - 14.50	3 6% - 19.50
CARDEN Mr J	1/ 5 20% - 2.00	: :	0 0% - 2.00	0 0% - 7.00	0 0% - 13.00	0 0% - 16.00
CAREY P* 9st 7lbs	2/ 29 7% + 14.00	: :	0 0% 0.00	0 0% 0.00	0 0% 0.00	0 0% 0.00
CARR P*	1/ 26 4% - 24.27	: :	0 0% - 1.00	0 0% - 2.00	0 0% 0.00	0 0% 0.00
CARROLL A 10st 0lbs	7/111 6% - 73.00	: :	9 5% - 100.92	10 6% - 102.85	7 5% - 92.50	17 11% - 45.86
CHAPMAN Mr M	1/ 5 20% + 6.00	: :	0 0% 0.00	0 0% 0.00	0 0% 0.00	0 0% 0.00
CHARLTON A 10st 0lbs	9/ 71 13% + 21.00	: :	0 0% - 43.00	9 10% - 43.10	9 11% - 36.23	14 13% - 39.81
CLARKE J*	1/ 41 2% - 36.50	: :	0 0% - 6.00	1 5% - 16.00	3 14% - 11.18	1 7% - 9.50
CLARKE Mr P	1/ 4 25% - 1.75	: :	0 0% - 8.00	1 13% + 7.00	0 0% - 16.00	0 0% - 16.00
CLAY Diane	1/ 18 6% - 14.75	: :	0 0% 0.00	3 20% + 1.00	12 9% - 31.36	5 5% - 34.50
CLIFFORD B M* 9st 7lbs	27/232 12% - 13.61	: :	9 8% - 23.02	4 11% - 1.00	0 0% - 4.00	0 0% 0.00
COLEMAN N 10st 0lbs	12/106 11% - 21.44	: :	4 4% - 71.00	6 6% - 72.52	23 10% - 14.46	15 11% + 40.75
COMERFORD K* 10st 4lbs	3/ 19 16% - 6.33	: :	0 0% - 27.00	1 33% + 3.00	0 0% - 1.00	0 0% 0.00
CORKELL J*	1/ 14 7% - 8.00	: :	12 17% + 49.13	3 19% - 0.67	0 0% - 5.00	0 0% 0.00

	1991/92 Wns Mts(%)	: 1990/91 Wns(%)	1989/90 Wns(%)	1988/89 Wns(%)	1987/88 Wns(%)
COWLEY S 10st 0lbs	2/ 39 5% - 23.50	0 0% : - 9.00	5 7% - 35.50	1 2% - 53.00	12 14% + 45.83
CROSSMAN D* 9st 8lbs	2/ 20 10% - 8.75	1 3% : - 25.00	2 7% - 17.50	5 19% + 1.50	0 0% - 7.00
CUMINGS Miss J	1/ 2 50% + 1.25	1 100% : + 2.00	0 0% 0.00	0 0% 0.00	0 0% 0.00
CURLING Miss P 10st 11lbs	4/ 16 25% + 1.71	2 29% : + 1.25	1 14% - 4.50	0 0% 0.00	1 8% - 8.00
CURRAN S* 9st 7lbs	2/ 70 3% - 61.17	4 10% : - 20.52	0 0% - 12.00	0 0% 0.00	0 0% 0.00
DACE L* 9st 7lbs	2/ 26 8% - 14.50	2 13% : - 6.00	0 0% - 1.00	0 0% 0.00	0 0% 0.00
DALRYMPLE Mr N	1/ 2 50% + 1.25	0 0% : 0.00	0 0% 0.00	0 0% 0.00	0 0% 0.00
DALTON B* 9st 7lbs	3/ 66 5% - 38.50	5 9% : - 2.00	1 6% + 3.00	0 0% 0.00	0 0% 0.00
DALTON Mr A	1/ 17 6% - 14.50	0 0% : - 5.00	0 0% 0.00	0 0% 0.00	0 0% 0.00
DARE Miss A	1/ 2 50% + 4.00	0 0% : 0.00	0 0% - 1.00	0 0% - 1.00	0 0% - 6.00
DARKE Mr R 9st 13lbs	6/ 41 15% + 60.00	0 0% : - 31.00	0 0% - 4.00	0 0% - 3.00	0 0% - 2.00
DASCOMBE T*	1/ 18 6% - 7.00	0 0% : 0.00	0 0% 0.00	0 0% 0.00	0 0% 0.00
DAVIES H 10st 1lbs	44/346 13% - 77.88	51 14% : - 122.50	60 15% + 0.90	50 11% - 83.49	33 9% - 65.52
DAVIES Judy* 9st 7lbs	6/ 73 8% + 15.00	0 0% : - 45.00	0 0% 0.00	0 0% 0.00	0 0% 0.00
DAVIES P*	1/ 62 2% - 50.00	1 3% : - 18.00	0 0% - 23.00	0 0% - 17.00	0 0% - 8.00
DAVIES S* 9st 11lbs	2/ 74 3% - 55.00	2 2% : - 69.00	7 7% - 48.87	8 11% - 2.50	6 6% - 52.75
DAVIS Mr R 9st 7lbs	10/ 89 11% + 29.63	3 7% : - 32.70	0 0% 0.00	0 0% 0.00	0 0% 0.00
DAWE N 10st 0lbs	2/ 46 4% - 34.50	2 4% : - 7.00	2 4% - 42.50	1 2% - 42.50	1 3% - 31.00
DAWSON Mrs J	1/ 1 100% + 2.00	0 0% : 0.00	0 0% - 1.00	1 50% - 0.33	0 0% - 2.00
DE HAAN B 9st 11lbs	4/114 4% - 72.75	10 9% : - 50.97	29 18% - 28.95	15 8% - 103.35	16 10% - 25.83
DEASLEY Mr S	1/ 1 100% + 5.00	0 0% : - 2.00	0 0% - 1.00	0 0% 0.00	0 0% 0.00
DENNIS C*	1/ 76 1% - 61.00	1 2% : - 35.50	4 4% - 99.13	11 7% - 76.79	11 9% - 61.67
DENNIS D* 10st 7lbs	2/ 23 9% - 1.00	1 6% : - 13.00	1 4% - 20.00	0 0% 0.00	0 0% 0.00

	1991/92 Wns Mts(%)	: 1990/91 : Wns(%)	1989/90 Wns(%)	1988/89 Wns(%)	1987/88 Wns(%)
DICKEN A* 9st 10lbs	15/ 49 31% - 2.21	: 2 25% : + 7.00	0 0% - 9.00	0 0% - 2.00	0 0% - 2.00
DOBBIN A* 9st 7lbs	14/ 76 18% + 21.26	: 0 0% : - 25.00	0 0% 0.00	0 0% 0.00	0 0% 0.00
DONOGHUE V*	1/ 14 7% - 5.00	: 0 0% : 0.00	0 0% 0.00	0 0% 0.00	0 0% 0.00
DONOHOE S* 9st 12lbs	2/ 58 3% - 32.50	: 8 11% : - 33.29	0 0% 0.00	0 0% 0.00	0 0% 0.00
DOOLAN K 10st 0lbs	6/100 6% - 78.53	: 7 8% : + 24.25	6 11% - 19.12	1 2% - 39.00	11 8% - 29.70
DOUGHTY N 10st 7lbs	44/232 19% - 81.35	: 96 28% : + 51.35	47 24% - 48.02	33 20% + 63.95	18 11% - 63.74
DOWLING B 10st 0lbs	7/109 6% - 70.67	: 14 10% : - 61.60	23 17% - 16.94	17 11% - 6.62	14 11% - 6.25
DRISCOLL J* 9st 9lbs	4/109 4% - 65.00	: 0 0% : - 6.00	1 20% + 8.00	0 0% 0.00	0 0% 0.00
DUFFY M*	1/ 4 25% - 0.50	: 0 0% : 0.00	0 0% 0.00	0 0% 0.00	0 0% 0.00
DUGGAN J	1/ 14 7% - 9.50	: 4 6% : - 42.89	3 5% - 22.00	4 5% - 43.06	3 3% - 83.50
DUGGAN Mr D 10st 7lbs	2/ 22 9% + 4.00	: 1 5% : + 31.00	2 12% - 3.50	0 0% - 6.00	0 0% - 3.00
DUN Mr J M	1/ 6 17% 0.00	: 0 0% : - 6.00	0 0% - 2.00	0 0% 0.00	0 0% 0.00
DUNWOODY R 10st 0lbs	137/715 19% - 171.85	: 127 20% : - 154.92	102 17% - 65.11	91 14% - 172.49	79 14% - 103.45
DURKAN Mr J 9st 10lbs	4/ 61 7% - 40.62	: 6 10% : - 48.00	7 17% - 10.60	1 25% + 4.00	0 0% 0.00
DWAN W J* 9st 7lbs	7/ 48 15% - 17.46	: 6 19% : + 12.38	1 8% - 4.00	1 11% + 6.00	0 0% - 1.00
DWYER M 10st 1lbs	73/380 19% - 101.57	: 81 21% : - 60.60	74 20% - 135.50	92 20% - 26.25	73 18% - 24.98
DYER Mr R	1/ 6 17% - 4.27	: 0 0% : - 3.00	0 0% - 2.00	0 0% 0.00	0 0% 0.00
EARLE S 10st 0lbs	8/221 4% - 154.17	: 16 6% : - 196.21	22 10% - 135.77	13 6% - 112.99	21 11% - 13.68
ECCLES S SMITH 10st 4lbs	21/155 14% - 51.49	: 56 24% : - 7.06	0 0% 0.00	0 0% 0.00	0 0% 0.00
EDWARDS Mr G	1/ 3 33% + 2.00	: 1 9% : - 3.50	0 0% - 7.00	0 0% - 7.00	0 0% - 3.00
ELEY T* 9st 7lbs	6/ 64 9% - 22.00	: 2 8% : - 4.50	1 8% - 1.00	0 0% 0.00	0 0% 0.00
ELLWOOD Maj O	1/ 4 25% + 3.50	: 1 25% : + 2.00	0 0% - 2.00	0 0% - 3.00	0 0% - 1.00
ERKENOV A	1/ 3 33% + 14.00	: 0 0% : 0.00	0 0% 0.00	0 0% 0.00	0 0% 0.00

	1991/92 Wns Mts(%)	: 1990/91 : Wns (%)	1989/90 Wns(%)	1988/89 Wns(%)	1987/88 Wns(%)
EVANS C 10st 2lbs	3/ 37 8% + 22.00	0 0% : - 32.00	3 6% - 35.75	1 2% - 31.00	1 2% - 41.00
EWART Mr C 10st 0lbs	2/ 10 20% + 1.25	1 13% : - 4.75	0 0% - 1.00	0 0% - 1.00	0 0% 0.00
FAHEY R 10st 0lbs	9/ 67 13% - 34.71	9 9% : - 39.27	18 12% - 55.41	29 13% - 12.45	0 0% - 64.00
FARRANT Mr A 10st 3lbs	3/ 31 10% - 18.75	13 18% : + 16.95	4 17% - 3.10	0 0% - 6.00	0 0% 0.00
FARRANT Mr R 8st 0lbs	7/ 81 9% - 21.17	3 8% : + 12.50	1 17% + 20.00	0 0% 0.00	0 0% 0.00
FARRELL Mrs A 9st 11lbs	4/ 60 7% - 43.32	7 22% : + 28.25	3 7% - 1.75	6 13% + 4.26	2 6% - 25.00
FARRELL P A 10 st 0lbs	5/ 80 6% - 40.62	7 11% : - 26.82	3 4% - 58.50	6 7% - 39.38	3 4% - 40.00
FARTHING Mr J 11st 9lbs	4/ 8 50% + 12.90	0 0% : - 2.00	0 0% 0.00	0 0% 0.00	0 0% 0.00
FELTON Mr M 11st 2lbs	4/ 24 17% - 9.34	1 17% : - 3.00	0 0% - 8.00	0 0% - 3.00	0 0% - 4.00
FITZGERALD M A* 9st 11lbs	38/265 14% + 62.15	11 15% : + 23.75	1 4% - 12.00	2 9% + 7.00	0 0% 0.00
FLANNIGAN A*	1/ 53 2% - 38.00	0 0% : - 6.00	0 0% 0.00	0 0% 0.00	0 0% 0.00
FORD Mr R 9st 8lbs	2/ 19 11% - 4.50	1 4% : - 21.75	3 13% - 6.25	0 0% - 12.00	2 11% + 37.50
FORSTER Miss S	1/ 7 14% - 2.50	1 10% : 0.00	0 0% 0.00	0 0% 0.00	0 0% 0.00
FORTT D* 9st 9lbs	3/ 22 14% - 8.00	0 0% : - 4.00	0 0% 0.00	0 0% 0.00	0 0% 0.00
FOSTER M* 9st 9lbs	21/138 15% - 28.70	35 30% : - 2.68	9 23% + 29.85	2 10% - 8.12	0 0% 0.00
FOX S* 9st 9lbs	2/ 36 6% - 29.50	0 0% : - 42.00	0 0% - 13.00	1 5% - 2.00	0 0% 0.00
FROST J 10st 1lbs	41/337 12% - 145.47	39 14% : - 71.16	46 15% - 86.88	41 14% - 46.32	30 13% + 21.93
FRY W* 9st 7lbs	3/ 48 6% - 29.17	4 21% : - 4.37	0 0% - 2.00	0 0% 0.00	0 0% 0.00
GALLAGHER D 9st 12lbs	16/206 8% - 90.02	12 5% : - 53.62	23 10% - 69.22	3 2% - 46.00	15 11% - 10.12
GARRITY R 10st 2lbs	17/170 10% - 66.04	14 10% : - 75.59	22 10% - 89.17	21 14% - 34.10	0 0% - 45.00
GRANT C 10st 0lbs	78/449 17% - 106.25	57 16% : - 92.37	94 23% - 87.28	39 20% - 57.72	80 16% - 129.14
GRANTHAM T 10st 0lbs	17/108 16% - 0.77	8 8% : - 66.75	6 9% - 42.78	4 4% - 77.47	11 10% - 44.54
GREENALL Mr J 11st 8lbs	11/ 44 25% + 18.87	3 9% : - 22.75	6 20% - 11.12	7 17% + 0.25	7 23% - 1.37

	1991/92 Wns Mts(%)	1990/91 Wns(%)	1989/90 Wns(%)	1988/89 Wns(%)	1987/88 Wns(%)
GREENE R* 9st 9lbs	14/142 10% + 35.75	8 5% - 111.50	12 11% - 39.65	2 3% - 48.75	0 0% - 10.00
GRIFFITH Mr A 11st 7lbs	2/ 12 17% - 4.67	1 11% - 6.25	1 20% - 1.50	2 22% + 28.50	0 0% - 5.00
GRIFFITHS Mr R	1/ 11 9% + 2.00	0 0% 0.00	0 0% 0.00	0 0% 0.00	0 0% 0.00
GUEST Richard 10st 0lbs	43/315 14% - 6.98	33 10% - 54.24	13 7% - 134.99	19 10% - 44.50	18 9% - 76.02
HACKING Mr P	1/ 13 8% - 10.12	1 9% - 8.90	2 20% + 36.00	5 31% - 3.06	4 31% + 13.83
HALE Mr R 9st 9lbs	5/ 37 14% - 15.21	4 15% - 10.17	0 0% - 22.00	0 0% - 30.00	2 18% + 9.00
HALLS J* 10st 0lbs	3/ 16 19% - 2.75	1 13% - 4.25	0 0% - 11.00	0 0% - 5.00	0 0% - 5.00
HAMBLY Mr A	1/ 32 3% - 24.50	2 11% + 4.50	2 13% - 10.99	0 0% - 16.00	0 0% - 18.00
HAMMOND Mr M	1/ 5 20% - 1.75	0 0% - 2.00	0 0% - 2.00	0 0% 0.00	0 0% 0.00
HANCOCK Mr C	1/ 27 4% - 12.00	0 0% - 12.00	0 0% - 14.00	0 0% - 4.00	0 0% 0.00
HANMER Mr G	1/ 15 7% - 8.50	2 20% - 2.90	0 0% - 6.00	2 2% - 59.00	0 0% - 21.00
HARDING-JONES Mr P 10st 11lbs	2/ 22 9% - 16.70	2 11% + 85.00	0 0% - 25.00	6 9% - 33.44	6 17% - 5.67
HARKER G	1/ 46 2% - 40.00	4 4% - 85.12	7 5% - 89.75	5 5% - 73.37	16 10% - 50.74
HARLEY P 10st 0lbs	3/ 88 3% - 45.00	0 0% - 53.00	5 4% - 87.75	3 4% - 50.00	2 6% - 26.00
HARRIS J A 10st 0lbs	4/ 86 5% - 61.50	10 11% + 15.50	2 3% - 43.00	3 3% - 63.37	1 1% - 86.00
HARTNETT K* 9st 7lbs	3/ 26 12% + 24.00	0 0% 0.00	0 0% 0.00	0 0% 0.00	0 0% 0.00
HARVEY L 10st 0lbs	25/252 10% - 62.35	42 15% - 43.84	25 12% - 3.57	11 7% - 57.61	17 8% - 64.83
HARVEY Mr A	1/ 10 10% - 6.00	0 0% - 3.00	6 33% + 21.08	3 20% - 3.25	0 0% - 6.00
HARWOOD Miss A 10st 0lbs	2/ 7 29% + 5.75	5 24% + 6.73	6 33% + 21.08	3 20% - 3.25	0 0% - 6.00
HAWKE N 10st 0lbs	12/165 7% - 86.34	15 12% + 30.97	17 12% - 64.33	18 15% - 43.35	12 16% + 9.74
HAWKINS C 10st 0lbs	4/ 91 4% - 54.60	7 6% - 74.70	11 8% - 45.37	12 7% - 66.17	17 7% - 81.17
HAZELL S*	1/ 24 4% - 20.75	0 0% - 14.00	1 7% - 11.50	0 0% 0.00	0 0% 0.00
HEAVER G* 9st 7lbs	2/ 27 7% - 16.70	1 7% + 6.00	1 8% - 10.90	0 0% - 25.00	1 3% - 23.00

	1991/92 Wns Mts (%)	: 1990/91 : Wns (%)	1989/90 Wns (%)	1988/89 Wns (%)	1987/88 Wns (%)
HENDERSON Mrs R 11st 2lbs	2/ 5 40% + 7.00	0 0% : - 1.00	0 0% 0.00	0 0% 0.00	0 0% 0.00
HICKMAN Mr A	1/ 6 17% - 1.67	2 5% : - 9.00	0 0% - 13.00	0 0% - 4.00	0 0% - 2.00
HIDE P* 9st 7lbs	8/ 89 9% - 11.40	1 50% : - 0.33	0 0% 0.00	0 0% 0.00	0 0% 0.00
HILL M	1/ 35 3% - 25.00	5 11% : - 23.25	12 18% - 15.79	0 0% - 11.00	5 11% + 1.87
HILL Mr A 11st 11lbs	3/ 9 33% + 4.15	1 100% : + 3.33	1 13% - 6.33	3 27% - 4.38	3 20% - 10.22
HOAD M* 10st 2lbs	3/ 35 9% - 27.37	10 11% : - 7.00	1 2% - 54.25	2 5% - 33.25	3 5% - 5.00
HOBBS Peter 10st 0lbs	31/261 12% - 89.46	9 24% : - 9.50	43 15% - 68.88	47 13% + 28.21	26 9% - 122.43
HODGE R* 9st 7lbs	24/199 12% - 68.80	19 17% : - 24.69	11 20% - 2.74	0 0% - 32.00	4 11% - 6.50
HODGSON S 10st 0lbs	9/ 71 13% + 60.70	8 9% : - 65.42	6 8% - 30.37	9 13% - 10.18	0 0% - 17.00
HOLLEY P 10st 0lbs	11/125 9% - 49.27	19 12% : + 16.13	11 9% - 67.23	22 14% + 37.70	6 7% - 34.60
HOLLOWELL Mr K	1/ 17 6% - 16.00	0 0% : - 6.00	0 0% 0.00	0 0% 0.00	0 0% 0.00
HOUGHTON Mr G J 9st 9lbs	4/ 28 14% + 52.50	7 18% : + 55.68	3 12% - 2.50	0 0% 0.00	0 0% 0.00
HOURIGAN Mr M P 9st 7lbs	24/ 95 25% + 62.79	0 0% : 0.00	0 0% 0.00	0 0% 0.00	0 0% 0.00
HUGHES P* 9st 7lbs	4/ 22 18% + 6.00	0 0% : 0.00	0 0% - 3.00	0 0% 0.00	0 0% 0.00
HUMPHREYS W 10st 0lbs	3/102 3% - 67.25	0 0% : - 119.00	6 5% - 81.00	4 3% - 93.60	14 7% - 75.62
HURST Mr W 10st 6lbs	2/ 4 50% + 7.50	0 0% : 0.00	0 0% 0.00	0 0% 0.00	0 0% 0.00
IRVINE W 10st 0lbs	10/199 5% - 115.95	12 6% : - 44.23	14 7% - 85.25	23 9% + 20.24	15 9% - 62.37
JARVIS T 10st 1lbs	2/ 37 5% + 2.00	0 0% : - 22.00	2 40% + 2.00	0 0% 0.00	0 0% - 6.00
JENKINS H	1/ 15 7% - 8.00	0 0% : 0.00	0 0% 0.00	0 0% 0.00	0 0% 0.00
JENKS Mr T	1/ 53 2% - 42.00	0 0% : - 13.00	0 0% - 5.00	0 0% 0.00	0 0% 0.00
JOHNSON B	1/ 6 17% + 4.00	0 0% : - 3.00	0 0% 0.00	0 0% 0.00	0 0% 0.00
JOHNSON K 10st 0lbs	12/137 9% - 72.57	0 0% : - 2.00	14 20% - 32.76	14 22% + 15.02	0 0% - 14.00
JOHNSON Mr P 10st 13lbs	2/ 22 9% - 12.75	0 0% : - 30.00	0 0% - 16.00	2 11% + 3.00	1 5% - 13.50

	1991/92 Wns Mts(%)	: 1990/91 Wns(%)	1989/90 Wns(%)	1988/89 Wns(%)	1987/88 Wns(%)
JONES A 10st 0lbs	3/ 48 6%	: 1 3%	2 6%	7 13%	3 4%
	- 34.25	: - 18.00	- 27.27	+ 1.60	- 44.50
JONES K 10st 0lbs	2/ 92 2%	: 2 2%	0 0%	1 2%	12 9%
	- 74.00	: - 87.00	- 76.00	- 57.00	- 13.37
JONES M 9st 11lbs	8/209 4%	: 11 6%	9 7%	12 8%	6 8%
	- 134.04	: - 94.00	- 63.30	- 67.75	- 30.12
JONES Mr T 11st 4lbs	3/ 23 13%	: 2 17%	2 13%	2 17%	1 20%
	- 4.00	: 0.00	- 3.75	- 5.75	+ 2.00
KAVANAGH J 9st 11lbs	23/179 13%	: 11 14%	0 0%	0 0%	0 0%
	- 7.63	: + 1.51	0.00	0.00	0.00
KEIGHTLEY S 10st 0lbs	9/ 76 12%	: 8 9%	5 5%	5 4%	3 2%
	- 7.63	: - 58.99	- 80.00	- 74.50	- 110.75
KENDALL Mrs M	1/ 16 6%	: 0 0%	0 0%	0 0%	0 0%
	+ 10.00	: - 9.00	- 13.00	- 8.00	- 15.00
KERSEY Susan*	1/ 29 3%	: 0 0%	1 2%	1 2%	1 2%
	- 16.00	: - 21.00	- 60.50	- 44.00	- 39.00
KNIGHT G 10st 0lbs	2/ 68 3%	: 0 0%	0 0%	0 0%	0 0%
	- 54.50	: - 2.00	0.00	0.00	0.00
KONDRAT A	1/ 5 20%	: 0 0%	0 0%	0 0%	0 0%
	+ 6.00	: - 6.00	0.00	0.00	0.00
LARNACH A* 9st 8lbs	11/100 11%	: 6 13%	3 21%	0 0%	0 0%
	- 34.18	: - 31.39	- 4.25	0.00	0.00
LAWRENCE I 10st 0lbs	15/163 9%	: 16 7%	21 10%	15 8%	7 9%
	+ 40.26	: - 100.58	- 30.53	- 27.87	- 17.68
LAWTHER Mr R	1/ 7 14%	: 1 14%	0 0%	0 0%	0 0%
	+ 1.50	: - 0.50	- 2.00	0.00	0.00
LAY Mr A 10st 12lbs	2/ 10 20%	: 0 0%	0 0%	0 0%	0 0%
	0.00	: 0.00	0.00	0.00	0.00
LEACH N* 9st 7lbs	5/ 57 9%	: 2 5%	0 0%	1 7%	0 0%
	- 29.95	: - 5.25	- 34.00	- 11.50	0.00
LEAHY D* 9st 7lbs	6/109 6%	: 2 5%	0 0%	0 0%	0 0%
	- 55.34	: - 21.50	0.00	0.00	0.00
LEECH J* 9st 11lbs	2/ 36 6%	: 2 4%	15 18%	10 14%	5 19%
	- 26.75	: - 39.00	- 11.08	- 11.87	- 5.38
LEECH P 10st 0lbs	2/ 49 4%	: 1 11%	4 13%	0 0%	0 0%
	- 39.17	: - 6.25	- 8.00	0.00	- 1.00
LEWIS Mr G	1/ 34 3%	: 0 0%	0 0%	0 0%	0 0%
	- 26.00	: 0.00	0.00	0.00	0.00
LITSTON Mrs J 10st 4lbs	2/ 10 20%	: 1 20%	0 0%	0 0%	0 0%
	+ 7.75	: - 1.50	- 3.00	0.00	2.00
LLEWELLYN C 10st 0lbs	53/382 14%	: 32 11%	19 10%	20 8%	41 11%
	- 15.43	: - 32.29	- 83.80	- 149.58	- 33.26
LODDER J 10st 0lbs	6/138 4%	: 18 9%	25 11%	10 13%	0 0%
	- 59.50	: - 92.99	- 102.50	- 31.80	0.00
LOWER J 10st 0lbs	6/ 45 13%	: 29 24%	49 33%	27 25%	11 9%
	- 9.50	: - 22.82	+ 2.46	+ 11.55	- 61.40

	1991/92 Wns Mts(%)	: 1990/91 Wns(%)	1989/90 Wns(%)	1988/89 Wns(%)	1987/88 Wns(%)
LYNCH M M 10st 0lbs	23/219 11% − 74.04	: 16 7% : − 123.29	17 10% − 81.21	12 8% − 41.37	0 0% 0.00
LYONS Gary 10st 2lbs	7/116 6% − 50.97	: 10 7% : − 70.75	31 15% − 88.80	8 5% − 54.67	0 0% 0.00
LYONS Mr S 9st 7lbs	16/127 13% − 30.00	: 1 6% : − 11.50	0 0% 0.00	0 0% 0.00	0 0% 0.00
MACTAGGART Mr D	1/ 22 5% + 12.00	: 2 8% : − 20.20	2 6% − 3.75	1 2% − 38.50	3 7% − 31.00
MADDOCK P* 9st 7lbs	2/ 11 18% + 32.00	: 0 0% : 0.00	0 0% 0.00	0 0% 0.00	0 0% 0.00
MAGUIRE A* 9st 9lbs	71/500 14% − 119.60	: 3 50% : + 20.00	0 0% 0.00	0 0% 0.00	0 0% 0.00
MANN N 10st 0lbs	16/152 11% − 78.52	: 27 13% : − 16.17	24 18% + 20.29	3 16% + 53.50	0 0% 0.00
MARLEY R 10st 0lbs	12/144 8% − 83.25	: 16 9% : − 86.89	11 7% − 113.03	21 14% − 124.23	20 13% − 23.12
MARQUIS Mr B	1/ 1 100% + 20.00	: 0 0% : 0.00	0 0% 0.00	0 0% 0.00	0 0% 0.00
MARSTON W* 9st 7lbs	16/140 11% − 24.68	: 4 7% : − 12.25	1 6% − 12.00	0 0% − 1.00	0 0% 0.00
MASON S*	1/ 40 3% − 36.00	: 1 4% : − 16.00	0 0% − 8.00	1 6% + 17.00	1 25% − 0.50
MATTHEWS D* 9st 11lbs	7/ 52 13% − 16.05	: 1 4% : − 15.00	0 0% − 13.00	0 0% 0.00	0 0% 0.00
MAUDE C 10st 0lbs	20/232 9% − 126.41	: 28 12% : − 17.32	12 9% − 55.89	3 10% − 12.50	0 0% − 7.00
MCCABE A*	1/ 21 5% − 17.50	: 1 5% : − 16.00	1 5% − 14.00	2 13% + 2.50	1 25% + 13.00
MCCABE J*	1/ 9 11% − 4.67	: 0 0% : − 6.00	0 0% 0.00	0 0% 0.00	0 0% 0.00
MCCAIN Jnr Mr D 10st 1lbs	3/ 61 5% − 33.50	: 5 11% : − 1.22	6 9% − 39.65	4 9% − 11.00	0 0% − 10.00
MCCARTHY J* 9st 10lbs	2/ 28 7% − 18.75	: 1 4% : − 18.00	2 15% − 2.00	0 0% 0.00	0 0% 0.00
MCCOURT G 10st 4lbs	102/506 20% + 32.80	: 83 19% : + 7.27	100 23% + 70.40	86 20% − 35.12	68 17% − 10.73
MCDERMOTT P	1/ 47 2% − 26.00	: 1 3% : − 28.00	7 8% − 36.04	5 5% − 37.80	0 0% − 60.00
MCFARLAND W 10st 0lbs	15/197 8% − 85.83	: 24 10% : − 55.95	26 12% − 35.24	23 14% − 33.19	2 4% + 10.50
MCGIFF B*	1/ 4 25% + 2.00	: 2 2% : − 82.62	18 17% − 14.05	9 32% + 24.83	0 0% − 5.00
MCGONAGLE M* 10st 0lbs	9/ 39 23% + 9.41	: 3 43% : + 11.75	1 17% 0.00	0 0% 0.00	0 0% 0.00
MCKEOWN Dale 10st 0lbs	16/113 14% − 11.35	: 17 14% : − 35.92	30 19% − 67.52	31 16% + 10.33	17 10% − 67.10

	1991/92 Wns Mts (%)	: 1990/91 : Wns (%)	1989/90 Wns (%)	1988/89 Wns (%)	1987/88 Wns (%)
MCKIE Mr I	1/ 4 25% - 1.75	2 40% + 11.50	0 0% 0.00	0 0% 0.00	0 0% 0.00
MCKINLEY E	1/ 40 3% - 38.80	7 9% - 50.87	0 0% - 17.00	3 9% 0.00	2 10% - 1.37
MCLAUGHLIN J 10st 0lbs	2/ 18 11% - 4.12	8 10% - 40.70	4 9% - 24.87	7 11% + 14.96	10 15% + 7.17
MCLOUGHLIN Mr P J 9st 7lbs	3/ 50 6% - 6.00	0 0% 0.00	0 0% 0.00	0 0% 0.00	0 0% 0.00
MCNEILL S 10st 0lbs	31/268 12% - 32.79	20 8% - 11.50	15 6% - 136.47	22 7% - 148.56	9 4% - 111.75
MEADE D* 9st 7lbs	2/ 45 4% - 24.50	0 0% - 12.00	0 0% - 10.00	0 0% 0.00	0 0% 0.00
MELLOR Mrs E	1/ 1 100% + 3.50	0 0% 0.00	0 0% 0.00	0 0% 0.00	0 0% 0.00
MEREDITH D* 9st 7lbs	13/100 13% + 10.33	2 5% - 24.00	2 10% - 9.50	0 0% 0.00	0 0% 0.00
MERRIGAN A 10st 0lbs	7/139 5% - 107.81	9 9% - 49.03	10 11% + 23.38	28 13% - 74.97	26 11% - 102.65
MIDGLEY P* 9st 12lbs	10/168 6% - 99.96	6 6% - 11.00	5 6% - 40.83	2 6% - 22.75	0 0% 0.00
MILES Mr N	1/ 7 14% + 14.00	0 0% 0.00	0 0% 0.00	0 0% 0.00	0 0% 0.00
MITCHELL Mr N	1/ 12 8% - 6.50	1 17% + 3.00	0 0% - 18.00	0 0% - 3.00	0 0% 0.00
MOFFATT D J* 9st 7lbs	15/145 10% - 62.51	3 4% - 60.38	1 6% - 10.00	0 0% 0.00	0 0% 0.00
MOLONEY M* 9st 9lbs	12/140 9% - 40.67	9 10% - 9.77	8 10% - 50.38	0 0% 0.00	0 0% 0.00
MONNIER Mr F 10st 10lbs	7/ 28 25% + 0.42	7 33% - 0.32	2 29% + 0.10	0 0% 0.00	0 0% 0.00
MOORE G 10st 0lbs	11/199 6% - 98.47	17 13% - 51.46	9 6% - 86.50	2 1% - 111.50	5 4% - 65.50
MOORE P*	1/ 11 9% 0.00	0 0% 0.00	0 0% 0.00	0 0% 0.00	0 0% 0.00
MORRIS Candy	1/ 29 3% - 26.50	1 3% - 28.50	2 5% - 27.50	3 6% - 13.00	0 0% 0.00
MORRIS D 10st 0lbs	9/143 6% - 76.04	15 12% - 1.48	6 6% - 74.12	4 3% - 66.50	16 9% - 122.57
MORRIS W	1/ 21 5% - 14.00	4 7% - 27.00	2 3% - 52.50	0 0% - 38.00	2 3% - 22.00
MORRISON Mr T	1/ 5 20% 0.00	0 0% - 3.00	0 0% - 2.00	1 50% + 0.50	0 0% - 4.00
MULHOLLAND A 10st 2lbs	3/ 41 7% - 16.75	5 9% + 4.50	7 9% - 27.54	9 10% - 8.00	11 13% - 14.02
MULLANEY L* 9st 7lbs	7/ 40 18% 5.17	3 19% + 15.25	0 0% 0.00	0 0% 0.00	0 0% 0.00

	1991/92 Wns Mts(%)	: 1990/91 : Wns(%)	1989/90 Wns(%)	1988/89 Wns(%)	1987/88 Wns(%)
MURPHY D J 10st 0lbs	48/326 15% - 109.97	: 29 11% : - 125.36	15 9% - 84.50	19 16% - 32.62	15 21% + 8.01
MURPHY E 10st 0lbs	8/ 76 11% - 44.63	: 10 12% : - 5.34	9 10% - 23.95	10 10% - 71.36	8 9% - 41.90
MURPHY Mr J 9st 7lbs	2/ 24 8% - 6.50	: 0 0% : 0.00	0 0% 0.00	0 0% 0.00	0 0% 0.00
MURPHY Mr P 9st 7lbs	1/ 11 9% + 56.00	: 0 0% : - 5.00	0 0% 0.00	0 0% 0.00	0 0% 0.00
MURTAGH F* 9st 7lbs	15/181 8% - 60.07	: 20 11% : - 41.05	0 0% - 23.00	2 9% - 14.67	0 0% 0.00
NASH Mrs P 9st 7lbs	8/ 53 15% - 0.36	: 2 15% : - 3.25	0 0% - 23.00	0 0% 0.00	0 0% 0.00
NEAVES J* 10st 0lbs	1/ 86 1% - 81.67	: 2 4% : - 45.00	3 20% + 30.00	0 0% 0.00	0 0% 0.00
NEWPORT Mr C	1/ 8 13% - 3.50	: 0 0% : - 6.00	1 50% + 5.50	0 0% - 3.00	0 0% 0.00
NIVEN P 10st 1lbs	105/400 26% - 40.17	: 86 20% : - 5.85	48 18% - 20.05	49 14% - 17.97	30 9% - 73.36
O'DWYER C 10st 0lbs	2/ 10 20% + 10.50	: 0 0% : - 9.00	0 0% - 3.00	3 7% - 24.50	0 0% - 1.00
O'HANLON J*	1/ 18 6% + 8.00	: 1 6% : - 12.00	0 0% - 3.00	0 0% - 13.00	0 0% - 22.00
O'HARA L 10st 0lbs	20/169 12% - 78.48	: 24 13% : - 60.23	10 8% - 60.50	21 16% + 1.63	0 0% - 32.00
O'HARE L* 9st 12lbs	2/ 27 7% - 12.25	: 2 11% : - 4.50	0 0% - 5.00	0 0% 0.00	0 0% 0.00
O'NEILL S J 10st 0lbs	14/212 7% - 140.01	: 13 5% : - 207.21	19 6% - 167.75	18 7% - 142.38	12 4% - 157.92
O'SULLIVAN D* 9st 9lbs	16/ 95 17% + 36.94	: 6 10% : + 3.76	4 7% - 41.00	10 15% - 1.87	1 8% - 7.50
OLIVER Jacqui 10st 0lbs	6/ 37 16% - 12.96	: 6 19% : + 7.50	0 0% 0.00	0 0% 0.00	0 0% 0.00
ORKNEY A 10st 0lbs	28/209 13% - 12.31	: 20 13% : + 3.70	11 8% - 72.37	4 3% - 87.00	4 3% - 64.00
OSBORNE J 10st 0lbs	76/412 18% - 65.40	: 62 18% : - 24.00	53 19% + 11.79	22 9% - 123.82	21 10% - 106.83
PARKER Mr A	1/ 10 10% - 8.00	: 0 0% : - 5.00	0 0% - 7.00	0 0% - 18.00	0 0% - 17.00
PERRETT M 10st 0lbs	22/200 11% - 77.15	: 58 21% : - 80.56	52 23% + 1.47	27 12% - 1.21	24 11% + 53.14
PITMAN M 10st 10lbs	35/185 19% - 9.76	: 27 18% : - 8.54	57 30% + 52.32	40 23% - 0.47	27 17% - 9.21
POTTS T	1/ 12 8% - 1.00	: 0 0% : - 13.00	2 9% + 4.00	0 0% - 14.00	0 0% - 2.00
POWELL B 10st 0lbs	35/326 11% - 70.11	: 38 8% : - 235.18	48 9% - 251.87	64 11% - 240.61	38 7% - 214.50

	1991/92 Wns Mts(%)	: 1990/91 Wns(%)	1989/90 Wns(%)	1988/89 Wns(%)	1987/88 Wns(%)
PRITCHARD Dr P 10st 0lbs	3/ 30 10% + 1.00	0 0% : - 16.00	2 9% - 17.87	1 100% + 5.00	1 100% + 0.91
PRITCHARD Mr J	1/ 15 7% - 4.00	0 0% : - 4.00	0 0% - 8.00	0 0% - 2.00	0 0% 0.00
PROCTER A* 9st 7lbs	4/ 49 8% - 21.50	1 25% : - 2.00	0 0% 0.00	0 0% 0.00	0 0% 0.00
PROTHEROE T*	1/ 17 6% - 9.50	1 33% : + 2.00	0 0% 0.00	0 0% 0.00	0 0% 0.00
PULLIN J* 9st 8lbs	5/ 65 8% - 13.00	1 7% : - 6.00	0 0% - 12.00	0 0% - 2.00	0 0% 0.00
QUINN J J 10st 0lbs	6/ 61 10% - 13.42	5 5% : - 15.25	10 8% - 56.75	9 6% - 85.75	5 5% - 77.04
RAILTON J 10st 0lbs	11/194 6% - 118.95	27 12% : - 32.08	21 9% - 147.98	18 8% - 17.72	4 7% - 42.75
RANGER Mr M 9st 7lbs	5/ 68 7% - 41.76	0 0% : - 29.00	0 0% - 9.00	0 0% - 2.00	0 0% 0.00
REED T 10st 3lbs	19/186 10% - 67.49	14 7% : - 105.00	14 7% - 4.79	11 7% - 82.50	16 10% - 1.02
REYNOLDS L*	1/ 18 6% - 12.50	0 0% : 0.00	0 0% 0.00	0 0% 0.00	0 0% 0.00
RICHARDS M 10st 0lbs	37/271 14% - 33.06	28 9% : - 111.05	25 12% - 46.89	30 13% + 45.22	7 6% - 15.90
RICHARDS P	1/ 37 3% - 20.00	0 0% : - 32.00	3 5% - 22.50	3 4% - 43.75	5 5% - 31.50
RICHMOND D* 9st 7lbs	7/ 51 14% - 8.06	7 13% : + 2.63	2 8% - 16.25	1 50% + 15.00	0 0% 0.00
RIMELL Mr M	1/ 28 4% - 19.50	1 8% : - 5.00	0 0% - 1.00	0 0% 0.00	0 0% 0.00
ROBERTSON G*	1/ 12 8% + 22.00	0 0% : - 11.00	0 0% - 11.00	0 0% - 8.00	0 0% - 2.00
ROBSON Miss P 9st 7lbs	5/ 52 10% - 19.54	1 5% : - 17.37	0 0% - 2.00	0 0% 0.00	0 0% - 1.00
ROWE G* 10st 0lbs	3/ 50 6% - 26.50	5 8% : + 34.00	2 22% - 0.25	0 0% - 4.00	0 0% - 4.00
RYAN C	1/ 23 4% + 11.00	2 5% : - 29.00	1 2% - 57.75	7 16% - 5.25	0 0% 0.00
RYAN J* 9st 11lbs	9/111 8% - 70.08	1 5% : - 17.00	11 16% - 24.20	1 5% - 14.00	2 20% - 2.00
SAMPLE Mr C	1/ 10 10% - 6.50	2 22% : + 9.62	1 7% - 11.75	2 7% - 11.50	2 9% - 9.50
SANSOME Mr A 10st 3lbs	5/ 27 19% + 4.25	1 5% : + 14.00	2 7% - 14.00	0 0% - 4.00	0 0% - 5.00
SCHOLFIELD Mr P	1/ 8 13% - 5.75	1 9% : - 4.00	0 0% - 5.00	0 0% - 12.00	2 11% - 9.50
SCUDAMORE P 10st 0lbs	175/513 34% - 7.90	141 33% : + 8.74	170 33% - 8.26	221 33% - 58.43	132 24% - 65.56

	1991/92 Wns Mts(%)	: 1990/91 : Wns(%)	1989/90 Wns(%)	1988/89 Wns(%)	1987/88 Wns(%)
SHARRATT M*	1/ 52 2% - 49.25	0 0% 0.00	0 0% - 10.00	0 0% - 23.00	0 0% - 8.00
SHERIDAN B	1/ 7 14% + 6.00	0 0% - 7.00	1 50% + 24.00	0 0% - 5.00	0 0% - 1.00
SHIELS Mr R 11st 7lbs	4/ 16 25% - 6.67	3 25% + 9.10	1 100% + 3.00	0 0% - 3.00	0 0% - 4.00
SHOEMARK I 9st 13lbs	7/ 97 7% - 59.62	3 3% - 66.00	11 17% - 37.40	4 4% - 74.83	15 10% - 15.05
SHORTT J 10st 2lbs	13/121 11% - 44.17	17 8% - 74.82	11 8% - 37.75	7 7% - 60.62	0 0% 0.00
SKYRME D 10st 0lbs	6/ 93 6% - 54.03	18 9% - 67.08	15 12% - 67.34	9 8% - 41.67	6 11% + 21.25
SLATTERY V* 9st 7lbs	5/181 3% - 114.50	7 6% - 61.00	3 4% - 58.67	6 9% - 31.24	0 0% - 2.00
SMITH A S 9st 11lbs	15/154 10% + 1.13	24 15% - 7.73	8 17% - 9.47	4 17% - 7.70	1 13% + 13.00
SMITH Mr J S	1/ 4 25% + 30.00	0 0% - 2.00	0 0% - 2.00	0 0% - 2.00	1 4% - 12.00
SMITH N* 9st 9lbs	8/155 5% - 32.50	10 7% + 5.75	14 9% - 83.41	3 4% - 67.00	5 8% - 33.12
SMITH V 10st 0lbs	2/ 35 6% - 2.00	2 4% - 32.00	5 7% - 5.30	0 0% - 26.00	0 0% - 4.00
SOUTHCOMBE Miss J	1/ 7 14% + 10.00	0 0% - 1.00	0 0% - 1.00	3 43% + 6.25	0 0% - 3.00
SQUIRE L*	1/ 17 6% - 12.50	0 0% 0.00	0 0% 0.00	0 0% 0.00	0 0% 0.00
STOKELL Ann* 10st 0lbs	3/ 27 11% + 31.00	0 0% - 7.00	1 4% - 21.00	0 0% - 19.00	0 0% - 6.00
STOREY B 10st 0lbs	40/334 12% - 81.38	20 7% - 155.16	32 11% - 23.69	30 9% - 129.00	25 7% - 207.93
STOREY Mr C	1/ 2 50% - 0.43	0 0% 0.00	0 0% 0.00	0 0% 0.00	0 0% 0.00
STRONGE R 10st 0lbs	10/126 8% - 3.75	3 3% - 67.50	2 5% - 37.25	9 9% - 8.87	4 2% - 171.50
SULLIVAN D* 9st 8lbs	2/ 7 29% + 7.50	0 0% - 2.00	0 0% - 10.00	1 5% - 15.00	0 0% 0.00
SUPPLE J A* 9st 7lbs	5/ 94 5% - 27.00	3 13% - 13.00	0 0% - 6.00	0 0% 0.00	0 0% 0.00
SUPPLE R 10st 0lbs	31/305 10% - 40.58	29 12% - 69.09	34 14% - 102.03	8 14% - 10.82	5 6% - 26.50
SWAN C F 10st 0lbs	2/ 16 13% + 1.63	1 8% - 11.09	1 8% - 3.50	2 22% + 15.00	0 0% - 1.00
SWIERS Mr S 10st 5lbs	3/ 61 5% - 50.25	12 11% - 39.62	10 11% - 28.24	12 16% - 19.06	2 5% - 4.00
SWINDLEHURST Mr D	1/ 13 8% + 13.00	1 25% + 3.00	0 0% - 5.00	0 0% - 7.00	0 0% - 5.00

	1991/92	:	1990/91	1989/90	1988/89	1987/88
	Wns Mts (%)	:	Wns (%)	Wns (%)	Wns (%)	Wns (%)
TAAFFE T J	1/ 8 13%	:	0 0%	1 11%	2 22%	1 13%
	+ 7.00	:	- 1.00	- 7.09	+ 3.63	- 1.00
TAYLOR S* 9st 7lbs	3/ 25 12%	:	0 0%	0 0%	0 0%	0 0%
	- 14.67	:	- 4.00	0.00	0.00	0.00
TEAL Mr R 10st 7lbs	3/ 8 38%	:	3 17%	0 0%	0 0%	0 0%
	- 0.83	:	- 4.50	- 8.00	- 7.00	- 1.00
TEGG D 10st 0lbs	19/231 8%	:	21 9%	12 7%	21 8%	23 11%
	- 107.57	:	- 19.12	- 117.13	- 76.59	+ 26.03
TELFER D*	1/ 12 8%	:	0 0%	1 3%	1 2%	3 10%
	+ 5.00	:	- 18.00	- 29.00	- 54.00	- 14.30
THOMSON G* 9st 12lbs	2/ 61 3%	:	1 4%	0 0%	0 0%	0 0%
	- 39.00	:	- 18.50	- 8.00	- 11.00	- 10.00
THORNTON Mr A 9st 12lbs	10/ 34 29%	:	0 0%	0 0%	0 0%	0 0%
	+ 12.23	:	- 3.00	0.00	0.00	0.00
THURLOW Miss J 9st 7lbs	4/ 42 10%	:	4 11%	3 16%	0 0%	1 10%
	- 7.92	:	- 6.50	- 2.67	- 13.00	- 1.00
TIERNEY E* 9st 7lbs	7/ 91 8%	:	6 8%	6 9%	0 0%	0 0%
	- 13.87	:	+ 23.63	+ 39.75	- 13.00	0.00
TITLEY J F* 9st 11lbs	2/ 9 22%	:	0 0%	0 0%	0 0%	0 0%
	+ 27.63	:	- 1.00	0.00	0.00	0.00
TORY A 10st 0lbs	26/188 14%	:	32 16%	15 12%	15 14%	1 2%
	- 70.67	:	+ 28.61	- 62.92	- 17.91	- 30.00
TOWNSEND Mr D	1/ 15 7%	:	2 10%	0 0%	0 0%	1 8%
	- 12.75	:	+ 15.50	- 9.00	- 18.00	- 6.50
TRELOGGEN Mr R 11st 2lbs	2/ 7 29%	:	0 0%	0 0%	0 0%	0 0%
	- 1.99	:	- 3.00	- 1.00	0.00	0.00
TURNER Miss Z	1/ 1 100%	:	0 0%	0 0%	0 0%	0 0%
	+ 7.00	:	0.00	0.00	0.00	0.00
TURNER S 10st 0lbs	6/109 6%	:	5 3%	25 9%	29 9%	14 11%
	- 77.50	:	- 109.62	- 63.42	- 61.20	+ 4.26
TUTTY Mr N	1/ 16 6%	:	1 7%	4 21%	0 0%	0 0%
	- 1.00	:	- 11.75	+ 3.19	- 13.00	- 13.00
TWOMEY J* 9st 7lbs	11/ 59 19%	:	7 20%	1 100%	0 0%	0 0%
	- 23.05	:	- 8.73	+ 5.00	0.00	0.00
UPTON G 10st 2lbs	5/142 4%	:	10 8%	13 14%	7 9%	4 13%
	- 58.33	:	- 70.07	- 9.90	- 23.50	- 8.50
VERLING P 9st 11lbs	5/ 72 7%	:	8 7%	5 5%	14 26%	3 8%
	- 37.87	:	- 39.75	- 72.45	+ 22.09	+ 5.00
VICKERY Mrs R	1/ 6 17%	:	2 50%	0 0%	1 14%	1 14%
	- 3.25	:	+ 2.38	- 1.00	- 3.00	+ 44.00
VIGORS Mr C	1/ 3 33%	:	0 0%	0 0%	0 0%	0 0%
	+ 8.00	:	0.00	0.00	0.00	0.00
VINCENT Lorna 10st 0lbs	10/ 75 13%	:	11 12%	5 13%	5 4%	4 5%
	+ 6.38	:	+ 12.00	- 19.63	- 71.00	- 43.50
WAGGOTT P* 9st 7lbs	4/ 68 6%	:	3 9%	0 0%	0 0%	0 0%
	- 42.97	:	0.00	- 2.00	0.00	0.00

	1991/92 Wns Mts(%)	1990/91 Wns(%)	1989/90 Wns(%)	1988/89 Wns(%)	1987/88 Wns(%)
WALES Mr W 11st 3lbs	2/ 6 33% - 0.40	0 0% - 3.00	2 25% - 0.20	0 0% - 2.00	0 0% - 4.00
WALL T 10st 0lbs	12/182 7% - 72.15	10 7% - 10.49	15 8% - 35.65	15 6% - 71.77	4 3% - 130.50
WALSH D*	1/ 20 5% - 15.00	0 0% 0.00	0 0% 0.00	0 0% 0.00	0 0% 0.00
WALTON Mr A 10st 0lbs	2/ 9 22% + 9.50	0 0% - 5.00	0 0% - 1.00	0 0% - 7.00	1 9% + 4.00
WARD P*	1/ 40 3% - 6.00	0 0% - 5.00	0 0% - 5.00	0 0% 0.00	0 0% 0.00
WARD THOMAS Mr C 10st 6lbs	3/ 12 25% + 6.00	2 33% + 7.50	0 0% 0.00	0 0% 0.00	0 0% 0.00
WEBB A 10st 0lbs	14/204 7% - 88.92	13 8% - 68.74	10 6% - 95.87	15 6% - 143.05	20 7% - 84.37
WEYMES Mr J	1/ 3 33% + 12.00	0 0% - 3.00	0 0% - 2.00	0 0% 0.00	0 0% 0.00
WHITAKER Michael	1/ 1 100% + 0.67	0 0% 0.00	0 0% 0.00	0 0% 0.00	0 0% 0.00
WHITE J 10st 0lbs	11/123 9% - 57.35	14 10% - 18.87	31 15% - 57.77	27 17% - 31.22	15 8% - 62.52
WILKINSON D 10st 0lbs	9/ 65 14% - 2.33	6 9% - 41.47	2 7% - 20.75	5 5% - 61.94	3 4% - 67.38
WILLIAMS P* 9st 12lbs	6/ 45 13% - 16.00	1 5% - 3.00	0 0% - 4.00	0 0% 0.00	0 0% 0.00
WILLIAMS S D* 9st 7lbs	9/ 71 13% - 2.37	3 11% - 12.00	5 33% + 6.00	0 0% 0.00	0 0% 0.00
WILLIAMSON N 10st 0lbs	33/203 16% - 46.92	33 17% + 12.64	20 15% - 11.09	1 25% - 0.75	0 0% 0.00
WILSON Mr C	1/ 10 10% + 11.00	0 0% - 1.00	0 0% - 4.00	0 0% - 9.00	0 0% - 9.00
WILSON Mr N 9st 7lbs	3/ 45 7% - 24.80	4 11% + 4.00	4 9% - 7.25	0 0% - 9.00	0 0% 0.00
WINGATE A* 9st 7lbs	3/ 20 15% + 13.38	0 0% - 9.00	0 0% 0.00	0 0% 0.00	0 0% 0.00
WINTLE Mr J	1/ 18 6% - 15.58	0 0% - 9.00	0 0% 0.00	0 0% 0.00	0 0% 0.00
WONNACOTT Mrs C	1/ 16 6% - 7.00	4 11% + 7.13	5 42% + 18.13	1 17% + 1.00	0 0% - 1.00
WOODS S 10st 0lbs	3/ 21 14% - 9.67	5 7% - 53.50	8 7% - 18.50	2 3% - 51.87	11 7% - 54.24
WORTHINGTON W 10st 0lbs	3/ 87 3% - 68.12	5 6% - 41.90	7 6% - 24.31	1 2% - 56.00	4 7% - 29.00
WYER L 10st 0lbs	35/221 16% - 70.44	44 18% - 45.76	33 12% - 67.26	36 16% - 60.54	30 13% - 93.29
WYNNE S* 9st 7lbs	12/129 9% - 41.11	6 13% - 20.90	0 0% 0.00	0 0% 0.00	0 0% 0.00

13 . A - Z of WINNING TRAINERS

Showing the record of wins, win% and level-stake over the past five years for every trainer to have had a winner in the 1991/92 season.

	1991/92 Wns Rns (%)	1990/91 : Wns (%)	1989/88 Wns (%)	1988/89 Wns (%)	1987/88 Wns (%)
ACONLEY Mrs V A North Yorks	12/ 98 12% - 27.62	10 21% : + 52.63	7 19% + 4.83	3 16% - 5.25	1 7% + 3.00
AKEHURST J Berkshire	5/ 50 10% - 33.00	6 15% : - 5.75	0 0% 0.00	0 0% 0.00	0 0% 0.00
AKEHURST R Surrey	17/137 12% - 53.62	35 16% : + 46.51	30 23% + 33.86	43 21% + 23.98	21 15% - 25.25
ALEXANDER H Co Durham	1/ 7 14% - 3.75	3 25% : - 4.38	2 20% + 3.00	0 0% - 12.00	1 25% + 17.00
ALLAN R Northumerland	10/ 52 19% - 27.41	3 6% : - 31.67	10 14% - 8.92	6 10% - 0.75	4 6% - 35.50
ALLEN C N Suffolk	1/ 27 4% - 22.67	1 6% : 0.00	2 13% + 11.00	2 10% - 2.00	0 0% - 14.00
ALLISON Miss K S Berkshire	2/ 10 20% + 7.25	0 0% : - 4.00	0 0% 0.00	0 0% 0.00	0 0% 0.00
ALNER R H Dorset	4/ 24 17% + 7.25	1 9% : - 2.00	2 100% + 3.04	0 0% 0.00	0 0% 0.00
ALSTON E J Lancashire	3/ 26 12% - 5.50	1 3% : - 26.75	5 17% + 6.50	0 0% - 54.00	2 3% - 32.75
ANDERSON K Dumfries	2/ 5 40% - 0.77	0 0% : - 1.00	0 0% - 1.00	0 0% 0.00	0 0% 0.00
ARBUTHNOT D W P Berkshire	2/ 8 25% + 16.50	1 50% : + 3.50	0 0% - 9.00	0 0% - 5.00	0 0% - 5.00
ARMYTAGE R C North Yorks	3/ 13 23% - 0.87	2 15% : - 5.87	2 8% - 11.00	1 5% + 1.00	7 5% - 88.29
AUSTIN Mrs S M North Yorks	3/ 34 9% - 8.50	0 0% : - 21.00	0 0% - 15.00	1 3% - 24.00	1 3% - 28.00
BAILEY K C Berkshire	38/250 15% - 20.91	33 17% : + 11.79	34 19% - 2.69	18 10% - 82.14	20 11% + 2.18
BAKER J H Devon	11/ 66 17% - 7.94	16 10% : - 74.90	15 13% + 32.71	15 15% + 15.71	14 16% + 31.50

	1991/92 Wns Rns(%)	1990/91 Wns(%)	1989/88 Wns(%)	1988/89 Wns(%)	1987/88 Wns(%)
BAKER Miss D J Northants	1/ 6 17% + 15.00	0 0% - 4.00	0 0% - 3.00	0 0% - 1.00	0 0% - 1.00
BAKER R J Devon	1/ 63 2% - 61.33	0 0% 0.00	0 0% 0.00	0 0% 0.00	0 0% 0.00
BALDING G B Dorset	53/368 14% - 7.25	48 14% - 167.12	42 11% - 138.33	59 16% - 2.20	40 11% - 104.35
BALDING I A Hampshire	12/ 36 33% + 0.73	4 44% + 5.00	5 38% + 19.40	1 33% - 1.60	1 8% - 7.50
BANKS J E Suffolk	6/ 16 38% + 10.12	0 0% 0.00	0 0% 0.00	0 0% 0.00	0 0% 0.00
BANKS M C Bedfordshire	1/ 19 5% - 2.00	2 10% - 2.50	1 8% - 5.00	0 0% - 1.00	2 13% + 11.00
BARBER R Dorset	5/ 11 45% + 12.65	0 0% - 1.00	0 0% - 1.00	0 0% 0.00	0 0% 0.00
BARCLAY Miss J E North Yorks	1/ 43 2% - 38.00	0 0% - 25.00	0 0% 0.00	0 0% 0.00	0 0% 0.00
BARCLAY Mrs A Gloucestershire	2/ 12 17% - 0.50	1 7% + 3.00	1 25% - 1.50	1 50% + 2.00	0 0% 0.00
BARKER MRS P A West Yorks	3/ 23 13% - 12.60	2 5% - 36.50	6 8% - 1.50	2 8% - 12.00	0 0% - 1.00
BARNES M A Cumbria	2/ 49 4% - 27.00	0 0% - 28.00	0 0% - 13.00	0 0% - 4.00	0 0% 0.00
BARONS D H Devon	25/233 11% - 62.84	34 16% + 22.17	40 17% - 11.62	36 12% - 63.49	29 11% - 65.95
BARRACLOUGH M F Warwicks	3/ 56 5% + 2.00	2 7% - 7.00	1 3% - 30.00	0 0% - 36.00	0 0% - 7.00
BARRON T D North Yorks	1/ 10 10% - 4.00	1 13% + 1.00	4 13% - 1.50	6 19% + 14.50	9 26% + 40.88
BARROW A Somerset	4/ 91 4% - 57.50	6 11% - 18.09	4 5% - 55.77	4 6% - 43.25	2 5% - 17.00
BARWELL C R Devon	2/ 31 6% - 21.50	2 5% + 31.00	0 0% 0.00	0 0% 0.00	0 0% 0.00
BATEY A C Northumberland	1/ 17 6% - 2.00	3 15% + 49.00	1 6% - 12.50	0 0% - 12.00	0 0% - 10.00
BEAUMONT P North Yorks	5/106 5% - 74.82	12 23% + 19.43	4 5% - 34.50	8 11% - 4.75	0 0% - 33.00
BEEVER C R Lincs	4/ 82 5% - 63.37	8 9% - 35.92	17 14% - 49.43	10 12% - 17.62	0 0% 0.00
BELL Mrs H North Yorks	1/ 5 20% - 0.67	1 25% - 1.75	1 33% + 1.50	0 0% 0.00	0 0% 0.00
BENTLEY W North Yorks	11/ 67 16% - 10.97	5 10% - 20.34	5 19% - 2.50	1 6% - 8.00	0 0% - 1.00
BERRY F Ireland	1/ 3 33% + 10.00	0 0% 0.00	0 0% 0.00	0 0% 0.00	0 0% 0.00
BERRY J Lancashire	2/ 14 14% - 8.15	4 29% + 3.50	1 10% - 3.00	3 38% + 1.63	1 4% - 25.37

	1991/92 Wns Rns(%)	1990/91 Wns(%)	1989/88 Wns(%)	1988/89 Wns(%)	1987/88 Wns(%)
BEVAN P J Staffordshire	9/111 8% - 34.75	3 7% : + 46.00	3 4% - 51.50	3 3% - 76.65	3 4% - 48.00
BILL T T Leicestershire	2/ 41 5% - 13.00	3 6% : - 37.00	8 12% - 41.01	6 9% + 22.90	8 6% - 71.75
BISHOP K Somerset	5/ 58 9% - 12.00	2 3% : - 70.00	1 2% - 50.90	5 6% - 50.00	16 13% + 49.57
BISHOP V R H'ford & Worcs	1/ 10 10% - 6.75	0 0% : - 3.00	0 0% - 2.00	1 10% - 2.00	1 6% - 12.50
BISSILL W H Nottinghamshire	4/ 10 40% + 15.95	1 8% : - 7.50	2 18% - 3.25	0 0% - 1.00	0 0% 0.00
BLAGBROUGH G D Wiltshire	1/ 2 50% + 1.25	0 0% : 0.00	0 0% 0.00	0 0% 0.00	0 0% 0.00
BLANSHARD M Berkshire	3/ 18 17% + 8.50	3 19% : + 8.50	1 20% + 10.00	0 0% - 4.00	0 0% 0.00
BLOCKLEY P A Staffordshire	2/141 1% - 124.67	10 8% : - 19.37	8 5% - 77.83	13 9% - 76.57	13 9% - 9.69
BLOOMFIELD D Cornwall	2/ 11 18% + 69.00	0 0% : - 3.00	3 23% + 13.75	1 13% - 4.75	1 9% - 7.00
BLOOR D R Warwicks	2/ 18 11% + 10.25	0 0% : - 26.00	2 15% + 2.10	0 0% - 19.00	1 5% + 6.00
BOSLEY J R Oxon	4/ 86 5% - 45.82	6 7% : - 30.62	5 8% - 42.00	2 4% - 33.00	3 5% - 38.17
BOSTOCK J R Norfolk	4/ 34 12% - 12.75	2 4% : - 44.75	2 6% - 18.00	0 0% - 30.00	0 0% 0.00
BOTTOMLEY J F North Yorks	6/ 26 23% + 19.83	1 13% : + 13.00	1 20% - 2.00	0 0% 0.00	0 0% 0.00
BOUSFIELD B Cumbria	2/ 15 13% + 3.50	0 0% : - 9.00	0 0% - 12.00	4 17% - 2.67	1 5% - 13.00
BOWEN S A Kent	2/ 7 29% + 12.50	0 0% : 0.00	0 0% - 1.00	0 0% - 2.00	0 0% - 3.00
BOWLES LEE Powys	3/ 31 10% - 12.00	0 0% : 0.00	0 0% 0.00	0 0% 0.00	0 0% 0.00
BRACKENBURY Mrs R Devon	2/ 10 20% - 1.33	2 17% : - 4.25	0 0% - 2.00	0 0% 0.00	0 0% 0.00
BRADBURNE Mrs S C Fife	9/ 93 10% - 14.00	9 9% : - 49.17	6 11% - 22.75	1 2% - 19.00	0 0% 0.00
BRADLEY J M Gwent	2/114 2% - 82.00	15 9% : - 63.74	4 4% - 71.00	12 7% - 104.90	16 10% - 2.56
BRAVERY G C Suffolk	4/ 14 29% + 1.75	0 0% : 0.00	0 0% 0.00	0 0% 0.00	0 0% 0.00
BRAZINGTON R G Gloucestershire	2/ 13 15% + 11.00	4 11% : + 41.00	2 7% - 23.67	2 5% - 29.50	5 11% + 97.00
BRENNAN O Nottinghamshire	13/188 7% - 61.87	15 11% : - 6.96	16 18% + 41.07	14 10% + 5.25	10 9% - 52.90
BREWIS R Northumberland	1/ 14 7% - 6.00	3 25% : + 0.88	1 17% + 3.00	3 14% - 10.80	4 17% + 1.00

	1991/92 Wns Rns (%)	1990/91 Wns (%)	1989/88 Wns (%)	1988/89 Wns (%)	1987/88 Wns (%)
BRIDGWATER K S Warwicks	6/107 6% - 48.50	12 15% + 56.25	8 12% - 26.32	3 5% + 0.25	2 3% - 35.50
BROAD C D Gloucestershire	4/101 4% - 82.87	5 6% - 13.17	1 2% - 40.67	0 0% 0.00	0 0% 0.00
BROOKS C P E Berkshire	29/169 17% - 50.25	27 13% - 99.53	56 27% + 6.65	41 21% - 51.26	0 0% 0.00
BROOKSHAW S A Shropshire	4/ 8 50% + 0.38	0 0% 0.00	0 0% 0.00	0 0% 0.00	0 0% 0.00
BROWN R L Gwent	1/ 8 13% - 4.50	0 0% - 4.00	1 8% - 9.50	3 27% - 5.49	0 0% - 10.00
BRYDON D A D North Yorks	2/ 4 50% + 9.00	2 67% + 3.86	1 50% + 3.00	0 0% 0.00	0 0% 0.00
BUCKLER R H Dorset	2/ 62 3% - 52.17	0 0% 0.00	1 50% + 11.00	0 0% - 2.00	0 0% 0.00
BUKOVETS J M Warwicks	1/ 31 3% - 26.67	1 3% - 21.00	6 13% - 19.25	6 14% - 11.92	1 2% - 37.50
BULWER-LONG W H Norfolk	1/ 3 33% - 0.25	0 0% - 2.00	1 33% + 3.00	0 0% - 2.00	0 0% - 3.00
BURCHELL D Gwent	18/126 14% + 2.43	18 16% - 18.77	11 13% - 38.32	12 11% - 30.79	14 16% - 5.87
BURGOYNE P Oxon	1/ 20 5% + 21.00	0 0% - 11.00	1 4% - 16.00	0 0% - 21.00	4 12% - 11.62
BURKE K R H'ford & Worcs	4/113 4% - 49.88	4 5% - 61.12	0 0% 0.00	0 0% 0.00	0 0% 0.00
BURNELL W M North Yorks	2/ 6 33% + 30.00	0 0% 0.00	0 0% 0.00	0 0% 0.00	0 0% 0.00
BUTLER P East Sussex	1/ 26 4% 0.00	3 5% - 52.25	1 2% - 43.50	2 2% - 66.00	3 3% - 33.00
BYCROFT N North Yorks	3/ 32 9% + 7.50	2 5% + 16.00	0 0% - 36.00	2 4% - 38.75	4 9% - 3.25
C-BROWN K O Hampshire	2/ 39 5% - 31.75	1 3% - 24.00	4 17% - 4.33	0 0% - 5.00	0 0% - 12.00
CAINE E M North Yorks	4/ 67 6% - 20.50	3 10% + 16.00	0 0% - 24.00	1 3% - 28.00	0 0% - 16.00
CALDWELL T H Lancashire	1/ 35 3% - 1.00	2 5% - 33.33	2 5% - 17.00	4 9% - 28.56	0 0% - 45.00
CALLAGHAN N A Suffolk	9/ 38 24% - 1.98	6 19% - 11.57	4 14% - 14.81	8 20% - 1.63	2 13% - 5.00
CALLOW R Somerset	3/ 39 8% - 4.00	4 12% + 10.50	2 7% - 8.00	1 5% + 32.00	0 0% 0.00
CALVER P North Yorks	3/ 14 21% + 7.00	2 14% - 3.50	0 0% - 3.00	0 0% - 2.00	1 25% - 1.25
CAMACHO M J North Yorks	2/ 7 29% + 9.00	0 0% - 5.00	1 5% + 6.00	0 0% - 10.00	4 29% + 1.26
CAMBIDGE B R Staffordshire	1/ 18 6% - 8.00	0 0% - 9.00	2 8% - 15.50	0 0% - 40.00	0 0% - 29.00

222 . A - Z of Winning Trainers

	1991/92 Wns Rns(%)	:	1990/91 Wns(%)	1989/88 Wns(%)	1988/89 Wns(%)	1987/88 Wns(%)
CAMPBELL I Suffolk	4/ 20 20% - 6.37	: : -	3 15% 5.50	2 10% - 13.50	5 13% - 5.50	3 7% - 5.50
CAMPION S W Lincs	2/ 8 25% + 1.50	: : +	1 9% 23.00	0 0% - 1.00	2 67% + 10.80	0 0% - 5.00
CANTILLON D Suffolk	1/ 9 11% - 5.25	: : -	0 0% 1.00	0 0% 0.00	0 0% 0.00	0 0% 0.00
CAREY D N Gwent	1/ 20 5% - 7.00	: : -	0 0% 2.00	0 0% - 5.00	1 10% + 24.00	0 0% - 9.00
CARTER W Surrey	5/ 43 12% + 14.00	: : -	1 7% 10.00	6 18% - 11.37	2 9% - 13.09	0 0% 0.00
CASEY R F Suffolk	1/ 3 33% + 3.50	: : -	2 18% 2.50	0 0% - 8.00	3 18% - 6.12	2 13% + 2.38
CASEY T Berkshire	10/101 10% - 47.17	: : -	9 9% 58.56	4 6% - 32.00	12 9% - 63.47	17 11% - 49.32
CHADWICK S Cumbria	5/ 28 18% + 7.08	: :	0 0% 0.00	2 29% - 1.67	0 0% - 5.00	0 0% 0.00
CHAMBERLAIN A J Wiltshire	1/ 27 4% - 17.00	: : +	2 7% 32.00	0 0% - 41.00	1 2% - 50.00	0 0% - 43.00
CHAMPION R Suffolk	1/ 34 3% - 28.50	: : -	2 6% 22.50	2 6% - 20.50	6 16% - 4.77	4 7% - 36.25
CHANNON M R Berkshire	6/ 50 12% - 12.74	: : -	8 15% 16.75	1 11% - 5.50	0 0% 0.00	0 0% 0.00
CHAPMAN M C Lincs	9/113 8% - 43.12	: : -	8 9% 26.02	4 4% - 72.29	10 7% - 79.82	6 4% - 84.67
CHARLES M J Warwicks	5/ 60 8% + 7.00	: : -	2 7% 9.00	1 3% - 33.90	0 0% - 20.00	0 0% - 28.00
CHARLES-JONES G F Oxon	7/ 56 13% - 4.25	: : -	0 0% 4.00	0 0% 0.00	0 0% 0.00	0 0% 0.00
CHARLTON J I A Northumberland	9/128 7% - 67.08	: : -	6 6% 51.12	8 10% - 42.50	5 5% - 58.25	10 10% - 44.70
CHATTERTON M G Nottinghamshire	1/ 4 25% + 1.00	: : +	2 33% 16.50	0 0% 0.00	0 0% 0.00	0 0% 0.00
CHEATLE J N Leicestershire	1/ 2 50% + 1.25	: : -	0 0% 2.00	0 0% 0.00	0 0% 0.00	0 0% 0.00
CHRISTIAN S H'ford & Worcs	19/ 96 20% + 12.30	: : +	12 15% 23.63	12 14% + 9.96	15 11% - 33.82	22 16% - 20.09
CHUGG J Oxon	2/ 25 8% + 4.00	: : -	6 20% 15.48	7 39% + 20.00	1 8% - 8.50	1 3% - 7.00
CHURCHES M R Somerset	1/ 9 11% - 5.00	: : -	1 8% 4.50	2 15% + 29.00	0 0% - 6.00	0 0% - 12.00
CLARKE Mrs Sarah West Sussex	1/ 9 11% - 4.50	:	0 0% 0.00	0 0% - 1.00	0 0% 0.00	0 0% 0.00
CLARKE Peter C East Sussex	1/ 18 6% - 15.75	: : -	0 0% 24.00	0 0% 0.00	0 0% 0.00	0 0% 0.00
CLAXTON Mrs P Northumberland	1/ 2 50% - 0.43	: :	1 50% 0.87	0 0% 0.00	0 0% 0.00	0 0% 0.00

	1991/92 Wns Rns(%)	1990/91 Wns(%)	1989/88 Wns(%)	1988/89 Wns(%)	1987/88 Wns(%)
CLAY Mrs L West Sussex	3/ 27 11% + 13.50	2 5% - 20.00	2 5% - 32.50	2 4% - 9.00	4 11% + 31.00
CLAY W Staffordshire	5/136 4% - 88.75	0 0% - 76.00	11 7% - 98.72	14 7% - 73.86	4 3% - 71.50
COATSWORTH G M R Northumberland	1/ 68 1% - 64.50	0 0% - 42.00	0 0% 0.00	0 0% 0.00	0 0% 0.00
COLE P F I Oxon	1/ 3 33% + 4.50	0 0% - 2.00	0 0% - 11.00	0 0% 0.00	0 0% 0.00
COLE S N Devon	1/ 16 6% - 3.00	0 0% - 16.00	0 0% - 27.00	0 0% - 4.00	2 7% - 20.75
COLLINGRIDGE H J Suffolk	1/ 22 5% - 15.00	2 7% - 7.00	0 0% - 17.00	1 5% - 9.00	1 5% - 5.00
COLLINSON J E Devon	1/ 14 7% + 37.00	0 0% - 7.00	0 0% 0.00	0 0% 0.00	0 0% 0.00
CORNER A S North Yorks	1/ 5 20% + 12.00	0 0% 0.00	0 0% - 2.00	0 0% 0.00	0 0% 0.00
COWLEY P M Gloucestershire	1/ 24 4% - 7.00	0 0% - 40.00	2 7% - 10.25	1 6% - 11.00	0 0% 0.00
CUMINGS K Devon	1/ 4 25% - 0.75	0 0% 0.00	0 0% 0.00	0 0% 0.00	0 0% 0.00
CUNNINGHAM T W North Yorks	1/ 25 4% - 10.00	3 7% + 3.00	3 4% - 44.50	5 7% - 53.59	1 1% - 64.00
CURLEY B J Suffolk	1/ 8 13% - 5.00	7 37% + 6.10	4 13% - 18.80	13 24% - 16.50	16 37% + 31.01
CURLING Miss P Somerset	3/ 5 60% + 8.38	0 0% 0.00	0 0% 0.00	0 0% 0.00	0 0% 0.00
CURTIS R Surrey	7/ 96 7% - 36.04	12 9% - 19.60	6 8% - 32.46	11 10% + 32.86	10 7% + 17.08
CUTHBERT T A K Cumbria	2/ 23 9% - 11.50	0 0% - 39.00	3 6% - 19.00	1 3% - 18.00	0 0% - 20.00
DALTON P T Staffordshire	3/ 43 7% + 17.00	5 12% + 11.75	0 0% 0.00	0 0% 0.00	0 0% 0.00
DAVIES J D J Kent	1/ 3 33% + 0.25	0 0% - 20.00	3 10% + 13.50	5 9% - 10.50	4 7% - 22.50
DAVIES M W Gwent	1/ 10 10% - 7.37	1 20% - 0.67	2 18% + 6.50	2 14% - 2.25	3 23% + 7.00
DAVISON A R Surrey	9/ 74 12% - 8.25	4 7% - 6.50	5 11% - 6.17	7 19% + 7.75	4 9% - 19.62
DAWE Mrs J C Somerset	1/ 14 7% - 9.50	0 0% 0.00	0 0% 0.00	0 0% 0.00	0 0% 0.00
DAWSON C Lincs	1/ 2 50% + 1.00	0 0% 0.00	0 0% - 1.00	1 50% - 0.33	0 0% - 2.00
DEACON D Gloucestershire	1/ 15 7% + 36.00	0 0% 0.00	0 0% 0.00	0 0% 0.00	0 0% 0.00
DEASLEY M J Surrey	1/ 1 100% + 5.00	0 0% 0.00	0 0% 0.00	0 0% 0.00	0 0% 0.00

	1991/92	1990/91	1989/88	1988/89	1987/88
	Wns Rns(%) :	Wns(%)	Wns(%)	Wns(%)	Wns(%)
DELAHOOKE J S Bucks	2/ 6 33% : - 2.60 :	0 0% 0.00	1 33% - 1.33	3 50% + 0.62	3 33% - 3.34
DENSON A W Surrey	2/ 34 6% : - 27.87 :	0 0% - 13.00	5 11% - 17.21	1 8% - 6.00	0 0% - 26.00
DICKIN R Gloucestershire	17/168 10% : - 14.42 :	15 7% - 36.75	6 5% - 83.05	11 8% - 55.50	10 9% - 18.12
DIXON M Surrey	1/ 15 7% : - 3.00 :	0 0% 0.00	0 0% 0.00	0 0% 0.00	0 0% 0.00
DOCKER Mrs J Warwicks	2/ 6 33% : + 4.00 :	0 0% 0.00	0 0% 0.00	0 0% 0.00	0 0% 0.00
DONNELLY T W Leicestershire	1/ 52 2% : - 49.37 :	2 4% - 40.00	0 0% - 26.00	0 0% - 36.00	1 4% - 9.00
DOUMEN F France	1/ 5 20% : + 6.00 :	0 0% - 6.00	0 0% 0.00	0 0% 0.00	0 0% 0.00
DOW S Surrey	24/ 85 28% : + 32.59 :	6 14% - 19.13	6 6% - 51.50	3 3% - 96.00	5 7% + 25.00
DREWE C J Oxon	2/ 20 10% : + 49.38 :	0 0% - 5.00	0 0% 0.00	0 0% 0.00	0 0% 0.00
DUFOSSE J W Dorset	1/ 12 8% : - 9.12 :	0 0% 0.00	0 0% 0.00	0 0% 0.00	0 0% 0.00
DUNN A J K Somerset	3/ 30 10% : - 18.00 :	3 12% - 16.18	1 11% - 6.50	2 20% + 6.50	0 0% - 3.00
DUNN N G H Somerset	1/ 6 17% : + 11.00 :	0 0% - 9.00	0 0% 0.00	0 0% 0.00	0 0% 0.00
EASTERBY M H North Yorks	42/203 21% : - 56.24 :	33 19% - 42.16	29 17% - 50.42	45 25% - 26.63	23 13% - 91.48
EASTERBY M W York	22/108 20% : + 7.50 :	18 19% - 13.64	10 9% - 79.43	22 15% - 44.99	18 19% - 20.52
EATON Miss J Lancashire	2/ 8 25% : + 15.75 :	0 0% - 15.00	0 0% - 19.00	0 0% - 27.00	4 20% - 3.12
ECKLEY M W H'ford & Worcs	2/ 29 7% : - 12.00 :	3 11% - 14.87	1 4% - 19.25	1 6% - 13.25	2 7% - 14.00
EDDY D Tyne & Wear	4/ 18 22% : - 0.75 :	1 20% - 0.50	0 0% 0.00	0 0% 0.00	0 0% 0.00
EDWARDS G F Somerset	2/ 6 33% : + 6.25 :	1 6% - 9.50	0 0% - 4.00	0 0% - 3.00	0 0% - 2.00
EDWARDS J A C H'ford & Worcs	39/260 15% : - 69.30 :	54 17% - 59.75	47 13% - 104.00	78 19% + 122.59	61 19% - 16.06
EDWARDS Mrs John Devon	1/ 3 33% : + 6.00 :	0 0% 0.00	0 0% 0.00	0 0% 0.00	0 0% 0.00
EGERTON C R Berkshire	4/ 29 14% : + 10.75 :	0 0% 0.00	0 0% 0.00	0 0% 0.00	0 0% 0.00
ELLIOTT J P D Hampshire	1/ 31 3% : - 28.50 :	5 10% + 3.25	1 1% - 64.00	0 0% - 49.00	0 0% - 51.00
ELLISON B North Yorks	3/ 34 9% : - 14.00 :	3 6% - 7.00	2 4% - 37.75	0 0% 0.00	0 0% 0.00

	1991/92 Wns Rns(%)	1990/91 Wns(%)	1989/88 Wns(%)	1988/89 Wns(%)	1987/88 Wns(%)
ELSEY C C Berkshire	1/ 11 9% + 10.00	1 3% - 24.00	1 3% - 30.43	0 0% - 2.00	0 0% 0.00
ELSEY C W C North Yorks	3/ 14 21% - 0.92	1 8% + 13.00	1 6% - 13.00	4 22% + 15.00	3 27% + 17.75
ELSWORTH D R C Hampshire	20/143 14% - 16.52	23 18% - 19.50	24 14% - 87.94	54 21% - 11.99	50 19% + 11.43
ENRIGHT G P East Sussex	1/ 57 2% - 50.00	5 11% - 27.21	6 8% - 26.00	6 8% - 1.82	5 8% + 2.50
ETHERINGTON T J Surrey	10/ 60 17% + 54.63	6 11% - 21.25	4 11% - 24.20	3 7% - 20.00	0 0% 0.00
EUBANK A Cumbria	3/ 4 75% + 10.29	0 0% - 4.00	0 0% - 2.00	1 20% + 10.00	0 0% - 8.00
EVANS Mrs Jill Clwyd	1/ 16 6% + 18.00	0 0% - 18.00	0 0% - 23.00	0 0% - 15.00	0 0% - 26.00
EVANS P D Powys	5/ 37 14% - 13.36	4 9% - 22.50	3 9% + 3.00	1 4% - 13.00	0 0% 0.00
EYRE J L West Yorks	2/ 34 6% - 21.75	4 10% - 17.09	8 29% + 9.46	0 0% 0.00	0 0% 0.00
FAIRHURST T North Yorks	2/ 36 6% - 28.25	0 0% - 21.00	3 7% - 33.07	5 11% - 3.25	2 9% - 13.25
FANSHAWE J Suffolk	3/ 10 30% + 0.13	1 25% + 13.00	0 0% 0.00	0 0% 0.00	0 0% 0.00
FELTON M J Somerset	4/ 13 31% + 1.66	1 50% + 1.00	0 0% 0.00	0 0% 0.00	0 0% 0.00
FFITCH-HEYES J East Sussex	6/ 82 7% - 32.75	2 3% - 58.00	15 15% - 43.08	12 9% - 89.09	8 8% - 55.25
FISHER R F Cumbria	3/ 55 5% - 26.75	1 2% - 43.67	8 14% - 9.75	6 8% - 32.06	8 10% - 28.12
FITZGERALD J G North Yorks	33/198 17% - 19.55	45 21% - 28.64	58 26% - 1.17	59 23% - 5.32	49 20% - 52.47
FLYNN P J Ireland	1/ 3 33% + 6.00	0 0% 0.00	0 0% 0.00	0 0% 0.00	0 0% 0.00
FORBES A L Staffordshire	3/ 38 8% + 2.75	1 10% - 5.50	0 0% 0.00	0 0% 0.00	0 0% 0.00
FORSTER Capt T A Oxon	44/273 16% + 26.28	37 17% - 13.99	23 13% - 39.67	34 15% - 3.77	38 13% - 49.20
FORT J R Co Durham	1/ 32 3% - 26.00	2 10% - 5.00	1 6% - 9.00	0 0% 0.00	0 0% 0.00
FOWLER A Leicestershire	1/ 11 9% - 1.00	0 0% - 15.00	4 19% - 8.37	2 12% - 4.37	1 5% - 14.50
FRANCIS M E D Berkshire	1/ 6 17% - 1.50	1 4% - 18.00	5 17% + 25.25	7 20% + 35.23	4 9% - 16.40
FRANKS D R Co Durham	1/ 34 3% - 32.27	0 0% 0.00	0 0% 0.00	0 0% 0.00	0 0% 0.00
FROST R G Devon	14/170 8% - 41.67	11 7% - 104.58	15 10% - 76.79	20 12% - 19.81	15 9% - 45.00

	1991/92 Wns Rns (%)	1990/91 Wns (%)	1989/88 Wns (%)	1988/89 Wns (%)	1987/88 Wns (%)
GANDOLFO D R Oxon	14/135 10% - 8.69	6 3% : - 127.02	14 9% - 81.80	8 5% - 74.75	13 7% - 124.52
GARRATON D T North Yorks	1/ 13 8% - 10.12	0 0% : 0.00	0 0% - 2.00	0 0% - 1.00	0 0% 0.00
GASELEE N A Berkshire	15/140 11% - 53.13	19 14% : - 21.13	19 13% - 6.31	13 10% - 5.00	24 16% + 58.68
GIFFORD J T West Sussex	49/389 13% - 150.20	62 14% : - 107.54	50 14% - 81.85	64 17% - 65.28	91 22% + 95.82
GILL H J North Yorks	1/ 10 10% - 6.87	1 11% : + 4.00	0 0% - 9.00	0 0% 0.00	0 0% 0.00
GLOVER J A Nottinghamshire	9/ 58 16% + 0.88	7 13% : - 33.52	13 23% + 10.23	3 8% - 8.17	4 14% - 13.70
GOODALL Robert Dorset	1/ 15 7% + 6.00	0 0% : - 4.00	2 20% + 19.25	0 0% 0.00	0 0% 0.00
GOODFELLOW Mrs J Borders	5/ 36 14% - 5.50	2 25% : + 8.73	1 4% - 21.25	2 7% - 13.00	2 6% - 22.50
GRAINGER Mrs P H'ford & Worcs	1/ 1 100% + 1.50	0 0% : 0.00	0 0% 0.00	0 0% 0.00	0 0% 0.00
GREEN Miss Z A Cumbria	1/ 22 5% - 17.00	0 0% : - 18.00	0 0% - 31.00	0 0% - 28.00	0 0% - 35.00
GRIFFITH Mrs J G Clwyd	2/ 7 29% + 0.33	1 13% : - 5.25	5 56% + 13.76	2 18% + 26.50	1 17% - 0.50
GRIFFITHS S G Dyfed	1/ 15 7% - 8.00	2 11% : - 10.25	1 10% + 91.00	3 27% + 15.00	0 0% - 7.00
GRISSELL D M East Sussex	5/ 77 6% - 47.92	14 18% : - 21.84	16 23% - 1.94	14 20% + 13.17	7 8% - 51.05
GUBBY B Surrey	2/ 7 29% + 2.00	0 0% : - 2.00	2 22% + 16.00	0 0% 0.00	0 0% 0.00
HAIGH W W North Yorks	3/ 20 15% - 7.00	4 14% : + 8.00	4 20% + 12.50	1 8% - 1.00	2 9% - 13.00
HAINE Mrs D Suffolk	6/ 91 7% - 70.84	14 22% : - 3.60	11 20% + 6.33	6 9% - 38.75	7 11% - 10.09
HALDANE J S Roxburghshire	1/ 42 2% - 38.00	1 3% : - 15.00	0 0% - 26.00	3 12% + 52.00	0 0% - 33.00
HALL Miss S E North Yorks	6/ 19 32% + 9.25	1 8% : - 2.00	2 29% + 10.50	0 0% - 7.00	1 8% - 10.09
HALLETT T B Cornwall	3/ 56 5% - 25.13	11 17% : - 15.42	13 13% - 14.87	2 3% - 51.00	3 4% - 72.28
HAM G A Somerset	9/145 6% - 82.58	13 10% : - 21.90	21 14% + 10.67	25 20% - 15.35	9 11% - 11.60
HAMILTON Mrs A Tyne & Wear	1/ 1 100% + 5.00	0 0% : - 11.00	0 0% - 3.00	0 0% - 9.00	0 0% - 21.00
HAMMOND M D North Yorks	35/228 15% - 79.16	31 15% : - 45.42	0 0% 0.00	0 0% 0.00	0 0% 0.00
HANNON R Wiltshire	4/ 20 20% - 6.00	1 20% : + 1.50	0 0% - 2.00	0 0% - 5.00	0 0% - 16.00

	1991/92 Wns Rns (%)	:	1990/91 Wns (%)	1989/88 Wns (%)	1988/89 Wns (%)	1987/88 Wns (%)
HANSON J West Yorks	1/ 18 6% - 10.00	:	1 8% - 8.75	6 21% + 1.68	2 8% - 2.20	5 16% + 0.50
HARDY W Nottinghamshire	1/ 3 33% - 0.37	:	0 0% - 6.00	0 0% - 9.00	0 0% - 12.00	0 0% - 5.00
HARRIS J L Leicestershire	6/ 84 7% - 41.00	:	6 8% + 1.50	3 4% - 45.00	2 2% - 100.00	2 3% - 36.00
HARRISON A North Yorks	2/ 23 9% - 11.75	:	1 3% - 33.50	0 0% 0.00	0 0% 0.00	0 0% 0.00
HARWOOD G West Sussex	16/ 78 21% - 27.64	:	13 21% - 6.56	19 37% + 49.14	6 18% + 0.25	5 100% + 17.93
HASLAM P C North Yorks	10/ 26 38% + 13.82	:	0 0% 0.00	0 0% 0.00	0 0% 0.00	0 0% 0.00
HAYNES H E Wiltshire	1/ 9 11% + 6.00	:	0 0% - 2.00	0 0% 0.00	0 0% 0.00	0 0% 0.00
HAYNES M J Surrey	7/ 30 23% + 0.50	:	3 18% + 2.75	4 13% - 13.17	1 13% + 13.00	0 0% - 15.00
HEDGER P R West Sussex	8/ 73 11% - 28.95	:	12 10% - 50.62	13 13% - 25.34	14 18% + 12.13	9 11% - 30.75
HELLENS J A Tyne & Wear	6/ 39 15% - 10.39	:	7 25% + 12.33	1 4% - 20.75	0 0% - 11.00	0 0% - 13.00
HEMBROW Mrs S J R Somerset	1/ 4 25% + 2.50	:	0 0% - 10.00	0 0% - 1.00	1 100% + 4.00	2 15% - 1.50
HENDERSON Mrs R G Devon	2/ 7 29% + 5.00	:	0 0% 0.00	0 0% 0.00	0 0% 0.00	0 0% 0.00
HENDERSON N J Berkshire	52/251 21% - 58.96	:	49 19% - 53.44	41 17% - 44.55	43 18% + 1.23	40 16% - 8.08
HERRIES LADY West Sussex	2/ 23 9% - 12.00	:	0 0% - 4.00	1 17% - 1.50	2 13% + 9.33	0 0% - 35.00
HEWITT Mrs A R Cheshire	4/ 35 11% + 0.88	:	3 8% - 22.00	1 5% - 17.50	2 7% + 7.00	6 30% + 16.12
HIDE A Suffolk	3/ 20 15% + 2.00	:	4 18% - 14.00	0 0% - 3.00	0 0% - 4.00	0 0% - 2.00
HILLS B W Berkshire	1/ 13 8% - 4.50	:	0 0% - 3.00	2 22% - 4.08	3 38% + 5.20	0 0% - 2.00
HOAD R P C East Sussex	3/ 40 8% - 32.37	:	6 26% + 25.50	1 3% - 26.25	2 5% - 35.25	2 5% + 8.00
HOBBS P J Somerset	51/283 18% - 31.00	:	33 13% - 106.85	45 18% - 0.74	24 9% - 85.50	22 9% - 31.10
HODGES R J Somerset	21/260 8% - 179.99	:	19 8% - 73.78	19 7% - 128.47	18 7% - 130.83	21 7% - 121.70
HOLDEN W Suffolk	3/ 20 15% - 8.42	:	0 0% - 9.00	1 6% - 4.00	4 22% + 0.25	0 0% - 16.00
HOLDER R J Avon	31/228 14% - 57.82	:	29 12% - 20.75	33 18% + 13.15	25 13% + 14.04	17 9% + 16.75
HOLLINSHEAD R Staffordshire	13/ 69 19% - 18.99	:	8 9% - 18.40	15 17% - 32.09	4 4% - 26.50	7 6% - 20.50

	1991/92	1990/91	1989/88	1988/89	1987/88
	Wns Rns (%) :	Wns (%)	Wns (%)	Wns (%)	Wns (%)
HOLLOWELL Kerry Northants	1/ 9 11% - 8.00	0 0% : - 6.00	0 0% 0.00	0 0% 0.00	0 0% 0.00
HORGAN C A Berkshire	2/ 41 5% - 30.00	3 14% : - 1.75	1 3% + 21.00	0 0% - 5.00	0 0% - 27.00
HORWOOD Miss J Oxon	1/ 6 17% + 11.00	0 0% : - 11.00	0 0% - 10.00	0 0% - 6.00	0 0% - 12.00
HOUGHTON R F J Oxon	5/ 23 22% + 41.32	6 22% : + 3.26	3 17% - 0.40	3 17% - 0.50	0 0% 0.00
HOWLING P Surrey	1/ 12 8% + 5.00	0 0% : - 6.00	1 2% - 14.00	0 0% - 57.00	1 1% - 77.00
HUBBARD G A Suffolk	1/ 4 25% + 63.00	0 0% : 0.00	15 14% + 1.38	15 10% - 16.01	6 7% - 29.25
HUTSBY H Warwicks	2/ 7 29% + 3.00	0 0% : - 10.00	1 14% + 10.00	1 17% - 2.25	0 0% - 4.00
JACKSON C F C H'ford & Worcs	1/ 24 4% - 9.00	0 0% : - 23.00	1 4% - 18.50	1 2% - 41.50	4 10% - 10.50
JAMES A P H'ford & Worcs	8/ 87 9% - 34.37	5 6% : - 52.37	7 8% + 20.25	2 2% - 88.67	0 0% - 58.00
JAMES C Berkshire	3/ 44 7% + 20.33	0 0% : - 28.00	0 0% - 20.00	0 0% - 13.00	0 0% - 31.00
JARVIS A P Oxon	2/ 35 6% + 4.00	0 0% : 0.00	0 0% 0.00	0 0% 0.00	0 0% 0.00
JARVIS M A Suffolk	2/ 7 29% + 0.25	0 0% : - 2.00	1 14% - 2.50	0 0% - 3.00	2 50% + 21.00
JEFFERSON J M North Yorks	3/ 37 8% - 6.00	5 10% : - 29.55	6 9% - 13.25	8 11% - 15.50	9 14% - 19.75
JEMMESON J D North Yorks	1/ 2 50% + 13.00	0 0% : - 1.00	0 0% - 1.00	0 0% 0.00	0 0% 0.00
JENKINS J R Herts	20/244 8% - 120.30	30 16% : + 61.99	31 13% - 25.47	29 10% - 115.33	24 9% - 143.54
JENNINGS Miss G S North Yorks	1/ 8 13% + 18.00	0 0% : 0.00	0 0% 0.00	0 0% 0.00	0 0% 0.00
JOHNSON J H Co Durham	21/131 16% + 12.88	10 9% : - 31.75	14 13% - 47.57	14 17% + 43.31	5 10% - 11.37
JOHNSTON M North Yorks	1/ 7 14% - 3.50	0 0% : - 7.00	1 10% - 6.00	0 0% 0.00	0 0% 0.00
JONES A P Herts	4/ 60 7% - 31.00	8 12% : + 49.39	2 5% - 11.67	0 0% 0.00	0 0% 0.00
JONES D HAYDN mid Glamorgan	2/ 5 40% + 8.00	0 0% : 0.00	3 15% - 5.25	1 9% + 15.00	0 0% - 29.00
JONES Mrs Gill E H'ford & Worcs	2/ 70 3% - 27.00	4 6% : + 9.50	3 6% - 18.00	4 5% - 30.30	1 3% - 35.50
JONES Mrs M A Berkshire	3/ 6 50% + 6.50	0 0% : 0.00	0 0% 0.00	0 0% 0.00	0 0% 0.00
JONES P J Wiltshire	4/ 57 7% - 40.00	3 6% : - 29.25	4 6% - 51.24	6 7% - 48.25	8 10% - 41.49

	1991/92 Wns Rns(%) :	1990/91 Wns(%)	1989/88 Wns(%)	1988/89 Wns(%)	1987/88 Wns(%)
JONES Paul Staffordshire	1/ 3 33% : + 0.25	3 6% - 29.25	0 0% 0.00	0 0% 0.00	0 0% 0.00
JONES T THOMSON Berkshire	23/130 18% : - 18.42	21 21% + 44.91	17 30% + 33.78	6 40% + 9.76	0 0% 0.00
JORDAN F H'ford & Worcs	5/136 4% : - 66.50	17 9% - 95.49	21 15% - 53.75	16 12% - 64.20	8 9% - 48.50
JORDAN Mrs J North Yorks	1/ 54 2% : - 51.25	3 11% + 7.50	0 0% 0.00	0 0% 0.00	0 0% 0.00
JOYNES Mrs P M Warwicks	3/ 68 4% : - 47.37	0 0% - 5.00	0 0% 0.00	0 0% 0.00	0 0% 0.00
JUCKES R T H'ford & Worcs	7/118 6% : - 90.12	6 9% - 13.50	3 4% - 61.75	3 2% - 102.00	2 3% - 7.50
KAVANAGH H M H'ford & Worcs	1/ 23 4% : - 15.50	0 0% 0.00	0 0% 0.00	0 0% 0.00	0 0% 0.00
KELLEWAY P A Suffolk	4/ 17 24% : - 2.11	4 17% 0.00	1 50% + 3.50	0 0% - 20.00	1 10% + 1.00
KELLY G P York	1/ 27 4% : - 20.00	0 0% - 3.00	0 0% - 16.00	0 0% - 15.00	0 0% - 37.00
KELLY P G Ireland	1/ 4 25% : + 3.50	0 0% 0.00	0 0% - 1.00	0 0% 0.00	0 0% 0.00
KEMP W T Borders	1/ 35 3% : - 31.75	1 2% - 29.00	2 3% - 53.25	6 5% - 93.87	10 5% - 87.02
KENDALL Mrs M A Cumbria	1/ 21 5% : + 5.00	0 0% - 7.00	0 0% - 14.00	0 0% - 10.00	0 0% - 16.00
KERSEY T South Yorks	1/ 35 3% : - 22.00	0 0% - 26.00	1 1% - 79.50	1 1% - 63.00	2 2% - 74.56
KETTLEWELL S E North Yorks	9/ 47 19% : - 3.10	5 14% - 13.46	11 26% + 30.78	2 11% + 1.50	0 0% - 6.00
KING J S Wiltshire	5/128 4% : - 68.00	16 14% + 38.27	16 13% - 47.58	16 12% - 24.67	7 6% - 62.96
KING Mrs A L M Warwicks	8/ 84 10% : - 30.00	2 2% - 77.00	2 5% - 22.50	2 3% - 16.00	2 3% - 58.00
KINSEY Mrs T R Cheshire	1/ 7 14% : - 0.50	0 0% - 5.00	0 0% - 1.00	0 0% 0.00	0 0% 0.00
KNIGHT Miss H C Oxon	14/171 8% : - 102.85	24 16% - 57.76	15 14% - 59.03	0 0% 0.00	0 0% 0.00
KNIGHT Mrs A Devon	2/103 2% : - 89.50	7 6% - 37.67	2 2% - 65.00	3 5% - 18.00	2 3% - 18.00
LAMYMAN Mrs S Lincs	1/ 12 8% : + 5.00	0 0% - 20.00	1 9% - 7.00	0 0% - 20.00	2 9% - 13.80
LAYLAND R Lancashire	1/ 7 14% : - 3.00	0 0% - 12.00	0 0% - 9.00	0 0% - 2.00	0 0% - 19.00
LEACH P Somerset	6/ 61 10% : - 19.54	4 7% - 45.25	2 3% - 60.12	1 6% - 12.00	0 0% 0.00
LEADBETTER S J Borders	5/ 46 11% : - 10.67	3 8% - 14.90	2 5% - 30.62	2 5% - 31.00	3 7% - 7.12

	1991/92 Wns Rns(%)	1990/91 : Wns(%)	1989/88 Wns(%)	1988/89 Wns(%)	1987/88 Wns(%)
LEE D North Yorks	1/ 9 11% - 5.25	0 0% : - 19.00	3 6% - 10.00	4 4% - 46.62	3 4% - 67.25
LEE R Powys	20/161 12% - 20.12	22 11% : - 74.39	37 18% + 33.69	29 16% + 42.33	19 16% + 7.11
LEIGH J P Lincs	3/ 61 5% - 50.27	5 8% : - 48.50	4 7% - 35.21	1 2% - 51.37	3 6% - 25.00
LITSTON Mrs J Somerset	1/ 9 11% + 6.00	0 0% : 0.00	0 0% 0.00	0 0% 0.00	0 0% 0.00
LUNGO L Dunfries	8/ 69 12% - 27.77	6 20% : - 2.74	0 0% 0.00	0 0% 0.00	0 0% 0.00
MACAULEY Mrs N Leicestershire	1/ 22 5% - 18.00	4 19% : - 7.00	1 14% - 5.20	0 0% - 1.00	0 0% - 9.00
MACKIE J Derbys	11/155 7% - 90.50	6 5% : - 77.58	18 16% + 22.42	11 15% + 9.83	1 3% - 27.00
MACTAGGART A H Borders	1/ 16 6% + 18.00	0 0% : - 3.00	0 0% - 3.00	0 0% - 6.00	0 0% - 13.00
MACTAGGART B Borders	1/ 36 3% - 28.00	1 6% : - 12.00	0 0% - 7.00	0 0% - 7.00	0 0% 0.00
MADGWICK M Hampshire	2/ 42 5% - 35.25	5 10% : - 17.17	2 4% - 32.00	4 6% - 40.50	8 14% + 33.63
MAKIN P J Wiltshire	1/ 6 17% + 3.00	1 20% : + 16.00	0 0% - 17.00	1 9% - 8.62	0 0% - 12.00
MANNERS W Tyne & Wear	2/ 4 50% + 0.21	0 0% : 0.00	0 0% 0.00	0 0% 0.00	0 0% 0.00
MCCAIN D Cheshire	9/124 7% - 36.89	8 8% : - 39.72	13 11% + 36.65	13 10% - 5.67	12 10% - 56.57
MCCONNOCHIE J C Warwicks	7/115 6% - 54.75	10 7% : - 56.70	7 8% - 36.75	0 0% 0.00	0 0% 0.00
MCCORMACK M Oxon	1/ 21 5% - 6.00	5 19% : + 4.38	4 21% - 5.69	3 11% - 8.50	0 0% - 18.00
MCCOURT M Oxon	6/ 47 13% - 9.16	9 22% : - 15.20	0 0% - 22.00	2 6% - 21.12	3 6% - 14.25
MCDONALD R Borders	3/ 16 19% + 6.00	0 0% : - 14.00	0 0% - 4.00	0 0% - 13.00	0 0% - 15.00
MCKENZIE-COLES W Somerset	1/ 25 4% - 12.00	0 0% : - 26.00	2 10% - 1.25	1 4% + 39.00	0 0% - 13.00
MCKIE Mrs I Berkshire	13/ 58 22% + 6.46	6 8% : - 41.75	7 12% + 2.50	6 14% - 12.87	3 4% - 65.75
MCMAHON B A Staffordshire	5/ 62 8% + 0.12	5 8% : - 31.49	11 21% + 7.27	8 10% - 8.79	8 19% - 19.50
MCMILLAN M D Gloucestershire	3/ 14 21% + 2.50	0 0% : - 2.00	0 0% 0.00	0 0% 0.00	0 0% 0.00
MEADE M Wiltshire	1/ 22 5% - 20.33	1 5% : - 9.00	2 25% + 17.00	0 0% 0.00	0 0% 0.00
MELLOR S Wiltshire	8/145 6% - 87.92	34 22% : - 37.26	21 21% + 58.29	11 11% - 34.99	6 5% - 50.00

	1991/92 Wns Rns (%)	1990/91 Wns (%)	1989/88 Wns (%)	1988/89 Wns (%)	1987/88 Wns (%)
MESSER-BENNETTS M Cornwall	2/ 5 40% + 2.25	0 0% 0.00	0 0% 0.00	0 0% 0.00	0 0% 0.00
MILLER C J VERNON Warwicks	2/ 26 8% - 17.25	0 0% - 35.00	2 5% - 30.75	2 8% - 13.50	2 6% - 26.20
MILLER N Co Durham	2/ 53 4% - 29.00	4 8% + 224.00	2 6% - 26.40	0 0% 0.00	0 0% 0.00
MILLMAN B R Devon	1/ 13 8% - 4.50	1 6% - 2.00	0 0% - 8.00	0 0% 0.00	0 0% 0.00
MINNS Mrs Sylvia H'ford & Worcs	1/ 26 4% - 11.00	0 0% - 14.00	0 0% - 10.00	0 0% - 4.00	1 13% + 5.00
MITCHELL N R Dorset	1/ 80 1% - 69.00	5 7% - 14.50	12 7% - 89.37	17 9% - 33.87	2 2% - 25.00
MITCHELL P Surrey	5/ 34 15% + 7.54	4 10% - 23.75	4 7% - 30.00	7 12% - 12.39	5 11% - 28.00
MOFFATT D Cumbria	7/ 73 10% - 35.51	3 5% - 50.38	3 5% - 44.25	5 5% - 48.50	10 8% - 59.56
MONTEITH P Lothian	23/107 21% + 13.29	17 18% + 1.50	10 14% - 5.21	6 6% - 52.50	5 6% - 65.62
MOORE A East Sussex	11/226 5% - 146.80	9 6% - 86.00	11 6% - 89.50	5 3% - 132.00	10 5% - 98.62
MOORE A L T Ireland	2/ 9 22% + 21.00	0 0% - 1.00	1 11% - 7.09	2 20% + 2.63	1 20% + 2.00
MOORE G M North Yorks	38/240 16% - 70.03	46 20% - 60.94	53 22% - 51.49	37 13% - 134.56	47 24% + 32.43
MOORE J S Hampshire	14/ 80 18% + 37.25	2 7% - 19.00	0 0% 0.00	0 0% 0.00	0 0% 0.00
MORGAN B C Staffordshire	5/ 40 13% - 2.25	0 0% - 23.00	4 15% - 6.50	2 5% - 21.37	3 5% - 49.37
MORGAN K A Leicestershire	8/114 7% - 30.50	15 12% - 24.25	12 9% - 75.52	20 13% - 68.21	11 8% - 62.74
MORRIS D Suffolk	1/ 9 11% - 6.12	0 0% - 5.00	0 0% - 5.00	0 0% 0.00	0 0% 0.00
MORRIS M F Ireland	1/ 7 14% - 4.37	1 14% - 5.09	1 11% - 0.50	0 0% - 8.00	0 0% - 6.00
MOSCROP Mrs E Tyne & Wear	1/ 4 25% + 2.00	0 0% 0.00	0 0% 0.00	0 0% 0.00	0 0% 0.00
MUGGERIDGE M P Wiltshire	5/ 64 8% - 36.00	2 5% - 4.00	0 0% 0.00	0 0% 0.00	0 0% 0.00
MUIR W R Berkshire	3/ 13 23% - 0.75	0 0% - 1.00	0 0% 0.00	0 0% 0.00	0 0% 0.00
MULLINS Seamus Hampshire	1/ 8 13% + 7.00	0 0% 0.00	0 0% 0.00	0 0% 0.00	0 0% 0.00
MURPHY F Suffolk	19/133 14% - 41.38	11 10% - 30.48	0 0% 0.00	0 0% 0.00	0 0% 0.00
MURRAY B W North Yorks	3/ 16 19% + 4.08	0 0% - 5.00	0 0% 0.00	0 0% 0.00	0 0% 0.00

	1991/92 Wns Rns (%) :	1990/91 Wns (%)	1989/88 Wns (%)	1988/89 Wns (%)	1987/88 Wns (%)
MURRAY Mrs A M Oxon	1/ 3 33% : - 0.75 :	0 0% 0.00	0 0% 0.00	0 0% 0.00	0 0% 0.00
MUSSON W J Suffolk	1/ 8 13% : + 13.00 :	4 17% - 0.50	3 14% - 11.07	0 0% - 16.00	2 8% - 8.00
NASH C T Oxon	9/ 89 10% : - 50.11 :	0 0% - 5.00	1 4% - 20.00	0 0% 0.00	0 0% 0.00
NAUGHTON M P North Yorks	3/ 24 13% : - 13.00 :	1 5% - 11.50	3 9% - 20.75	5 6% - 50.67	11 8% - 68.00
NAUGHTON T Surrey	1/ 12 8% : - 7.50 :	0 0% - 2.00	0 0% 0.00	0 0% 0.00	0 0% 0.00
NEEDHAM J L Shropshire	1/ 18 6% : - 3.00 :	0 0% - 15.00	0 0% - 5.00	0 0% - 25.00	0 0% - 30.00
NELSON W M Dumfries	2/ 4 50% : + 18.00 :	0 0% - 1.00	0 0% - 2.00	0 0% - 6.00	0 0% 0.00
NICHOLLS P F Somerset	10/100 10% : - 47.54 :	0 0% 0.00	0 0% 0.00	0 0% 0.00	0 0% 0.00
NICHOLSON D Gloucestershire	63/329 19% : - 41.37 :	55 20% - 58.88	42 16% - 22.01	39 11% - 163.05	50 15% - 49.73
NORTON J South Yorks	1/ 40 3% : - 36.50 :	0 0% - 20.00	2 5% - 26.25	0 0% - 10.00	1 3% - 36.27
NORTON S G South Yorks	1/ 11 9% : - 4.00 :	1 8% - 6.50	2 18% + 12.00	0 0% - 5.00	0 0% - 4.00
O'LEARY R North Yorks	8/ 77 10% : - 23.08 :	9 17% - 5.62	2 5% - 30.00	0 0% - 6.00	1 3% - 26.00
O'MAHONY F J Surrey	4/ 22 18% : + 3.67 :	1 4% + 7.00	1 5% - 15.00	3 13% - 2.00	0 0% 0.00
O'NEILL J J Cumbria	26/155 17% : - 55.88 :	27 15% - 57.25	34 16% - 58.85	29 19% - 28.39	14 11% - 39.87
O'NEILL M Lancashire	2/ 62 3% : - 56.50 :	8 21% + 21.38	2 9% + 11.00	0 0% - 2.00	0 0% 0.00
O'NEILL O Gloucestershire	4/ 81 5% : - 22.00 :	5 10% - 27.00	4 5% - 50.67	10 7% - 100.17	19 21% + 75.56
O'SHEA J G M Warwicks	5/ 38 13% : - 25.44 :	1 3% - 1.00	3 10% - 13.37	0 0% 0.00	0 0% 0.00
O'SULLIVAN R J West Sussex	14/ 56 25% : + 0.94 :	6 11% + 2.76	6 10% - 38.65	13 14% - 20.62	16 14% - 39.67
OLD J A B Wiltshire	21/ 75 28% : + 66.73 :	10 10% - 11.30	2 3% - 39.50	9 6% - 66.44	6 4% - 29.87
OLDROYD G R North Yorks	3/ 45 7% : - 22.50 :	2 4% - 40.00	3 7% - 27.50	2 5% - 36.50	2 13% + 2.25
OLIVER J K M Borders	3/ 87 3% : - 45.00 :	4 4% - 83.50	4 5% - 53.67	7 12% + 21.75	6 7% - 59.82
OLIVER Mrs S Staffordshire	10/ 71 14% : - 14.46 :	14 15% - 18.62	10 15% + 4.23	12 13% - 32.60	16 16% + 13.09
OWEN JUN E H Clwyd	2/ 27 7% : + 11.50 :	1 3% - 18.00	3 7% - 29.75	2 3% - 44.50	4 5% - 36.27

	1991/92 Wns Rns (%) :	1990/91 Wns (%)	1989/88 Wns (%)	1988/89 Wns (%)	1987/88 Wns (%)
P-GORDON G A Suffolk	4/ 34 12% : - 3.67	6 14% : - 19.75	5 20% - 3.25	5 16% - 20.56	1 8% - 9.62
PALLING B South Glamorgan	3/ 39 8% : + 20.00	0 0% : - 31.00	3 6% - 36.75	1 2% - 25.00	1 2% - 50.00
PARK IAN Co Cleveland	2/ 12 17% : + 0.50	1 20% : + 12.00	0 0% - 7.00	0 0% - 13.00	0 0% - 12.00
PARKER C Dumfries	7/116 6% : - 67.40	8 9% : - 37.37	2 4% - 24.00	9 11% - 12.95	8 10% - 14.75
PARKER R Surrey	1/ 2 50% : + 2.33	0 0% : - 1.00	0 0% 0.00	0 0% 0.00	0 0% 0.00
PARKES J North Yorks	4/ 73 5% : - 10.00	3 3% : - 81.80	14 10% - 76.05	11 12% - 36.37	1 1% - 99.50
PARROTT Mrs H Gloucestershire	5/ 72 7% : - 35.34	4 6% : - 33.50	5 8% - 31.09	2 8% - 9.00	1 7% - 5.00
PAYNE S G Cumbria	1/ 34 3% : 0.00	1 3% : - 32.00	3 8% - 9.00	0 0% - 50.00	2 4% - 16.00
PEARCE J Suffolk	4/ 23 17% : - 4.24	3 7% : - 28.95	2 5% - 32.87	4 11% - 22.56	7 17% + 9.58
PENFOLD G W Devon	2/ 4 50% : + 6.25	3 30% : + 0.85	1 20% - 2.50	0 0% - 1.00	1 17% - 2.00
PERRATT Miss L A Strathclyde	15/100 15% : - 28.14	0 0% 0.00	0 0% 0.00	0 0% 0.00	0 0% 0.00
PERRIN Mrs J Herts	1/ 19 5% : - 14.50	0 0% 0.00	0 0% 0.00	0 0% 0.00	0 0% 0.00
PERRY J Oxon	1/ 1 100% : + 7.50	0 0% 0.00	0 0% 0.00	0 0% 0.00	0 0% 0.00
PICKERING J A Leicestershire	2/ 26 8% : - 4.00	1 3% : - 24.00	1 3% - 30.00	2 40% + 8.33	0 0% - 4.00
PIPE M C Devon	224/839 27% : - 60.90	230 29% : - 4.02	224 35% - 13.72	208 37% + 72.72	129 25% - 24.28
PITMAN Mrs J Berkshire	50/333 15% : - 69.40	43 15% : - 58.34	93 28% + 77.17	62 22% + 23.10	45 15% - 29.79
PLOWRIGHT Mrs G S South Yorks	1/ 12 8% : - 8.25	2 15% : + 1.00	1 7% - 6.00	2 22% + 12.00	1 10% - 1.50
POPHAM C L Somerset	3/100 3% : - 87.46	16 9% : - 115.87	17 10% - 89.78	20 15% + 9.79	12 9% - 69.21
POTTS A W S Humberside	1/ 13 8% : - 2.00	0 0% : - 18.00	2 11% + 8.00	0 0% - 17.00	0 0% - 18.00
PREECE B Shropshire	5/ 88 6% : - 55.47	4 4% : - 90.00	22 18% - 29.90	10 8% - 78.41	9 9% - 68.17
PRICE G M Powys	1/ 13 8% : + 21.00	0 0% : - 7.00	0 0% - 6.00	1 10% + 5.00	0 0% - 7.00
PRICE R J H'ford & Worcs	8/ 67 12% : + 12.30	3 13% : + 38.25	1 14% + 4.00	0 0% - 2.00	0 0% - 5.00
PRICE William Gwent	1/ 28 4% : - 13.00	1 2% : - 54.00	1 2% - 40.00	2 4% - 43.50	0 0% - 37.00

	1991/92	1990/91	1989/88	1988/89	1987/88
	Wns Rns(%) :	Wns(%)	Wns(%)	Wns(%)	Wns(%)
PRITCHARD Dr P Gloucestershire	3/ 29 10% : + 2.00 :	0 0% - 58.00	1 8% - 9.12	0 0% 0.00	1 100% + 0.91
PRITCHARD P A Warwicks	3/ 71 4% : - 24.00 :	0 0% - 58.00	0 0% - 54.00	5 9% + 8.50	0 0% - 91.00
PURCELL M Ireland	1/ 1 100% : + 33.00 :	0 0% 0.00	0 0% 0.00	0 0% 0.00	0 0% 0.00
RAMSDEN Mrs J R North Yorks	6/ 30 20% : - 2.68 :	7 19% - 12.71	4 21% - 3.00	1 20% - 1.00	0 0% - 3.00
RATCLIFF Mrs A E Warwicks	1/ 15 7% : + 6.00 :	0 0% - 15.00	0 0% - 25.00	0 0% - 16.00	0 0% - 10.00
REED W G Northumberland	3/ 46 7% : - 15.25 :	2 8% - 10.50	2 6% - 4.00	1 2% - 42.50	4 8% + 9.00
REID A S Beds	3/ 52 6% : - 2.00 :	1 4% - 19.00	1 2% - 44.00	0 0% - 3.00	0 0% 0.00
RETTER Mrs J G Devon	24/124 19% : + 94.76 :	11 15% + 11.66	3 4% - 26.00	11 15% + 3.38	1 4% - 13.00
REVELEY Mrs G R Co Cleveland	99/323 31% : - 0.88 :	58 26% + 37.69	41 29% + 53.87	23 12% - 61.42	26 14% - 53.41
RICHARDS G W Cumbria	67/409 16% : - 90.01 :	118 24% - 14.31	78 21% - 62.08	69 20% - 57.63	72 20% - 64.62
RICHARDS Grenville Powys	1/ 27 4% : - 14.00 :	0 0% - 19.00	0 0% - 4.00	0 0% - 1.00	0 0% 0.00
RICHMOND B Lincs	2/ 45 4% : - 33.17 :	3 5% - 51.25	3 7% - 35.12	2 5% - 19.00	2 3% - 37.50
ROBERTS J D Somerset	3/ 46 7% : + 8.00 :	4 4% - 57.09	7 8% - 24.25	3 5% 0.00	3 5% - 51.70
ROBINSON M H B Oxon	7/ 57 12% : - 14.66 :	7 7% - 42.37	8 10% - 28.57	13 21% + 12.14	7 13% - 32.17
ROBSON T L A Northumberland	1/ 5 20% : - 1.75 :	0 0% - 10.00	0 0% - 5.00	1 17% + 3.00	0 0% - 9.00
RODFORD P R Dorset	3/ 57 5% : + 14.00 :	1 2% - 39.00	0 0% - 42.00	0 0% - 76.00	2 4% - 43.00
ROE G Devon	1/ 12 8% : + 3.00 :	0 0% - 20.00	1 4% - 8.00	0 0% 0.00	0 0% 0.00
ROE GRAEME Gloucestershire	3/ 17 18% : - 5.25 :	0 0% - 32.00	1 4% - 25.00	0 0% 0.00	0 0% 0.00
ROTHWELL B S Humberside	7/ 61 11% : + 106.00 :	0 0% 0.00	0 0% 0.00	0 0% 0.00	0 0% 0.00
ROWE R West Sussex	7/ 96 7% : - 59.50 :	0 0% 0.00	0 0% 0.00	0 0% 0.00	0 0% 0.00
RYALL B J M Somerset	2/ 22 9% : - 6.50 :	1 14% + 60.00	0 0% - 3.00	0 0% - 5.00	0 0% - 2.00
RYAN M J Suffolk	7/ 47 15% : - 20.58 :	9 15% - 10.50	11 28% + 4.80	8 17% - 4.66	8 23% + 1.68
SAMPLE Major W N Northumberland	1/ 13 8% : - 9.50 :	4 36% + 17.12	2 40% + 15.25	0 0% - 11.00	0 0% - 3.00

	1991/92 Wns Rns (%)	:	1990/91 Wns (%)	1989/88 Wns (%)	1988/89 Wns (%)	1987/88 Wns (%)
SANDERS Miss B Surrey	18/ 84 21% - 22.89	: +	9 19% 7.25	14 25% - 11.63	8 15% - 19.50	9 17% - 17.27
SAUNDERS M S Northants	1/ 14 7% + 3.00	:	0 0% 0.00	0 0% 0.00	0 0% 0.00	0 0% 0.00
SAUNDERS Miss C Somerset	9/ 35 26% + 19.83	:	0 0% 0.00	0 0% - 1.00	0 0% 0.00	0 0% 0.00
SCUDAMORE M H'ford & Worcs	3/ 34 9% - 15.00	: +	7 21% 108.00	2 7% - 19.00	2 5% - 29.75	0 0% - 53.00
SHERWOOD O Berkshire	48/227 21% - 69.45	:	56 21% - 25.39	58 19% - 42.68	53 21% + 30.49	42 17% - 14.70
SHERWOOD S E Berkshire	17/125 14% + 8.11	:	12 14% - 24.30	0 0% 0.00	0 0% 0.00	0 0% 0.00
SHOREY D J H'ford & Worcs	1/ 4 25% + 9.00	:	0 0% - 2.00	0 0% - 1.00	0 0% 0.00	0 0% - 4.00
SIMPSON R Wiltshire	9/ 47 19% - 3.31	:	3 7% - 20.00	3 5% - 40.00	3 12% + 3.00	6 8% - 22.25
SLY Mrs P Cambs	5/ 36 14% - 5.50	: +	3 9% 2.00	1 4% - 17.00	0 0% - 21.00	3 8% - 4.50
SMART B Berkshire	3/ 30 10% + 16.00	:	1 3% - 26.00	2 4% - 39.00	6 5% - 82.13	4 3% - 80.50
SMITH C Lincs	5/ 78 6% - 51.76	:	0 0% - 60.00	0 0% - 36.00	0 0% - 1.00	0 0% - 2.00
SMITH C A H'ford & Worcs	2/ 35 6% - 18.50	:	0 0% 0.00	0 0% 0.00	0 0% 0.00	0 0% 0.00
SMITH D E S Gloucestershire	1/ 5 20% + 29.00	:	0 0% 0.00	0 0% 0.00	0 0% 0.00	0 0% 0.00
SMITH D MURRAY Berkshire	13/ 77 17% + 8.46	:	0 0% 0.00	0 0% 0.00	0 0% 0.00	0 0% 0.00
SMITH Denys Co Durham	19/129 15% - 51.07	:	21 14% - 33.33	13 9% - 99.00	20 11% - 50.45	26 14% - 84.81
SMITH J P Staffordshire	2/ 35 6% + 27.00	:	1 5% - 5.00	1 4% - 18.00	1 3% - 11.00	0 0% - 35.00
SMITH Mrs S J West Yorks	12/108 11% + 113.50	:	2 4% - 40.50	0 0% - 4.00	0 0% 0.00	0 0% 0.00
SMITH N A Staffordshire	2/ 49 4% - 39.17	: +	1 2% 5.00	3 6% - 20.00	1 8% + 14.00	0 0% - 16.00
SMITH SIDNEY J Northants	2/ 8 25% + 1.00	: +	2 40% 9.00	0 0% 0.00	0 0% 0.00	0 0% 0.00
SMYTH R V Surrey	1/ 2 50% + 0.50	:	2 9% - 13.00	2 14% + 16.00	3 23% - 1.83	1 7% - 3.00
SOMERLEYTON Lord Norfolk	1/ 4 25% 0.00	:	0 0% 0.00	0 0% 0.00	0 0% 0.00	0 0% 0.00
SOWERSBY M E Gloucestershire	1/ 7 14% - 3.75	:	0 0% 0.00	0 0% 0.00	0 0% 0.00	0 0% 0.00
SPEARING J L Warwicks	7/ 86 8% - 52.12	:	9 10% - 19.87	4 5% - 51.00	6 5% - 111.57	15 9% + 2.75

	1991/92 Wns Rns(%) :	1990/91 Wns(%)	1989/88 Wns(%)	1988/89 Wns(%)	1987/88 Wns(%)
STEPHENSON W A Co Durham	101/539 19% : − 88.59	83 16% : − 199.56	116 22% − 86.43	90 16% − 160.33	93 15% − 162.84
STIRK Mrs M K North Yorks	5/ 9 56% : + 16.50	4 31% : + 18.75	0 0% − 3.00	0 0% 0.00	0 0% − 5.00
STOREY F S Cumbria	1/ 19 5% : + 7.00	1 9% : + 15.00	0 0% − 10.00	2 15% − 2.25	0 0% − 15.00
STOREY W Co Durham	6/ 76 8% : − 42.03	6 8% : − 19.75	9 16% − 9.32	4 6% 0.00	7 7% − 69.50
STRINGER A P North Yorks	3/ 29 10% : + 18.25	2 6% : − 21.25	2 6% − 22.25	1 6% − 5.00	1 8% − 8.25
SUTCLIFFE J Surrey	4/ 17 24% : + 3.21	0 0% : − 5.00	2 12% − 12.83	3 18% + 16.50	0 0% 0.00
SWINBANK Mrs A North Yorks	1/ 10 10% : + 11.00	0 0% : 0.00	0 0% 0.00	0 0% 0.00	0 0% 0.00
SWINDLEHURST D G Cumbria	2/ 15 13% : + 15.00	2 29% : + 34.00	0 0% − 4.00	0 0% − 5.00	0 0% − 3.00
SYCKELMOORE Mrs L Wiltshire	1/ 2 50% : + 3.50	0 0% : − 2.00	1 25% + 13.00	0 0% 0.00	0 0% 0.00
TATE M H'ford & Worcs	1/ 19 5% : − 11.00	1 3% : − 7.00	2 6% − 19.50	3 8% − 11.00	2 7% − 16.50
TATE T P North Yorks	8/ 67 12% : − 23.62	9 15% : − 18.66	9 19% − 14.90	5 20% − 8.71	1 6% − 13.62
TAYLOR Mrs S Northumberland	2/ 23 9% : − 2.00	0 0% : − 9.00	0 0% − 1.00	0 0% − 1.00	0 0% 0.00
TETLEY Mrs P A Surrey	1/ 13 8% : + 13.00	0 0% : − 18.00	0 0% − 10.00	0 0% 0.00	0 0% 0.00
THOMAS J D South Glamorgan	2/ 55 4% : − 38.50	2 3% : − 47.00	0 0% − 41.00	0 0% 0.00	2 14% − 1.12
THOMPSON R Lincs	4/ 31 13% : − 0.50	2 9% : + 33.00	0 0% − 34.00	3 11% + 9.50	3 11% + 2.00
THOMPSON V Northumberland	2/ 89 2% : − 54.00	0 0% : − 19.00	0 0% − 20.00	2 2% − 69.00	6 5% − 60.50
THORNE Miss J Somerset	2/ 26 8% : − 8.00	1 2% : − 17.00	2 6% − 22.50	1 3% − 31.50	1 3% − 24.00
THORNER G Oxon	5/ 52 10% : + 18.50	2 5% : + 36.00	0 0% − 28.00	0 0% − 42.00	1 1% − 69.50
THORNTON C W North Yorks	10/ 47 21% : + 4.55	15 28% : − 0.79	4 10% − 31.12	6 14% − 19.83	8 26% + 14.75
TINKLER C North Yorks	2/ 12 17% : − 5.59	2 13% : + 2.50	5 17% − 11.08	5 21% + 5.63	7 21% + 2.25
TINKLER N North Yorks	38/163 23% : − 12.15	29 16% : − 66.43	49 24% − 26.00	54 27% − 28.69	16 22% − 24.76
TOMPKINS M H Suffolk	15/ 86 17% : − 5.89	25 21% : + 3.03	17 28% + 27.66	7 18% − 9.80	2 8% − 13.90
TOWNSEND R D Kent	1/ 15 7% : − 12.75	3 13% : + 16.75	0 0% − 13.00	1 5% − 15.50	1 7% − 7.50

	1991/92 Wns Rns(%)	:	1990/91 Wns(%)	1989/88 Wns(%)	1988/89 Wns(%)	1987/88 Wns(%)
TRICKEY M J Devon	1/ 3 33% + 2.00	: :	0 0% 0.00	0 0% 0.00	0 0% 0.00	0 0% 0.00
TRIETLINE C C Warwicks	14/151 9% - 46.93	: :	10 8% - 79.79	4 4% - 87.67	8 5% - 79.45	9 5% - 82.37
TRIGG Mrs H Hampshire	2/ 4 50% + 3.50	: :	0 0% 0.00	0 0% 0.00	0 0% 0.00	0 0% 0.00
TUCK J Gloucestershire	2/ 14 14% - 3.67	: :	0 0% 0.00	0 0% 0.00	0 0% 0.00	0 0% 0.00
TUCKER D R Devon	1/ 21 5% - 13.00	: :	0 0% - 25.00	0 0% - 34.00	3 5% - 14.00	2 3% - 26.00
TURNELL Andrew Oxon	18/113 16% + 10.82	: :	7 9% - 39.00	16 15% + 16.44	11 8% - 65.09	19 13% - 33.24
TURNER J M Suffolk	3/ 9 33% + 4.30	: :	4 36% + 34.50	1 17% + 3.00	0 0% - 1.00	1 10% - 7.50
TURNER J R North Yorks	1/ 5 20% + 6.00	: :	0 0% - 8.00	0 0% - 9.00	1 7% + 53.00	0 0% - 11.00
TURNER W G M Dorset	8/110 7% + 1.50	: :	1 2% - 36.00	6 11% - 30.50	3 4% - 52.25	2 3% - 50.37
TWISTON-DAVIES N Gloucestershire	31/224 14% - 31.90	: :	19 12% - 11.39	8 14% + 7.01	2 12% + 6.00	3 14% - 1.25
UPSON JOHN R Northants	24/161 15% - 40.70	: :	27 20% - 12.56	22 16% - 55.32	0 0% 0.00	0 0% 0.00
USHER M D I Berkshire	5/ 48 10% - 30.00	: :	1 3% - 34.67	0 0% - 19.00	2 9% - 15.25	5 13% - 11.25
VERGETTE Mrs G Cambs	1/ 2 50% + 2.33	: :	1 50% - 0.43	3 100% + 3.55	0 0% 0.00	0 0% 0.00
VICKERY Mrs R A Somerset	1/ 5 20% - 2.25	: :	0 0% 0.00	0 0% 0.00	0 0% 0.00	0 0% 0.00
VIGORS Mrs Fiona Berkshire	1/ 1 100% + 10.00	: :	0 0% 0.00	0 0% 0.00	0 0% 0.00	0 0% 0.00
VOORSPUY R East Sussex	2/ 35 6% - 27.00	: :	2 5% - 33.25	4 13% - 16.80	5 12% - 13.75	0 0% - 22.00
WAINWRIGHT J S North Yorks	2/ 24 8% - 10.75	: :	0 0% - 29.00	2 7% - 14.00	0 0% - 3.00	1 5% - 11.00
WALEY-COHEN R B Oxon	1/ 8 13% + 18.00	: :	0 0% - 9.00	1 13% - 2.50	3 23% + 94.00	0 0% - 4.00
WALFORD T D York	1/ 3 33% - 0.80	: :	0 0% - 9.00	0 0% - 8.00	0 0% - 2.00	0 0% - 3.00
WALTON F T Northumberland	3/ 48 6% - 31.77	: :	5 11% - 31.60	8 18% - 19.12	4 11% - 25.40	4 8% - 16.50
WALTON Mrs K North Yorks	2/ 3 67% + 0.75	: :	0 0% 0.00	0 0% 0.00	0 0% 0.00	0 0% 0.00
WALWYN Mrs F Berkshire	2/ 81 2% - 69.75	: :	15 13% - 26.18	18 17% - 13.32	15 14% - 47.98	24 16% + 10.67
WARNER Peter Gloucestershire	2/ 15 13% - 1.58	: :	0 0% 0.00	0 0% 0.00	0 0% 0.00	0 0% 0.00

	1991/92 Wns Rns (%)	:	1990/91 Wns (%)	1989/88 Wns (%)	1988/89 Wns (%)	1987/88 Wns (%)
WARNER W J Northants	2/ 8 25% + 3.75	: :	0 0% 0.00	0 0% 0.00	0 0% 0.00	0 0% 0.00
WEAVER R J Leicestershire	3/ 43 7% - 28.12	: :	3 9% - 22.12	6 12% + 12.50	2 4% - 36.00	1 4% + 24.00
WEBBER J Oxon	16/ 99 16% + 1.49	: :	9 8% - 46.67	9 10% - 26.00	15 10% - 44.70	20 12% - 19.97
WEEDON C Surrey	7/ 74 9% - 9.00	: :	5 7% - 28.00	11 25% + 17.55	1 3% - 27.00	3 15% + 1.50
WELLS Mrs H S Dumfries	1/ 4 25% + 1.00	: :	0 0% 0.00	1 8% - 3.00	0 0% - 3.00	0 0% 0.00
WELLSTEAD H Dorset	3/ 4 75% + 2.56	: :	0 0% 0.00	0 0% 0.00	0 0% 0.00	0 0% 0.00
WHARTON J Leicestershire	7/ 64 11% - 9.39	: :	10 19% - 0.86	6 14% - 2.00	4 7% - 12.63	1 3% - 9.00
WHEELER E A Berkshire	2/ 44 5% - 29.50	: :	2 7% - 12.67	6 16% - 38.67	2 4% - 37.00	2 5% - 8.50
WHILLANS A C Borders	2/ 24 8% - 2.00	: :	0 0% - 7.00	0 0% - 1.00	0 0% - 3.00	0 0% 0.00
WHITAKER R M West Yorks	1/ 37 3% - 11.00	: :	0 0% - 38.00	3 6% - 23.75	5 6% - 34.25	6 13% - 1.75
WHITE J Bucks	39/183 21% - 26.31	: :	20 12% - 63.42	16 11% - 87.27	14 12% - 38.65	0 0% 0.00
WHITE K Shropshire	6/ 83 7% - 15.00	: :	3 4% - 58.12	8 11% + 11.50	6 9% - 28.25	6 8% - 32.37
WHITE Mrs R K Wiltshire	1/ 4 25% + 1.50	: :	0 0% 0.00	0 0% 0.00	0 0% 0.00	0 0% 0.00
WHITFIELD Miss A Berkshire	1/ 6 17% + 7.00	: :	0 0% - 13.00	0 0% - 1.00	0 0% - 2.00	0 0% 0.00
WHITING H A T Co Durham	1/ 17 6% - 2.00	: :	2 7% - 14.75	1 14% - 3.00	0 0% 0.00	0 0% - 1.00
WIKE D R Somerset	1/ 6 17% + 11.00	: :	1 25% + 17.00	0 0% 0.00	0 0% 0.00	0 0% 0.00
WILKINS R C Avon	2/ 4 50% + 1.01	: :	0 0% 0.00	0 0% 0.00	0 0% 0.00	0 0% 0.00
WILKINSON B E North Yorks	6/ 75 8% - 47.62	: :	5 6% - 62.18	8 12% + 8.23	5 7% - 41.00	7 11% - 24.44
WILKINSON M J Oxon	4/ 71 6% - 34.50	: :	3 4% - 36.00	2 2% - 96.50	4 4% - 72.58	6 6% - 21.25
WILLIAMS C N Suffolk	1/ 8 13% - 5.00	: :	0 0% - 3.00	0 0% - 11.00	0 0% - 3.00	0 0% - 3.00
WILLIAMS D L Berkshire	2/ 51 4% - 31.00	: :	0 0% - 5.00	5 5% - 65.21	1 1% - 57.00	4 5% + 7.00
WILLIAMS Mrs S D Somerset	2/ 28 7% - 20.50	: :	2 5% + 6.00	0 0% - 10.00	0 0% - 1.00	0 0% - 2.00
WILLIAMS W R Devon	1/ 32 3% - 28.75	: :	1 7% + 7.00	2 5% - 16.00	0 0% - 33.00	0 0% - 40.00

	1991/92 Wns Rns (%)	1990/91 : Wns (%)	1989/88 Wns (%)	1988/89 Wns (%)	1987/88 Wns (%)
WILLIS H Hampshire	1/ 31 3% + 20.00	1 4% : - 21.00	0 0% - 19.00	1 3% - 25.50	0 0% - 5.00
WILSON A J Gloucestershire	6/100 6% - 49.80	6 7% : - 15.00	8 8% - 26.58	3 3% - 85.75	10 10% - 20.68
WILSON Capt J H Lancashire	2/ 14 14% + 22.38	0 0% : - 12.00	0 0% 0.00	0 0% 0.00	0 0% 0.00
WILSON D A Surrey	2/ 29 7% 0.00	1 3% : - 11.00	2 7% - 18.00	2 5% - 20.50	3 6% - 25.75
WILTON Miss S J Staffordshire	8/106 8% - 50.25	4 5% : - 72.63	17 11% - 70.94	22 13% + 0.66	12 9% - 7.25
WINTLE D J Gloucestershire	5/108 5% - 71.33	4 5% : - 55.75	5 5% - 81.37	10 6% - 124.30	15 12% - 20.91
WONNACOTT Mrs J Devon	5/ 97 5% - 53.50	6 6% : - 81.02	16 16% - 0.56	0 0% - 19.00	3 8% - 17.37
WOODHOUSE R D E York	6/ 67 9% - 41.12	4 8% : - 17.00	4 6% - 46.43	4 11% - 12.15	5 6% - 44.50
WOODMAN S West Sussex	4/ 28 14% - 8.87	3 20% : + 12.50	2 6% - 5.75	1 3% - 33.50	0 0% - 63.00

14 . TRAINERS TO FOLLOW

Following particular trainers on selected occasions based on past performance can be a profitable system. Trainers have their methods, techniques and habits, and these are reflected in their results. Therefore statistical returns are not just a record, but an actual indication of how different stables operate, showing where and when they strike form.

The "Blue Chip" portfolio is not a staking plan because it would take far too much time to be a practical proposition. Rather, it sets out to see how a very rough-and-ready plan actually works, to get some idea of how a better thought-out portfolio might fare. Readers will be able to find many more interesting (and profitable) staking plans for themselves.

The first principle of the portfolio is that whether or not it makes a profit, it should perform better than indiscriminate following. Providing this is the case more often than not, then there is validity to the whole idea of a system based on statistical pointers.

The Blue Chip portfolio is so named because it takes the top five trainers of the previous year, and nominally invests £1 wherever one of the five's record over the past five years suggests greatest likelihood of profitability.

In his best selling book *Value Betting*, professional punter Mark Coton wrote that if asked to give a single piece of advice on how punters could make their betting more successful, he would offer the suggestion that they *"choose a stable to follow"*.

Mark goes on to qualify that broad statement, of course; he certainly doesn't advocate blindly following a chosen stable - the quickest way to the poor house, bar "doubling up" systems. Rather, he suggests that by following a stable closely one can learn a good deal about the way it operates - its strengths and weaknesses, the 'reliables' in the yard, the type of race it does well in, and so on. After a while, he says, you get to develop a feel for when, where and which horses are likely to go in - a valuable edge in the battle to beat the bookmaker.

It's a strategy which is the thinking behind the "Blue Chip" portfolio. As ever, though, it's not quite as simple as just listing the months, venues, race-types etc that our selected trainers do well in - if only it was!

With a fourth level stakes loss in as many years, the folly of even that strategy is cruely exposed. Perhaps "Blue Chip" is a misnomer for the portfolio; but then if we are being pedantic about these things, you would have to say that the categories selected are those which the five "don't do as badly in"!

Whichever way you choose to look at it, the fact remains that careful analysis of the breakdown of a stable's record, coupled with a developed "feel" for the way it operates, can reap dividends.

Our selected trainers and categories are not gospel by any means. Although making sorry reading in themselves, they are printed for what they are worth; and that worth is proven by the difference between the losses made by selective staking and that by staking blindly - the latter being far greater.

But just limiting losses is hardly a reason in itself to even consider this strategy. However, taking it one step further, and using it in conjunction with a developed feel for a stable's performance, *then* it is possible to give yourself the edge.

You can, of course, devise your own portfolio. *Backing Trainers*, published by Aesculus Press, is an excellent publication for doing so, listing as it does a full statistical breakdown of some 40 top stables.

So to last year's results:

M. PIPE

Runners	in November	+	10.28
	in April	−	6.87
Runners	Novice Hurdles	+	8.55
	Novice Chases	−	6.31
	in Sellers	−	37.09
Runners	at Bangor	−	9.83
	at Chepstow	+	12.73
	at Haydock	−	6.90
	at Leicester	−	7.24
	at Newton Abbot	−	15.39
	at Newbury	+	11.88
	at Uttoxeter	+	28.22
	at Wolverhampton	−	12.55
Portfolio	....	−	30.52
Stable	....	−	60.90
(Balance	....	+	30.38)

W. STEPHENSON

Runners	in Handicap Chases	−	12.94
	in Sellers	+	2.00
Portfolio	....	−	10.94
Stable	....	−	88.59
(Balance	....	+	77.65)

MRS G. REVELEY

Runners	in September	+	6.80
	in February	−	7.56
Runners	in Handicap Hurdles	−	7.22
	in Novice Chases	−	3.16
	in Handicap Chases	−	13.29

Runners	at Market Rasen	-	1.99
	at Sedgefield	+	0.40
Portfolio	....	-	26.02
Stable	....	-	0.88
(Balance	....	-	25.14)

G. RICHARDS

Runners	in July/August	-	11.75
Runners	at Ayr	-	2.77
	at Cartmel	-	7.38
	at Hexham	+	1.88
	at Kelso	+	19.31
	at Wetherby	-	6.42
Portfolio	....	-	7.13
Stable	....	-	90.01
(Balance	....	+	82.88)

J. GIFFORD

Runners	in September	-	0.37
	in October	-	16.85
Runners	at Ascot	-	17.25
	at Chepstow	-	5.62
	at Cheltenham	-	11.83
	at Fontwell	-	15.99
	at Warwick	+	0.20
Portfolio	....	-	67.71
Stable	....	-	150.20
(Balance	....	+	82.49)

TOTAL PORTFOLIO	-	**142.32**
TOTAL STABLE	-	**390.58**
BALANCE	+	**248.26**

Had you staked a pound on every Gordon Richards' runner throughout the 1991/92 season, your losses come June would have amounted to £90.01. However, limiting stakes to the categories in the portfolio would have reduced that loss to a mere £7.13. But by exercising the type of judgement expounded in the first part of this chapter, it would almost certainly have been possible to turn even that small loss into a profit - and with any sort of luck at all, a fairly worthwhile one.

Richards showed a very healthy level-stakes profit of £19.31 with his runners at Kelso throughout the season, while at Hexham a profit of £1.88 was made, a sum which could be added to a five-year overall profit of £17.39 at the Northumberland course

He was less successful than in previous years with his early season runners, showing a loss of £11.75 throughout July and August, but judicious evaluation of his overall portfolio would have meant a profitable year for followers of Gordon Richards.

Much the same could be said about Arthur Stephenson. An overall level-stakes loss of £88.59 - which in itself was an improvement for the yard compared to recent years - could be limited to just £10.94 by provident use of the portfolio, although that would have bets limited to runners in just two types of race: Handicap Chases and Sellers.

Not surprisingly, followers of Martin Pipe would have much more scope for laying a bet, given the number of options in his portfolio. November again proved a profitable month, with a £10.28 level-stakes profit boosting a £5.16 five-yearly total. Pipe's novice hurdlers complimented his training methods by showing a profit of £8.55 throughout the season. But sellers, once a modest source of success for the Wellington yard, proved a graveyard last season, showing a loss of £37.09.

But it is the courses at which Pipe traditionally does well which makes for the most interesting reading. Uttoxeter, probably because of its quality racing and relatively high prizemoney, is often a target for Pipe runners, and a profit of

£28.22 last season keeps the course ahead of the likes of Chepstow, Newbury and Haydock, other tracks where he also does well. Wolverhampton, a source of rich pickings in the past, returned a disappointing loss of £12.55 last season.

For followers of Josh Gifford, however, it was a case of "damage limitation". A whacking £150.20 overall loss from all his runners, was limited to under half that by using the portfolio. However, one shining star emerged in the shape of his N.H. Flat record, which showed a profit of £30.00 during 1991/92.

The biggest disappointment for the portfolio was in managing to turn a very creditable loss of 88p for Mary Reveley into one totalling £26.02. In a statistical record littered with level-stake profits, we managed to miss most of them. However, unlike yourself, we are obliged by the nature of things to bet blind. You, on the other hand, can be more selective - a strategy which we hope this chapter demonstrates.

This year four of the top five trainer are the same as last year, David Nicholson is the newcomer whilst Josh Gifford drops out. Here are the categories which seem to be the ones to concentrate on - according to their five year records! The criteria for selection remains the same as usual:- any level-stake profit of £10 or more over five years in any month or race type, or £15 profit at any course shown in *Backing Trainers*, is followed to a level-stake.

MONTH	RACE TYPE	COURSE

M PIPE

November	Novice Hurdles	Chepstow
April	Novice Chases	Haydock
May/June	Handicap Chases	Newbury
	Sellers	Uttoxeter
		Wolverhampton
		Worcester

W STEPHENSON

September   Newcastle
October

G REVELEY

September   Handicap Chases   Market Rasen
October   Sedgefield
December
February

G RICHARDS

April   Hexham
                                                      Kelso

D NICHOLSON

                   Novice Chases   Cheltenham
                   Sellers

As usual, we will give a full report on this portfolio next year.

Leading Trainers by Month 1991/92 :
July/August/September

			Total Wins	Runs	(	%	)	Hurdles Wins	Runs	Chases Wins	Runs	Stake
1	(2)	Pipe M C	:	30	73	(41.1)	16	51	14	22	- 8.45
2	(40)	Tinkler N	:	13	21	(61.9)	10	17	3	4	+ 17.69
3	(4)	Hobbs P J	:	13	38	(34.2)	5	22	8	16	- 0.60
4	(8)	White J	:	10	41	(24.4)	7	26	3	15	- 11.20
5	(64)	Hammond M D	:	9	23	(39.1)	8	22	1	1	+ 1.59
6	(1)	Richards G W	:	9	41	(22.0)	9	31	0	10	- 20.52
7	(14)	Forster Capt T A	:	7	16	(43.8)	3	8	4	8	+ 4.21
8	(3)	Stephenson W A	:	7	41	(17.1)	5	19	2	22	- 8.23
9	(26)	Baker J H	:	6	9	(66.7)	3	5	3	4	+ 11.93
10	(--)	O'Sullivan R J	:	6	10	(60.0)	5	7	1	3	+ 14.11
11	(--)	Easterby M H	:	6	14	(42.9)	4	12	2	2	+ 15.83
12	(10)	Upson John R	:	6	23	(26.1)	3	6	3	17	- 8.21
13	(--)	Ryan M J	:	5	12	(41.7)	2	8	3	4	+ 1.42
14	(32)	Juckes R T	:	5	26	(19.2)	5	24	0	2	- 10.12
15	(62)	Smith Denys	:	5	28	(17.9)	2	21	3	7	- 9.40
16	(73)	Kettlewell S E	:	4	8	(50.0)	3	7	1	1	+ 8.57
17	(--)	Perratt Miss L A	:	4	8	(50.0)	2	4	2	4	+ 0.13
18	(49)	Moffatt D	:	4	9	(44.4)	2	7	2	2	+ 5.99
19	(--)	O'Shea J G M	:	4	10	(40.0)	2	7	2	3	+ 1.06
20	(--)	Gandolfo D R	:	4	14	(28.6)	3	11	1	3	+ 12.81

Leading Trainers by Month 1987-92 :
July/August/September

			Total Wins	Runs	(	%	)	Hurdles Wins	Runs	Chases Wins	Runs	Stake
1		Pipe M C	:	153	372	(41.1)	95	276	58	96	- 19.58
2		Stephenson W A	:	61	270	(22.6)	45	157	16	113	+ 4.88
3		Richards G W	:	58	188	(30.9)	42	128	16	60	+ 2.34
4		Hobbs P J	:	39	148	(26.4)	24	95	15	53	+ 2.09
5		Tinkler N	:	32	103	(31.1)	23	90	9	13	- 8.09
6		Reveley Mrs G R	:	32	118	(27.1)	17	88	15	30	+ 11.83
7		White J	:	31	108	(28.7)	25	72	6	36	- 11.79
8		Jenkins J R	:	26	159	(16.4)	12	121	14	38	- 29.78
9		Smith Denys	:	24	128	(18.8)	13	93	11	35	- 38.45
10		Baker J H	:	23	79	(29.1)	14	62	9	17	+ 36.09
11		Moore G M	:	23	107	(21.5)	14	87	9	20	- 19.15
12		O'Neill J J	:	20	83	(24.1)	15	67	5	16	- 15.38
13		Bradley J M	:	19	129	(14.7)	14	72	5	57	- 25.41
14		Forster Capt T A	:	18	50	(36.0)	11	24	7	26	+ 17.82
15		Holder R J	:	18	83	(21.7)	11	66	7	17	- 12.82
16		FitzGerald J G	:	17	53	(32.1)	9	36	8	17	- 3.89
17		O'Sullivan R J	:	17	59	(28.8)	11	41	6	18	+ 25.86
18		Balding G B	:	17	90	(18.9)	10	62	7	28	- 5.59
19		Gandolfo D R	:	16	94	(17.0)	14	62	2	32	- 23.65
20		Clay W	:	16	128	(12.5)	5	92	11	36	+ 30.89

Leading Trainers by Month 1991/92 : October

			Total Wins	Runs	(	%	)	Hurdles Wins	Runs	Chases Wins	Runs	Stake
1	(2)	Pipe M C	:	21	57	(36.8)	12	40	9	17	- 0.64
2	(10)	Reveley Mrs G R	:	16	33	(48.5)	8	18	8	15	+ 13.95
3	(1)	Stephenson W A	:	16	45	(35.6)	9	23	7	22	+ 21.18
4	(11)	Moore G M	:	7	14	(50.0)	5	11	2	3	+ 9.38
5	(13)	Balding G B	:	6	28	(21.4)	4	18	2	10	- 7.09
6	(6)	Richards G W	:	6	29	(20.7)	3	9	3	20	- 15.01
7	(9)	Gifford J T	:	6	32	(18.8)	1	15	5	17	- 16.85
8	(--)	Bailey K C	:	5	15	(33.3)	5	11	0	4	+ 3.87
9	(8)	Nicholson D	:	5	17	(29.4)	1	3	4	14	- 0.02
10	(--)	Forster Capt T A	:	5	18	(27.8)	2	6	3	12	+ 12.23
11	(20)	Twiston-Davies N	:	5	21	(23.8)	4	12	1	9	- 3.34
12	(--)	Lee R	:	4	7	(57.1)	4	7	0	0	+ 7.50
13	(--)	Monteith P	:	4	10	(40.0)	1	6	3	4	- 2.76
14	(92)	Tompkins M H	:	4	12	(33.3)	3	11	1	1	- 0.63
15	(--)	Tinkler N	:	4	13	(30.8)	2	11	2	2	- 3.38
16	(--)	Gandolfo D R	:	4	18	(22.2)	1	6	3	12	+ 19.50
17	(17)	Hobbs P J	:	4	21	(19.1)	4	15	0	6	- 14.77
18	(5)	Hammond M D	:	4	23	(17.4)	1	17	3	6	- 2.83
19	(--)	Balding I A	:	3	3	(100.0)	3	3	0	0	+ 1.36
20	(36)	Harwood G	:	3	4	(75.0)	2	2	1	2	+ 7.00

Leading Trainers by Month 1987-92 : October

		Total Wins	Runs	(	%	)	Hurdles Wins	Runs	Chases Wins	Runs	Stake
1	Pipe M C	:	77	228	(33.8)	37	160	40	68	- 30.65
2	Stephenson W A	:	71	267	(26.6)	48	158	23	109	+ 25.83
3	Reveley Mrs G R	:	37	131	(28.2)	16	77	21	54	+ 25.85
4	Gifford J T	:	37	176	(21.0)	17	90	20	86	- 8.96
5	Moore G M	:	33	87	(37.9)	20	67	13	20	+ 10.48
6	Barons D H	:	32	151	(21.2)	16	79	16	72	+ 42.80
7	Richards G W	:	28	160	(17.5)	16	77	12	83	- 54.45
8	Hobbs P J	:	22	143	(15.4)	17	95	5	48	- 0.62
9	Balding G B	:	21	143	(14.7)	13	96	8	47	- 27.17
10	FitzGerald J G	:	19	63	(30.2)	12	40	7	23	+ 3.08
11	Nicholson D	:	19	94	(20.2)	7	41	12	53	+ 0.44
12	Edwards J A C	:	19	95	(20.0)	10	48	9	47	+ 39.86
13	Lee R	:	17	55	(30.9)	12	33	5	22	+ 65.21
14	Frost R G	:	17	97	(17.5)	9	63	8	34	- 6.10
15	Easterby M H	:	16	95	(16.8)	7	57	9	38	- 27.64
16	Brooks C P E	:	15	62	(24.2)	7	26	8	36	- 9.92
17	O'Neill J J	:	15	65	(23.1)	8	41	7	24	- 14.26
18	Hammond M D	:	13	48	(27.1)	7	35	6	13	+ 5.20
19	Sherwood O	:	13	67	(19.4)	5	33	8	34	- 22.29
20	Forster Capt T A	:	13	92	(14.1)	9	41	4	51	- 26.52

Leading Trainers by Month 1991/92 : November

			Total Wins	Runs	(%)	Hurdles Wins	Runs	Chases Wins	Runs	Stake
1	(1)	Pipe M C	:	27	101	(26.7)	15	70	12	31	+ 10.28
2	(5)	Richards G W	:	16	81	(19.8)	10	38	6	43	- 3.61
3	(16)	Reveley Mrs G R	:	14	66	(21.2)	7	40	7	26	- 26.60
4	(3)	Gifford J T	:	14	89	(15.7)	10	44	4	45	- 25.78
5	(11)	FitzGerald J G	:	13	55	(23.6)	10	46	3	9	+ 29.35
6	(8)	Stephenson W A	:	13	79	(16.5)	6	36	7	43	- 21.93
7	(10)	Balding G B	:	12	65	(18.5)	7	38	5	27	+ 26.09
8	(2)	Nicholson D	:	11	61	(18.0)	4	27	7	34	- 2.43
9	(7)	Edwards J A C	:	10	32	(31.3)	6	18	4	14	+ 35.54
10	(4)	Sherwood O	:	10	43	(23.3)	6	20	4	23	+ 0.25
11	(--)	Twiston-Davies N	:	10	45	(22.2)	6	23	4	22	- 0.64
12	(13)	Moore G M	:	9	38	(23.7)	5	24	4	14	+ 5.93
13	(6)	Easterby M H	:	9	40	(22.5)	4	26	5	14	- 3.66
14	(74)	Pitman Mrs J	:	8	52	(15.4)	4	41	4	11	+ 17.10
15	(14)	Gaselee N A	:	7	21	(33.3)	1	10	6	11	+ 0.87
16	(9)	Henderson N J	:	7	31	(22.6)	3	16	4	15	- 13.54
17	(12)	Forster Capt T A	:	7	48	(14.6)	3	21	4	27	- 19.04
18	(--)	McCain D	:	6	17	(35.3)	1	6	5	11	+ 27.86
19	(25)	Holder R J	:	6	50	(12.0)	6	40	0	10	- 14.63
20	(--)	Etherington T J	:	5	12	(41.7)	4	10	1	2	+ 71.75

Leading Trainers by Month 1987-92 : November

		Total Wins	Runs	(%)	Hurdles Wins	Runs	Chases Wins	Runs	Stake
1	Pipe M C	:	111	324	(34.3)	62	220	49	104	+ 42.63
2	Richards G W	:	75	351	(21.4)	50	179	25	172	- 25.81
3	Gifford J T	:	66	325	(20.3)	34	166	32	159	- 11.03
4	Stephenson W A	:	60	346	(17.3)	37	180	23	166	- 77.75
5	Nicholson D	:	57	274	(20.8)	32	140	25	134	- 29.77
6	Easterby M H	:	51	195	(26.2)	24	124	27	71	- 20.20
7	Sherwood O	:	49	198	(24.8)	25	105	24	93	- 0.07
8	FitzGerald J G	:	42	191	(22.0)	30	128	12	63	+ 39.03
9	Edwards J A C	:	42	217	(19.4)	23	116	19	101	+ 17.14
10	Balding G B	:	40	259	(15.4)	22	157	18	102	- 54.41
11	Moore G M	:	37	180	(20.6)	14	117	23	63	- 10.91
12	Forster Capt T A	:	31	175	(17.7)	15	80	16	95	- 17.37
13	Gaselee N A	:	30	94	(31.9)	14	51	16	43	+ 71.26
14	Reveley Mrs G R	:	30	161	(18.6)	13	98	17	63	- 39.18
15	Brooks C P E	:	29	130	(22.3)	12	67	17	63	- 37.55
16	Henderson N J	:	29	146	(19.9)	16	91	13	55	- 59.73
17	Tinkler N	:	28	123	(22.8)	16	106	12	17	- 24.70
18	Elsworth D R C	:	25	132	(18.9)	13	100	12	32	- 56.70
19	Akehurst R	:	23	125	(18.4)	10	98	13	27	- 19.11
20	Barons D H	:	22	174	(12.6)	14	110	8	64	- 59.82

Leading Trainers by Month 1991/92 : December

		Total Wins	Runs	(%)	Hurdles Wins	Runs	Chases Wins	Runs	Stake
1 (3)	Reveley Mrs G R	17	42	(40.5)	11	31	6	11	+ 33.24
2 (22)	Nicholson D	15	55	(27.3)	9	25	6	30	- 5.82
3 (1)	Pipe M C	15	72	(20.8)	11	48	4	24	- 23.39
4 (27)	Stephenson W A	12	62	(19.4)	3	27	9	35	+ 10.12
5 (26)	Sherwood O	10	33	(30.3)	9	20	1	13	- 4.71
6 (21)	Pitman Mrs J	10	49	(20.4)	3	28	7	21	- 21.14
7 (4)	Henderson N J	9	30	(30.0)	8	20	1	10	+ 0.15
8 (15)	Balding G B	8	53	(15.1)	5	25	3	28	- 6.88
9 (70)	Hobbs P J	6	28	(21.4)	1	10	5	18	+ 16.00
10 (19)	Elsworth D R C	6	30	(20.0)	1	20	5	10	+ 12.88
11 (6)	Edwards J A C	6	31	(19.4)	1	9	5	22	- 2.27
12 (--)	White J	5	19	(26.3)	3	17	2	2	- 3.87
13 (25)	O'Neill J J	5	26	(19.2)	3	13	2	13	+ 10.25
14 (18)	Hammond M D	5	34	(14.7)	1	22	4	12	- 10.33
15 (2)	Richards G W	5	46	(10.9)	2	19	3	27	- 27.39
16 (8)	Gifford J T	5	49	(10.2)	4	25	1	24	- 22.83
17 (33)	Christian S	4	9	(44.4)	3	7	1	2	+ 4.00
18 (55)	Retter Mrs J G	4	13	(30.8)	2	9	2	4	+ 51.75
19 (60)	Easterby M W	4	15	(26.7)	1	8	3	7	+ 27.50
20 (10)	Tinkler N	4	16	(25.0)	4	15	0	1	+ 11.00

Leading Trainers by Month 1987-92 : December

		Total Wins	Runs	(%)	Hurdles Wins	Runs	Chases Wins	Runs	Stake
1	Pipe M C	106	353	(30.0)	61	225	45	128	- 25.63
2	Pitman Mrs J	63	281	(22.4)	35	184	28	97	+ 67.14
3	Gifford J T	55	341	(16.1)	32	183	23	158	- 25.07
4	Richards G W	50	269	(18.6)	34	136	16	133	-109.46
5	FitzGerald J G	48	232	(20.7)	31	145	17	87	- 46.09
6	Nicholson D	43	257	(16.7)	25	131	18	126	- 55.07
7	Reveley Mrs G R	41	156	(26.3)	21	109	20	47	+ 35.22
8	Sherwood O	39	206	(18.9)	24	127	15	79	- 68.75
9	Edwards J A C	39	240	(16.3)	24	132	15	108	- 56.77
10	Henderson N J	37	155	(23.9)	24	85	13	70	+ 16.96
11	Stephenson W A	37	301	(12.3)	18	136	19	165	-120.27
12	Balding G B	34	279	(12.2)	20	163	14	116	-109.94
13	Tinkler N	31	130	(23.9)	18	108	13	22	+ 2.75
14	Barons D H	28	217	(12.9)	22	132	6	85	- 63.98
15	Easterby M H	27	169	(16.0)	16	108	11	61	- 94.31
16	Elsworth D R C	27	180	(15.0)	13	124	14	56	- 13.69
17	Forster Capt T A	26	189	(13.8)	17	82	9	107	- 37.44
18	Akehurst R	24	153	(15.7)	9	120	15	33	- 7.16
19	Moore G M	21	156	(13.5)	9	108	12	48	- 54.66
20	Brooks C P E	19	116	(16.4)	8	64	11	52	- 31.25

Leading Trainers by Month 1991/92 : January

		Total Wins	Runs	(%)	Hurdles Wins	Runs	Chases Wins	Runs	Stake
1	(1) Pipe M C	: 18	94	(19.2)	13	69	5	25	- 39.91
2	(2) Reveley Mrs G R	: 12	39	(30.8)	6	20	6	19	- 6.14
3	(--) Dow S	: 11	19	(57.9)	9	17	2	2	+ 24.11
4	(24) Pitman Mrs J	: 10	49	(20.4)	7	30	3	19	- 20.30
5	(--) Sanders Miss B	: 9	27	(33.3)	6	23	3	4	+ 4.52
6	(11) Nicholson D	: 9	43	(20.9)	7	21	2	22	- 3.56
7	(10) Richards G W	: 9	53	(17.0)	6	32	3	21	+ 8.10
8	(14) Brooks C P E	: 6	22	(27.3)	3	13	3	9	+ 0.25
9	(--) Tinkler N	: 6	24	(25.0)	3	19	3	5	+ 1.68
10	(15) Elsworth D R C	: 6	30	(20.0)	4	19	2	11	- 2.75
11	(3) Sherwood O	: 6	32	(18.8)	3	17	3	15	- 20.13
12	(25) Forster Capt T A	: 6	36	(16.7)	3	15	3	21	+ 32.75
13	(19) Easterby M W	: 5	11	(45.5)	3	4	2	7	+ 9.12
14	(35) White J	: 5	18	(27.8)	5	14	0	4	+ 4.75
15	(23) Henderson N J	: 5	25	(20.0)	3	10	2	15	- 1.60
16	(5) Mellor S	: 5	30	(16.7)	5	19	0	11	+ 6.83
17	(--) Johnson J H	: 4	12	(33.3)	2	8	2	4	+ 30.00
18	(33) Old J A B	: 4	13	(30.8)	3	9	1	4	+ 16.38
19	(20) Jones T Thomson	: 4	13	(30.8)	2	9	2	4	+ 2.16
20	(--) Moore J S	: 4	15	(26.7)	2	13	2	2	- 1.75

Leading Trainers by Month 1987-92 : January

		Total Wins	Runs	(%)	Hurdles Wins	Runs	Chases Wins	Runs	Stake
1	Pipe M C	: 91	374	(24.3)	57	259	34	115	- 33.93
2	Pitman Mrs J	: 51	219	(23.3)	29	139	22	80	- 31.91
3	Gifford J T	: 39	248	(15.7)	16	118	23	130	- 31.19
4	Richards G W	: 37	188	(19.7)	26	103	11	85	- 11.09
5	Elsworth D R C	: 36	163	(22.1)	22	113	14	50	+ 18.81
6	Sherwood O	: 36	186	(19.4)	19	116	17	70	+ 13.38
7	FitzGerald J G	: 35	167	(21.0)	20	109	15	58	- 39.08
8	Moore G M	: 32	161	(19.9)	15	102	17	59	- 26.70
9	Stephenson W A	: 32	268	(11.9)	22	135	10	133	-126.58
10	Reveley Mrs G R	: 30	126	(23.8)	15	79	15	47	- 7.82
11	Henderson N J	: 29	183	(15.9)	16	103	13	80	- 48.91
12	Nicholson D	: 28	209	(13.4)	19	108	9	101	- 63.06
13	Forster Capt T A	: 26	191	(13.6)	16	78	10	113	- 34.27
14	Balding G B	: 26	238	(10.9)	15	139	11	99	-101.45
15	Jenkins J R	: 25	170	(14.7)	20	145	5	25	- 12.82
16	O'Neill J J	: 24	125	(19.2)	12	86	12	39	- 11.91
17	Edwards J A C	: 24	184	(13.0)	12	82	12	102	- 32.90
18	Tinkler N	: 23	126	(18.3)	11	106	12	20	- 2.68
19	Brooks C P E	: 22	111	(19.8)	13	68	9	43	- 21.62
20	Mellor S	: 21	118	(17.8)	11	66	10	52	- 8.56

Leading Trainers by Month 1991/92 : February

			Total Wins	Runs	(%)	Hurdles Wins	Runs	Chases Wins	Runs	Stake
1	(1)	Pipe M C	:	29	129	(22.5)	20	88	9	41	- 27.52
2	(8)	Henderson N J	:	12	49	(24.5)	7	30	5	19	+ 3.47
3	(13)	Reveley Mrs G R	:	10	43	(23.3)	8	27	2	16	- 7.56
4	(2)	Pitman Mrs J	:	10	60	(16.7)	6	38	4	22	+ 4.01
5	(18)	Jones T Thomson	:	9	27	(33.3)	8	23	1	4	+ 13.26
6	(15)	Sherwood O	:	9	41	(22.0)	5	24	4	17	- 11.65
7	(39)	Balding G B	:	9	49	(18.4)	5	26	4	23	+ 28.32
8	(3)	Gifford J T	:	9	64	(14.1)	5	40	4	24	- 14.54
9	(--)	Holder R J	:	8	40	(20.0)	5	29	3	11	- 8.30
10	(9)	Nicholson D	:	8	64	(12.5)	7	32	1	32	- 18.29
11	(--)	Easterby M H	:	6	29	(20.7)	5	19	1	10	- 11.95
12	(40)	Barons D H	:	6	31	(19.4)	3	18	3	13	+ 3.50
13	(6)	Richards G W	:	6	45	(13.3)	4	22	2	23	- 19.44
14	(86)	Dow S	:	5	19	(26.3)	2	16	3	3	- 4.00
15	(--)	White J	:	5	24	(20.8)	2	15	3	9	+ 3.56
16	(11)	Brooks C P E	:	5	29	(17.2)	3	17	2	12	- 1.62
17	(--)	Murphy F	:	5	31	(16.1)	4	9	1	22	- 0.50
18	(--)	Trietline C C	:	5	33	(15.2)	4	20	1	13	+ 11.33
19	(41)	Moore G M	:	5	42	(11.9)	2	25	3	17	- 16.15
20	(--)	Kelleway P A	:	4	8	(50.0)	1	5	3	3	+ 6.89

Leading Trainers by Month 1987-92 : February

		Total Wins	Runs	(%)	Hurdles Wins	Runs	Chases Wins	Runs	Stake
1	Pipe M C	:	89	364	(24.5)	49	250	40	114	- 44.41
2	Pitman Mrs J	:	63	230	(27.4)	31	141	32	89	+ 16.70
3	Gifford J T	:	36	284	(12.7)	22	163	14	121	-119.14
4	Henderson N J	:	35	176	(19.9)	20	116	15	60	+ 22.08
5	Elsworth D R C	:	31	167	(18.6)	20	126	11	41	- 26.20
6	FitzGerald J G	:	30	167	(18.0)	19	114	11	53	- 39.12
7	Sherwood O	:	30	183	(16.4)	20	113	10	70	- 57.34
8	Balding G B	:	27	207	(13.0)	15	117	12	90	- 40.29
9	Nicholson D	:	26	218	(11.9)	18	117	8	101	- 83.80
10	Richards G W	:	25	174	(14.4)	13	93	12	81	- 81.81
11	Edwards J A C	:	24	187	(12.8)	14	100	10	87	- 93.84
12	Reveley Mrs G R	:	23	108	(21.3)	14	65	9	43	+ 14.44
13	Akehurst R	:	23	115	(20.0)	12	91	11	24	+ 70.56
14	Moore G M	:	20	154	(13.0)	9	102	11	52	- 78.26
15	Brooks C P E	:	17	97	(17.5)	6	40	11	57	- 27.93
16	Stephenson W A	:	17	230	(7.4)	10	111	7	119	-150.77
17	Jones T Thomson	:	16	53	(30.2)	13	42	3	11	+ 7.02
18	Easterby M H	:	16	83	(19.3)	9	49	7	34	- 19.57
19	Mellor S	:	16	92	(17.4)	6	48	10	44	+ 15.49
20	Lee R	:	16	118	(13.6)	10	57	6	61	- 1.62

Leading Trainers by Month 1991/92 : March

			Total				Hurdles		Chases			
			Wins	Runs	(	%)	Wins	Runs	Wins	Runs		Stake
1	(1)	Pipe M C	:	28	117	(23.9)	12	78	16	39	-	5.09
2	(12)	Henderson N J	:	10	52	(19.2)	6	38	4	14	-	5.98
3	(28)	Stephenson W A	:	8	42	(19.1)	7	22	1	20	+	3.23
4	(17)	Nicholson D	:	8	48	(16.7)	3	21	5	27	-	7.74
5	(72)	Brooks C P E	:	7	23	(30.4)	4	12	3	11	+	1.89
6	(5)	Sherwood O	:	7	29	(24.1)	4	17	3	12	-	2.46
7	(4)	Edwards J A C	:	7	39	(18.0)	3	16	4	23	+	0.80
8	(32)	Easterby M H	:	6	21	(28.6)	6	16	0	5	+	2.88
9	(10)	Barons D H	:	6	27	(22.2)	1	15	5	12	+	15.75
10	(6)	Forster Capt T A	:	6	42	(14.3)	2	18	4	24	-	7.37
11	(7)	Gifford J T	:	6	51	(11.8)	4	30	2	21	-	8.21
12	(71)	Hobbs P J	:	5	24	(20.8)	2	11	3	13	+	14.80
13	(61)	Jenkins J R	:	5	27	(18.5)	4	16	1	11	+	2.50
14	(16)	Twiston-Davies N	:	5	36	(13.9)	5	23	0	13	+	29.33
15	(2)	Richards G W	:	5	41	(12.2)	4	22	1	19	-	13.92
16	(--)	Dow S	:	4	7	(57.1)	2	5	2	2	+	17.98
17	(--)	Saunders Miss C	:	4	9	(44.4)	3	3	1	6	+	26.25
18	(--)	Price R J	:	4	12	(33.3)	3	11	1	1	+	7.80
19	(21)	Old J A B	:	4	13	(30.8)	3	11	1	2	+	23.50
20	(45)	Lungo L	:	4	13	(30.8)	1	10	3	3	-	0.02

Leading Trainers by Month 1987-92 : March

			Total				Hurdles		Chases			
			Wins	Runs	(	%)	Wins	Runs	Wins	Runs		Stake
1	Pipe M C	:	119	469	(25.4)	69	324	50	145	+	6.42	
2	Richards G W	:	50	265	(18.9)	32	163	18	102	-	31.89	
3	Edwards J A C	:	45	235	(19.2)	25	119	20	116	+	42.93	
4	Sherwood O	:	44	185	(23.8)	21	115	23	70	+	36.48	
5	Stephenson W A	:	43	265	(16.2)	31	124	12	141	-	58.61	
6	Pitman Mrs J	:	39	260	(15.0)	22	168	17	92	-	46.82	
7	Henderson N J	:	36	225	(16.0)	19	151	17	74	-	54.07	
8	Gifford J T	:	33	305	(10.8)	18	165	15	140	-	46.52	
9	Nicholson D	:	31	206	(15.1)	14	99	17	107	-	24.83	
10	Forster Capt T A	:	28	209	(13.4)	17	80	11	129	+	57.93	
11	Balding G B	:	28	286	(9.8)	12	168	16	118	-	40.69	
12	Barons D H	:	27	188	(14.4)	8	100	19	88	+	67.19	
13	Brooks C P E	:	22	100	(22.0)	11	45	11	55	-	34.27	
14	Moore G M	:	21	139	(15.1)	11	90	10	49	-	40.97	
15	Easterby M H	:	20	101	(19.8)	14	63	6	38	-	2.09	
16	Reveley Mrs G R	:	19	93	(20.4)	9	52	10	41	-	10.31	
17	Mellor S	:	19	105	(18.1)	9	52	10	53	-	12.75	
18	Akehurst S	:	18	115	(15.7)	9	84	9	31	-	7.96	
19	Elsworth D R C	:	18	170	(10.6)	13	120	5	50	-	45.97	
20	Hobbs P J	:	16	154	(10.4)	8	95	8	59	-	4.65	

Leading Trainers by Month 1991/92 : April

			Total Wins	Runs	(%)	Hurdles Wins	Runs	Chases Wins	Runs	Stake
1	(1)	Pipe M C :	20	92	(21.7)	11	63	9	29	- 6.87
2	(--)	Reveley Mrs G R :	15	38	(39.5)	7	19	8	19	+ 4.79
3	(6)	Stephenson W A :	13	90	(14.4)	4	45	9	45	- 33.71
4	(9)	Bailey K C :	9	33	(27.3)	2	15	7	18	+ 80.75
5	(17)	Hobbs P J :	7	32	(21.9)	3	16	4	16	+ 1.20
6	(10)	Pitman Mrs J :	7	52	(13.5)	4	34	3	18	- 5.25
7	(--)	Upson John R :	6	19	(31.6)	4	9	2	10	+ 22.50
8	(26)	Barons D H :	6	39	(15.4)	3	27	3	12	- 3.47
9	(2)	Richards G W :	6	51	(11.8)	3	25	3	26	+ 11.41
10	(19)	Monteith P :	5	15	(33.3)	2	8	3	7	+ 7.25
11	(55)	Hodges R J :	5	17	(29.4)	5	10	0	7	+ 0.76
12	(60)	Dickin R :	5	26	(19.2)	4	15	1	11	+ 3.50
13	(7)	Forster Capt T A :	5	28	(17.9)	2	8	3	20	- 1.00
14	(32)	Nicholson D :	5	29	(17.2)	4	16	1	13	+ 2.54
15	(5)	Balding G B :	5	43	(11.6)	2	26	3	17	- 21.27
16	(--)	Old J A B :	4	11	(36.4)	2	9	2	2	+ 15.38
17	(--)	Bevan P J :	4	13	(30.8)	2	7	2	6	+ 22.50
18	(--)	Perratt Miss L A :	4	20	(20.0)	4	20	0	0	+ 4.00
19	(--)	Johnson J H :	4	21	(19.1)	3	12	1	9	+ 2.83
20	(31)	Henderson N J :	4	37	(10.8)	3	27	1	10	- 24.55

Leading Trainers by Month 1987-92 : April

		Total Wins	Runs	(%)	Hurdles Wins	Runs	Chases Wins	Runs	Stake
1	Pipe M C :	108	380	(28.4)	55	240	53	140	+ 30.61
2	Stephenson W A :	50	380	(13.2)	24	165	26	215	-149.41
3	Richards G W :	47	270	(17.4)	26	139	21	131	+ 36.19
4	Edwards J A C :	43	293	(14.7)	22	154	21	139	- 68.18
5	Balding G B :	34	230	(14.8)	15	144	19	86	- 52.15
6	Pitman Mrs J :	31	215	(14.4)	16	129	15	86	- 8.60
7	Bailey K C :	29	162	(17.9)	13	102	16	60	+ 64.40
8	Sherwood O :	29	179	(16.2)	13	115	16	64	+ 0.71
9	Henderson N J :	27	200	(13.5)	14	129	13	71	- 30.29
10	Hobbs P J :	25	166	(15.1)	14	105	11	61	- 12.18
11	Nicholson D :	25	179	(14.0)	16	87	9	92	- 41.29
12	Gifford J T :	25	228	(11.0)	12	114	13	114	- 77.99
13	FitzGerald J G :	24	99	(24.2)	14	59	10	40	+ 43.46
14	Reveley Mrs G R :	20	104	(19.2)	11	71	9	33	- 37.96
15	Barons D H :	20	154	(13.0)	12	97	8	57	+ 17.24
16	Moore G M :	17	126	(13.5)	12	85	5	41	- 39.00
17	Tinkler N :	16	66	(24.2)	8	52	8	14	- 19.97
18	Turnell Andrew :	15	79	(19.0)	5	45	10	34	- 21.47
19	Forster Capt T A :	15	95	(15.8)	7	34	8	61	+ 0.75
20	O'Neill J J :	15	97	(15.5)	10	73	5	24	+ 27.74

Leading Trainers by Month 1991/92 : May/June

		Total				Hurdles		Chases		
		Wins	Runs	(	%)	Wins	Runs	Wins	Runs	Stake
1	(1) Pipe M C	:	36	104	(34.6)	23	87	13	17	+ 40.69
2	(2) Stephenson W A	:	26	72	(36.1)	10	34	16	38	+ 28.70
3	(44) Reveley Mrs G R	:	9	33	(27.3)	4	19	5	14	- 5.79
4	(--) Hammond M D	:	6	13	(46.2)	5	12	1	1	+ 14.28
5	(18) Edwards J A C	:	6	27	(22.2)	4	16	2	11	- 3.95
6	(29) Balding G B	:	6	30	(20.0)	3	18	3	12	- 6.30
7	(--) Easterby M H	:	5	11	(45.5)	2	6	3	5	+ 2.23
8	(--) Bentley W	:	5	12	(41.7)	2	9	3	3	+ 16.63
9	(3) Richards G W	:	5	22	(22.7)	3	12	2	10	- 9.63
10	(5) Bailey K C	:	5	31	(16.1)	2	13	3	18	- 6.99
11	(90) Easterby M W	:	4	8	(50.0)	3	6	1	2	+ 6.80
12	(25) Retter Mrs J G	:	4	10	(40.0)	2	7	2	3	+ 34.13
13	(45) Chapman M C	:	4	14	(28.6)	3	10	1	4	+ 17.50
14	(22) Hobbs P J	:	4	16	(25.0)	4	11	0	5	+ 4.66
15	(--) White J	:	4	21	(19.1)	4	14	0	7	- 5.08
16	(46) Hewitt Mrs A R	:	3	6	(50.0)	1	4	2	2	+ 25.38
17	(50) Harwood G	:	3	6	(50.0)	0	2	3	4	+ 11.13
18	(52) Christian S	:	3	12	(25.0)	2	8	1	4	+ 9.60
19	(48) O'Neill J J	:	3	16	(18.8)	2	9	1	7	- 3.87
20	(4) Henderson N J	:	3	18	(16.7)	2	12	1	6	- 14.21

Leading Trainers by Month 1987-92 : May/June

		Total				Hurdles		Chases		
		Wins	Runs	(	%)	Wins	Runs	Wins	Runs	Stake
1	Pipe M C	:	161	473	(34.0)	99	354	62	119	+ 44.34
2	Stephenson W A	:	112	390	(28.7)	62	197	50	193	- 45.07
3	Richards G W	:	34	126	(27.0)	14	70	20	56	- 12.67
4	Edwards J A C	:	33	156	(21.2)	16	81	17	75	+ 12.68
5	Tinkler N	:	25	68	(36.8)	18	56	7	12	- 9.64
6	Henderson N J	:	25	104	(24.0)	13	58	12	46	+ 14.49
7	Bailey K C	:	20	108	(18.5)	9	63	11	45	- 29.58
8	Moore G M	:	17	77	(22.1)	10	59	7	18	- 25.42
9	Gifford J T	:	17	84	(20.2)	9	50	8	34	- 1.07
10	Holder R J	:	15	62	(24.2)	7	43	8	19	+ 48.46
11	Reveley Mrs G R	:	15	71	(21.1)	6	42	9	29	- 16.22
12	Balding G B	:	15	86	(17.4)	7	57	8	29	+ 12.44
13	Morgan K A	:	15	96	(15.6)	4	71	11	25	- 11.06
14	Brennan O	:	15	105	(14.3)	8	81	7	24	+ 1.09
15	FitzGerald J G	:	14	32	(43.8)	10	21	4	11	+ 17.83
16	Casey T	:	14	73	(19.2)	6	51	8	22	- 6.93
17	Gaselee N A	:	13	65	(20.0)	8	28	5	37	- 1.88
18	O'Neill J J	:	13	71	(18.3)	9	46	4	25	- 23.45
19	Hobbs P J	:	13	83	(15.7)	9	50	4	33	- 7.93
20	Bradley J M	:	13	100	(13.0)	12	57	1	43	+ 43.08

Leading Trainers in order of Winning Favourites 1991/92

				No.of Favs	(%)	Wns	No of Favs	(%)	%Wng Favs	Stake
1	(1)	Pipe M C	: 839	336	(40.1)	224	152	(67.9)	45.2	- 15.67
2	(7)	Reveley Mrs G R	: 323	136	(42.1)	99	66	(66.7)	48.5	+ 14.25
3	(3)	Stephenson W A	: 539	111	(20.6)	101	45	(44.6)	40.5	- 11.74
4	(5)	Nicholson D	: 329	82	(24.9)	63	39	(61.9)	47.6	+ 12.97
5	(2)	Richards G W	: 409	92	(22.5)	67	31	(46.3)	33.7	- 23.52
6	(14)	Henderson N J	: 251	77	(30.7)	52	30	(57.7)	39.0	- 10.81
7	(11)	Sherwood O	: 227	62	(27.3)	48	28	(58.3)	45.2	+ 3.35
8	(16)	Hobbs P J	: 283	47	(16.6)	51	27	(52.9)	57.5	+ 19.01
9	(12)	Pitman Mrs J	: 333	73	(21.9)	50	26	(52.0)	35.6	- 12.67
10	(21)	Tinkler N	: 163	55	(33.7)	38	25	(65.8)	45.5	+ 2.49
11	(15)	Easterby M H	: 203	58	(28.6)	42	25	(59.5)	43.1	+ 1.02
12	(6)	Balding G B	: 368	69	(18.8)	53	25	(47.2)	36.2	- 6.00
13	(9)	Gifford J T	: 389	56	(14.4)	49	22	(44.9)	39.3	- 6.64
14	(19)	Bailey K C	: 250	40	(16.0)	38	19	(50.0)	47.5	+ 8.34
15	(4)	Edwards J A C	: 260	50	(19.2)	39	19	(48.7)	38.0	- 2.05
16	(48)	White J	: 183	36	(19.7)	39	18	(46.2)	50.0	+ 9.35
17	(17)	Forster Capt T A	: 273	49	(18.0)	44	17	(38.6)	34.7	+ 1.71
18	(8)	Moore G M	: 240	50	(20.8)	38	16	(42.1)	32.0	- 15.61
19	(20)	Brooks C P E	: 169	38	(22.5)	29	15	(51.7)	39.5	+ 2.29
20	(13)	FitzGerald J G	: 198	45	(22.7)	33	15	(45.5)	33.3	- 10.36

Leading Trainers in order of Winning Favourites 1987-92

			Runs	No.of Favs	(%)	Wins	No of Favs	(%)	%Wng Favs	Stake
1	Pipe M C		: 3337	1507	(45.2)	1015	724	(71.3)	48.0	+ 6.30
2	Stephenson W A		: 2717	564	(20.8)	483	257	(53.2)	45.6	- 1.46
3	Richards G W		: 1991	491	(24.7)	404	203	(50.3)	41.3	- 35.21
4	Pitman Mrs J		: 1545	381	(24.7)	293	154	(52.6)	40.4	- 4.31
5	Edwards J A C		: 1645	387	(23.5)	279	144	(51.6)	37.2	- 29.93
6	FitzGerald J G		: 1136	339	(29.8)	244	131	(53.7)	38.6	- 37.99
7	Tinkler N		: 828	283	(34.2)	186	130	(69.9)	45.9	- 2.71
8	Reveley Mrs G R		: 1068	318	(29.8)	247	129	(52.2)	40.6	- 14.27
9	Balding G B		: 1818	324	(17.8)	242	127	(52.5)	39.2	- 3.50
10	Gifford J T		: 2011	361	(18.0)	316	127	(40.2)	35.2	- 40.85
11	Sherwood O		: 1278	343	(26.8)	257	125	(48.6)	36.4	- 33.51
12	Nicholson D		: 1554	315	(20.3)	249	120	(48.2)	38.1	- 23.21
13	Moore G M		: 1187	289	(24.4)	221	117	(52.9)	40.5	- 24.68
14	Easterby M H		: 896	275	(30.7)	172	111	(64.5)	40.4	- 10.69
15	Henderson N J		: 1249	320	(25.6)	225	110	(48.9)	34.4	- 37.64
16	Brooks C P E		: 777	212	(27.3)	153	89	(58.2)	42.0	- 0.87
17	Elsworth D R C		: 969	202	(20.9)	171	82	(48.0)	40.6	- 10.98
18	Hobbs P J		: 1310	178	(13.6)	175	73	(41.7)	41.0	+ 0.47
19	Forster Capt T A		: 1182	215	(18.2)	176	69	(39.2)	32.1	- 13.71
20	O'Neill J J		: 825	154	(18.7)	130	65	(50.0)	42.2	- 0.10

15 . NATIONAL HUNT SIRES

by

Robert Carter
(I.R.B.)

ARDROSS (1976)
b. Run the Gantlet - Le Melody by Levmoss.

Won 14 of his 24 races (12-21f), including Ascot Gold Cup twice and Prix Royal Oak, and runner-up to Akiyda in 1982 Arc. Stud 1983. Sire of Karinga Bay, Filia Ardross, Aahsaylad, Arden, Bean King and St. Ninian but never stood much chance of establishing himself as a flat sire. All the same, he was 53rd on the list in 1991, one place below Shirley Heights and just above the likes of Be My Guest and Sharpo. Changed homes twice (1990/91), while being realigned as a jumping stallion, and is now in Bedfordshire. Miocamen won the Gran Premio di Merano in 1990 and became the first chaser to be voted Horse of the Year in Italy in a long while. Arden, Burgoyne and Macarthur are his best over jumps to date in Britain, while the four-year-old Avro Anson won both his races over hurdles in 91/92.

BEAU CHARMEUR (1968-87)
b. Le Fabuleux - Cymbale by Soleil Levant.

Won eight (7.5-15f). Stud, in Italy 1973, Ireland 1981. Sire of Laura's Beau, Willsford, Beau Pari, French Goblin, Hitchcock, Lacken Beau, Smooth Escort, Sparkling Flame and Sweet Charmer. Covered a maximum of 32 mares but they produced enough talent, like the

Irish-trained pair, Ballykilty and Future Hero, to keep him in the limelight for a few years yet.

BLACK MINSTREL (1974)
b. Luthier - Innocent Air by Court Martial.

Won seven (7-8f), mainly on soft ground. Half-brother to Arlington Million winner, Perrault, whose son, Kiichi, won the 1990 Galway Plate. Stud 1982 and has been consistently popular, covering 82 mares (56 foals) in 1990. Southern Minstrel and Tildarg are his best to date but many minor winners lifted him to 29th leading sire in 91/92.

BUCKSKIN (1973)
b. Yelapa - Bete a Bon Dieu by Herbager.

Won ten (10.5-20f) including Prix du Cadran (twice), Prix Jean Prat, Jockey Club Cup, Doncaster Cup and Henry II Stakes. Very game, but best on soft and had problems with both his feet and his forelegs for much of his career. Stud in England 1980 and Ireland from 1982, where he has covered between 104 and 174 mares each year to 1990. Black Moccasin, Buckshee Boy, Buckskin's Best, Buck Up, Hotplate and Rawhide were his best early winners over jumps. Black Humour, Flashy Buck, Johnny's Turn, My View and Cheltenham bumper winner Turning Trix all did well in the first half of 92. Buckskin has had plenty of success in bumpers and, with 443 foals born between 1987 and 1991, has every chance of taking his place among the leading sires (he was 7th in 91/92).

CALLERNISH (1977-89)
br. Lord Gayle - Azurine by Chamossaire.

Won two (9.5 & 12f). Stud 1981. Full-brother to dual Oaks winner Blue Wind. Sire of Arctic Call, Green Willow, The Proclamation, Mweenish, Call Me Later, Cushinstown, Final Tub and Lake Teereen. Also of On The Twist, who beat Arctic Call for a Callernish 1-2 in the Mildmay, and St. Donavint, who made a winning debut in a valuable bumper at Galway in July. Was just becoming popular with breeders, covering 86 mares in 1988 (51 foals) and 138 (103 foals) in his final season. Has an excellent percentage of winners to runners. His success, and that of Strong

Gale, has fuelled a fashion for sons of their sire, who died in July 92. Arctic Lord covered 66 mares, Aristocracy 71, Executive Perk 260 (153 foals) and Lord Americo 88 in 1990 while Henrietta Knight paid 22,000gns for Elegant Lord, a winning four-year-old Irish point-to-pointer, from one of Lord Ha Ha's tiny crops, in June 1992.

CARLINGFORD CASTLE (1980)
ch. Le Bavard - Rachel Ruysch by Skymaster.

Won two (10 & 12f), including Gr.2 Gallinule. Also 3l second to Teenoso in Derby and 3/4l + sh hd third to Sun Princess in St. Leger, both run on soft going. Runner-up in three group races (14 & 16f) at four but disappointed and, although the lack of soft ground may have been the key factor, his temperament was questioned. Stud 1985. Covered 168 mares in 1987 (103 foals, including a colt from Gold Cup winner, Glencaraig Lady) but only 88 (61 foals) in 1988, 77 (53 foals) in 1989 and 60 (36 foals) in 1990. Needs to make more of a mark on the racecourse very soon and Jamalade looks a promising chaser in Ireland.

CELTIC CONE (1967-92)
ch. Celtic Ash - Fircone by Mossborough.

Won nine on flat, including Yorkshire Cup and Queen Alexandra Stakes. Second in Ascot Gold Cup. Won five over hurdles but, although he was a fine stayer on the flat, he was best at two miles over timber, winning only one of his four attempts over longer trips. Stud 1974 and was the best N.H. stallion in Britain until his retirement in 1991 (his last crop, born that year, comprised only five foals from 28 mares covered). Responsible for Bitofabanter, Celtic Chief, Celtic Ryde, Celtic Shot, Combs Ditch, Cruising Altitude, Latent Talent, Laundryman, Observer Corps, Pipers Copse, Royal Cedar, Ryde Again, Sip of Orange, Stan's Pride and Trefelyn Cone.

CRASH COURSE (1971-88)
b. Busted - Lucky Stream by Persian Gulf.

Won five (10-20f), including Doncaster Cup and Ascot Stakes. Ran badly in only outing on soft. Stud 1977. Sire of Ballyhane, Captain Dibble, Castle King, Conclusive, Course Hunter, Dalkey Sound, Eastshaw, Esha Ness, Jodami, Kittinger, Maid of Money, Remedy the Malady, Romany King and The Langholm Dyer. Fourth leading stallion of 91/92. An unraced four-year-old was the show champion at Doncaster in May, and then was sold for 31,000gns, while a member of his final crop (3ys) made 22,000gns at Fairyhouse in June.

DEEP RUN (1966-87)
ch. Pampered King - Trial By Fire by Court Martial.

Won four (7.9-12f), including Beresford Stakes. Second in Dewhurst (to Ribofilio) and Irish St. Leger. Won one hurdle, at Doncaster, when trained by Fred Rimell. Stud 1971. Sire of Golden Cygnet, Dawn Run, Amarach, Aonoch, Aquilifer, Ararun, Attitude Adjuster, Bob Tisdall, Cahervillahow, Chrysaor, Cool Sun, Cuddy Dale, Danny Harrold, Daring Run, Deep Gale, Deep Idol, Deep Sensation, Deep South, Dis Train, Egypt Mill Prince, Ekbalco, Fifty Dollars More, Golden Friend, Granville Again, Half Free, Highfrith, Knockelly Castle, L'Ane Rouge, Local Whisper, Mole Board, Morley Street, Ri-Na-Rithann, Run and Skip, Run For Free, Rose Ravine, Skipping Tim, Slalom, Slieve Felim, Sound Judgement, Take No Trash, Vazon Bay, Waterloo Boy, Whatever You Like, Whip Along and many other fine performers. But also sire of huge numbers of foals, including 141 from 224 mares covered in 1986, his final full season. His last crop, of 85 foals from 101 mares, was born in 1988. With his remarkable fertility, it is no surprise that he has been champion stallion so many times. His progeny earned over £300,000 more than the runner-up, Strong Gale, in 91/92 and he will dominate the scene for a few more years yet. Deep Run has proved a great sire but the managers of many other stallions have drawn the doubtful lesson from his success that their horse's best chance is to cover the maximum number of mares possible. His half-brother, Abednego (1974 by Allangrange) stands in Northern Ireland. A winner twice (10 & 12f), he has sired several fair jumpers like Repeat The Dose and Cokenny Boy.

DERRING ROSE (1975)
b. Derring-Do - Bandi Rosa by Relko.

Won on the flat in France (12f) and Britain (the 13f Aston Park Stakes) and seven times over hurdles, at up to $3^{1}/4$m. Also has an excellent pedigree. But anyone who saw him attempting to pull himself up in the middle of races on more than one occasion, only to be bullied and cajoled into renewed effort by John Francome, might be surprised that the owners of 101 mares took a gamble on him in 1989 and of 85 (57 foals) in 1990. Stud 1982 in Ireland. Only covered 100 mares in his last four seasons there (85-88) but good racecourse results revived his career when he was moved to England. Dara Dub, Daring Prince, Grey Danube and The Committee are his best to date. Daring March (sire of March On, a big winner over hurdles in France, and Tom Clapton), Derrylin (Royal Derbi, Kesslin, Old Dundalk, Smith's Cracker, Southernair and Tebitto), Dominion (Hopscotch, My Dominion and Sprowston Boy) and High Top are good flat stallions by Derring-Do, which also sire smart jumpers.

FURRY GLEN (1971-87)
b. Wolver Hollow - Cleftess by Hill Gail.

Won five (5-9f) including Irish 2,000. Stud 1975 but stood 1982 in Italy, where he sired Chiasso Forte and Vicario di Bray. Also sire of Abbey Glen, Athy Spirit, Change The Act, Clara Mountain, Danny Connors, Glen Cherry, Good Team, Jennycomequick, Macroom, Mass Appeal, Shannon Glen, Toby Tobias and Very Very Ordinary. With plenty of young horses, like the dual Irish bumper winner, Big Matt, coming on, he is sure of several more years at the top.

GENERAL IRONSIDE (1973)
gr. Sea Hawk II - Come Dancing by Northern Dancer.

Won three (7-16f), including the Queen's Vase. Stud 1979, in Ireland, but did not race after his 2nd in 1976 Irish St. Leger. Did not cover in 1988/89 and had only two mares, both of which produced foals, in 1990. Blitzkrieg, Haepenny Well and Motivator have been his best to date while Off The Bru looked a promising stayer when third in the '92 Scottish Grand National.

GOOD THYNE (1977)
b. Herbager - Foreseer by Round Table.

Half-brother to two stud successes, Caerleon and Vision. Won three

(12-15f) and 2nd in Irish St. Leger. Stud 1983. Sire of Mighty Mogul, New York Rainbow, Nodform and Paco's Boy. Covered 103 mares (82 foals) in 1988, 93 (64 foals) in 1989 and 78 (54 foals) in 1990.

GUNNER B. (1973)
ch. Royal Gunner - Sweet Councillor by Privy Councillor.

Won 15 (6-12f) out of 33, including Eclipse, Prince of Wales's and a trio of Gr.3s. Second in Benson and Hedges Gold Cup. Stud, in England, 1979. Sent to Germany 1983 (where he sired a lot of winners but nothing of much note) and returned 1988. Sire of Royal Gait, K-Battery (now at stud in Northumberland), Star of a Gunner, Accuracy, Baluchi, Gilderdale, Jim Thorpe, Sir Crusty and Swingit Gunner. Covered 83 mares (53 foals) in 1989 and 62 (40 foals) in 1990 and the Champion Hurdle victory of Royal Gait will have done his popularity no harm.

HENBIT (1977)
b. Hawaii - Chateaucreek by Chateaugay.

Won four of his eight races (8-12.3f) and unbeaten in three in his classic year, when he cracked his off-fore cannon bone whilst winning the Derby. Spent three months in his box and showed little in two outings at four. Stud, in Ireland, 1982 and has sired several group race winners. Re-advertised as a sire of jumpers after the victory of Kribensis in the 1988 Triumph. Sired 72 foals in 1990 from 118 mares. Relocated in Co. Cork that year and made to work even harder, covering 192 mares who produced 116 foals. Kribensis and Sybillin remain his best.

IDIOT'S DELIGHT (1970-91)
b. Silly Season - Dolphinet by Big Game.

Won five (6-10.5f) and third in Cambridgeshire. Stud 1976 in England. Very consistent and was in the top ten in the sires' list four out of five seasons between 85/86 and 89/90, followed by an 11th place in 90/91. However, he fell to 21st in 91/92. Cavvie's Clown, Clever Folly, Easter Lee, Good for a Laugh, Ida's Delight, Jester's Prospect, Mr Moonraker, Prideaux Boy, Saffron Lord, Sea Merchant, Simple Pleasure and Vulrory's Clown are among his many smart performers, most of whom are best at two miles.

KAMBALDA (1970-91)
b. Right Royal V - Opencast by Mossborough.

Won five (16-20f) including Ascot Stakes. Stud 1976. Sire of Miinnehoma, Barton Bank, Cautious Pete, John O'Dee, Kamadoor, Nassau Royale and Right Regent. The 64 mares (48 foals), which he covered in 1990, was his largest book since 1986. Ninth leading stallion in 91/92 and should have more good seasons.

KEMAL (1971-87)
b. Armistice - Ilrem by Prudent.

Won four (15 or 15.5f) and second in Prix du Cadran. Best on soft. Half-brother to other smart French stayers Guadanini and Ti King. Stud, in Northern Ireland, from 1978 and in the Republic for his final season (1987), during which he covered 158 mares. Since they produced 111 foals, it will be some years before we hear the last of him. Rhyme 'n Reason, Farmlea Boy, Kissane, Outside Edge, Queensway Boy and The Bakewell Boy are his best to date.

KINGLET (1970)
b. Pampered King - War Ribbon by Anwar.

Won four (8.5-12f) and was one of Bustino's pacemakers in 'the race of the century'. Dam produced many winners, including a full-brother, Czar Alexander, who was a top horse in the USA in 69/70. By the same sire as Deep Run and Pitpan. Stud 1978. Sire of Brown Windsor, Gallic King, King Credo, Marsh King, Mossmorran and Risk A Bet.

KING'S RIDE (1976)
b. Rarity - Ride by Sovereign Path.

Won six (8-12f) including 1980 Lincoln H'cap. Stud 1983 in Ireland. Sire of Alekhine, Bawnmore Lad, Carobee, Kindly King, King's Curate, Ounavarra Creek and Tipping Tim. Popular at the sales and set a record for a 3yo store when Paul Nicholls gave 58,000gns, for a brother to Alekhine and Carobee, at Doncaster in May. Finished 13th in 91/92, and can be relied on for further racecourse success.

LE BAVARD (1971)
ch. Devon - Lueur Doree by Le Haar.

Won five (11-20f), including Prix du Cadran, Prix Jean Prat (15f) and Prix Berteux (15f). Also 2nd in Ascot Gold Cup. Stud 1978. Sire of Carlingford Castle (see above) and of Abba Lad, Bankers Benefit, Barney Burnett, Bartres, Dis Fiove, Fair Child, Flying Ferret, Keep Talking, Kildimo, Mr. Gossip, Perris Valley, Shannon Spray, Shilgrove Place and Young Bavard. Runner-up on the sires' list in 85/86 and third in each of the next three seasons. Disappointing since but has plenty of young horses, like La Princesse, winner of both her bumpers, to lift him back to the top.

LE MOSS (1975)
ch. Le Levanstell - Feemoss by Ballymoss.

Won 11 (14-22f) including two Ascot Gold Cups, Goodwood Cups and Doncaster Cups. Stud 1981 but not promoted as a sire of jumpers until 1984. Sire of Waterfield (Gr. placed on flat) but his future lies with his jumpers. He covered 805 mares between 1984 and 1988 so whole troops of them will be reaching the course in the next few seasons. Mossy Fern and Sendai won good races in 91/92 but early results have not been too encouraging and his book fell to 82 mares (51 foals) in 1989 and 64 mares (38 foals) in 1990.

MANDALUS (1974)
b. Mandamus - Laminate by Abernant.

Won 13 (6-10f) for Sir Mark Prescott and was placed in four staying events, including the Queen Alexandra Stakes, after moving to Ireland. Stud 1980. Sire of Henry Mann, Long Engagement, Mandavi, Mandraki Shuffle, Polar Nomad, Springholm and Undaunted while his sire (also best at a mile) was responsible for Pearlyman. Showed remarkable fertility, getting 205 foals from 251 mares covered in 1988/89. Not quite so good with 77 foals from 101 mares in 1991 but still has plenty of young horses to come on. Maneree, Easby Mandrina and Tallywagger were among those showing promise last season.

MONKSFIELD (1972-89)

b. Gala Performance - Regina by Tulyar.

Won five (7.5-16f) flat, including his only race at two, and 14 over hurdles. Won 1978 and 79 Champion Hurdles and second in '77 and '80. Also won Templegate Hurdle (2m 5½f) twice. Stud 1980. His US-bred sire was imported as a flat stallion but was also responsible for West Tip. Capable of siring smart flat horses like Villa d'Orleans (Gr. placed at a mile in France and Italy). Toranfield, Bishop's Staff, Grand Habit, Judge's Fancy, Leap Field and Ross Venture are his best jumpers to date and he finished 22nd in 91/92. Other useful performers should emerge, but success is likely to be limited by the small number of mares he covered and, reportedly, the lack of scope of many of his offspring.

NEARLY A HAND (1974)

b. Busted - Petite Chou by Hook Money.

Won five (12-16f), including Newbury Autumn Cup, and 3rd in Cesarewitch. Injured and went to stud, in Dorset, 1978 but returned for two 2nds from three runs on flat in '79 before retiring permanently. Sire of Beech Road, Silent Surrender, Teletrader and Tom Caxton. Had his busiest season with 66 mares (37 foals) in '90.

NICHOLAS BILL (1975)

ch. High Line - Centro by Vienna.

Won eight (8-16f), including Gr.2 Geoffrey Freer and Princess of Wales's. Stud 1982. High Line (d. 1992), a top-class flat sire, is also responsible for smart jumpers like Bobsline, Heighlin, High Knowl, Highland Bounty and Muse, as well as being the damsire of such stars as Morley Street and Blazing Walker. Nicholas Bill has also sired some useful flat horses while Ghofar, One For The Pot and Tancred Sand are his best over jumps.

OATS (1973-90)

b. Northfields - Arctic Lace by Arctic Chevalier.

Won five (7-13.4f), including Jockey Club Stakes, Ormonde Stakes and Blue Riband Trial. Derby 3rd and St. Leger 4th. Stud 1978, in Ireland, and in England 1984. Sire of Wing and a Prayer, Against the Grain, Prime Oats, Atkinsons, Big James, Bizage Motors, Flakey Dove and Midnight Train. Covered around 75 mares each year to 1989 (one 1991 foal from his only mare before he died) and there should be plenty more useful jumpers to come.

ORCHESTRA (1974)
ch. Tudor Music - Golden Moss by Sheshoon.

Gr.2 winner at two, three and four years and Gr.3 at five. Won seven (8-12f), including John Porter, Nijinsky and Beresford Stakes. Also 2nd in Irish St. Leger, 3rd William Hill Futurity and 4th Irish Derby. Stud 1980. Sire of Pat's Jester, Robert's Rhapsody, String Player and Vanton. Very prolific sire, with 272 foals born between '89-'91. Popular at the sales.

OVER THE RIVER (1974)
ch. Luthier - Medenine by Prudent.

Won one (10f) flat and three good 4yo hurdles in France. Stud 1980. Sire of Cool Ground, Astral River, Leagaune, Over The Deel, Over The Edge, Over The Road, Riska's River, River Bounty, River Tarquin, Thar-an-Bharr, Travel Over and Zeta's Lad. His progeny will never be renowned for their speed but he is popular with breeders and buyers. Reached the top when Cool Ground won the Gold Cup and is clearly one of the top chasing sires of the 90s. Third in 91/92 when 87% of his earnings were contributed by chasers.

PITPAN (1969)
b. Pampered King - Pitter Patter by Kingstone.

Half-brother to Hotfoot (sire of Flown) and by the sire of Deep Run. Won three (8-9f) in France and three hurdles, when trained by Fulke Walwyn, in Britain. Stud, in Ireland, 1975. Moved to England 1987 but not as popular as might have been expected, covering 28 mares (17 foals) in '89 and 20 (11 foals) in '90. Sire of Afford A King, Danish Flight, Randolph Place, Spider's Well, Burnt Oak, Edenspring, Espy, Garamycin, Knockbrack, Master Bob, Oppidan, Pan Arctic, Park Rainbow and Tartan Trix.

POLITICO (1967-91)

b. Right Royal V - Tendentious by Tenerani.

Won five (7-12.3f), including Chester Vase, and 3rd to Nijinsky in St. Leger. Sire of Allerlea, Durham Edition, Lauderdale Lad, Political Pop and Stearsby. Party Politics confirmed Politico's reputation as a sire of smart staying chasers with victory in the Grand National. Covered 14 mares (ten foals) in 1990.

PRINCE REGENT (1966)

br. Right Royal V - Noduleuse by Nosca.

Won six (5-12f), including Irish Derby and Prix Lupin. Unlucky 3rd to Blakeney in Derby. Stud 1971 but spent 79-82 in France. Out of fashion and covering few mares in recent years but still capable of getting smart jumpers like Remittance Man, Cybrandian, Gay George, Lulav, Mountebor and Tinryland. Was 11th leading sire in 91/92.

PROVERB (1970-84)

ch. Reliance II - Causerie by Cagire II.

Won five (12-21f) including Goodwood Cup (twice), Doncaster Cup and Chester Vase. Second in Ascot Gold Cup. Stayed well enough to win Goodwood Cup at three. Big, strong horse who was best on fast ground. Stud 1976. Sire of Bishopdale, By The Way, Catch Phrase, Envopak Token, I've Topped It, Lean Ar Agaidh, Multum In Parvo, Newtown Gazette, Proverb Prince, Proverity, Righthand Man, Third In Line and Topsham Bay.

RAISE YOU TEN (1960-84)

br. Tehran - Visor by Combat.

Won four (10-21f) including Goodwood, Doncaster and Yorkshire Cups. Stud 1965. Sire of Baies, Brunton Park, Comeragh King, Gallaher, Get Out Of Me Way, Oketee, Super Nova, Tenfores, Ten of Spades, Ten Plus, Ten Up, The Dealer and Twin Oaks. Not quite a back number yet and also an important sire of dams.

RANDOM SHOT (1967-83)

b. Pirate King - Time and Chance by Supreme Court.

Won six (11.7-20f) including Ascot Gold Cup (awarded race after Rock Roi failed a dope test). Stud 1973. Sire of Fane Ranger, Garrison Savannah, Jinxy Jack, Random Leg, Random Prince, Randoss and W Six Times.

RELKINO (1973-89)
b. Relko - Pugnacity by Pampered King.

Won four (6-10.5f) including Benson and Hedges Gold Cup and Lockinge. Second in Derby and Champion. Stud 1978, in England, but bought by National Stud in 1984 and relocated as a jumping stallion in Oxfordshire. Sire of Bespoke, Flight Hill, Relatively Easy, Roark and Silk Thread.

ROSELIER (1973)
gr. Misti IV - Peace Rose by Fastnet Rock.

Won one (10f) on flat and three, including Grande Course de Haies d'Auteuil (3m 1½f), over hurdles, in France. Brother to Roseliere, winner of Prix de Diane and Vermeille and dam of Ile de Bourbon and Rose Bowl. Half-brother to another Irish-based stallion, Peacock. Stud 1981. Sire of Carvill's Hill, Graiguenamon, Night Session, No One To Blame, One More Knight, Royal Athlete, Stay On Tracks and Torrent Bay. A leading candidate for the mantle of Deep Run, both at stud, with 397 foals in 89/91 from 606 mares, and on the course (14th leading sire of 91/92).

ROYAL FOUNTAIN (1977)
br. Royalty - Fountain by Reform.

Won three (8-11.7f). Stud 1982 in Northumberland. Sire of smart chasers Carrick Hill Lad and Kings Fountain. Gaining in popularity and his book rose each year from 1987 (42-55-60-89) to 1990, resulting in a total of 166 foals, 61 of them in 1991.

RYMER (1971)
b. Reliance II - Piave by Alcide.

Won two (8 & 10f), including Brigadier Gerard Stakes. Bred to stay further but showed nothing in three attempts at 12f. Stud 1979. Sire of a champion filly on the flat in Venezuela and of Fourth of July,

Jennie Pat, Merry Jane, Merry Junior, Poetic Gem and Rymster over obstacles. Wellwotdouthink, unbeaten in three bumpers, and Lucky Crisis, 15l winner in similar company on his only appearance, could soon be joining that list.

SCALLYWAG (1973)
gr. Sea Hawk II - Scammell by Dante.
Won two (10 & 12f) of five and 3rd in St. Leger. Stands 17.2hh and was lengthy in proportion, having trouble fitting in the stalls. Won over 10f at two. Stud 1977, in England. Sire of Another City, Better Times Ahead, Border Rambler, Lucky Rascal, Salehurst, Scally Owen, Sword Beach, The Grey Bomber, The Man Himself and Tom's Little Bet. Covered 40 mares (30 foals) in 1990.

SEXTON BLAKE (1975)
gr. Blakeney - Mayo Blues by Abernant.
Won five (7-12f), including Gr.2 Champagne Stakes plus Gordon, Westbury and Seaton Delaval, all Gr.3. Stud 1980. Sire of good flat performers like Ala Hounak and Jung (Group winner in Italy) and of Sir Blake. Likely to make more of a mark over jumps. Blakeney is the sort of good class middle distance sire, who always produces some good jumpers, most recently Thetford Forest. (Niniski, Ile de Bourbon and Kris were the pick of this type last season). Roscoe Blake, another son of Blakeney, who was exported to Italy in 1986, after six years at stud in England, left Docklands Express, Goodshot Rich and Lothian Captain behind.

SHEER GRIT (1978-90)
b. Busted - Abettor by Abernant.
Won 3 (7-12f) and was Group placed from two to four, including 3rd to Beldale Flutter and Shergar in William Hill Futurity and a dead-heat 3rd in the Goodwood Cup. Also 6th of 18 to Shergar in the Derby. Stud 1984. Died early in the 1990 covering season (5 foals from 6 mares). Never one of the most popular stallions (1989 was easily his busiest year with 65 mares) but Clay County and Cock Cockburn came out of his first two crops and there should be

more talent on the way. Shernazar, another son of Busted, has sired useful hurdlers like Chirkpar, Cheering News and Larnaca.

STRONG GALE (1975)
br. Lord Gayle - Sterntau by Tamerlane.

Won six (7-11f) and in the frame in 15 Group races. Stud 1982 and sired Very Strong, Gr.3 winning two-year-old in Italy, in his second crop. Covered 468 mares 1984-86 and 194 (next highest 168 by Carlingford Castle) in 87, producing a phenomenal 151 foals to add to 345 in the previous three years. Overtaken by Roselier (216) in 88 but still covered 206 mares, who produced 163 live foals. Again second to Roselier in 1989 but his 200 mares produced an exceptional 168 foals. Worked less hard in 1990, with 161 mares, but his fertility was as high as ever, with 135 foals. In spite of these huge numbers, he now reigns supreme in the sale rings and 42 horses by him, including six foals and 11 yearlings, topped five figures in 1991, while 12 of their elders beat 20,000gns. Retained most of his popularity in the weaker market of 1992 and Nicky Henderson paid 40,000gns for an unraced four-year-old at Doncaster in May. Alone Success and Nos Na Gaoithe gave him a good start over jumps and each year has seen the emergence of new stars. Brief Gale, Force Seven, Gale Again, Soft Day, Strong Case and Travado are the latest additions to a list which includes Cab On Target, Edberg, File Concord, Fragrant Dawn, Full Strength, Galevilla Express, Guesswork, Katabatic, Minorette's Girl, Rongale, Southerly Buster, Strong Gold and Wink Gulliver. Runner-up to Deep Run in 91/92 and many more young stars are on the way.

THE PARSON (1968-90)
b. Aureole - Bracey Bridge by Chanteur II.

Only ran four times. Second, beaten ½l, in the Dante and 10l sixth behind Mill Reef in the Derby. Never raced again. Stud 1972. Sire of Brittany Boy, Church Warden, Delius, Direct, Eton Rouge, Fifth Amendment, Forest Ranger, Hassle Money, Hill of Slane, Killone Abbey, Lucky Baloo, Miriam's Fancy VI, Mixed Blends, Mount Parson, Nancy Myles, Navallus VI, Over The Counter, Parsons Green, Red Cleric, Steeple View, The Breener, Trapper John, Very

Promising, Western Dandy and Won't Be Gone Long. Josh Gifford paid 68,000gns (still an English record for a 4yo store) at Doncaster in 1989. The following year The Parson established the Irish record (equalled 12 months later) when Mouse Morris paid 65,000gns for another 4yo (later named Aaronic) at Fairyhouse. Covered only eight mares (six foals) before his death in 1990 but was sire of 141 foals in the previous two years so he is sure to keep his place among the leaders (he was 6th in 91/92) for a few years yet. Holy Joe, Jodi's Money, Monsieur Le Cure, Nathalie's Fancy, Open The Gate and Shuil Ar Agaidh are the sort which guarantee that much.

TORUS (1976)
b. Ribero - Lighted Lamp by Sir Gaylord.

Won two (7 & 12f) and 2nd to Niniski in Irish St. Leger. Half-brother to King Luthier, Rolfe and other good winners. Stud 1981. Sire of Abbreviation, Bradbury Star, Fatal Hesitation, Howe Street, Little Toro and The Gooser. Has high fertility (301 foals from 401 mares in 1988-91) and is popular with buyers.

16 . RACECOURSES

Fence Ratings

Each course's fences are rated in order of difficulty, based on a survey of top jump jockeys carried out by the Racing Post. Brackets indicate half points (e.g. Kempton +++(+) is rated more testing than average)

+++++	=	Difficult
++++	=	Testing
+++	=	Average
++	=	Moderate
+	=	Easy

Standard of Racing

The standard of racing at each course has been evaluated by a combination of the average prize per race (see p.316) and feature meetings/races. Brackets indicate either half points or departures from the norm (e.g. Newcastle ££(££) indicates generally moderate standards but at times very good).

£££££	=	Excellent
££££	=	Very Good
£££	=	Good
££	=	Moderate
£	=	Poor

NOTE:
* after a meeting at Lingfield and Southwell denotes all weather racing.
All-weather Course Statistics are given at the back of this section

ASCOT

Despite the high quality of Ascot's National Hunt programme, jump racing at the Berkshire track has never enjoyed quite the same popularity as its flat counterpart. The vast stands are hard to fill and a long way from the action, while the makeshift winter parade ring does not enhance the ambience.

Nevertheless, a succession of well-planned fixtures makes the sport top class. United House Group Day (Oct), H & T Walker Gold Cup (Nov), SGB Day (Dec) and Charterhouse Day (Feb) all boast excellent cards, including the HSS Hurdle in December. The Hurst Park and Reynoldstown Novice Chases are usually won by high-class sorts, while there is a staying hurdlers' 'triple crown' of the Long Walk (Dec), Fernbank (Feb) and Letherby & Christopher (April) Hurdles.

The track itself has a triangular right-hand circuit of one and three quarter miles and is essentially a galloping course. There are ten stiff fences and novices are often found out by one of the far side downhill fences approaching Swinley Bottom. The straight contains two fences, followed by a stiff, uphill run-in of 240-yards guaranteed to test the character of any horse. Good jumping is essential, as is stamina, since the track becomes particularly testing when the going is soft or worse.

FENCES: ++++   **RACING: £££££**

MEETINGS
Oct 21st, Nov 20th & 21st, Dec 19th, Jan 15th & 16th, Feb 10th, Mar 31st, Apr 7th, Apr 27th (10 days)

ENQUIRIES
Capt. The Hon ENC Beaumont CVO, DL, The Ascot Authority, Ascot Racecourse, Ascot, Berks, SL5 7JN. Tel: (0344) 22211

COURSE STATISTICS 1987-92

	Total W/R	(%)	Hurdles Nov	Hcp	Chases Nov	Hcp	Level Stake
Top Trainers							
Pipe M C	23/ 90	25.5	8/27	8/36	2/ 9	5/18	- 0.05
Gifford J T	21/143	14.6	7/48	2/28	6/33	6/34	- 6.00
Balding G B	15/104	14.4	7/35	3/39	2/11	3/19	- 26.02
Pitman Mrs J	12/ 48	25.0	4/22	4/18	3/ 5	1/ 3	+ 31.80
Elsworth D R C	12/ 54	22.2	3/18	4/19	3/10	2/ 7	+ 21.03
Sherwood O	10/ 52	19.2	4/21	2/15	3/ 8	1/ 8	- 15.45
Top Jockeys							
Scudamore P	27/115	23.4	11/37	8/30	4/19	4/29	- 9.31
Osborne J	15/ 68	22.0	5/24	5/15	4/11	1/18	+ 13.99
Dunwoody R	15/123	12.2	2/37	4/27	4/24	5/35	- 28.98
Perrett M	11/ 53	20.7	2/18	3/15	2/ 8	4/12	+ 22.00
Hobbs Peter	10/ 42	23.8	1/11	3/ 6	3/12	3/13	+ 9.88
Frost J	10/ 54	18.5	8/25	2/14	0/ 8	0/ 7	- 13.73

Favourites Records

Autmn	H:	43.6%	2m	Hdl:	33.1%	2m	Chs:	40.1%	Hvy : 16.7%
	C:	37.2%	2.5m	Hdl:	37.2%	2.5m	Chs:	23.6%	Sft : 26.0%
Wintr	H:	30.4%	3m	Hdl:	28.9%	3m	Chs:	22.5%	Gd-Sft: 21.7%
	C:	30.4%	3.5m	Hdl:	0.0%	3.5m	Chs:	0.0%	Gd : 29.7%
Sprng	H:	23.9%	Nov	Hdl:	33.6%	Nov	Chs:	26.5%	Gd-Fm : 38.1%
	C:	16.7%	Hcp	Hdl:	31.6%	Hcp	Chs:	30.1%	Fm/Hd : 30.8%

Total : 30.8%   L/Stake : - 63.27   Lngst Wng Run: 5   Lngst Lsg Run: 19

AYR

Scotland's premier course enjoys a fine reputation amongst racegoers and professionals alike. The quality of racing is moderate on the whole, due to its relative isolation from the main training centres, but the excellent facilities and hospitable management make for a pleasant atmosphere. Scottish Grand National Day in April is the chief fixture and the two day meeting also includes the Scottish Champion Hurdle and the Future Champions Novices Chase. With travelling in mind, most of the meetings are over two days.

The course is one of the fairest in Britain. It comprises a flat left-hand circuit measuring one and a half miles. There are nine fences in all with three in the long straight, followed by a run-in of 210-yards. The obstacles are quite stiff, particularly the penultimate fence, which is a formidable open ditch. The excellent drainage means that the going is seldom very soft or heavy and, indeed, there is a popular belief that if racing is not possible at Ayr then it is not possible anywhere else in Britain. The course would appear to suit strong gallopers but when conditions are firm, Ayr becomes one of the fastest tracks in the land.

FENCES: +++(+)   **RACING: ££(£)**

MEETINGS
Oct 10th, Nov 13th & 14th, Jan 2nd, 21st, 30th, Feb 12th & 13th, Mar 12th & 13th, Apr 16th & 17th (12 days)

ENQUIRIES
Mr Mark Kershaw, Western Meeting Club, Racecourse Office, 2 Whitletts Road, Ayr, KA8 OJE. Tel: (0292) 264179

COURSE STATISTICS 1987-92

Top Trainers	Total W/R	(%)	Hurdles Nov	Hcp	Chases Nov	Hcp	Level Stake
Richards G W	51/250	20.4	15/81	6/52	17/60	13/57	+ 14.31
Moore G M	29/130	22.3	17/54	6/31	4/24	2/21	- 19.83
Stephenson W A	18/114	15.7	0/25	1/ 5	9/38	8/46	- 9.14
Reveley Mrs G R	50/30	30.0	7/24	4/16	3/ 7	1/ 3	+ 4.45
Bradburne Mrs S C	10/ 60	16.6	0/15	1/13	3/17	6/15	+ 16.50
Naughton M P	10/ 69	14.4	0/22	8/35	0/ 2	2/10	- 14.42
Top Jockeys							
Doughty N	28/127	22.0	10/50	5/26	7/36	6/15	+ 53.55
Storey B	26/169	15.3	4/51	6/28	10/45	6/45	- 44.88
McCourt G	21/ 83	25.3	6/34	2/16	7/18	6/15	+ 1.21
Niven P	21/116	18.1	9/35	7/30	3/27	2/24	- 10.55
Wyer L	15/ 93	16.1	7/38	5/24	3/20	0/11	- 42.96
Dwyer M	14/ 79	17.7	4/25	4/22	3/14	3/18	- 20.64

Favourites Records

Autmn	H:	27.1%	2m	Hdl:	38.6%	2m	Chs:	48.8%	Hvy : 43.5%
	C:	53.7%	2.5m	Hdl:	25.0%	2.5m	Chs:	43.5%	Sft : 33.9%
Wintr	H:	42.1%	3m	Hdl:	44.6%	3m	Chs:	39.6%	Gd-Sft: 41.4%
	C:	39.7%	3.5m	Hdl:	0.0%	3.5m	Chs:	33.3%	Gd : 36.2%
Sprng	H:	35.0%	Nov	Hdl:	38.1%	Nov	Chs:	43.8%	Gd-Fm : 53.9%
	C:	38.6%	Hcp	Hdl:	34.3%	Hcp	Chs:	41.7%	Fm/Hd : 0.0%

Total : 39.3% L/Stake : - 26.78 Lngst Wng Run: 7 Lngst Lsg Run: 8

BANGOR-ON-DEE

Bangor is the only racecourse in North Wales and enjoys considerable popularity despite the poor quality of the racing. Fixtures are all one day affairs, with those in October and April boasting the best cards, the latter mainly thanks to the sponsorship of the McAlpine family.

The track itself is unusual since its one and a half miles includes no straight, as such, but instead a succession of tight bends. It is relatively flat, with minor undulations, and its proximity to the River Dee means the track can be watered even in conditions of drought. The nine fences are quite easy with the exception of one open ditch approaching the final turn, which claimed half the total casualities at the track last year. The so called 'paddock bend' is very sharp indeed and the course is ideal for front runners despite the long run-in of 325-yards.

FENCES: ✦✦(✦)   **RACING: £**

MEETINGS
Oct 10th, Oct 30th, Nov 27th, Dec 16th, Feb 12th, Mar 10th, Mar 27th, Apr 17th, Apr 30th, May 15th. Jul 30th (11 days)

ENQUIRIES
P W Ockleston Esq., Bangor on Dee Races Ltd, Chorlton Hall, Malpas, Cheshire ST14 7ET Tel: (0948) 860438

COURSE STATISTICS 1987-92

Top Trainers	Total W/R	(%)	Hurdles Nov	Hcp	Chases Nov	Hcp	Level Stake
Pipe M C	26/ 74	35.1	13/41	4/ 8	6/12	3/13	+ 10.97
Richards G W	22/ 96	22.9	4/31	1/ 5	7/27	10/33	- 29.52
Edwards J A C	16/ 74	21.6	7/27	1/10	6/19	2/18	- 1.08
Jordan F	13/ 69	18.8	2/29	9/26	1/ 7	1/ 7	+ 30.29
Stephenson W A	11/ 52	21.1	1/13	0/ 5	3/12	7/22	- 11.53
Ham G A	8/ 30	26.6	1/ 6	3/ 8	1/ 5	3/11	+ 98.88
Top Jockeys							
Scudamore P	20/ 64	31.2	9/31	3/ 9	4/12	4/12	- 4.64
Grant C	17/ 48	35.4	6/16	1/ 8	4/ 9	6/15	+ 10.68
Doughty N	13/ 48	27.0	4/19	1/ 3	5/14	3/12	- 16.55
Lodder J	12/ 73	16.4	1/27	8/24	2/10	1/12	+ 19.38
McCourt G	11/ 54	20.3	3/22	1/11	5/11	2/10	+ 13.05
O'Neill S J	10/118	8.4	4/44	1/16	2/30	3/28	- 75.15

Favourites Records

Autmn	H:	34.6%	2m	Hdl:	40.8%	2m	Chs:	36.5%	Hvy :	0.0%
	C:	38.3%	2.5m	Hdl:	27.1%	2.5m	Chs:	40.2%	Sft :	38.2%
Wintr	H:	39.7%	3m	Hdl:	27.8%	3m	Chs:	35.9%	Gd-Sft:	16.7%
	C:	16.1%	3.5m	Hdl:	0.0%	3.5m	Chs:	0.0%	Gd :	37.0%
Sprng	H:	35.2%	Nov	Hdl:	35.3%	Nov	Chs:	40.9%	Gd-Fm :	43.2%
	C:	44.5%	Hcp	Hdl:	36.5%	Hcp	Chs:	33.2%	Fm/Hd :	32.5%
Total	**:**	**36.2%**	**L/Stake :**		**- 38.09**	**Lngst Wng Run:**	**5**	**Lngst Lsg Run:**	**13**	

CARLISLE

The very moderate quality of the sport at Carlisle should not be allowed to detract from what is a delightful country course set amongst the Lakeland hills of Cumbria. There is generally a fixture each month throughout the season with a two day meeting over Easter.

The course itself, a right-hander of about one mile five furlongs in length, is one of the stiffest in the country. It is pear-shaped and distinctly undulating, with a very severe uphill run-in of some 300-yards. There are nine well-built obstacles of no great difficulty but, when the ground is soft or worse, the course becomes one for a long-striding galloper with bottomless reserves of stamina and courage.

FENCES: ✚✚(✚)   **RACING: £**

MEETINGS
Oct 9th, Nov 9th, Nov 26th, Dec 30th, Jan 18th, Feb 9th, Mar 11th, Apr 10th, Apr 12th (9 days)

ENQUIRIES
Mrs Anne Bliss, Carlisle Racecourse Co Ltd, Grandstand Office, The Racecourse, Blackwell, Carlisle. Cumbria, CA2 4TS. Tel: (0228) 22973

COURSE STATISTICS 1987-92

	Total W/R	(%)	Hurdles Nov	Hcp	Chases Nov	Hcp	Level Stake
Top Trainers							
Richards G W	30/158	18.9	7/74	1/19	8/27	14/38	- 34.59
Stephenson W A	18/146	12.3	4/58	2/18	7/33	5/37	- 50.85
O'Neill J J	16/105	15.2	8/49	3/16	1/16	4/24	- 36.59
Moore G M	13/ 62	20.9	6/24	4/13	2/13	1/12	- 25.60
Parker C	12/ 90	13.3	7/42	0/13	2/14	3/21	- 11.00
Edwards J A C	9/ 27	33.3	4/12	1/ 3	2/ 8	2/ 4	+ 14.05
Top Jockeys							
Doughty N	20/ 77	25.9	6/35	3/ 9	5/16	6/17	+ 11.64
Niven P	19/ 81	23.4	4/32	3/10	3/16	9/23	+ 12.31
Storey B	16/143	11.1	6/56	0/23	3/24	7/40	- 20.99
Dwyer M	14/ 71	19.7	4/30	4/12	2/10	4/19	- 13.65
Wyer L	10/ 44	22.7	5/16	2/ 8	2/12	1/ 8	+ 13.20
Doolan K	10/ 57	17.5	6/24	3/16	0/ 8	1/ 9	+ 27.30

Favourites Records

Autmn	H:	37.9%	2m	Hdl:	34.0%	2m	Chs:	32.8%	Hvy : 38.6%
	C:	40.6%	2.5m Hdl:		35.9%	2.5m Chs:		54.3%	Sft : 36.8%
Wintr	H:	37.8%	3m	Hdl:	43.8%	3m	Chs:	42.9%	Gd-Sft: 32.4%
	C:	36.5%	3.5m Hdl:		0.0%	3.5m Chs:		23.3%	Gd : 36.3%
Sprng	H:	29.6%	Nov	Hdl:	39.8%	Nov	Chs:	55.6%	Gd-Fm : 45.3%
	C:	45.7%	Hcp	Hdl:	28.3%	Hcp	Chs:	31.9%	Fm/Hd : 40.4%

Total : 37.8%   L/Stake : - 24.04   Lngst Wng Run: 6   Lngst Lsg Run: 8

CARTMEL

Those that visit this small Cumbrian racetrack, set in attractive wooded parkland, would probably argue that there is far too little racing at Cartmel. There are only five days racing scheduled for the whole of 1992, and those are spread over two fixtures, one on the Spring Bank holiday in late May, the other in late August.

This tight, undulating course is left-handed and measures just over one mile. The feature here is the six stiff fences, which although severe for a minor track, do not claim as many victims as might be expected, largely since the ground is usually good. The run-in includes a separate chute, missing out the fences on the back turn, and with half-mile from the last is the longest in the country. Despite this, the approach to the line is mainly on the turn, as is most of the course, and thus favours handy, adaptable animals rather than strong gallopers.

FENCES: +++(+)   **RACING: £**

MEETINGS
May 26th, May 29th, May 31st, Aug 28th & 30th (5 days)

ENQUIRIES
Major T R Riley, Cartmel Steeplechase Ltd., Estate Office, Lowther, Penrith, Cumbria, CA10 2HG Tel: (09312) 378

COURSE STATISTICS 1987-92

	Total W/R	(%)	Hurdles Nov	Hcp	Chases Nov	Hcp	Level Stake
Top Trainers							
Stephenson W A	17/ 62	27.4	4/17	3/14	5/15	5/16	+ 3.27
Richards G W	14/ 36	38.8	1/13	2/ 6	6/ 9	5/ 8	+ 0.60
Chapman M C	13/ 85	15.2	3/30	6/43	3/ 6	1/ 6	- 36.62
Pipe M C	9/ 27	33.3	4/13	4/12	1/ 2	0/ 0	- 3.58
Smith Denys	8/ 28	28.5	4/10	2/ 8	1/ 4	1/ 6	+ 7.72
White J	7/ 47	14.8	3/16	2/12	2/12	0/ 7	- 27.08
Top Jockeys							
Grant C	13/ 47	27.6	7/17	0/14	3/ 7	3/ 9	- 8.07
McCourt G	9/ 20	45.0	1/ 6	3/ 6	3/ 5	2/ 3	- 0.23
Dwyer M	9/ 27	33.3	2/12	3/10	3/ 3	1/ 2	- 0.79
Doughty N	8/ 17	47.0	1/ 8	2/ 3	3/ 3	2/ 3	+ 9.40
Supple R	4/ 20	20.0	0/ 7	3/ 8	0/ 2	1/ 3	+ 9.07
Moffatt D J*	4/ 21	19.0	1/11	3/10	0/ 0	0/ 0	- 7.75

Favourites Records

Autmn	H:	46.3%	2m	Hdl:	51.5%	2m	Chs:	60.9%	Hvy	:	0.0%
	C:	55.0%	2.5m Hdl:	0.0%	2.5m	Chs:	61.9%	Sft	:	33.3%
Wintr	H:	0.0%	3m	Hdl:	25.9%	3m	Chs:	45.5%	Gd-Sft:	75.0%
	C:	0.0%	3.5m Hdl:	0.0%	3.5m	Chs:	0.0%	Gd	:	39.6%
Sprng	H:	42.7%	Nov	Hdl:	48.7%	Nov	Chs:	73.3%	Gd-Fm :	50.0%
	C:	60.0%	Hcp	Hdl:	41.2%	Hcp	Chs:	40.0%	Fm/Hd :	49.4%

Total : 49.3%   L/Stake : - 2.44   Lngst Wng Run: 8   Lngst Lsg Run: 9

CATTERICK

One of the smaller and more unremarkable courses in the country, Catterick nevertheless attracts reasonable crowds, partly due to its situation just off the A1. There are no fixtures of any real note, but what there are, are well spread throughout the winter months.

The circuit itself is left-handed, and is basically oval-shaped, measuring a mile and a quarter. It is essentially sharp, with the course turning most of the way, with undulations adding some variety. The eight fences are notoriously easy, and a very poor education for a novice, who might make a string of errors but remain on his feet, learning next to nothing. The run-in is 240-yards, and the track firmly favours the nippy, front-running type.

FENCES: ✚   **RACING: £**

MEETINGS
Oct 24th, Nov 21st, Nov 23rd, Dec 2nd, Dec 18th, Dec 31st, Jan 1st, Jan 22nd & 23rd, Feb 13th, Feb 25th, Mar 10th (12 days)

ENQUIRIES
Mr J F Sanderson, The Catterick Racecourse Co Ltd., First Floor, Ebor Court, Westgate, Leeds, LS1 4ND Tel: (0532) 422221

COURSE STATISTICS 1987-92

	Total W/R	(%)	Hurdles Nov	Hcp	Chases Nov	Hcp	Level Stake
Top Trainers							
Stephenson W A	23/151	15.2	4/68	1/17	2/20	16/46	- 42.21
Richards G W	21/ 90	23.3	4/34	0/ 7	8/22	9/27	- 1.49
Moore G M	18/ 86	20.9	8/45	8/25	2/11	0/ 5	- 11.05
FitzGerald J G	18/102	17.6	7/60	0/ 9	7/15	4/18	- 25.23
Reveley Mrs G R	14/ 66	21.2	6/26	5/13	2/11	1/16	+ 7.21
Tinkler N	13/ 51	25.4	5/24	8/23	0/ 2	0/ 2	- 4.85
Top Jockeys							
Dwyer M	26/120	21.6	10/50	6/27	7/19	3/24	- 17.07
Doughty N	17/ 74	22.9	4/30	2/13	5/18	6/13	+ 48.10
Grant C	15/118	12.7	4/42	1/26	0/20	10/30	- 43.49
Wyer L	14/108	12.9	4/45	3/21	6/22	1/20	- 22.95
Niven P	12/111	10.8	5/46	2/19	1/20	4/26	- 54.03
Storey B	11/105	10.4	3/37	0/16	3/22	5/30	- 36.90

Favourites Records

Autmn	H:	34.4%	2m	Hdl:	33.4%	2m	Chs:	40.5%	Hvy :	0.0%
	C:	35.0%	2.5m	Hdl:	0.0%	2.5m	Chs:	0.0%	Sft :	35.4%
Wintr	H:	27.0%	3m	Hdl:	25.9%	3m	Chs:	36.5%	Gd-Sft:	29.4%
	C:	41.2%	3.5m	Hdl:	0.0%	3.5m	Chs:	57.1%	Gd :	32.5%
Sprng	H:	52.2%	Nov	Hdl:	30.4%	Nov	Chs:	46.4%	Gd-Fm :	39.2%
	C:	38.9%	Hcp	Hdl:	34.8%	Hcp	Chs:	34.6%	Fm/Hd :	30.8%
Total	**:**	**35.4%**	**L/Stake :**		**- 41.01**	**Lngst Wng Run:**	**6**	**Lngst Lsg Run:**	**12**	

CHELTENHAM

Set in an outstanding natural amphitheatre at the foot of Cleeve Hill, Cheltenham has every reason to be regarded as the premier National Hunt course in Britain with the highlight of the jumping calendar, the three day Festival meeting in mid-March. Every fixture is a good one, backed up by excellent facilities and knowledgeable crowds.

Cheltenham has two undulating left-handed courses, the Old and the New. The former is a one and a half mile oval, with nine stiff fences, only one of which is jumped in the final straight, leaving a tough uphill run-in of 350-yards. The New course is slightly longer with 10 fences, leaving the Old course at the furthest point from the stands. Two fences are jumped in the straight where the run-in is 237-yards.

Both circuits are most testing. The fences are stiff but well-constructed and universally regarded as being inviting to jump but harsh on mistakes. The notorious third last fence, as the horses come down the hill before the turn into the straight, finds out many, as does the fence before it at the top of the hill. The last half-mile is uphill all the way and countless races have been transformed on that final slog to the line, particularly when conditions are soft underfoot.

FENCES: ✚✚✚✚   **RACING: £££££**

MEETINGS
Oct 1st, Oct 14th, Nov 13th, 14th & 15th, Dec 11th & 12th, Dec 31st, Jan 1st, Jan 30th, Mar 16th, 17th & 18th, Apr 21st & 22nd, May 5th (16 days)

ENQUIRIES
E W Gillespie Esq., The Steeplechase Co (Cheltenham) Ltd., Prestbury Park, Cheltenham, Glos. GL50 4SH Tel: (0242) 513014

COURSE STATISTICS 1987-92

	Total W/R	(%)	Hurdles Nov	Hcp	Chases Nov	Hcp	Level Stake
Top Trainers							
Pipe M C	52/241	21.5	27/94	10/71	6/24	9/52	- 38.24
Gifford J T	34/214	15.8	4/65	9/37	9/30	12/82	+ 26.65
Nicholson D	32/166	19.2	12/52	2/18	6/32	12/64	+ 18.34
Balding G B	22/124	17.7	7/40	6/34	5/18	4/32	+ 44.99
Henderson N J	17/ 94	18.0	6/36	3/24	3/11	5/23	+ 8.01
Barons D H	13/ 59	22.0	2/18	2/ 5	4/ 9	5/27	+ 68.00
Top Jockeys							
Scudamore P	44/210	20.9	17/74	7/50	7/25	13/61	- 76.55
Dunwoody R	40/236	16.9	14/73	5/52	6/33	15/78	- 17.68
Frost J	14/ 75	18.6	7/35	5/19	1/ 7	1/14	- 14.36
Hobbs Peter	11/ 74	14.8	3/26	4/14	2/ 9	2/25	+ 6.98
Osborne J	11/ 92	11.9	4/31	3/25	2/11	2/25	- 22.33
McCourt G	10/ 93	10.7	3/31	2/27	2/13	3/22	+ 51.25

Favourites Records									
Autmn	H:	41.2%	2m Hdl:	30.7%	2m Chs:	50.5%	Hvy	:	25.0%
	C:	46.5%	2.5m Hdl:	38.5%	2.5m Chs:	35.4%	Sft	:	33.8%
Wintr	H:	37.9%	3m Hdl:	35.1%	3m Chs:	27.7%	Gd-Sft:		26.7%
	C:	30.6%	3.5m Hdl:	0.0%	3.5m Chs:	33.3%	Gd	:	25.6%
Sprng	H:	21.4%	Nov Hdl:	36.3%	Nov Chs:	45.9%	Gd-Fm	:	46.5%
	C:	33.8%	Hcp Hdl:	30.2%	Hcp Chs:	31.9%	Fm/Hd	:	41.8%
Total	:	35.2%	L/Stake :	- 38.82	Lngst Wng Run:	5	Lngst Lsg Run:		10

CHEPSTOW

Situated in beautiful countryside in Piercefield Park, yet only a mile from the M4, Chepstow has much to recommend it for those reasons alone. While it stages both flat and jumping programmes, the latter enjoy far more popularity and, indeed, are of rather higher quality, despite occasional lack of numbers.

The Coral Welsh Grand National meeting in late December is the highlight of the calendar. The February meeting, quite often lost to the weather, features the Foodbrokers Persian War Novices Hurdle and the Weathercall Rising Stars Chase. The other main meeting in early March suffers from its proximity to the Cheltenham Festival. The Welsh Champion Hurdle is run here in April.

The left-handed track basically consists of two long straights and two sharp turns. It measures nearly two miles round, with many changing gradients, and 11 moderately stiff fences, of which the fourth last claims more than its fair share of victims. There are many changing gradients but few obstacles that continually catch horses out. The five furlong straight with five fences and a 240-yard run-in sounds daunting, particularly when it is soft underfoot, but front runners have always done well here.

FENCES: +++(+)   **RACING: £££(£)**

MEETINGS
Oct 3rd, Nov 7th, Dec 5th, Dec 28th Jan 12th, Jan 26th, Feb 6th, Feb 20th, Mar 13th, Mar 20th, Apr 12th & 13th, May 11th (13 days)

ENQUIRIES
Rodger D Farrant Esq., Tylers Farm, Gravel Hill Road, Goose Green, Yate, Nr Bristol, BS17 5BN Tel: (0291) 622260

COURSE STATISTICS 1987-92

Top Trainers	Total W/R	(%)	Hurdles Nov	Hcp	Chases Nov	Hcp	Level Stake
Pipe M C	57/183	31.1	15/56	12/59	15/27	15/41	+ 31.07
Pitman Mrs J	23/114	20.1	7/39	9/31	6/23	1/21	+ 12.22
Gifford J T	15/ 83	18.0	6/29	3/20	1/10	5/24	+ 29.38
Barons D H	14/ 94	14.8	4/31	2/21	1/15	7/27	+ 8.75
Balding G B	11/ 95	11.5	3/24	0/30	3/15	5/26	- 35.04
Edwards J A C	10/ 61	16.3	7/24	0/ 9	1/11	2/17	- 4.42
Top Jockeys							
Scudamore P	50/132	37.8	15/46	9/32	13/25	13/29	+ 35.46
Pitman M	19/ 77	24.6	7/30	5/16	6/20	1/11	+ 27.72
Dunwoody R	13/ 88	14.7	3/30	2/20	5/17	3/21	- 26.79
Powell B	12/ 78	15.3	2/23	1/14	3/20	6/21	+ 6.04
Hawke N	8/ 39	20.5	2/ 8	2/11	1/10	3/10	+ 24.50
Osborne J	8/ 46	17.3	3/19	1/11	2/ 8	2/ 8	- 5.75

Favourites Records

Autmn H:	32.1%	2m	Hdl:	42.7%	2m	Chs:	37.5%	Hvy :	39.8%
C:	32.1%	2.5m	Hdl:	37.0%	2.5m	Chs:	36.1%	Sft :	33.0%
Wintr H:	38.3%	3m	Hdl:	18.3%	3m	Chs:	45.8%	Gd-Sft:	48.0%
C:	36.2%	3.5m	Hdl:	0.0%	3.5m	Chs:	38.1%	Gd :	32.2%
Sprng H:	34.5%	Nov	Hdl:	36.5%	Nov	Chs:	39.3%	Gd-Fm :	30.6%
C:	46.2%	Hcp	Hdl:	34.1%	Hcp	Chs:	40.0%	Fm/Hd :	54.2%

Total : 37.4%   L/Stake : - 6.43   Lngst Wng Run: 6   Lngst Lsg Run: 10

DONCASTER

Doncaster's jump programme inevitably suffers by comparison with the flat racing at Town Moor, although the December meeting featuring the Freebooter Novices Chase sees some good sport, as does the January fixture which, when allowed to take place by the elements, offers the William Hill Golden Spurs Handicap Chase and the Rossington Main Novices Hurdle.

The pear-shaped track is essentially flat and left-handed, measuring about two miles. It is ideal for the long-striding horse, with easy turns and a run in of over a furlong. The fences are possibly too easy and many riders do not care for them since they ride like hurdles and sometimes enable a horse to get away with errors. Beware of the novice who has scraped round at Doncaster when he comes up against tougher obstacles.

FENCES: ✦(✦)　　　　　　　　　　　　　　　　　　　　　**RACING: £££(£)**

MEETINGS
Dec 11th & 12th, Jan 29th, Feb 24th, Mar 6th, Mar 8th (6 days)

ENQUIRIES
J F Sanderson Esq., Doncaster Racecourse, Grand Stand, Leger Way, Doncaster, DN2 6BB. Tel: (0302) 320066/7

COURSE STATISTICS 1987-92

	Total W/R	(%)	Hurdles Nov	Hcp	Chases Nov	Hcp	Level Stake
Top Trainers							
Edwards J A C	13/ 43	30.2	3/17	0/ 7	4/ 6	6/13	+ 21.93
Reveley Mrs G R	10/ 43	23.2	4/17	3/16	0/ 6	3/ 4	+ 8.20
Stephenson W A	8/ 55	14.5	1/13	0/ 6	1/15	6/21	- 19.54
Lee R	7/ 19	36.8	1/ 5	0/ 1	3/ 7	3/ 6	+ 16.17
FitzGerald J G	7/ 42	16.6	4/21	0/ 6	1/ 4	2/11	- 12.52
Easterby M W	6/ 17	35.2	3/ 6	2/ 8	0/ 1	1/ 2	+ 7.25
Top Jockeys							
Niven P	15/ 54	27.7	5/14	4/18	1/12	5/10	+ 19.08
McCourt G	9/ 34	26.4	1/11	3/13	4/ 6	1/ 4	- 6.55
Dwyer M	7/ 43	16.2	1/16	1/ 9	1/16	3/11	- 14.82
Dowling B	6/ 12	50.0	1/ 3	0/ 0	3/ 5	2/ 4	+ 18.17
Marley R	5/ 29	17.2	1/13	2/ 8	1/ 5	1/ 3	- 10.83
Grant C	5/ 49	10.2	1/13	0/12	1/10	3/14	- 30.54

Favourites Records

Autmn	H:	0.0%	2m	Hdl:	45.3%	2m	Chs:	47.9%	Hvy :	0.0%
	C:	0.0%	2.5m	Hdl:	41.9%	2.5m	Chs:	35.7%	Sft :	33.3%
Wintr	H:	44.0%	3m	Hdl:	34.6%	3m	Chs:	54.0%	Gd-Sft:	16.7%
	C:	46.2%	3.5m	Hdl:	0.0%	3.5m	Chs:	44.4%	Gd :	38.4%
Sprng	H:	38.6%	Nov	Hdl:	47.1%	Nov	Chs:	60.7%	Gd-Fm :	47.9%
	C:	36.7%	Hcp	Hdl:	37.0%	Hcp	Chs:	31.4%	Fm/Hd :	55.0%

Total : 43.7%　**L/Stake : + 4.64**　**Lngst Wng Run: 4**　**Lngst Lsg Run: 9**

EDINBURGH

Musselburgh racecourse is situated on the Firth of Forth with Muirfield's famous golf course a seven iron away. The sea air and sandy soil mean that the going at the track is seldom heavy and the cry often goes up North of the Border that racing "could have taken place at Edinburgh" when more fashionable fixtures have been lost to the weather in the South.

The track is flat and right-handed and measures approximately 11 furlongs. The eight fences are just about the easiest in Britain although the ones down the far side come pretty close together and place a premium on quick and accurate jumping. With the turns tight into the bargain, the course favours the handy, nippy type of runner.

FENCES: ✛   **RACING: ££(£)**

MEETINGS
Dec 7th, Dec 12th, Dec 21st, Jan 8th, Jan 15th, Feb 4th, Feb 19th, Feb 27th (8 days)

ENQUIRIES
Mr Mark Kershaw, Lothian Racing Syndicate Ltd, Racecourse Office, 2 Whitletts Road, Ayr, KA8 OJE Tel: (0292) 264179

COURSE STATISTICS 1987-92

	Total W/R	(%)	Hurdles Nov	Hcp	Chases Nov	Hcp	Level Stake
Top Trainers							
Reveley Mrs G R	17/ 69	24.6	7/28	1/15	4/15	5/11	- 14.01
FitzGerald J G	15/ 50	30.0	4/29	1/ 3	7/11	3/ 7	- 9.57
Stephenson W A	14/ 98	14.2	1/31	2/18	2/22	9/27	- 62.04
Smith Denys	12/ 50	24.0	4/19	0/11	4/11	4/ 9	- 3.92
Tinkler N	11/ 38	28.9	6/21	4/13	1/ 1	0/ 3	- 3.18
Moore G M	9/ 59	15.2	5/26	3/22	1/ 7	0/ 4	- 31.25
Top Jockeys							
Niven P	25/104	24.0	9/41	0/18	8/24	8/21	+ 22.06
Dwyer M	22/ 68	32.3	9/30	2/12	7/16	4/10	+ 26.31
McCourt G	19/ 55	34.5	8/23	7/17	2/10	2/ 5	+ 6.18
Grant C	17/ 74	22.9	2/27	2/17	5/13	8/17	- 29.23
Orkney A	10/ 36	27.7	2/16	3/ 5	3/11	2/ 4	+ 66.00
Storey B	9/ 87	10.3	5/40	0/15	1/21	3/11	- 19.25

Favourites Records							
Autmn H:	0.0%	2m Hdl:	45.4%	2m Chs:	50.0%	Hvy :	0.0%
C:	0.0%	2.5m Hdl:	41.7%	2.5m Chs:	43.8%	Sft :	0.0%
Wintr H:	38.6%	3m Hdl:	16.0%	3m Chs:	58.1%	Gd-Sft:	37.5%
C:	51.6%	3.5m Hdl:	0.0%	3.5m Chs:	0.0%	Gd :	47.8%
Sprng H:	0.0%	Nov Hdl:	42.1%	Nov Chs:	46.7%	Gd-Fm :	42.0%
C:	0.0%	Hcp Hdl:	32.6%	Hcp Chs:	56.3%	Fm/Hd :	0.0%
Total :	**44.2%**	**L/Stake :**	**+ 6.66**	**Lngst Wng Run:**	**5**	**Lngst Lsg Run:**	**7**

EXETER

Otherwise known as Haldon, Devon and Exeter is a favourite with racegoers as much for its friendly atmosphere as for its attractive situation on the fringes of Dartmoor. Racing begins early in the season here with a popular two day fixture in August and, while there is plenty of racing throughout the year, there are no events of any great significance.

The track is hilly and tricky, measuring almost two miles. The right-handed circuit is laid out in a long oval with a reasonably stiff uphill run-in of 300-yards. The position of the 11 fences is varied between the summer and winter courses, the winter one having four in each straight and the summer one five in the back straight and three in the home straight. This is not a suitable venue for the long-striding galloper although the home straight and run-in are certainly a test of character when the going is soft

FENCES: ✦✦(✦)   RACING: £

MEETINGS
Oct 13th, Oct 23rd, Nov 3rd, Nov 24th, Dec 4th, Jan 1st, Mar 24th, Apr 28th, May 3rd (9 days)

ENQUIRIES
R Merton Esq., Exeter Steeplechase Ltd, The Racecourse, Haldon, Nr Exeter, Devon.
Tel: (0392) 832599

COURSE STATISTICS 1987-92

	Total W/R	(%)	Hurdles Nov	Hcp	Chases Nov	Hcp	Level Stake
Top Trainers							
Pipe M C	106/265	40.0	65/145	22/70	9/23	10/27	- 1.12
Balding G B	26/110	23.6	9/42	10/35	3/11	4/22	+ 35.89
Hobbs P J	26/141	18.4	9/62	5/34	6/27	6/18	- 9.01
Frost R G	16/112	14.2	4/55	3/19	5/21	4/17	+ 3.46
Baker J H	15/ 78	19.2	6/43	5/22	2/ 7	2/ 6	- 16.37
Barons D H	10/108	9.2	3/56	2/18	1/18	4/16	- 55.70
Top Jockeys							
Scudamore P	87/180	48.3	53/87	15/41	10/24	9/28	+ 42.66
Frost J	25/140	17.8	6/57	4/29	8/26	7/28	+ 1.33
Hobbs Peter	17/105	16.1	8/45	2/27	5/22	2/11	- 27.28
Guest Richard	14/ 84	16.6	5/37	6/23	1/11	2/13	- 4.75
Powell B	14/153	9.1	3/67	3/39	3/20	5/27	- 80.24
Foster M*	8/ 26	30.7	6/14	1/11	0/ 0	1/ 1	- 0.27
Favourites Records							

Autmn	H:	48.0%	2m	Hdl:	43.2%	2m	Chs:	50.7%	Hvy : 52.8%
	C:	46.7%	2.5m	Hdl:	45.7%	2.5m	Chs:	50.0%	Sft : 33.0%
Wintr	H:	29.1%	3m	Hdl:	0.0%	3m	Chs:	31.3%	Gd-Sft: 30.4%
	C:	50.0%	3.5m	Hdl:	0.0%	3.5m	Chs:	83.3%	Gd : 37.7%
Sprng	H:	40.5%	Nov	Hdl:	50.2%	Nov	Chs:	41.9%	Gd-Fm : 48.5%
	C:	30.3%	Hcp	Hdl:	32.1%	Hcp	Chs:	43.3%	Fm/Hd : 48.9%
Total :		43.2%	L/Stake :	- 52.78		Lngst Wng Run: 11			Lngst Lsg Run: 17

FAKENHAM

Not far from Sandringham and just eight miles from the Norfolk coast, Fakenham is a popular course with holiday makers. The management run a caravan and camping site throughout the summer and invests the profits in the racecourse facilities.

The course is square-shaped, left-handed and undulating with a circuit of just a mile. The six fences are considered to be the easiest in the country with the one in the finishing straight followed by an uphill run-in of 200-yards. The open ditch is the only obstacle that demands extra care.

The track has recently been reshaped and widened to eliminate the sharp bends but it still favours the handy, free running jumper and is against a long-striding individual. It is noted for good going in wet weather thanks to the excellent drainage.

FENCES: ✚   RACING: £

MEETINGS
Oct 19th, Dec 18th, Feb 19th, Mar 19th, Apr 12th, May 31st (6 days)

ENQUIRIES
P B Firth Esq, 6 Hayes Lane, Fakenham, Norfolk, NR21 9ER. Tel: (0328) 862388

COURSE STATISTICS 1987-92

	Total W/R	(%)	Hurdles Nov	Hcp	Chases Nov	Hcp	Level Stake
Top Trainers							
Jenkins J R	10/ 45	22.2	0/ 5	6/24	2/ 6	2/10	- 2.17
Brooks C P E	8/ 20	40.0	3/ 7	3/ 4	1/ 3	1/ 6	+ 19.54
Ryan M J	6/ 18	33.3	2/ 7	3/ 8	0/ 0	1/ 3	+ 15.50
Tompkins M H	5/ 14	35.7	1/ 5	4/ 9	0/ 0	0/ 0	+ 1.91
Champion S	5/ 39	12.8	1/ 4	2/ 8	0/10	2/17	- 8.50
Vergette Mrs G	4/ 4	100.0	0/ 0	0/ 0	1/ 1	3/ 3	+ 6.50
Top Jockeys							
Carroll A	7/ 43	16.2	0/ 9	5/23	1/ 3	1/ 8	- 9.87
Dunwoody R	6/ 27	22.2	0/ 6	3/13	1/ 4	2/ 4	+ 1.17
Armytage Mr M	5/ 14	35.7	2/ 2	1/ 4	1/ 3	1/ 5	- 4.70
McLaughlin J	5/ 22	22.7	1/ 6	3/12	0/ 1	1/ 3	+ 4.50
Harding-Jones Mr	5/ 28	17.8	0/ 5	1/ 3	3/12	1/ 8	- 11.20
Durkan Mr J	4/ 11	36.3	1/ 2	1/ 4	0/ 0	2/ 5	+ 5.57

Favourites Records

Autmn	H:	25.0%	2m	Hdl:	31.3%	2m	Chs:	56.3%	Hvy : 0.0%
	C:	50.0%	2.5m	Hdl:	17.7%	2.5m	Chs:	48.5%	Sft : 33.3%
Wintr	H:	29.2%	3m	Hdl:	0.0%	3m	Chs:	41.4%	Gd-Sft: 32.0%
	C:	43.8%	3.5m	Hdl:	0.0%	3.5m	Chs:	0.0%	Gd : 37.2%
Sprng	H:	30.2%	Nov	Hdl:	29.7%	Nov	Chs:	48.5%	Gd-Fm : 91.7%
	C:	48.9%	Hcp	Hdl:	28.5%	Hcp	Chs:	46.7%	Fm/Hd : 16.7%

Total : 37.2% L/Stake : - 22.52 Lngst Wng Run: 7 Lngst Lsg Run: 8

FOLKESTONE

Situated at Westenhangen some seven miles west of Folkestone, the course provides popular sport for the Kent locals on the rare occasions that National Hunt racing takes place.

The oval track is right-handed and undulating with a circumference of about 11 furlongs. There are eight friendly fences per circuit, two of which are in the straight, and a run-in of 220-yards on the jump course and 250-yards on the hurdle course.

This is a fairly simple track which suits an adaptable sort of animal rather than one abundantly endowed with stamina.

FENCES: ✚   **RACING: £(£)**

MEETINGS
Nov 23rd, Dec 15th, Dec 31st, Jan 19th, Feb 17th, Feb 24th, Mar 10th May 11th (8 days)

ENQUIRIES
C E Griggs Esq, Pratt & Company, 11 Boltro Road, Haywards Heath, Sussex, RH16 1BP. Tel: (0444) 441111

COURSE STATISTICS 1987-92

	Total W/R	(%)	Hurdles Nov	Hcp	Chases Nov	Hcp	Level Stake
Top Trainers							
Gifford J T	16/ 96	16.6	6/38	1/ 6	4/21	5/31	- 35.96
Grissell D M	11/ 40	27.5	5/21	1/ 3	3/11	2/ 5	+ 27.68
Akehurst R	9/ 39	23.0	7/30	0/ 3	1/ 4	1/ 2	+ 29.85
Jenkins J R	6/ 41	14.6	2/19	2/ 9	0/ 4	2/ 9	+ 8.25
Sherwood O	5/ 30	16.6	1/12	0/ 4	3/12	1/ 2	- 0.12
Forster Capt T A	5/ 38	13.1	1/ 9	0/ 0	2/15	2/14	+ 18.75
Top Jockeys							
Davies H	12/ 66	18.1	6/34	1/ 7	3/15	2/10	+ 2.18
Murphy D J	9/ 49	18.3	3/25	3/ 5	2/ 9	1/10	- 3.10
Richards M	7/ 37	18.9	2/11	1/ 6	2/11	2/ 9	+ 28.63
Powell B	7/ 37	18.9	1/17	0/ 3	3/ 8	3/ 9	+ 6.44
Hobbs Peter	5/ 31	16.1	1/13	0/ 1	3/ 7	1/10	- 12.59
Llewellyn C	5/ 36	13.8	2/13	0/ 3	1/12	2/ 8	+ 20.25

Favourites Records

Autmn	H:	10.0%	2m	Hdl:	31.7%	2m	Chs:	61.1%	Hvy :	44.5%
	C:	27.8%	2.5m	Hdl:	80.0%	2.5m	Chs:	31.8%	Sft :	16.7%
Wintr	H:	33.1%	3m	Hdl:	32.2%	3m	Chs:	0.0%	Gd-Sft:	35.3%
	C:	36.2%	3.5m	Hdl:	0.0%	3.5m	Chs:	29.8%	Gd :	37.3%
Sprng	H:	54.6%	Nov	Hdl:	31.2%	Nov	Chs:	33.9%	Gd-Fm :	26.9%
	C:	29.3%	Hcp	Hdl:	37.5%	Hcp	Chs:	32.5%	Fm/Hd :	52.5%
Total :		**33.2%**	**L/Stake :**		**- 23.36**	**Lngst Wng Run:**		**5**	**Lngst Lsg Run:**	**10**

FONTWELL PARK

Picturesquely situated between Goodwood and Chichester, this unusual track is popular with trainers and public alike although newcomers can be forgiven a certain amount of confusion during the steeplechases.

The hurdle course is a left-handed oval, about a mile in circumference, with four flights and is straightforward enough, if on the tight side for some. The chase course, though, is a figure-of-eight with a water-jump, an open ditch and five fences all constructed on the 'X' of the figure-of-eight. There is a 230-yard run-in which is uphill and slightly to the left. This is unquestionably a course for specialists who must be handy and adaptable.

FENCES: ✚(✚) RACING: £(£)

MEETINGS
Oct 12th, Oct 28th, Dec 1st, Dec 30th, Jan 18th, Feb 8th, Feb 22nd, Mar 23rd, Apr 15th, May 3rd, May 31st (11 days)

ENQUIRIES
C E Griggs Esq, Pratt & Company, 11 Boltro Road, Haywards Heath, Sussex, RH16 1BP. Tel: (0444) 441111

COURSE STATISTICS 1987-92

	Total W/R	(%)	Hurdles Nov	Hcp	Chases Nov	Hcp	Level Stake
Top Trainers							
Gifford J T	44/195	22.5	16/79	8/33	7/34	13/49	+ 8.19
Pipe M C	38/ 98	38.7	18/44	8/29	6/13	6/12	+ 7.76
Balding G B	16/ 88	18.1	5/37	1/17	5/15	5/19	− 36.21
Akehurst R	15/ 64	23.4	6/29	8/29	0/ 1	1/ 5	+ 20.20
Hobbs P J	14/ 44	31.8	7/23	0/ 1	1/ 8	6/12	+ 10.39
Grissell D M	12/ 62	19.3	3/30	2/ 9	3/12	4/11	+ 5.69
Top Jockeys							
Scudamore P	28/ 77	36.3	16/40	5/22	4/ 6	3/ 9	− 3.34
Davies H	20/122	16.3	7/55	3/18	1/13	9/36	+ 11.44
Frost J	16/ 63	25.4	5/24	2/13	7/15	2/11	− 18.74
Hobbs Peter	15/ 68	22.0	3/25	3/ 9	3/16	6/18	+ 3.93
McKeown Dale	12/ 74	16.2	8/43	4/24	0/ 4	0/ 3	+ 3.25
Richards M	12/ 91	13.1	5/40	3/16	1/16	3/19	− 37.37

Favourites Records

Autmn	H:	37.8%	2m	Hdl:	0.0%	2m	Chs:	0.0%	Hvy :	61.1%
	C:	52.3%	2.5m Hdl:	39.8%	2.5m	Chs:	49.6%	Sft :	33.7%
Wintr	H:	34.4%	3m	Hdl:	36.7%	3m	Chs:	0.0%	Gd-Sft:	48.2%
	C:	51.6%	3.5m Hdl:	0.0%	3.5m	Chs:	48.5%	Gd :	44.2%
Sprng	H:	47.6%	Nov	Hdl:	39.7%	Nov	Chs:	57.2%	Gd-Fm :	45.0%
	C:	43.8%	Hcp	Hdl:	38.6%	Hcp	Chs:	44.0%	Fm/Hd :	41.5%

Total : 43.5% L/Stake : + 26.96 Lngst Wng Run: 7 Lngst Lsg Run: 10

HAYDOCK PARK

Undoubtedly the premier track in the north-west, Haydock Park is a most attractive venue. First class facilities, combined with the fact that the area is somewhat starved of good racing, means that excellent crowds turn up for the better fixtures. The main meetings are in January and early March. The early January fixture features the Newton Chase and later in the month there is the Peter Marsh chase and a Champion Hurdle Trial which generally attracts the leading Northern trained hurdlers. The March fixture suffers from the proximity of Cheltenham, particularly the Greenalls Gold Cup Chase, which is steadily on the decline, although the Timeform Chase and the Victor Ludorum Hurdle provide good back-up.

The course itself, a left-handed oval of about 13 furlongs, is one of the fairest in the country. It is flat and, although the bends are somewhat sharp on the hurdle course, Haydock is essentially a galloping track. The ten stiff fences are among the toughest in the land, but well-regarded by the jockeys. They are evenly spaced along the front and back stretches and there is a testing run-in of two furlongs. The nature of the fences occasionally leads to small, select fields in the better chases but this seldom detracts from the quality of the sport.

FENCES: ✛✛✛✛   **RACING: £££(£)**

MEETINGS
Nov 11th, Nov 18th & 19th, Dec 9th & 10th, Jan 9th, Jan 23rd, Feb 26th & 27th, May 3rd (10 days)

ENQUIRIES
C H Barnett Esq, Haydock Park Racecourse Co Ltd, Newton le Willows, Merseyside, WA12 0HQ. Tel: (0942) 727345/727731

COURSE STATISTICS 1987-92

	Total W/R	(%)	Hurdles Nov	Hcp	Chases Nov	Hcp	Level Stake
Top Trainers							
Pipe M C	49/129	37.9	18/39	9/33	7/20	15/37	+ 20.48
Richards G W	24/101	23.7	1/38	2/13	9/20	12/30	+ 2.63
O'Neill J J	9/ 56	16.0	2/28	6/21	1/ 3	0/ 4	- 13.66
McCain D	9/ 70	12.8	3/30	0/ 9	2/18	4/13	+ 6.61
Brooks C P E	8/ 31	25.8	1/ 9	0/ 8	4/ 6	3/ 8	+ 6.07
FitzGerald J G	8/ 53	15.0	4/23	1/10	0/ 3	3/17	- 13.79
Top Jockeys							
Scudamore P	42/107	39.2	17/40	5/23	9/17	11/27	+ 29.85
Doughty N	20/ 69	28.9	1/25	2/13	7/14	10/17	+ 16.03
McCourt G	16/ 90	17.7	1/31	3/23	4/18	8/18	- 2.68
Dwyer M	16/103	15.5	5/39	4/29	3/15	4/20	- 38.27
Bradley G	10/ 47	21.2	5/20	0/13	4/ 8	1/ 6	+ 7.46
Dunwoody R	9/ 57	15.7	3/22	1/12	2/ 9	3/14	- 10.59

Favourites Records

Autmn	H:	45.5%	2m	Hdl:	33.8%	2m	Chs:	51.9%	Hvy	:	51.0%
	C:	63.6%	2.5m	Hdl:	54.0%	2.5m	Chs:	51.3%	Sft	:	51.2%
Wintr	H:	46.2%	3m	Hdl:	52.3%	3m	Chs:	56.8%	Gd-Sft:		45.5%
	C:	52.0%	3.5m	Hdl:	0.0%	3.5m	Chs:	60.0%	Gd	:	45.6%
Sprng	H:	36.7%	Nov	Hdl:	52.7%	Nov	Chs:	56.8%	Gd-Fm	:	33.3%
	C:	46.7%	Hcp	Hdl:	29.8%	Hcp	Chs:	52.1%	Fm/Hd	:	33.3%

Total : 48.0%   L/Stake : + 21.65   Lngst Wng Run: 5   Lngst Lsg Run: 7

HEREFORD

The course is situated in pleasant surroundings a mile from the Cathedral city of Hereford. Attendances are seldom high, probably because the standard of the runners is poor, but the track is certainly popular with trainers and the fields here are generally above average in size.

Hereford's right-handed circuit of a mile and a half, with a 300-yard run-in, is virtually square. The turns are easier than appears the case from a course diagram with the exception of the home turn which is on falling ground and quite sharp. There are nine stiffish fences, the one after the winning post needing to be negotiated on the turn, making an excellent test for a jumper.

FENCES: +++   **RACING: £**

MEETINGS
Oct 23rd, Nov 3rd, Nov 25th, Dec 4th, Dec 22nd, Feb 15th, Mar 6th, Apr 3rd, Apr 12th, May 1st, May 12th, May 27th, May 31st (13 days)

ENQUIRIES
John Williams Esq., Hereford Racecourse Co Ltd., Shepherds Meadow, Lane Head, Eaton Bishop, Hereford, HR2 9UA Tel: (0981) 250436

COURSE STATISTICS 1987-92

Top Trainers	Total W/R	(%)	Hurdles Nov	Hcp	Chases Nov	Hcp	Level Stake
Pipe M C	37/124	29.8	18/64	9/36	6/14	4/10	- 27.39
Nicholson D	18/ 62	29.0	9/27	0/ 1	3/13	6/21	+ 13.12
Edwards J A C	15/ 84	17.8	3/36	1/ 5	6/18	5/25	- 0.38
Holder R J	13/ 62	20.9	6/42	1/ 9	4/ 6	2/ 5	- 0.82
Burchell D	11/ 43	25.5	4/21	6/16	0/ 2	1/ 4	+ 0.68
Barons D H	11/ 48	22.9	5/19	0/ 7	2/12	4/10	+ 10.23
Top Jockeys							
Dunwoody R	23/ 96	23.9	9/37	1/21	7/20	6/18	+ 3.30
Scudamore P	22/ 67	32.8	9/34	6/15	4/ 9	3/ 9	- 15.20
Burchell D J	13/ 49	26.5	4/24	8/18	0/ 3	1/ 4	+ 6.01
Tegg D	12/ 77	15.5	2/24	3/23	3/15	4/15	+ 13.25
Osborne J	10/ 20	50.0	5/ 8	0/ 5	4/ 5	1/ 2	+ 14.71
McNeill S	10/ 58	17.2	5/26	4/11	1/ 9	0/12	+ 32.00

Favourites Records

Autmn	H:	35.9%	2m Hdl:	35.0%	2m Chs:	59.8%	Hvy :	45.0%
	C:	42.2%	2.5m Hdl:	44.9%	2.5m Chs:	42.0%	Sft :	34.8%
Wintr	H:	40.9%	3m Hdl:	13.6%	3m Chs:	41.8%	Gd-Sft:	45.3%
	C:	50.0%	3.5m Hdl:	0.0%	3.5m Chs:	0.0%	Gd :	38.5%
Sprng	H:	32.4%	Nov Hdl:	34.4%	Nov Chs:	48.9%	Gd-Fm :	33.8%
	C:	47.3%	Hcp Hdl:	36.8%	Hcp Chs:	42.8%	Fm/Hd :	42.1%
Total :		**39.6%**	**L/Stake :**	**- 35.38**	**Lngst Wng Run:**	**9**	**Lngst Lsg Run:**	**9**

HEXHAM

Of all the 'gaffs' as the smaller tracks are often called, Hexham is without peer in terms of situation and charm. It is perched high above the Northumbrian border country in a natural bowl that allows an excellent view of the action and the breathtaking scenery. The major drawback is the weather, or rather the wind, which is seldom less than gusting and very chilly. The spectator has little protection from the elements, natural or otherwise and, consequently, there are no fixtures in January or February.

The left-handed track is extremely testing, particularly when the going is very soft. The rectangular mile and a half circuit contains ten very easy fences. The long back straight slopes quite sharply downhill and there follows a steep climb to the winning post with a run-in of 250-yards that flattens out in front of the stands. The finish is actually on a separate spur, containing one fence that many jockeys consider the easiest in Britain. A poor jumper will enjoy Hexham but one lacking in stamina certainly will not.

FENCES: ++   **RACING: £**

MEETINGS
Oct 2nd, Oct 15th, Nov 6th, Nov 25th, Dec 11th, Mar 18th, Mar 29th, Apr 24th & 26th, May 1st, May 29th & 31st (12 days)

ENQUIRIES
S C Enderby Esq., Hexham Steeplechase Co Ltd., The Riding, Hexham, Northumberland, NE46 4PF Tel: (0434) 606881

COURSE STATISTICS 1987-92

	Total W/R	(%)	Hurdles Nov	Hcp	Chases Nov	Hcp	Level Stake
Top Trainers							
Stephenson W A	44/219	20.0	7/93	6/25	12/49	19/52	- 52.85
Richards G W	30/125	24.0	12/52	4/17	10/32	4/24	+ 28.14
Moore G M	29/101	28.7	19/47	5/27	4/19	1/ 8	- 3.62
Reveley Mrs G R	16/ 77	20.7	3/26	5/16	5/25	3/10	- 1.53
Monteith P	13/ 51	25.4	1/12	7/14	3/21	2/ 4	+ 20.91
Hammond M D	9/ 51	17.6	4/21	0/ 7	1/13	4/10	- 22.00
Top Jockeys							
Grant C	36/155	23.2	7/52	1/29	10/35	18/39	- 11.29
Niven P	19/116	16.3	2/39	5/24	5/33	7/20	- 19.15
Dwyer M	16/ 74	21.6	4/27	5/22	4/14	3/11	- 13.85
Storey B	16/187	8.5	2/56	0/42	4/45	10/44	- 96.92
Doughty N	14/ 57	24.5	4/23	2/10	7/17	1/ 7	+ 8.56
O'Hara L	12/ 72	16.6	4/28	4/18	1/12	3/14	+ 1.76

Favourites Records

Autmn	H:	45.3%	2m	Hdl:	40.8%	2m	Chs:	35.2%	Hvy : 25.0%
	C:	34.4%	2.5m	Hdl:	42.7%	2.5m	Chs:	31.6%	Sft : 29.6%
Wintr	H:	44.4%	3m	Hdl:	29.8%	3m	Chs:	40.3%	Gd-Sft: 37.8%
	C:	22.2%	3.5m	Hdl:	0.0%	3.5m	Chs:	33.3%	Gd : 34.2%
Sprng	H:	36.6%	Nov	Hdl:	42.6%	Nov	Chs:	38.0%	Gd-Fm : 43.9%
	C:	38.0%	Hcp	Hdl:	35.9%	Hcp	Chs:	34.2%	Fm/Hd : 45.7%

Total : 38.3% L/Stake : - 38.36 Lngst Wng Run: 8 Lngst Lsg Run: 10

HUNTINGDON

Huntingdon's rather featureless racecourse is seldom well attended, save for Bank Holidays. Many of the fixtures are on weekdays and the sport and facilities are some way short of top-class. On the plus side, the Cambridgeshire course is conveniently placed just off the A1 and the excellent drainage ensures that there is almost always decent jumping ground. The two and a half mile Sidney Banks Hurdle in February is the major event of the season. February also sees the Chatteris Fen Hurdle, a good Triumph Hurdle trial.

The track itself is a right-handed oval of approximately one and a half miles. It is flat, with easy turns, and with the ground generally on the fast side, the runners need to be able to maintain a good gallop. The nine fences are moderately easy with the exception of the two in the straight. The penultimate, in particular, finds out many a novice. The flat 200-yard run-in holds few terrors but horses seldom have a chance to get a breather here, so staying is the name of the game.

FENCES: ++   **RACING: £(£)**

MEETINGS
Oct 24th, Nov 13th, Nov 24th, Dec 2nd, Dec 26th, Jan 28th, Feb 11th, Feb 23rd, Mar 17th, Apr 12th, Apr 19th, May 13th, May 31st (13 days)

ENQUIRIES
Mr R G Thomas, Huntingdon Steeplechases Ltd., Brampton Racecourse, Huntingdon, Cambs PE18 8NN. Tel: (0480) 453373 / 454610

COURSE STATISTICS 1987-92

Top Trainers	Total W/R	(%)	Hurdles Nov	Hcp	Chases Nov	Hcp	Level Stake
Gifford J T	21/103	20.3	7/34	3/12	8/26	3/31	- 10.03
Pitman Mrs J	14/ 58	24.1	8/28	0/ 5	5/17	1/ 8	+ 3.10
Murphy F	14/ 61	22.9	2/13	1/ 7	3/15	8/26	+ 5.29
Nicholson D	14/ 70	20.0	4/26	1/ 3	5/18	4/23	- 10.01
Balding G B	11/ 72	15.2	3/27	3/15	3/16	2/14	- 38.93
Hubbard G A	11/ 92	11.9	1/22	3/15	3/26	4/29	- 17.37
Top Jockeys							
Dunwoody R	23/143	16.0	7/55	2/32	8/24	6/32	- 44.22
Murphy D J	16/ 93	17.2	3/41	3/25	4/11	6/16	- 37.82
Davies H	13/ 97	13.4	2/35	5/14	1/21	5/27	- 47.46
Pitman M	10/ 34	29.4	5/16	0/ 3	4/10	1/ 5	+ 13.94
White J	9/ 40	22.5	3/16	1/ 5	1/ 6	4/13	- 7.38
Perrett M	9/ 45	20.0	6/25	0/ 7	1/ 4	2/ 9	+ 40.74

Favourites Records

Autmn H:	31.5%	2m Hdl:	31.9%	2m Chs:	32.1%	Hvy :	0.0%
C:	45.2%	2.5m Hdl:	31.0%	2.5m Chs:	45.3%	Sft :	39.6%
Wintr H:	28.1%	3m Hdl:	47.4%	3m Chs:	46.3%	Gd-Sft:	39.5%
C:	47.5%	3.5m Hdl:	0.0%	3.5m Chs:	0.0%	Gd :	34.7%
Sprng H:	38.1%	Nov Hdl:	36.7%	Nov Chs:	44.4%	Gd-Fm :	39.2%
C:	34.5%	Hcp Hdl:	27.0%	Hcp Chs:	40.4%	Fm/Hd :	34.4%
Total :	**37.1%**	**L/Stake : - 54.91**		**Lngst Wng Run: 6**		**Lngst Lsg Run: 13**	

KELSO

Situated somewhat remotely in the heart of the Scottish Border country, Kelso is attended in the main by the local farming and hunting community. Crowds are small but knowledgeable, and a friendly, professional atmosphere prevails. Chases tend to be of a higher quality than the hurdle races here, partly due to the nature of the smaller hurdle track.

Kelso possesses two left-handed circuits, the chase course measuring one mile 600-yards, and the very sharp hurdle course measuring a mile and 330-yards. The nine fences are no stiffer than average, but are well-constructed and ride excellently according to the jockeys.

The back stretch of the chase course is gently downhill, with two tricky fences, but the uphill run-in of 440-yards, most of it on an elbow, is very testing. The tight nature of some of the turns, particularly the one after the stands, make the course unsuitable for the long-striding type, but courage and stamina is at a premium for the tiring final slog to the line.

FENCES: ✦✦(✦)   **RACING: £**

MEETINGS
Oct 3rd, Oct 17th, Nov 4th, Nov 12th, Nov 30th, Dec 17th, Jan 13th, Feb 5th, Mar 5th, Mar 24th, Apr 5th, Apr 28th (12 days)

ENQUIRIES
R M Landale Esq., Kelso Races Ltd., c/o John Sales & Partners, 18-20 Glendale Road, Wooler, Northumberland NE71 6DW. Tel: (0668) 81611

COURSE STATISTICS 1987-92

	Total W/R	(%)	Hurdles Nov	Hcp	Chases Nov	Hcp	Level Stake
Top Trainers							
Richards G W	40/158	25.3	14/64	4/21	9/30	13/43	+ 30.05
Stephenson W A	39/252	15.4	9/96	7/37	7/59	16/60	- 80.28
Reveley Mrs G R	27/106	25.4	11/49	6/22	1/16	9/19	+ 6.01
Moore G M	19/ 98	19.3	10/47	4/27	4/16	1/ 8	- 12.99
Monteith P	12/ 79	15.1	3/32	1/22	4/16	4/ 9	- 22.90
Hammond M D	9/ 41	21.9	5/19	0/ 8	2/ 6	2/ 8	+ 1.67
Top Jockeys							
Niven P	29/133	21.8	12/56	3/21	5/31	9/25	- 18.57
Doughty N	28/ 91	30.7	15/45	3/12	6/19	4/15	+ 14.64
Grant C	21/140	15.0	2/50	4/22	5/34	10/34	- 75.24
Dwyer M	15/ 92	16.3	5/40	2/16	5/19	3/17	- 28.68
O'Hara L	13/ 69	18.8	1/33	2/13	3/10	7/13	+ 3.37
Storey B	13/163	7.9	3/69	2/21	4/36	4/37	- 87.89

Favourites Records

Autmn H:	36.4%	2m Hdl:	33.9%	2m Chs:	35.2%	Hvy :	32.1%
C:	44.3%	2.5m Hdl:	42.5%	2.5m Chs:	0.0%	Sft :	44.1%
Wintr H:	33.8%	3m Hdl:	32.0%	3m Chs:	56.0%	Gd-Sft:	35.7%
C:	44.2%	3.5m Hdl:	0.0%	3.5m Chs:	13.3%	Gd :	26.9%
Sprng H:	31.7%	Nov Hdl:	34.0%	Nov Chs:	54.1%	Gd-Fm :	57.7%
C:	48.9%	Hcp Hdl:	34.6%	Hcp Chs:	39.9%	Fm/Hd :	50.0%

Total : 39.2%   L/Stake : - 23.73   Lngst Wng Run: 7   Lngst Lsg Run: 9

KEMPTON PARK

Kempton Park is now hard to match in terms of facilities, access and indeed quality of racing, but one element is rather lacking: atmosphere. The track very much epitomises its suburban surroundings, just off the M3, although there is a tremendous buzz on Boxing Day, where large crowds turn up for the King George.

The sport is of a high standard at almost every fixture. The Charisma Gold Cup in October starts the season off, but it, and almost everything else, is dwarfed by the two-day Christmas meeting featuring the King George VI Rank Chase and the Top Rank Christmas Hurdle the day after. January and February provide the Lanzarote Hurdle, the Tote Placepot (4yo) Hurdle, the valuable Racing Post Handicap Chase and the three-mile Rendlesham Hurdle.

The track itself is a flat right-hander, triangular in shape, measuring one mile five and a half furlongs. The circuit boasts ten fences, well-constructed and quite a stiff, but fair test of a jumper, with a run-in of 175-yards. Some of the turns are tight, and the course is essentially sharp in nature, favouring front-runners. The very long run, on the turn, between the last obstacle on the far side and the first in the straight, places the emphasis firmly on speed.

FENCES: +++(+)   **RACING: ££££(£)**

MEETINGS
Oct 17th, Oct 29th, Nov 18th, Dec 26th, Dec 28th, Jan 22nd & 23rd, Feb 26th & 27th (9 days)

ENQUIRIES
Major R M O Webster, United Racecourses (Holdings) Ltd., Kempton Park Racecourse, Sunbury-on Thames, Middx TW16 5AQ. Tel: (0932) 782292

COURSE STATISTICS 1987-92

Top Trainers	Total W/R	(%)	Hurdles Nov	Hcp	Chases Nov	Hcp	Level Stake
Gifford J T	20/138	14.4	3/40	4/31	9/33	4/34	- 43.22
Sherwood O	19/ 72	26.3	7/24	3/21	9/20	0/ 7	+ 7.33
Elsworth D R C	18/ 86	20.9	4/36	3/19	6/12	5/19	+ 6.96
Henderson N J	16/ 77	20.7	8/29	0/12	6/18	2/18	- 18.11
Pipe M C	11/ 54	20.3	6/23	2/14	1/ 7	2/10	- 13.44
Pitman Mrs J	11/ 59	18.6	5/28	4/18	0/ 6	2/ 7	- 17.48
Top Jockeys							
Dunwoody R	27/129	20.9	6/43	4/27	10/30	7/29	- 25.98
Osborne J	18/ 88	20.4	7/36	2/13	8/21	1/18	- 16.29
Scudamore P	13/ 86	15.1	7/33	2/21	3/19	1/13	- 39.14
McCourt G	12/ 68	17.6	6/24	4/19	1/15	1/10	+ 5.07
Powell B	11/ 91	12.0	1/30	0/12	4/24	6/25	- 45.14
Frost J	8/ 43	18.6	5/20	2/ 7	1/11	0/ 5	- 8.90

Favourites Records

Autmn H:	31.9%	2m	Hdl:	37.3%	2m	Chs:	55.3%	Hvy :	30.8%
C:	51.1%	2.5m	Hdl:	33.0%	2.5m	Chs:	39.4%	Sft :	28.6%
Wintr H:	35.4%	3m	Hdl:	25.0%	3m	Chs:	38.9%	Gd-Sft:	37.7%
C:	39.9%	3.5m	Hdl:	0.0%	3.5m	Chs:	0.0%	Gd :	42.9%
Sprng H:	0.0%	Nov	Hdl:	37.7%	Nov	Chs:	51.7%	Gd-Fm :	33.1%
C:	0.0%	Hcp	Hdl:	29.3%	Hcp	Chs:	37.4%	Fm/Hd :	48.5%

Total : 38.8%   L/Stake : - 7.54   Lngst Wng Run: 5   Lngst Lsg Run: 10

LEICESTER

Surrounded as it is by some of the best-known hunts in the country, among others the Quorn and the Fernie, the quality of steeplechasing at this rather characterless track is very moderate. Moreover, unlike its flat counterpart, the pulse cannot be quickened by the occasional presence of a Henry Cecil-trained classic aspirant. That said, the facilities at the Midlands venue are good, and its central location attracts good-sized fields from all over the country.

The circuit itself is rectangular, a right-hander measuring one and three-quarter miles, but is essentially two long, undulating straights. The ten fences are quite severe, but the chief feature is an uphill finish of three furlongs and three fences, which takes its toll when underfoot conditions are poor. The 250-yard run-in takes in a slight elbow on the chase course, which often leads to Stewards' Enquiries due to tired horses becoming slightly unbalanced in finishes.

FENCES: +++   **RACING: £**

MEETINGS
Nov 16th, Nov 20th, Dec 31st, Jan 1st, Jan 12th, Jan 25th, Feb 3rd, Feb 18th, Mar 1st Mar 9th (10 days)

ENQUIRIES
D C Henson Esq, Leicester Racecourse Co Ltd, 2 Lower Mounts, Northampton NN1 3DE. Tel: (0604) 30757 (office) / (0533) 716515 (racecourse)

COURSE STATISTICS 1987-92

	Total W/R	(%)	Hurdles Nov	Hcp	Chases Nov	Hcp	Level Stake
Top Trainers							
Pitman Mrs J	29/ 85	34.1	8/37	1/11	15/23	5/14	+ 33.14
Pipe M C	25/ 65	38.4	14/31	3/13	7/12	1/ 9	+ 7.49
Sherwood O	7/ 31	22.5	3/16	1/ 3	2/ 7	1/ 5	+ 11.94
Lee R	7/ 37	18.9	0/ 9	0/ 5	5/10	2/13	+ 1.40
Old J A B	6/ 35	17.1	0/ 3	2/ 7	1/ 7	3/18	+ 59.30
Tompkins M H	5/ 14	35.7	3/10	2/ 4	0/ 0	0/ 0	+ 5.30
Top Jockeys							
Pitman M	24/ 62	38.7	7/29	1/ 5	12/17	4/11	+ 39.85
Scudamore P	20/ 56	35.7	13/28	3/12	3/ 7	1/ 9	- 10.81
Dunwoody R	10/ 67	14.9	4/29	1/10	2/13	3/15	- 35.28
Osborne J	8/ 48	16.6	5/21	0/11	1/ 6	2/10	+ 30.57
Eccles S Smith	7/ 26	26.9	6/17	0/ 4	1/ 3	0/ 2	+ 19.75
Richards M	7/ 40	17.5	4/15	2/12	1/ 8	0/ 5	+ 6.70

Favourites Records

Autmn	H:	28.8%	2m Hdl:	32.6%	2m Chs:	39.7%	Hvy :	39.1%
	C:	39.5%	2.5m Hdl:	33.3%	2.5m Chs:	45.7%	Sft :	36.6%
Wintr	H:	36.1%	3m Hdl:	56.3%	3m Chs:	42.0%	Gd-Sft:	38.7%
	C:	42.4%	3.5m Hdl:	0.0%	3.5m Chs:	0.0%	Gd :	41.5%
Sprng	H:	0.0%	Nov Hdl:	32.6%	Nov Chs:	46.8%	Gd-Fm :	32.8%
	C:	46.7%	Hcp Hdl:	32.4%	Hcp Chs:	38.7%	Fm/Hd :	50.0%

Total : 38.6% L/Stake : - 32.21 Lngst Wng Run: 8 Lngst Lsg Run: 10

LINGFIELD PARK

Lingfield Park is an attractive, leafy course set in the Kent/Surrey borderland, and the progressive management have rightly been rewarded by ever-increasing crowds over the last few years. However, the jumping here is undoubtedly inferior in quality to the Flat, maybe partly due to the tricky nature of the course itself.

The circuit is a conically shaped, left-hander of approximately a mile and a quarter, with the main feature being the gradients. The most notable of these is a tight downhill turn into the straight, itself measuring four furlongs, before a comparatively short run-in of 200-yards. The ten fences are no stiffer than average, but the fourth last is apt to catch out novices. The turns and gradients do not suit many horses and course specialists, usually handy types, are worth following here. The going, which is often on the soft side, can become particularly holding.

The All-Weather track is left handed, one and a quarter miles round, generally flat with a very gradual descent from five furlongs to one and a half furlongs out. The Equitrack surface consists of graded sand particles encapsulated in a synthetic binder. The portable plastic hurdles are very easy.

FENCES: ♦♦(♦)   **RACING: ££**

MEETINGS
Dec 12th, Dec 21st, Jan 5th* & 6th Jan 11th & 12th*, Jan 21st*, Jan 25th & 26th*, Feb 2nd*, Feb 5th, Feb 9th*, Feb 16th*, Feb 23rd*, Mar 2nd*, Mar 9th*, Mar 16th*, Mar 19th & 20th (10 days AW, 9 days Turf)

ENQUIRIES
Mr A W Sunley Esq, Lingfield Park (1991) Ltd, Racecourse Road, Lingfield, Surrey, RH7 6PQ Tel: (0342) 834800

TURF COURSE STATISTICS 1987-92 *(All-Weather Statistics p.317)*

	Total W/R	(%)	Hurdles Nov	Hcp	Chases Nov	Hcp	Level Stake
Top Trainers							
Akehurst R	16/ 69	23.1	10/36	4/21	2/ 7	0/ 5	+ 37.91
Sanders Miss B	14/ 38	36.8	1/11	12/25	1/ 2	0/ 0	+ 12.21
Gifford J T	11/ 73	15.0	2/20	2/12	3/22	4/19	- 24.92
Pitman Mrs J	10/ 34	29.4	3/ 9	6/17	0/ 4	1/ 4	- 5.00
Pipe M C	9/ 43	20.9	4/17	0/13	4/ 7	1/ 6	- 18.74
Jenkins J R	9/ 64	14.0	0/11	9/45	0/ 4	0/ 4	- 26.37
Top Jockeys							
Scudamore P	9/ 44	20.4	3/21	0/ 6	5/ 9	1/ 8	- 23.61
McKeown Dale	9/ 46	19.5	7/26	2/15	0/ 2	0/ 3	+ 30.57
Davies H	9/ 60	15.0	1/20	2/10	4/18	2/12	+ 44.54
Perrett M	7/ 46	15.2	1/24	0/ 7	5/ 8	1/ 7	+ 13.78
Osborne J	6/ 25	24.0	3/12	0/ 4	1/ 3	2/ 6	+ 1.60
White J	5/ 22	22.7	0/ 3	0/ 2	1/ 8	4/ 9	+ 8.78

Favourites Records

Autmn H:	50.0%	2m	Hdl:	33.3%	2m	Chs:	41.2%	Hvy :	30.2%
C:	0.0%	2.5m	Hdl:	46.8%	2.5m	Chs:	46.5%	Sft :	29.8%
Wintr H:	37.1%	3m	Hdl:	50.0%	3m	Chs:	25.0%	Gd-Sft:	25.0%
C:	33.6%	3.5m	Hdl:	0.0%	3.5m	Chs:	0.0%	Gd :	36.6%
Sprng H:	39.3%	Nov	Hdl:	28.3%	Nov	Chs:	46.1%	Gd-Fm :	55.6%
C:	40.4%	Hcp	Hdl:	41.6%	Hcp	Chs:	26.7%	Fm/Hd :	0.0%

Total   : 37.5%   L/Stake : - 35.28   Lngst Wng Run: 6 Lngst Lsg Run: 7

LIVERPOOL

Home of the world's greatest steeplechase, the Grand National, Aintree has a tremendous atmosphere for its 3-day meeting, and the festival is becoming a serious rival to Cheltenham. The Grand National is obviously the centrepiece, but the rest of the programme has been well thought out and there are a battery of top events which help to attract our very best jumpers, all the more so when the meeting comes three weeks after Cheltenham. This year sees a new meeting in November, which promises to bring more good racing to Liverpool.

Aintree comprises two left-handed courses. The National course is two and a quarter miles in extent and flat throughout. Its feature is the 16 unique, and exceptionally stiff, fences, including the legendary Becher's Brook and the Chair, although the former has been adapted after the two deaths there in the 1989 National. After jumping 30 fences, the National finishers are confronted by a very long run-in of 494-yards, including the famous elbow. All in all, the National circuit is probably the most searching test of a steeplechaser to be found in the world.

The Mildmay course is a one and a half mile rectangle with eight relatively soft fences, and some quite sharp turns. Front-runners are favoured here, and with the relatively short run-in of 260-yards, few animals are able to win if they are too far off the pace turning into the straight.

FENCES: National ✚✚✚✚✚; Mildmay ✚✚   **RACING: ££££££**

MEETINGS
Nov 21st, Apr 1st, 2nd & 3rd (4 days)

ENQUIRIES
John Parrett Esq, Aintree Racecourse Co Ltd, Ormskirk Road, Aintree, Liverpool LP9 5AS. Tel: (051) 523 2600

COURSE STATISTICS 1987-92

	Total W/R	(%)	Hurdles Nov	Hcp	Chases Nov	Hcp	Level Stake
Top Trainers							
FitzGerald J G	5/ 21	23.8	1/ 4	3/ 6	1/ 3	0/ 8	+ 40.00
Balding G B	5/ 33	15.1	3/12	1/ 7	0/ 1	1/13	+ 15.10
Pitman Mrs J	5/ 44	11.3	2/17	0/ 6	2/ 4	1/17	+ 13.50
Hubbard G A	3/ 10	30.0	0/ 0	0/ 0	2/ 4	1/ 6	+ 93.00
Moore A L T (Ire)	3/ 13	23.0	0/ 2	1/ 2	1/ 2	1/ 7	+ 14.63
Elsworth D R C	3/ 18	16.6	1/ 4	0/ 4	0/ 3	2/ 7	0.00
Top Jockeys							
Dunwoody R	7/ 47	14.8	2/16	1/ 6	1/ 7	3/18	+ 25.54
Frost J	3/ 12	25.0	2/ 5	0/ 2	0/ 1	1/ 4	+ 23.30
Pitman M	3/ 21	14.2	1/11	0/ 2	2/ 4	0/ 4	+ 18.50
Dwyer M	3/ 28	10.7	0/ 6	3/ 9	0/ 3	0/10	− 2.00
Byrne D	2/ 3	66.6	1/ 1	0/ 1	1/ 1	0/ 0	+ 32.00
Dowling B	2/ 6	33.3	0/ 1	0/ 1	2/ 2	0/ 2	+ 21.00

Favourites Records								
Autmn H:	0.0%	2m Hdl:	19.7%	2m Chs:	30.0%	Hvy :	0.0%
C:	0.0%	2.5m Hdl:	35.7%	2.5m Chs:	20.5%	Sft :	30.0%
Wintr H:	0.0%	3m Hdl:	20.0%	3m Chs:	32.0%	Gd-Sft:	25.4%
C:	0.0%	3.5m Hdl:	0.0%	3.5m Chs:	0.0%	Gd :	26.4%
Sprng H:	25.0%	Nov Hdl:	25.0%	Nov Chs:	43.1%	Gd-Fm :	28.6%
C:	25.8%	Hcp Hdl:	25.0%	Hcp Chs:	17.6%	Fm/Hd :	25.0%
Total :	25.4%	L/Stake :	− 13.87	Lngst Wng Run:	3	Lngst Lsg Run:	10

LUDLOW

Originally dedicated to Flat racing, this pretty Shropshire track now hosts National Hunt sport only, for which its intimate atmosphere is much better suited. Traditionally races are mid-week, and while the quality of the fixtures is not high, crowds are both sizeable and knowledgeable. The open-air rooftop stand offers an excellent view of every obstacle on the course.

The circuit itself is a right-handed oval of approximately a mile and a half. The hurdle course runs along the outside of the chase track and has somewhat easier turns. Ludlow is flat, and basically a fast track, but the eight stiffish fences require sound jumping, and the long run-in of 450-yards becomes very testing when the ground is soft. Despite the sharp turns on the chase course, long-striding animals rarely experience any difficulty here.

FENCES: +++   **RACING: £**

MEETINGS
Oct 8th, Oct 16th, Nov 19th, Dec 2th, Dec 14th, Jan 20th, Feb 10th, Mar 4th, Mar 26th, Apr 7th, Apr 23rd, May 3rd (12 days)

ENQUIRIES
B R Davies Esq., Ludlow Race Club Ltd, Shepherds Meadow, Eaton Bishop, Lane Head, Hereford HR2 9UA Tel: (0981) 250436

COURSE STATISTICS 1987-92

Top Trainers	Total W/R	(%)	Hurdles Nov	Hcp	Chases Nov	Hcp	Level Stake
Pipe M C	22/ 93	23.6	15/55	3/18	3/12	1/ 8	- 31.48
Edwards J A C	15/ 90	16.6	5/42	1/ 6	5/20	4/22	- 15.25
Forster Capt T A	11/ 59	18.6	1/18	0/ 6	5/15	5/20	+ 0.35
Nicholson D	11/ 66	16.6	5/28	0/ 8	1/14	5/16	- 5.42
Lee R	10/ 59	16.9	2/22	2/12	2/11	4/14	- 8.60
Jordan F	10/ 78	12.8	3/33	7/34	0/11	0/ 0	- 19.46
Top Jockeys							
Scudamore P	15/ 67	22.3	9/33	1/ 9	2/ 9	3/16	- 17.46
Dunwoody R	12/ 74	16.2	8/34	0/ 9	1/16	3/15	- 18.52
Lodder J	8/ 55	14.5	2/19	6/26	0/ 8	0/ 2	- 7.05
Llewellyn C	8/ 63	12.7	1/24	0/ 9	1/12	6/18	- 10.00
Powell B	7/ 29	24.1	2/ 8	0/ 7	2/ 8	3/ 6	- 0.03
Davies H	7/ 52	13.4	1/17	1/ 9	4/12	1/14	- 24.42

Favourites Records

Autmn	H:	47.2%	2m	Hdl:	40.4%	2m	Chs:	46.6%	Hvy : 0.0%
	C:	53.9%	2.5m	Hdl:	37.5%	2.5m	Chs:	39.1%	Sft : 21.4%
Wintr	H:	41.1%	3m	Hdl:	37.5%	3m	Chs:	38.5%	Gd-Sft: 26.0%
	C:	38.8%	3.5m	Hdl:	0.0%	3.5m	Chs:	0.0%	Gd : 43.0%
Sprng	H:	34.1%	Nov	Hdl:	41.7%	Nov	Chs:	36.9%	Gd-Fm : 38.3%
	C:	33.6%	Hcp	Hdl:	35.9%	Hcp	Chs:	43.0%	Fm/Hd : 45.9%

Total : 39.9%   L/Stake : + 6.29   Lngst Wng Run: 6   Lngst Lsg Run: 10

MARKET RASEN

Market Rasen, set in rather featureless country north of Lincoln, is well respected amongst professionals and racegoers alike for its progressive management. It stages racing on the first and last days of the National Hunt season with plenty of fixtures in between. The quality of the racing is mostly moderate although it includes a quite valuable Grand National Trial and Novice Chase in its' February/March meeting.

The right-handed oval circuit measures one and a quarter miles and is slightly undulating, with a run-in of 220-yards. The bends are fairly sharp, especially the one turning into the back straight where, in wet conditions, some horses have problems in keeping their feet. The eight fences are all easy and a horse making an error usually gets away with it, often without losing much impetus. The long striding galloper is at a disadvantage here for it is the handy sort that is principally favoured.

FENCES: +   **RACING: £**

MEETINGS
Oct 9th, Nov 6th, Nov 21st, Dec 26th, Jan 7th, Jan 16th, Feb 27th, Mar 12th, Apr 12th, Apr 24th, May 8th, Jun 5th, Jul 31st (13 days)

ENQUIRIES
Major C L Moore, Market Rasen Racecourse Ltd., Legsby Road, Market Rasen, Lincs, LN8 3EA. Tel: (0637) 843434

COURSE STATISTICS 1987-92

	Total W/R	(%)	Hurdles Nov	Hcp	Chases Nov	Hcp	Level Stake
Top Trainers							
Stephenson W A	31/158	19.6	3/54	3/15	6/44	19/45	- 41.48
FitzGerald J G	29/110	26.3	12/62	5/10	4/11	8/27	- 5.35
Tinkler N	24/ 76	31.5	6/37	15/34	2/ 3	1/ 2	- 20.82
Pipe M C	23/ 63	36.5	15/36	2/16	4/ 6	2/ 5	- 10.04
Easterby M W	18/ 69	26.0	9/37	2/15	3/ 9	4/ 8	+ 1.90
Reveley Mrs G R	17/ 51	33.3	3/20	2/ 7	9/12	3/12	+ 22.01
Top Jockeys							
McCourt G	30/ 84	35.7	7/29	14/30	5/12	4/13	+ 3.48
Dwyer M	25/ 96	26.0	10/41	7/21	3/13	5/21	- 4.46
Niven P	23/108	21.3	4/39	3/22	8/20	8/27	+ 53.64
Grant C	22/ 74	29.7	4/22	3/10	6/18	9/24	+ 5.03
Brennan M	19/141	13.4	3/42	6/40	1/25	9/34	+ 31.00
Byrne D	16/ 84	19.0	9/32	4/26	2/12	1/14	- 17.92

Favourites Records

Autmn H:	38.7%	2m	Hdl:	39.1%	2m	Chs:	39.7%	Hvy	:	50.0%
C:	42.5%	2.5m	Hdl:	32.7%	2.5m	Chs:	34.6%	Sft	:	30.3%
Wintr H:	32.0%	3m	Hdl:	34.4%	3m	Chs:	47.8%	Gd-Sft:		32.1%
C:	34.2%	3.5m	Hdl:	0.0%	3.5m	Chs:	0.0%	Gd	:	39.4%
Sprng H:	37.8%	Nov	Hdl:	43.7%	Nov	Chs:	49.5%	Gd-Fm:		36.6%
C:	42.4%	Hcp	Hdl:	28.1%	Hcp	Chs:	33.7%	Fm/Hd:		46.8%
Total :	**38.9%**	**L/Stake :**		**- 88.05**	**Lngst Wng Run:**		**6**	**Lngst Lsg Run:**		**12**

NEWBURY

The easily accessible Berkshire circuit, is among the most popular in the country, especially with trainers. Its situation close to Lambourn guarantees fields combining quality and quantity for most of the fixtures, the more so as the track is fair and galloping. Facilities are excellent, if slightly antiquated, and the atmosphere is a pleasant mixture of town and country.

The October fixture whets the appetite for the tremendously popular Hennessy Cognac Gold Cup day in late November. Next the Year End meeting features the Save & Prosper Mandarin Chase, the L'Oreal Handicap Hurdle and the Challow Novices Hurdle. The remaining meetings in February and March are also popular and provide more quality racing.

The oval track is left-handed and one and three quarter miles in circumference. The circuit is slightly undulating and contains 11 stiff fences. The cross fence before the straight is always tricky and the straight itself, five furlongs long with four fences, tests both horse and rider. The run-in is 255-yards and when the ground is soft, the track becomes most arduous. The long-striding individual is favoured but the easy turns and wide-open spaces ensure the course being good for all types.

FENCES: +++++   **RACING: ££££**

MEETINGS
Oct 23rd, Nov 4th, Nov 27th, Nov 28th, Jan 2nd Jan 4th, Feb 12th & 13th, Mar 5th & 6th, Mar 26th & 27th (12 days)

ENQUIRIES
Maj Gen J D G Pank CB, Newbury Racecourse Plc, The Racecourse, Newbury, Berks RG14 7NZ. Tel: (0635) 40015

COURSE STATISTICS 1987-92

	Total W/R	(%)	Hurdles Nov	Hcp	Chases Nov	Hcp	Level Stake
Top Trainers							
Pipe M C	26/ 84	30.9	11/34	5/23	3/ 8	7/19	+ 30.01
Elsworth D R C	24/133	18.0	12/63	5/36	1/16	6/18	- 0.40
Sherwood O	23/112	20.5	11/54	0/17	7/20	5/21	- 19.20
Henderson N J	22/127	17.3	6/52	2/24	8/21	6/30	- 42.92
Nicholson D	18/108	16.6	6/41	0/12	4/18	8/37	- 21.93
Gifford J T	16/175	9.1	5/66	1/30	6/34	4/45	- 93.59
Top Jockeys							
Dunwoody R	44/212	20.7	14/81	7/31	10/31	13/69	+ 1.89
Scudamore P	34/143	23.7	9/58	5/24	7/19	13/42	- 26.94
Osborne J	24/116	20.6	8/47	1/16	10/23	5/30	- 21.25
Perrett M	17/ 79	21.5	7/41	5/17	0/ 2	5/19	+ 12.52
McCourt G	14/ 73	19.1	4/34	5/20	4/10	1/ 9	+ 20.00
Davies H	13/ 90	14.4	0/31	1/10	2/14	10/35	- 26.12
Favourites Records							

Autmn H:	41.5%	2m Hdl:	33.7%	2m Chs:	46.6%	Hvy :	25.0%
C:	44.8%	2.5m Hdl:	44.0%	2.5m Chs:	37.3%	Sft :	36.8%
Wintr H:	43.1%	3m Hdl:	37.4%	3m Chs:	41.1%	Gd-Sft:	37.5%
C:	39.8%	3.5m Hdl:	0.0%	3.5m Chs:	40.0%	Gd :	41.2%
Sprng H:	25.5%	Nov Hdl:	35.7%	Nov Chs:	46.2%	Gd-Fm :	42.9%
C:	35.7%	Hcp Hdl:	38.4%	Hcp Chs:	37.9%	Fm/Hd :	20.0%
Total :	**38.6%**	**L/Stake :**	**- 20.48**	**Lngst Wng Run:**	**5**	**Lngst Lsg Run:**	**11**

NEWCASTLE

Newcastle racecourse is attractively sited in the middle of 1000 acre Gosforth Park, part of which is a wild-life sanctuary, and is one of Northern England's premier jumping tracks. The main criticism from a racegoers point of view is that the grandstand is set well back so as to accommodate large summer crowds, leaving the winter spectator somewhat isolated from the action.

The jumping is generally of good quality and the fields are above average in size. Principal events staged here are the Bellway Homes Fighting Fifth Hurdle in November, the marathon Tote Eider Chase over four miles in February, and the Newcastle Brown Top of the North Novices Hurdle final in May.

Newcastle's pear-shaped circuit is left-handed and one and three quarter miles round. The 11 fences are among the toughest in the country with the obstacle before the straight standing out. The steadily rising home straight of half a mile with its furlong run-in becomes a real slog when conditions are heavy, which is the case more often than not. The galloping type is generally favoured here and the non-stayer will be found out.

FENCES: ++++   **RACING: ££(££)**

MEETINGS
Oct 21st, Nov 7th, Nov 28th, Dec 1st, Dec 19th, Jan 16th, Feb 20th, Mar 20th, Mar 22nd, May 8th (10 days)

ENQUIRIES
M Hills, High Gosforth Park plc, High Gosforth Park, Newcastle upon Tyne NE3 5HP. Tel: (091) 236 2020 / 5508

COURSE STATISTICS 1987-92

	Total W/R	(%)	Hurdles Nov	Hcp	Chases Nov	Hcp	Level Stake
Top Trainers							
Stephenson W A	61/260	23.4	12/87	5/31	18/55	26/87	+ 15.61
Easterby M H	20/ 84	23.8	6/26	5/21	5/19	4/18	- 23.05
Johnson J H	15/ 71	21.1	4/27	1/14	1/12	9/18	- 2.70
FitzGerald J G	14/ 63	22.2	3/24	3/13	2/10	6/16	+ 9.45
Moore G M	14/ 75	18.6	7/32	1/21	5/16	1/ 6	+ 3.10
Richards G W	13/107	12.1	3/35	1/23	8/21	1/28	- 61.53
Top Jockeys							
Grant C	40/159	25.1	10/58	5/27	11/30	14/44	+ 40.43
Storey B	22/163	13.5	6/59	2/23	8/38	6/43	- 55.65
Niven P	17/128	13.2	9/53	2/27	2/21	4/27	- 32.68
Wyer L	16/ 88	18.1	6/34	3/21	3/16	4/17	- 18.52
Reed T	16/117	13.6	3/48	0/10	6/34	7/25	- 20.67
Dwyer M	15/ 91	16.4	5/41	1/23	3/16	6/11	- 37.59

Favourites Records

Autmn	H:	46.0%	2m Hdl:	49.3%	2m Chs:	53.3%	Hvy :	0.0%
	C:	49.6%	2.5m Hdl:	26.0%	2.5m Chs:	30.3%	Sft :	30.0%
Wintr	H:	38.0%	3m Hdl:	41.2%	3m Chs:	54.9%	Gd-Sft:	50.8%
	C:	31.2%	3.5m Hdl:	0.0%	3.5m Chs:	26.7%	Gd :	42.1%
Sprng	H:	38.9%	Nov Hdl:	45.0%	Nov Chs:	48.0%	Gd-Fm :	36.8%
	C:	49.7%	Hcp Hdl:	34.9%	Hcp Chs:	39.8%	Fm/Hd :	42.9%

Total : 41.9%   L/Stake : - 15.20   Lngst Wng Run: 7   Lngst Lsg Run: 8

NEWTON ABBOT

Newton Abbot is very much a holiday track, being within close range of Torbay and within easy reach of the M5. As well as sharing the opening day of the jump season with Market Rasen, this small, rather humdrum course has the distinction of staging more days jump racing (excluding All-Weather) than any other in the land. Meetings are rarely abandoned as the area is favoured with above average weather throughout the year. The overall standard of runner is moderate but there is no lack of support from the West Country trainers who like to make hay while the sun shines early in the season before their more illustrious rivals have slipped into top gear.

The circuit is a tight, flat left-hander. At only nine furlongs in circumference it is one of the smallest courses around. It's seven fences are comparatively easy, although the second in the back straight causes problems for the unwary. The eight tight turns and short run-in favour the nippy type of horse and a front-runner should do well here.

FENCES: ++   **RACING: £(£)**

MEETINGS
Oct 6th, Oct 27th, Nov 17th, Dec 14th, Dec 26th, Jan 5th, Jan 28th, Feb 16th, Mar 17th, Apr 10th, 12th, 20th & 30th, May 4th, May 12th, Jul 31st (16 days)

ENQUIRIES
P G Masterson, Newton Abbot Races Ltd, The Racecourse, Kingsteignton Road, Newton Abbot, Devon TQ12 3AF. Tel: (0626) 53235

COURSE STATISTICS 1987-92

	Total W/R	(%)	Hurdles Nov	Hcp	Chases Nov	Hcp	Level Stake
Top Trainers							
Pipe M C	130/368	35.3	48/132	27/133	25/45	30/58	+ 4.13
Hobbs P J	22/114	19.3	6/49	7/19	3/28	6/18	- 19.35
Baker J H	18/ 97	18.5	7/39	9/45	1/ 6	1/ 7	+ 33.89
Barons D H	18/138	13.0	3/49	6/23	2/38	7/28	- 67.12
Holder R J	17/102	16.6	3/46	6/32	4/12	4/12	+ 5.13
Hodges R J	13/134	9.7	4/36	5/52	1/18	3/28	- 20.17
Top Jockeys							
Scudamore P	98/222	44.1	37/84	19/61	18/32	24/45	+ 29.06
Powell B	20/206	9.7	6/72	6/51	3/32	5/51	-108.43
McCourt G	17/ 60	28.3	6/27	4/16	2/ 6	5/11	+ 7.97
Coleman N	17/104	16.3	2/37	10/40	1/12	4/15	+ 33.93
Hobbs Peter	16/ 94	17.0	3/37	2/15	5/26	6/16	- 19.17
Frost J	16/166	9.6	5/66	1/28	7/34	3/38	-108.78

Favourites Records

Autmn H:	39.2%	2m Hdl:	36.1%	2m Chs:	32.7%	Hvy :	44.6%
C:	44.7%	2.5m Hdl:	32.6%	2.5m Chs:	60.7%	Sft :	37.2%
Wintr H:	33.1%	3m Hdl:	0.0%	3m Chs:	0.0%	Gd-Sft:	28.5%
C:	51.1%	3.5m Hdl:	43.5%	3.5m Chs:	49.0%	Gd :	40.1%
Sprng H:	32.2%	Nov Hdl:	41.7%	Nov Chs:	48.9%	Gd-Fm :	40.6%
C:	46.4%	Hcp Hdl:	30.1%	Hcp Chs:	44.9%	Fm/Hd :	42.1%

Total : 40.0% L/Stake : - 73.50 Lngst Wng Run: 10 Lngst Lsg Run: 10

NOTTINGHAM

Situated alongside the River Trent, with the Colwick Hill trees providing a pleasant backdrop, Nottingham racecourse does not reflect the rather plain area in which it is located. The sport, along with the prize-money offered, is only modest, but events such as the City Trial Hurdle and the Nottinghamshire Novices Chase in February help swell the attendance.

The track itself is an oval left-hander of about a mile and a half, and perfectly flat. The turns are easy, too, and while the chase course is not testing, it suits galloping types ideally, all the more so because of the long five-furlong straight, containing four fences and a run-in of 240-yards. The obstacles are generally quite easy, but the third last, an open ditch, is the most likely stumbling block to a clear round.

FENCES: ++   **RACING: ££**

MEETINGS
Nov 14th, Nov 26th, Dec 4th, Dec 19th, Jan 2nd, Jan 26th, Feb 2nd, Feb 20th, Mar 2nd, Mar 23rd (10 days)

ENQUIRIES
Mr T Hiscocks, Nottingham Racecourse Co Ltd, Colwick Park, Colwick Road, Nottingham NG2 4BE. Tel: (0602) 580620

COURSE STATISTICS 1987-92

	Total W/R	(%)	Hurdles Nov	Hcp	Chases Nov	Hcp	Level Stake
Top Trainers							
Pipe M C	13/ 49	26.5	7/25	5/17	1/ 6	0/ 1	- 0.15
FitzGerald J G	11/ 53	20.7	3/28	0/ 8	3/ 4	5/13	- 16.28
Henderson N J	10/ 29	34.4	2/ 7	1/ 9	5/ 9	2/ 4	+ 6.80
Tinkler N	8/ 41	19.5	2/27	6/14	0/ 0	0/ 0	- 4.51
Nicholson D	8/ 47	17.0	1/18	1/ 4	2/10	4/15	- 14.25
Reveley Mrs G R	6/ 24	25.0	2/ 6	2/ 6	2/ 4	0/ 8	- 1.28
Top Jockeys							
McCourt G	20/ 77	25.9	6/30	7/21	2/13	5/13	+ 64.12
Dunwoody R	14/ 80	17.5	3/29	2/20	5/15	4/16	- 14.27
Scudamore P	13/ 47	27.6	5/18	2/11	4/11	2/ 7	- 9.84
Dwyer M	13/ 64	20.3	3/29	2/13	3/ 8	5/14	- 13.49
Niven P	8/ 40	20.0	3/12	2/11	3/10	0/ 7	- 0.28
Railton J	7/ 32	21.8	2/10	1/ 5	0/ 6	4/11	+ 2.20
Favourites Records							
Autmn H:	37.2%	2m	Hdl:	39.5%	2m	Chs:	45.6%	Hvy :	27.8%
C:	48.4%	2.5m	Hdl:	0.0%	2.5m	Chs:	0.0%	Sft :	33.3%
Wintr H:	37.5%	3m	Hdl:	26.2%	3m	Chs:	36.5%	Gd-Sft:	28.4%
C:	26.7%	3.5m	Hdl:	30.0%	3.5m	Chs:	6.3%	Gd :	32.0%
Sprng H:	20.0%	Nov	Hdl:	36.8%	Nov	Chs:	44.4%	Gd-Fm :	43.3%
C:	47.1%	Hcp	Hdl:	32.8%	Hcp	Chs:	27.9%	Fm/Hd :	59.1%
Total :	**35.1%**	**L/Stake :**	**- 38.20**	**Lngst Wng Run:**	**3**	**Lngst Lsg Run:**	**9**

PERTH

As well as being Britain's northernmost jumping track, Perth Hunt also has claims to being one of the most picturesque, set as it is amongst the wooded parklands of Scone Palace. Because of its wintry location, fixtures are limited to Spring and Autumn, with a popular meeting in late August. The sport is modest, but the quaint stands and intimate atmosphere means that there are few more relaxed environments for racing.

The circuit is an oblong shaped, right-hander, measuring a mile and a quarter. The chief feature is the very sharp bends, where the steering has to be good or important ground can be lost. The eight fences are modest, and do not really test a horse's jumping ability. Since the water-jump in front of the stands is omitted on the final circuit, the run-in is quite long at 300-yards, but overall, Perth suits adaptable types, and is emphatically against long-striding gallopers.

FENCES: ✚(✚)   **RACING: £**

MEETINGS
Apr 21st, 22nd, & 23rd, May 12th & 13th, May 19th (6 days)

ENQUIRIES
Miss J I C Grant, The Perth Hunt, Penrose Hill, Moffat, Dumfriesshire, DG10 9BX
Tel: (0683) 20131

COURSE STATISTICS 1987-92

	Total W/R	(%)	Hurdles Nov	Hcp	Chases Nov	Hcp	Level Stake
Top Trainers							
Richards G W	31/187	16.5	4/68	7/42	8/30	12/47	- 74.15
Stephenson W A	28/126	22.2	3/39	7/19	8/29	10/39	- 22.30
Moore G M	16/ 66	24.2	6/30	5/23	2/ 6	3/ 7	- 9.82
Reveley Mrs G R	11/ 37	29.7	5/14	3/13	3/ 6	0/ 4	- 9.53
Monteith P	11/ 66	16.6	1/26	3/19	2/15	5/ 6	- 1.47
Tinkler N	10/ 24	41.6	5/13	3/ 7	2/ 4	0/ 0	+ 4.03
Top Jockeys							
Dwyer M	24/ 92	26.0	7/40	5/19	6/10	8/23	- 12.15
Grant C	24/116	20.6	5/44	2/21	6/20	11/31	- 8.56
Niven P	20/ 81	24.6	10/31	5/15	2/19	3/16	+ 3.13
McCourt G	15/ 46	32.6	6/17	6/13	2/10	1/ 6	+ 10.94
Doughty N	15/ 79	18.9	1/33	3/11	4/18	7/17	- 14.32
O'Hara L	10/ 51	19.6	1/17	3/16	1/ 7	5/11	- 3.62

Favourites Records

Autmn	H:	42.2%	2m Hdl:	38.6%	2m Chs:	45.5%	Hvy	:	0.0%
	C:	49.7%	2.5m Hdl:	36.1%	2.5m Chs:	52.9%	Sft	:	41.7%
Wintr	H:	0.0%	3m Hdl:	38.6%	3m Chs:	54.2%	Gd-Sft:		45.4%
	C:	0.0%	3.5m Hdl:	0.0%	3.5m Chs:	0.0%	Gd	:	41.4%
Sprng	H:	33.3%	Nov Hdl:	42.5%	Nov Chs:	55.4%	Gd-Fm	:	50.3%
	C:	51.4%	Hcp Hdl:	32.7%	Hcp Chs:	47.1%	Fm/Hd	:	33.3%

Total : 43.4%   L/Stake : + 8.53   Lngst Wng Run: 9   Lngst Lsg Run: 12

PLUMPTON

Situated just north-east of Brighton, Plumpton is very much a course for the 'regulars', be they equine or human. The sport is only ever modest, but the fields are of a good size for such a small track, and there is plenty of racing throughout the year. The good crowds give it the atmosphere of a point-to-point.

The track is a quirky rectangular left-hander measuring only nine furlongs in circumference. It has steep undulations and an uphill home straight, but the bends are very tight. The seven fences are no stiffer than they should be for this grade of track, but the two plain fences down the far side sometimes pose problems. Despite the steep run-in of 200-yards, the course is not a testing one. It is tricky, though, for both horse and rider, and favours course specialists, usually adaptable types.

FENCES: ✦(✦)   **RACING: £**

MEETINGS
Oct 20th, Nov 2nd, Nov 25th, Dec 8th, Dec 29th, Jan 13th, Feb 1st, Feb 15th, Mar 1st, Mar 15th, Mar 22nd, Apr 10th Apr 12th, (13 days)

ENQUIRIES
C E Griggs Esq., Pratt & Company, 11 Boltro Road, Haywards Heath, Sussex
RH16 1BP Tel: (0444) 441111

COURSE STATISTICS 1987-92

	Total W/R	(%)	Hurdles Nov	Hcp	Chases Nov	Hcp	Level Stake
Top Trainers							
Akehurst R	23/ 72	31.9	19/45	3/21	1/ 2	0/ 4	+ 20.32
Ffitch-Heyes J	22/201	10.9	3/50	16/106	1/23	2/22	-105.46
White J	21/ 98	21.4	3/28	5/23	2/17	11/30	- 7.01
Pitman Mrs J	19/ 48	39.5	7/24	2/ 5	5/12	5/ 7	+ 17.34
Jenkins J R	14/ 84	16.6	7/34	4/33	2/13	1/ 4	- 25.00
Grissell D M	13/ 75	17.3	2/29	4/15	2/16	5/15	- 18.00
Top Jockeys							
Davies H	20/104	19.2	4/40	4/23	2/14	10/27	- 15.17
McKeown Dale	18/ 96	18.7	9/51	8/33	0/ 5	1/ 7	- 0.30
Dunwoody R	17/ 86	19.7	8/37	3/19	2/15	4/15	- 20.52
Perrett M	16/105	15.2	8/45	3/25	2/15	3/20	- 19.06
Pitman M	14/ 35	40.0	6/19	0/ 1	4/ 9	4/ 6	+ 11.51
Scudamore P	12/ 43	27.9	5/21	1/ 9	6/12	0/ 1	- 14.68

Favourites Records

Autmn	H:	47.8%	2m	Hdl:	44.3%	2m	Chs:	38.6%	Hvy	:	35.2%
	C:	32.3%	2.5m	Hdl:	33.8%	2.5m	Chs:	32.7%	Sft	:	29.3%
Wintr	H:	33.6%	3m	Hdl:	0.0%	3m	Chs:	39.1%	Gd-Sft:		37.5%
	C:	38.9%	3.5m	Hdl:	0.0%	3.5m	Chs:	0.0%	Gd	:	37.0%
Sprng	H:	36.7%	Nov	Hdl:	50.0%	Nov	Chs:	37.2%	Gd-Fm	:	40.3%
	C:	41.8%	Hcp	Hdl:	33.9%	Hcp	Chs:	36.9%	Fm/Hd	:	51.6%
Total	**:**	**39.7%**	L/Stake	:	- 13.87	Lngst Wng Run:		6	Lngst Lsg Run:		8

SANDOWN PARK

Sandown combines accessibility, high-class racing, superb facilities and a tremendous atmosphere on the big days, in no small way due to the regular presence of Desert Orchid. The modern stand offers a first-class view of the chase course, and the whole track is compact and easy to get around.

The racing is virtually always good, although prone to small fields at times. Most meetings have competitive feature races, the William Hill Handicap Hurdle (December), the Mildmay/Cazalet Chase (January) and the Agfa Diamond Handicap Chase being amongst them. The popular Whitbread in May ends the season in style.

The track is a right-handed oval of about one mile five furlongs, with a tough climb to the finish from the home turn. The bends are easy, but the eleven fences certainly are not, particularly the three Railway fences. They come in quick succession, and are a tricky test of any jumper, with races often being won or lost here. The 300-yard uphill run-in sees many a transformation, with horses often tiring rapidly in the closing stages, especially when the ground is soft or worse. Sandown suits long-striding horses, and Cheltenham is perhaps its only peer as a test of stamina and jumping ability.

FENCES: ✛✛✛✛(✛)   **RACING: ££££**

MEETINGS
Oct 31st, Dec 4th & 5th, Jan 9th, Feb 6th, Feb 18th & 19th, Mar 12th & 13th, Mar 30th, Apr 24th (11 days)

ENQUIRIES
Miss K Winterborne, United Racecourses (Holdings) Ltd, The Racecourse, Esher, Surrey, KT10 9AJ. Tel: (0372) 463072/464348

COURSE STATISTICS 1987-92

	Total W/R	(%)	Hurdles Nov	Hcp	Chases Nov	Hcp	Level Stake
Top Trainers							
Gifford J T	31/188	16.4	8/73	6/33	11/40	6/42	- 33.24
Pipe M C	16/ 63	25.4	6/19	6/17	0/ 3	4/24	+ 13.98
Brooks C P E	15/ 56	26.7	2/13	3/ 7	4/12	6/24	+ 8.89
Nicholson D	15/ 78	19.2	1/24	0/ 5	2/ 9	12/40	- 22.40
Henderson N J	12/ 72	16.6	8/42	0/10	2/ 5	2/15	- 19.78
Walwyn Mrs F	10/ 40	25.0	0/ 9	0/ 4	1/ 3	9/24	+ 47.18
Top Jockeys							
Dunwoody R	25/126	19.8	6/36	2/27	3/17	14/46	- 16.53
Scudamore P	18/ 71	25.3	8/23	5/14	2/12	3/22	+ 6.33
Osborne J	14/ 71	19.7	5/26	2/16	3/ 9	4/20	- 0.62
Murphy D J	10/ 50	20.0	2/16	1/12	5/11	2/11	- 10.13
Perrett M	9/ 54	16.6	1/20	3/14	1/ 7	4/13	- 7.58
Davies H	9/ 73	12.3	0/26	1/10	1/ 8	7/29	- 34.58

Favourites Records

Autmn H:	39.7%	2m	Hdl:	35.7%	2m	Chs:	51.3%	Hvy :	28.6%
C:	43.8%	2.5m	Hdl:	32.4%	2.5m	Chs:	48.1%	Sft :	44.8%
Wintr H:	31.9%	3m	Hdl:	0.0%	3m	Chs:	30.0%	Gd-Sft:	42.1%
C:	47.7%	3.5m	Hdl:	0.0%	3.5m	Chs:	26.9%	Gd :	34.1%
Sprng H:	36.4%	Nov	Hdl:	40.2%	Nov	Chs:	45.9%	Gd-Fm :	41.5%
C:	33.9%	Hcp	Hdl:	26.4%	Hcp	Chs:	39.2%	Fm/Hd :	57.1%
Total :	**38.2%**	**L/Stake :**		**- 17.36**	**Lngst Wng Run:**		**6**	**Lngst Lsg Run:**	**11**

SEDGEFIELD

Although its location suggests otherwise, being bang in the middle of Middlesborough, Darlington and Durham, Sedgefield is set in attractive country surroundings. The lack of quality of the racing is compensated by the frequency of the fixtures, second only to Newton Abbot in their regularity. The vast majority of these are on Tuesdays, where crowds are surprisingly good, largely because facilities have improved in the last few years.

The track is an undulating oval left-hander measuring a mile and a quarter. It is essentially sharp in character, with tight turns, and seven quite easy fences. Unusually, the final obstacle is an open ditch, and this is followed by a punishing uphill run-in of 525-yards, so long because the water jump is omitted on the finishing circuit. The uphill finish is preceded by a steep downhill run from the second last, making atmospheric viewing since the horses are silhouetted against the sky as they come into view. The longer chases are a severe test of stamina when the ground is heavy.

FENCES: ++   **RACING: £**

MEETINGS
Oct 13th, Oct 28th, Nov 10th, Nov 20th, Dec 8th, Dec 26th, Jan 6th, Jan 27th, Feb 2nd, Feb 17th, Feb 23rd, Mar 9th, Mar 16th, Mar 27th, Apr 6th, Apr 20th, May 4th, May 14th, (18 days)

ENQUIRIES
D McW Riley Esq, Sedgefield Steeplechase Co Ltd, 23a The Green, Billingham, Cleveland, TS23 1ES. Tel: (0642) 557081

COURSE STATISTICS 1987-92

	Total W/R	(%)	Hurdles Nov	Hcp	Chases Nov	Hcp	Level Stake
Top Trainers							
Stephenson W A	69/343	20.1	13/122	8/49	18/83	30/89	-112.46
Reveley Mrs G R	41/177	23.1	14/58	8/48	11/37	8/34	+ 20.32
Moore G M	26/131	19.8	11/48	5/45	4/22	6/16	- 7.93
Smith Denys	26/188	13.8	7/76	7/51	6/27	6/34	- 39.23
Easterby M H	25/ 94	26.6	5/34	7/22	7/18	6/20	+ 11.54
FitzGerald J G	17/ 57	29.8	7/25	3/12	2/ 7	5/13	+ 18.14
Top Jockeys							
Grant C	51/237	21.5	8/69	11/58	9/48	23/62	- 66.52
Niven P	43/233	18.4	12/81	6/54	15/53	10/45	- 7.98
Dwyer M	34/153	22.2	19/69	5/40	2/18	8/26	+ 4.06
Wyer L	25/108	23.1	5/40	7/26	8/19	5/23	+ 24.74
Merrigan A	16/121	13.2	4/52	1/13	7/34	4/22	- 42.59
Garrity R	14/ 89	15.7	4/44	5/20	1/13	4/12	- 5.07
Favourites Records							

Autmn H:	38.9%	2m	Hdl:	35.2%	2m	Chs:	50.9%	Hvy :	0.0%
C:	57.0%	2.5m	Hdl:	34.9%	2.5m	Chs:	47.1%	Sft :	54.2%
Wintr H:	30.3%	3m	Hdl:	0.0%	3m	Chs:	0.0%	Gd-Sft:	45.3%
C:	45.1%	3.5m	Hdl:	41.5%	3.5m	Chs:	47.9%	Gd :	38.4%
Sprng H:	36.9%	Nov	Hdl:	40.0%	Nov	Chs:	48.0%	Gd-Fm :	40.6%
C:	42.8%	Hcp	Hdl:	31.7%	Hcp	Chs:	48.5%	Fm/Hd :	40.6%

Total : 41.4% L/Stake : - 8.43 Lngst Wng Run: 7 Lngst Lsg Run: 8

SOUTHWELL

Just outside the charming town of the same name, N.E. of Nottingham, Southwell epitomises the minor jumping course in England. The standard of both the amenities and racing is not high, but fixtures are frequent and the fields are usually a good size.

A left-handed, triangular circuit of approximately a mile and a quarter, Southwell is essentially a sharp track with tight bends, particularly the home turn on the hurdles course. The seven fences are of average difficulty, but unevenly spaced, with the two before the straight coming in quick succession before a tight turn, these two obstacles claimed three-quarters of all the fallers at the track last year, and races are often decided before they turn into the straight. The 250-yard run-in should hold no terrors, and the track favours the nippy, quick-jumping type.

The All Weather track is a left handed oval of ten furlongs with a three furlong straight. The surface is Fibresand which consists of a blended mixture of silica sand and synthetic fibres set on a reinforced sub-base. The hurdles are not very substantial. There is going to be a try-out over fences in November 1991 in an effort to expand the range of All Weather racing.

FENCES: ✚✚(✚)   **RACING: £**

MEETINGS
Oct 5th, Oct 10th, Oct 17th, Jan 6th*, Jan 13th*, Jan 20th*, Jan 27th*, Feb 3rd*,
Feb 10th*, Feb 17th*, Feb 24th*, Mar 3rd*, Mar 10th*, Mar 13th, May 3rd, May 12th,
May 22nd (10 days AW, 7 days Turf)

ENQUIRIES
R Muddle Esq, The RAM Racecourses Ltd, Rolleston, Southwell, Notts., NG25 0TS.
Tel: (0636) 814481

COURSE STATISTICS 1987-92 (All-Weather Statistics p.317)

	Total W/R	(%)	Hurdles Nov	Hcp	Chases Nov	Hcp	Level Stake
Top Trainers							
FitzGerald J G	17/ 58	29.3	5/15	5/19	3/ 9	4/15	+ 6.00
Pipe M C	16/ 47	34.0	1/12	12/24	3/10	0/ 1	- 10.36
Preece B	13/ 47	27.6	0/ 7	11/32	0/ 4	2/ 4	+ 9.33
Upson John R	12/ 30	40.0	0/ 1	0/ 0	6/17	6/12	+ 29.04
Richards G W	12/ 40	30.0	2/ 6	3/ 9	2/13	5/12	+ 8.94
Edwards J A C	12/ 47	25.5	0/ 6	0/ 5	8/24	4/12	- 13.11
Top Jockeys							
Dwyer M	26/101	25.7	3/28	16/38	5/17	2/18	+ 54.62
McCourt G	19/ 64	29.6	6/14	8/28	3/14	2/ 8	+ 25.67
Niven P	12/ 78	15.3	1/18	2/16	4/21	5/23	- 28.43
Supple R	11/ 46	23.9	1/ 7	0/ 6	5/17	5/16	+ 12.78
Brennan M	9/ 88	10.2	2/21	0/21	2/21	5/25	- 23.97
Osborne J	8/ 43	18.6	2/13	1/13	4/ 8	1/ 9	- 7.97
Favourites Records							

Autmn H:	43.5%	2m Hdl:	39.0%	2m Chs:	48.7%	Hvy :	36.7%
C:	43.3%	2.5m Hdl:	34.0%	2.5m Chs:	47.4%	Sft :	26.5%
Wintr H:	32.7%	3m Hdl:	34.6%	3m Chs:	40.2%	Gd-Sft:	33.3%
C:	52.1%	3.5m Hdl:	0.0%	3.5m Chs:	62.5%	Gd :	41.7%
Sprng H:	34.9%	Nov Hdl:	27.5%	Nov Chs:	45.3%	Gd-Fm :	41.0%
C:	43.8%	Hcp Hdl:	40.3%	Hcp Chs:	43.9%	Fm/Hd :	44.4%
Total : 40.0%	**L/Stake : - 38.03**		**Lngst Wng Run: 6**		**Lngst Lsg Run: 12**		

STRATFORD-ON-AVON

Situated just outside the tourist-populated town of Stratford itself, the actual setting is somewhat plain. Nevertheless, it draws good sized crowds, and the lay-out of the stands and enclosures means there is excellent viewing and usually a good atmosphere. Hunter chases are a strong point here, of a much higher standard than the rest of the racing, and culminate in the popular Horse and Hound Cup day at the end of the season.

The track itself is a fairly sharp, flat left-hander measuring a mile and a quarter. The eight fences are not very testing, and neither is the going in general, since the good drainage usually ensures decent jumping ground. There is only one fence in the short home straight, with a further run-in of 200-yards. It is a tight, fast course in nature, much of it on the turn, and unsuitable for galloping types.

FENCES: ✛✛   **RACING: £(£)**

MEETINGS
Oct 17th, Oct 29th, Nov 24th, Dec 29th, Feb 6th, Mar 6th, Mar 25th, Apr 17th, May 14th, May 21st, Jun 4th, & 5th, (12 days)

ENQUIRIES
Mrs A L N Gale, Stratford on Avon Racecourse Co Ltd, Luddington Road, Stratford on Avon, Warwicks CV37 9SE. Tel (0789) 267949/269411

COURSE STATISTICS 1987-92

	Total W/R	(%)	Hurdles Nov	Hcp	Chases Nov	Hcp	Level Stake
Top Trainers							
Pipe M C	21/ 92	22.8	12/36	8/40	0/ 5	1/11	- 0.14
Forster Capt T A	16/ 58	27.5	4/18	0/ 4	3/14	9/22	+ 62.58
Edwards J A C	13/ 57	22.8	1/15	3/ 7	6/23	3/12	+ 26.60
Richards G W	12/ 29	41.3	1/ 4	0/ 3	5/ 9	6/13	+ 1.88
Pitman Mrs J	12/ 62	19.3	6/20	2/18	2/12	2/12	- 2.82
FitzGerald J G	11/ 28	39.2	3/ 9	1/ 2	6/ 7	1/10	+ 18.63
Top Jockeys							
Dunwoody R	17/106	16.0	7/32	4/24	2/19	4/31	+ 11.24
McCourt G	16/ 82	19.5	5/30	7/28	3/17	1/ 7	- 14.45
Scudamore P	14/ 60	23.3	8/24	4/16	0/ 9	2/11	- 19.99
Dwyer M	12/ 60	20.0	3/17	1/15	5/11	3/17	- 19.87
Llewellyn C	11/ 62	17.7	2/19	1/13	2/14	6/16	+ 19.50
Doughty N	9/ 24	37.5	0/ 3	0/ 2	4/ 8	5/11	- 4.06

Favourites Records

Autmn	H:	31.3%	2m	Hdl:	31.7%	2m	Chs:	40.6%	Hvy	:	16.7%
	C:	45.4%	2.5m	Hdl:	0.0%	2.5m	Chs:	0.0%	Sft	:	32.1%
Wintr	H:	29.7%	3m	Hdl:	30.5%	3m	Chs:	38.1%	Gd-Sft:		44.1%
	C:	44.4%	3.5m	Hdl:	50.0%	3.5m	Chs:	37.7%	Gd	:	36.4%
Sprng	H:	33.0%	Nov	Hdl:	36.8%	Nov	Chs:	41.3%	Gd-Fm	:	30.8%
	C:	31.6%	Hcp	Hdl:	27.0%	Hcp	Chs:	37.0%	Fm/Hd	:	38.9%

Total : 35.1%   L/Stake : - 42.57   Lngst Wng Run: 5   Lngst Lsg Run: 12

TAUNTON

Taunton racecourse, although not particularly well appointed, benefits from panoramic views of the Blackdown and Quantock hills. This rustic track is popular with the local trainers in particular, both because of its proximity and its fairness, but the quality of the sport in general is distinctly moderate. The fixtures are evenly spaced, and the Christmas meeting in particular attracts a good crowd.

The track is an elongated oval, measuring a mile and a quarter, and the eight easy fences are taken right-handed. The turns are easy, and although there is a steady rise from the home turn to the finish, the straight, with its three fences and a run-in of 150-yards, is not too daunting. Despite the fact that the fences do not help to educate a horse, it is otherwise a very fair test.

FENCES: ✦(✦)   **RACING: £**

MEETINGS
Oct 15th, Nov 12th, Nov 26th, Dec 10th, Dec 30th, Jan 21st, Feb 18th, Mar 15th, Apr 1st, Apr 16th, Apr 23rd (11 days)

ENQUIRIES
Lt Col A G M Shewen, Taunton Racecourse Co Ltd, Orchard Portman, Taunton, Somerset TA3 7BL. Tel: (0823) 337172/275575

COURSE STATISTICS 1987-92

	Total W/R	(%)	Hurdles Nov	Hcp	Chases Nov	Hcp	Level Stake
Top Trainers							
Pipe M C	58/202	28.7	31/94	15/61	8/24	4/23	- 2.72
Hodges R J	25/180	13.8	7/64	5/56	5/29	8/31	+ 22.72
Holder R J	14/ 70	20.0	7/42	4/18	2/ 7	1/ 3	+ 54.33
Popham C L	13/108	12.0	4/31	5/27	1/24	3/26	- 32.42
Hobbs P J	10/ 85	11.7	7/38	1/17	1/16	1/14	+ 5.53
Barons D H	8/ 53	15.0	1/19	2/13	1/ 9	4/12	+ 21.75
Top Jockeys							
Scudamore P	40/111	36.0	23/56	8/23	7/19	2/13	- 4.72
Powell B	19/164	11.5	4/62	3/37	4/30	8/35	- 38.15
Frost J	9/ 88	10.2	2/34	2/24	3/14	2/16	+ 23.93
Perrett M	8/ 27	29.6	6/16	0/ 1	1/ 3	1/ 7	+ 30.27
Mann N	8/ 34	23.5	4/17	4/14	0/ 1	0/ 2	+ 11.25
Tory A	8/ 49	16.3	2/16	1/10	4/14	1/ 9	+ 10.50

Favourites Records

Autmn	H:	30.4%	2m	Hdl:	36.2%	2m	Chs:	34.9%	Hvy : 19.4%
	C:	41.2%	2.5m	Hdl:	35.5%	2.5m	Chs:	30.8%	Sft : 46.2%
Wintr	H:	46.6%	3m	Hdl:	58.3%	3m	Chs:	44.5%	Gd-Sft: 39.5%
	C:	36.1%	3.5m	Hdl:	0.0%	3.5m	Chs:	63.6%	Gd : 31.9%
Sprng	H:	36.0%	Nov	Hdl:	43.8%	Nov	Chs:	45.3%	Gd-Fm : 44.6%
	C:	45.5%	Hcp	Hdl:	27.1%	Hcp	Chs:	38.0%	Fm/Hd : 39.4%

Total : 38.7%   L/Stake : - 0.13   Lngst Wng Run: 7   Lngst Lsg Run: 12

TOWCESTER

Easily accessible from the M1, Towcester racetrack is set in very attractive surroundings at Easton Neston, south of Northampton. Although racing is generally of a moderate nature, good horses are often sent here, and attendances are relatively high. Spectators are treated to an excellent view of the racing, particularly the last three parts of a mile as the runners begin the uphill finish.

Towcester is one of the few square circuits in the country, a right-hander of a mile and three-quarters in circumference. The back stretch is slightly downhill, but the last three quarters of a mile is uphill, and very punishing when the ground is soft. Indeed, the 200-yard run-in has seen many a race turned on its head as the leaders began to tire. Of the ten fences, of average difficulty, the two in the downhill stretch away from the stands frequently cause problems. The steep climb to the home turn really puts a premium on stamina, and overall Towcester is one of the most testing tracks in the country.

FENCES: ✚✚(✚)   **RACING: £**

MEETINGS
Oct 7th, Nov 12th, Nov 21st, Dec 5th, Dec 17th, Jan 8th, Feb 4th, Feb 16th, Mar 11th, Apr 10th Apr 12th, May 3rd, May 11th, May 28th (14 days)

ENQUIRIES
F P Brangwyn Esq, Towcester Racecourse Co Ltd, Easton Neston, Towcester, Northants, NN12 7HS Tel: (0327) 53414

COURSE STATISTICS 1987-92

	Total W/R	(%)	Hurdles Nov	Hcp	Chases Nov	Hcp	Level Stake
Top Trainers							
Sherwood O	15/ 50	30.0	8/21	1/ 4	4/14	2/11	+ 12.64
McKie Mrs I	14/ 71	19.7	0/26	3/12	5/22	6/11	- 3.04
Casey T	14/108	12.9	5/44	3/29	4/17	2/18	- 32.25
Henderson N J	13/ 60	21.6	4/26	0/ 3	4/16	5/15	+ 18.21
Forster Capt T A	13/ 98	13.2	0/20	1/ 6	6/26	6/46	+ 36.23
Balding G B	12/ 92	13.0	1/21	3/19	4/27	4/25	- 39.49
Top Jockeys							
Dunwoody R	21/154	13.6	4/50	4/31	4/32	9/41	- 80.58
Llewellyn C	17/112	15.1	4/37	3/18	5/27	5/30	+ 29.65
White J	12/ 54	22.2	2/18	2/10	4/13	4/13	+ 9.09
Beggan R J	11/ 63	17.4	1/17	3/19	3/12	4/15	+ 12.50
Harvey L	11/ 90	12.2	1/32	3/22	3/21	4/15	+ 7.21
Scudamore P	10/ 49	20.4	4/22	2/ 8	1/ 8	3/11	- 8.08

Favourites Records

Autmn	H:	34.7%	2m Hdl:	34.1%	2m Chs:	38.8%	Hvy :	38.5%
	C:	25.7%	2.5m Hdl:	39.0%	2.5m Chs:	34.1%	Sft :	27.5%
Wintr	H:	31.8%	3m Hdl:	20.0%	3m Chs:	29.0%	Gd-Sft:	29.5%
	C:	37.3%	3.5m Hdl:	0.0%	3.5m Chs:	0.0%	Gd :	29.3%
Sprng	H:	36.1%	Nov Hdl:	35.1%	Nov Chs:	36.5%	Gd-Fm:	38.0%
	C:	33.3%	Hcp Hdl:	33.5%	Hcp Chs:	31.0%	Fm/Hd:	43.0%

| **Total** : | **33.8%** | **L/Stake** : | **- 46.32** | **Lngst Wng Run:** | 5 | **Lngst Lsg Run:** | 12 |

UTTOXETER

Located in mid-Staffordshire, not far from the Peak district, Uttoxeter racecourse is an increasingly popular venue with a pleasant rural setting. The management have brought about a definite improvement in amenities over the last few years, and in any case the layout of the course and the position of the stands mean that viewing is excellent. The racing is generally moderate, but the Midlands (Ansells) Grand National meeting in March, as well as other Bank Holiday fixtures, are well supported.

The course itself is an oval left-hander, slightly undulating, and just over a mile and a quarter in circumference. The bends are easy, and the flat home straight, with a run-in of 170-yards, is not particularly testing. Neither are the eight fences, although the two in the straight can cause problems, likewise the third last, an open ditch. The track puts the emphasis on speed, and favours front-runners.

FENCES: ✚✚(✚)　　　　　　　　　　　　　　　　　　　　　　**RACING: £**

MEETINGS
Oct 3rd, Oct 15th, Nov 5th, Dec 3rd, Dec 18th & 19th, Jan 29th, Feb 13th, Mar 20th, Apr 10th & 12th, May 6th, May 31st, Jun 2nd, (14 days)

ENQUIRIES
Major D McAllister, Uttoxeter Leisure & Development Co Ltd, The Racecourse, Wood Lane, Uttoxeter, Staffs ST14 8BD. Tel: (0889) 562561

COURSE STATISTICS 1987-92

	Total W/R	(%)	Hurdles Nov	Hcp	Chases Nov	Hcp	Level Stake
Top Trainers							
Pipe M C	38/104	36.5	19/38	12/41	3/ 8	4/17	+ 57.93
Edwards J A C	20/113	17.7	8/44	2/15	5/20	5/34	- 6.82
Webber J	14/ 60	23.3	4/20	0/ 2	3/14	7/24	+ 18.05
Richards G W	14/ 85	16.4	0/29	1/10	3/16	10/30	- 46.20
Stephenson W A	13/ 82	15.8	0/19	2/11	6/21	5/31	- 29.23
Wilton Miss S J	12/116	10.3	4/48	7/58	1/ 5	0/ 5	- 44.12
Top Jockeys							
Scudamore P	28/ 77	36.3	13/30	7/20	5/12	3/15	+ 21.57
McCourt G	19/ 89	21.3	7/40	8/32	0/ 5	4/12	+ 5.97
Dunwoody R	18/106	16.9	8/39	5/33	3/15	2/19	- 26.85
Dwyer M	12/ 68	17.6	4/26	1/19	2/ 6	5/17	- 23.20
Doughty N	10/ 51	19.6	1/21	1/ 6	2/10	6/14	- 26.85
Llewellyn C	10/ 53	18.8	2/20	2/14	3/11	3/ 8	- 10.11

Favourites Records

Autmn	H:	34.6%	2m	Hdl:	32.1%	2m	Chs:	52.9%	Hvy : 7.1%
	C:	43.1%	2.5m Hdl:		30.5%	2.5m Chs:		45.3%	Sft : 36.0%
Wintr	H:	25.0%	3m	Hdl:	39.2%	3m	Chs:	40.0%	Gd-Sft: 41.5%
	C:	30.4%	3.5m Hdl:		0.0%	3.5m Chs:		32.1%	Gd : 30.3%
Sprng	H:	34.8%	Nov	Hdl:	29.4%	Nov	Chs:	46.9%	Gd-Fm : 47.6%
	C:	43.4%	Hcp	Hdl:	37.1%	Hcp	Chs:	36.8%	Fm/Hd : 38.0%

Total : 36.6% L/Stake : - 48.12 Lngst Wng Run: 8 Lngst Lsg Run: 8

WARWICK

One of the oldest racecourses in Britain, Warwick is located in comparatively urban surroundings, although there are some pleasant views from the enclosures. Jump racing, like the flat sport on offer here, is moderate in quality, but usually attracts good fields. Brooke Bond Oxo National day is particularly popular with the public.

The track itself is almost triangular, measuring one and three-quarter miles in circumference. The ten fences are jumped left-handed, and there are a number of undulations, which allied to the sharp bends, make this a tricky course. In addition, the fences are relatively stiff for a small track, and the five in the back straight are jumped in quick succession. The home straight is short, with a run-in of 240-yards, and the circuit undoubtedly favours handiness and acceleration in a horse.

FENCES: +++(+)   **RACING: £(£)**

MEETINGS
Oct 31st, Nov 17th, Nov 28th, Dec 7th, Dec 30th, Jan 9th, Jan 23rd, Feb 9th, Feb 24th, Mar 4th, May 8th, May 22nd (12 days)

ENQUIRIES
P McNeile Esq, Warwick Racecourse Co Ltd, Hampton Street, Warwick CV34 6HN.
Tel: (0926) 491553

COURSE STATISTICS 1987-92

	Total W/R	(%)	Hurdles Nov	Hcp	Chases Nov	Hcp	Level Stake
Top Trainers							
Pipe M C	36/124	29.0	10/57	11/33	8/14	7/20	- 12.21
Pitman Mrs J	16/ 87	18.3	9/42	0/19	3/15	4/11	+ 27.61
Nicholson D	14/ 86	16.2	7/40	1/ 7	3/16	3/23	- 16.24
Akehurst R	11/ 49	22.4	7/22	1/16	1/ 7	2/ 4	+ 2.01
Sherwood O	11/ 61	18.0	7/27	0/10	3/16	1/ 8	- 11.86
Gifford J T	10/ 35	28.5	3/12	4/10	2/10	1/ 3	+ 63.20
Top Jockeys							
Scudamore P	29/ 97	29.9	9/43	11/23	7/16	2/15	- 10.42
Dunwoody R	19/128	14.8	7/50	1/28	4/22	7/28	- 59.99
Pitman M	10/ 36	27.7	7/16	0/ 7	2/ 9	1/ 4	+ 37.73
McCourt G	9/ 63	14.2	4/31	1/11	2/15	2/ 6	- 17.19
Perrett M	8/ 29	27.5	1/10	2/ 7	2/ 3	3/ 9	+ 3.16
Llewellyn C	8/ 80	10.0	1/35	0/12	3/14	4/19	- 27.75

Favourites Records							
Autmn	H:	35.6%	2m Hdl:	34.0%	2m Chs:	45.3%	Hvy : 28.6%
	C:	38.6%	2.5m Hdl:	20.6%	2.5m Chs:	50.0%	Sft : 32.3%
Wintr	H:	24.7%	3m Hdl:	0.0%	3m Chs:	33.0%	Gd-Sft: 35.9%
	C:	39.3%	3.5m Hdl:	0.0%	3.5m Chs:	21.9%	Gd : 30.5%
Sprng	H:	33.6%	Nov Hdl:	30.7%	Nov Chs:	44.1%	Gd-Fm : 42.7%
	C:	46.7%	Hcp Hdl:	28.8%	Hcp Chs:	39.0%	Fm/Hd : 34.3%
Total :		**34.9%**	**L/Stake :**	**- 39.12**	**Lngst Wng Run:**	**5**	**Lngst Lsg Run: 14**

WETHERBY

Although hard by the A1, Wetherby is essentially a country course just south-east of Harrogate, and within easy range of the training centre at Malton. It is generally popular with leading Northern trainers, because it provides a fair test of a jumper, but this changed last year due to the extreme severity of the fences, which many thought had been rebuilt. Crowds are good, and the racing, although generally moderate, is improved by some good chases, notably the Bobby Renton Novices Chase (Oct), the Charlie Hall Chase (Nov) and the Rowland Meyrick Chase in the New Year.

The track is left-handed, oval in shape, and a mile and a half in circumference. There are slight undulations, but with easy turns and a comparatively short run-in, the circuit is a very fair test of a free-running, long-striding galloper. The nine fences are now rated the stiffest in the country bar only the Grand National obstacles, with the second last in particular often singled out as a very intimidating obstacle. The hurdle course is altogether sharper, putting a greater emphasis on speed.

FENCES: ✚✚✚✚✚   **RACING: ££(£)**

MEETINGS
Oct 14th, Oct 30th & 31st, Nov 17th, Dec 5th, Dec 26th, Dec 28th, Jan 14th, Feb 6th, Mar 3rd, Apr 12th & 13th, May 5th, May 31st (14 days)

ENQUIRIES
G M Hanson Esq, Wetherby Steeplechase Committee Ltd, The Racecourse, York Road, Wetherby, West Yorks, LS22 5EJ. Tel: (0937) 62035

COURSE STATISTICS 1987-92

	Total W/R	(%)	Hurdles Nov	Hcp	Chases Nov	Hcp	Level Stake
Top Jockeys							
Dwyer M	33/184	17.9	10/74	13/45	3/23	7/42	– 33.91
Grant C	30/208	14.4	4/76	4/47	6/35	16/50	– 85.64
Wyer L	24/120	20.0	9/43	6/35	4/15	5/27	– 47.49
Niven P	22/147	14.9	6/67	4/35	4/18	8/27	– 35.57
McCourt G	21/ 86	24.4	12/39	4/22	0/ 9	5/16	+ 34.54
Doughty N	13/ 60	21.6	3/25	2/ 7	7/14	1/14	– 17.29
Top Trainers							
Stephenson W A	43/293	14.6	6/96	2/33	10/54	25/110	– 73.07
Richards G W	29/130	22.3	11/41	2/19	11/25	5/45	+ 7.70
Easterby M H	25/134	18.6	7/51	6/37	5/14	7/32	– 43.24
FitzGerald J G	21/104	20.1	7/51	6/20	3/ 8	5/25	– 6.63
Easterby M W	16/ 82	19.5	9/46	2/21	2/ 7	3/ 8	– 26.74
Tinkler N	16/ 86	18.6	11/55	4/26	0/ 0	1/ 5	+ 2.58

Favourites Records

Autmn	H:	42.3%	2m	Hdl:	32.7%	2m	Chs:	39.0%	Hvy : 0.0%
	C:	26.3%	2.5m	Hdl:	46.5%	2.5m	Chs:	24.2%	Sft : 40.8%
Wintr	H:	31.7%	3m	Hdl:	32.9%	3m	Chs:	43.4%	Gd-Sft: 23.8%
	C:	42.7%	3.5m	Hdl:	0.0%	3.5m	Chs:	0.0%	Gd : 36.2%
Sprng	H:	35.8%	Nov	Hdl:	41.3%	Nov	Chs:	44.7%	Gd-Fm : 47.5%
	C:	37.9%	Hcp	Hdl:	29.0%	Hcp	Chs:	30.5%	Fm/Hd : 37.0%

Total : 36.0%   L/Stake : – 57.60   Lngst Wng Run: 5   Lngst Lsg Run: 14

WINCANTON

Half-way between Frome and Yeovil, in the attractive East Somerset countryside, Wincanton racecourse is a very popular venue, all the more so because the standard of sport has increased over the past few years. Not too far west to discourage the Lambourn contingent, and obviously well suited to the needs of the West Country handlers, fields are generally good, as are the facilities. Most meetings are mid-week, with the valuable Kingwell Hurdle and Jim Ford Challenge Cup in February the undoubted highlight of the season here.

Essentially a galloping course, Wincanton comprises an oval right-hander of about eleven furlongs. Minor undulations include a slight rise passing the stands, and a comparable decline on the turn into the home straight. The bends are easy, and are moved each meeting to ensure a good racing surface. The nine fences are quite stiff, but there are no major pitfalls for the good jumper, and the short 190-yard run-in favours the front-running types.

FENCES: +++(+)   **RACING: £(£)**

MEETINGS
Oct 8th, Oct 22nd, Nov 5th, Nov 19th, Dec 26th, Jan 14th, Jan 29th, Feb 11th, Feb 25th, Mar 11th, Mar 25th, Apr 12th, May 7th (13 days)

ENQUIRIES
R I Renton Esq, Wincanton Races Co Ltd, Wincanton Racecourse, Wincanton, Somerset, BA9 8BJ Tel: (0963) 32344

COURSE STATISTICS 1987-92

Top Trainers	Total W/R	(%)	Hurdles Nov	Hcp	Chases Nov	Hcp	Level Stake
Pipe M C	33/112	29.4	16/57	7/30	8/15	2/10	- 0.41
Elsworth D R C	27/120	22.5	5/52	5/22	8/17	9/29	- 1.86
Pitman Mrs J	20/ 57	35.0	8/25	4/ 8	6/13	2/11	+ 55.81
Nicholson D	16/ 76	21.0	6/28	1/ 4	5/18	4/26	- 9.37
Hodges R J	14/204	6.8	2/63	1/54	3/33	8/54	-108.04
Sherwood O	12/ 48	25.0	4/17	2/10	4/ 9	2/12	- 4.02
Top Jockeys							
Dunwoody R	31/148	20.9	11/65	4/25	9/27	7/31	+ 13.38
Scudamore P	30/ 83	36.1	14/37	6/19	6/17	4/10	+ 33.23
Powell B	18/177	10.1	4/64	1/33	6/36	7/44	- 42.94
Davies H	13/ 85	15.2	6/34	3/12	1/12	3/27	+ 57.63
Pitman M	11/ 29	37.9	4/12	1/ 3	5/ 8	1/ 6	+ 23.11
Bradley G	10/ 56	17.8	4/26	0/ 7	2/ 6	4/17	- 21.49

Favourites Records

Autmn	H:	35.0%	2m Hdl:	36.8%	2m Chs:	29.0%	Hvy	:	0.0%
	C:	53.3%	2.5m Hdl:	0.0%	2.5m Chs:	40.1%	Sft	:	46.0%
Wintr	H:	35.2%	3m Hdl:	35.9%	3m Chs:	37.5%	Gd-Sft:		35.6%
	C:	26.6%	3.5m Hdl:	0.0%	3.5m Chs:	0.0%	Gd	:	32.0%
Sprng	H:	39.4%	Nov Hdl:	42.0%	Nov Chs:	44.6%	Gd-Fm	:	40.0%
	C:	29.2%	Hcp Hdl:	27.1%	Hcp Chs:	31.4%	Fm/Hd	:	39.6%
Total	:	**36.5%**	**L/Stake :**	**- 38.69**	**Lngst Wng Run:**	**5**	**Lngst Lsg Run:**		**12**

WINDSOR

Situated between Windsor and Maidenhead, and within easy reach of London, the crowds tend to be good for the jumping here, although they have yet to match the popularity of the evening flat racing in summer. Again, the accessibility means good fields, with quantity rather than quality being the byword. Nevertheless, the New Year's Day Hurdle, and the Fairlawne Chase in February help raise the standard.

Windsor is laid out in a figure of eight pattern, almost entirely flat, and measuring a mile and six furlongs in circumference. The bends are quite sharp, and although the long finishing straight helps redress the balance, the track is ideally suited to the nippy type of horse. There are nine fences in all, seven on the larger upper loop, and two in the lower loop, and they are very easy.

FENCES: ✚(✚)   RACING: ££

MEETINGS
Nov 7th, Nov 16th, Dec 3th, Jan 1st, Jan 20th, Feb 3rd, Feb 20th, Mar 8th (8 days)

ENQUIRIES
R Knight, Windsor Racing Ltd, The Racecourse, Windsor, Berks SL4 5JJ.
Tel: (0753) 865234 / 864726

COURSE STATISTICS 1987-92

	Total W/R	(%)	Hurdles Nov	Hcp	Chases Nov	Hcp	Level Stake
Top Trainers							
Pitman Mrs J	12/ 49	24.4	8/29	1/ 7	3/10	0/ 3	+ 0.11
Henderson N J	11/ 37	29.7	7/20	0/ 4	4/ 7	0/ 6	+ 4.05
Sherwood O	9/ 34	26.4	3/15	1/ 6	4/ 8	1/ 5	+ 2.50
Akehurst R	9/ 45	20.0	4/26	3/12	1/ 4	1/ 3	+ 8.21
Hobbs P J	8/ 45	17.7	2/19	1/ 4	3/ 9	2/13	- 14.50
Hedger P R	7/ 33	21.2	2/13	1/10	3/ 6	1/ 4	- 3.62
Top Jockeys							
Osborne J	11/ 52	21.1	3/21	2/11	3/ 8	3/12	+ 5.99
Richards M	9/ 66	13.6	4/30	1/12	3/14	1/10	- 29.52
Moore G	9/ 93	9.6	2/36	4/22	2/20	1/15	- 13.42
Pitman M	8/ 25	32.0	6/18	0/ 2	2/ 3	0/ 2	+ 0.98
Dunwoody R	8/ 57	14.0	5/30	0/12	2/ 7	1/ 8	- 36.78
Hobbs Peter	6/ 48	12.5	4/24	1/ 4	1/13	0/ 7	- 27.37

Favourites Records

Autmn H:	35.0%	2m Hdl:	40.2%	2m Chs:	25.0%	Hvy : 0.0%
C:	26.7%	2.5m Hdl:	0.0%	2.5m Chs:	36.7%	Sft : 17.4%
Wintr H:	40.2%	3m Hdl:	34.8%	3m Chs:	29.3%	Gd-Sft: 34.1%
C:	26.4%	3.5m Hdl:	0.0%	3.5m Chs:	21.4%	Gd : 40.9%
Sprng H:	41.7%	Nov Hdl:	41.9%	Nov Chs:	51.4%	Gd-Fm : 34.1%
C:	54.6%	Hcp Hdl:	35.1%	Hcp Chs:	16.0%	Fm/Hd : 33.3%
Total :	**34.9%**	**L/Stake :**	**- 20.53**	**Lngst Wng Run:**	**4**	**Lngst Lsg Run: 9**

WOLVERHAMPTON

Despite being located in the Black Country, itself not renowned for its beauty, the course at Wolverhampton is quite pleasant, and easily accessible. Unfortunately, the large local population do not support racing here, and crowds are small. Fields are not though, and while the average runner is only moderate, the contestants in Wolverhampton's principal event, the Champion Hurdle trial, provide a welcome change from the usual mediocrity.

The track is a triangular left-hander, of a mile and a half in length. It is level throughout, with eight fairly stiff fences, particularly the first in the straight. The straight itself is four furlongs in length, with a shortish run-in of 180-yards. While the bends on the hurdle course are on the tight side, the chase course is well suited to the long-striding type.

FENCES: +++   **RACING: £(£)**

MEETINGS
Nov 2nd, Nov 9th, Nov 23rd, Dec 26th & 28th, Jan 4th Jan 27th, Feb 8th, Feb 22nd, Mar 8th, Mar 19th (11 days)

ENQUIRIES
M J Legge Esq, Wolverhampton Racecourse Plc, Gorsebrook Road, Wolverhampton, West Midlands, WV6 0PE. Tel: (0902) 24481

COURSE STATISTICS 1987-92

	Total W/R	(%)	Hurdles Nov	Hcp	Chases Nov	Hcp	Level Stake
Top Trainers							
Pipe M C	24/ 72	33.3	12/29	4/20	4/14	4/ 9	+ 41.70
Nicholson D	13/ 60	21.6	3/22	0/ 7	7/18	3/13	+ 14.06
Edwards J A C	11/ 62	17.7	3/18	2/10	3/18	3/16	- 28.62
Pitman Mrs J	10/ 48	20.8	7/26	2/ 8	0/ 6	1/ 8	- 5.38
Holder R J	10/ 56	17.8	3/24	5/12	2/12	0/ 8	+ 28.50
Lee R	10/ 60	16.6	2/20	1/ 7	3/18	4/15	+ 43.68
Top Jockeys							
Scudamore P	25/ 73	34.2	11/31	5/14	4/14	5/14	+ 26.83
Dunwoody R	22/110	20.0	6/36	4/23	8/30	4/21	+ 8.98
Lynch M M	9/ 41	21.9	1/11	1/ 6	4/13	3/11	- 5.87
Wall T	7/ 80	8.7	1/32	3/20	3/19	0/ 9	+ 21.80
Williamson N	6/ 27	22.2	4/12	0/ 2	1/ 9	1/ 4	+ 9.19
Pitman M	6/ 30	20.0	5/19	1/ 4	0/ 4	0/ 3	- 15.97

Favourites Records

Autmn H:	27.2%	2m Hdl:	31.1%	2m Chs:	33.3%	Hvy :	33.3%
C:	32.9%	2.5m Hdl:	28.9%	2.5m Chs:	31.5%	Sft :	40.4%
Wintr H:	34.9%	3m Hdl:	33.3%	3m Chs:	34.6%	Gd-Sft:	32.7%
C:	29.2%	3.5m Hdl:	0.0%	3.5m Chs:	0.0%	Gd :	30.3%
Sprng H:	25.9%	Nov Hdl:	34.1%	Nov Chs:	37.5%	Gd-Fm :	26.1%
C:	40.0%	Hcp Hdl:	25.4%	Hcp Chs:	26.9%	Fm/Hd :	38.5%

Total : 31.6%   L/Stake : - 56.29   Lngst Wng Run: 3   Lngst Lsg Run: 14

WORCESTER

While actually near the middle of the cathedral city of Worcester itself, the racetrack is attractively sited alongside the banks of the River Severn, which makes it prone to flooding. The fields are sizeable, as are the crowds, who are not put off by the unfortunate positioning of the stands making part of the course out of sight. Fixtures are plentiful, and many of them take place on Wednesdays.

The track is a long oval measuring thirteen furlongs, flat throughout with easy, sweeping left-handed turns. The nine fences are no more difficult than average, although an open ditch down the back stretch occasionally causes problems. The home straight is a long one, with four fences, and a run-in of 220-yards, and is well-suited to the galloping type. A number of trainers, not all of them local, consider the easy turns and well-constructed fences make an excellent introduction for a novice.

FENCES: ++(+)   **RACING: £(£)**

MEETINGS
Oct 10th, Oct 24th, Nov 11th, Nov 30th, Dec 9th, Jan 7th, Feb 17th, Mar 3rd, Mar 24th, Mar 31st, Apr 14th, Apr 24th, May 8th, May 19th, (14 days)

ENQUIRIES
J H A Bennett Esq, Ryall Cottage, Ryall, Upton on Severn, Worcester, WR8 0PN Tel: (068-46) 2033 (home) / (0905) 25364 (office)

COURSE STATISTICS 1987-92

	Total W/R	(%)	Hurdles Nov	Hcp	Chases Nov	Hcp	Level Stake
Top Jockeys							
Scudamore P	52/154	33.7	20/58	14/37	7/22	11/37	- 4.67
Dunwoody R	35/232	15.0	10/79	4/44	6/41	15/68	- 31.80
Davies H	17/132	12.8	7/50	3/27	0/23	7/32	- 17.29
McCourt G	15/ 96	15.6	5/39	8/26	1/13	1/18	- 11.27
Powell B	15/179	8.3	2/54	1/28	7/43	5/54	- 82.50
Earle S	12/107	11.2	1/34	0/22	8/26	3/25	- 44.95
Top Trainers							
Pipe M C	51/143	35.6	24/56	14/53	5/17	8/17	+ 22.87
Sherwood O	22/ 69	31.8	8/28	4/11	5/13	5/17	+ 57.64
Holder R J	19/ 82	23.1	3/30	6/22	2/ 5	8/25	+ 26.26
Nicholson D	19/115	16.5	4/46	0/ 8	4/15	11/46	+ 1.67
Balding G B	17/116	14.6	6/46	4/29	3/12	4/29	- 39.96
Forster Capt T A	16/ 86	18.6	3/26	1/ 4	2/13	10/43	- 2.41

Favourites Records

Autmn H:	39.6%	2m	Hdl:	43.2%	2m	Chs:	39.8%	Hvy :	33.3%
C:	43.6%	2.5m	Hdl:	35.4%	2.5m	Chs:	36.1%	Sft :	39.1%
Wintr H:	32.7%	3m	Hdl:	28.0%	3m	Chs:	43.8%	Gd-Sft:	29.0%
C:	23.9%	3.5m	Hdl:	0.0%	3.5m	Chs:	41.7%	Gd :	35.2%
Sprng H:	40.3%	Nov	Hdl:	37.7%	Nov	Chs:	46.2%	Gd-Fm :	41.7%
C:	43.1%	Hcp	Hdl:	39.8%	Hcp	Chs:	36.7%	Fm/Hd :	45.4%

Total :   39.3%   L/Stake : + 1.15   Lngst Wng Run: 8 Lngst Lsg Run: 10

LINGFIELD-AW COURSE STATISTICS 1990-92

	Total W/R	(%)	Hurdles Nov	Hcp	Chases Nov	Hcp	Level Stake
Top Trainers							
Dow S	16/ 34	47.0	5/15	11/19	0/ 0	0/ 0	+ 17.46
Sanders Miss B	13/ 44	29.5	6/18	7/26	0/ 0	0/ 0	- 6.69
Jenkins J R	10/ 43	23.2	2/10	8/32	0/ 0	0/ 1	- 17.62
White J	8/ 28	28.5	3/10	5/18	0/ 0	0/ 0	+ 15.56
McCourt M	7/ 14	50.0	1/ 3	6/11	0/ 0	0/ 0	+ 5.57
Old J A B	5/ 12	41.6	0/ 1	5/11	0/ 0	0/ 0	+ 15.48
Top Jockeys							
Dicken A*	15/ 30	50.0	5/13	10/17	0/ 0	0/ 0	+ 22.79
Maguire A*	14/ 46	30.4	8/23	6/23	0/ 0	0/ 0	- 4.00
McKeown Dale	9/ 31	29.0	4/17	5/14	0/ 0	0/ 0	+ 14.23
Grantham T	3/ 5	60.0	0/ 1	3/ 4	0/ 0	0/ 0	+ 2.48
Webb A	3/ 6	50.0	1/ 3	2/ 3	0/ 0	0/ 0	+ 10.13
Bates A*	3/ 6	50.0	1/ 2	2/ 4	0/ 0	0/ 0	+ 5.40

Favourites Records

Autmn H:	0.0%	2m	Hdl:	50.6%	2m	Chs:	0.0%	Hvy :	0.0%
C:	0.0%	2.5m	Hdl:	46.9%	2.5m	Chs:	100.0%	Sft :	0.0%
Wintr H:	49.6%	3m	Hdl:	54.6%	3m	Chs:	0.0%	Gd-Sft:	0.0%
C:	100.0%	3.5m	Hdl:	0.0%	3.5m	Chs:	0.0%	Gd :	0.0%
Sprng H:	50.0%	Nov	Hdl:	40.7%	Nov	Chs:	0.0%	Gd-Fm :	0.0%
C:	0.0%	Hcp	Hdl:	52.7%	Hcp	Chs:	100.0%	Fm/Hd :	0.0%

Total : 49.9% L/Stake : + 13.00 Lngst Wng Run: 7 Lngst Lsg Run: 5

SOUTHWELL-AW COURSE STATISTICS 1990-92

	Total W/R	(%)	Hurdles Nov	Hcp	Chases Nov	Hcp	Level Stake
Top Trainers							
Hollinshead R	15/ 60	25.0	6/22	9/38	0/ 0	0/ 0	- 13.74
Pipe M C	12/ 43	27.9	3/13	8/27	1/ 3	0/ 0	- 3.87
Harris J L	9/ 65	13.8	1/17	8/48	0/ 0	0/ 0	+ 29.50
Tompkins M H	7/ 24	29.1	1/ 4	6/20	0/ 0	0/ 0	+ 7.25
Aconley Mrs V A	6/ 18	33.3	1/ 3	5/15	0/ 0	0/ 0	+ 18.00
Weaver R J	6/ 32	18.7	1/ 4	5/28	0/ 0	0/ 0	- 4.12
Top Jockeys							
Wynne S*	7/ 42	16.6	7/26	0/16	0/ 0	0/ 0	- 22.76
Campbell R	4/ 9	44.4	2/ 4	2/ 5	0/ 0	0/ 0	+ 16.08
Burchell D J	4/ 12	33.3	2/ 3	1/ 6	1/ 2	0/ 1	- 2.93
Lyons Gary	4/ 20	20.0	1/15	3/ 5	0/ 0	0/ 0	+ 13.00
Harris J A	4/ 33	12.1	1/19	3/14	0/ 0	0/ 0	+ 34.00
Keightley S	3/ 7	42.8	3/ 5	0/ 2	0/ 0	0/ 0	+ 6.50

Favourites Records

Autmn H:	37.9%	2m	Hdl:	38.4%	2m	Chs:	40.0%	Hvy :	0.0%
C:	50.0%	2.5m	Hdl:	39.5%	2.5m	Chs:	40.0%	Sft :	0.0%
Wintr H:	37.0%	3m	Hdl:	35.2%	3m	Chs:	50.0%	Gd-Sft:	0.0%
C:	25.0%	3.5m	Hdl:	0.0%	3.5m	Chs:	0.0%	Gd :	0.0%
Sprng H:	44.4%	Nov	Hdl:	42.5%	Nov	Chs:	50.0%	Gd-Fm :	0.0%
C:	100.0%	Hcp	Hdl:	37.0%	Hcp	Chs:	37.5%	Fm/Hd :	0.0%

Total : 38.6% L/Stake : - 12.21 Lngst Wng Run: 6 Lngst Lsg Run: 8

17 . PRINCIPAL STATISTICS

PRIZE MONEY DISTRIBUTION BY COURSE

		Races	Win - £	Place-£	Total - £	Average	Pos by Av.
1	Cheltenham	94	1,080,148	687,514	1,767,662	18,223	(2)
2	Ascot	56	449,643	235,730	685,373	12,461	(3)
3	Newbury	69	423,715	217,976	641,691	7,640	(7)
4	Liverpool	20	382,097	231,422	613,519	30,707	(1)
5	Sandown Park	54	381,450	214,501	595,951	9,168	(5)
6	Kempton Park	55	350,637	193,819	544,456	9,899	(4)
7	Chepstow	64	327,488	166,795	494,283	6,029	(8)
8	Wetherby	87	278,696	138,548	417,244	5,151	(10)
9	Uttoxeter	95	271,115	130,626	401,741	3,901	(14)
10	Haydock Park	56	239,739	133,411	373,150	8,481	(6)
11	Newton Abbot	116	259,710	107,585	367,295	2,915	(33)
12	Market Rasen	111	242,432	104,396	346,828	3,303	(18)
13	Worcester	107	231,994	103,270	335,264	3,105	(23)
14	Ayr	76	211,530	110,294	321,824	5,455	(9)
15	Wincanton	75	217,157	103,924	321,081	4,225	(13)
16	Newcastle	65	209,215	97,409	306,624	4,319	(12)
17	Warwick	68	202,808	96,411	299,219	4,337	(11)
18	Bangor	79	202,524	90,941	293,465	3,261	(20)
19	Sedgefield	99	198,410	84,884	283,294	2,983	(31)
20	Devon/Exeter	88	184,583	84,192	268,775	3,089	(25)
21	Stratford	86	173,691	75,038	248,729	3,071	(27)
22	Huntingdon	87	170,626	75,946	246,572	3,083	(26)
23	Towcester	71	171,851	74,199	246,050	3,001	(30)
24	Hereford	94	170,257	75,372	245,629	2,641	(40)
25	Fontwell	83	172,217	73,149	245,366	2,696	(38)
26	Kelso	71	167,294	76,340	243,634	3,432	(17)
27	Taunton	69	154,105	69,650	223,755	2,906	(34)
28	Southwell-AW	107	158,058	64,243	222,301	2,059	(44)
29	Perth	61	144,215	62,719	206,934	3,089	(24)
30	Plumpton	90	141,768	60,041	201,809	2,374	(43)
31	Leicester	60	136,921	58,357	195,278	3,201	(22)
32	Carlisle	51	133,099	56,288	189,387	2,668	(39)
33	Ludlow	63	129,226	55,771	184,997	2,606	(41)
34	Lingfield-AW	83	126,961	51,579	178,540	1,962	(45)
35	Wolverhampton	58	120,580	54,524	175,104	2,919	(32)
36	Lingfield	38	117,760	53,715	171,475	3,898	(15)
37	Windsor	39	115,951	51,797	167,748	3,289	(19)
38	Nottingham	55	114,878	49,060	163,938	3,214	(21)
39	Catterick	51	109,782	46,328	156,110	2,439	(42)
40	Southwell	49	103,918	45,424	149,342	3,048	(28)
41	Hexham	81	100,229	43,313	143,542	1,889	(46)
42	Edinburgh	45	89,690	39,762	129,452	2,815	(35)
43	Doncaster	43	88,263	38,881	127,144	3,740	(16)
44	Folkestone	37	83,848	36,460	120,308	2,734	(37)
45	Fakenham	32	62,409	28,196	90,605	3,020	(29)
46	Cartmel	30	58,983	23,496	82,479	2,749	(36)

TOP RACES 1991/92

			Dist	To Winner £
1 (2)	MARTELL GRAND NATIONAL CHASE	L'pool	4m 4f	99,943
2 (1)	TOTE CHELTENHAM GOLD CUP	Chelt	3m 2f	98,028
3 (3)	SMURFIT CHAMPION HURDLE	Chelt	2m	80,065
4 (4)	QUEEN MOTHER CHAMPION CHASE	Chelt	2m	63,390
5 (5)	WHITBREAD GOLD CUP CHASE	S'down	3m 5f	57,400
6 (8)	KING GEORGE VI RANK CHASE	Kempt	3m	44,170
7 (6)	`SUN ALLIANCE' NOVICES' CHASE	Chelt	3m	43,507
8 (10)	MUMM MELLING CHASE	L'pool	2m 4f	42,341
9 (7)	BONUSPRINT STAYERS' HURDLE	Chelt	3m 1f	40,535
10 (14)	HENNESSY COGNAC GOLD CUP	Newb	3m 2f	37,462
11 (9)	W'FORD ARKLE CHAL. TRPHY. CHASE	Chelt	2m	37,345
12 (13)	WM HILL SCOTTISH NATIONAL CHASE	Ayr	4m 120yds	36,950
13 (12)	`SUN ALLIANCE' NOVICES' HURDLE	Chelt	2m 4f	34,152
14 (17)	MACKESON GOLD CUP H'CAP CHASE	Chelt	2m 4f	33,100
15 (15)	TRAFALGAR HOUSE SUPREME NOV HDLE	Chelt	2m	32,096
16 (16)	DAILY EXPRESS TRIUMPH HURDLE	Chelt	2m	31,991
17 (24)	RACING POST HANDICAP CHASE	Kempt	3m	31,875
18 (18)	CASTLEFORD CHASE	Wthby	2m 50yds	31,730
19 (19)	TOP RANK CHRISTMAS HURDLE	Kempt	2m	31,520
20 (21)	VICTOR CHANDLER H'CAP CHASE	Ascot	2m	30,438
21 (-)	TOTE GOLD TROPHY (H'CAP HURDLE)	Newby	2m 100yds	30,405
22 (-)	CORAL GOLDEN H'CAP HURDLE (FINAL)	Chelt	3m 1f	28,840
23 (-)	H & T WALKER GOLD CUP H'CAP CHASE	Ascot	2m 4f	27,344
24 (11)	NEWTON CHASE	Hayd	2m 4f	27,310
25 (20)	MARTELL AINTREE HURDLE	L'pool	2m 4f	26,948
26 (22)	RITZ CLUB NATIONAL HUNT H'CAP CHASE	Chelt	3m 1f	26,805
27 (-)	A F BUDGE GOLD CUP (H'CAP CHASE)	Chelt	2m 4f	26,524
28 (-)	CHARTERHOUSE MERC. H'CAP CHASE	Ascot	3m	25,146
29 (30)	BUTLINS FELTHAM NOVICES' CHASE	Kempt	3m	24,260
30 (34)	GREENALLS GOLD CUP HANDICAP CHASE	Hayd	3m 4f	24,086
31 (26)	CATHCART CHALLENGE CUP (CHASE)	Chelt	2m 4f	24,075
32 (-)	CORAL WELSH NATIONAL H'CAP CHASE	Chepst	3m 6f	23,654
33 (-)	ANSELLS NATIONAL HANDICAP CHASE	Uttox	4m	23,108
34 (-)	MARTELL CUP CHASE	L'pool	3m 1f	23,065
35 (-)	MUMM MILDMAY NOVICES' CHASE	L'pool	3m 1f	21,948

TOP EARNERS OF UK PRIZEMONEY 1991/92

		Runs	Wins	Plcs	Win-£	Place-£	TOTAL-£
1	REMITTANCE MAN	5	4	1	129,881	8,183	138,064
2	COOL GROUND	8	3	1	130,659	1,888	132,547
3	PARTY POLITICS	5	1	3	99,943	23,872	123,815
4	WATERLOO BOY	7	4	3	88,998	22,866	111,864
5	KINGS FOUNTAIN	7	4	2	87,095	5,683	92,778
6	ROYAL GAIT	4	3	1	86,738	1,776	88,514
7	DOCKLANDS EXPRESS	7	1	6	31,875	55,977	87,852
8	BRADBURY STAR	9	7	1	66,122	16,192	82,314
9	THE FELLOW	2	1	1	44,170	35,647	79,817
10	KATABATIC	6	3	3	39,340	36,833	76,173
11	TOPSHAM BAY	8	3	2	70,022	1,480	71,502
12	WHATEVER YOU LIKE	6	2	4	5,352	65,990	71,342
13	CAPTAIN DIBBLE	7	3	4	49,269	17,649	66,918
14	ROMANY KING	7	3	4	16,224	48,102	64,326
15	YOUNG POKEY	5	3	2	56,757	5,472	62,229
16	TIPPING TIM	11	4	2	46,690	13,542	60,232
17	THETFORD FOREST	7	5	1	51,134	2,625	53,759
18	RODEO STAR	8	5	2	46,388	5,239	51,627
19	NOMADIC WAY	4	1	3	40,535	10,248	50,783
20	ROYAL DERBI	7	3	3	32,495	16,478	48,973
21	MIINNEHOMA	3	3	0	48,268	0	48,268
22	MY YOUNG MAN	9	6	3	41,814	5,299	47,113
23	SABIN DU LOIR	5	3	1	46,296	487	46,783
24	GRAN ALBA	4	2	2	40,805	5,579	46,384
25	CHATAM	2	2	0	45,446	0	45,446
26	ANOTHER CORAL	6	1	4	33,100	12,266	45,366
27	PAT'S JESTER	4	2	2	32,793	11,450	44,243
28	MORLEY STREET	3	2	1	42,514	1,388	43,902
29	CARVILL'S HILL	3	2	1	40,384	3,208	43,592
30	GRANVILLE AGAIN	5	4	0	41,547	0	41,547
31	LAURA'S BEAU	3	1	1	23,108	18,379	41,487
32	ARCTIC CALL	6	2	2	18,992	22,368	41,360
33	COMBERMERE	9	4	2	36,821	2,032	38,853
34	FLOWN	3	2	1	37,586	796	38,382
35	DANNY HARROLD	7	2	4	32,558	5,134	37,692

TOP TRAINERS BY EARNINGS 1991/92

		Runs	Wins	Plcs	Win-£	Place-£	Total - £
1 (1)	Pipe M C	839	224	240	724,763	202,009	£ 926,772
2 (7)	Henderson N J	251	52	90	337,840	163,520	£ 501,360
3 (9)	Nicholson D	329	63	115	363,233	119,330	£ 482,563
4 (5)	Balding G B	368	53	132	318,215	133,166	£ 451,381
5 (3)	Stephenson W A	539	101	161	262,564	100,194	£ 362,758
6 (2)	Richards G W	409	67	121	241,977	107,374	£ 349,351
7 (16)	Reveley Mrs G R	323	99	104	240,021	78,799	£ 318,820
8 (8)	Gifford J T	389	49	113	218,079	96,606	£ 314,685
9 (13)	Bailey K C	250	38	78	194,084	114,550	£ 308,634
10 (4)	Pitman Mrs J	333	50	103	203,570	98,346	£ 301,916
11 (6)	Sherwood O	227	48	70	200,086	85,110	£ 285,196
12 (-)	Twiston-Davies N	224	31	57	148,187	63,778	£ 211,965
13 (-)	Gaselee N A	140	15	37	140,642	42,253	£ 182,895
14 (-)	Brooks C P E	169	29	46	147,863	31,116	£ 178,979
15 (11)	Elsworth D R C	143	20	49	72,162	104,553	£ 176,715
16 (19)	Forster Capt T A	273	44	63	124,476	48,548	£ 173,024
17 (20)	Easterby M H	203	42	76	98,700	66,814	£ 165,514
18 (12)	Edwards J A C	260	39	76	119,595	43,267	£ 162,862
19 (-)	Hobbs P J	283	51	75	109,707	39,200	£ 148,907
20 (-)	Tinkler N	163	38	38	113,957	33,567	£ 147,524

TOP TRAINERS BY WINS 1991/92

		Wins	Runs (%)	2nd	3rd	4th	Unpl	£-Stake
1 (1)	Pipe M C	224	839 (26.7)	120	87	29	379	- 60.90
2 (3)	Stephenson W A	101	539 (18.7)	73	67	21	277	- 88.59
3 (5)	Reveley Mrs G R	99	323 (30.7)	57	43	4	120	- 0.88
4 (2)	Richards G W	67	409 (16.4)	64	42	14	222	- 90.01
5 (7)	Nicholson D	63	329 (19.2)	51	47	17	151	- 41.37
6 (10)	Balding G B	53	368 (14.4)	57	51	21	186	- 7.25
7 (9)	Henderson N J	52	251 (20.7)	50	29	10	110	- 58.96
8 (18)	Hobbs P J	51	283 (18.0)	37	25	15	155	- 31.00
9 (13)	Pitman Mrs J	50	333 (15.0)	38	50	19	176	- 69.40
10 (4)	Gifford J T	49	389 (12.6)	52	51	10	227	- 150.20
11 (6)	Sherwood O	48	227 (21.2)	35	25	8	111	- 69.45
12 (14)	Forster Capt T A	44	273 (16.1)	27	28	8	166	+ 26.28
13 (19)	Easterby M H	42	203 (20.7)	36	32	8	85	- 56.24
14 (-)	White J	39	183 (21.3)	22	25	6	91	- 26.31
15 (8)	Edwards J A C	39	260 (15.0)	33	33	10	145	- 69.30
16 (-)	Tinkler N	38	163 (23.3)	15	18	4	88	- 12.15
17 (11)	Moore G M	38	240 (15.8)	29	24	12	137	- 70.03
18 (20)	Bailey K C	38	250 (15.2)	36	27	14	135	- 20.91
19 (-)	Hammond M D	35	228 (15.4)	35	31	5	122	- 79.16
20 (12)	FitzGerald J G	33	198 (16.7)	24	25	2	114	- 19.55

TOP TRAINERS BY FIVE YEAR EARNINGS

		1987/8-£	1988/9-£	1989/0-£	1990/1-£	1991/2-£	TOTAL-£
1	Pipe M C	360,081	683,653	792,545	1,203,734	926,772	3,966,785
2	Stephenson W A	302,742	354,186	479,016	459,067	362,758	1,957,769
3	Gifford J T	425,408	397,006	362,592	371,707	314,685	1,871,398
4	Balding G B	198,965	406,974	292,333	379,034	451,381	1,728,687
5	Richards G W	221,586	193,732	437,521	524,591	349,351	1,726,781
6	Elsworth D R C	475,120	432,452	351,658	267,532	176,715	1,703,477
7	Pitman Mrs J	129,911	211,410	519,988	437,957	301,916	1,601,182
8	Nicholson D	267,708	231,196	247,984	344,368	482,563	1,573,819
9	Henderson N J	128,697	229,136	275,124	372,098	501,360	1,506,415
10	Sherwood O	213,360	204,124	291,246	373,422	285,196	1,367,348
11	Edwards J A C	293,218	383,360	232,927	252,810	162,862	1,325,177
12	FitzGerald J G	210,993	228,941	288,521	226,816	142,765	1,098,036
13	Bailey K C	86,794	101,053	282,250	248,548	308,634	1,027,279
14	Barons D H	139,983	116,387	209,174	277,431	147,053	890,028
15	Brooks C P E	0	169,247	256,243	172,138	178,979	776,607
16	Easterby M H	107,027	148,781	175,307	174,429	165,514	771,058
17	Reveley Mrs G R	58,310	61,116	97,222	211,875	318,820	747,343
18	Forster Capt T A	141,081	153,873	102,830	175,439	173,024	746,247
19	Hobbs P J	89,924	96,621	237,474	155,530	148,907	728,456
20	Moore G M	127,136	86,048	145,120	180,030	125,676	664,010

TOP TRAINERS BY FIVE YEAR WINS

		1986/7 Wns Rns	1987/8 Wns Rns	1988/9 Wns Rns	1989/0 Wns Rns	1990/1 Wns Rns	Total Wins Runs
1	Pipe M C	129 / 511	208 / 566	224 / 639	230 / 782	224 / 839	1015 / 3337
2	Stephenson W A	93 / 605	90 / 549	116 / 519	83 / 505	101 / 539	483 / 2717
3	Richards G W	72 / 364	69 / 351	78 / 374	118 / 493	67 / 409	404 / 1991
4	Gifford J T	91 / 422	64 / 384	50 / 365	62 / 451	49 / 389	316 / 2011
5	Pitman Mrs J	45 / 304	62 / 279	93 / 335	43 / 294	50 / 333	293 / 1545
6	Edwards J A C	61 / 319	78 / 402	47 / 353	54 / 311	39 / 260	279 / 1645
7	Sherwood O	42 / 241	53 / 250	58 / 299	56 / 261	48 / 227	257 / 1278
8	Nicholson D	50 / 336	39 / 347	42 / 265	55 / 277	63 / 329	249 / 1554
9	Reveley Mrs G R	26 / 186	23 / 198	41 / 141	58 / 220	99 / 323	247 / 1068
10	FitzGerald J G	49 / 242	59 / 258	58 / 222	45 / 216	33 / 198	244 / 1136
11	Balding G B	40 / 373	59 / 371	42 / 366	48 / 340	53 / 368	242 / 1818
12	Henderson N J	40 / 243	43 / 244	41 / 247	49 / 264	52 / 251	225 / 1249
13	Moore G M	47 / 196	37 / 277	53 / 242	46 / 232	38 / 240	221 / 1187
14	Tinkler N	16 / 74	54 / 198	49 / 207	29 / 186	38 / 163	186 / 828
15	Forster Capt T A	38 / 292	34 / 231	23 / 171	37 / 215	44 / 273	176 / 1182
16	Hobbs P J	22 / 255	24 / 264	45 / 250	33 / 258	51 / 283	175 / 1310
17	Easterby M H	23 / 173	45 / 182	29 / 166	33 / 172	42 / 203	172 / 896
18	Elsworth D R C	50 / 263	54 / 255	24 / 177	23 / 131	20 / 143	171 / 969
19	Barons D H	29 / 268	36 / 304	40 / 230	34 / 215	25 / 233	164 / 1250
20	Brooks C P E	0 / 0	41 / 193	56 / 206	27 / 209	29 / 169	153 / 777

TOP JOCKEYS BY U.K. WINS 1991/92

			Wins	Runs (%)	2nd	3rd	4th	Unpl		Stake
1	(1)	Scudamore P	175	513 (34.1)	79	52	19	188	-	7.90
2	(2)	Dunwoody R	137	715 (19.2)	128	108	28	314	-	171.85
3	(4)	Niven P	105	400 (26.3)	65	46	12	172	-	40.17
4	(5)	McCourt G	102	506 (20.2)	75	54	25	250	+	32.80
5	(9)	Grant C	78	449 (17.4)	62	55	20	234	-	106.25
6	(7)	Osborne J	76	412 (18.5)	66	45	19	206	-	65.40
7	(6)	Dwyer M	73	380 (19.2)	46	43	11	207	-	101.57
8	(--)	Maguire A*	71	500 (14.2)	69	56	18	286	-	119.60
9	(20)	Llewellyn C	53	382 (13.9)	41	42	15	231	-	15.43
10	(24)	Murphy D J	48	326 (14.7)	43	39	7	189	-	109.97
11	(3)	Doughty N	44	232 (19.0)	38	18	7	125	-	81.35
12	(11)	Davies H	44	346 (12.7)	26	31	11	234	-	77.88
13	(18)	Guest Richard	43	315 (13.7)	37	26	16	193	-	6.98
14	(14)	Frost J	41	337 (12.2)	50	51	17	178	-	145.47
15	(41)	Storey B	40	334 (12.0)	38	53	12	191	-	81.38
16	(76)	Fitzgerald M A*	38	265 (14.3)	38	29	5	155	+	62.15
17	(26)	Richards M	37	271 (13.7)	32	27	10	165	-	33.06
18	(27)	Pitman M	35	185 (18.9)	23	31	13	83	-	9.76
19	(12)	Wyer L	35	221 (15.8)	44	23	12	107	-	70.44
20	(15)	Powell B	35	326 (10.7)	34	42	19	196	-	70.11

TOP JOCKEYS BY EARNINGS 1991/92

			Mnts	Wins	Plcs	Win- £	Place-£		Total - £
1	(1)	Dunwoody R	715	137	264	673,265	250,116	£	923,381
2	(2)	Scudamore P	513	175	154	686,769	164,611	£	851,380
3	(5)	Osborne J	412	76	132	443,217	157,727	£	600,944
4	(3)	McCourt G	506	102	153	415,559	125,540	£	541,099
5	(86)	Maguire A*	500	71	143	303,599	135,652	£	439,251
6	(9)	Niven P	400	105	123	269,525	104,489	£	374,014
7	(25)	Llewellyn C	382	53	97	271,754	76,063	£	347,817
8	(10)	Grant C	449	78	138	222,251	86,261	£	308,512
9	(19)	Murphy D J	326	48	89	188,480	95,477	£	283,957
10	(6)	Dwyer M	380	73	100	167,110	78,036	£	245,146
11	(21)	Guest Richard	315	43	77	137,984	105,144	£	243,128
12	(11)	Pitman M	185	35	64	165,298	72,352	£	237,650
13	(4)	Doughty N	232	44	65	168,954	67,126	£	236,080
14	(17)	Tory A	188	26	64	174,117	58,749	£	232,866
15	(17)	Frost J	337	41	121	134,217	94,247	£	228,464
16	(14)	Davies H	346	44	68	185,342	40,587	£	225,929
17	(23)	Bradley G	294	29	82	155,615	69,201	£	224,816
18	(27)	Richards M	271	37	69	139,526	33,916	£	173,442
19	(36)	Storey B	334	40	104	103,555	65,619	£	169,174
20	(8)	Perrett M	200	22	49	91,633	76,606	£	168,239

TOP JOCKEYS BY FIVE YEAR WINS

		1987/8 Wns Mts	1988/9 Wns Mts	1989/0 Wns Mts	1990/1 Wns Mts	1991/2 Wns Mts	Total Wins Mnts
1	Scudamore P	132/558	221/663	170/523	141/421	175/513	839/2678
2	Dunwoody R	79/582	91/671	102/604	127/644	137/715	536/3216
3	McCourt G	68/405	86/426	100/434	83/436	102/506	439/2207
4	Dwyer M	73/398	92/455	74/379	81/377	73/380	393/1989
5	Grant C	80/485	39/192	94/425	57/348	78/449	348/1899
6	Niven P	30/327	49/340	48/264	86/424	105/400	318/1755
7	Doughty N	18/167	33/161	47/194	96/349	44/232	238/1103
7	Davies H	33/357	50/462	60/406	51/376	44/346	238/1947
9	Osborne J	21/218	22/240	53/277	62/354	76/412	234/1501
10	Powell B	38/517	64/582	48/550	38/451	35/326	223/2426
11	Frost J	30/233	41/284	46/301	39/277	41/337	197/1432
12	Pitman M	27/159	40/172	57/191	27/146	35/185	186/ 853
13	Perrett M	24/210	27/234	52/228	58/271	22/200	183/1143
14	Wyer L	30/239	36/227	33/270	44/248	35/221	178/1205
15	Llewellyn C	41/379	20/260	19/191	32/288	53/382	165/1500
16	Bradley G	38/233	34/215	30/207	26/222	29/294	157/1171
17	Hobbs Peter	26/292	47/349	43/278	9/ 37	31/261	156/1217
18	Storey B	25/334	30/333	32/298	20/269	40/334	147/1568
19	Richards M	7/112	30/226	25/208	28/296	37/271	127/1113
20	Murphy D J	15/ 73	19/116	15/164	29/255	48/326	126/ 934

TOP AMATEUR RIDERS

		Wins	Runs (%)	2nd	3rd	4th	Unpl		Stake
1	Hourigan Mr M P	24	95 (25.3)	10	8	0	53	+	62.79
2	Armytage Mr M	21	79 (26.6)	13	5	5	35	+	20.03
3	Lyons Mr S	16	127 (12.6)	21	16	2	72	-	30.00
4	Greenall Mr J	11	44 (25.0)	8	3	2	20	+	18.87
5	Thornton Mr A	10	34 (29.4)	8	2	0	14	+	12.23
5	Davis Mr R	10	89 (11.2)	3	9	0	67	+	29.63
7	Alner Mr R	8	25 (32.0)	1	1	0	15	+	15.43
7	Nash Mrs P	8	53 (15.1)	9	5	6	25	-	0.36

TOP OWNERS

		Wins		Win - £	Best Horse		Win - £
1	Whitcombe Manor Racing	13	£	153,343	Cool Ground	£	130,659
2	J E Collins	4	£	129,881	Remittance Man	£	129,881
3	M R Deeley	5	£	122,098	Waterloo Boy	£	88,998
4	P Piller	39	£	114,214	Stay on Tracks	£	20,650
5	Mrs D Thompson	1	£	99,943	Party Politics	£	99,943
6	E J Banks	4	£	87,095	Kings Fountain	£	87,095
7	Sheikh Mohammed	3	£	86,738	Royal Gait	£	86,738
8	Mrs J Mould	10	£	83,130	Tipping Tim	£	46,690
9	M L Marsh	6	£	80,837	Topsham Bay	£	70,022

18 . PRINCIPAL RECORDS

CHAMPION TRAINERS 1952-1992

		Winning Horses	Races Won	Value £
1952/53	M V O'Brien	4	5	15,515
1953/54	M V O'Brien	7	8	14,274
1954/55	H R Price	24	47	13,888
1955/56	W Hall	18	41	15,807
1956/57	N Crump	19	39	18,495
1957/58	F T T Walwyn	14	35	23,013
1958/59	H R Price	29	52	26,550
1959/60	P V F Cazalet	25	58	22,270
1960/61	T F Rimell	28	58	34,811
1961/62	H R Price	34	64	40,950
1962/63	K Piggott	4	6	23,091
1963/64	F T T Walwyn	30	59	67,129
1964/65	P V F Cazalet	34	82	36,153
1965/66	H R Price	29	65	42,276
1966/67	H R Price	34	73	41,222
1967/68	Denys Smith	26	55	37,944
1968/69	T F Rimell	32	62	38,344
1969/70	T F Rimell	35	77	61,864
1970/71	F T Winter	29	73	69,739
1971/72	F T Winter	31	72	62,863
1972/73	F T Winter	37	85	79,066
1973/74	F T Winter	41	89	101,781
1974/75	F T Winter	39	81	74,205
1975/76	T F Rimell	30	40	111,740
1976/77	F T Winter	31	75	85,202
1977/78	F T Winter	44	90	145,915
1978/79	M H Easterby	24	55	156,681
1979/80	M H Easterby	31	75	215,173
1980/81	M H Easterby	34	70	234,993
1981/82	M W Dickinson	32	84	296,028
1982/83	M W Dickinson	42	120	358,837
1983/84	M W Dickinson	30	86	266,146
1984/85	F T Winter	43	85	218,978
1985/86	N Henderson	27	46	162,234
1986/87	N Henderson	38	67	222,949
1987/88	D Elsworth	24	50	358,891
1988/89	M Pipe	87	208	683,653
1989/90	M Pipe	95	224	668,660
1990/91	M Pipe	96	230	1,194,865
1991/92	M Pipe	98	224	724,442

CHAMPION JOCKEYS 1951-1991

		Wins			Wins
1952/53	F Winter	121	1972/73	R Barry	125
1953/54	R Francis	76	1973/74	R Barry	94
1954/55	T Molony	67	1974/75	T Stack	82
1955/56	F Winter	74	1975/76	J Francome	96
1956/57	F Winter	80	1976/77	T Stack	97
1957/58	F Winter	82	1977/78	J J O'Neill	149
1958/59	T Brookshaw	83	1978/79	J Francome	95
1959/60	S Mellor	68	1979/80	J J O'Neill	117
1960/61	S Mellor	118	1980/81	J Francome	105
1961/62	S Mellor	80	1981/82=	J Francome	120
1962/63	K Gifford	70	1981/82=	P Scudamore	120
1963/64	J Gifford	94	1982/83	J Francome	106
1964/65	T Biddlecombe	114	1983/84	J Francome	131
1965/66	T Biddlecombe	102	1984/85	J Francome	101
1966/67	J Gifford	122	1985/86	P Scudamore	91
1967/68	J Gifford	82	1986/87	P Scudamore	123
1968/69=	B R Davies	77	1987/88	P Scudamore	132
1968/69=	T Biddlecombe	77	1988/89	P.Scudamore	221
1969/70	B R Davies	91	1989/90	P.Scudamore	170
1970/71	G Thorner	74	1990/91	P Scudamore	141
1971/72	B R Davies	89	1991/92	P Scudamore	175

CHAMPION AMATEUR RIDERS 1951-1991

1952/53	Mr A H Moralee	2	1972/73	Mr R Smith	56
1953/54	Mr A H Moralee	22	1973/74	Mr A Webber	21
1954/55	Mr A H Moralee	16	1974/75	Mr R Lamb	22
1955/56=	Mr R McCreery	13	1975/76=	Mr P Greenall	25
1955/56=	Mr A H Moralee	13	1975/76=	Mr G Jones	25
1956/57	Mr R McCreery	23	1976/77	Mr P Greenall	27
1957/58	Mr J Lawrence	18	1977/78	Mr G Sloan	23
1958/59	Mr J Sutcliffe	18	1978/79	Mr T G Dun	26
1959/60	Mr G Kindersley	22	1979/80	Mr O Sherwood	29
1960/61	Sir W Pigott-Brown	28	1980/81	Mr P Webber	32
1961/62	Mr A Biddlecombe	30	1981/82	Mr D Browne	28
1962/63	Sir W Pigott-Brown	20	1982/83	Mr D Browne	33
1963/64	Mr S Davenport	32	1983/84	Mr S Sherwood	28
1964/65	Mr M Gifford	15	1984/85	Mr S Sherwood	30
1965/66	Mr C Collins	24	1985/86	Mr T Thomson Jones	25
1966/67	Mr C Collins	33	1986/87	Mr T Thomson Jones	19
1967/68	Mr R Tate	30	1987/88	Mr T Thomson Jones	15
1968/69	Mr R Tate	17	1988/89	Mr P Fenton	18
1969/70	Mr M Dickinson	23	1989/90	Mr P McMahon	15
1970/71	Mr J Lawrence	17	1990/91	Mr K Johnson	24
1971/72	Mr W foulkes	26	1991/92	Mr M Hourigan	24

PAST WINNERS OF THE CHAMPION HURDLE

1991

Morley Street	7-12-00	J Frost	4-1
Nomadic Way	6-12-00	R Dunwoody	9-1
Ruling	5-12-00	P Niven	50-1

Trainer of Winner: G B Balding

1990

Kribensis	6-12-00	R.Dunwoody	95-40
Nomadic Way	5-12-00	P.Scudamore	8-1
Past Glories	7-12-00	J.J.Quinn	150-1

Trainer of Winner: M.R.Stoute

1989

Beech Road	7-12-00	R.Guest	50-1
Celtic Chief	6-12-00	G.McCourt	6-1
Celtic Shot	6-12-00	P.Scudamore	8-1

Trainer of Winner: G B Balding

1988

Celtic Shot	5-12-00	P Scudamore	7-1
Classical Charm	5-12-00	K Morgan	33-1
Celtic Chief	5-12-00	R Dunwoody	5-2F

Trainer of Winner: Fred Winter

1987

See You Then	7-12-00	S Smith Eccles	11-10
Flatterer	8-12-00	J Fishback	10-1
Barnbrook Again	6-12-00	S Sherwood	14-1

Trainer of Winner: N Henderson

1986

See You Then	6-12-00	S Smith Eccles	5-6
Gaye Brief	9-12-00	P Scudamore	14-1
Nohalmdun	5-12-00	J J O'Neill	20-1

Trainer of Winner: N Henderson

1985

See You Then	5-12-00	S Smith Eccles	16-1
Robin Wonder	7-12-00	J J O'Neill	100-1
Stans Pride	8-11-09	S Morshead	100-1

Trainer of Winner: N Henderson

1984

Dawn Run	6-11-00	J J O'Neill	4-5
Cima	6-12-00	P Scudamore	66-1
Very Promising	6-12-00	S Morshead	16-1

Trainer of Winner: P Mullins, in Ireland

1983

Gaye Brief	6-12-00	R Linley	7-1
Boreen Prince	6-12-00	M Madden	50-1
For Auction	7-12-00	C Magnier	3-1

Trainer of Winner: Mrs M Rimell

1982

For Auction	6-12-00	C Magnier	40-1
Broadsword	5-12-00	P Scudamore	100-30
Ekbalco	6-12-00	D Goulding	7-2

Trainer of Winner: M Cunningham

1981

Sea Pigeon	11-12-00	J Francome	7-4
Pollardstown	6-12-00	P Blacker	9-1
Daring Run	6-12-00	T Walsh	8-1

Trainer of Winner: M H Easterby

1980

Sea Pigeon	10-12-00	J J O'Neill	13-2
Monksfield	8-12-00	D T Hughes	6-5
Bird's Nest	10-12-00	A Turnell	11-1

Trainer of Winner: M H Easterby

1979

Monksfield	7-12-00	D T Hughes	9-4
Sea Pigeon	9-12-0.	J J O'Neill	6-1
Beacon Light	8-12-00	J Francome	22-1

Trainer of Winner: D McDonogh in Ireland

1978

Monksfield	6-12-00	T Kinane	11-2
Sea Pigeon	8-12-00	F Berry	5-1
Night Nurse	7-12-00	C Tinkler	3-1

Trainer of Winner: D McDonogh in Ireland

1977

Night Nurse	6-12-00	P Broderick	15-2
Monksfield	5-12-00	T Kinnane	15-1
Dramatist	6-12-00	W Smith	6-1

Trainer of Winner: M H Easterby

1976

Night Nurse	5-12-00	P Broderick	2-1
Birds Nest	6-12-00	A Turnell	100-30
Flash Imp	7-12-00	R Mann	40-1

Trainer of Winner: M H Easterby

1975

Comedy of Errors	8-12-00	K White	11-8
Flash Imp	6-12-00	T Stack	12-1
Tree Tangle	6-12-00	A Turnell	10-1

Trainer of Winner: T F Rimell

1974

Lanzarote	6-12-00	R Pitman	7-4
Comedy of Errors	7-12-00	W Smith	4-6
Yenisei	7-12-00	H Beasley	100-1

Trainer of Winner: F Winter

1973

Comedy of Errors	6-12-00	W Smith	8-1
Easby Abbey	6-12-00	R Barry	20-1
Captain Christy	6-12-00	H Beasley	85-40

Trainer of Winner: T F Rimell

1972

Bula	7-12-00	P Kelleway	8-11
Boxer	5-11-12	J Uttley	25-1
Lyford Cay	8-12-00	D Cartwright	66-1

Trainer of Winner: F Winter

PAST WINNERS OF THE CHELTENHAM GOLD CUP

1991

Garrison Savannah	8-12-00	M Pitman	16-1
The Fellow	6-12-00	A Kondrat	28-1
Desert Orchid	12-12-00	R Dunwoody	4-1

Trainer of Winner: Mrs J Pitman

1990

Norton's Coin	9-12-00	G.McCourt	100/1
Toby Tobias	8-12-00	M.Pitman	8/1
Desert Orchid	11-12-00	R.Dunwoody	10/11F

Trainer of Winner: S.G.Griffiths

1989

Desert Orchid	10-12-00	S.Sherwood	5-2
Yahoo	8-12-00	T.Morgan	25-1
Charter Party	11-12-00	R.Dunwoody	14-1

Trainer of Winner: D R C Elsworth

1988

Charter Party	10-12-00	R Dunwoody	10-1
Cavvies Clown	8-12-00	S Sherwood	6-1
Beau Ranger	10-12-00	P Scudamore	33-1

Trainer of Winner: D Nicholson

1987

The Thinker	9-12-00	R Lamb	13-2
Cybrandian	9-12-00	C Grant	25-1
Door Latch	9-12-00	R Rowe	9-1

Trainer of Winner: W A Stephenson

1986
Dawn Run	8-11-09	J J O'Neill	15-8
Wayward Lad	11-12-00	G Bradley	8-1
Forgive'n'Forget	9-12-00	M Dwyer	7-2

Trainer of Winner: P Mullins in Ireland

1985
Forgive'n'Forget	8-12-00	M Dwyer	7-1
Righthand Man	8-12-00	G Bradley	15-2
Earls Brig	10-12-00	P Tuck	13-2

Trainer of Winner: J FitzGerald

1984
Burrough Hill Lad	8-12-00	P Tuck	7-2
Brown Chamberlain	9-12-00	J Francome	5-1
Drumlargan	10-12-00	F Codd	16-1

Trainer of Winner: Mrs J Pitman

1983
Bregawn	9-12-00	G Bradley	10-3
Captain John	9-12-00	D Goulding	11-1
Wayward Lad	8-12-00	J J O'Neill	6-1

Trainer of Winner: M Dickinson

1982
Silver Buck	10-12-00	R Earnshaw	8-1
Bregawn	8-12-00	G Bradley	18-1
Sunset Crisp	8-12-00	C Grant	100-1

Trainer of Winner: M Dickinson

1981
Little Owl	7-12-00	A J Wilson	6-1
Night Nurse	10-12-00	A Brown	6-1
Silver Buck	9-12-00	T Carmody	7-2

Trainer of Winner: M H Easterby

1980
Master Smudge	8-12-00	R Hoare	14-1
Mac Vidi	15-12-00	P Leach	66-1
Approaching	9-12-00	B R Davies	11-1

Trainer of Winner: A Borrow

1979
Alverton	9-12-00	J J O'Neill	5-1
Royal Mail (NZ)	9-12-00	P Blacker	7-1
Aldaniti	9-12-00	R Champion	40-1

Trainer of Winner: M H Easterby

1978
Midnight Court	7-12-00	J Francome	5-2
Brown Lad	12-12-00	T Carberry	8-1
Master H	9-12-00	R Crank	18-1

Trainer of Winner: F Winter

1977

Davy Lad	7-12-00	D T Hughes	14-1
Tied Cottage	9-12-00	T Carberry	20-1
Summerville	11-12-00	J King	15-1

Trainer of Winner: M O'Toole (Ireland)

1976

Royal Frolic	7-12-00	J Burke	14-1
Brown Lad	10-12-00	T Carberry	13-8
Colebridge	12-12-00	F Berry	12-1

Trainer of Winner: T F Rimell

1975

Ten Up	8-12-00	T Carberry	2-1
Soothsayer	8-12-00	R Pitman	28-1
Bula	10-12-00	J Francome	5-1

Trainer of Winner: J Dreaper in Ireland

1974

Captain Christy	7-12-00	H Beasley	7-1
The Dikler	11-12-00	R Barry	5-1
Game Spirit	8-12-00	T Biddlecombe	20-1

Trainer of Winner: P Taaffe in Ireland

1973

The Dikler	10-12-00	R Barry	9-1
Pendil	8-12-00	R Pitman	4-6
Charlie Potheen	8-12-00	T W Biddlecombe	9-2

Trainer of Winner: F Walwyn

1972

Glencaraig Lady	8-12-00	F Berry	6-1
Royal Toss	10-12-00	N Wakley	22-1
The Dikler	9-12-00	B Brogan	11-1

Trainer of Winner: F Flood in Ireland

PAST WINNERS OF THE GRAND NATIONAL

1991

Seagram	11-10-06	N Hawke	12-1
Garrison Savannah	8-11-01	M Pitman	7-1
Auntie Dot	10-10-04	M Dwyer	50-1

Trainer of Winner: D H Barons

1990

Mr Frisk	11-10-06	M.Armytage	16/1
Durham Edition	12-10-09	C.Grant	9/1
Rinus	9-10-04	N.Doughty	13/1

Trainer of Winner: K.C.Bailey

1989

Little Polveir	12-10-03	J.Frost	28-1
West Tip	12-10-11	R.Dunwoody	21-1
The Thinker	11-11-10	S.Sherwood	10-1

Trainer of Winner: G B Balding

1988

Rhyme 'N' Reason	9-11-00	B Powell	10-1
Durham Edition	10-10-09	C Grant	20-1
Monanore	11-10-04	T J Taaffe	33-1

Trainer of Winner: D Elsworth

1987

Maori Venture	11-10-13	S Knight	28-1
The Tsarevich	11-11-05	J White	20-1
Lean Ar Aghaidh	10-10-00	G Landau	14-1

Trainer of Winner: A Turnell

1986

West Tip	9-10-11	R Dunwoody	15-2
Young Driver	9-10-00	C Grant	66-1
Classified	10-10-03	S Smith Eccles	22-1

Trainer of Winner: M Oliver

1985

Last Suspect	10-11-05	H Davies	50-1
Mr Snugfit	8-10-00	P Tuck	12-1
Corbiere	10-11-10	P Scudamore	9-1

Trainer of Winner: T Forster

1984

Hallo Dandy	10-10-02	N Doughty	13-1
Greasepaint	9-11-02	T Carmody	9-1
Corbiere	9-12-00	B de Haan	16-1

Trainer of Winner: G W Richards

1983

Corbiere	8-11-04	B de Haan	13-1
Greasepaint	8-10-07	C Magnier	14-1
Yer Man	8-10-00	T V O'Connell	80-1

Trainer of Winner: Mrs J Pitman

1982

Grittar	9-11-05	C Saunders	7-1
Hard Outlook	11-10-01	A Webber	50-1
Loving Words	9-10-11	R Hoare	16-1

Trainer of Winner: F Gilman

1981

Aldaniti	11-10-13	R Champion	10-1
Sparton Missile	9-11-05	M J Thorne	8-1
Begg's Royal Mail	11-11-07	P Blacker	16-1

Trainer of Winner: J Gifford

1980

Ben Nevis	12-10-12	C Fenwick	40-1
Rough and Tumble	10-10-11	J Francome	11-1
The Pilgarlic	12-10-04	R Hyett	33-1

Trainer of Winner: T Forster

1979

Rubstic	10-10-00	M Barnes	25-1
Zongalero	9-10-05	B R Davis	20-1
Rough and Tumble	9-10-07	J Francome	14-1

Trainer of Winner: S J Leadbetter

1978

Lucius	9-10-00	B R Davies	14-1
Sebastian V	10-10-01	R Lamb	25-1
Drumroan	10-10-00	G Newman	50-1

Trainer of Winner: G W Richards

1977

Red Rum	12-11-08	T Stack	9-1
Churchtown Boy	10-10-00	M Blackshaw	20-1
Eyecatcher	11-10-01	C Read	18-1

Trainer of Winner: D McCain

1976

Rag Trade	10-10-12	J Burke	14-1
Red Rum	11-11-10	T Stack	10-1
Eyecatcher	10-10-07	B Fletcher	28-1

Trainer of Winner: T F Rimell

1975

L'Escargot	12-11-03	T Carberry	13-2
Red Rum	10-12-00	B Fletcher	7-2
Spanish Steps	12-10-03	W Smith	20-1

Trainer of Winner: D L Moore in Ireland

1974

Red Rum	9-12-00	B Fletcher	11-1
L'Escargot	11-11-13	T Carberry	17-2
Charles Dickens	10-10-00	A Turnell	50-1

Trainer of Winner: D McCain

1973

Red Rum	8-10-05	B Fletcher	9-1
Crisp (Aus)	10-12-00	R Pitman	9-1
L'Escargot	10-12-00	T Carberry	11-1

Trainer of Winner: D McCain

1972

Well To Do		9-10-01	G Thorner	14-1
Gay Trip		10-11-09	T Biddlecombe	12-1
Black Secret	=3	8-11-02	S Barker	14-1
General Symons	=3	9-10-00	P Kiely	40-1

Trainer of Winner: T Forster

19 . BETTING GUIDE

Parts of this guide are changed every edition (Naps Table), and parts are changed periodically or simply updated.

TYPES OF BET

WIN ONLY:
Just that.

EACH WAY (E/W):
Equal stakes to Win and Place. Half the stake is to Win Only and half the stake is Place, for which the following rates apply:

5 to 7	runners - 1/4 odds 1st or 2nd		All Races
8 to 11	runners - 1/5 odds 1st, 2nd or 3rd		All Races
12 to 15	runners - 1/4 odds 1st, 2nd or 3rd		Handicaps
16+	runners - 1/4 odds 1st, 2nd, 3rd or 4th	Handicaps

TO WIN AND PLACE:
Stake to Win, with lower amount to Place - e.g. £50 Win + £20 Place ("50 over 20"). Commonly used when the Place bet is required only to recover the original stake.

COMPUTER STRAIGHT FORECAST (CSF):
Selection of the first two past the post in correct order. Payment made to a complicated formula, dividends declared in £1 units and include stake.

REVERSED FORECAST:
Selection of the first two past the post in any order. Twice the stake required for full dividend.

TRICAST:
Selection of first three past the post in correct order. Winnings determined by computer, as with CSF.

DOUBLE:
Stake invested on two selections in different races, any returns from the first being automatically reinvested.

DOUBLE STAKES ABOUT:
Two bets involving two selections in different events - e.g. £2 A, £2 B, Double Stakes About (DSA). Total stake £4. £2 A any to come £4 B; £2 B any to come £4 A.

E/W MULTIPLE BETS:
Half the stake to Win Only, winnings plus stake being automatically reinvested to Win; half the stake to Place Only,

winnings plus stake automatically reinvested to Place.

E/W EQUALLY DIVIDED MULTIPLE BETS
("EACH WAY ALL EACH WAY"):
All winnings plus stake from Win or Place bets automatically reinvested with half returns to Win and half to Place.

TREBLE:
Stake invested on three selections in different races, winnings plus stake being cumulatively reinvested. Win or E/W.

TRIXIE
Three selections in three doubles and a treble. 4 bets.

PATENT:
As Trixie but with three single bets as well. 7 bets.

YANKEE:
Four selections fully permed, including one fourfold, four trebles and six doubles. 11 bets.

LUCKY FIFTEEN:
As Yankee but with four single bets as well. 15 bets.

CANADIAN OR SUPER YANKEE:
Five selections fully permed, including a fivefold, five fourfolds, ten trebles and ten doubles. 26 bets.

HEINZ:
Six selections fully permed, including a sixfold, six fivefolds, 15 fourfolds, 20 trebles and fifteen doubles. 57 bets.

GOLIATH OR SUPER HEINZ:
Seven selections fully permed, including a sevenfold, seven sixfolds, 21 fivefolds, 35 fourfolds, 35 trebles and 21 doubles.

ANY TO COME OR IF CASH:
A specified part of any returns from one selection staked on another selection. Any number of selections may be included.

STOP AT A WINNER:
Selections listed in any order (not necessarily by time) with equal or variable investment on each and instruction to the bookmaker to stop at the first winner listed, making any remaining instruction void.

COVER TO WIN:
Wagering to win a specific amount, stake dependent on S.P.

PARI-MUTUEL:
The Tote system operated for races abroad. Usually, but not always, accepted by bookmakers.

POOLS OPERATED BY THE TOTE

All dividends declared to a £1 stake. Minimum dividend £1.10 except in the Placepool when the minimum dividend is £1 if the calculated dividend falls below 70p.

Win: On all races. Minimum stake £2. Deduction 16%.

Place: 1st or 2nd in races of 5-7 runners
1st, 2nd or 3rd in races of 8+ runners
1st, 2nd, 3rd or 4th in handicaps of 16+ runners
Minimum stake £2. Scale of deduction 24%.

Dual Forecast: Select the first two past the post in either order for races with 3+ runners. Minimum stake £2. Scale of deduction 29%.

Jackpot: Winners of the first six races at selected meetings. When the pool is not won on the last day of the meeting it is carried over to the next Jackpot meeting. Minimum stake £1 and 10p+ lines accepted in permutations of £1 and over. Deduction is 26%.

Placepot: As above with place bet rules. Deduction is 26%.

NB. *On some courses and in some enclosures the minimum stake is £1.*

			PERMUTATION TABLE						
SELS	**2**	**3**	**4**	**5**	**6**	**7**	**8**	**9**	
2	1	-	-	-	-	-	-	-	1
3	3	1	-	-	-	-	-	-	4
4	6	4	1	-	-	-	-	-	11
5	10	10	5	1	-	-	-	-	26
6	15	20	15	6	1	-	-	-	57
7	21	35	35	21	7	1	-	-	120
8	28	56	70	56	28	8	1	-	247
9	36	84	126	126	84	36	9	1	502

BETTING TAX

Removal of on-course betting tax was a wholly positive step for Racing and can take credit for accelerating the recent increase in course attendance in the face of the ever more attractive facilities offered by betting shops. Long may they both flourish in this new positive environment for the sport.

For practical purposes, though, the incentive affects very few on a financial level. For most it is an added inducement to make the effort to go and join the fun and maximising on winnings. But, the majority of betting will always be done off-course and anybody wanting to play the game with a chance of winning must take into account the effect of tax on their off-course bets.

Before studying the effects, a simple explanation of the options available is needed. Backers can pay tax in two ways: either on the stake or on any winnings. Consider the following example of the sort to be seen in betting offices across the land:

£10 on a 5-1 winner tax not paid on

Stake	= £10	
Return	= £60 - £6 (10% tax)	= £54
Profit	= £44	

£10 on a 5-1 winner tax paid on

Stake	= £10 + £1 (10% tax)	= £11
Return	= £60	
Profit	= £49	

For just £1 a winning backer who pre-pays tax makes £5 more profit than one who doesn't. However, how many 5-1 bets go down for every success, how many times has that £1 been paid unnecessarily? The answer for most is more than the five to be gained from a winning bet because otherwise bookmakers would not be in business.

Any backer finding a 5-1 winner once to every five losers (or 2-1 to every two losers ... etc.) will be losing the same whether pre-paying tax or not. Using the above example one invests £66 for a return of £60, the other £60 for a return of

£54: a loss of £6 in both cases.

But for the majority, who pay for the pleasure of being involved in the game, pre-paying tax is a waste of money. The simple rule is that those who make a profit out of the game should always pre-pay tax, those who don't shouldn't.

But it is not that simple. The natural optimism of backers has a way of short-circuiting memory. And also many backers, even if able to own up to a dubious past record, tend to believe they can and will make betting pay tomorrow. As this possibility is one of the attractions of race betting it must figure in any decision about how to pay tax.

A logical rule of thumb, then, is that if a backer takes betting seriously with a view to profit that is enough to justify payment of tax on stake.

Those who accept losses as being fair payment for the pleasure of involvement and the odd win, and those who look upon racing as a stimulating form of doing the pools would be better off paying on their returns. However, the racing-pools player might just as well up the stakes and pre-pay tax because if that six-figured Heinz ever came in, it would be infuriating to have lost out on £10,000 for want of an extra 60p at source - or whatever.

So despite the fact that most would be better off not pre-paying tax, the racing game is such that most backers probably should stump up. And as most do anyway, it is worth looking at the implications.

THE EFFECT OF TAX

Obtaining good value is everything. A backer knows when he is getting this when, whatever the number of his winners, his betting account is profitable. Luck will always play a significant part in racing, but there are a great many areas in which skill can be brought profitably to play. Of these the skill to know good value will, by definition, be successful.

Betting tax undermines good value. The table shows just how much. Odds of 10-1 imply that any winnings will be ten times the stake. This is not so, because it takes an investment of £1.10 to get a return of £11 (stake plus winnings) and so the actual bet is £1.10 invested to win (profit) £9.90 which comes to a 9-1 return.

With odds-on the effect of tax becomes crippling. A favourite whom the market assesses as having a 1-2 chance will pay at odds of just 4-11 after tax, little better than half the "true" odds. At 2-9 the backer is getting exactly half the odds posted (the actual return being 1-9) and from then on it gets worse until at 1-10 even a winning bet becomes a losing one!

Now that there is no on-course betting tax there have been, and will continue to be, the occasional posting in excess of 1-10 and where this happens off-course backers will get their stake returned on single bets on the basis that you can't lose if you can't win (although the bookmaker is a loser every time in this situation as they have to declare the tax on the bet). In multiple bets, returns are worked out in the ordinary way, though were an extraordinary situation to arise such as negative double, then stakes would be returned.

Speaking of multiple bets, this is the one area where the effect of tax is minimised because it is only being paid once, and all re-investment of stake plus winnings are free of tax.

REAL RETURNS AT 10% TAX PREPAID
(taken to the nearest fraction)

ODDS POSTED	REAL ODDS	ODDS POSTED	REAL ODDS	ODDS POSTED	REAL ODDS
1-9	1-99	3-1	105-40	12-1	43-4
1-5	1-11	7-2	3-1	16-1	29-2
1-3	4-19	4-1	7-2	20-1	18-1
1-2	4-11	5-1	9-2	25-1	45-2
4-6	1-2	6-1	21-4	33-1	30-1
Evs	4-5	7-1	25-4	50-1	45-1
6-4	5-4	8-1	100-14	66-1	60-1
2-1	7-4	9-1	8-1	100-1	91-1
5-2	11-5	10-1	9-1		

FIELD MONEY TABLE FOR £100 BOOK

The odds against successfully forecasting the roll of a die would be one chance in six, or 5-1 against. Ask a bookmaker for odds and he will quote you 9-2 against. This would give him a 10% margin, or "over-round" on his book, which allows him to stay in business and offer his services to the public.

The ability to mentally calculate the over-round of any book is a great advantage to a backer. There are races, particularly the big competitive handicaps, where the over-round is so large that it appears impossible to find a runner quoted at a price at or above its actual chance of winning. On the other hand sometimes the margin is in the backers' favour, which is to say it is small enough for there to be value bets.

When calculating the over-round percentage it is worth remembering that there are times when, although the margin appears high, for practical purposes it can be quite reasonable for the backer. This happens when there are a number of "rags" (outsiders) in the field, who are typically marked up at a 33-1, just in case a well-disguised coup is attempted, but whose real chance may be 100-1. Excluding these from calculations often reveals the over-round for the principal contenders is fair. Of course one of the rags could spring a surprise, but far less often than expressed by their odds (see Favourites Records, Odds Report p.182).

Some backers like to stake to win a precise amount. In addition to showing bookmakers' margins the following table also shows how much a backer needs to invest to win a hundred pounds (or a thousand, a tenner or a single pound with a shifting of the decimal point). Just look at the figure to the left or right of the odds (depending on whether the selection is odds-on or odds against) and that is the amount in pounds and pence needed to get a return (including stake) of a hundred.

ODDS AGAINST	PRICE	ODDS ON	ODDS AGAINST	PRICE	ODDS ON
50.00	Evens	50.00	20.00	4-1	80.00
47.62	11-10	52.38	18.18	9-2	81.82
44.44	5-4	55.56	16.67	5-1	83.33
42.11	11-8	57.89	15.39	11-2	84.61
40.00	6-4	60.00	14.29	6-1	85.71
38.10	13-8	61.90	12.50	7-1	87.50
36.36	7-4	63.64	11.11	8-1	89.89
34.78	15-8	65.22	9.09	10-1	90.91
33.33	2-1	66.67	7.69	12-1	92.31
30.77	9-4	69.23	5.88	16-1	94.12
28.67	5-2	71.43	4.76	20-1	95.24
26.67	11-4	73.33	3.85	25-1	96.15
25.00	3-1	75.00	2.94	33-1	97.06
23.08	10-3	76.92	1.96	50-1	98.04
22.22	7-2	77.78	0.99	100-1	99.01

SPORTING LIFE/CORAL JUMPS NAPS TABLE

For the Sporting Life Challenge Cup and £1,000 with £500 for the runner-up.
Co-sponsored by Coral Bookmakers. Reproduced by courtesy of the Sporting Life.
Awarded for the period November 13, 1991 to March 20, 1992, both dates inclusive.

		W	L	NR	Lngst Seq. Wnrs	Lngst Seq. Lsrs	£ Level Stake
1	Western Daily Press *Bob Watts*	50	49	5	6	7	+ 30.13
2	Daily Mirror *Newsboy*	32	68	4	3	8	+ 25.74
3	Wolverhampton Express & Star *John Sexton*	31	62	7	4	10	+ 24.22
4	Daily Express *The Scout*	42	51	11	4	4	+ 23.05
5	Daily Star *Tony Lewis*	27	65	12	5	13	+ 3.35
6	Newcastle Journal *Underhand*	24	69	11	2	9	+ 2.42
7	Sporting Life *Form*	30	66	8	3	9	- 0.67
8	Sun *Templegate*	39	56	9	5	5	- 2.65
9	Sporting Life *Man On The Spot*	31	66	7	4	11	- 3.04
0	Western Mail *Alan Keyte*	53	48	3	5	5	- 3.29
0	Northern Echo *Janus*	41	58	5	5	6	- 3.80
0	Scottish Daily Express *Scotia*	36	58	10	7	7	- 4.66
0	Racing And Football Outlook	25	70	9	3	8	- 8.28
0	Weekender *Dick Hunter*	30	65	9	4	12	- 9.38
0	Sunday Mail *Rockavon*	32	61	9	5	7	- 9.69
0	Western Morning News *Jeffrey Ross*	26	71	7	3	14	- 10.08
0	The Herald *Martin Gale*	25	67	11	5	15	- 10.29
0	Today *Henry Rix*	17	76	11	4	10	- 10.31
0	Coventry Eve. Telegraph *Jimmy Marshall*	24	71	7	3	10	- 10.60
0	Raceform Update *Longbow*	30	66	8	4	8	- 12.30
0	Sunday Telegraph *Whistler*	36	62	6	3	8	- 13.70
0	Daily Mail *Robin Goodfellow*	32	66	6	4	12	- 14.76
0	Sheffield Star *Fortunatus*	30	63	6	3	7	- 16.43
0	News Of The World *Pegasus*	25	68	9	4	15	- 16.51
0	Daily Telegraph *Tony Stafford*	25	75	4	2	9	- 17.17
0	Guardian *Richard Baerlein*	23	73	7	3	9	- 18.81
0	The Times *Mandarin*	38	62	4	4	6	- 20.42
0	Sporting Life *Northern View*	18	74	8	2	24	- 21.46
0	Sporting Life *Nick Deacon*	23	75	6	3	8	- 21.97
0	The Independent *Paul Hayward*	20	76	7	3	12	- 22.70
0	Daily Record *Garry Owen*	29	70	5	4	11	- 23.82
0	Sunday Mirror *Phil Davies*	20	76	8	2	15	- 25.25
0	Birmingham Post *Veritas*	26	73	4	2	11	- 26.92
0	The Scotsman	17	75	12	3	12	- 27.08
0	Sporting Life *Augur*	24	71	9	3	14	- 27.46
0	Racing Post *Diomed*	23	70	11	2	9	- 27.95
0	Yorkshire Post *The Duke*	22	73	9	2	12	- 30.86
0	East Anglian Daily Times *Crusader*	21	76	7	2	9	- 31.64
0	Daily Post *Roy David*	18	78	7	2	10	- 42.96

Past Winners

			W	L	NR	Profit
1990/91	Martin Gale	Glasgow Herald	37	55	10	£ 42.45
1989/90	Tony Stafford	Daily Telegraph	41	56	9	£ 42.20
1988/89	John Karter	The Independent	34	74	6	£ 40.15
1987/88	Nick Deacon	Sporting Life	43	49	4	£ 45.74

WEIGHT FOR AGE TABLES

HURDLE RACES
Allowance assessed in lbs, which 3 & 4-y-o will receive from 5-y-o and upwards.

	Age	JAN	FEB	MAR	APR	MAY	JUN
2 m	4	12	10	8	6	5	5
2½m	4	13	11	9	7	6	6
3 m	4	14	12	10	8	7	7

	Age	JUL	AUG	SEP	OCT	NOV	DEC
2 m	3	20	20	18	17	16	14
	4	3	3	3	1	-	-
2½m	3	21	21	19	18	17	15
	4	3	3	2	1	-	-
3m	3	23	23	21	19	18	16
	4	4	4	3	2	1	-

STEEPLECHASES
Allowance assessed in lbs, which 4 & 5-y-o will receive from 6-y-o and upwards.

	Age	JAN	FEB	MAR	APR	MAY	JUN
2 m	5	10	9	8	7	6	6
2½m	5	11	10	9	8	7	7
3 m	5	12	11	10	9	8	8

	Age	JUL	AUG	SEP	OCT	NOV	DEC
2 m	4	15	15	14	13	12	11
	5	3	3	2	1	-	-
2½m	4	16	16	15	14	13	12
	5	4	4	3	2	1	-
3 m	4	17	17	16	15	14	13
	5	5	5	4	3	2	1

RULES GOVERNING BETTING

ALWAYS READ YOUR BOOKMAKER'S RULES.
In every office the rules of the establishment should be clearly displayed and backers are bound by these terms. There are variations between one firm and another and it is up to the backer to acquaint himself with those of the office (or credit firm) patronised.

Dead-Heats.
In a dead-heat for first place stake money on each of the horses concerned will be divided by the number of runners in the dead-heat and full odds paid on the remaining stake.

In a dead-heat for second any place stakes are halved in races of six or seven runners.

In a dead-heat for third any place stakes are halved, unless the first four home are being paid.

In a dead-heat for fourth place stakes are halved and full odds are paid on the remaining stake.

Incorrect Staking.
Understaked bets are usually settled on a proportional basis, though some smaller bookmakers have different methods. With overstaking, settlement is made in accordance with instructions, with excess sums being refunded.

Tattersalls Rule 4(c).
When a horse is withdrawn without coming under starters' orders and there is insufficient time to make a new book, winning returns (exclusive of stake) are subject to deductions that vary according to the odds of the withdrawn horse(s).

If the odds are greater than 14-1 no deduction is made

For odds between			inc. deduct	in the £.
10-1	and	14-1	inc. deduct 5p	in the £.
6-1	and	9-1	inc. deduct 10p	in the £.
9-2	and	11-2	inc. deduct 15p	in the £.
10-3	and	4-1	inc. deduct 20p	in the £.
5-2	and	3-1	inc. deduct 25p	in the £.
15-8	and	9-4	inc. deduct 30p	in the £.
13-8	and	7-4	inc. deduct 35p	in the £.

For odds between	Evs	and	6-5	inc. deduct	45p	in the £.
For odds between	5-4	and	6-4	inc. deduct	40p	in the £.
For odds between	20-21	and	5-6	inc. deduct	50p	in the £.
For odds between	4-5	and	4-6	inc. deduct	55p	in the £.
For odds between	8-13	and	4-7	inc. deduct	60p	in the £.
For odds between	8-15	and	4-9	inc. deduct	65p	in the £.
For odds between	2-5	and	1-3	inc. deduct	70p	in the £.
For odds of	3-10 or longer odds on deduct				75p	in the £.

If more than one horse is withdrawn a maximum of 75p in the £. may be deducted.

Non-Runners.

If a selection is withdrawn not under orders the bet is void and stakes are either returned or are re-invested (as with multiple or speciality bets). This includes ante-post bets struck on the day. Selections withdrawn under orders are losing bets.

Backing Favourites.

Practically all bookmakers will accept win bets (single or multiple) on unnamed first, second or third favourites.

When there are two joint-favourites of unnamed first, second or third favourites receive full odds to one third the stake.

Where there is a dead-heat between two equal favourites, backers of unnamed first or second favourites receive full odds to a quarter of the stake on both horses. When a dead-heat concerns only one of two equal favourites backers of unnamed first and second favourites receive full odds to one quarter of the stake.

If the favourite is withdrawn not under orders and Rule 4(c) applies, backers of unnamed favourites generally get their stakes returned, though in speciality bets different provision is made.

Disputes.

The *Green Seal* service operated by the *Sporting Life* is the most simple channel open to punters wishing arbitration and in all simple cases at least bookmakers abide by their judgement. The Tattersalls' Committee is the official body for settling any dispute related to horse-race betting.

READY RECKONER

Showing returns before tax **STAKE**

S.P.	10p	20p	25p	50p	£1.00	£5.00
1-3	.13	.27	.33	.67	1.33	6.67
2-5	.14	.28	.35	.70	1.40	7.00
4-9	.14	.29	.36	.72	1.44	7.22
1-2	.15	.30	.38	.75	1.50	7.50
4-7	.16	.31	.39	.79	1.57	7.86
8-13	.16	.32	.40	.81	1.62	8.08
4-6	.17	.33	.42	.83	1.67	8.33
8-11	.17	.35	.43	.86	1.73	8.64
4-5	.18	.36	.45	.90	1.80	9.00
5-6	.18	.37	.46	.92	1.83	9.17
10-11	19	.38	.48	.95	1.91	9.55
Evens	20	.40	.50	1.00	2.00	10.00
11-10	21	.42	.53	1.05	2.10	10.50
6-5	.22	.44	.55	1.10	2.20	11.00
5-4	.23	.45	.56	1.13	2.25	11.25
11-8	.24	.48	.59	1.19	2.38	11.88
6-4	.25	.50	.63	1.25	2.50	12.50
13-8	.26	.53	.66	1.31	2.63	13.13
7-4	.28	.55	.69	1.38	2.75	13.75
15-8	.29	.58	.72	1.44	2.88	14.38
2-1	.30	.60	.75	1.50	3.00	15.00
9-4	.33	.65	.81	1.63	3.25	16.25
5-2	.35	.70	.88	1.75	3.50	17.50
11-4	.38	.75	.94	1.88	3.75	18.75
3-1	.40	.80	1.00	2.00	4.00	20.00
10-3	.43	.87	1.08	2.17	4.33	21.67
7-2	.45	.90	1.13	2.25	4.50	22.50
4-1	.50	1.00	1.25	2.50	5.00	25.00
9-2	.55	1.10	1.38	2.75	5.50	27.50
5-1	.60	1.20	1.50	3.00	6.00	30.00
11-2	.65	1.30	1.63	3.25	6.50	32.50
6-1	.70	1.40	1.75	3.50	7.00	35.00
13-2	.75	1.50	1.88	3.75	7.50	37.50
7-1	.80	1.60	2.00	4.00	8.00	40.00
15-2	.85	1.70	2.13	4.25	8.50	42.50
8-1	.90	1.80	2.25	4.50	9.00	45.00
17-2	.95	1.90	2.38	4.75	9.50	47.50
9-1	1.00	2.00	2.50	5.00	10.00	50.00
10-1	1.10	2.20	2.75	5.50	11.00	55.00
11-1	1.20	2.40	3.00	6.00	12.00	60.00
12-1	1.30	2.60	3.25	6.50	13.00	65.00
14-1	1.50	3.00	3.75	7.50	15.00	75.00
16-1	1.70	3.40	4.25	8.50	17.00	85.00
20-1	2.10	4.20	5.25	10.50	21.00	105.00
25-1	2.60	5.20	6.50	13.00	26.00	130.00
33-1	3.40	6.80	8.50	17.00	34.00	170.00

20 . ADDRESS BOOK

GENERAL ADDRESSES

J.A. Allen & Co.,
'The Horseman's Bookshop', 1 Lower Grosvenor Place, London
SW1W OEL. Tel: 071-828 8855/834 5606

Amateur Riders Association of Great Britain,
c\o The Hon. Johnny Greenall, Premier House, P.O. Box 27, Loushers
Lane, Warrington, Cheshire WA4 6RQ. Tel: 0925 33500

Animal Health Trust,
P.O. Box 5, Newmarket, Suffolk CB8 7DW. Tel: 0638 661111

B.O.L.A. (Betting Office Licensees Association),
Francis House, Francis Street, London SW1P 1DE. Tel: 071-630 0667

British Racing School,
Snailwell Road, Newmarket, Suffolk CB8 7NU. Tel: 0638 665103

Brooke Hospital For Sick Animals,
British Columbia House, 1 Regent Street, London SW1. Tel: 071-930 0210

Equine Research Station,
Balaton Lodge, Snailwell Road, Newmarket, Suffolk. Tel: 0638 661111

European Breeders' Fund,
Stanstead House, The Avenue, Newmarket, Suffolk CB8 9AA.
Tel: 0638 661321

Gamblers Book Services,
18 Coleswood Road, Harpenden, Herts AL5 1EQ. Tel: 0582 761264

Horseracing Advisory Council,
52 Grosvenor Gardens, Victoria, London SW1W OAU. Tel: 071-730 4540

Horserace Betting Levy Board,
52 Grosvenor Gardens, Victoria, London SW1W OAU. Tel: 071-730 4540.

Horserace Totalisator Board,
Tote House, 74 Upper Richmond Road, Putney, London SW15 2SU.
Tel: 081-874 6411

Horserace Writers and Reporters Association,
59 Blenheim Road, Horsham, West Sussex RH12 4AQ. Tel: 0403 60831

Injured Jockeys' Fund,
P.O. Box, 9 Newmarket, Suffolk CB8 8JG. Tel: 0638 662246

International League for the Protection of Horses,
P.O. Box 166, 67a Camden High Street, London NW1. Tel: 071-388 1449

International Racing Bureau,
Alton House, 117 High Street, Newmarket, Suffolk CB8 9AG.
Tel: 0638 668881

The Jockey Club,
42 Portman Square, London W1H OEN. Tel: 071-486 4921

The Jockeys' Association of Great Britain,
39 Kingfisher Court, Hambridge Road, Newbury, Berkshire RG14 5SJ.
Tel: 0635 44102

National Association for the Protection of Punters (NAPP),
P.O.Box 1329, London SW1V 2HY.

National Association of Bookmakers,
Tolworth Tower (Fourth Floor), Ewell Road, Surbiton, Surrey KT6 7EL.
Tel: 081-390 8222

National Horseracing Museum,
99 High Street, Newmarket, Suffolk CB8 8JL. Tel: 0638 667333

National Stud,
Newmarket, Suffolk CB8 0XE. Tel: 0638 663464

National Trainers Federation,
42 Portman Square, London W1H OAP. Tel: 071-935 2055

Pride Of Place, Racing Books & Memorabilia,
P.O.Box 70, Chorley, Lancs PR6 7SB. Tel: 0772 36720/724337

Racecourse Association,
Winkfield Road, Ascot, Berkshire SL5 7HX. Tel: 0344 25912

Racecourse Technical Services,
88 Bushey Road, Raynes Park, London SW20 OJH. Tel: 081-947 3333

Racehorse Owners' Association,
42 Portman Square, London W1H 9FF. Tel: 071-486 6977

Race Vision Videos,
P.O. Box 142, Jubilee Estate, Foundry Lane, Horsham, West Sussex
RH13 5FJ. Tel: 0403 61554/5

Northern Racing School,
The Stables, Rossington Hall, Bawtry Road, Doncaster, S Yorks DN11 0HN.
Tel: 0302 865462

Stable Lads Welfare Trust,
Clifton House, 121 High Street, Newmarket, Suffolk CB8 9AJ.
Tel: 0638 560763

S.I.S.
Satellite Information Services, Satellite House, 17 Corsham Street, London
N1 6DR. Tel: 071-253 2232

Tattersalls Committee,
P.O. Box 13, 19, Wilwyne Close, Grosvenor Road, Caversham, Reading
RG4 OEP. Tel: 0734 461757

The Thoroughbred Breeders' Association,
Stanstead House, The Avenue, Newmarket, Suffolk CB8 9AA.
Tel: 0638 661321

Turf Newspapers Bookshop,
18 Clarges Street, Mayfair, London W1. Tel: 071-499 4391

Weatherbys,
42 Portman Square, London W1H OEN. Tel: 071-486 4921/486 4715
Sanders Road, Wellingborough, Northants NN8 4BX. Tel: 0933 440077

RACING CLUBS

FEDERATION OF BRITISH RACING CLUBS.

General Information Line: 0836 405998

Chairman: George Harris, 219, Burton Road, West Didsbury, Manchester M20 8NA. Tel: 061 448 1441

Secretary: Ricki Peacock, 4 Bosley Crescent, Wallingford, Oxon OX10 9AS. Tel: 0491 32399

Treasurer: Allan Forrow, 15 Cullum Close, Swanton Morley, Norfolk NR20 4LZ. Tel: 0362 637503

ANGLIAN RACING CLUB
Allan Forrow, 15 Cullum Close, Swanton Morley, Norfolk NR20 4LZ.
Tel: 0362 637503

BEDFORDSHIRE & DISTRICT RACE CLUB.
Mike Perkins, 100 North Road, Hertford, Herts SG14 2BZ. Tel: 0992 550002

CHELTENHAM & THREE COUNTIES RACE CLUB.
Anne Jones, 2 Southern Road, Leckhampton, Cheltenham, Glos GL53 9AN.
Tel: 0242 512700

DONCASTER ANNUAL MEMBERS CLUB.
General Manager, Doncaster Racecourse, Leger Way, Doncaster DN2 6BB.
Tel: 0302 320066/7/8

EAST MIDLANDS RACING CLUB.
Dave Richards, 26 Brendon Road, Wollaton, Nottingham. Tel: 0602 281624

FAKENHAM RACECOURSE SUPPORTERS CLUB
Ivor Jordan, 119 Newmarket Road, Cambridge. Tel: 0223 66795

LONDON RACING CLUB.
Claire Willerton, London Racing Club, 71 Belvedere Court, Dryburgh
Road, Putney, London SW15 6HY.

NORTH EAST RACING CLUB.
Allan Kelly, 11 Camelot Close, Northdene Park, Seaham, Durham
SR7 7AN. Tel: 091 581 6523

NORTH WEST RACING CLUB.
John Bryan, 38 West End, Penwortham, Preston, Lancs PR1 0JD.
Tel: 0772 745539

THE RACEGOERS CLUB.
Flagstaff House, High Street, Twyford, Berks RG10 9AE. Tel: 0734 341666

THE RACING CLUB OF IRELAND.
The Secretary, 1d Brighton Road, Foxrock Village, Dublin 18.

SCOTTISH RACING CLUB.
Richard Harrold, 57 Woodside Street, New Stevenston, Motherwell,
Scotland ML1 4JY. Tel: 0698 832494

SOUTH WEST RACING CLUB.
The South West Racing Club, c/o Newton Abbot Racecourse,
Kingsteignton Road, Newton Abbot, Devon. Tel: 0626 773475

WEST BERKSHIRE RACING CLUB.
Katy Peacock, 4 Bosley Crescent, Wallingford, Oxon OX10 9AS.
Tel: 0491 32399

WEST MIDLANDS RACING CLUB.
Chris Pitt, 17 Cross Farm Road, Harborne, Birmingham B17 0NB.
Tel: 021 426 1877

YORKSHIRE RACING CLUB.
Mrs Cindy West, 19 Horward Avenue, Halton, Leeds LS15.

PRINCIPAL FORM GUIDES

COMPUTER RACING FORM.
Racing Research, 21 Upper Green Lane, Hove Edge, Brighouse, West
Yorkshire HD6 2NZ. Tel: 0484 710979

FUTUREFORM.
82 Girton Road, Cambridge CB3 0LN. Tel: 0223 276243.

JUNIORATOR.
3 Withdean Hall, The Approach, Brighton, East Sussex BN1 6WN.
Tel: 0273 565411.

PROFESSIONAL SPORTING BUREAU LTD.
Ascot House, 29a High Street, Ascot, Berks SL5 7HG. Tel: 0344 872929

RACEFORM.
Compton, Newbury, Berkshire RG16 0NL. Tel: 0635 578080.

SPORTING LIFE PUBLICATIONS.
Orbit House, 1 New Fetter Lane, London EC4A 1AR. Tel: 071-822 2068

SUPERFORM.
Furlong Press, 116 High Street, Shoreham, West Sussex BN4 5BD.
Tel: 0273 452441

TIMEFORM.
Timeform House, Halifax, W. Yorkshire HX1 1XE. Tel: 0422 330330

COMPUTER BASED SERVICES

BRIMARDON COMPUTER RACING SERVICE
75 Cockerton Green, Darlington DL3 9EG. Tel: 0325 288483

CLASS FORM RACING DATA
16 Farleigh Crescent, Swindon, Wilts SN3 1JY. Tel: 0793 693321

COURSEMASTER
Intraset Ltd., 10 Woodside Avenue, Clayton-le-Woods, Chorley, Lancs PR6
7QF. Tel: 0490 3284

DATAFORM LIMITED
Po Box 137D, New Malden, Surrey, KT3 6QW. TEL: 081 336 0057

NEDDYBANK FORMGUIDE
Neddybank, 168 High Street, Newmarket, Suffolk CB8 9AQ. Tel: 0638
561155

OEM COMPUTER SYSTEMS
Rugby Microcentre, 9-11 Regent Street, Rugby CV21 2PE. Tel: 0788 570522

RACEBASE
7 Colyton Road, East Dulwich, London. SE22 0NE. Tel: 081 693 3454

THE RACING EXCHANGE
165 The Sycamores, Milton, Cambridge. CB4 4ZH. Tel: 0223 440474

NEWSPAPERS AND PERIODICALS

What Tipster
Dayshields Ltd., Hammerain House, Harrogate, HG2 8ER. Tel: 0423 870805

Pacemaker Update International (monthly magazine)
Sires for 1992 (annual)
The Thoroughbred Breeder (Monthly)
Haymarket Publishing, Lancaster Gate, London W2 3LP. Tel: 071-413 4544

Bloodstock Sales Review & Stud Register (annual)
Hobsons Publishing plc., Bateman Street, Cambridge CB2 1LZ
Tel: 0223 354551

Directory of the Turf (annual)
Kilijaro Ltd, Douglas Lodge, 9 Cheveley Road, Newmarket, Suffolk CB8
8AD. Tel: 0638 662745

Ruffs Guide to the Turf (annual)
The Sporting Life (daily)
Weekender (weekly)
Mirror Group Newspapers Ltd., Orbit House, 1 New Fetter Lane, London
EC4A 1AR. Tel: 071 822 2068

Racing and Football Outlook (weekly)
Outlook Press, 63-67 Tabernacle Street, London EC2A 4AH.
Tel: 071-490 1212

Racing World Video Magazine (monthly)
1 Hughes Mews, 143 Chatham Road, London SW11 6HJ. Tel: 071-924 4066

Horses In Training (annual)
Racing Ahead (annual magazine)
Raceform Handicap Book (weekly)
Raceform Ltd., Compton, Newbury, Berkshire RG16 0NL.
Tel: 0635 578080.

Racing Post (daily)
Racing Post, Cannon House, 120 Coombe Lane, Raynes Park, London
SW20 0BA. Tel: 081-879 3377.

Odds On (monthly)
Rowton Press Ltd, PO Box 10, Oswestry, Shropshire SY10 7QR.
Tel: 0691 70 444/445

The Irish Field (weekly)
The Irish Field, 11-15 D'Olier Street, Dublin 2, Eire. Tel: 010 353 1 6792022.

Irish Racing Annual (Annual)
Smurfit Publications, 126 Lower Baggot Street, Dublin 2, Eire.
Tel: 010 353 1 608264.

Programme Books
Racing Calendar (weekly)
Registered Names of Horses (biennial)
Rules of Racing (annual)
The Stallion Book (annual)
The Statistical Record (4-times a year + supplements)
Weatherbys, Sanders Road, Wellingborough, Northants NN8 4BX.
Tel: 0933 440077

21. DIRECTORY OF WINNING HORSES

The Directory of Winning Horses includes all the two thousand or so horses that won last year, giving their full form over two years. Form here is taken to mean any occasion that prizemoney is earned on the assumption that in such cases the horse will be trying hard and therefore producing the sort of performance that indicates ability. This is not always the case, but as a general rule it holds good.

Using the Directory is simple and informative. It gives an at-a-glance appraisal of racing character which will often pin-point significant details.

Backers can use the Directory alongside their daily newspaper or on its own. Very often vital clues about whether a selection is able to stay, act on the going or is up to the required standard are revealed. As the season progresses, providing the backer has access to 1992/93 form, the Directory becomes ever more useful, building a concise picture of the strengths of proven performers.

NOTES

The HANDICAP RATINGS shown to the right of the horse name is as at the 22/08/92

HUR = Hurdle Rating   CHS = Chase Rating

All distances are rounded to the nearest furlong.

The dash ("-") indicates the new season

The figures shown in bold type in the form range denote form over the jumps; light type denotes form over hurdles.

GOING ABBREVIATIONS

H	=	Heavy	G	=	Good
S	=	Soft	M	=	Medium or Good-Firm
Y	=	Yielding or Good-Soft	F	=	Firm-Hard
W	=	All Weather Track			

	CHS/HUR	TRAINER	FORM RANGE
A LAD INSANE	98/ --	Bailey K C	24M⁴ 24W² 20W³ 24M⁴ 25F¹ 24G³ 22M² - 20M¹ 25F² 25M¹ 25M⁴ 24M³ 25M⁴
ABBENOIR	--/ 92	Kendall Mrs M	- 16G¹
ABBOT OF FURNESS	115/110	Richards G W	16G² 16H¹ 16G² 16G¹ 18S¹ - 16Y¹ 20S¹
ABERCROMBY CHIEF	93/ --	Oliver J K M	20Y³ 24Y² - 20G⁴ 24S² 24H¹ 24Y¹
ABERFOYLE	--/ 81	Kelleway P A	- 16Y¹ 20W¹ 22W² 20W¹ 20W² 20W²
ABEROY	81/ 76	Ryan M J	24M³ 17F² 25M² 24G³ 22G¹ 20M⁴ - 22F¹ 22M³ 22F¹ 21M³ 18G⁴ 16G² 20G³
ABIGAIL'S DREAM	--/ 80	Jenkins J R	16W³ 16W¹ 20W¹ 16W³ 16M² - 16G² 20G¹ 20M² 18W²
ABINGDON FLYER	--/ 80	Pipe M C	- 16W³ 20W¹ 16W³
ABLE PLAYER	--/ 94	Thornton C W	- 18W² 16Y¹ 16G⁴ 16G¹ 16G²
ABNEGATION	--/108	Johnson J H	20G² - 16G¹ 20G¹ 16G² 20G¹
ABSAILOR	--/ --	Bradburne Mrs	20G³ - 16G² 17G² 24M¹
ABSALOM'S LADY	--/123	Balding G B	- 17S³ 18G¹ 16G³ 16Y³ 16G¹ 17G² 19G²
ABSENT RELATIVE	--/ --	Sanders Miss B	- 16G¹ 18Y² 16W¹
ABU MUSLAB	--/101	Edwards G F	20G² 17M³ 16M¹ 17M³ 18W² 16M³ - 17G¹ 17G³ 16W¹
ACE OF DIAMONDS	--/ 71	Storey F S	20Y² 16S¹ 16H² - 16M² 20F² 20M³ 18G³ 20M¹ 18S³ 20Y²
ACE OF SPIES	125/ --	Jones Mrs Gill	29S² 26G² 24M⁴ 24M¹ - 24G³ 28G¹
ACHILTIBUIE	83/ --	Richards G W	17G² 16M² 20F² 16F¹ 16F³ - 20M² 16F² 20F³ 17F³ 17M¹ 17M² 16G³
ACRE HILL	122/ --	Henderson N J	16G¹ 16Y² 16G² 20G³ 16G¹ - 16G² 16M⁴ 16M² 16M² 17F¹
ACROW LINE	--/ 96	Burchell D	21G² 17H³ - 20G² 22S¹ 20W³ 24S¹ 24G² 26S¹
ACROW LORD	--/ --	Pipe M C	19F³ - 18F³ 16F¹
ADELINE LYNN	--/ 75	Tinkler N	16M³ 16Y¹ 16G² 16M² 16M² - 17F² 17G¹ 16G² 17M²
AFFAIR OF HONOUR	--/103	O'Neill J J	- 16Y² 16S³ 20S¹ 20M¹
AFRICAN SAFARI	--/ --	Smith Mrs S J	16F² 16M¹ 16Y⁴ 16G³ - 16M¹ 16M²
AGARB	--/ 80	Bailey K C	- 25G¹
AINSTY FOX	--/ --	Ellison B	20G² 20M³ 20Y¹ 20G² 16S² 16G⁴ 16Y² - 20S² 26Y³ 25M² 20S² 20G¹ 16F¹
AL FROLIC	--/ 85	Monteith P	16G² 16G¹ - 16M³ 18G² 16F¹ 16M³
AL HASHIMI	138/ --	Nicholson D	20G¹ 20M² 20G² 16G² 20G¹ 20S² 20Y³ 16G¹ 22G⁴ - 16M² 16M² 16G² 16G¹ 16G¹
AL MUTAHM	--/137	Old J A B	- 16M² 16G² 16G² 16G³
AL SABAK	--/ --	Miller N	- 16S² 20Y¹ 18W² 27F²
AL SAHIL	--/ --	White J	- 17S³ 18G¹
AL-KHALIDA	--/ --	Hodges R J	- 18F² 20F³ 16G¹
ALAN BALL	81/ --	Wilton Miss S	16S³ - 16G¹ 16G³
ALBERTITO	--/105	Hollinshead R	- 21G³ 16Y¹ 16G¹
ALKINOR REX	114/ --	Harwood G	17S⁴ 16Y⁴ 16H¹ 16G² - 16G¹ 16G¹ 24Y¹
ALL AFLOAT	90/ --	Forster Capt T	20S² 20Y⁴ 24H - 22G¹
ALL GREEK TO ME	--/ --	Thornton C W	- 16G¹
ALL PRESENT	--/ --	Akehurst R	- 16Y¹

	CHS/HUR	TRAINER	FORM RANGE
ALL WELCOME	--/100	Moore G M	16G^1 18S^2 16S^2 16S^1 16G^1 - 16G^1 16Y^3 18F^1 16G^4 16G^3
ALREEF	--/110	Jones T Thomso	16G^2 16Y^1 18W^1 16Y^1 - 16W^1
ALTON BAY	--/ 70	Haine Mrs D	- 16F^1 17F^1 16F^2 16G^2 20G^1
ALWAYS ALEX	--/ 76	Evans P D	- 17G^2 17G^1 16G^2
ALWAYS REMEMBER	--/ --	Hobbs P J	- 17G^1
AMADORA	--/ 71	Pipe M C	17M^2 16F^2 16M^2 - 19G^1 16G^1
AMARI KING	121/ --	Forster Capt T	16G^1 16Y^1 17Y^2 16M^1 - 16G^1 16G^3 16G^3 16M^3 16M^1 16G^2 16G^2
AMBASSADOR	122/ --	Pipe M C	- 16Y^1 16M^3
AMBLESIDE HARVEST	--/ 97	O'Neill J J	- 20S^1 20S^3
AMBROSE	--/109	Houghton R F J	16S^2 16G^2 16M^3 - 16M^1 16G^1 20G^3
AMBUSCADE	--/130	Reveley Mrs G	- 20G^3 22F^1 22M^1 20S^3 22G^1
AMIGOS	--/100	Mitchell P	- 16G^1 16G^2 16G^2
AMONG FRIENDS	93/ --	Balding G B	16M^3 - 20G^2 19G^1 20G^3 20M^2 20G^2 20G^2 22G^1 20G^4 20G^3
AMOUR ROYAL	--/ 97	Sherwood O	- 16S^1
ANDERSON ROSE	--/ 60	Wilson Capt J	- 16M^2 16M^2 18W^1
ANDORRA	98/ --	FitzGerald J G	- 20Y^1 16Y^2 25M^1
ANDRELOT	--/ 85	White K	16M^2 16G^3 16G^1 - 16G^4 16G^3 21M^2 20W^3 16S^2 16M^1 16S^3
ANDREWS MINSTREL	--/ --	Jenkins J R	- 16G^2 16W^1 16W^2
ANGELICA PARK	--/ 97	Wharton J	16M^2 - 24M^1 25M^3 20G^1
ANGELS KISS	--/ 88	Pipe M C	- 16Y^3 16M^1
ANNICOMBE RUN	--/120	Lee R	20G^2 21G^1 22S^2 24S^3 20S^1 - 19G^2 20Y^3 21G^1 20G^1
ANNIE DE POMME	--/ --	Twiston-Davies	20M^3 - 20M^1
ANOTHER CORAL	137/ --	Nicholson D	16G^2 16M^2 20M^1 16M^4 20G 20G^1 16Y^3 - 21M^2 20G^1 20M^2 20G^3 20G^4
ANOTHER CRUISE	--/ 85	Price R J	20M^1 - 16M^3 16G^1
ANTICO NATIVO	--/100	Dow S	- 16M^2 16W^2 16W^2 16W^1 16W^1 16W^2
APOLLO KING	--/115	Mitchell P	18F^4 20F^2 20M^2 20M^1 - 20F^1 20F^2 20G^2 20M^1 22G^2 20M^2
APPLIANCEOFSCIENCE	--/ 90	Reid A S	16M^2 16G^2 16G^1 16Y^2 16Y^4 16M^2 - 16G^1
ARABIAN BOLD	--/115	Henderson N J	- 16W^3 16G^1 16M^3 16S^1
ARABIAN SULTAN	--/123	Pipe M C	- 16M^1 17F^1 19M^1 21G^1 18M^1 16M^2 20G^1 17G^2 21G^1
ARCOT	--/ --	Glover J A	- 16G^1 16G^2 16G^1
ARCTIC BARON	91/ --	Dawe Mrs J C	21M^4 24M^1 - 28M^3 25M^2 25F^2 26M^1
ARCTIC CALL	153/ --	Sherwood O	24M^1 26M^1 24Y^1 25G^2 - 24G^2 29M^1 24M^1 29M^2
ARCTIC SKYLIGHT	--/119	Richards G W	20G^3 16M^1 - 18S^1 16G^1 16G^3
ARCTIC TEAL	111/ --	Sherwood O	24G^3 20Y^1 20S^4 22G^4 20G^2 20G^1 - 22M^2 24G^1 24Y^1 26G^1
ARD T'MATCH	--/ 95	Forbes A L	- 26G^4 24G^1 28G^3 24G^3
ARDBRIN	120/ --	Tate T P	20G^1 20G^1 20Y^1 24Y^2 - 20Y^1 20G^2 20G^3
ARDCRONEY CHIEF	--/ 95	Gandolfo D R	16G^2 - 16G^1 16G^2 16G^4 16S^3
ARDIE	--/ --	Oliver Mrs S	- 16Y^3 20G^1 20G^2
ARMAGRET	120/ --	Wilkinson B E	25M^2 22S^3 20G^1 20G^2 24G^4 20S^3 - 22F^2 20G^1 20M^1 20G^1 20G^3 22G^2 20G^4
ARPAL FOREVER	85/ --	Allan R	16M^3 16S^3 - 16Y^1 22F^3 16G^2
ARR EFF BEE	--/ 79	Smith J P	- 19G^1 19G^2
ARTFUL ABBOT	104/ --	Sherwood S E	- 20G^1 20M^2 24M^1 24G^3

	CHS/HUR	TRAINER	FORM RANGE
ARTFUL ARTHUR	--/ 61	McConnochie J	- 24G¹
ARTHUR'S MINSTREL	--/105	Stephenson W A	- 16M¹ 16Y³ 20G¹ 20G¹ 20M²
ARTHURS STONE	--/ 82	Brennan O	16S¹ 16Y³ 16S² - 16Y³ 16Y³ 16G¹
ASHFOLD COPSE	--/118	Harwood G	16G¹ - 16G⁴ 16M² 21G¹ 20G³ 20G² 24S¹
ASK FRANK	112/ --	Balding G B	22G³ - 18G³ 24S¹ 24G⁴ 26H¹
ASSAGLAWI	110/ --	Knight Miss H	20G¹ 20G¹ 22G² 24M¹ 24G³ - 24G³ 24G¹
ASTON AGAIN	--/ 92	Moore G M	- 16G² 16F¹ 20G³ 16M¹ 16G²
ASTRABEE	--/ --	Wharton J	16M¹ 20M² 20M² 22M² - 22M¹
ASTROAR	--/ --	Perry J	- 25F¹
ASWAMEDH	--/ 90	Hobbs P J	- 16G² 20G¹
AT PEACE	--/ 99	White J	- 16M¹ 17S³ 17G³ 16M³ 16G² 16W¹ 16M¹
AUCTION LAW	113/ --	Barons D H	- 26G² 25G³ 25G¹ 24G¹ 25G²
AUGUST FOLLY	78/ --	Price R J	- 16M³ 16Y³ 20M¹ 16G² 20M⁴
AUNTIE DOT	138/ --	Webber J	21M² 22G² 20G¹ 20Y² 20Y³ 20S³ 20S³ 36Y³ 20G¹ 22M¹ - 22G³ 24G¹ 20G¹ 20G² 24G⁴
AUTONOMOUS	--/ --	Allen C N	20Y³ - 20M² 18F¹ 24W²
AUVILLAR	--/ 77	O'Neill O	- 17S² 16G² 20G³ 20G¹ 19G³
AVIATION SUPPORT	--/ --	Buckler R H	- 26F¹
AVONBURN	97/ --	Hedger P R	- 20G¹ 24G³ 24M² 21M¹ 21M¹ 20M⁴ 20F² 24S¹
AVONMOUTHSECRETARY	97/ --	Holder R J	19F¹ 19M¹ 25M³ - 25M¹ 24F² 25M¹ 22G¹ 25M¹ 25G¹ 20G²
AVRO ANSON	--/ 97	Camacho M J	- 16M¹ 16F¹
AZUREUS	--/ 86	Perratt Miss L	- 16M¹ 16M¹
AZUSA	96/ --	Hammond M D	18F¹ 16F¹ 17F¹ 16F⁴ - 24M¹ 25G² 20M¹ 24G³ 25M³ 28G¹ 26M²
BACK BEFORE DARK	--/ --	Monteith P	16S¹ 20G³ 20H² - 20M² 24G² 24F¹ 26M² 20G¹ 22G¹ 20Y²
BAD TRADE	109/ --	Stephenson W A	16F² 24F³ 20G¹ 20Y² 20M² 20S¹ 16M³ 20S⁴ 20M⁴ 22Y⁴ - 20Y² 20G² 20S¹ 20G³ 20Y¹
BAHRAIN QUEEN	--/ 76	Smith C	- 17F² 16F² 19G¹ 22M¹
BAKHTARAN	--/107	King Mrs A L M	16Y² - 16M¹ 17M² 16G² 16M¹ 16G² 16F²
BALAAT	--/ 90	Chapman M C	- 16S² 20M¹ 17G² 17M³ 17M¹
BALASANI	--/132	Pipe M C	- 16G¹ 21G³
BALLERINA ROSE	--/ 84	O'Neill O	- 16G¹ 17S² 16Y³ 16M³
BALLINROSTIG	--/ --	Smith Denys	20G⁴ 27Y⁴ 25G² 25G¹ - 24M¹ 24M² 24M¹
BALLYANTO	--/ 88	Holder R J	- 20Y¹ 16Y³ 24F³
BALLYEDEN	--/ --	Messer-Bennett	- 25G³ 25S¹ 27Y¹ 25G³
BALLYLORD	--/ 83	O'Neill J J	18H² - 20S³ 20G³ 16Y¹ 20G¹ 18S³ 16Y¹ 16H³
BALLYSTATE	--/ 90	James C	- 16G¹ 16Y³ 16Y³ 17M² 22M¹
BALZAC BOY	--/ --	Pitman Mrs J	- 16G¹
BANBRIDGE	123/ --	Nicholson D	16G¹ 16M¹ 19G² 19G² 16Y³ 16G³ - 16G³ 17G¹ 16M² 16M¹ 16M² 16M¹ 16M²
BAND OF HOPE	--/ 65	Clay W	- 16S³ 20W² 18W³ 16G² 16M¹
BANK VIEW	--/141	Tinkler N	- 16G⁴ 16G³ 16Y¹ 16G⁵ 16G² 20G⁴
BANKER'S GOSSIP	103/ --	Nicholson D	25G¹ 25M¹ 22M¹ 24M¹ 24G³ 24Y² 25Y¹ 25Y⁴ - 25M⁴ 24M¹ 24M¹ 24M² 24M¹ 25G²
BANKROLL	--/ 97	Hobbs P J	- 16M³ 20F¹ 16M³ 21M³

	CHS/HUR	TRAINER	FORM RANGE
BANNISTER	--/ 96	Pipe M C	17G³ - 17F¹ 17M¹ 19G¹ 21G¹
BARGE BOY	--/110	Old J A B	17G² 16M¹ 16M³ - 16M¹ 17G² 16G¹ 17M¹ 16G⁴ 16Y³
BARKIN	94/ --	Richards G W	20S³ 24S² 27Y² 24S¹ 24H¹ - 32G¹ 33G⁴
BARON SAFEGUARD	--/ --	Kemp W T	- 25G² 21G¹ 22Y² 22G³
BARRICA	--/ 80	Nicholson D	16G² 16M³ - 16M¹ 16Y³ 16M¹
BARRY WINDOW	--/ --	Pipe M C	- 17Y¹
BARTON BANK	--/130	Nicholson D	- 16H¹ 20S² 21G² 25G¹
BARTRES	--/ --	Smith D Murray	22G³ - 20G¹ 21G³
BAS DE LAINE	--/122	Sherwood O	- 16G¹ 16Y² 17G² 16M⁴ 16G³ 16M¹ 20G¹ 20S³
BASILEA	114/ --	Forster Capt T	20S⁴ - 16M¹ 19G³ 20G¹
BAVARD BAY	94/ --	Richards G W	- 22S¹ 20G²
BAY TERN	--/100	Easterby M H	- 20M³ 16G² 16M² 16G³ 16M³ 16G³ 16Y² 25M³ 20G¹ 20F¹
BAYDON STAR	--/113	Pitman Mrs J	- 16G² 16G¹ 16G¹ 20G²
BE MY ERA	--/ 78	Denson A W	- 16W¹
BE SURPRISED	80/ --	Moore A	16G¹ 16S⁴ - 20G¹ 20M³ 21M²
BEACHY HEAD	--/115	Thornton C W	- 16G¹ 16H¹ 20G¹
BEAN KING	--/116	Henderson N J	- 16G¹ 16Y²
BEAR'S PICNIC	--/ --	Easterby M H	- 20F¹ 20F¹
BEAU ROSE	--/ --	Trietline C C	24F¹ 26M¹ 24M² 24F² 25F² - 24G¹
BEAUCHAMP FIZZ	--/ --	Pipe M C	- 16Y³ 16G² 19G² 17M¹
BEAUFAN	--/ 73	Jackson C F C	- 16G¹
BEAUMOOD	--/ 99	Tinkler C	20G³ - 16Y² 20G¹ 25M² 24G³
BEE GARDEN	--/ --	Litston Mrs J	16G³ 16G³ 20Y² 22Y⁴ 19H² 16G² - 20G¹ 20Y³ 19G²
BEEBOB	--/123	Pipe M C	- 16Y¹ 16G² 16G¹
BEECH ROAD	135/ --	Balding G B	16G¹ 20Y³ 18Y² - 17G³ 17G¹ 20Y¹ 16G² 20G²
BEL COURSE	97/ --	Webber J	16F¹ 24M² - 16F¹ 24M¹ 16M³ 21F² 20G² 24Y² 25M⁴ 25G²
BELDINE	--/ --	Monteith P	16G¹ 16S² 16G¹ 16G¹ - 16G³ 17M³ 16G³ 16G¹
BELLEZZA	--/ --	Moore A	12Y² - 20Y¹
BELMOUNT CAPTAIN	123/ --	Balding G B	- 24M¹ 24G² 25G¹ 32G² 25G¹
BELSALAAMA	--/ 69	Moore G M	- 16M¹ 16Y¹ 20M⁴
BELTANE THE SMITH	--/ 94	Dunn N G H	16M³ 16M³ - 17G¹ 17G²
BEN HEAD	80/ --	Forster Capt T	- 24S¹ 26G⁴
BEN TIRRAN	79/ --	Lamyman Mrs S	- 16M⁴ 16M¹ 20M⁴
BENDICKS	79/ --	Moore A	17G⁴ 16S² 16G³ - 16G² 16G¹ 16G² 16G²
BERESFORDS GIRL	92/ --	Holder R J	22M¹ 22G³ - 21M² 24G³ 21Y² 27G¹ 26S³ 24G³
BERTIE BOY	98/ --	Reveley Mrs G	- 24M¹ 20Y¹ 22G¹ 26G⁴
BESCABY BOY	--/118	Wharton J	- 17M² 16M¹
BETTY HAYES	93/ --	Alner R H	22M² 22M³ 22G³ 24H¹ 27M² - 25M¹ 25G⁴ 24Y³ 24Y²
BIBENDUM	--/104	Waley-Cohen R	- 16G¹ 16Y⁴
BICKERMAN	--/ --	Spearing J L	16M³ 16M³ 16F² 16Y³ 16G² - 16M¹
BIGHAYIR	--/100	Pipe M C	- 16M² 17G² 17M¹ 18H³ 16S¹ 17G³ 16G¹ 16S¹
BIGSUN	--/ --	Nicholson D	24G² 28M² 29M³ 25Y² - 24M⁴ 28G³ 29G¹
BILLY BATHGATE	--/ --	Henderson N J	- 16G² 16Y³ 16M² 16M¹ 16F¹
BILLY BORU	--/ --	Davison A R	- 16Y¹
BISHOPDALE	130/ --	Stephenson W A	24G⁴ 24G⁴ 24F³ - 24G¹ 24S⁴ 24F¹ 24S¹ 26C¹ 26M³

	CHS/HUR	TRAINER	FORM RANGE
BISHOPS ISLAND	--/124	Nicholson D	- 21G[3] 21Y[1] 20S[2] 25G[3]
BIT OF A CLOWN	101/--	McKie Mrs I	25G[4] 25G[2] 25G[2] 25Y[3] 25S[2] 25Y[1] 32Y[3] - 21M[1] 25G[1] 25G[3] 28M[2] 25Y[1] 29Y[4] 25Y[2]
BITOFABANTER	--/--	Moore A L T (I	- 16G[1]
BLACK HUMOUR	123/--	Brooks C P E	16G[3] 16M[3] 20G[1] - 16G[1] 16G[1] 20G[4] 16G[1] 20G[1] 20G[4]
BLACK SAPPHIRE	--/123	Tompkins M H	16Y[2] 22Y[1] 22G[2] - 21G[1]
BLACK SPUR	93/--	Charlton J I A	20G[4] 25M[3] - 20G[3] 24G[2] 24S[1] 26S[3] 25G[3] 24G[3] 24F[2]
BLACKDOWN	--/ 78	Weedon C	- 17M[3] 16G[3] 16G[3] 16M[1]
BLACKSBURG	--/--	FitzGerald J G	16M[2] 16F[1] 16G[2] 16S[2] 16G[1] 16Y[1] 17G[1] - 16G[1] 16M[1]
BLAKE'S PROGRESS	--/ 91	Pipe M C	20W[1] 16F[1] 17F[3] - 18F[1] 17F[2] 20M[2] 17F[1] 20W[2]
BLAKES SON	104/--	Easterby M W	16G[2] 17G[3] 24Y[1] - 25G[2] 20Y[1] 16G[3] 20G[2] 20G[2]
BLUE BUCCANEER	91/--	Forster Capt T	16Y[3] - 16Y[2] 16Y[1] 16G[1]
BLUE DISC	--/ 89	Beever C R	- 18W[1] 20W[1] 18W[3] 16W[1]
BLUEBERRY KING	--/--	Turnell Andrew	- 20G[3]
BLUSTERY FELLOW	--/--	Chugg J	- 20M[1]
BOBBIE STACK	--/--	O'Neill J J	17F[3] 16F[2] 16F[1] 16M[1] 16G[3] 20F[2] 20M[2] 16M[3] 16G[2] 16G[3] 24Y[1] 20Y[1] 20G[1] - 16G[2] 20Y[1] 20S[2]
BOLANEY BOY	--/149	O'Neill J J	24M[2] 22Y[3] 20S[1] 22S[1] - 24Y[3] 24Y[1] 20G[1]
BOLD CHOICE	--/104	Frost R G	20M[3] 20W[3] - 16G[1] 16G[2] 16M[1] 16G[2]
BOLD IN COMBAT	83/--	Casey T	- 20M[2] 24F[2] 26G[1] 24G[1] 26G[3]
BOLGHERI	--/ 67	Tinkler N	- 16S[1] 20G[2]
BOLL WEEVIL	--/--	Sherwood O	- 16G[1]
BOLLIN PATRICK	--/112	Easterby M H	- 16M[1] 20S[1] 20G[2] 20Y[1]
BOLLIN WILLIAM	--/--	Easterby M H	- 16G[3] 16M[2] 16Y[3] 16Y[1]
BOLLINGER	--/ 67	Gifford J T	17M[2] 16S[1] 16Y[2] - 20G[1] 18S[2]
BONANZA	--/118	Reveley Mrs G	20Y[1] 16S[1] 16G[1] 16Y[1] - 26Y[3] 20G[1] 20M[1] 20F[2] 20F[2]
BONNIE DUNDEE	--/--	Edwards J A C	- 25G[2] 24G[1] 24M[2] 24G[3]
BOOK OF GOLD	--/--	Gifford J T	16M[1] 16M[1] 21Y[4] 17G[2] 16Y[6] - 16G[2] 17G[3] 20G[2] 20S[1] 20M[2]
BOOKCASE	--/117	Elsworth D R C	16G[1] 16M[2] - 16M[1] 16G[1]
BOOM TIME	90/--	Henderson N J	21Y[2] - 20G[4] 24G[1] 25G[2]
BORACEVA	125/--	Balding G B	27G[2] 24G[1] 27Y[2] 33M[4] - 20G[4] 26G[1] 30Y[6] 32G[3] 29G[2] 25G[3] 32S[5] 25G[3]
BORDER ARCHER	94/--	Hobbs P J	27G[2] - 22G[3] 20G[1] 22G[2] 26Y[1]
BOREEN JEAN	87/--	Bridgwater K S	16G[2] 16M[1] 20F[3] - 22G[3] 24Y[1] 24G[2] 25G[2] 20Y[3]
BOREEN OWEN	105/--	O'Neill J J	26G[3] 25Y[3] 24S[1] 24H[2] 24M[4] - 32G[2] 26S[3] 24S[1] 32Y[2]
BOSTON ROVER	96/--	Brennan O	16M[2] 16M[1] - 16G[2] 16M[2] 16G[2] 16S[1] 17G[2] 16G[1] 17F[3] 16G[3]
BOTTLES	--/120	Banks J E	- 16M[1] 16G[4]
BOUNDEN DUTY	121/--	Harwood G	- 16G[1] 17M[2] 16Y[1] 16G[6] 17F[1]
BOW HANDY MAN	99/--	Smith Denys	20S[2] 24S[1] 24M[2] 25G[1] 24S[2] 28S[3] 24H[3] 25G[3] 24M[3] - 28G[1] 32Y[3] 27M[3]
BOY PAINTER	--/ 73	Johnson J H	- 16M[1]
BRACKENFIELD	--/--	Hammond M D	- 18G[1] 17M[1]
BRADBURY STAR	145/--	Gifford J T	20G[3] 25M[2] 20G[1] 21Y[4] 16Y[6] 20Y[4] - 16G[1] 20M[1] 20G[1] 20M[1]

	CHS/HUR	TRAINER	FORM RANGE
			20G¹ 20M² 24G² 25G¹
BRANDESTON	--/ --	Murphy F	20M³ 20G¹ 20S² - 20M¹ 20M³ 21M¹
BRAVE BUCCANEER	--/ --	Smith D Murray	- 16G¹ 16Y⁴
BRAVE DEFENDER	97/ --	White J	20M³ 24W² - 21F⁴ 21M¹ 24M¹
BRAVE SETANTA	--/ --	O'Mahony F J	25G³ 20S² 24G² 24G³ 24G²
			25M³ 24G³ - 22F² 25M¹ 24M¹ 25M¹
BRAVO STAR	--/ 86	Rodford P R	- 19M³ 20M¹
BREAK THE CHAIN	--/128	Stephenson W A	20M² 20M¹ 20F¹ 20G⁴ 22Y¹
			20G² 20Y³ 20H² 22M¹ 22M⁴
			20F¹ 22F¹ - 20M³ 20Y² 24Y⁴ 22M¹
BREENAMORE	--/ --	Clarke Mrs Sar	20F² - 20G² 20Y² 20G¹
BRIDGETOWN LAD	81/ --	Meade M	20S³ - 16G⁴ 16S² 19G³ 16Y³ 16M² 16F³
BRIEF ENCOUNTER	98/ --	Nicholls P F	- 26S² 20Y¹ 24S²
BRIEF GALE	--/ --	Gifford J T	- 16Y¹
BRIERY FILLE	--/ --	Hide A	16G³ 17M² 16G² 16W² 16W¹ - 16W¹ 16W³ 16W² 16Y²
BRIG'S GAZELLE	92/ --	Park Ian	16M⁴ 20G³ 24G¹ - 25M² 26G² 25G¹ 28G² 27M² 27M¹
BRIGADIER BILL	--/ 78	Reveley Mrs G	16G³ - 16F¹
BRINKWATER	--/ --	White J	16M¹ 19F³ 24G¹ 17F³ 25M² - 16F¹ 16F¹
BROCTUNE GREY	--/108	Reveley Mrs G	24G² 26S⁴ 24M² 24G³ 25Y³
			24Y³ - 24G² 24Y³ 20Y¹ 20G¹ 24G¹
BROMPTON ROAD	99/ --	Lee R	- 26S¹
BRONZE FINAL	--/ --	Gifford J T	20M¹ 19S¹ 20S¹ - 20G¹
BROOM ISLE	--/ 70	Knight Mrs A	- 17F² 17G¹
BROUGHTON MANOR	102/ --	Retter Mrs J G	- 24G³ 26G³ 19M¹ 19M¹ 21Y³ 21G¹ 20S²
BROWN SAUCE	--/ --	Henderson N J	- 16M² 16Y² 16M¹
BROWN WINDSOR	145/ --	Henderson N J	- 25M¹
BRUNSWICK BLUE	--/ 74	Sutcliffe J	- 16W¹ 16W² 20W² 16W² 16W¹
BUCK OWENS	--/ --	Johnson J H	- 25M¹ 20F³
BUCK WILLOW	119/ --	Gifford J T	17G² 16Y² - 20M¹ 20G¹ 16M¹ 20G³ 20Y²
BUCKINGHAM GATE	--/ 84	Gandolfo D R	- 22G² 21G¹ 18M⁴
BUCKLE IT UP	88/ --	Mactaggart A H	- 24H¹ 24Y⁴
BUCKRA MELLISUGA	--/100	Stephenson W A	- 16F² 16Y¹ 16M¹ 19M¹
BUD'S BET	--/ 69	McConnochie J	- 16M¹ 17M¹
BUDDINGTON	91/ --	Forster Capt T	16G³ 22Y¹ 21G⁴ 22S² - 24S² 26Y¹
BUMBLES FOLLY	115/ --	Nicholls P F	- 25Y² 25G³ 21G¹
BUONARROTI	--/106	Old J A B	- 21Y¹ 20Y²
BURGOYNE	--/141	Easterby M H	16S² 20G¹ 22Y² 21Y² 22G³
			25Y² 24G³ - 25G¹ 24Y² 24G² 21G² 25G⁴
BURGUNDY BOY	--/ --	Jarvis A P	- 21Y¹
BURN BRIDGE	--/ 91	Hammond M D	- 16F³ 16M² 20M¹ 16G²
BURNT FINGERS	115/ --	White J	19G¹ 16G² 22F³ 22G¹ - 16S¹ 16M¹ 21M¹
BURSANA	--/ 75	Spearing J L	16Y³ - 16G³ 16M¹
BUSY MITTENS	--/ --	Mullins Seamus	- 25G¹ 25Y³ 24G² 24G²
BUTLER'S TWITCH	--/ --	Sherwood O	- 16G¹
BUTLERS PET	92/ --	Hallett T B	16G⁴ 16G³ 17S³ 16G⁴ - 16Y¹
BY FAR	--/ 72	O'Neill O	- 16M¹
CAB ON TARGET	--/150	Reveley Mrs G	16G¹ 20G¹ 20S¹ 20G¹ - 24G¹ 24Y¹ 20G¹ 24M²

	CHS/HUR	TRAINER	FORM RANGE
CABIN HILL	--/ 84	Christian S	16G³ - 19Y¹
CACHE FLEUR	124/ --	Pipe M C	- 20Y¹ 24Y² 20G³ 20M¹ 25G¹ 24Y³ 20G¹
CADDY	105/ --	Christian S	- 24M¹ 24M³ 25M³ 21G¹ 26F³
CADENCY	--/105	Tompkins M H	- 16G¹ 16S⁴ 16M¹
CADFORD GIRL	--/ --	Turner W G M	22M² - 18F¹
CAINSBRIDGE QUEEN	--/ 83	Jones Mrs Gill	- 22M² 22M¹
CALABRESE	120/ --	Henderson N J	- 24G² 26G¹ 26S² 26Y¹ 26G¹ 25S³
CALAPAEZ	106/ --	Sanders Miss B	20Y² 20Y² 20G² 20G² - 16G¹ 24G² 20G¹ 20M¹
CALL ME EARLY	87/ --	Turnell Andrew	- 16G³ 20S³ 16Y³ 16G¹ 16G²
CAMDEN BELLE	84/ --	Muggeridge M P	17M³ 17G¹ 16Y³ - 21M³ 21M⁴ 17G² 25G³ 24M⁴ 21G³ 25G¹
CAMDEN KNIGHT	--/ 94	Bycroft N	16G¹ 16M¹ - 20G³ 20G¹ 16G²
CAME DOWN	95/ --	Hodges R J	16M² 16M² 24M² 16G¹ 19Y⁴ 16G¹ 16S² 17H³ 16F¹ - 16M¹ 16M³ 16M³ 16G¹
CAMPSEA-ASH	127/ --	Murphy F	20G² 16M¹ 16F³ - 16M¹ 17P² 16G¹ 16M³ 16G³ 16G⁴ 16Y² 16M⁴ 16M³
CANDY CONE	81/ --	Brewis R	- 25M² 24H¹
CANDY TUFF	--/116	Reveley Mrs G	- 22Y¹ 24G¹ 22F¹
CANFORD PALM	--/ --	Felton M J	29M⁴ 24G² 35Y² 25H³ - 24G¹
CANNY CHRONICLE	--/135	Tompkins M H	- 16G¹ 16G¹ 16G⁴
CANOSCAN	--/ 88	Herries Lady	16G³ - 16G³ 16Y² 16G¹ 16M² 16G² 22G³
CAPABILITY BROWN	--/132	Pipe M C	16S¹ 16M⁴ 16M¹ 16S² 22G² - 20Y¹ 20Y¹ 25G¹ 24G¹
CAPRICORN KING	--/ --	McCain D	16W³ - 16S¹
CAPTAIN DIBBLE	136/ --	Twiston-Davies	20G² 25Y² 20Y¹ - 22G¹ 20M² 24Y¹ 24G² 20G² 24G⁵ 33G¹
CAPULET	--/ 85	James C	19G² 22Y³ 20Y³ - 19G¹
CARABALI DANCER	--/ 76	Garraton D T	- 16W¹ 16W²
CARBISDALE	127/ --	Reveley Mrs G	20G² 20S⁴ - 22M¹ 20G¹ 22M¹ 20M²
CARBONATE	--/ 96	Buckler R H	19M² 16M³ - 16G² 19M¹ 20M⁴ 18Y⁴ 16G³ 17M²
CARELESS KISS	--/ 83	Moore A	- 16G¹ 16G³ 16Y¹
CARFAX	--/ 91	Hoad R P C	24M⁴ 21G¹ - 20W¹ 24W² 22W¹
CARIBBEAN PRINCE	--/ 91	McCourt M	- 16G³ 17Y¹ 16G³ 16M¹
CAROBEE	--/142	Nicholson D	- 16G¹ 16Y³ 16S¹ 16Y¹ 16S¹ 16Y¹
CAROGROVE	--/ --	O'Shea J G M	16M³ 21M² - 20M³ 25F¹ 25M² 24G² 24M¹ 25M⁴
CAROLE'S KING	--/ --	Carter W	- 16M¹ 17F²
CAROLES CLOWN	--/ 89	Haynes M J	20W² 20W² 20W³ - 20W¹ 20W³ 18W³ 18W² 20W²
CAROMANDOO	--/ 95	Murray B W	- 16G² 16Y¹ 16G¹
CAROUSEL CALYPSO	--/ 79	Hammond M D	16G³ 24G¹ 25G¹ 24Y² 22M¹ - 26Y¹
CAROUSEL ROCKET	97/ --	Hammond M D	25H³ 20G² 24M¹ - 26Y² 28G³ 24S² 33G¹
CARSWELL'S CHOICE	--/ 78	Fisher R F	- 21S² 20G³ 22W¹ 22W³
CARVILL'S HILL	--/ --	Pipe M C	- 24Y¹ 30Y¹ 26G⁵
CASIENNE	--/ 74	Holder R J	- 16G³ 16G¹ 16M¹ 19M² 19G³ 16G²
CASPIAN MIST	--/ 85	Pipe M C	- 16G¹ 18G²
CASTELLANI	--/ 81	Eckley M W	- 16M³ 16M¹ 16M¹
CASTIGLIERO	--/116	Brooks C P E	- 20G² 24Y¹ 20S¹ 24Y¹
CASTLE DIAMOND	--/ 85	Kavanagh H M	- 21M¹

	CHS/HUR	TRAINER	FORM RANGE
CASTLE KING	100/ --	Stephenson W A	- 22F² 20G² 20M² 20G¹ 20F¹ 20G¹ 20G³
CASTLE SECRET	--/136	Burchell D	19M¹ 22M¹ 22M¹ - 20Y⁴ 20M¹ 25Y² 16G²
CASTLEACRE	--/ 67	Smith C A	- 16G¹
CASTLEBAY LAD	--/ 95	Old J A B	- 21Y³ 24S¹ 24Y¹
CATCH THE CROSS	115/ --	Pipe M C	20F² 20F² 23G² 20M¹ 23G¹ 21G¹ 20G¹ 21S² 24Y⁴ 24M⁴ 27M¹ 22F² 20S⁴ - 20S⁴ 20M¹ 20G² 20M¹ 20M² 24G³ 20S¹ 24G¹ 26M⁴
CAVALIER CROSSETT	--/ --	Caine E M	16G¹ 16G² 16G³ 16Y¹ 20S³ 16S² 16G³ 20G² 16M¹ - 16G¹ 16G¹ 20M³ 16G³ 16M³ 16G¹ 16H¹ 16Y³
CAXTON	--/ 88	Moore G M	- 16G² 16M¹
CAZAUDEHORE	--/ --	Robinson M H B	20W¹ - 20W² 24W¹ 20W¹ 20W² 24W³
CEDAR RUN	75/ --	Charles-Jones	- 16G³ 17S² 25G³
CELTIC BREEZE	--/105	Naughton M P	22S² - 22S² 24G² 22G¹ 24Y¹ 24H¹ 20G³
CELTIC CATCH	--/ 70	Bosley J R	- 16M¹
CELTIC DIAMOND	87/ --	Retter Mrs J G	22S² 22H² - 24M¹ 24M²
CELTIC HAMLET	82/ --	Davison A R	- 24G² 26G¹
CELTIC LEISURE	--/ --	Vickery Mrs R	- 21G¹ 20G²
CELTIC SHOT	--/ --	Brooks C P E	24G¹ 24S¹ 24Y¹ 24Y⁴ 25G¹ 25Y⁴ - 24G¹ 24G²
CENTENARY STAR	106/ --	Reveley Mrs G	20W² 20G¹ 20Y² 22S² 24Y³ 24G³ - 20S² 22G³ 19G³ 20M¹ 17F² 20Y¹ 22M¹
CHAFOLD COPSE	--/ --	Harwood G	16F² - 16G¹ 16G¹
CHAIN SHOT	96/ --	Easterby M H	16Y⁴ 16M¹ 16M² - 16M² 17G² 16M¹ 16G¹
CHAMPAGNE LAD	--/131	Gifford J T	18F² 18G² 16S¹ - 18G¹ 21G¹ 20G⁴
CHANCERY BUCK	--/ --	Balding G B	24M² 26M¹ 24G¹ 26M³ 25M¹ 24G³ 25M² - 26G² 25M¹ 24G²
CHANGE THE ACT	107/ --	Sherwood O	16G¹ 16M² 16Y¹ - 16F² 20G¹ 20G¹
CHANGE THE NAME	94/ --	Rothwell B S	24G¹ 24G² 28G³ 27G² - 25M¹ 22G²
CHARCOAL BURNER	--/ 68	Callow R	- 17S¹
CHARLIE'S DARLING	--/ 92	White J	- 16M³ 20W¹ 20W³ 22G³ 20G³
CHARLOTTE'S EMMA	--/ 93	Goodfellow Mrs	- 20M³ 20F² 22F¹ 22G¹ 20F² 22S¹ 20M³
CHARMED I'M SURE	--/ 72	Holder R J	17Y³ 20Y³ - 18M¹ 16G²
CHARMING GALE	--/ 67	Bradburne Mrs	- 16G³ 24F¹
CHASMARELLA	--/ 89	Davison A R	16M³ 16G³ 18S³ - 22M¹ 24G¹ 22G³
CHATAM	--/152	Pipe M C	- 26G² 26G¹
CHEEKY FOX	--/ 91	Bosley J R	16S³ 16G³ 19G³ - 21G¹ 24G² 22M² 18G³
CHEERFUL TIMES	--/125	McMahon B A	20G⁴ 16G¹ - 17G² 16G² 16S¹ 16G¹ 16M² 16G² 16G² 16G²
CHERRY CHAP	85/ --	Holden W	- 17G² 16G¹ 16G² 17F¹
CHERRYKINO	109/ --	Forster Capt T	16G¹ 22G¹ 24G¹ - 22G¹ 18Y¹
CHESAPEAKE BAY	85/ --	Balding G B	- 16F¹ 16G³ 16M³ 17F³
CHESWOLD	--/ --	Taylor Mrs S	20M² 16G³ 16M³ 20M⁴ 20M² - 17F³ 16M³ 20F¹
CHICAGO'S BEST	--/ 70	Burgoyne P	- 16G¹
CHIEF IRONSIDE	108/ --	Burchell D	- 16G² 19Y² 16G⁴ 16W¹

	CHS/HUR	TRAINER	FORM RANGE
CHILD OF THE MIST	--/113	Sherwood O	$16G^2$ - $19G^1$ $20S^1$ $20G^4$ $20Y^2$ $22G^2$
CHIMAYO	--/ 67	Hedger P R	- $16F^3$ $18F^1$ $18W^2$ $20W^3$ $18G^3$ $17Y^2$ $20G^2$
CHIMES OF THE DAWN	--/ --	Burchell D	- $16M^3$ $17S^1$
CHIPCHASE	--/ 88	Wilkinson B E	$24F^2$ $25M^2$ $20F^3$ $20G^2$ $24M^4$ - $20G^1$
CHOCTAW	86/ --	Beaumont P	$20Y^1$ $25G^3$ $20S^2$ $20H^3$ $22F^3$ $20F^3$ - $20G^3$ $25G^3$ $28G^1$ $24G^2$
CHOICE CHALLANGE	107/ --	Hammond M D	$24F^1$ $16F^2$ $20M^1$ $24G^1$ $16G^3$ $20Y^1$ - $20M^1$
CHUCK CURLEY	--/ --	Curley B J	- $16M^1$
CHUCKLESTONE	--/ 99	King J S	$22F^1$ $21F^1$ $24M^3$ $25F^2$ - $24M^1$
CIRCULATION	94/ --	McCain D	- $16G^1$ $16Y^4$ $16Y^2$ $16S^2$ $17G^1$ $20G^4$
CITY ENTERTAINER	--/ --	Goodall Robert	$25Y^4$ $20Y^4$ $24G^3$ - $20G^1$ $24G^3$ $24G^4$
CITY INDEX	78/ --	Smith N A	- $16G^3$ $16W^2$ $18W^1$ $22W^2$ $20W^2$ $19F^3$ $17F^3$
CIXI	--/ --	Pipe M C	- $16F^2$ $17F^1$
CLASSIC ACCOUNT	--/ 74	Akehurst J	- $18W^1$
CLASSIC STATEMENT	--/119	Lee R	$20G^3$ $16G^3$ $17Y^3$ $25Y^1$ - $24M^1$ $23M^3$ $24M^1$ $24G^2$ $24S^4$
CLAY COUNTY	125/ --	Allan R	$16G^2$ $16G^1$ $16G^3$ $16G^2$ $16H^2$ $16G^4$ - $16M^1$ $17F^1$ $16G^1$ $17G^1$ $16G^1$ $16G^2$
CLEANING UP	88/ --	Gandolfo D R	$16Y^4$ $20S^3$ $20G^4$ $19G^2$ $20M^2$ - $18F^1$ $20M^1$
CLEVER FOLLY	135/ --	Richards G W	$16F^2$ $20M^5$ $16G^5$ $16G^4$ $20M^2$ $16G^2$ $16G^4$ $16M^2$ $17G^1$ - $16M^2$ $20M^1$ $16M^1$ $20M^1$ $17F^1$ $16G^1$ $21M^1$ $16G^1$ $16M^1$ $16G^2$ $17M^1$
CLEVER SHEPHERD	102/ --	Hobbs P J	$24G^3$ - $20M^3$ $18G^1$ $20G^2$ $25M^1$ $25G^1$ $26G^2$ $24M^2$ $25G^2$
CLIFFALDA	108/ --	Richards G W	- $24S^3$ $22Y^1$ $24G^1$ $25M^2$
CLOVERMILL	--/ 70	Bentley W	- $16Y^3$ $20F^2$ $18Y^1$ $16Y^3$ $20G^1$ $20F^1$
COASTING	--/ 92	Balding G B	$16M^2$ - $20G^3$ $21G^1$
COE	101/ --	Akehurst R	$16M^1$ $18F^3$ $16M^2$ $16G^2$ - $20G^3$ $21G^3$ $20G^3$ $21G^3$ $21G^1$ $20G^1$ $20G^1$ $22M^3$
COKENNY BOY	--/133	Pitman Mrs J	$16Y^2$ $16Y^3$ $16G^3$ $16Y^2$ $21Y^1$ $20S^2$ - $18G^3$ $22M^1$ $21G^1$
COLONEL O'KELLY	83/ --	Barons D H	- $25G^3$ $25G^4$ $18Y^4$ $20G^1$ $24Y^2$ $26G^4$
COLORADO INSIGHT	--/ 66	Aconley Mrs V	- $17F^1$ $16G^1$ $16M^2$
COMANECI	--/ 75	Akehurst J	- $16W^2$ $16W^2$ $16G^1$
COMBERMERE	--/ --	Frost R G	$24Y^1$ $20G^2$ $25Y^3$ - $21M^2$ $25G^1$ $25M^2$ $30G^1$ $24M^1$ $29Y^1$
COMEDY ROAD	97/ --	Lee R	- $25G^1$
COMING ALIVE	--/ 93	Stephenson W A	- $16Y^2$ $20M^1$
COMMANCHE SIOUX	--/ 60	Morgan K A	- $16Y^1$
CONA GLEN	108/ --	Forster Capt T	- $26F^3$ $26G^1$ $25M^1$ $24G^1$
CONE LANE	--/ 80	Gubby B	- $16M^1$ $16W^3$ $16G^1$
CONNATE	--/ --	Barber R	- $21H^1$ $20G^1$
CONSTRUCTION	--/ 77	Edwards J A C	$22F^3$ - $20F^1$ $20G^3$ $20F^3$
CONTACT KELVIN	--/ --	Bycroft N	$16M^3$ $16G^4$ $16F^2$ $25G^3$ $24M^3$ $16G^1$ $20S^3$ $20M^4$ - $20M^1$
COOL CLOWN	--/ --	Pipe M C	- $17G^1$
COOL GROUND	167/ --	Balding G B	$28S^3$ $30G^2$ $25G^1$ $26G^4$ - $29G^3$ $30G^1$ $28Y^1$ $26G^1$

	CHS/HUR	TRAINER	FORM RANGE
COOLE DODGER	103/ --	Ham G A	17S² 16Y² - 17S¹ 17M³ 16G² 20S⁴ 21G¹ 21M¹
COPPER MINE	--/115	Sherwood O	16G³ 16F³ - 16S² 16G¹ 16M¹ 16G² 16G¹ 18M²
CORN LILY	--/ --	Reveley Mrs G	16G³ - 17G¹ 16G¹
CORNET	125/ --	Smith Denys	20G³ 16Y¹ 16G⁴ 16H³ 16G² 16G¹ 16S³ 16M¹ 16M¹ 16M¹ - 16M³ 20G² 16G³ 16G¹ 16M¹ 20G¹ 24G¹
COSMIC DANCER	--/102	Hide A	16M² 18G³ 20W¹ 20W¹ 22W¹ - 20M¹ 24M²
COSMIC RAY	90/ --	Aconley Mrs V	16Y³ 16S¹ 17G¹ 16M¹ - 17F³ 16M² 17G² 16M² 16G² 20F¹ 16M² 16M³
COUGHLANS RUN	97/ --	Forster Capt T	20G³ 20G³ - 20G¹
COULTON	--/146	Easterby M W	12S² - 20M¹ 20G³ 20S¹ 20G¹ 20G¹
COUNTERBID	--/ 96	Edwards J A C	- 16M¹ 16G¹ 19G¹
COUNTESS BLAKENEY	--/ --	Butler P	- 16G¹
COUNTORUS	--/ --	Johnson J H	- 16G¹ 24G¹
COUNTRY CAP	89/ --	Townsend R D	20M² 24Y³ 20Y³ - 20Y³ 26G² 24G¹ 18Y⁴ 25M³
COUNTRY DIARY	--/ --	Balding G B	19G² 20G¹ 22M¹ - 20M³ 25G¹ 21M³ 18G² 22G² 27M¹ 24G²
COUNTRY MEMBER	108/ --	Turnell Andrew	16G² - 20G¹ 20G² 25G¹ 25G²
COURAGE-MON-BRAVE	--/ --	P-Gordon G A	- 18F¹
COURT RAPIER	88/ --	Parrott Mrs H	16M³ 17F³ 16G² 21F² 16G² 16G⁴ 16M⁴ 17F¹ 19F² - 19F¹ 16M³ 19M¹ 21M² 18G³
COUTURE STOCKINGS	--/100	Mackie J	22G¹ - 22M³ 24G¹ 20G²
CRABBY BILL	--/102	Sanders Miss B	- 20G² 20W² 22W¹ 22W³
CRAZY DAISY	--/ --	Turner W G M	- 16Y³ 16G¹
CRAZY HORSE DANCER	--/ 78	Jordan F	- 16G² 20G¹
CRAZY RIVER	--/109	Pitman Mrs J	16M³ 18F¹ 16M² 16G² - 19Y³ 20G¹ 22G¹ 24G²
CREAM AND GREEN	--/ 75	White K	- 16G² 16G¹ 16G¹ 16G³
CREEAGER	--/103	Wharton J	17M² 20Y³ - 20G⁴ 24G¹ 22G³
CRIMSON CLOUD	--/ --	Tinkler N	- 16G¹ 16G³
CROCK-NA-NEE	105/ --	Richards G W	20M² 25Y⁴ 20G³ - 20G⁴ 25M³ 20G¹ 16S² 20S³ 20S² 20S¹
CROSSHOT	--/107	McDonald R	16S³ 16H² - 16M¹ 16G² 18S³ 16S¹ 16G¹ 16H²
CROSSOFSPANCILHILL	85/ --	Trietline C C	16G³ 25M¹ 25M⁴ - 25M² 24F³ 16G² 20G⁴ 19G⁴ 25G¹ 27G³
CRYSTAL HEIGHTS	--/116	Retter Mrs J G	- 22G⁴ 21G¹ 24G³
CRYSTAL SPIRIT	--/154	Balding I A	16M¹ 16G² 20Y¹ 20G¹ 20Y¹ 20Y² - 20M³ 24M² 21G¹ 25G³
CUDDY DALE	--/ --	Murphy F	20M³ 20G³ 20G³ 24Y² 25G³ - 18G² 20M² 24G² 24M¹ 20M¹
CULLANE	--/ --	Saunders Miss	- 20G¹ 25G³ 18G¹
CURAHEEN BOY	--/ --	Trietline C C	20H³ 25S² - 20G³ 19G³ 25S³ 20G¹ 20G³ 22G³ 19G¹ 25M²
CURIOUS FEELING	--/ 83	Bosley J R	19M² 16W¹ 16W¹ 16W² 16F² 19G³ - 16W³ 16M² 16W¹
CURRENT EXPRESS	--/128	Henderson N J	16M² 16M² - 16G¹ 16G⁵ 16Y¹
CUSHINSTOWN	--/ --	Pipe M C	- 25G¹
CYPHRATE	140/ --	Pipe M C	- 16Y¹ 17G² 16G¹ 16G⁴ 16G² 16Y¹ 16G¹
D'OR'S GEM	91/ --	Bevan P J	20M¹ 20Y³ 20G² 20G⁴ 20M³ - 20S³ 18G² 22M¹ 22W¹ 24G¹
DAGAZ	--/ 98	Edwards J A C	16S² 16G¹ - 16G¹ 21G² 20G⁴

	CHS/HUR	TRAINER	FORM RANGE
DAISY GIRL	--/ --	Mackie J	- 16M¹ 16M² 16F³
DAKYNS BOY	--/ --	Edwards J A C	16G³ 12S¹ - 20S⁴ 16S¹
DALE PARK	--/104	Tinkler N	16G³ 20G⁴ - 18Y³ 18S¹
DALKEY SOUND	136/ --	Reveley Mrs G	20G³ 20Y¹ 22G¹ 25G¹ 24Y¹ - 22M¹ 26M¹ 25M² 33G² 24Y¹
DALLISTON	--/ 94	Walwyn Mrs F	- 16G² 16Y¹
DAMERS CAVALRY	111/ --	Lee R	- 24M² 26G³ 24G³ 26M¹
DAN MARINO	90/ --	Pipe M C	- 24G¹ 18Y³
DANCING LEGEND	--/ 66	Parkes J	- 16Y² 16S³ 17G² 16W³ 16Y¹
DANCING NORTH	--/ --	Allan R	- 16F³ 20F¹
DANCING OATS	--/ 96	Bailey K C	16W³ - 16M² 22G¹
DANCING PADDY	--/105	C-Brown K O	- 16Y² 17S¹ 18Y¹ 16Y³ 16G³ 18G³
DANCING RIVER	105/ --	Stephenson W A	16M² 16M³ - 16F² 20M¹ 20F² 17M² 20M¹ 17M⁴ 17G¹ 20M² 17F¹ 20M²
DANCING SENSATION	--/ --	Wharton J	- 16M³ 17M¹
DANNY CONNORS	--/ --	O'Neill J J	20Y¹ 20G¹ 16Y³ 21Y³ 20Y³ 18S⁴ 25Y¹ - 20G¹
DANNY HARROLD	130/ --	Pitman Mrs J	16G² 21G² - 20S¹ 20G³ 20G² 24G³ 24M¹ 20G²
DANTE'S VIEW	--/106	Hedger P R	- 16M¹ 16M²
DANZA HEIGHTS	--/ --	Reveley Mrs G	- 16F¹ 18F¹
DARA DOONE	--/132	Akehurst R	16G¹ 16G¹ 17S¹ 16G³ 16S¹ 20S² - 16G² 16S² 20Y¹ 20G¹ 20G³
DARI SOUND	--/ 89	FitzGerald J G	- 16M¹ 16G³
DARING CLASS	--/ 69	Rodford P R	- 16M¹
DARK DAWN	--/ --	Stephenson W A	- 20Y² 20G¹
DARK HONEY	--/102	Dow S	- 24G¹ 21G¹ 22G³ 21G²
DAT TRAIN	96/ --	Pitman Mrs J	- 20Y³ 18Y² 20M² 24G¹ 18G³
DAUNOU	--/ 99	Christian S	- 16M¹ 16G² 16G³ 16G³ 20W²
DAVID'S DUKY	125/ --	Reid A S	- 18Y⁴ 29G³ 29G¹ 33G¹
DAWADAR	--/102	Tinkler N	- 20M¹ 24G¹ 20G¹ 20G²
DAWSON CITY	--/145	Easterby M H	16G² 16M¹ 16M¹ 16G³ - 16G³ 16M² 16Y² 20Y¹ 20G² 20G² 20S¹
DAYS OF THUNDER	--/ --	White J	- 16G¹ 16G²
DE VALERA	--/ --	Bentley W	- 16F¹ 16F³ 16F³ 20M² 16G³ 24M¹
DEADLINE	82/ --	Leigh J P	16Y² 20G¹ 17Y² 22Y² 16Y³ - 20S³ 24G¹ 18G³
DEADLY CHARM	117/ --	Nicholson D	- 16G² 16G¹ 16G¹ 16G² 16M² 16M² 20M³ 20M³ 21G² 19M¹
DEB'S BALL	--/130	Moffatt D	17F¹ 16M¹ 16Y² 16F³ - 16M¹ 17S¹ 20G¹ 16G² 16Y³ 22M³ 22S²
DECCAN PRINCE	--/ 60	Tucker D R	- 17F¹
DEEP COLONIST	121/ --	Tate T P	- 24S² 25G⁴ 28Y¹ 24Y¹ 24S¹ 24G⁴
DEEP DARK DAWN	--/ 68	Upson John R	16M¹ 17F² 16F¹ 16F³ 20M² 20Y³ 16F³ - 16M¹ 17G¹ 16M² 17M¹
DEEP SENSATION	133/ --	Gifford J T	16G¹ 16G³ 18Y⁴ - 17G¹ 16M¹ 16G² 16G¹ 16G⁴
DEEP SPARTACUS	--/ --	Stephenson W A	21G² - 24G² 20Y¹
DEEPKY	--/ --	Pipe M C	- 16M² 16G³ 18W¹ 16G¹ 16G¹
DEER CREST	--/ --	Bulwer-Long W	- 25M¹ 24G² 24F³
DEERNESS SPOOK	--/ --	Jones T Thomso	17G¹ 16F¹ 16F¹ 16M² - 17F¹ 16M³
DELGANY RUN	--/ --	Knight Miss H	- 22G² 18G¹

	CHS/HUR	TRAINER	FORM RANGE
DEPLETE	--/ --	Nicholson D	16F³ - 20M¹
DERAB	--/ --	Sherwood S E	- 18Y³ 16G³ 16G² 20S² 16S¹
DERISBAY	124/ --	Pipe M C	- 17G¹ 18G² 17G¹ 17G³
DERRING BUD	--/ --	Smith D Murray	- 22W¹
DERRINORE	--/ --	Johnson J H	- 16F³ 20P¹
DERRYMORE BOY	89/102	Ffitch-Heyes J	- 18G¹ 25G²
DESPERATE	--/ --	Twiston-Davies	- 20Y¹ 24W² 22G¹ 24S²
DEXTRA DOVE	--/104	Hobbs P J	- 16M¹ 16G³ 16G¹
DIAMOND CUT	--/125	Pipe M C	- 16M² 16G³ 17G¹ 16M² 18M¹ 17G¹ 16G¹ 16M¹ 16M¹
DIAMOND FORT	--/ --	Shorey D J	25S³ - 25Y¹
DIANES DESTINY	103/ --	Upson John R	17F¹ 24G¹ 24Y¹ - 24F² 24M¹ 24M² 22G² 20G³
DINNER SUIT	--/ --	Grainger Mrs P	20M² - 25P¹
DIRECT	103/ --	Edwards J A C	- 24S¹
DIRECT INTEREST	82/ --	Smith Denys	20P² 24F³ 16M¹ 20G³ 20G³ 20P² - 17P¹ 16M¹ 25S¹ 20P³ 16M¹ 20P³ 20G² 24M² 24G³ 24F³
DIRECTOR'S CHOICE	--/100	Carter W	- 20M¹
DIVINE CHARGER	83/ --	Leadbetter S J	16Y⁴ - 17G¹ 16M⁴ 16M⁴
DIZZY	--/108	Monteith P	- 16G² 16Y¹ 16G² 16Y¹ 16Y¹ 16G¹ 16G¹
DJEBEL PRINCE	--/ 81	Egerton C R	- 16G² 16G¹ 17Y³
DO BE BRIEF	100/ --	Pitman Mrs J	16G³ 24G² 24Y⁴ 24Y¹ - 21G¹ 20G¹
DOCKLANDS EXPRESS	165/ --	Bailey K C	24G² 24G¹ 25G³ 24Y¹ 29G¹ 22G¹ - 24G² 26G³ 24G² 20G⁵ 24M¹ 26G³ 36Y⁴
DODGER DICKINS	--/ 92	Hollinshead R	- 24M¹ 24M² 22G³
DOLIKOS	--/ 84	Jefferson J M	- 18S¹
DOMAIN	--/ 80	Weaver R J	- 16M¹ 16W¹
DON KEYDROP	93/ --	Sanders Miss B	- 22W³ 24W² 24W¹ 26M³
DON VALENTINO	--/ --	Pitman Mrs J	- 21S¹ 16G¹
DONNA DEL LAGO	--/ 87	Casey T	22F¹ - 21M¹ 20F¹
DONTPUSHME	78/ --	Ellison B	- 16M² 16M³ 16G¹
DOOLAR	--/ 95	Dalton P T	- 16M¹ 16M⁴ 16Y² 16G²
DOONLOUGHAN	101/ --	Balding G B	20M² - 20M² 19M² 18F² 18G² 21F² 26G¹ 24G⁴ 20G² 18G¹ 26F¹
DORMERS DELIGHT	--/ 57	Pipe M C	- 16M² 17Y¹ 20G³
DORNVALLEY LAD	76/ --	Garraton D T	20F² - 17F¹ 16F³
DOUBLE SILK	--/ --	Wilkins R C	- 25G² 25G² 24G¹ 25Y¹
DOUBLE TRICKS	--/ 85	Burchell D	24M⁴ - 26S² 25G³ 24G¹ 20W³
DR BULASCO	--/ 86	Smith D Murray	- 16W¹ 18W³ 16W²
DR ROCKET	--/ 96	Dickin R	16G¹ 16G⁴ 16S³ 16Y³ 17H² 16G¹ 16G¹ 16M³ 16G³ 17S² 16Y¹ 16G⁴ 16Y² 17H³
DREAMCOAT	--/ --	Hobbs P J	- 20M¹
DRIVING FORCE	--/ --	McCourt M	17M³ 16F² 17M¹ 18G² 16G² 16W¹ 20W¹ 22W¹ 22W¹ 20G² - 16M¹ 19F¹ 21F³
DUAL IMAGE	--/ --	FitzGerald J G	12S³ 16S¹ 16M¹ - 16G¹ 16G³
DUBALEA	80/ --	Haldane J S	16S³ - 17G³ 16G² 16F¹ 17F³
DUBIOUS JAKE	100/ --	Woodhouse R D	20S² 20S¹ 25S² 25S³ - 28Y² 24S³ 32Y¹ 24Y²
DUBLIN FLYER	--/ 99	Forster Capt T	- 22Y¹ 25G¹
DUHARRA	--/121	Elsworth D R C	- 16Y³ 16G¹ 16G²
DUKE OF MONMOUTH	--/146	Sherwood S E	- 16Y¹ 16G³ 16Y³ 16G¹
DUN GAY LASS	--/ --	Claxton Mrs P	26G² 24M¹ - 24Y¹
DUNBRODY ABBEY	--/ --	Barons D H	- 24F¹

	CHS/HUR	TRAINER	FORM RANGE
DUNCAN	--/ --	Saunders Miss	$20Y^3$ $24S^2$ $25Y^2$ - $22G^1$ $25G^2$ $20M^1$
DUNRAVEN ROYAL	--/ --	Curtis R	$27G^2$ $27S^2$ $28Y^2$ $26S^1$ - $26F^2$
DURHAM EDITION	--/ --	Stephenson W A	$24G^1$ $24G^4$ $25G^4$ $36Y^6$ $29G^6$ $26G^4$ - $24F^2$ $30G^1$
DUSTY MILLER	--/133	Sherwood S E	$16M^1$ $16G^2$ $16G^1$ $16S^2$ $20G^2$ - $21G^2$ $16S^3$ $16G^1$
DUTCH BLUES	--/ 76	Austin Mrs S M	- $16Y^1$
EASBY MANDRINA	--/ 87	Kettlewell S E	- $16G^1$ $17G^1$ $16Y^1$
EAST RIVER	77/ --	Balding G B	$22M^1$ $20M^2$ $22S^3$ - $20G^1$ $24G^3$ $24G^2$ $24M^3$ $26G^4$ $25M^4$ $21F^3$ $24F^4$ $20F^4$
EASTER LEE	87/ --	Dufosse J W	$16S^2$ $20F^1$ $24M^3$ - $16Y^3$ $20G^2$ $26F^2$
EASTERN DESTINY	--/ --	Griffith Mrs J	$25Y^1$ $24S^3$ - $19G^1$ $25S^3$ $24G^3$
EASTERN MAGIC	--/ 82	Akehurst J	- $16W^2$ $16W^2$ $16M^1$ $16W^2$
EASTSHAW	132/ --	Forster Capt T	$20G^1$ $20Y^1$ $20G^2$ - $21M^1$ $25G^3$ $20M^4$ $20M^1$ $25G^2$ $20G^3$
EASY BUCK	--/118	Gaselee N A	$16G^1$ $16G^2$ - $16Y^1$ $16G^1$ $18G^2$ $16G^4$ $16M^3$
EBONY GALE	--/ --	Pitman Mrs J	- $20Y^2$ $16G^3$ $24S^1$ $25G^3$
EBONY SWELL	98/ --	Campion S W	$22G^1$ - $24G^4$ $24G^1$ $24G^2$ $18G^1$ $18G^2$
ECOSSAIS DANSEUR	--/ 90	Spearing J L	- $16G^3$ $16M^1$ $16M^1$ $16M^1$
EDBERG	130/ --	Johnson J H	$16G^1$ $16G^2$ $16Y^3$ $20G^2$ $16G^1$ $16Y^2$ $16G^2$ $20M^4$ $16M^1$ $20G^2$ $24Y^2$ - $17G^1$ $16G^2$
EGYPT MILL PRINCE	--/126	Pitman Mrs J	$16G^1$ $16G^1$ $20Y^5$ - $16G^2$ $16G^1$ $16M^1$ $16G^3$
EIGHT SPRINGS	111/ --	Pipe M C	$20G^1$ - $20M^1$
ELDER PRINCE	--/121	Easterby M H	$16G^1$ $16Y^1$ $16Y^1$ $16S^1$ $16Y^1$ $16G^1$ $16Y^1$ $16Y^3$ - $16Y^1$ $17M^4$ $16G^2$ $20G^4$
ELFAST	135/ --	Webber J	- $16G^2$ $16M^2$ $16S^3$ $16G^2$ $16G^1$ $20G^1$ $16S^2$ $22M^3$
EMERALD SUNSET	--/100	Davison A R	$20G^1$ - $20G^1$ $24G^1$ $25G^1$ $22G^3$ $24G^3$
EMERITUS	--/ --	Bentley W	$16M^3$ $20Y^2$ - $20M^2$ $24F^1$ $20F^1$
EMSEE-H	103/ --	Murphy F	$16G^3$ $20Y^2$ $22Y^3$ $16G^2$ $20G^3$ - $22F^2$ $20M^1$ $24M^2$ $16G^3$ $17G^2$ $17M^1$ $16G^1$ $16Y^1$
ENBORNE LAD	--/100	Enright G P	$24S^3$ - $21Y^1$
ENFANT DU PARADIS	--/ 69	Evans P D	- $16G^1$
ENSHARP	88/ --	Leigh J P	- $17M^3$ $17M^2$ $16F^4$ $17G^2$ $16M^1$
ENTERTAINMENT PARK	--/ 55	Preece B	$16F^3$ - $16M^1$ $22W^3$
ERIC'S TRAIN	--/ 76	Pitman Mrs J	- $16M^1$ $16M^2$
ERME EXPRESS	--/ --	Retter Mrs J G	- $26G^1$
EROSTIN FLOATS	--/ --	Upson John R	$25G^2$ $24F^1$ - $26M^3$ $22M^1$
ERRANT KNIGHT	109/ --	Pipe M C	- $16G^1$ $20G^2$ $20S^1$ $20S^1$ $21G^1$ $20G^1$
ESPY	137/ --	Brooks C P E	$20M^1$ $20G^2$ $24Y^1$ $20S^4$ $24G^3$ - $20M^1$ $25M^1$ $24G^2$
EVENING RAIN	93/ --	Hodges R J	$19G^3$ $20W^3$ $17H^1$ $17Y^2$ $19G^1$ $17F^1$ - $17M^2$ $16G^2$ $16G^2$ $17H^2$ $16S^3$ $17G^2$ $17M^1$ $16G^3$
EVER SMILE	--/ --	Pipe M C	- $19F^1$ $20M^1$ $17F^2$
EVERALDO	--/141	Henderson N J	- $21G^1$ $24S^1$ $25Y^3$ $20G^2$
EXPENSIVE LARK	--/ --	Smith D E S	- $24G^2$ $24M^1$
EXPLOSIVE SPEED	--/103	Hammond M D	- $16G^3$ $20M^2$ $16G^2$ $16G^2$ $16G^1$ $16M^1$
FAARIS	--/ --	Grissell D M	$19F^4$ $20M^1$ - $20M^2$ $20G^1$ $20G^4$

	CHS/HUR	TRAINER	FORM RANGE
FACILITY LETTER	--/ 93	Moore G M	16G² 16F² 16M¹ 16F¹ - 16F³ 20F² 20G² 16G³ 16G¹
FACT OR FICTION	--/ --	Sanders Miss B	- 18W¹ 20W¹
FAIR CROSSING	--/102	Brooks C P E	- 16G³ 16Y² 16M² 21G¹
FAIR PLUME	--/ --	Barons D H	- 16M¹
FAIR PROSPECT	--/ --	Hobbs P J	16S¹ 20S² - 20M¹
FAIRFIELDS CONE	--/ 85	Dickin R	- 20G³ 18G¹
FAIRWAYS ON TARGET	--/111	Reveley Mrs G	16F¹ 16G² 16G¹ - 20M¹ 20G² 20Y² 21G¹
FALCON FLIGHT	--/104	Simpson R	- 16G¹ 16G¹ 16Y² 16M¹ 17G¹ 16G²
FALSE ECONOMY	106/ --	Edwards J A C	22Y³ 24G³ - 26G³ 24S³ 18G¹ 18G¹ 24G³ 25G³ 24S¹ 25G²
FAMILY LINE	--/ 82	Perratt Miss L	- 16G³ 16H¹ 18Y² 16Y² 16M³
FANLIGHT	--/ 93	Akehurst R	- 16Y² 16Y¹
FAR OVER STRUY	--/ --	Sherwood O	16G³ 20G² 20G² 16M¹ - 16M² 20G² 16G¹ 20G¹ 20M² 17G³ 16G¹
FAR SENIOR	120/ --	Bailey K C	21M¹ - 21F¹ 25M¹ 20G¹ 20G² 25M¹ 24G⁴ 20G³ 20G⁴ 25M⁴
FAR TOO LOUD	--/ 90	Gaselee N A	16M³ 17S² - 21G¹ 19G³ 22Y³ 22W² 17G³ 16G¹
FARMLEA BOY	115/ --	Balding G B	19G¹ 20G⁴ 24G¹ 20G¹ 24G¹ 20G² 21Y³ 20G³ 20M¹ 24M¹ - 22G² 24G² 24M² 20M² 25G³ 24G³ 25G² 25M¹
FARRANRORY	--/ --	Warner Peter	- 25M¹ 24M⁴ 26G²
FAST CRUISE	85/ --	Owen Jun E H	16G³ 16S¹ - 16G¹ 20M³ 20Y³ 20S³ 20G³ 24G¹
FAST THOUGHTS	--/ 95	Gandolfo D R	16Y² 16Y³ 16G¹ - 17M¹ 16S² 21G¹
FATHER JOHN	--/ --	Muggeridge M P	- 19F³ 26F¹ 25F² 24M²
FATHER PADDY	79/ --	Nash C T	- 16M³ 17M³ 16M⁴ 16M⁴ 16G² 16M¹ 20M³
FEARSOME	--/ 82	Wonnacott Mrs	18F³ 16F³ 17G² - 17S² 17S¹ 17H¹ 16G³ 17S² 18G² 18F³
FEATHER YOUR NEST	97/ --	Bailey K C	- 16Y³ 16G¹ 16G² 16G³ 16G²
FENCE JUDGE	100/ --	Forster Capt T	25Y¹ 25Y² - 26G³ 25G² 25G¹ 26G²
FENTON LAKE	--/ --	P-Gordon G A	- 16M¹ 17M² 16M³
FENWICK	--/ 83	Stephenson W A	- 16H¹ 20S³ 20Y³
FESTIVAL FANCY	--/ 95	Reveley Mrs G	- 22G¹ 22S² 25M³ 25G¹
FETTUCINE	--/104	Stephenson W A	- 24G³ 24F³ 24H² 24Y³ 24G¹ 24Y² 25M²
FIBREGUIDE TECH	--/ --	Kinsey Mrs T R	24M³ 22M² 20S² - 25M¹
FIDDLE A LITTLE	97/ --	Murphy F	20Y³ - 16G³ 24G⁴ 20G² 20F¹ 20G¹
FIDDLERS PIKE	--/ --	Henderson Mrs	26M² - 25Y¹ 25Y¹ 24G² 26Y²
FIDDLERS THREE	102/ --	Forster Capt T	20S³ - 20G³ 26G¹ 26G¹
FIDWAY	--/150	Jones T Thomso	16M¹ 16G¹ 16G² - 16M⁴ 16M⁴ 16M⁴ 16G¹ 16G¹ 16G⁴ 16G³
FIEFDOM	--/ 86	Storey W	- 20M⁴ 16G⁴ 20G¹ 20F³ 20F³
FIERCE	--/ 82	Jenkins J R	- 16F¹ 18G²
FIFTH AMENDMENT	123/ --	Pitman Mrs J	16G² 22Y³ 21Y¹ 24Y¹ - 24G³ 25G¹ 20Y² 21M² 24G⁴ 24Y¹ 24M³ 25G⁴
FIFTH ATTEMPT	--/ --	Vergette Mrs G	22Y¹ 21G² - 18M¹
FIGHT TO WIN	--/112	Balding I A	- 16G² 17M¹ 20G¹ 21S³
FIGHTING CHRISTINE	--/ --	Stubbs Mrs L	- 16M¹ 17G²
FIGHTING FINISH	--/ --	Stephenson W A	20S⁴ 16S³ 16Y⁴ 20Y¹ 16H² 20G³ 20G² 24G⁴ 20F¹ - 20G¹

	CHS/HUR TRAINER	FORM RANGE
FIGHTING JESSICA	103/ -- Upson John R	20G¹ 19Y⁴ 25G¹ 24G² 25G³ 24Y³ 24G² - 25S³ 24Y³ 24G³ 24G¹ 22Y³ 20Y² 20S² 21G³ 18G¹ 26G³
FINAL CHANT	--/ -- Brydon D A D	25G¹ 24Y¹ 26S⁴ - 24Y² 26G¹ 24G¹
FINAL SPRING	--/ -- Warner Peter	21G⁴ - 22G² 24G² 18G³ 18Y² 24M³ 20G¹ 25P²
FINE WARRIOR	--/ 66 Clay W	20G³ - 16M² 20M² 20M³ 20M¹ 19F³ 22W³
FINELY BALANCED	--/ 97 Curtis R	- 19G² 22Y¹
FINGERS CROSSED	--/ 74 Brennan O	16F³ 20M³ 24G² 24F¹ - 24G¹ 20M² 28M² 21M² 22S³
FINO	--/ 98 Pitman Mrs J	- 16M¹ 20G² 21G² 22G² 24M¹
FIRE AT WILL	102/-- Forster Capt T	20S² 25Y¹ 24S² - 18Y² 25Y¹ 25Y²
FIRM PRICE	--/109 Reveley Mrs G	24G² 24G² 25M¹ - 22M² 26G¹ 24Y² 27M³
FIRST LORD	--/101 Aconley Mrs V	24W¹ - 24M² 26S¹ - 24W¹ 24G² 24G³ 24Y¹ 25G² 25M²
FIRST STAGE	--/ 89 O'Shea J G M	16G³ - 17F¹ 17F¹ 16Y¹ 20F²
FISHKI	--/116 Hammond M D	16S¹ 16H³ 20S¹ - 24Y¹ 24Y²
PIT FOR FIRING	98/-- Elsworth D R C	- 25G² 20M³ 21G⁴ 25F² 20M²
PIT THE BILL	--/ 82 Wainwright J S	- 16G⁴ 16M¹ 16M¹
FIVE LAMPS	--/107 Dickin R	16Y³ 20W³ 18W² 20W¹ 16Y¹ 16G³ 20G³ - 16M² 18W² 16S² 16M² 16G¹ 16G¹ 16G² 16Y¹ 16G³
FIVELEIGH BUILDS	--/106 Upson John R	- 21G³ 24G³ 20S¹ 18G¹ 24G¹ 24M³
FLAKEY DOVE	--/130 Price R J	16Y³ 20S⁴ 21G¹ 17Y³ - 16S¹ 20Y² 17M¹ 16S² 16G¹ 16G¹ 16G³
FLASHTHECASH	--/ -- Balding G B	- 22F¹
FLASS VALE	--/ 88 Fairhurst T	- 16F³ 20F¹ 18G³ 20M² 22M²
FLEURCONE	--/ 98 White K	16F³ 16M² 16G³ 16F³ - 16G³ 21G¹ 20M³
FLIGHT HILL	115/ -- Reveley Mrs G	16M¹ 16Y³ - 16M² 20G² 20M² 20G² 20G¹ 20G¹ 20G¹ 20G³
FLIGHTY GUEST	--/ 66 Reveley Mrs G	- 16F² 18F² 16G²
FLORET	--/104 Pipe M C	- 17M¹ 20Y² 17G² 16G¹ 19M¹
FLOWING RIVER	--/ 90 Allan R	- 16G¹ 16M¹ 16G²
FLOWN	--/140 Henderson N J	- 16M¹ 16G¹ 16Y⁴
FLOYD	--/ -- Elsworth D R C	26M¹ 16G² 24Y¹ - 24M¹
FLY THE WIND	--/ -- Pipe M C	- 20M¹ 18G¹ 26F¹
FLYER'S NAP	--/102 Alner R H	- 24S² 24Y¹ 24S¹
FLYING FERRET	--/ -- Pipe M C	- 17M⁴ 19M¹
FLYING SPEED	--/111 Pipe M C	- 17M¹ 16S⁴ 16G¹ 17F¹ 19F¹
FOCUS ON POSTER	82/-- Webber J	20Y³ 20G⁴ 20M² - 24M¹
FOGAR	84/ -- White J	- 16M² 16G¹ 17F²
FOODBROKER FLYER	--/ -- Akehurst R	- 20G² 20G¹
FOR HEAVEN'S SAKE	--/ 95 Preece B	- 20F¹ 20M² 26F¹ 22G³
FOR THE GRAIN	130/ -- Nicholson D	16G¹ 16M¹ - 16G³ 16G² 16S² 16G¹ 20M¹
FORBEARANCE	--/ -- Reveley Mrs G	- 16M¹
FORCED MARCH	--/ -- Balding G B	- 18G¹
FOREST FAWN	--/ 79 Wheeler E A	- 16G¹ 16G³ 16G³ 17S¹ 16G² 16G²
FOREST SUN	--/148 Balding G B	- 16Y³ 16G³ 24M¹ 25G⁶ 20G³
FORWARD GLEN	--/108 Stephenson W A	- 16F¹ 20G² 20F¹ 24Y² 22M³

	CHS/HUR	TRAINER	FORM RANGE
FOUR TRIX	128/ --	Richards G W	22G⁴ 25S³ 32S³ - 20G⁴ 22S¹
FOURTH IN LINE	--/ --	Edwards J A C	- 16S¹
FOX CHAPEL	--/105	FitzGerald J G	- 16G¹ 16Y³ 16G¹ 17G¹
FOYLE FISHERMAN	125/ --	Gifford J T	16S³ 20Y¹ - 26G² 25M¹ 24Y¹ 24M⁴
FRAGRANT DAWN	122/ --	Elsworth D R C	16M⁴ 16M⁴ - 16M¹ 16G⁴ 16M¹ 16G⁵
FRANCISCAN	--/ 87	Preece B	16S¹ 22W² 20W¹ - 20Y¹ 25F³
FREE EDUCATION	--/ --	Hedger P R	- 16G¹
FREE FORM	--/ 64	Weedon C	- 18F³ 16F¹
FREE MINX	--/ 85	Aconley Mrs V	- 20W¹ 22W³
FREE NATIVE	--/ --	Reveley Mrs G	- 16G¹
FREELINE FINISHING	116/ --	Henderson N J	- 16Y¹ 16G² 16G¹ 20S² 16G³
FREEZING	--/ 65	Simpson R	- 16G¹ 17M¹ 16G² 20W²
FRESH-MINT	--/ 90	Hobbs P J	- 19G² 20W² 17Y¹
FRISKNEY DALE LAD	--/ 80	Reveley Mrs G	16F² - 16M¹ 16Y³
FRONT PAGE	--/ 80	Akehurst J	16S¹ - 16S¹ 16M⁴
FROSTY RECEPTION	--/ 92	Baker J H	20M³ 17F¹ - 17F¹ 17F¹ 20W² 20W³
FU'S LADY	--/ --	Pipe M C	16F¹ 20M⁶ 19G³ 24G⁴ 16G¹ 16G¹ - 16M¹
FULL MONTY	--/ 98	Smith Denys	20F¹ 16Y³ 16S² 18W² - 16S³ 22W² 18W² 20G² 20Y¹ 16G² 16M² 17M¹
FUN MONEY	--/ --	Wilson A J	- 16M¹ 16G³
FUNAMBULIEN	--/ --	Pipe M C	- 17M¹ 16G³ 17M²
FURRY KNOWE	102/ --	Walwyn Mrs F	16M¹ 16M³ 17M¹ - 20G³ 20G² 22S² 22M¹
FUSSY LADY	--/ 80	McKie Mrs I	16G³ - 16M¹ 16Y³ 21M³
FUTURE KING	--/ 86	Jarvis A P	- 17M³ 16H³ 17G¹ 18G³
G W SUPERSTAR	--/ --	Balding G B	22G² 24G² 22G³ - 24Y² 25G¹
G'IME A BUZZ	--/ --	Pipe M C	- 16G¹
GALAXY HIGH	--/115	Leach P	16S² - 16Y² 16G² 16M² 16G¹ 16S² 17Y¹
GALE AGAIN	125/ --	Stephenson W A	- 19M² 22M¹ 16G² 20M¹ 20G³ 16F¹ 16Y² 20M¹
GALLANT EFFORT	--/ 91	Dow S	- 16G² 16G³ 16M⁴ 20W¹ 20W³ 18W¹ 18W¹
GALLATEEN	--/102	Richards G W	- 16G² 16G² 16G² 16G² 16M¹ 20G² 16H² 16M⁴ 16G¹
GALLOWAY RAIDER	--/ 86	Smith Denys	20G² 18Y² 16M¹ 20M² 16G³ 20M³ - 17G³ 16F¹ 20M² 27F² 24G³ 17M¹
GALWAY STAR	--/126	Pipe M C	- 17M² 16G² 17F¹ 16G¹
GAMBLING ROYAL	132/ --	Nicholson D	- 24G¹ 25Y¹ 26G¹ 24S¹ 25G¹ 25G³
GANGER CAMP	--/ --	White J	- 18F¹
GARDA'S GOLD	--/ 82	Dickin R	16Y³ - 16G² 17S¹ 16S¹
GAY RUFFIAN	--/133	Burchell D	20G¹ 20S² 21G³ 20S¹ - 16G¹ 20S⁴ 16G²
GEE-A	113/ --	Hubbard G A	20F¹ 20F¹ 22G³ 16Y⁴ 20Y⁴ 20Y³ - 18G⁴ 20G³ 18G³ 22Y¹ - 25G² 25G⁴ 24G¹ 25G³
GENERAL HARMONY	85/ --	Jennings Miss	
GENERAL HIGHWAY	--/ --	Chugg J	24G² 25Y¹ 25Y² - 26G¹ 25Y⁴
GENERAL JAMES	--/ --	Gifford J T	20F³ 16M¹ 16G³ 16G³ 16G¹ 16G¹ - 16G² 20G¹
GENERAL MERCHANT	85/ --	Hodges R J	24G⁴ 19Y¹ - 17S² 20G² 21G² 18Y¹ 20Y³ 17M¹ 25G⁴ 26M¹
GENERAL PERSHING	111/ --	Richards G W	16S³ 20Y² 24M¹ 24G² 20F¹ 20M¹ 24M² - 16M¹
GEOSTAR	--/ --	Leigh J P	16G¹ 16M¹ 17M¹ 20G³ 20Y⁴ -

	CHS/HUR	TRAINER	FORM RANGE
			20M¹
GINA'S CHOICE	--/ 66	Pritchard P A	16F³ - 17M² 16F¹ 16M²
GINA-DIANE	--/ --	Dow S	- 20W² 16M⁴ 16W¹ 16W¹ 16W¹
GIPSY DAWN	--/ --	Barwell C R	16G¹ 16G⁴ - 16G² 20G² 20G¹
GIVEMEACALL	--/ --	Tinkler N	- 16M² 16M¹ 17M¹
GLADTOGETIT	--/ --	Gandolfo D R	22Y³ 24Y² 20S³ 20S² 20S² - 22G¹ 24G¹
GLEBELANDS GIRL	--/ 67	Rowe R	18G² 16G¹ 16G¹ 17Y² - 25G³ 17H³ 18G² 18Y³ 24Y³
GLEN CHERRY	98/ --	Forster Capt T	17H³ - 22G² 24M¹ 25G³ 20M¹ 25G³
GLEN LOCHAN	--/ --	Jemmeson J D	- 25G¹
GLEN RUN	--/ --	Layland R	- 16G³ 16Y¹
GLENBROOK D'OR	106/ --	Wilson A J	21G² - 25S⁴ 26G¹ 26S² 24G⁴
GLENGOOLE	--/ --	Smart B	- 19F¹ 21G² 21M³
GLENGRIFFIN	--/ 85	Gifford J T	- 21Y² 22M¹
GLOVE PUPPET	--/ 89	Balding G B	23Y² - 19G¹
GO TALLY-HO	--/ 70	O'Neill J J	- 16G³ 16F² 16G² 16M³
GOLD MEDAL	--/111	Pipe M C	- 16M² 19M³ 16S¹ 16G¹ 17Y¹ 16G¹
GOLDEN ARCTIC	--/111	Henderson N J	- 18G³ 21G³ 25G¹ 20S²
GOLDEN ASSET	--/ --	Reveley Mrs G	- 24M¹
GOLDEN CELTIC	--/120	Knight Miss H	20G¹ 20S² 20S³ 20G¹ 20M⁴ - 20G² 20G¹ 20G⁴
GOLDEN COAST	--/ --	Elsworth D R C	- 16W¹
GOLDEN FREEZE	139/ --	Pitman Mrs J	22G² - 19Y¹ 20G⁴ 20M³ 20G³ 20Y³ 20G² 22S³
GOLDEN GUNNER	--/ 83	McCourt M	- 17M¹ 16W¹ 16Y¹
GOLDEN MOSS	--/110	Ffitch-Heyes J	- 22G² 22G¹ 20G¹
GOOD FOR A LOAN	--/ 88	Lee R	- 16M¹ 16G² 16G¹
GOOD PROFILE	--/122	Moore G M	- 16Y¹ 16Y¹ 16G¹ 16G¹ 16G¹ 16Y³
GOOD TONIC	130/ --	Etherington T	16G³ 20S¹ 20S³ 20G² 20G² 17Y³ 20M¹ 21G² - 20G¹ 20G¹ 20G³ 22G⁴ 20G² 20G¹ 20G³
GOOD WORD	--/ --	Vigors Mrs Fio	- 20Y¹
GOODSHOT RICH	102/ --	Brooks C P E	- 16Y³ 20G² 21G³ 24Y¹ 18Y³
GOSPEL ROCK	--/100	Calver P	- 16M¹ 20G³
GRACE CARD	--/120	Reveley Mrs G	- 22H¹ 26G² 24G¹ 24Y¹
GRAN ALBA	--/159	Hannon R	- 16G² 16Y¹ 16M¹ 16G²
GRAND FRERE	--/ 90	Pipe M C	19M³ - 16M² 17M¹ 17G¹ 17F¹ 16G²
GRANGE BRAKE	--/ 85	Twiston-Davies	16M¹ 16G² - 22G¹ 20Y¹ 20S³ 24G³
GRANNY PRAY ON	90/ --	Balding G B	21S² 21Y² - 19G⁴ 17S³ 26S¹ 25Y³
GRANVILLE AGAIN	--/160	Pipe M C	20G² 16Y¹ 16Y¹ 16Y¹ 16Y² 16S¹ - 20M¹ 16Y¹ 16G¹ 16G¹
GRANVILLEWATERFORD	121/ --	Sherwood S E	16G¹ 16G² 16Y⁴ 20G¹ 20G¹ - 20G² 20G¹ 24G³ 20G²
GREAT ASPECT	--/ 99	Rowe R	16H³ - 16Y¹ 16Y² 18Y³
GREAT FUN	--/ 66	Ramsden Mrs J	- 16S³ 16M¹
GREAT MILL	--/111	Bailey K C	16M² 20M¹ 16Y² 20Y⁴ 22G² 20G² 19F¹ 22M¹ - 20M² 23M³ 18G¹ 21G³
GREAT POKEY	82/ --	Corner A S	- 16M¹
GREAT SALING	--/ 95	Jordan P	- 16S¹
GREEN ISLAND	90/ --	Dunn A J K	- 17F¹ 17G² 17F¹ 17F¹ 17S² 17G³
GREEN SILVER	99/ --	Lungo L	20G³ 16F² 22G² 20Y¹ 20W³ 20Y³ - 24G¹ 25M¹ 24Y¹ 20Y³

	CHS/HUR	TRAINER	FORM RANGE
GREEN WILLOW	123/ --	Gifford J T	17G² - 16G² 16S¹
GREEN'S CASSATT	--/ --	Brisbourne W M	- 16W¹ 16W²
GREEN'S VAN GOYEN	--/109	Akehurst R	- 16Y¹ 16G¹ 16M² 20Y² 16S³
GREENHEART	130/ --	Stephenson W A	16M¹ 20G⁴ 16M¹ 16G¹ 16G⁴
			17G⁴ 17M¹ 16G⁴ 20F¹ 17G⁴ -
			16M¹ 16G¹ 16G² 16G¹ 16Y⁴
			16G⁴ 17M²
GREENHILL RAFFLES	97/ --	Hobbs P J	16Y³ - 16W¹ 17F¹ 16G¹
GREENHILLS PRIDE	92/ --	Jenkins J R	- 18M² 20F¹ 16G⁴ 20Y² 20W¹
			18Y³
GREY MERLIN	--/ 79	Taylor Mrs S	16Y¹ 16S³ 16Y³ - 18S¹ 16Y³
			18Y³
GREY MINSTREL	99/ --	Smith Denys	- 16G³ 16Y² 16G¹ 16Y³ 20H¹
			20H¹ 25G²
GREY RUM	--/ --	Lee R	16M² 16M⁴ - 16G¹ 19Y³
GREY SONATA	--/ 79	Popham C L	17F¹ 16F³ 17F³ 17M³ 20W³
			18W³ 20W² 17Y² - 17F² 17G¹
GREYFRIARS BOBBY	--/103	Retter Mrs J G	- 20G⁴ 22G² 16G¹ 19Y²
GREYSBY	85/ --	Brennan O	17Y³ - 24G² 22G¹ 24G⁴
GRONDOLA	--/ 73	Burchell D	17G¹ - 16M² 16W² 16W¹ 16S³
			16G³
GROOMSMAN	--/ 99	McKie Mrs I	18W¹ - 25M² 22W² 22W¹ 24W²
			22W³
GUEST PLAYER	--/ 79	Naughton T	16W¹ - 20F² 17S² 16Y² 16M¹
GUIBURN'S NEPHEW	121/ --	Hobbs P J	20M¹ 17M³ 20M² 20Y¹ 16M² -
			20G² 20G³ 17G¹ 20G⁴ 20G⁴
			25G²
GUILD STREET	--/ --	Jones Paul	- 20M¹
GULSHA	--/ --	Twiston-Davies	17G³ 16Y¹ 17H¹ 20Y⁴ - 16G¹
GUNNER STREAM	90/ --	Holder R J	- 20M⁴ 25M¹
GUNNER'S FLIGHT	--/ --	Wellstead H	- 25G¹ 25G¹
GYMCRACK STARDOM	--/106	Easterby M H	- 16G¹ 20G²
GYMCRACK GAMBLE	--/ 75	Easterby M H	- 16S² 16M² 16G² 16G³ 16F¹
			16M²
GYMCRAK SOVEREIGN	--/ 98	Easterby M H	- 16G³ 16M² 16W² 16W¹ 16W¹
			16W¹ 18Y¹
HAGLER	--/ 89	Bousfield B	27M² - 16M² 16Y¹ 20M¹
HALF BROTHER	122/ --	Pitman Mrs J	20S³ 20G³ 21G¹ 22G³ - 20G³
			20Y³ 20G¹ 20S² 20G³
HALKOPOUS	--/130	Tompkins M H	- 16G¹ 16M¹ 16G² 16Y²
HALLOW FAIR	--/ --	Horgan C A	- 17F³ 16M¹
HANGOVER	--/120	Lee R	- 16G³ 16G¹ 16Y¹ 16G³ 16Y³
HARD STUFF	--/ --	Nicholson D	16M³ 16Y² - 16M⁴ 20G³ 20M¹
			16Y² 20G¹
HARD TO GET	--/ 70	Barraclough M	16G³ - 20M² 20M³ 20W³ 16G¹
			17G¹ 16G¹
HARD TO HOLD	--/ 86	Esden D	20G¹ 20Y³ 20M³ - 22G² 20M²
			21M³ 20S¹ 24G³ 21S²
HARLEY	--/ --	Eaton Miss J	20S⁴ - 24Y¹ 24M² 24S² 24S¹
HARPLEY	--/ 87	Kettlewell S E	- 16M² 16G¹ 17G² 20G² 24Y¹
			20F²
HARRY LIME	--/ 80	Pipe M C	17M² - 17M³ 22M¹
HASHAR	--/110	Elsworth D R C	- 16M¹ 16M³
HASTY DIVER	88/ --	Old J A B	24G³ 24Y¹ 25G² - 24M¹
HAWTHORN BLAZE	--/114	Elsworth D R C	17G¹ 16Y³ - 16G⁴ 16G¹ 21G¹
HAWWAR	--/ 70	King Mrs A L M	- 22W² 24W¹ 22W³
HE WHO DARES WINS	111/ --	Stephenson W A	24G² 24G² 24S² 24H² 24G¹
			24F² 24G² 26M² - 25F¹ 24M¹
			24G³ 28G² 28G⁴ 26S³ 25G²
			26G³ 24F¹ 24G² 24F²
HEADIN' ON	87/ --	Joynes Mrs P M	24M³ 22G¹ 22G³ 24M² 20M⁴

	CHS/HUR	TRAINER	FORM RANGE
			22M⁴ 16G⁴ - 17F⁴ 22F² 20F¹ 25M³ 20F³ 19F³
HEARD IT BEFORE	--/ 56	Hoad R P C	- 20M¹ 17G²
HEDGEHOPPER	--/ --	Weedon C	- 16W¹ 16G³
HELIOPSIS	--/ 90	Hammond M D	- 16Y² 16G² 16G¹ 16G² 18Y¹
HELMAR	--/ --	Jordan F	- 17S¹ 16M³
HENBURY HALL	--/ 79	Reveley Mrs G	- 16G¹ 16M³
HENRY MANN	135/ --	Christian S	20Y⁴ 24G¹ - 20Y¹ 20Y² 25G² 26Y²
HERE HE COMES	--/ --	Akehurst R	16S³ - 16G¹ 16G¹
HEY COTTAGE	120/ --	McCain D	20S² 24M⁴ - 20Y³ 20S² 20G¹ 20Y³
HEY JOE	--/ 69	Monteith P	- 20G¹
HI-RISE LADY	82/ --	Gaselee N A	22M⁴ - 25M¹
HICKELTON LAD	87/ --	Williams D L	21G⁴ 16M³ - 20M¹ 22M³ 16G³ 16M³ 16G⁴ 20G² 16M³
HIDDEN COVE	--/ --	Balding I A	- 16M¹ 16M¹
HIDDEN QUIVER	--/ --	Reveley Mrs G	- 16G¹
HIGH ALLTITUDE	--/ --	Moore G M	- 16G¹ 16H¹
HIGH BARON	--/ 93	Alner R H	- 16S² 16M¹
HIGH GRADE	--/ 95	Dow S	- 18G² 16G¹ 16G³ 18W¹ 20W¹ 18Y²
HIGH IMP	--/ --	Leach P	16M³ 16P³ 19M³ 16S³ 17M³ 17F³ - 17P¹ 17M⁴
HIGH MARINER	--/ 67	Burke K R	- 16Y¹ 16G³
HIGH PADRE	--/ 92	FitzGerald J G	- 20G¹
HIGHFIELD PRINCE	--/ --	O'Leary R	16P³ 16Y³ 17G¹ 16M³ 16M¹ 16P² - 16F³ 16M² 16P¹ 17M³ 16F⁴
HIGHLAND ECHO	--/ --	Edwards Mrs Jo	- 25G² 26P¹
HIGHLY DECORATED	--/ --	Johnson J H	- 16G¹
HILL BEAGLE	--/ 78	Clay W	16M¹ 16M² 16M² 16W² 19P² - 16M³ 20M² 18W² 20W³ 20W³ 16W¹
HIRAM B BIRDBATH	--/110	Glover J A	16P² 16W² 20W² 20W¹ 20W¹ 20W² 16W² - 16M² 20M¹ 20P¹ 20W²
HOGMANAY	--/ --	Casey R F	- 17F⁴ 16M¹
HOLD COURT	--/ 72	Callaghan N A	- 16W¹
HOLDENBY	--/103	FitzGerald J G	- 16M¹ 17M³
HOLT PLACE	--/103	Smith N A	20P¹ 17M² - 24M³ 22W³ 20W¹ 20W³
HOLTERMANN	100/ --	Clay Mrs L	- 16M¹ 16G⁴ 17G³ 16G¹ 17F⁴ 20G² 21P²
HOLY JOE	--/128	Wilson A J	22Y³ 25Y⁴ 20M³ - 21G² 24M³ 18F² 22S³
HOMME D'AFFAIRE	--/ --	O'Sullivan R J	20F¹ 21M⁴ 20G² 20G² - 22F¹ 21P¹
HONDEGHEM	--/ --	Elsey C W C	- 17M³ 16F¹ 16S¹
HONEST WORD	--/ --	Pipe M C	16Y¹ - 18Y¹
HORNBLOWER	--/ 90	Easterby M H	16G² 16S² - 20Y³ 20M² 17G¹ 20F² 20M³
HOTPLATE	123/ --	McCain D	20G² 26G² 26G¹ 28G¹ 32S⁴ - 20S³ 28G¹
HOUXTY LAD	91/ --	Charlton J I A	20G² 24G¹ - 25G¹
HOWE STREET	123/ --	Johnson J H	- 16M¹ 16G³ 20G⁴ 20G¹
HUGLI	--/ 96	Sherwood S E	16G³ 16G² 20M³ 19M¹ - 18M² 22M² 24M¹
HUMDECOLA	--/ --	Preece B	20W³ 25Y⁴ - 24G³ 24G³ 24M¹ 24P²
HUNTING GROUND	--/ 89	Harwood G	- 17F¹ 18F¹

	CHS/HUR	TRAINER	FORM RANGE
HUNTWORTH	125/ --	Pipe M C	24F¹ 24G³ 25M² 24M¹ 29M² 26S² 26M² 25M¹ - 25G³ 26G⁴ 26F² 26M¹
HURRICANE BLAKE	--/ --	Cantillon D	- 16W¹
HUSO	--/ 89	Haslam P C	- 16M¹ 16M¹ 22M¹
HYPNOTIST	--/ 93	Bentley W	- 16M³ 16M² 20G⁵ 16M² 17M² 20F² 16G³ 16Y¹ 20M³
I KID YOU NOT	95/ --	O'Neill J J	- 20G¹
IAMA ZULU	87/ --	Hobbs P J	17M³ 16M² 20M² 17M³ 16G³ - 16M² 24M² 21S⁴ 21M¹
IBN ZAMAN	--/ 57	Carey D N	- 17G¹
ICARUS	115/ --	Easterby M H	- 16M¹ 20G³ 20G¹ 17G¹ 16M³ 20G³ 20M⁴
IDA'S DELIGHT	124/ --	Charlton J I A	24G³ 24M² 20G² 20G² 20G² 24F² - 24F² 20G⁵ 20Y¹ 20M³ 20Y² 20M⁴ 24G³ 20G² 24G¹ 20G¹ 24M¹
ILEWIN	--/ 86	Jenkins J R	- 16M² 16G² 16G¹ 16W² 20G³ 18W² 18W² 16G¹ 16G¹ 16M¹
IMPERTAIN	82/ --	Cunningham T W	16G⁴ 20M¹ 16M⁴ 22F⁴ 20G⁴ 20F² 24M² - 24F² 24M³ 20G¹
IN THE SPOTLIGHT	--/ 71	Curtis R	- 18G¹ 18Y³ 20G³
INNOCENT PRINCESS	--/ 81	Barons D H	- 16G² 16G³ 19G² 19G³ 18F¹
INTEGRITY BOY	--/ 93	O'Leary R	16F¹ 16F² 17M³ 16M¹ 16M² 18G¹ 20Y² 20S² 20S¹ 20W² - 20F³ 22M² 20G¹ 24M² 20G² 22W³
INTERIM LIB	114/ --	Bradburne Mrs	21G² 22Y² 16H¹ 20G³ 17M⁴ 20G¹ 22F¹ 20G³ - 24M⁴ 16G¹ 20G² 16M³ 20Y¹ 17S¹ 16S² 16H² 22S⁴ 20G¹
INTERPRETATION	--/104	Henderson N J	- 16M³ 16G² 16M² 20M¹ 22G³
INTO THE FUTURE	--/ 62	Stringer A P	- 17F³ 16G¹ 17F¹
INTO THE GLEN	93/ --	Stephenson W A	21G³ 20Y³ - 24F² 24G³
INVASION	92/ --	Brennan O	22M¹ - 20G¹ 25G³
INVERINATE	--/ 95	Lungo L	- 24M³ 25M¹ 20S³ 20S¹ 24H³
INVERTIEL	--/ --	Monteith P	16G² - 16M¹
INVITE D'HONNEUR	--/ 81	Oliver Mrs S	- 16G³ 20G¹ 20W³
IRISH EMERALD	--/102	Bravery G C	- 16G³ 16G³ 16G¹ 16G¹ 16M¹
IRISH GENT	--/ 92	Stephenson W A	- 22M² 27M² 24G³ 24F¹
ISABEAU	--/103	Morgan K A	17M¹ - 16G² 22M¹ 20G³ 22G² 24M³ 18G² 16G³ 20M¹ 26S²
ISCA'S SON	--/ --	FitzGerald J G	- 16M¹
ISLAND JETSETTER	107/ --	FitzGerald J G	17M² 16F² 16F² 16G³ 17M¹ 16G² 16G¹ 16M¹ - 17F¹ 17F² 16Y¹ 16G¹ 16G²
ISOBAR	--/ 81	Chapman M C	25F² 17F³ 24G⁴ 24G⁴ 24M¹ 22M³ 21F¹ 21G³ - 25S⁴ 24M³ 25M¹ 19M²
ITALIAN TOUR	--/ 78	Plowright Mrs	20F¹ - 19M¹
ITS ALL VERY FINE	85/ --	Forster Capt T	19M² 20M¹ 22G² - 20M¹ 19M²
ITS NEARLY TIME	101/ --	Brackenbury Mr	22S² 22G² 22S¹ 21G² - 22G⁴ 21S² 16G¹ 16G³ 16S¹
IXOR	92/ --	Nash C T	- 24G² 24G² 24G⁴ 24G² 24G¹ 20Y¹
J BRAND	--/ 93	Moore J S	- 16W² 18Y¹ 16Y¹ 20G¹ 16G² 16Y²
JAAEZ	--/ --	Swinbank Mrs A	- 24G¹
JADIDH	--/ 77	Dawe Mrs J C	- 17G¹ 20M⁴ 22G¹ 24G²
JAILBREAKER	--/105	Millman B R	16G² 16G¹ - 16M² 18G¹ 22G⁴
JAKARRDI	--/105	Pitman Mrs J	16Y² - 16G¹

	CHS/HUR	TRAINER	FORM RANGE
JALINGO	--/ --	Makin P J	16S¹ - 16G¹
JAMES THE FIRST	--/ --	Nicholls P F	- 16W² 16W¹
JAMESTOWN BOY	--/ --	P-Gordon G A	- 17M¹ 18G³ 16G¹
JAN-RE	--/ 95	Murphy F	- 20W¹ 20W¹ 20W¹ 16G²
JARRWAH	--/ 64	Spearing J L	- 20W¹
JAY-DEE-JAY	--/ 88	Davies J D J	24W³ 20M² - 20M¹
JEASSU	--/ --	Wilson A J	16M¹ 20G³ 16M² - 20G³ 16Y² 21G¹ 21S⁴ 20G¹ 20G³ 18F²
JEFFERBY	--/ 87	Glover J A	14Y² 16W¹ - 16G² 24G¹ 20Y²
JENPAT	--/ --	Tinkler N	- 16F¹ 16M¹
JESTERS PROSPECT	114/ --	Goodfellow Mrs	22Y¹ 24S⁴ 20S¹ - 20M² 20G² 20Y³ 16S¹ 16H³
JIMMY MAC JIMMY	--/ 70	Perratt Miss L	- 18S¹
JIMMY THE GILLIE	--/108	Christian S	- 16G¹ 16S² 16M¹
JIMSTER	93/ --	Nash C T	- 26G² 24S² 24Y⁴ 24M¹ 20M¹
JINGA	--/100	Herries Lady	- 17G¹ 22W²
JINXY JACK	--/148	Richards G W	16Y¹ 16S³ 16S¹ 16M¹ 16G¹ - 16G¹ 16G³ 16G¹ 16Y¹ 16G¹ 16G²
JODAMI	141/ --	Beaumont P	16S¹ 16G² 20G¹ 20S¹ 20G¹ 22M¹ - 22M¹ 24S¹ 25G¹ 24M² 25G²
JOHNNY'S SLIPPER	88/ --	Stephenson W A	17G⁴ 16S² - 24G¹ 24G³ 22S² 26Y⁴
JOKERS PATCH	--/ 77	Holder R J	- 22Y¹
JUMBY BAY	--/ 80	Johnston M	16Y² - 16W¹
JUNIOR PARKER	--/ --	Edwards J A C	24Y² - 22G⁴ 24G¹ 25G² 20S³
JURZ	--/100	Baker J H	- 16Y¹
JUST A WONDER	--/ 68	Christian S	16M³ - 17F³ 18M² 16Y³ 22W² 21M¹ 22M³
JUST AS HOPEFUL	--/119	Barons D H	- 20M¹
JUST AS I AM	--/ --	Christian S	21Y¹ - 24G¹
JUST BLAKE	--/ 99	Roberts J D	22M¹ 22M¹ 22M³ - 18F³ 20F² 20G³ 22G¹
JUST FRANKIE	97/ --	Reveley Mrs G	21G⁴ - 16F² 16M³ 16F¹ 16G² 17M² 16G¹ 16M² 16F²
K-BRIGADE	--/ --	Elsey C W C	- 20Y³ 16G² 16G¹
KAGRAM QUEEN	--/ --	Reveley Mrs G	- 16M¹
KAHER	--/105	Callaghan N A	- 16M¹ 16G¹ 16M⁴ 16G²
KALOGY	--/ --	Retter Mrs J G	- 21G³ 16M¹
KALZARI	--/ 63	Deacon D	- 16W³ 16G¹
KAMBALDA RAMBLER	105/ --	Parker C	22S¹ - 16Y⁴ 16G² 20G³ 20S¹ 25G³ 20S³ 16H¹ 20Y³
KAMEO STYLE	85/ --	Jordan F	20M⁴ 20F 25G² 24S¹ 25M² 25F³ 24M³ - 24M³ 20S¹
KANNBANIYA	--/ 91	Holden W	- 20Y² 20G¹ 18G³
KANNDABIL	--/116	Tinkler N	17M² 16M³ 16S² 16S¹ 16S² 16Y¹ 16G² - 16G³ 16S¹ 20G² 16G¹
KANOOZ	--/ 70	Mellor S	- 22W³ 20W¹ 20G³
KARAKTER REFERENCE	128/ --	O'Sullivan R J	19M⁴ 24F¹ 24M¹ 25G² 24M² 20Y² 24Y³ 25G¹ - 21F² 25M¹ 25M⁴
KASHAN	--/ 98	Henderson N J	- 16G¹ 16G³
KATABATIC	167/ --	Turnell Andrew	16S¹ 20G² 16Y³ 20G¹ 16Y¹ 20S² - 16Y¹ 24Y³ 20G² 16G² 16G¹ 20Y¹
KATESVILLE	--/ --	Bowles Lee	- 25G² 26G³ 24G² 26Y¹ 24G¹
KAYPARK	--/102	Pipe M C	- 16G¹ 16Y²
KAYTAK	--/100	Jenkins J R	- 16M² 16G² 16G¹ 18M²
KEEN VISION	--/ 91	Arbuthnot D W	- 16G¹ 16G³ 16W¹

	CHS/HUR	TRAINER	FORM RANGE
KEEP OUT OF DEBT	--/109	Gifford J T	- 18G¹ 22M¹ 21G² 22G²
KEEP TALKING	129/ --	Jones T Thomso	24G³ - 20G¹ 25G³ 24M¹ 24M¹ 32G¹
KEEPOFF-THE-GRASS	--/102	Upson John R	- 25F¹ 24G²
KELLING	--/ --	Retter Mrs J G	- 16S¹
KELLYANN	--/ --	Ham G A	24M² 17M² 25S² - 20G³ 21M³ 24G² 24G¹ 27M²
KENILWORTH LAD	--/ --	Reveley Mrs G	- 16M¹ 16Y¹
KENTISH PIPER	103/ --	Gaselee N A	16G¹ 16G¹ 16M³ - 17M² 20M² 21F¹ 22M¹ 22M² 24G³
KETTI	--/116	Williams D L	16M³ 16G¹ 20Y³ 16Y² - 16G⁴ 16G⁴ 16Y³ 21G⁴ 16G¹ 24Y²
KIBREET	--/113	Elsworth D R C	16M¹ 16M² 16Y¹ 16S² - 16M³ 17M⁴ 16M¹
KILCASH	--/110	Hedger P R	- 16G² 16G² 18M³ 16S¹ 18G¹
KILDIMO	142/ --	Smith Mrs S J	24G² 24M⁴ 25G⁴ 25G³ 26G⁵ - 24Y² 24G³ 24M¹ 28T²
KILHALLON CASTLE	97/ --	Twiston-Davies	19Y¹ 16G³ 17H² 17Y² 20F³ - 20G³ 24M² 25G¹ 20Y³ 24S³ 25G² 22M²
KILIAN MY BOY	--/ --	Kelly P G (Ire	- 24G¹ 16M³
KILKNOCKIN	--/ --	Stephenson W A	21S² 24Y¹ 25G³ - 26Y¹
KILLBANON	129/ --	Trietline C C	24M¹ 24M¹ 24G² 24G¹ 24G¹ 25G³ 25Y³ 25Y³ - 26G¹ 24G³ 24G³
KILTONGA	--/ 69	Leach P	- 17G¹
KIND'A SMART	92/ --	Morgan K A	16M² 16S¹ 16S³ 16M³ - 16M³ 17G¹ 17G¹ 17G² 17M⁴ 17G¹
KING CREDO	--/125	Woodman S	16G¹ 16Y¹ - 18G¹ 16G³ 16G¹
KING NEON	--/ --	Delahooke J S	20S³ 24G² 20M² 20S² - 18G² 20G³ 24F¹
KING OF SHADOWS	--/ 92	Hollinshead R	22W¹ 22W¹ - 20W¹ 20W¹ 20W¹ 24W³ 20W¹
KING OF THE LOT	130/ --	Nicholson D	- 16G² 20Y³ 16G¹ 20G³ 16G¹ 16M¹
KING WILLIAM	--/ 91	Spearing J L	16F¹ 16F¹ 17M² 20W² 16G² 17F¹ - 16M¹ 16M³ 16F¹
KING'S CURATE	125/ --	Mellor S	22S² 21G² 24G² 24G¹ 24Y¹ 21G² 25Y¹ - 20G² 25Y¹ 25G² 25G⁴
KING'S RARITY	--/ 87	Wilson A J	- 16G¹ 16G²
KING'S SHILLING	--/ 82	Oliver Mrs S	- 16W¹ 16G³ 16M¹ 16G²
KINGS FOUNTAIN	153/ --	Bailey K C	16G³ 16G¹ 20G⁴ 16F¹ 20M¹ 20M¹ 20M¹ - 20G³ 20G¹ 20M¹ 24Y² 25G¹ 25Y¹
KINLET VISION	--/ 66	Oliver J K M	- 18F² 16G³ 20Y¹ 20W³ 16F²
KINO	--/ 91	Sherwood S E	16Y¹ 16G² 19M³ 16G³ - 16G¹ 16Y¹ 18Y¹ 16G² 16S³
KINTARO	--/ --	Smith D Murray	- 16F¹ 17G³
KIR	--/ 93	Franks D R	- 16G¹ 16G⁴ 20M² 20M¹
KIRSTY'S BOY	121/ --	Perratt Miss L	22Y² 25S² 24M² 24G² 24G¹ 24M¹ 24M¹ - 20M¹ 24Y² 25M² 24F⁴ 25G¹ 24G¹ 24F³
KISSANE	108/ --	Broad C D	19G³ 16G³ 17Y⁴ 20G³ - 19G² 20M² 24G³ 16M³ 19Y¹ 19Y² 20G¹ 20G¹
KISU KALI	--/ 73	Ffitch-Heyes J	- 16G³ 16M¹ 16M²
KNIGHT IN SIDE	--/ 88	Callow R	- 16G² 16M¹ 17M² 17M¹
KNIGHT OIL	127/ --	Sherwood O	- 20G² 20G¹ 24G¹ 24G⁴
KNIGHT'S SPUR	--/ 94	Webber J	- 16G² 16G² 16G¹ 16G³ 16G² 16Y⁴

	CHS/HUR	TRAINER	FORM RANGE
KNIGHTON COOMBE	--/105	Forster Capt T	- 17G¹ 16G³ 19Y¹
KNOCK KNOCK	--/ --	Balding I A	16Y³ - 16M¹ 16M¹
KNOCKUMSHIN	--/ --	Smith Sidney J	20S¹ 24M³ 22G² 20M¹ - 20G² 20Y² 16G² 25M¹ 25G¹
KONVEKTA CONTROL	--/ --	O'Neill J J	- 18S¹
KOVALESKIA	--/ 70	Wilson D A	- 20W¹
KRONPRINZ	--/ 73	Trietline C C	- 16G² 16G² 17G² 16G¹ 17G¹
L'UOMO PIU	92/ --	Barrow A	- 17M¹ 16M² 17G⁴ 16S³
LA CIENAGA	--/125	Balding G B	20F¹ 20M¹ 20G² 16G³ 16G³ - 16G¹ 18G³ 16G²
LA PEREET	--/ 50	Richmond B	- 16W³ 17G¹ 16Y³ 16G³
LA PRINCESSE	--/ --	Christian S	- 16Y¹ 16Y¹
LA RAPTOTTE	--/ 85	Charles M J	16M¹ - 16M¹ 16G¹ 16W² 16W² 16W¹ 16W³ 17Y² 16M²
LACIDAR	115/ --	Johnson J H	20G¹ 24Y³ 24G² - 20Y⁴ 20G¹ 24F² 20G² 20F³ 20M²
LADY POLY	--/ 69	Sanders Miss B	- 16W³ 16M¹ 16W³ 18W¹ 20W² 20W¹ 20W³ 16M³
LADY TOKEN	82/ --	Gill H J	20G¹ 20M² 24G² - 22G³ 20G² 20G² 24M¹ 24Y⁴ 20G³ 24F²
LAFKADIO	--/ --	Chapman M C	16F³ 17M¹ 16M² 17Y² 17G³ 25F¹ 22M³ - 22F¹ 25G³ 23M²
LAHARNA GIRL	--/ 58	Oldroyd G R	- 18F² 20F¹
LAKE MISSION	102/ --	Sherwood S E	- 19M³ 20G¹ 20G² 20S² 21G²
LAKE TEEREEN	--/122	Rowe R	19M¹ 20G¹ 20G² 21Y¹ 20G³ 16Y¹ 16M³ - 20M² 24Y⁴ 20M¹ 22G¹
LAMBSON	--/ 82	Whitaker R M	- 18G¹ 16G⁴ 16M²
LANDSKER OATS	--/ 86	Sly Mrs P	- 20G¹ 25M² 27F¹
LANDSKI	--/ --	Storey W	20S² 18M¹ - 16M² 16M¹ 20M¹ 20Y² 20M² 16G² 16F³ 20G²
LANE LAD	--/ 61	Wonnacott Mrs	- 16W¹ 18W² 17F²
LAPIAFFE	94/ --	Hodges R J	22S³ 24M² 24Y³ 24G⁴ 22G³ 24G² - 20Y¹ 24M¹
LARKSMORE	80/ --	Baker Miss D J	20S³ - 24M¹
LAST 'O' THE BUNCH	139/ --	Richards G W	16F¹ 16G¹ 16G¹ 16Y¹ 16S¹ 16S³ - 16G² 16S¹ 16Y² 16G² 20G³ 20Y¹ 24Y³
LAST EXTRAVAGANCE	--/ --	Churches M R	24M² 20S³ 24G² - 24G¹ 20G⁴
LASTING MEMORY	--/ 84	Frost R G	16Y² 16F³ - 19F³ 24M³ 23M¹ 24G⁴
LATENT TALENT	125/ --	Sherwood S E	22G² 22G² 24Y¹ - 24G¹ 25G¹ 25M² 24G² 24G³ 24G³
LAUNDRYMAN	125/ --	Mellor S	16G³ 19Y¹ 20G¹ 20S¹ 20Y¹ 20S¹ - 20Y³ 20G¹ 20G¹
LAURA'S BEAU	--/ --	Berry F (Ire)	24Y⁵ - 32S¹ 36Y³
LAURIE-O	105/ --	Reveley Mrs G	20M¹ 20Y¹ 20G⁴ 20S¹ - 24M² 24G³ 20M² 20Y¹ 20M¹
LAVA FALLS	--/ 89	Banks M C	- 16F² 18W³ 16G¹
LE CHAT NOIR	110/ --	Grissell D M	20M¹ 24G⁴ 16G¹ 20G¹ 22M¹ - 20Y² 16G³ 16G¹
LE GRAND MAITRE	102/ --	Roe Graeme	21G² 27G⁴ 24M² 24G³ 25Y² 28G² - 28M¹ 24M² 24F² 25G¹ 25Y¹
LE PICCOLAGE	--/ --	Henderson N J	16Y² - 20M¹ 20G¹
LEACROFT	91/ --	Haigh W W	16M² 16W³ 16G³ 16G³ 16W¹ 16W³ 16G⁴ 16M⁴ 16G² - 16M¹ 16G¹ 16W² 16W¹
LEGAL BEAGLE	--/118	Harwood G	16G¹ 16Y¹ 16G⁶ 20M⁴ 16G² - 21G² 24M² 25G¹
LEIGH BOY	96/ --	Moore G M	- 16G¹ 16G² 16G⁴ 20M² 20G⁴

	CHS/HUR	TRAINER	FORM RANGE
LEINTHALL FOX	--/ --	Needham J L	- 16S¹
LETTERFORE	--/ 90	Upson John R	22S² - 22G² 16Y¹ 24S³ 24Y¹
LEVY FREE	--/ 98	Reveley Mrs G	- 20G³ 25M¹
LIADETT	--/130	Pipe M C	- 16G⁴ 20Y⁴ 16G² 20G¹ 18Y¹ 16G² 20G¹ 16G³
LIFT AND LOAD	--/116	Hannon R	- 16Y¹ 20G¹
LIGHT VENEER	--/117	Jones Mrs M A	16F³ - 16G¹ 16G² 17G² 20G¹ 20G¹
LIGHTWATER AGAIN	91/ --	Hammond M D	16G¹ 16S⁴ 16Y¹ 16G³ - 16S¹
LILY SUGARS	--/ 62	Juckes R T	- 17M³ 18F¹ 17M² 20W³
LINE DRUMMER	--/ --	Kelleway P A	- 16W² 16W¹
LISA ROSA	--/ 69	Wilton Miss S	- 16G¹ 16G³ 16G³
LISLARY LAD	--/ 76	Bowles Lee	- 20G² 20G¹ 22Y⁴ 24M³
LITTLE TOM	81/ --	King J S	- 17M² 20M⁴ 16M² 16G³ 17Y¹
LIVE ACTION	--/ --	Knight Miss H	- 16G¹ 16S³
LIVE IN HOPE	91/ --	Smith D Murray	- 20M¹ 19G⁴ 16Y³ 16G⁴
LOBRIC	--/102	Jenkins J R	- 20G³ 22M² 21G³ 18G¹
LOCAL CUSTOMER	90/ --	Hammond M D	20G¹ 24G² 20M² - 22F¹ 20G⁴ 24G³ 20M¹ 20G⁴
LOCH BLUE	--/ --	Dow S	- 20G¹ 18G¹
LOCH DUICH	--/ 72	Baker R J	- 16G³ 16G¹ 17G²
LOCHEART LADY	--/ --	Stringer A P	- 17G¹
LOCHERRE	--/ 82	Brennan O	16W¹ 16W² 20W³ - 20W² 22W¹
LOGAMIMO	115/ --	Hellens J A	16G¹ 16S³ 16Y¹ 16W¹ 16W¹ 16G¹ - 16M² 16F² 16M² 16M¹ 16G¹ 17G² 16M² 20M¹ 20M⁴
LOOKSEE	--/ --	Easterby M H	- 17F¹
LORD FUTURE	--/ 60	Potts A W	- 16G¹
LOTHIAN CAPTAIN	--/ --	Richards G W	18G¹ 16G¹ 16G² 16G³ 20Y² 16Y¹ 16S¹ 20M² 17F² 24G¹ - 24M² 22M³
LOTHIAN PILOT	--/ --	Lungo L	- 16G² 20G¹
LOVE ANEW	--/110	Sherwood O	- 16G¹ 16M² 16G³ 16G²
LUCKY CRISIS	--/ --	Nicholls P F	- 16W¹
LUCKY LANE	87/ --	Hobbs P J	17M³ - 26F¹ 22F¹ 24M¹ 22F¹ 25M³ 24G⁴ 25G²
LUKE'S BRAVE BOY	--/ --	Hide A	- 16M³ 16G² 16Y¹ 16G³
LUMBERJACK	112/ --	FitzGerald J G	- 20G³ 20Y³ 20S² 20G³ 16G¹ 20M³
LUPY MINSTREL	93/ --	Parker C	18F³ 22G² 20G¹ - 24M¹ 24M³ 24S³ 24Y¹ 22G¹ 25F³
LUSTREMAN	--/ --	Channon M R	16F³ - 16M¹
LUSTY LAD	--/119	Haynes M J	16W² 16W² 16W¹ 18W¹ 20M¹ - 16M¹ 16G² 16M¹ 20M³ 18G¹ 16W³ 18W¹
LYNEMORE	--/ --	Forster Capt T	16M² 16G¹ 16M² - 22M¹ 24M¹ 24G³
LYPHAR DANCER	--/ 84	Haslam P C	- 17S¹ 18G¹ 16G² 16W³
LYPHENTO	122/ --	Gifford J T	- 16Y³ 20G¹ 20Y³ 20M¹ 20G³
M I BABE	100/ --	McKie Mrs I	16G¹ 16S² - 16M¹ 20G³ 16Y¹ 16Y¹
MACARTHUR	123/ --	Easterby M W	16M² 16G⁴ 16G² 16Y¹ 16S¹ 16Y³ 20Y¹ - 16M² 17G¹ 20M² 16G¹ 16Y¹ 16G³
MACEDONAS	--/ 87	Casey T	- 16Y¹ 16G³ 16F³
MACHO MAN	91/ --	O'Neill J J	16G¹ 16Y¹ - 16S² 22Y⁴ 24H³ 22S² 20S⁴ 20Y⁴ 20G¹ 20F³
MAD CASANOVA	94/ --	Sherwood O	20S¹ 21Y⁴ - 20M³ 25Y¹ 26G³ 24G³ 26G² 20Y¹ 20S² 25G³
MADRAJ	--/ 94	Baker R J	- 16M¹ 17G² 17F² 16F¹
MAELKAR	--/137	O'Neill J J	- 25Y⁴ 24S¹

	CHS/HUR	TRAINER	FORM RANGE
MAGGIES LAD	--/ --	Codd L J	- 17F¹ 17G²
MAGIC AT DAWN	--/ --	Moore G M	- 20M¹ 22F³
MAGIC SOLDIER	--/ --	Richards G W	16G⁴ 18S² 16Y² - 16M² 21S¹ 16M¹ 20M²
MAGNUS PYM	--/109	Balding G B	- 17G³ 17G¹ 17Y³
MAILCOM	--/102	Pitman Mrs J	- 16G² 20Y² 20Y¹ 20S³
MAJOR EFFORT	--/ 83	Sherwood O	16G¹ 20G² - 16G¹ 16M³
MAJOR IVOR	--/ 73	Reveley Mrs G	- 16G¹ 16M²
MAJOR KINSMAN	87/ --	Lee R	- 20S¹ 20S³ 20Y²
MAJOR MATCH	122/ --	Forster Capt T	- 21F³ 24F¹ 22G¹ 24G¹ 25G³
MAN FROM MARS	--/ 84	Hobbs P J	- 16M² 24M¹ 22W¹
MAN OF MYSTERY	--/ 86	Trietline C C	- 18Y² 21Y¹
MAN'S BEST FRIEND	--/100	Tate T P	16S³ - 24S³ 22S³ 20S¹ 24H³
MANDER'S WAY	103/ --	Knight Miss H	22G² 24S² - 20M² 22S¹ 26H² 24G¹ 20G³
MANDIKA	--/ 89	Jarvis M A	- 22Y¹ 22G²
MANDRAKI SHUFFLE	--/ --	Sherwood O	24M¹ 25G² 26G¹ 25G³ 25Y¹ 24Y² 32Y⁴ - 21M¹ 25M²
MANENDA	--/ 92	Nicholson D	17G¹ 17G² - 16G² 22G² 22G¹
MANGROVE MIST	--/ 87	Monteith P	- 18F³ 16M² 16G² 16F¹ 20F¹
MANHATTAN BOY	--/ 85	Ffitch-Heyes J	20F² 20W³ - 16G¹ 16G² 18F³
MANHATTAN CHASE	106/ --	Richards G W	20G³ 20Y⁴ 24G¹ 24S¹ 25H² - 25H¹ 24Y³
MANY A SLIP	--/ --	Walford T D	- 24F² 24G³ 24G⁴
MANZOOR SAYADAN	--/ --	Simpson R	- 16G¹
MAPLE DANCER	110/ --	Sherwood O	- 16M¹ 17M³ 16M² 16G¹ 16G¹ 16G² 20G²
MARA ASKARI	--/ 83	Harris J L	- 16W³ 16W¹ 18W² 20G³ 16W¹
MARCELLINA	88/ --	Alston E J	20G² 20G² 20G² 20S³ - 22G³ 25G¹ 24G¹
MARDOOD	--/106	Kersey T	- 17G³ 17M³ 19G¹ 16G³ 16G³ 20G⁴
MAREJO	111/ --	Walton F T	16S² 17M³ 16G¹ 16S² 16Y⁴ 16M² 16F³ 16M³ 17G² - 16M¹ 22G⁴ 17S² 16M³ 16M² 16F² 17S³ 16G³ 16F¹
MARINERS MIRROR	--/118	Scudamore M	16G¹ 16M³ 16G¹ 16S³ 19Y¹ - 18Y² 16S¹ 20G¹
MARINERS SECRET	--/ 88	Brazington R G	- 18W² 20W¹ 20W²
MARK KYBO	103/ --	O'Sullivan R J	- 22G³ 25M¹ 24G¹ 26M¹ 25G¹
MARKET LEADER	99/ --	Lee R	16M¹ 16F² 16M³ 17G³ 19F¹ - 17F² 19M¹ 19F² 20G²
MARLBOROUGH LADY	--/ 59	Knight Mrs A	16G² - 18F² 17F³ 19G²
MARLIN DANCER	--/114	Sanders Miss B	- 22G¹ 16M¹ 20W¹ 20W¹ 20W³ 21G²
MAROUAT	--/ --	Brooks C P E	22W¹ 20G² - 20M¹ 21F⁴ 25M² 25G³ 20M³
MARSH KING	--/ --	Hobbs P J	24G² 25G³ - 20M¹
MARSHLANDER	--/ --	Gandolfo D R	24S³ 24M³ 25M² - 26G¹
MARTELL SPIRIT	--/ --	Barons D H	- 16Y¹ 16G¹
MARTHA'S SON	--/ 97	Forster Capt T	- 16G¹ 16G²
MARTIN'S FRIEND	87/ --	Bloomfield D	- 20Y³ 20G⁴ 20M¹
MARTIN'S LAMP	--/ --	Gifford J T	- 16G¹
MARTIYA	--/ 60	Balding G B	- 16W¹
MASAI MARA	--/ --	Haslam P C	- 16M¹ 16G¹
MASHUM	--/ 69	Batey A C	- 22Y³ 20Y¹ 24F³
MASTER CORNET	91/ --	Rothwell B S	- 24G¹ 24G³ 24G² 24M²
MASTER DANCER	--/105	Jones T Thomso	16M¹ 16G² 16Y¹ 16G³ 16F² 16G² - 20M¹ 22W² 24W¹ 20W³ 22W³ 24M¹ 24W³
MASTER FOODBROKER	--/111	Elsworth D R C	- 20M¹ 16G³

	CHS/HUR	TRAINER	FORM RANGE
MASTER GLEASON	--/ --	Pipe M C	26G² 24M⁴ - 20G² 20Y¹ 26G²
MASTER GLEN	--/ --	Oldroyd G R	- 16M² 16G¹ 16Y²
MASTER OATS	97/ --	Bailey K C	- 20G² 24G¹ 26M²
MASTER OF TROY	--/ 92	Parker C	- 16G² 21Y³ 16S³ 18Y¹ 20F³
MASTER OFTHE HOUSE	--/ 91	Hammond M D	16M³ 16M² - 17F² 16G¹ 16M¹
			16M³ 16G² 16G² 16G¹ 16G¹
MASTER SALESMAN	97/ --	Rothwell B S	16G¹ 16G⁴ 16Y¹ 20Y² 16G²
			16G⁴ 16Y³ - 16M¹ 16G² 16M³
			16G¹ 17G¹ 16M²
MASTER WILLIAM	--/ 73	Edwards J A C	- 25F³ 20F² 22F¹
MASTER'S CROWN	--/ 75	Chapman M C	- 16W² 16W¹ 16G² 17F¹
MAUDLINS CROSS	99/ --	Reveley Mrs G	16M¹ 17G² 16G¹ 16Y² 16G¹
			16G³ - 16M¹ 17M¹ 16M² 16M¹
			16G²
MAY SQUARE	--/ 80	Bailey K C	- 16G¹ 16G³
MAYFAIR MINX	--/115	Christian S	16Y⁴ 16F³ 19M¹ 21M¹ 22M² -
			21M¹ 24G¹ 20M¹ 21G³
MAZMOOR	--/ --	Eubank A	- 16G² 17G¹ 16G¹ 16M¹
MEADOWVALE	90/ --	FitzGerald J G	- 20M¹
MEAT THE FOULKES	98/ --	Collinson J E	- 26G² 21S³ 26H² 26S¹
MEGA BLUE	91/ --	Aconley Mrs V	16M³ 16Y² 16G³ - 17G² 16G²
			16G³ 20S⁴ 16G³ 17G¹
MELICUS	--/ --	Egerton C R	- 19G¹ 18Y¹
MEMBERS' REVENGE	114/ --	Christian S	16G⁴ 16M¹ 19F¹ 16G² - 16Y²
			20G² 20M¹
MERANDI SPECIAL	--/ 85	Thomas J D	17M³ 17M³ - 19M² 17F¹ 19M²
			17M¹ 16M² 16S⁴ 16G²
MERANO	--/ --	Easterby M W	- 20G¹ 24Y¹
MERCHANT OF VENICE	--/ 90	Tompkins M H	- 18W¹ 16Y³
MERRY MASTER	110/ --	Armytage R C	16S³ 16F² 20G³ 25G¹ 25Y³
			24Y¹ - 20G² 24G³ 20S¹ 24S¹
			22Y³ 20S¹ 33G⁴
METAL OISEAU	--/ 94	Moore J S	- 16G¹ 18G¹ 16Y¹ 16G¹ 16G²
MIAMI BEAR	--/102	Berry J	20G³ 20G¹ 20G¹ 20G¹ 20W¹
			22W³ 18W³ 20M³ - 20F³ 20G³
			16W² 20M⁴ 20W¹
MIC-MAC EXPRESS	--/ --	Syckelmoore Mr	- 20G¹
MICHAELS DAWN	--/ 76	Ffitch-Heyes J	- 21M¹
MICK'S TYCOON	--/ 74	Pipe M C	- 22G¹ 20G³ 20M²
MIDDLEWICK	--/ 81	Christian S	- 16S¹ 16G³ 17F² 16G¹
MIDFIELDER	105/ --	Hobbs P J	16M² 16M² 21G² 18M¹ 16M¹
			16M³ - 17M¹ 21M¹ 17G² 16M⁴
			21M⁴ 22M²
MIDLAND LAD	--/ 94	Eyre J L	20W³ 20G³ 20M³ - 20M³ 24G²
			24S¹
MIG	--/ --	Reveley Mrs G	20G² 20G¹ 20W³ - 22M² 20G¹
MIGHTY FALCON	119/ --	Elsworth D R C	17G⁴ 20Y⁴ 24S³ 24Y² 24S²
			24H¹ 21M¹ 20M² - 21M¹ 20G⁴
			20G⁴ 20S³ 25G¹
MIGHTY MOGUL	--/116	Pitman Mrs J	- 16Y² 16Y¹ 20S¹ 16S³
MIINNEHOMA	147/ --	Pipe M C	- 26S¹ 24G¹ 24G¹
MILFORD QUAY	142/ --	Pipe M C	- 16Y¹ 17G¹ 20G¹
MILITARY BAND	--/ 93	Retter Mrs J G	- 24G³ 17G² 21M¹
MILITARY SECRET	93/ --	Stephenson W A	- 20F¹ 26M¹ 20G² 24M² 27Y²
MILS MIJ	--/127	Cuthbert T A K	20G² - 20G¹ 18Y¹ 20G⁴
MINDY	--/ 53	Callaghan N A	- 16G³ 16Y² 16G³ 16G¹
MINERS LUCK	--/ --	Nicholson D	16Y³ - 20G¹ 25G¹
MINT-MASTER	81/ --	McKie Mrs I	16F² - 17F³ 16M⁴ 24G⁴ 22M¹
			25Y³ 24G⁴ 20M²
MISS BOBBY BENNETT	--/124	Pipe M C	- 16G¹ 20M¹ 20W³ 16G⁶ 20Y¹
			16Y¹ 20S¹ 16G⁴

	CHS/HUR	TRAINER	FORM RANGE
MISS FERN	91/ --	Dickin R	21Y⁴ 19Y² 25G³ 20M¹ 22G³ 17M³ 16H⁴ 25G² 20M⁴ 20P³ - 20M³ 24G¹ 27M³ 20G¹ 26M²
MISS LAWN	--/ 87	Burchell D	- 20W¹ 20W¹
MISS MANGAROO	--/ --	Reveley Mrs G	- 20G¹
MISS MOODY	--/ 63	Bradley J M	- 16W¹
MISS PURBECK	--/ 94	Retter Mrs J G	- 17S¹ 16Y³ 18Y¹ 21M⁴ 17S¹
MISSING MAN	101/ --	Gifford J T	24G² 25G⁴ 25G⁴ 27M¹ - 25G² 25G¹
MISTER BUTLER	--/ --	Blagbrough G D	22F³ 26G³ 24G¹ - 24F² 24F¹
MISTER CHRISTIAN	108/ --	Nicholls P F	- 25M³ 27Y⁴ 26S¹ 30G³ 26Y² 28Y³
MISTER ED	122/ --	Curtis R	26G¹ 25M¹ 26G² 25Y¹ 29S⁴ 27Y⁴ 24G¹ - 24G¹ 26G³ 26G³ 28G²
MISTER FEATHERS	96/ --	King J S	19G² 22M² - 20M² 16M¹ 20G¹ 19P²
MISTER GEBO	100/ --	Edwards J A C	20M¹ 20G² 24G¹ 22G² 24M¹ - 24M² 24M¹ 25M² 22M² 26F¹ 21F¹ 26M¹
MISTER MAJOR	--/112	Balding G B	- 18G² 16G¹ 16S³ 16G¹ 16S² 20G³
MISTER MOODY	86/ --	Johnson J H	- 24S¹ 20Y³ 16S² 24H³ 24Y¹
MISTER TICKLE	105/ --	Twiston-Davies	22M¹ - 20Y⁴ 18Y² 22G¹ 25Y¹
MISTRESS ROSS	--/ 72	Thorner G	19G² 22F³ - 19M² 25M¹ 21G¹ 24G³ 25G² 21M³
MISTY GLOW	--/ --	Haigh W W	- 16S³ 16G¹
MIZYAN	--/ --	Banks J E	- 16W¹ 16W¹
MO ICHI DO	--/ 74	Wilton Miss S	20M¹ - 24G¹ 24F² 22M³
MODIFY	--/ --	Harwood G	- 17F¹
MOHELI	--/ 74	Holder R J	- 20M¹ 22S²
MOLOJEC	--/ --	Retter Mrs J G	- 17G¹ 17F² 22M¹
MOMENT OF TRUTH	137/ --	Monteith P	20G² 17G¹ 16M¹ 17G¹ 17Y¹ 16G¹ 17M¹ 16M¹ - 20M¹ 20G¹ 20M¹ 16M² 16M¹ 16G³ 20G² 16Y³ 16G⁴ 16G⁴ 16G¹
MOMSER	--/ --	Ryan M J	16G² 16Y¹ 16S⁴ 16G¹ - 16M¹ 19M¹ 20P²
MONARU	--/105	Reveley Mrs G	- 22F³ 28M¹ 25G¹ 25M¹ 24G² 27M¹ 25F¹
MONDAY CLUB	--/112	Tuck J	16G¹ 16G² 16G¹ 16S² 17Y² 16M² - 16M¹ 17G³ 16G² 16G³ 16F² 16M²
MONK'S MISTAKE	99/ --	Lee R	16Y¹ - 16G¹ 16G² 16G³
MONSIEUR LE CURE	--/ --	Edwards J A C	- 16G¹
MONTALINO	99/ --	Gifford J T	16M² - 16M¹ 16G² 16G³ 24M¹
MONTEBEL	--/120	Twiston-Davies	- 16G¹ 20G¹ 20M¹ 16G¹
MONTELADO	--/ --	Flynn P J (Ire	- 16G¹
MONTGOMERY	78/ --	McKenzie-Coles	24M³ - 25G² 25F¹
MONUMENTAL LAD	118/ --	Parrott Mrs H	16S¹ 16G⁵ 17Y¹ 20Y³ - 16G² 20G¹ 20Y² 20G³ 16G³ 16Y³ 20G¹
MOOR SCOPE	--/ --	White Mrs R K	- 25Y¹
MOORFIELD LADY	90/ --	Wilkinson B E	- 16M³ 16G³ 16Y¹ 16Y¹ 17G³
MORE BY LUCK	--/ 72	Holder R J	- 16Y³ 19G¹
MORLEY STREET	--/158	Balding G B	20M¹ 20G² 20M² 21G¹ 16Y¹ 20Y¹ - 20G¹ 16G⁶ 20G¹
MOSSY FERN	110/ --	Sherwood O	22G¹ 20G⁴ - 20G¹ 20G¹ 24M¹ 24M³ 26G²
MOTTRAM'S GOLD	--/ 92	Retter Mrs J G	- 16G¹ 19G¹ 16G¹ 19M²
MOUNT ARGUS	--/ --	Brookshaw S A	24S¹ 26G¹ 20M⁴ - 24Y² 24Y¹

	CHS/HUR	TRAINER	FORM RANGE
			26Y¹ 26G² 24G¹
MOUNTAIN CABIN	--/ 72	Smith D Murray	25G⁴ - 25M² 20G¹
MOUNTAIN KINGDOM	--/120	Tinkler N	- 16G² 20M¹ 20G³ 20M² 16G²
			20M² 16G¹ 24M¹
MOUNTSHANNON	--/ 87	Trietline C C	- 16G³ 16G³ 16G³ 20G¹
MOZE TIDY	89/ --	Rowe R	20G¹ 21M³ 20G⁴ 21Y² 20G⁴ -
			22G³ 20G¹ 24G³ 20G³
MR BOSTON	125/ --	Woodhouse R D	16M¹ - 22M¹ 22G² 25G¹ 25G¹
			24G¹ 30M¹ 32S² 24G³
MR ENTERTAINER	133/ --	Gaselee N A	20G² 20Y¹ 20Y¹ 20Y⁴ - 20M²
			20G¹ 20M¹ 25Y⁴ 22M⁴
MR FELIX	81/ --	Champion R	16F² 16F³ - 16G³ 17G² 16M⁴
			16G¹
MR FLUTTS	--/ --	Tuck J	- 20M¹
MR FRISK	--/ --	Bailey K C	25M¹ 24M¹ - 24G¹ 29G² 29M⁴
			25G⁴
MR GOSSIP	--/125	Henderson N J	24M³ 28G¹ 26Y¹ 26G³ 26M³
			26G² - 25G² 24Y³ 24G² 24Y¹
			25G² 25G⁴ 24S⁴
MR LION	--/102	Balding G B	16Y¹ - 18S¹ 19G² 25G³ 26Y¹
MR MONDAY	--/ --	Stephenson W A	- 25M¹
MR OPTIMISTIC	--/ 87	O'Neill J J	- 16G¹ 20S³ 18S³ 20S² 16S²
			20Y¹
MR SEAGULL	--/ --	Hembrow Mrs S	16M³ - 17F¹ 21M²
MR TITTLE TATTLE	--/ 72	Bailey K C	- 22M³ 19M¹
MR VERGETTE	94/ --	Nicholson D	16G² - 20M¹ 20G³
MR WOODCOCK	--/129	Reveley Mrs G	16G¹ 16G¹ 16G² 16G¹ - 16M¹
			16F¹ 20M¹ 16Y³ 20G³
MRS JAWLEYFORD	--/ 85	Smith C	- 16W² 16W³ 16W² 16H¹ 17Y¹
MRS PEOPLEATER	--/ --	Weedon C	16Y¹ 18S¹ 20Y² - 17S¹
MUBAARIS	--/ 93	Richmond B	28G² 27Y² 24W² 22W¹ - 25G²
			20W¹ 20W³ 28M³ 20W³ 20W¹
MUBIN	--/ --	Elsey C C	- 16M¹ 16G⁴
MUDAHIM	--/140	Broad C D	17M¹ 16S² 19Y² 16S¹ - 16S²
			16G¹ 21S³ 24G⁴
MUGONI BEACH	--/105	Pipe M C	16S¹ - 16G³ 20Y³ 24G¹ 20Y³
			24Y³
MULBANK	--/ 88	Hobbs P J	- 17M¹ 16G³ 20S³
MULTIHANDS	--/ 79	Wharton J	- 20W³ 20W¹ 16W³
MUSE	--/126	Elsworth D R C	16G² 16G³ 16Y² - 16G¹ 20Y¹
			16M² 24G² 20G²
MUSICAL MONARCH	--/ 85	Nicholls P F	- 17G³ 18S¹
MUTARE	139/ --	Henderson N J	20G² 25Y⁶ - 18Y¹ 24G¹ 24G²
MY ALIBI	--/ 80	Carter W	- 16W³ 16W² 16G¹
MY CHIARA	--/100	Bevan P J	- 20Y³ 20G² 20W³ 20W² 19G¹
			24G¹ 22G²
MY KEY SILCA	--/ 90	Nash C T	20Y³ - 16M¹ 18Y¹ 18G¹
MY SWAN SONG	--/ 68	Smith J P	17M³ 16S³ 17M² - 17G¹ 19G²
			16G³
MY VIEW	--/142	Purcell M (Ire	- 25G¹
MY YOUNG MAN	156/ --	Brooks C P E	17G¹ 17G¹ 16Y⁶ - 16G² 17S¹
			16G¹ 17G¹ 16M¹ 16G¹ 17G⁴
			16G¹ 20G³
MYVERYGOODFRIEND	82/ --	Turnell Andrew	- 16G¹ 21M³
NAMASTE	--/ --	Rowe R	- 16G¹
NANDA MOON	--/ 65	Thornton C W	- 16M¹ 16G² 16M² 17M¹ 20G⁴
NATIVE CROWN	--/ --	Perratt Miss L	- 16Y² 20G³ 24G¹
NATIVE PRIDE	--/113	Bailey K C	- 16M¹ 16Y¹ 20Y¹ 20G¹ 20G⁶
NAUGHTY NICKY	--/ --	Bishop K	24M² 26M² 25M³ 26M⁴ - 24G¹
NAUTICAL JOKE	106/ --	Stephenson W A	24G² 28M⁴ 24M³ 25M³ 24S³
			25G³ 24S⁴ 24M² - 24M² 24M¹

	CHS/HUR	TRAINER	FORM RANGE
			24M¹ 24G¹ 20G³ 25G³ 25M¹
			25M³ 24M¹ 24M¹
NEEDWOOD LEADER	76/ --	Pritchard Dr P	- 16M¹ 16M²
NEEDWOOD MUPPET	--/109	Morgan B C	- 16H² 16G³ 16G¹ 20G¹ 22G¹
NEEDWOOD SPRITE	--/ 92	Morgan B C	19G³ 16G³ - 16G¹ 19Y³ 18M¹
NEGATORY	--/105	Chapman M C	- 17G² 24Y¹ 17G¹ 22G²
NETHERBRIDGE	77/ --	Gandolfo D R	- 24F¹ 21M² 26G³ 20M¹ 25G³
			26G² 20M⁴
NEVADA GOLD	--/ 93	Minns Mrs Sylv	- 22G³ 16G³ 16G¹
NEVER A PENNY	87/ --	Elliott J P D	24M³ 19M³ 27F³ 19M¹ - 18F²
			18F¹ 18F² 20M² 21M³ 26M³
			20G² 18F²
NEW HALEN	117/ --	James A P	22G¹ 20M³ 24M⁴ 20M¹ 20G¹
			20G³ - 19M² 20G⁴ 20S² 25M¹
			22M¹ 20M⁴
NEW MENDOZA	--/ --	Richards Grenv	25F³ - 24S¹
NEW YORK RAINBOW	--/ --	Henderson N J	16Y² 16Y² 16G³ - 16G¹ 16M¹
			16G¹ 16G⁴
NEWLANDS-GENERAL	--/ --	FitzGerald J G	17G³ - 16G¹ 16Y¹
NICHOLAS MARK	--/ 77	FitzGerald J G	- 17M² 16F¹
NICKLE JOE	--/106	Tate M	21Y² 16Y² 20G³ - 20S³ 20G³
			20G¹
NICKNAVAR	86/ --	Tetley Mrs P A	- 20G² 20Y⁴
NIGHT GUEST	101/ --	Monteith P	16F² 20G¹ - 17S¹
NIGHT OF MADNESS	--/ --	Hanson J	- 17M¹ 16Y²
NIJMEGEN	--/ --	FitzGerald J G	- 16G³ 16S¹ 16G²
NIKITAS	--/ 92	Whitfield Miss	- 16G¹ 17S² 16M²
NINEOFUS	120/ --	Easterby M H	18G¹ 16G¹ 20G¹ 17M¹ 16G¹
			16M³ 20M⁴ - 16F² 16G² 20M¹
			20M¹ 25G¹
NINEPINS	--/ --	Moore A L T (I	- 20G¹
NISHKINA	--/ 80	Easterby M H	- 17F² 16F¹ 16F¹ 17F¹ 16M¹
			20G³
NO BONUS	--/106	Baker J H	16G² 16W³ 16F¹ 17F³ - 17F¹
			17F¹ 17F¹ 16M³
NO ESCORT	--/ --	Saunders Miss	- 24G¹ 25G²
NOBLE BID	--/ 83	Wilton Miss S	- 20M² 20M¹ 20F³ 24G¹
NOBLE EYRE	89/ --	Gandolfo D R	17Y¹ 16M¹ 16G¹ - 17M¹ 16M⁴
			16G³
NOBLE INSIGHT	--/ 96	Pipe M C	16M³ - 16G³ 16M³ 16Y² 16M²
			18G¹ 16F¹ 16M¹
NOBLE VISION	--/ --	Pipe M C	- 26Y² 22W¹
NOBLE YEOMAN	--/ 96	Dickin R	- 17S¹ 17Y¹
NODDLE	--/ 90	Lungo L	- 16M² 16M⁴ 20G² 18S² 20M¹
			20G³ 22W¹
NODFORM	--/ --	Gifford J T	21M³ 20G² 20G³ 20G³ 25S² -
			21M³ 20G² 20G¹ 20G¹
NODFORM WONDER	--/101	Eddy D	16F¹ - 16M² 20F¹ 24G³
NOEL LUCK	--/ --	King Mrs A L M	16S¹ 19G³ 20Y² 24M¹ 26G² -
			26G³ 24G¹
NOMADIC WAY	--/161	Hills B W	- 16M² 16M² 20G³ 25G¹
NON PERMANENT	--/ --	Rothwell B S	21G³ - 16M¹ 20M¹
NONE SO BRAVE	--/122	Akehurst R	- 16G¹ 16M¹ 16Y² 16G¹ 16M⁴
NORDIC DELIGHT	--/ 93	Pipe M C	16G¹ 18M² - 16M¹ 17F¹ 17G³
			19M² 16G² 18W¹ 16S¹ 16Y²
NORMAN CONQUEROR	111/ --	Jones T Thomso	16M³ 17M¹ 20Y³ - 16M¹ 20Y¹
			20G³ 20G² 20G¹
NORQUAY	--/ --	Tinkler N	- 16G¹
NORSTOCK	--/ 98	White J	16W¹ 16S² 16M² 16G³ 19F³
			16M² - 19F² 18F¹ 18G¹ 18G³
			16G³ 18G¹ 16G¹ 18G¹ 20W¹

	CHS/HUR	TRAINER	FORM RANGE
NORTH PRIDE	--/ 70	Payne S G	- 16M¹
NORTHANTS	--/115	Storey W	20G¹ 20S¹ - 20G² 18S¹ 20H²
NORTHERN GUNNER	--/ --	Robinson M H B	16G² 16M² 16G³ - 16F² 20M⁴
NORTHERN JINKS	105/ --	Dickin R	16G⁴ 21S² 20Y⁴ - 20G³ 21Y¹
			20Y¹ 20Y²
NORTHERN LION	95/ --	Thompson R	16W³ 16M¹ 16M⁴ - 17F¹ 17M¹
			16G² 17G⁴ 16Y¹ 17G⁴ 16G³
			16F¹
NORTHERN MEADOW	97/ --	Chadwick S	- 24F¹ 24F⁴ 24M³ 26S¹ 28G³
			20S¹ 24Y¹ 24G⁴ 24M² 24F¹
NORTHERN NATION	--/ 76	Clay W	- 16M² 16G¹ 16W¹ 16M³
NORTHERN VILLAGE	--/ 97	Dow S	16G³ - 16G³ 18W¹ 20W¹ 21G¹
NORTHUMBRIAN KING	--/ --	Walton Mrs K	16F¹ 20F² 20F¹ 17M¹ 21F¹
			20F² 22G² 20G² - 24M² 24G¹
			24G¹
NORVAL	--/100	Reveley Mrs G	20Y² 22Y¹ 20G¹ 24S¹ 20S²
			24G² - 22G⁴ 24S¹ 28Y³
NOVA SPIRIT	--/ 71	Saunders M S	- 18H¹
NTOMBI	--/ 93	Bishop V R	- 20Y² 20Y¹
NUT TREE	--/ 78	Wike D R	16F³ 16M¹ - 20W¹ 20W²
OAK PARK	--/ 96	Pickering J A	- 16M² 16M³ 16G¹ 16G³ 16G¹
OASIS	--/ --	Bishop K	17F² 17F² - 17F³ 18F¹
OBELISKI	84/ --	Haslam P C	16W³ 22W³ 20W¹ 20S⁴ - 20M³
			16M² 16G¹ 16Y⁴ 16G⁴
OBIE'S TRAIN	--/ 96	Pitman Mrs J	16Y² - 16G¹ 16M³
ODSTONE PEAR	--/ 86	Leach P	24M³ - 22G¹ 24W² 22W³
OFF PISTE	--/ --	Henderson N J	- 16G¹
OFF THE BRU	106/ --	Bradburne Mrs	24G³ - 22M³ 25G¹ 20M³ 24M³
			25Y³ 25G⁴ 28Y⁴ 33G³ 24Y⁴
			24G⁴
OFFICER CADET	--/ 93	Curtis R	- 17M² 22G¹ 20Y³
OFFICER GROWLER	93/ --	Haine Mrs D	16G² 16S¹ 16S¹ 16G¹ - 18G¹
			20G³ 20M³ 20G² 21M³
OK CORRAL	104/ --	White J	- 21G³ 16G¹ 20G¹ 20G¹ 20S¹
			24G¹
OL DE LOIR	--/ 66	Nicholson D	- 16G¹ 16Y³ 19G³
OLD APPLEJACK	123/ --	Johnson J H	20F¹ 24G³ 20S¹ 20G¹ 20G⁴
			24Y⁴ 24F⁴ - 20F¹ 24G⁴ 20G⁴
			20G³ 20M¹ 25M² 20M² 24F¹
OLD NICK	101/ --	Bell Mrs H	24G¹ - 25M¹
OLD PEG	--/ 73	Easterby M H	- 16Y² 16W² 17M¹ 16F¹ 16Y³
			17M¹
OLE OLE	--/ --	Moscrop Mrs E	- 26Y² 24Y¹ 24M³
OLIVERS HILL	--/ 94	Trietline C C	16G² 16F³ - 17M¹ 18M¹ 16F¹
OLVESTON	--/104	Nicholls P F	- 19G² 16Y¹
ON THE HOOCH	89/ --	Bradburne Mrs	22G¹ - 22G⁴ 16Y¹ 20M³
ON THE PROWL	--/ 91	Pipe M C	- 16Y¹ 22G³ 22M³
ON THE TWIST	--/ --	Murphy F	24S¹ 24S³ 24Y¹ 28S⁴ 25Y⁴
			25S⁴ - 24G¹ 25G¹ 24M⁴
ONCE STUNG	--/ --	Stephenson W A	- 24F² 26Y¹ 24S² 24G³ 32Y¹
			26Y¹ 24M¹ 26G²
ONE MORE DREAM	--/ --	Balding G B	- 16G² 16M¹
ONE MORE KNIGHT	--/116	McKie Mrs I	20G³ 24G² 22Y¹ - 24M¹ 24Y²
ONE TO NOTE	--/ 86	Muggeridge M P	16S³ 17H² - 16Y¹ 17H²
ONENINEFIVE	--/ 64	Ham G A	- 17M³ 21M¹
ONEUPMANSHIP	--/121	Elsworth D R C	16Y³ 16G¹ 16S¹ - 16M⁴ 16G¹
ORCHIPEDZO	82/ --	Dickin R	16G³ - 16M³ 16G³ 20M¹ 24Y⁴
			16M³
ORIEL DREAM	--/ 78	Fisher R F	16S¹ - 22G¹
OSMOSIS	--/ --	Smith D Murray	- 17M¹
OTTERBURN HOUSE	100/ --	FitzGerald J G	24M¹ 22Y¹ 25Y³ - 24G¹ 24M²

	CHS/HUR	TRAINER	FORM RANGE
			$26G^1$ $24G^2$
OUBLIER L'ENNUI	--/ --	Barons D H	- $20G^1$ $20M^2$ $20G^2$
OUNAVARRA MILL	--/104	Smith D Murray	- $18S^1$ $28G^2$
OUR MARTHA	--/ --	Roberts J D	- $16G^1$ $17G^2$
OUR NOBBY	124/ --	Elsworth D R C	$20M^3$ $20G^2$ $21G^1$ - $21S^1$ $18Y^1$ $24G^1$ $20G^4$
OUR SLIMBRIDGE	--/ 80	Williams C N	- $16G^1$ $16G^3$
OUTSIDE EDGE	130/ --	Pipe M C	$26G^3$ $28S^2$ $32Y^2$ $26S^1$ $25G^3$ - $26S^3$ $30G^4$ $26Y^1$
OVER THE DEEL	100/ --	Stephenson W A	$16G^1$ $20G^2$ $24M^3$ $20Y^2$ $25G^1$ $27M^1$ - $24Y^1$ $26M^1$ $26G^2$ $27M^1$ $27M^3$ $28Y^2$ $24F^2$ $24M^2$
OWEN	88/ --	Smart B	- $20G^3$ $20G^4$ $20Y^3$ $20G^2$ $24F^2$
PACIFIC GEM	80/ --	Curtis R	- $18G^3$ $16G^2$ $16M^2$ $16M^3$ $16G^2$ $17G^4$ $16M^1$
PACIFIC SOUND	103/ --	Smith Mrs S J	$20M^2$ - $20G^1$ $25G^1$ $24M^2$ $24Y^2$ $20S^1$ $24S^2$ $20G^1$
PACO'S BOY	119/ --	Pipe M C	$24G^3$ $24G^4$ $25H^1$ $24Y^2$ $24S^3$ $20S^3$ $20S^3$ $25F$ - $20G^1$ $22G^1$ $25Y^3$ $24G^2$ $29M^5$
PACTOLUS	--/129	Christian S	- $20M^1$ $24G^2$
PADAVENTURE	104/ --	Reveley Mrs G	$18G^2$ $20G^2$ $16S^2$ $20Y^1$ $20Y^1$ - $24S^3$ $25G^2$ $20G^1$ $26M^1$
PADDY HAYTON	--/ --	Leadbetter S J	$27S^1$ $24Y^1$ $27M^1$ - $25G^1$ $24G^1$ $27F^1$ $24F^2$ $26G^2$
PADDY TEE	--/ 67	Pipe M C	- $16M^1$ $16M^2$
PADIORD	--/ 89	Wintle D J	- $22G^3$ $20M^1$
PADRIGAL	--/ --	Cheatle J N	- $18Y^1$ $18G^3$
PALACE GARDENS	81/ --	Bradley J M	$21G^1$ - $24F^3$ $25M^4$ $20G^1$
PALANQUIN	--/ 84	Reed W G	$24G^3$ $24G^2$ $24G^1$ $20F^1$ $20F^3$ $20M^2$ $22M^3$ - $24G^1$ $24G^1$
PALM READER	115/ --	Stephenson W A	$16Y^1$ $16G^4$ $20M^1$ $20F^1$ $22G^2$ $22M^1$ - $20F^1$ $17F^1$ $20M^1$ $20G^3$ $20F^1$ $20M^1$ $20M^1$
PALMAHALM	--/ --	Anderson K	- $24G^1$ $26G^3$ $25M^1$
PALMER'S GOLD	--/ --	Caldwell T H	- $24M^1$
PALMRUSH	83/ --	Thornton C W	- $17M^3$ $16G^1$ $16M^3$ $20M^2$
PAMBER PRIORY	113/ --	Jones T Thomso	$20G^3$ $22G^2$ $24G^4$ $25Y^2$ $25G^2$ - $24Y^1$ $26Y^2$ $25G^1$ $25Y^3$
PANATHINAIKOS	--/ 81	Ham G A	- $22M^2$ $20W^1$
PANDESSA	--/ 88	Reveley Mrs G	- $18G^1$ $16G^2$ $16M^3$ $16W^1$ $16W^3$ $16M^2$ $20F^1$
PANDORA'S PRIZE	--/ 67	Bailey K C	- $20Y^1$
PANICO	--/ 79	Hall Miss S E	- $16W^1$
PANT LLIN	--/ 74	Jordan F	$17M^1$ $16M^1$ $16F^2$ - $16M^2$ $16M^1$
PANTECHNICON	90/ --	Barrow A	$17F^1$ $16M^1$ - $19M^3$ $16M^2$ $17M^1$ $16M^3$ $17G^4$ $19F^1$ $16G^3$ $17M^2$
PANTOMINE PRINCE	96/ --	Thornton C W	- $17G^3$ $16M^1$ $16G^3$
PAPERWORK BOY	--/ --	Easterby M H	$16G^1$ $16M^1$ $20S^2$ - $16G^1$
PARBOLD HILL	--/ 65	Burke K R	- $18W^1$
PARIS OF TROY	--/109	Twiston-Davies	- $16W^1$ $16S^1$ $16G^2$ $19G^1$
PARSON'S THORNS	--/ --	Brooks C P E	$16G^1$ $16Y^1$ $20S^3$ - $20G^1$ $20G^1$ $16Y^1$
PARSONS GREEN	--/ --	Henderson N J	$24G^4$ $22Y^1$ $24G^1$ $24Y^4$ $24G^1$ - $24G^1$ $25G^2$
PARSONS PLEASURE	87/ --	Wilkinson M J	- $20G^4$ $24G^2$ $25M^2$ $24S^1$ $24G^2$
PARTY POLITICS	152/ --	Gaselee N A	$24G^1$ $24S^2$ $26Y^1$ $25S^1$ - $26G^2$ $30Y^2$ $28Y^2$ $36Y^1$
PARTY PRINCE	--/ 90	Weedon C	- $16S^3$ $16G^1$
PASHTO	--/113	Henderson N J	$16Y^1$ - $16G^3$ $19Y^1$ $21G^3$ $22G^2$
PASSED PAWN	--/ 97	Pipe M C	- $17G^1$ $18G^1$ $16G^3$ $16G^1$ $16S^1$

	CHS/HUR	TRAINER	FORM RANGE
			20G² 19M³ 18G² 16G³ 24M²
PASSO ALL'ERTA	75/ --	Deacon D	- 17S³ 16Y¹ 17M² 16S³
PASTORAL PRIDE	--/ --	Curling Miss P	- 20G¹ 21G¹ 16Y¹
PAT'S JESTER	150/ --	Richards G W	22G¹ 22G² 25S² 20Y¹ - 20G¹
			20G¹ 20Y² 20G³
PATRICK'S STAR	--/ 88	Bridgwater K S	- 16M³ 16G¹ 20M³
PAY TO DREAM	--/ 70	Weaver R J	- 16M² 16M² 20M¹ 20W¹ 18W³
PEACE KING	--/122	Harwood G	16M¹ 16G¹ 16M² 16M² 18M¹
			16M³ - 16M¹ 16M⁴ 16G³ 16G³
			16G¹
PEACEWORK	--/ --	Reveley Mrs G	16M² 16Y³ 16Y³ 16S² 16M²
			17M³ - 20F³ 20P² 16F¹ 20G¹
			20G³ 22G³ 20F²
PEAJADE	93/ --	Nicholson D	23M³ 22S¹ - 20G³ 24Y¹ 26G⁴
PEAK DISTRICT	--/ 84	Bridgwater K S	16G¹ 16W¹ 16G² - 16W² 16W¹
			16W¹
PEANUTS PET	--/131	Tate T P	20G² 16M¹ 21S³ - 16G³ 16G¹
			16M¹ 16G³ 17P¹
PEATSWOOD	--/109	Channon M R	- 17S¹ 20M²
PECHE D'OR	--/ 87	Haynes H E	16M² - 21G¹
PENLLYNE'S PRIDE	--/ --	Juckes R T	16F¹ 16F³ 20M¹ 19F¹ 16M¹
			16M³ 20W³ 20W² 20F² - 17S²
			17P¹ 20M¹
PEOPLE'S CHOICE	92/ --	Mitchell N R	20S⁴ 20M⁴ 21G⁴ - 19G³ 25M²
			25M¹
PERE BAZILLE	--/ 81	Nicholls P F	17G¹ 16M³ - 17F¹ 19M²
PERFECT STRANGER	--/ --	Hallett T B	- 26P² 24M² 25F⁴ 24M¹
PERJURY	--/ --	Eddy D	- 16S¹ 16G³ 16M¹ 16G¹
PERROQUET	--/ --		20G² -
PERSIAN HOUSE	--/105	Jefferson J M	16Y¹ 16G³ 16S² 16Y² 16G⁴ -
			20G¹ 20G² 20Y³ 16Y¹
PERSUASIVE	--/101	Perratt Miss L	16Y³ 16H² 16G² - 16G¹ 16G² 16M²
			16S² 16G³ 16G¹ 16G² 16G³
PETOSKU	--/107	Twiston-Davies	- 17M³ 16S¹ 17S³ 20G² 16S¹
			16S² 20G²
PETTY BRIDGE	--/120	James A P	22G³ 24S² 24G³ 25G² 24H²
			24G² 24M² 24G³ 26M¹ - 23M²
			22G¹ 25G⁴ 22M² 24G⁴ 26Y³
			21S¹ 24Y¹
PHALAROPE	--/ 68	Harris J L	- 17M³ 17G² 16G¹ 16G¹
PHAROAH'S LAEN	130/ --	Pipe M C	- 26G² 26G¹
PHILLIMAY	87/ --	Lee R	- 17G¹
PHISUS	--/ --	Henderson N J	- 17F¹
PHOENIX GOLD	--/ --	FitzGerald J G	- 22G¹
PICADOR	--/ --	Hobbs P J	20M¹ 25M⁴ 25M¹ 26G¹ - 19G¹
			21M¹
PICK ROUNDSTONE	90/ --	Gifford J T	16S² 20G³ - 16G³ 16G² 17G¹
			17P²
PIMS GUNNER	--/105	Burchell D	- 16G³ 16G¹ 16M³ 16W¹ 16G²
			16M³
PINATA	--/105	Pitman Mrs J	16S¹ - 16G¹
PINEMARTIN	106/ --	Richards G W	16M¹ 16G² 21M¹ 17F¹ 22M¹
			16M¹ 20G¹ 16M³ 16M³ 20S³
			20Y³ 20M⁴ 16F² 16G⁴ 17P¹
			16M⁴ - 16M² 16F² 16M¹ 16M²
			24F¹ 20G² 28G² 25M¹ 16G²
			21P¹
PINISI	--/ 78	Burke K R	- 21M¹ 21G³
PINK GIN	--/ 94	Hall Miss S E	18F² 16S¹ - 16M¹ 16Y⁴ 20W¹
			20W¹ 20Y²
PINTAIL BAY	--/ 80	Brooks C P E	- 17G² 16M¹

	CHS/HUR	TRAINER	FORM RANGE
PLAGUE O'RATS	80/ --	Frost R G	- 19F⁴ 25M¹ 20M³
PLASTIC SPACEAGE	110/ --	Old J A B	16G⁴ 16S³ 21G³ 20S³ 20G⁴ 20G¹ 25G³ - 16G¹ 18H² 20G¹ 20Y¹ 20G¹
PLAT REAY	115/ --	Forster Capt T	16S³ 16Y³ 20G¹ - 20S³ 16G³ 22G¹ 20S³ 20S¹
PLATINUM ROYALE	--/ 92	Pipe M C	- 18F²
PLATONIC AFFAIR	--/ 80	Wilson D A	21G¹ 21M² 21M³ 16M³ - 20M³ 16Y¹ 16Y²
PLAUSIBLE	--/ 93	Moore J S	- 22M² 19M¹ 16M² 22M² 21F¹
PLAY THE BLUES	--/ 78	Frost R G	- 18W³ 16M¹ 16S² 20W² 17F¹ 16F²
PLAYFUL JULIET	--/ --	Cambidge B R	- 22W¹
PLAYPEN	97/ --	Frost R G	17Y² 17M² 17M² 27M¹ - 22P² 26F¹ 25F¹ 24M² 25M² 25M² 18Y² 24G² 21G³
PLENTY CRACK	--/ 99	Mactaggart B	25S⁴ 25H¹ 28S⁵ - 26S¹ 25G³ 33G⁶
POACHER'S DELIGHT	--/ 91	Retter Mrs J G	17G² - 19G³ 24G¹ 24M³
POETIC GEM	119/ --	Smith Mrs S J	17S³ 16Y² 18H¹ 16G¹ 16M¹ - 20G³ 16G¹ 16G³ 20G¹ 16G⁶ 16M⁴ 20G² 20S¹ 20Y⁴
POLAR REGION	--/121	FitzGerald J G	20M¹ 24M¹ - 24G¹ 24F¹
POLECROFT	--/ 90	Burchell D	- 25G¹ 20Y¹ 16G³
POLISHING	--/110	Barker Mrs P A	- 16Y¹ 16G¹ 16M³ 16G¹ 20G³
POLITICAL ISSUE	--/ --	Robson T L A	22Y³ - 24S¹
POLLOCK	--/105	Pipe M C	- 17P³ 16W³ 16G² 19M¹ 16Y¹ 18G² 16G³
POLYGONUM	--/ --	Burnell W M	- 22G¹ 18G² 24G¹ 24G³
POLYPLATE	--/ 65	Ryan M J	- 16G³ 22G² 20P¹
POP SONG	79/ --	Roe G	17M⁴ 26G⁴ - 26F¹
POPPADOM	--/ 68	Turner J R	16F³ - 20M¹
PORTAVOGIE	85/ --	Parker C	20G⁴ 24G² 16G² 24S¹ 22S³ 24H³ - 24M² 24G² 24Y² 24G¹ 24G³
PORTER'S SONG	--/ --	Hutsby H	19Y³ 24M⁴ - 20G³ 19G¹ 16G¹
PORTONIA	85/ --	Reveley Mrs G	- 24G² 24G⁴ 27Y¹ 24G³ 24F¹
POSITIVE ACTION	79/ --	Barnes M A	- 16M¹ 17G⁴ 16M³
POSTAGE STAMP	--/116	Pearce J	- 20G¹ 20G¹ 20G⁴ 18M¹ 22M¹
PRAGADA	--/148	Pipe M C	24S² 24G¹ 27G¹ 24G² 24G¹ 25Y³ - 25G² 24G¹
PRAIRIE STORM	--/ --	Etherington T	25Y⁴ 25M² 25G¹ 24G³ 27M² - 24M³ 26G² 26M¹
PRECIOUS BOY	--/ --	Burke K R	16Y¹ 16H² 16G¹ 16Y¹ 16Y² 16G¹ - 16G¹ 16Y²
PREDESTINE	--/ 75	Madgwick M	- 16G² 16G¹ 16G¹
PREMIER PRINCESS	--/119	Ham G A	20M¹ 25M¹ 27G¹ 20S² 20M³ - 20P² 27F¹ 19G³ 22M¹ 22M³ 20M³ 28G¹ 24G³
PREOBLAKENSKY	--/119	Richards G W	- 16G¹ 20G¹ 20G¹ 20Y¹ 20G¹ 18Y¹
PRESENT TIMES	--/ 91	Moore A	16G¹ 16G¹ - 16M³ 16M¹ 16G³
PRIME DISPLAY	--/130	Sherwood O	- 20G¹ 21G² 24G¹ 24M³
PRIMITIVE SINGER	--/102	Pipe M C	- 16M¹ 16M³ 16Y¹ 16Y⁴ 20G³
PRINCE METTERNICH	111/ --	Hammond M D	24G¹ - 20G¹ 24F² 24F² 24M² 25G²
PRINCESS MOODYSHOE	--/ 87	Pipe M C	- 16G³ 16G² 19M¹ 19G¹ 17G¹
PRIVATE AUDITION	105/ --	Murphy F	- 17G³ 16Y⁴ 24G² 20G¹
PROPERO	--/138	Gifford J T	- 16Y¹ 18Y²
PROSEQUENDO	--/ 85	Dixon M	- 16Y¹
PROVERBIAL LUCK	--/ --	Saunders Miss	24M³ 24G⁴ 24M¹ 24G² 26M³ -

	CHS/HUR	TRAINER	FORM RANGE
PURBECK DOVE	87/ --	Parrott Mrs H	24M¹ 25Y² 26Y⁴ 24F² - 20S² 20G² 20G¹
QAJAR	83/ --	Bailey K C	- 16Y² 24M¹
QUAI D'ORSAY	--/ 89	O'Mahony F J	20G¹ - 20G¹ 18G³
QUALITAIR SOUND	--/123	Bottomley J F	- 16G² 17G¹ 16W¹ 16M¹ 16Y⁴
QUIDEST	80/ --	Fowler A	- 24G⁴ 25M⁴ 24F²
QUIET DAWN	--/ 80	King J S	- 22G¹
RAAWI	--/ 79	Norton L	- 16G³ 17M³ 20M¹
RADICAL LADY	119/ --	Moore G M	20S⁴ 24G² 24S² 28M¹ 26S¹ 24S² 24Y¹ 25G² 26G¹ - 20Y¹ 20Y¹ 33G² 25G² 20S¹ 26G³ 26M²
RADICAL VIEWS	--/ --	Murray Mrs A M	- 25G⁴ 20Y¹
RAFIKI	--/ 90	Retter Mrs J G	16Y¹ - 20Y³ 16G² 16G³ 17S¹
RAG TIME BELLE	--/ --	Charles-Jones	16G¹ 16M¹ 16M¹ 16M³ - 16M¹ 16G¹ 16M¹ 17G⁴
RAGE	--/ 68	Easterby M H	16G³ - 16F¹
RAGOREY	--/ --	Stephenson W A	- 24G¹ 24G¹ 22M¹ 22G¹ 24Y⁴ 25G¹
RAGTIME	--/ 90	Reid A S	16G² 16Y³ - 16Y² 20Y¹ 19Y² 16W³ 16S² 16Y³ 25F²
RAIN MARK	--/ --	Chatterton M G	20S¹ 24Y⁴ 24G³ 22M¹ - 20G¹
RAISE AN ARGUMENT	--/ --	Docker Mrs J	24Y⁴ 24Y² - 21G² 26G¹ 22Y² 22G¹ 24G³
RAITH HOMES	81/ --	Richards G W	16S³ - 16G¹
RAMBLING SONG	114/ --	Forster Capt T	19G¹ 20S³ - 21G² 21G² 21G¹
RANDAMA	--/ 73	Wintle D J	- 18W² 20F¹
RANDOLPH PLACE	--/144	Richards G W	20G¹ 20S¹ 25Y³ 20G¹ - 22G¹ 16Y³ 25G⁵
RAPID SLANE	--/ --	Stephenson W A	- 16G³ 16M¹ 16G¹ 20G¹ 16Y³
RARE BID	91/ --	Hodges R J	- 25M² 24F³ 24M³ 25G⁴ 24G³ 21G³ 24Y³ 25F³ 20M¹ 20M²
RARE LUCK	92/ --	Jones P J	20F³ 25G³ 16Y⁴ 16H³ 25G³ 24M² - 24G⁴ 25G¹ 25M¹ 25Y¹
RARFY'S DREAM	--/ 88	Banks J E	- 16W¹ 16W³ 16W¹ 16W¹
RATHER GORGEOUS	--/ --	Wilson Capt J	16W³ - 20G¹
RATHMORE	--/ 86	Gaselee N A	- 24Y³ 25M¹
RATHVINDEN HOUSE	--/ 94	Jones T Thomso	- 16G² 18G² 21G¹
RATIFY	--/ 90	Knight Miss H	- 16M² 16G¹
RAWAAN	--/106	Tinkler N	- 17F¹ 17M¹ 16G¹ 16F¹ 16G² 16M³ 16M¹ 16M²
RE-RELEASE	98/ --	Pipe M C	20M² 17Y¹ 20G³ 20S¹ - 17G¹ 20Y² 20Y² 20S¹ 17G²
REAL CLASS	110/ --	Richards G W	- 24G¹ 20G¹ 24Y¹ 20Y¹ 25G⁴
RED CRESCENT	--/ --	Jenkins J R	- 16M¹
RED RING	--/107	Webber J	16S¹ 16Y² 16M² - 16G² 21G³ 21G² 16Y¹ 16S² 16Y¹
RED RONDO	100/ --	Edwards J A C	16G¹ 19G¹ 16M¹ 16S³ 19Y¹ 20M² 20G³ - 20G³ 18G³ 20M³ 25G² 24Y¹ 24M³ 20G³
REDGRAVE GIRL	--/ --	Bishop K	16M³ 16M² 17M¹ 16M² - 17G² 17Y¹ 17M³ 16M²
REEF LARK	--/ 73	Hellens J A	16S¹ 16S¹ 20G³ - 20M¹ 20G³
REELING	--/ 70	Leach P	16F³ - 16F¹
REFERRAL FEE	--/ --	Kelly G P	- 16M¹
REPUTE	--/ --	Pipe M C	- 22F¹ 22F¹ 25F²
REGAL ESTATE	88/ --	Moffatt D	16S² 18S² 16H¹ 22S³ - 16S³ 20G⁴ 24Y¹
REGAN	--/ 73	Barclay Miss J	- 22W¹ 25M²
REGENT CROSS	101/ --	Reed W G	- 16Y² 16G¹ 20G¹
RELEKTO	--/ --	Felton M J	- 16G¹ 20Y¹ 20Y¹ 16Y²

	CHS/HUR	TRAINER	FORM RANGE
RELIEF MAP	--/ 87	Parkes J	16G³ 16Y³ 16Y² 17G¹ – 20F³ 18F³ 20W³ 16G³ 16S² 18Y¹ 17G²
REMITTANCE MAN	168/ --	Henderson N J	16G¹ 20M¹ 20M¹ 20Y¹ 20Y¹ 16Y¹ – 20G¹ 24G² 20G¹ 16G¹ 20G¹
REPEAT THE DOSE	129/ --	Etherington T	20G³ 20G¹ 20Y¹ 20Y³ – 24G² 22G³ 20S¹ 20G¹ 20G³
REVARO	89/ --	Ramsden Mrs J	16G² 16S² 16G³ – 16M⁴ 16M¹
REVE DE VALSE	--/122	Smith Denys	– 18G¹ 16G³
REVE EN ROSE	--/ 83	McMillan M D	16S³ – 19M¹ 16G¹ 17M²
REVTON	--/ --	Dalton P T	– 16M¹
RHODE ISLAND RED	87/ --	Moore A	– 26M⁴ 25M³ 25G¹ 26G⁴ 26M¹
RHOMAN COIN	--/ 75	Rothwell B S	– 17G³ 16Y¹
RIBOKEYES BOY	--/ 71	Davison A R	16G² 16M³ – 16G¹ 16G²
RICH REMORSE	--/ --	Curtis R	24G¹ 25M² 24Y³ – 24M¹ 24G³
RICHARDSON	--/ --	FitzGerald J G	– 16G³ 16M¹
RICMAR	--/ 86	Retter Mrs J G	– 19G³ 19M⁴ 20M¹
RIDWAN	--/101	Morgan K A	16G³ – 20G² 20Y¹ 24S³
RING OF FORTUNE	--/108	Pipe M C	– 17G¹ 16G² 16G² 16S² 16G¹ 16S² 20Y¹ 20G¹ 22M²
RINGMORE	95/ --	Parkes J	– 16Y¹ 17M³ 16Y² 20M³ 16G² 16M² 17M²
RIO HAINA	102/ --	Forster Capt T	20S³ – 20M³ 22M¹ 24G¹
RIVA	--/ --	Barons D H	– 16M¹
RIVA'S TOUCH	79/ --	King Mrs A L M	– 16F² 17F¹ 18F¹ 16M⁴ 17M³ 16M³
RIVER BOUNTY	118/ --	Upson John R	22G² 20S¹ 16Y² – 20G² 20G¹ 20G⁴ 24M¹ 24G² 24G¹ 24G² 25G² 20G²
RIVER HOUSE	105/ --	Stephenson W A	20G² 24G² 24G¹ 25G² 20G¹ 24G¹ 22Y³ 22F² 24F² – 20S¹ 24M³ 24M¹ 20G² 24G² 24G² 20G² 20G³ 20G² 20M³
RIVER PEARL	--/ 91	Richards G W	– 20G¹ 20Y¹
RIVERAIN	--/ 67	Barron T D	– 16M¹
RIVERSIDE BOY	123/ --	Pipe M C	20Y³ 23Y¹ 24G¹ 21Y¹ 24S¹ 24Y² – 24G² 24S¹
RIVERTINO	94/ --	Mitchell P	– 20M³ 20G³ 24G¹ 26G³ 24M²
ROAD TO RICHES	--/ --	Jones T Thomso	16G¹ – 17G¹ 20G⁴
ROARK	--/ --	Willis H	– 20Y¹
ROBBIE BURNS	--/ --	Smyth R V	20S³ 16G² – 16M¹
ROCCO	--/118	Pitman Mrs J	– 16Y¹ 21G¹ 20M³ 20G³
ROCKTOR	118/ --	Barons D H	– 24G² 26G¹ 25G² 25G² 26G¹
RODEO STAR	--/136	Tinkler N	– 20G³ 16G¹ 16Y¹ 16G¹ 16M¹ 16G¹ 16G²
ROLLING BALL	--/ --	Pipe M C	– 20Y¹
ROMAN DART	91/ --	Scudamore M	16G¹ 16S¹ 16Y² – 16W¹ 16G⁴
ROMANY KING	145/ --	Balding G B	22G³ 17Y³ 20G¹ 20Y¹ 20S¹ 20Y³ 20Y² 20Y¹ 20G³ – 24G¹ 24G² 21G¹ 24G³ 24M³ 25G⁴ 36Y²
ROMOLA NIJINSKY	--/ 57	Evans P D	– 16M¹
RONANS BIRTHDAY	110/ --	Hobbs P J	20M⁴ 20S¹ 24M² 25G¹ 24G¹ – 20G¹ 20G³ 25Y⁴ 24G¹
RONOCCO	--/ --	Williams Mrs S	17F³ 16F² 17M¹ 17F² – 17F³ 16F³ 17F³ 16M¹ 17M² 16M² 16G³
ROSCOE BOY	--/ --	Dawson C	– 18G¹
ROSE LANCASTER	80/ --	Hallett T B	– 21Y⁴ 26G² 26G¹
ROSE TABLEAU	--/100	Wells Mrs H S	– 16G³ 17G² 20M³ 22S¹

	CHS/HUR	TRAINER	FORM RANGE
ROSE-LANE	--/ --	Saunders Miss	- 22G¹ 25Y² 24M³ 24M⁴
ROSES HAVE THORNS	--/ --	Morris D	- 16G³ 16G³ 16W¹ 16W³
ROSGILL	--/103	Mitchell P	- 16G² 16M¹ 16G⁴
ROSS VENTURE	125/ --	Edwards J A C	16G¹ 16G¹ 16S⁴ 17G¹ 16M² 19M¹ 20M¹ - 20G² 20M¹ 20G³ 20M¹ 20G² 25M² 25G¹
ROSSVILLE	91/ --	Charlton J I A	20G³ - 16G⁴ 16Y³
ROSTHERNE	--/ --	O'Leary R	16Y³ 22M² 22F² - 22F¹
ROSTREAMER	--/104	Bravery G C	22G³ 25Y² 22Y³ 28S¹ - 27M¹ 27G²
ROTHKO	--/117	Smith Mrs S J	- 22G² 20G² 24G¹ 21S⁴
ROUGH QUEST	132/ --	Etherington T	- 20G² 20G² 25S² 24G⁴ 20G⁴
ROUSILLON TO BE	--/ 76	Sanders Miss B	- 18G³ 19G¹
ROW REE	--/ --	Hobbs P J	- 16G¹ 16G¹
ROWHEDGE	--/ 78	Perrin Mrs J	18M¹ 22M¹ 20M² 16F² 16G² 16G³ - 16G³ 16G³ 20G¹
ROWLANDSONS JEWELS	130/ --	Smith D Murray	30G³ 25Y¹ - 24M¹ 24M¹ 29M³ 24M² 29M⁴
ROXALL CLUMP	106/ --	Bailey K C	16Y² 16Y³ 16Y¹ 17H⁴ - 16G² 16G³ 16G² 18G¹ 16M¹ 26M² 16M³ 20G²
ROYAL BATTERY	123/ --	Barons D H	- 34M³ 28Y¹ 26Y⁴ 28G¹ 32S⁶
ROYAL DERBI	--/145	Callaghan N A	16G² 16M⁴ 16G¹ 16G⁴ 16G³ - 16G² 16G¹ 16M¹ 16M¹ 16M² 16G²
ROYAL GAIT	--/ --	Fanshawe J	- 16G² 16G¹ 16G¹ 16G¹
ROYAL SAXON	--/ 86	Knight Miss H	- 20G¹ 21G¹
ROYAL SQUARE	--/125	Harwood G	- 18G³ 20G¹ 24G⁴ 21G⁴
RUBIKA	118/ --	Mellor S	- 24Y² 32G¹ 33G² 33G⁴
RUBINS BOY	--/ 89	Sherwood S E	24M² - 24G³ 22G¹
RUFUS	--/100	Edwards J A C	- 24G² 24S¹ 24Y¹
RULING DYNASTY	--/ 96	Usher M D I	18F¹ 16M³ 18M³ - 18F¹ 17G¹ 18F¹ 18G² 19M¹ 20W³ 16W²
RUN BY JOVE	81/ --	White J	- 18F³ 18F³
RUN FOR FREE	136/ --	Pipe M C	20Y¹ 16G¹ 20G² 21Y¹ 25Y² 20Y³ - 20G⁴ 24G¹ 26H¹ 20S¹ 20Y¹ 24G² 25G³
RUN FOR NICK	--/ 90	Green Miss Z A	- 17G³ 16Y² 16M¹ 16G³ 16F¹
RUN PET RUN	92/ --	Monteith P	- 22H² 20H¹ 20S¹ 16Y²
RUN UP THE FLAG	--/ 77	Gifford J T	- 16M¹ 16G³
RUPPLES	79/ --	Chapman M C	16Y³ - 17F¹ 17F² 17G² 19F² 19M³ 17M¹
RUSHING WILD	127/ --	Barber R J	- 26G² 24G¹
RUSTY MUSIC	--/ 77	Brown R L	- 19G³ 25G¹
RUSTY ROC	--/117	Davies M W	16M¹ 16Y³ - 16G¹ 16S³ 17M³
RUTHS PRIDE	--/ 67	Price G M	- 16G¹
RYDE AGAIN	135/ --	Pitman Mrs J	26M² 20G⁴ 24Y² 16G² - 20G¹ 20G¹ 20Y² 24G¹
SABAKI RIVER	108/ --	Retter Mrs J G	16G² 16S¹ 16G¹ - 17G² 22M² 17G¹
SABIN DU LOIR	157/ --	Pipe M C	- 21M¹ 17G¹ 20G¹ 20G⁶
SACRE D'OR	109/ --	Mackie J	- 16S¹ 16M³ 16G² 20G² 20G¹ 20S² 19G²
SAFETY	--/105	White J	- 16F¹ 16M² 16M¹ 17G² 16W¹ 18W² 16W¹ 16W¹
SAFFAAH	--/100	Muir W R	- 16G¹ 16G¹
SAGART AROON	--/ --	Pipe M C	- 26G¹
SAILOR BLUE	--/ 93	Turnell Andrew	- 16M¹ 16S² 21G³
SAILOR BOY	--/ 97	Akehurst R	18F³ - 16M³ 18W¹ 16W³ 18W³ 20W¹ 22W²
SAINT BENE'T	--/ 70	Haslam P C	- 16G¹

	CHS/HUR	TRAINER	FORM RANGE
SALAMANDER JOE	103/ --	Nicholson D	16G³ 16G¹ 20G² 16G³ 22G³ 21M¹ - 25M¹ 24G⁴ 25M¹ 24G² 30M²
SALCOMBE HARBOUR	89/ --	Nicholls P F	- 24G⁴ 20G³ 25G² 20Y¹ 20G³
SALLY'S DOVE	--/ 75	Price R J	- 16Y¹
SALLY'S GEM	--/104	White J	20M² - 22G¹ 22G³ 22G¹ 20G² 24G²
SALWAN	--/135	Bevan P J	- 16G¹ 16G¹ 16G¹ 16G⁵ 16Y¹
SAM SHORROCK	95/ --	Thorner G	25G¹ 28G² 26Y² - 26S³ 26Y³ 26G¹ 25G¹ 25G²
SAN FERNANDO	--/122	Gifford J T	- 16Y² 16Y¹ 20S²
SAN FRANCISCO JOE	--/ 85	Denson A W	- 16W¹ 16W² 18W³
SAN LORENZO	--/ 95	Bailey K C	- 16G³ 16G⁴ 16G² 16G¹ 16G¹ 16G¹ 16M²
SAN OVAC	--/ --	Brooks C P E	20M² 24F² 20F⁴ 25G⁴ - 21G³ 25M¹ 26G² 20G²
SANAWI	--/ 66	James A P	16F¹ 16S³ 20W² 16M³ 20Y² - 20W³ 16M³ 19M¹ 20G³ 17G²
SAND CASTLE	--/ 68	Howling P	20W¹ - 22M¹
SAND-DOLLAR	--/108	Old J A B	16W² - 16M³ 16G³ 16W³ 19F¹ 17M¹ 17F²
SANDHURST PARK	--/ 97	Holder R J	19M³ - 16S¹ 16G¹ 16Y²
SANDHURST TYPE	--/ --	Chamberlain A	- 17F¹
SANDMOOR PRINCE	81/ --	Pritchard Dr P	- 17F² 17F⁴ 24G² 17G³ 20G² 16G³ 19G³ 20W¹ 22W³ 20F¹
SANDY'S BEACON	--/ 97	FitzGerald J G	14M³ 17G³ - 20G² 24Y³
SANSOOL	--/ --	Whillans A C	- 24H¹ 26G² 25G²
SANTARAY	--/ 98	Mackie J	12S¹ - 16G² 16G¹ 16G¹ 16M⁴
SANTELLA BOBKES	81/ --	Barnes M A	- 20F² 20M² 24G¹
SARTORIUS	--/115	Jones T Thomso	26F² 16G⁴ - 16G² 16M³ 16G¹ 16Y¹
SASKIA'S HERO	--/ --	Bottomley J F	- 16W¹
SASKIA'S REPRIEVE	--/ 95	Bottomley J F	- 16M¹ 20W³ 16G³
SASKIA'S SILVER	--/ --	Bottomley J F	- 16M¹
SAWDUST JACK	--/ --	Easterby M W	17Y¹ 16S³ 16Y³ 16S¹ 16Y² 17M² - 16M¹
SCAPIN	--/ 90	Forster Capt T	- 18G¹
SCENT OF BATTLE	--/ --	Haynes M J	- 16Y² 16Y¹ 16Y¹ 16Y⁴
SCENTED GODDESS	--/ 66	Moore J S	- 16M² 16M² 16W² 16W³ 16W² 18W¹
SCHWEPPES TONIC	--/ 87	Price William	16G³ 20G² 18S² 18W³ - 16G¹ 16G² 16G³
SCOTONI	--/100	O'Sullivan R J	- 17F³ 16F³ 16G² 16W³ 16W¹ 18W² 16W¹ 16W¹
SCOTTISH GOLD	--/ 91	Perratt Miss L	- 24S¹ 24G²
SEA BUCK	--/100	Balding G B	- 22G¹ 21G³ 24S⁴ 24Y²
SEA ISLAND	118/ --	Pipe M C	19Y² 16Y² 16H¹ 16G¹ 20Y¹ 20M³ - 24G² 22G² 20Y² 25G² 24Y¹ 20G²
SEA TROUT	--/107	Horwood Miss J	20S³ - 22G¹
SEAL PRINCE	--/ --	Penfold G W	- 25G² 24M¹
SEATON GIRL	--/ 79	Frost R G	17G³ 19M¹ 17F² 21M⁴ 17Y¹ 17Y² 17Y⁴ - 17S¹
SEBEL HOUSE	85/ --	McCain D	19Y⁴ - 16S¹ 20S³ 20G⁴ 24S²
SECRET CASTLE	--/ --	Easterby M H	- 16M¹
SECRET FINALE	--/ 72	Fort J R	24G¹ 24S² 26G³ 27S¹ 24Y³ - 24G¹ 26G² 25G²
SECRET LIASON	--/ 75	Turner W G M	16M² 17F³ - 16S¹ 16G²
SECRET SUMMIT	--/ 90	Forbes A L	- 17F¹ 16F³ 20F² 16F³ 16G¹ 16W¹ 18W¹
SENATOR OF ROME	--/107	Balding G B	24M¹ 24M² 24G³ 24G³ 24Y⁴

	CHS/HUR	TRAINER	FORM RANGE
			$25G^2$ $25G^3$ – $24G^3$ $25G^2$ $25G^1$ $24G^2$ $25M^2$ $20M^2$
SENATOR SNUGFIT	--/113	Easterby M W	– $20M^4$ $24M^4$ $25G^1$ $24S^1$ $24S^2$ $27Y^1$ $28G^3$
SENDAI	--/110	Gifford J T	– $16G^1$ $16M^1$ $20Y^1$ $20G^1$ $21S^1$
SEON	--/ 84	Bentley W	– $16M^2$ $18S^3$ $18Y^1$ $18G^2$ $16G^1$ $16G^1$ $16M^2$
SEQUESTRATOR	--/ 70	Evans P D	$16F^2$ – $17F^2$ $16M^1$ $17M^3$ $16F^1$
SERGEANT AT ARMS	--/ --	Davison A R	– $18F^1$
SERPHIL	--/ 60	Smith Mrs S J	– $16M^1$
SET THE STANDARDS	--/ 82	Whillans A C	– $17S^3$ $16F^3$ $18G^2$ $16M^1$ $16Y^2$ $17G^3$ $16F^4$ $16G^4$
SETTER COUNTRY	113/ --	Hodges R J	$17G^3$ $20M^2$ $16G^1$ $16G^1$ $16G^3$ $16G^3$ $16G^2$ $16Y^2$ – $16G^1$ $17G^4$ $16G^1$ $16M^1$ $16M^2$
SEVEN SONS	--/ 95	Turner W G M	$16F^3$ $16G^1$ $16M^3$ $16M^3$ – $17F^3$ $18F^2$ $16F^1$ $16M^2$ $16G^1$ $16M^2$
SEVENTH LOCK	--/ 95	Sherwood O	$20S^3$ $16Y^3$ – $19M^1$ $20G^3$ $22W^2$
SEXY MOVER	--/ 85	Storey W	$16G^1$ $16F^3$ – $16M^2$ $17G^1$ $16G^3$ $18F^3$
SHADES OF PEACE	--/ --	Rodford P R	– $17G^3$ $17G^2$ $17S^1$ $16W^3$ $16G^3$
SHADEUX	--/108	Wonnacott Mrs	$16M^4$ – $19F^2$ $17S^1$ $22M^1$
SHADOW RUN	--/ --	Dickin R	$16G^3$ $16S^2$ $16G^2$ – $16G^2$ $16Y^1$ $20G^2$ $20Y^1$ $16S^4$
SHADOWS OF SILVER	--/ --	McMahon B A	– $16G^1$ $16Y^2$
SHAH'S CHOICE	--/ --	Popham C L	$22Y^3$ $22Y^1$ $22M^3$ $24M^2$ – $17M^4$ $20M^1$
SHALCHLO BOY	--/ --	Hodges R J	$17M^3$ – $17F^4$ $21F^2$ $17G^4$ $24G^1$ $25M^2$ $24G^2$ $24G^3$
SHAMANA	121/ --	Nicholson D	$16M^2$ $16M^1$ $16G^2$ $16M^3$ $16M^2$ – $16G^1$ $17G^1$ $16G^1$ $17G^2$ $16Y^1$ $20G^4$
SHAMSHOM AL ARAB	--/ 72	Carter W	– $16F^3$ $16G^2$ $16M^1$ $16W^3$
SHANBALLY BOY	102/ --	Henderson N J	– $24G^1$
SHANNAGARY	115/ --	Hodges R J	$21M^2$ $21F^3$ $20M^3$ $17Y^3$ $20G^1$ $17G^1$ – $21M^1$ $21M^3$ $21G^2$ $19G^1$ $21G^4$ $21G^1$
SHAR EMBLEM	--/ --	Dow S	– $20W^3$ $20W^1$ $22W^1$
SHAREEF STAR	--/ 74	Blanshard M	– $20Y^3$ $20W^2$ $16S^1$ $19G^2$
SHARINSKI	78/ --	Juckes R T	– $16F^2$ $20F^1$
SHARP ORDER	--/ --	Wilton Miss S	– $20M^1$ $20M^3$ $20M^4$ $16M^1$ $16Y^1$
SHARPGUN	89/ --	Moore A	– $16G^3$ $16G^2$ $16G^1$ $16Y^3$ $16G^2$ $16G^1$ $16M^2$
SHAWWAL	--/ 81	O'Leary R	– $16W^3$ $16G^1$ $16W^2$ $18Y^2$
SHEARMAC STEEL	--/ --	Bridgwater K S	– $16G^1$
SHEEP STEALER	--/ --	FitzGerald J G	– $16W^1$
SHEEPHAVEN	--/ --	Etherington T	$20Y^4$ $24S^3$ – $24G^1$
SHEER JEST	--/ --	Warner W J	– $25M^2$ $24G^2$ $22M^1$ $26G^1$
SHELTON ABBEY	86/ --	Stephenson W A	– $20F^3$ $24M^1$ $24S^4$
SHEPHERD'S HYMN	92/ --	Aconley Mrs V	$24M^3$ $24M^3$ – $24M^2$ $27F^1$ $28M^2$ $27F^1$ $24G^2$ $26G^1$ $27M^2$ $32G^3$ $24M^4$ $25G^3$ $24F^1$
SHIKARI KID	--/ 83	Blockley P A	– $16G^3$ $16M^1$ $16G^3$ $16W^2$ $16S^2$ $16Y^1$
SHILINSKI	--/ 85	Moore G M	– $26Y^1$ $26G^3$
SHIPWRIGHT	94/ --	Retter Mrs J G	$25F^2$ – $20M^2$ $24M^3$ $20S^1$ $17M^1$
SHOON WIND	125/ --	Hammond M D	$24G^3$ $20G^2$ $20H^1$ $20H^1$ $25G^3$ – $24G^1$ $24Y^2$ $24G^1$
SHOULD NEVER BE	102/ --	Jenkins J R	– $20M^2$ $25M^2$ $20M^1$
SHRADEN LEADER	83/ --	Bailey K C	– $24G^1$ $24M^1$
SHU FLY	--/124	Oliver Mrs S	– $16G^2$ $16M^1$ $16G^1$ $16G^3$ $16G^1$

	CHS/HUR	TRAINER	FORM RANGE
			16G⁴
SHUIL SAOR	--/ --	Smith Mrs S J	- 20Y¹ 20G³
SIBERIAN BREEZE	--/ 70	Glover J A	- 17M² 16M¹ 16S² 20W²
SIBTON ABBEY	105/ --	Murphy F	20F¹ 22M³ 25M¹ - 16M³ 24G¹ 24G² 24G¹
SIGNOR SASSIE	--/ 83	Tinkler N	- 20G¹ 16S¹ 16F³
SIKERA SPY	108/ --	Hewitt Mrs A R	16G⁴ 20M¹ 20M² 20M¹ - 20Y² 20G² 20G³ 20S³ 25G¹ 24G¹ 20M¹
SILK DEGREES	--/107	Storey W	20M³ 18F¹ - 16M³ 22G² 20G¹ 20M² 20M¹
SILLARS STALKER	--/ 86	Ramsden Mrs J	- 16M¹ 16G¹ 17M¹ 16G¹
SILLIAN	--/109	Hewitt Mrs A R	16S² 20G¹ 16Y³ 20M² 20M² - 20S³ 16M¹
SILVER CANNON	94/ --	Voorspuy R	- 18F² 18F² 20G³ 18F³
SILVER HELLO	88/ --	Perratt Miss L	16G³ - 16G³ 20G⁴ 16G¹ 24G³ 20F¹ 20M³
SILVER KING	--/ --	Pipe M C	- 16Y¹
SILVER STICK	--/ 85	Easterby M W	- 22G¹ 20F¹ 20M¹
SILVER STRINGS	--/ 77	Palling B	18W² 20W² 20W³ 22G¹ - 19G² 16Y² 20G³ 16G³ 16G³ 18W¹
SIMONE'S SON	--/ 75	Barnett G	- 16G¹ 16G²
SIMPLE PLEASURE	--/ 94	Stirk Mrs M K	17F⁴ 22G² 24G⁴ 24Y⁴ 20G¹ 16Y¹ 16G² 20Y⁴ 16Y¹ 16M¹ - 16M² 16G¹ 16M¹ 16G¹ 18F¹ 16S¹ 16Y²
SIMPSON	--/117	Old J A B	17M¹ - 16G¹ 20G¹ 20S¹ 25G⁴
SINGING SAM	90/ --	Edwards J A C	14M¹ - 16G¹
SINGLE SHOOTER	--/ --	O'Sullivan R J	- 17G¹ 16G¹ 16G⁴
SINGLESOLE	91/ 90	Sly Mrs P	16G³ 20S¹ 20Y³ 20G² - 18Y² 20M² 20G¹ 24G¹ 20F³
SIR CRUSTY	--/121	O'Neill O	25F¹ 25F³ 25M¹ - 24Y⁴ 24S¹
SIR NODDY	103/ --	Miller C J Ver	19G³ 20S² - 24M⁴ 20M¹ 19G² 25M¹ 20G²
SIR PETER LELY	--/110	Hammond M D	18Y¹ 16Y² 16F⁴ 16F¹ - 16G² 17M¹ 16G¹
SIRE NANTAIS	--/ --	Burke K R	- 20G¹ 16S¹ 25G⁴
SIRISAT	--/ --	Hollowell Kerr	- 18G⁴ 22M¹ 24F¹
SIRRAH JAY	133/ --	Balding G B	20S³ 20G³ 20S¹ 20Y¹ 20S² 21G¹ 20G³ - 16G¹ 18G² 20Y¹ 16M¹ 20G² 20G² 20M²
SKELETOR	--/105	Tate T P	16G¹ 16G¹ 16Y¹ - 16G¹ 16Y² 18S³ 16G² 16Y²
SKINNHILL	97/ --	Jones T Thomso	20Y¹ 20H¹ 20G¹ 20G¹ 24M⁴ - 20G⁴ 25G⁴ 24M¹ 24M³ 20G³
SKIPPING TIM	125/ --	Pipe M C	21M¹ 20M¹ 20F¹ 20G¹ 25G¹ 20S¹ 20Y¹ 21G¹ 24S⁴ 21M³ 22M² - 26G¹ 25G¹ 18M¹
SKOLERN	--/ 94	Harrison A	16S³ - 16F⁴ 16M¹ 16M¹
SKOMAL	--/ 91	Bowen S A	- 16F¹ 16G¹
SKYGRANGE	--/ --	Turner J M	26F¹ - 24G¹ 26G² 25M¹ 24M¹
SLAVI	--/102	Pipe M C	- 17H¹ 16G¹ 16Y¹ 20G³
SLIPPERY MAX	88/ --	Juckes R T	16G² 17G³ - 20M³ 17S² 16F² 20F¹ 17G¹ 16M¹ 16S³ 17G³ 16G² 16M² 16G⁴ 20F²
SMALLMEAD LAD	--/ 63	Gandolfo D R	- 20G¹
SMARTIE EXPRESS	102/ --	Hodges R J	- 21F³ 21M² 19G² 21M² 26G⁴ 19M² 20M² 19M² 24G³ 21M² 20S¹ 21F¹ 20M¹
SMARTIE LEE	--/ --	Cole P F I	- 20G¹
SMILE AGAIN	--/ --	Knight Miss H	17M¹ 16M² 17M² - 16F⁴ 16F¹

	CHS/HUR	TRAINER	FORM RANGE
			17F¹
SMOOTH ESCORT	104/ --	Haine Mrs D	24G² 24S² 24G² 24S² 32Y¹ - 26G¹ 26M⁴
SMOOTH START	81/ --	James A P	19M² 16F³ - 20M¹ 19M³ 24F⁴ 20G³ 24G¹ 24M²
SNEAKAPENNY	120/ --	Bailey K C	26M² 24G³ 25Y² 24M³ 22G¹ - 18Y¹ 18G¹
SNITTON LANE	--/103	Edwards J A C	16G³ 16M³ 16M² - 20G² 16G¹ 18Y¹ 16G¹ 21M¹
SNOOKER TABLE	--/ 69	Williams W R	20M⁴ 16M³ - 16M¹ 18M¹ 17F² 17F³ 18M³
SNOWDRIFTER	--/ 74	Tompkins M H	13W² - 16G³ 16M¹
SNOWFIRE CHAP	113/ --	Reveley Mrs G	24Y² 27Y¹ 24G¹ 28Y¹ 28Y² 28M² 28Y³ 24S¹ - 26G³ 30G³ 26G¹ 25G² 28G³ 27M¹
SNOWY LANE	--/114	Pipe M C	- 16Y² 20G³ 16Y¹ 16G²
SNUGGLE	--/ --	Tompkins M H	16M⁴ 16G² 16W² 16W² 16W¹ 16W¹ 16W¹ 16W¹ - 16M⁴ 18W¹
SOCIETY GUEST	--/100	Turnell Andrew	16Y³ 16S³ 16F¹ 16M³ - 16G¹ 16G¹ 16G³
SODA POPINSKI	--/ 83	Campbell I	- 16W¹ 16W³
SOLAR CLOUD	82/ --	Charles M J	22G² 20M⁴ 21Y² 21M³ 20M³ - 20F¹ 20M² 20M³ 25M³ 20S¹ 21M³
SOLID	--/ 76	Jenkins J R	- 16G³ 16W¹
SOLID FUEL	--/ 87	Moffatt D	- 20F¹ 24Y² 24S² 25G³ 24Y³ 25F³
SOLITARY REAPER	--/ 67	Beever C R	18F² 16M¹ 16M² 16G² 20W³ 20W³ 20M² - 20F¹ 20F³ 18G¹
SOLO SAIL	--/ --	Weedon C	- 16M¹
SOLSTICE BELL	--/ 80	Voorspuy R	18F² 20F² 19F² 22M² - 18F² 18F¹ 19M² 18W³
SONALTO	78/ --	Williams D L	20M³ 20F² 20Y³ - 25G² 26F⁴ 20F¹
SONG OF SIXPENCE	--/122	Balding I A	- 16Y³ 16M² 16M¹ 16M¹ 16M²
SOONER STILL	119/ --	Edwards J A C	26G² 25Y³ 28G² 25M¹ 24Y² 26G² 26G¹ - 26G² 25G¹ 24Y¹ 24M³ 28Y⁴ 29Y²
SOUTH CROSS	84/ --	Moore G M	- 16Y¹ 17G⁴ 20G¹
SOUTHERN MINSTREL	125/ --	Stephenson W A	16M³ - 20G³ 20Y³ 24G⁴ 20Y⁴ 17M¹
SOUTHERN SUPREME	--/ --	Gifford J T	22G¹ 22M¹ - 21M¹
SOUTHERNAIR	111/ --	Jenkins J R	19M¹ 20G² 20M³ - 18G¹ 20M³ 20G²
SOVEREIGN NICHE	--/ 61	Miller N	- 16W² 16G¹ 16F³ 16H² 20F³
SOVEREIGN SOUND	--/ 98	Turnell Andrew	- 16G¹ 16G²
SPACE CAPTAIN	--/ --	Moore G M	- 16G¹ 16G¹
SPACE FAIR	126/ --	Lee R	20G³ - 20M³ 20G² 20G¹ 17G¹ 16G³ 16Y⁴
SPACIAL	--/ --	Gaselee N A	- 16G⁴ 16G¹ 21G¹ 20G⁴
SPANISH WHISPER	--/ 80	Bostock J R	16G² 16G¹ 16G² - 16G¹ 16G¹ 16G¹ 16M³
SPARK OF PEACE	95/ --	Blockley P A	20S³ 24Y³ - 24G⁴ 20G³ 16H¹ 16H³ 19G⁴ 16S²
SPARROW HALL	--/ --	FitzGerald J G	- 16W² 16W¹
SPARTAN DANCER	--/ --	Trickey M J	- 25S² 21G¹ 21F²
SPARTAN RANGER	--/ --	Hammond M D	16S² - 16G³ 20G¹
SPARTAN SPRITE	--/ --	Somerleyton Lo	- 24G³ 26G¹
SPEAKERS CORNER	--/ --	Sowersby M E	27S³ 24G³ - 26G¹ 26Y³
SPECIAL ACCOUNT	--/ --	Barwell C R	- 16W¹
SPEECH	--/ --	Stephenson W A	24M³ 21F¹ 21F¹ 20F¹ 27F¹

NAME	CHS/HUR	TRAINER	FORM RANGE
			24M^2 27M^3 24F^1 25M^1 22G^4
			16S^1 20M^3 20F^2 16G^2 20F^1
			24M^3 – 24M^1 26M^2 20M^2 20F^2
			24M^2 20G^3
SPHINX	--/ --	Bostock J R	16G^2 – 16W^1
SPICE MERCHANT	82/ --	Gaselee N A	16G^2 – 17F^2 19M^1 17G^2
SPINNING	--/120	Balding I A	– 16G^1 16M^1 16G^1 16G^3
SPLITTHEDIFFERENCE	102/ --	Barclay Mrs Al	22M^3 24G^2 – 24M^1 24M^2 24M^1
SPORTING IDOL	--/ 84	Burke K R	16M^3 16S^2 16G^3 16W^3 20W^1
			16W^1 16W^1 16W^1 16M^2 – 17F^3
			19F^1 18W^2
SPORTING MARINER	--/ --	Bloor D R	24Y^3 20G^3 25M^2 – 24M^1 22Y^1
			24S^3
SPREE CROSS	97/ --	Stephenson W A	– 16S^1 20M^4 17M^3 16Y^3 17F^4
			16G^1 16G^4
SPRING COTTAGE	--/ 85	Hardy W	24Y^2 – 22M^2 19F^1 24M^2
SPRING FUN	--/ --	Wellstead H	– 25G^1
SPRING TO GLORY	--/ 77	Pipe M C	– 16G^3 17G^2 17M^1
SPRING TO IT	--/112	Pipe M C	– 16F^3 24M^1 24F^1 24G^1 24G^1
			24M^1
SPRINGALEAK	127/ --	Sherwood O	16G^1 21Y^3 16Y^1 16Y^1 20M^1 –
			21M^1 20G^1 18Y^1 24G^1 25S^1
			24G^6
SPRINGDALE HALL	--/ --	Easterby M W	– 17M^1 17G^2
SPRINGHOLM	--/ --	Nicholson D	19G^2 16G^2 17M^1 17G^3 16Y^3 –
			17M^1 16G^2 16M^2
SPROWSTON BOY	--/124	Perratt Miss L	24G^4 – 24G^2 25M^1
SPRUCER	103/ --	McKie Mrs I	20Y^3 – 24G^2 20G^1 16Y^1 25Y^1
SRIVIJAYA	--/105	Reveley Mrs G	16Y^2 16M^1 16G^4 17G^2 – 16G^2
			17F^2 16G^3 16G^1 16G^3 17M^2
STAGE PLAYER	--/113	Wilton Miss S	18F^1 16F^2 16M^4 24M^1 20M^2
			21M^2 25M^2 – 18F^2 19F^1 18G^2
			21G^1 20M^4
STAGS FELL	97/ --	Moore G M	16M^1 16Y^2 – 20F^1 20M^1 16G^2
STANDARD ROSE	--/ 85	Channon M R	20G^2 24W^3 – 18M^1
STANE STREET	--/ 68	Forster Capt T	– 16G^3 16Y^3 17M^3 16G^1 19M^2
			16G^3
STANWAY	--/ --	Joynes Mrs P M	16M^2 16M^1 – 17F^2 16F^1 16F^2
			16F^1 20F^2 16F^3 16M^3
STAR OATS	--/ 75	Richards G W	– 16M^2 17G^1 18S^2 16G^3
STAR OF THE GLEN	--/ 92	Pitman Mrs J	20W^3 – 16G^3 16G^1 17G^1 16G^1
STAR QUEST	--/109	Jenkins J R	– 20M^1
STAR SEASON	--/ --	Holder R J	20G^3 18G^1 17S^2 16G^1 16G^2 –
			21S^1 20G^2 19G^1 19G^1 20G^1
STAR'S DELIGHT	150/ --	Pipe M C	16M^1 17G^1 16Y^1 16Y^1 16G^1 –
			21G^1 20Y^1 16G^6
STAREMBER LAD	--/ --	Cumings K	24Y^1 – 24G^1 24G^2
STATAJACK	--/115	Elsworth D R C	– 16G^1 16G^2
STATED CASE	--/111	Easterby M H	– 20Y^2 20S^1 24G^2 27G^1
STATELY LOVER	108/ --	Grissell D M	20S^1 20S^3 – 20G^1 20M^3
STAUNCH FRIEND	--/138	Tompkins M H	– 16Y^2 16G^1 16Y^2
STAUNCH RIVAL	--/ 90	Thorner G	– 16F^3 16F^2 16M^2 17G^1 17M^3
			21M^2 22M^3 21G^2 20Y^3
STAY AWAKE	105/ --	O'Neill J J	16Y^2 16Y^2 16M^1 16M^3 – 16M^1
			17G^1 16F^1 17M^1 16M^2 16G^2
			16M^1 16G^4 16M^3
STAY ON TRACKS	128/ --	Stephenson W A	20M^2 24M^2 24M^1 24S^2 24S^3
			24Y^3 25Y^3 – 26G^3 24M^2 25G^2
			24Y^3 24Y^1 30M^1 33G^3 29M^6
STEELE JUSTICE	--/ --	Manners W	– 24F^1 24G^2 24M^1
STEEPLE JACK	--/ 89	Bishop K	– 17Y^3 16Y^1

	CHS/HUR	TRAINER	FORM RANGE
STEPFASTER	100/ --	Stephenson W A	22M² 20M³ 20F¹ 24M¹ - 20M² 25S² 27F³ 27F² 22G³ 20H³ 20G¹ 20M¹ 20G¹
STEVEADON	--/108	Callaghan N A	- 16G¹ 16M² 16G² 16G¹
STIRLING EXPRESS	104/ --	Mackie J	16M¹ 18G³ 16G² - 16M¹ 17G⁴ 17M¹ 16G²
STONE FLAKE	--/110	Kelleway P A	- 16W¹ 16W¹ 20G³ 20Y³
STORM ALERT	98/ --	Turnell Andrew	- 16G² 16G¹
STORM ORPHAN	--/ 78	Sanders Miss B	- 20W² 16W¹ 16W¹ 16W² 16W² 16W³ 16W³
STORMHEAD	--/ --	Hall Miss S E	- 17M² 16F¹
STORMWATCH	--/ 84	Gandolfo D R	- 22G¹ 20G³ 24M⁴
STORMY DREAMS	--/104	Reveley Mrs G	16G¹ 16S² - 16G² 22G¹ 20G²
STRAIGHT LACED	--/ 71	Clarke Peter C	- 16W² 20W¹ 16G³ 16G³ 16M³ 17F³
STRANDS OF GOLD	--/ --	Pipe M C	- 24S¹
STRANGELY QUIET	--/ --	Donnelly T W	16G³ 16M⁴ 22G⁴ 17M⁴ - 20M⁴ 17F² 16M⁴ 16G³ 17M³ 16G¹
STRATH ROYAL	--/ --	Brennan O	- 16G¹
STREET KID	--/ 94	Houghton R F J	- 16M¹ 17Y²
STRONG APPROACH	110/ --	Charlton J I A	16F⁴ 22G² 16G² - 20M² 16G³ 24M² 20G¹ 20S⁴ 20G²
STRONG VIEWS	--/ 86	Stephenson W A	- 16G³ 16Y¹ 16M³ 16M¹ 16M¹
STYLISH GENT	--/ 93	Tinkler N	- 16M¹ 16Y² 16G¹
SUKAAB	--/ 96	Ryall B J M	16G² 20G³ 16M³ 16Y³ 20G³ 25Y³ 20F³ - 16M¹ 16M² 16M¹ 17G³ 17G³ 18S³ 19M² 21G³ 22M³
SULUK	--/108	Hollinshead R	- 18W¹ 22W¹ 18W¹ 16W¹ 20W¹ 20W¹
SUNBEAM TALBOT	107/ --	Jones A P	25G⁴ 26G³ - 26G¹ 24Y³ 24G¹ 27S¹ 24G⁴ 26G⁴
SUNDAY PUNCH	--/ 93	Gifford J T	16Y³ - 16M³ 16Y² 20G¹ 22G⁴
SUNSET AGAIN	--/101	Balding G B	24M² - 18G³ 24M⁴ 25F¹
SUNSET AND VINE	--/116	Dow S	16M⁴ - 22G¹ 20G³ 18G¹ 20S¹
SUNSET REINS FREE	--/ 87	Alston E J	16G³ - 16G¹ 17G³
SUNSET ROCK	--/ --	FitzGerald J G	- 16G² 16W¹
SUPER MALT	--/ 78	Allison Miss K	- 18F³ 17F³ 18F³ 16W¹ 18G¹ 16S²
SUPER RITCHART	--/ 92	Palling B	- 16G¹ 16G¹
SUPERIOR FINISH	--/103	Pitman Mrs J	16Y¹ - 20G¹ 20S³
SURE METAL	135/ --	McCain D	20G¹ 18G³ 20G² 16M³ 16Y¹ 20G⁴ - 16G¹ 16G¹ 16M³ 16Y² 16S³
SUREFOOT SILLARS	--/ 86	Brennan O	16G¹ - 16G³ 20W² 22W² 22W¹
SUREN	--/ 96	Weedon C	20M³ 20M² 20W² 20W¹ - 22G⁴ 18G² 22G² 20Y¹ 22G²
SWAN WALK	--/ 87	Macauley Mrs N	- 16G¹ 16Y²
SWEET CITY	--/111	Richards G W	16S² 16S¹ 20G² - 16Y¹ 20G³ 20Y² 20H¹ 24G³
SWEET DUKE	--/105	Twiston-Davies	- 18G¹ 16M³ 24Y¹ 20S² 20Y²
SWEET GLOW	--/140	Pipe M C	- 17F³ 23M¹ 20M² 24G² 18S³ 24M¹ 24G¹ 24M¹ 24G³
SWIFT SWORD	--/ --	Reveley Mrs G	- 16M² 16G¹ 16M³ 16G¹ 16G² 16G²
SWILLY EXPRESS	--/ 98	Christian S	17Y³ 17G³ - 16G³ 19Y³ 18S¹ 21M³ 17S³
SWORD BEACH	125/ --	Easterby M H	16S⁴ 20G² 24F¹ - 20M³ 20G² 20G³ 20G¹ 24M³ 20M¹
SYBILLIN	--/149	FitzGerald J G	16G² 16G¹ - 16G¹ 16G¹ 16M³ 16G³

	CHS/HUR	TRAINER	FORM RANGE
SYDMONTON	--/103	Henderson N J	- 16G² 16G¹
SYLVIA BEACH	--/ --	Holder R J	- 16Y¹
TACO	--/ --	McMillan M D	- 24M¹ 25M³ 25M²
TAGMOUN CHAUFOUR	80/ --	Barrow A	- 26M³ 26G³ 34M⁴ 26G² 26G¹
TAKE ISSUE	--/115	Sutcliffe J	- 20G¹ 16G² 16M² 18W¹ 16W² 16W³
TAKE TWO	--/ 90	White J	- 16W¹ 16W¹ 17M¹
TAKEMETHERE	101/ --	Pipe M C	21F¹ 21M³ 22M¹ - 17F¹ 19M³ 17M² 21F² 20M³ 20G¹ 26G⁴
TALL MEASURE	--/ 88	Swindlehurst D	16F³ - 16F¹ 20F¹
TALLYWAGGER	--/111	Moore G M	- 16F¹ 16F² 16G² 20M³ 22G³ 22S³ 20G¹
TALUS	--/ 83	Bosley J R	- 16M³ 16F¹
TAMISE	--/ --	White J	16M¹ 17G² - 17G¹ 17F² 22M¹
TANFIRION BAY	--/ 88	Hedger P R	- 18G² 16G² 16M¹ 16G² 16G² 22F¹
TAPAGEUR	--/ --	Pipe M C	16S¹ 17Y² 16M² 17M¹ 21M¹ 22G¹ 20M¹ - 16M¹
TAPATCH	--/ 92	Moore G M	- 16M¹ 16H³ 16F² 16F¹ 16G¹ 17M² 17M²
TARKOVSKY	--/107	Lee R	18G² 20Y² 24S³ 21S⁴ 24S¹ - 24Y¹ 24Y²
TARMON	--/ 70	Barrow A	- 16M¹ 17M³ 16G³
TAROUDANT	--/ --	Holder R J	- 22G¹
TARTAN TRADEMARK	119/ --	Richards G W	20G² 25G¹ 22M¹ 24M¹ 27M¹ 24G² 24G³ 24G³ 22M³ - 26M¹
TASMAN OAK	--/ --	Oliver Mrs S	- 17G¹ 18F¹
TASMIM	--/ --	Moore G M	- 17F¹ 17M¹ 16F¹
TAYLORMADE BOY	--/107	Smith Denys	16G⁴ 16M² - 20F¹
TAYLORS CASTLE	--/ 66	Cole S N	17M³ - 16G³ 17G³ 16G¹ 16Y²
TEAM CHALLENGE	120/ --	Pitman Mrs J	26Y⁴ 25G² 25G² 27Y¹ 28S⁶ - 25M¹ 25G⁴ 25M⁴ 26Y¹
TEAPLANTER	--/ --	Saunders Miss	24G¹ 25Y¹ 24G² 25Y¹ 25F¹ 24M¹ 26S² - 18Y¹ 24G¹
TEL E THON	--/ 82	Jones P J	- 16W² 16W³ 17F¹ 16M²
TELL YOU WHAT	--/ 73	Casey T	- 17M¹
TENTER CLOSE	--/ 96	Hammond M D	- 22F¹ 20M¹ 20M² 24G¹
TERAO	--/ --	Pipe M C	16G¹ - 22Y³ 20S¹ 20S¹
TEWTRELL LAD	88/ --	Bukovets J M	26M² 26G⁴ - 20W² 24G¹ 26M³ 18G³
TEXAN CLAMOUR	--/ 95	Moore J S	- 16W² 20W¹ 20W² 17Y¹ 19M² 18G¹ 16G³
THATS THE BUSINESS	--/ --	Balding G B	19M³ 22Y² - 26M¹
THE ANTARTEX	115/ --	Richards G W	16S² 16H² 16G³ 16S¹ 20S² 22Y³ - 16G³ 20G² 20Y⁴ 22S¹ 16S¹
THE BLUE BOY	--/108	Pipe M C	- 17F¹ 17F¹ 17F¹ 17M¹ 17G¹ 16M¹ 16G¹ 16G² 16M² 20M² 17G¹
THE CITY MINSTREL	92/ --	Edwards J A C	17S³ 22Y³ - 24M¹ 24M² 26M²
THE DEMON BARBER	--/136	Richards G W	20S³ 25F¹ 20Y¹ 24M¹ 24M¹ - 24M¹ 20G² 26G² 20S² 24G¹ 20G³
THE FELLOW	166/ --	Doumen F (Fra)	- 24G¹ 26G²
THE FORTIES	103/ --	Bill T T	25Y³ 26G³ 26M³ 26G² - 26G¹ 24M³ 25G⁴ 34M⁴ 30M³
THE GREEN FOOL	--/ 80	Thompson V	- 16Y¹
THE GREEN STUFF	100/ --	Upson John R	16G¹ 16F² 16G¹ 16G⁴ 16F³ - 16G³ 17G² 16G¹ 16M¹ 16G³ 17G¹ 16F²
THE HIDDEN CITY	--/ 90	Trietline C C	- 16M² 16G¹ 16G⁴ 16G² 16G²

	CHS/HUR	TRAINER	FORM RANGE
			16G¹
THE HILL	--/ 73	Smart B	- 22W¹
THE ILLYWHACKER	129/ --	Pitman Mrs J	22G¹ 24Y³ 21Y⁴ 20S³ - 21G⁴
			21G² 20G¹ 20G¹ 20G¹
THE LAGER LOUT	--/ --	Parker R	- 20G¹
THE LAUGHING LORD	--/105	Stephenson W A	22F¹ - 22F³ 20F¹ 16H¹ 20M¹
			22S¹
THE LEGGETT	130/ --	Pipe M C	16S³ 20Y³ 20S¹ 20Y³ 24Y¹ -
			24G⁴ 20G² 24Y² 24G¹ 25M²
			26G² 18Y³ 29M³
THE LIGHTER SIDE	--/ 94	Charles M J	16M³ 20W² 22W² - 18F² 24W³
			20W² 20M³ 20W² 24W¹
THE MAGUE	--/ 89	Houghton R F J	- 16F¹ 18F¹ 16F² 16G³
THE MALTKILN	--/ --	Hammond M D	27Y³ 25M¹ 25Y³ - 24F¹ 24M²
			20S¹
THE MOSSES	--/ --	Forster Capt T	16Y⁴ - 20M¹ 24S¹
THE MOTCOMBE OAK	--/ --	Anderson K	- 26Y¹
THE QUOHEE	--/ --	Baker J H	24M³ - 24F² 26F² 25M⁴
THE SHADE MATCHER	--/107	Richards G W	- 22S¹ 24S²
THE SHY CONTROLLER	--/ --	Pitman Mrs J	16Y³ - 16S³ 16G¹ 16Y² 16G¹
			16G³
THE SLATER	--/ 99	Turner W G M	16G² - 16M² 16G² 16M¹ 16G¹
			16G¹ 16Y³
THE TARTAN SPARTAN	--/ --	Wilkinson M J	- 24M² 25M¹
THE WIDGET MAN	--/140	Gifford J T	18G² 16G¹ 16S¹ 16Y¹ - 20G¹
			21G¹ 20M² 25G³
THE YANK	--/ 82	Hammond M D	16F¹ 16M³ - 22F³ 24S³ 24M¹
			24F¹
THETFORD FOREST	--/ --	Nicholson D	- 16G¹ 16G³ 16M¹ 16M³ 21S¹
			20G¹
THEY ALL FORGOT ME	82/ --	Casey T	16F³ 16G¹ 17Y³ 16S³ 16Y²
			22Y³ 20W³ 16M³ 17G³ 22F¹ -
			16F³ 18F¹ 20F² 20W³ 20G²
			16M³ 18G² 18G⁴ 16M¹ 18Y³
			16Y³
THIN RED LINE	--/ 90	Jenkins J R	16F² 20M² - 16M³ 20F³ 16G¹
			16M²
THIRD IN LINE	120/ --	Edwards J A C	- 24M¹ 24M¹ 24G⁴ 25M² 25M¹
THISTLEHOLM	--/ 98	Nelson W M	- 20S¹ 20G¹
THREE LAKES	--/ 81	Griffiths S G	16F¹ 16M³ 16G³ - 16Y¹ 16G²
THREEOUTOFFOUR	--/127	Brennan O	22Y² 17G⁴ 16Y¹ 22G¹ 20G²
			20M² - 19G² 21Y¹ 24F² 25Y¹
			24Y³ 24M²
TIBER MELODY	85/ --	Rothwell B S	26M³ - 25G¹ 25G⁴ 25G³ 24M³
			26F²
TIGER CLAW	--/112	Hodges R J	- 17M¹ 16G¹
TIGERS PET	99/ --	Bissill W H	17M³ 18W² 16F² 16G² 22G²
			17G³ 17M³ 17M¹ - 16M¹ 17M²
			17F³ 16W¹ 16G¹ 16F³ 19F¹
			16G²
TILDEBO	112/ --	Webber J	16S³ 20G² 16F² 16G² 16M¹
			16G³ - 16F³ 16M¹ 16M¹ 16M²
			16G⁴ 16G¹ 16Y² 16Y¹ 16Y³
			20M¹ 16F²
TILDEN PARK	82/ --	Bevan P J	- 20G¹ 20G² 18G⁴
TIMID	--/ 86	Pipe M C	- 17F² 17F³ 16M¹ 17G¹ 20Y³
TIMUR'S KING	--/ 84	Mellor S	- 16Y¹ 24S³
TIMURS DOUBLE	--/ 97	Sample Major W	18S¹ 22M¹ 16S¹ 18S¹ 22M³ -
			18S¹ 18S² 22S³ 20Y²
TINAS LAD	90/ --	Edwards J A C	20M¹ 16G¹ - 20M¹ 20M¹
TINRYLAND	133/ --	Henderson N J	- 20G⁴ 16M² 20M¹ 16G² 16G¹

	CHS/HUR	TRAINER	FORM RANGE
TIPP DOWN	--/ 89	Smith D Murray	- 16Y¹ 17S² 16S³ 16Y²
TIPP MARINER	--/ 95	Grissell D M	22Y³ - 16Y¹
TIPPING TIM	128/ --	Twiston-Davies	25G⁴ 20Y³ 20S¹ 19G¹ 20M⁴ 20G¹ - 20G⁴ 24G¹ 20G³ 24G¹ 25G¹ 25Y²
TO BE FAIR	--/ 85	Hobbs P J	- 17F² 17F³ 19M¹ 16M²
TOBACCO ROAD	--/ 65	Ham G A	- 16M³ 17F² 16F¹
TOBY TOBIAS	157/ --	Pitman Mrs J	24Y² 25G² - 21G² 24G⁴ 21G¹ 24G¹ 26G⁴
TOCHENKA	77/ --	Juckes R T	17S² 27M³ - 20F¹ 22F² 20M² 22G² 19G¹ 24Y³ 20M⁴ 20G⁴
TOM BIR	107/ --	Turnell Andrew	25G³ 24S⁴ 24G² 24Y¹ 24M² 24M¹ - 22G¹ 25M² 20G¹ 24G³ 20S³ 18G²
TOM CLAPTON	--/115	Pipe M C	16G³ 16W¹ 16M¹ 16Y¹ 16M¹ 16G¹ 16M¹ - 19G¹ 20M⁴ 16G² 16Y¹ 18Y¹ 17M¹ 16M² 16M¹
TOM TROUBADOUR	118/ --	Gifford J T	20M² 21M¹ - 20G² 24G¹ 24G¹
TOMAHAWK	--/113	Holder R J	16S¹ - 16M¹ 16S¹ 16M¹ 16G¹ 16G²
TONY MURPHYS MAN	--/ --	Upson John R	16F² 16G¹ - 20F¹ 19M⁴ 20F²
TOOGOOD TO BE TRUE	--/ --	Easterby M H	- 16G¹
TOP IT ALL	--/ 64	Ryan M J	- 16M³ 16G¹ 16G² 16G³
TOP JAVALIN	--/ 96	Barons D H	- 16M³ 17G³ 17S¹ 17H¹
TOP VILLAIN	--/ 89	Rothwell B S	16G³ - 16F¹ 17M³ 16S³ 16W¹ 16W²
TOPEKA EXPRESS	--/ 88	Tinkler C	- 16M¹
TOPSAWYER	--/ --	Hall Miss S E	- 17M¹
TOPSHAM BAY	140/ --	Barons D H	25M¹ 24G¹ 28M¹ 25M² - 29G⁴ 24G² 26G¹ 26Y¹ 29M¹
TORRE TRADER	80/ --	Frost R G	- 16F³ 22F³ 20W¹
TORRENT BAY	120/ --	Egerton C R	- 24F¹
TOUCHING STAR	98/ --	Hobbs P J	- 16M³ 16G³ 17G¹ 17Y² 16G¹ 16M¹
TOWNY BOY	--/ 78	Clay Mrs L	17Y² - 16Y³ 16G³ 18F¹
TRANSMIT	--/ 95	O'Neill M	- 20M¹ 20Y² 21G² 20G³
TRAPPER JOHN	--/ --	Morris M F (Ir	25M¹ - 24Y³ 24G¹ 24G²
TRAVADO	--/120	Henderson N J	16Y¹ - 16Y¹ 16G¹ 20G²
TRAVEL OVER	122/ --	Lee R	24M⁴ 25G¹ 24Y² 26G² - 25G² 25G¹
TREE POPPY	--/113	Brooks C P E	21S¹ 24Y³ 20G⁴ - 20G³ 20G¹ 16G³
TRES AMIGOS	--/ 89	Johnson J H	16F² 16G² 16Y³ 16M¹ 16F³ 16G³ 17G⁴ 16G³ - 20G³ 16H³ 20F¹ 20M² 20F²
TRESIDDER	115/ --	Easterby M W	16M¹ 17G¹ - 16G³ 16M² 16M³ 20M² 16G² 16M¹ 17M¹ 17G³ 16M² 16G¹
TREVAYLOR	109/ --	Hobbs P J	- 19M³ 16S² 16G¹ 16S¹ 17S¹ 17G¹
TREWITHIEN	--/ 90	Barons D H	- 17G² 17G¹ 18F³
TRIBAL RULER	88/ --	McCain D	20M³ 16G² 16S² 20G³ - 20G² 20G³ 24G¹ 25M² 24M²
TRIBUTE TO YOUTH	100/ --	Nicholson D	- 16G² 16G² 16G³ 17M¹ 16G² 16G³ 16G³ 17G³ 16G¹ 16M¹
TRIMLOUGH	--/121	Dalton P T	16S⁴ - 16M¹
TRIPLE WITCHING	--/121	Pitman Mrs J	- 16G³ 16Y¹ 16Y¹ 24G¹ 24G³ 20G⁴ 25G³
TRIREME	--/ --	White J	- 20M¹
TRISTAN'S COMET	--/ 75	Harris J L	16F³ 16W² 16M³ 16W¹ 18W¹ - 20W² 16W³ 20W¹ 20W³

	CHS/HUR	TRAINER	FORM RANGE
TROJAN CALL	--/ 80	Rowe R	16G² 16M² - 18G² 16G¹ 16G²
TROJAN ENVOY	--/ --	Carter W	- 18G¹ 16M³ 16G⁴
TROODOS	--/ 81	Austin Mrs S M	- 16F² 16M³ 20M¹ 25M¹
TROUT ANGLER	111/ --	Channon M R	- 26S¹
TRUBLION	108/ --	Mellor S	- 16G⁶ 16Y² 16G²
TRUISM	--/107	Retter Mrs J G	16M³ 17M¹ - 17S³ 16Y² 17G¹
TRUSS	--/ 72	Smith C A	- 16G¹
TRUSTY FRIEND	117/ --	Edwards J A C	20G¹ 24G² 25G¹ 25Y² - 26G²
			24S³ 24G² 26G¹ 26G²
TRYUMPHANT LAD	--/ --	Deasley M J	26G² 27M² 27G³ 27H² 25M³ -
			26G¹
TUG OF GOLD	125/ --	Nicholson D	22G² 24G⁴ 22G⁴ 25G¹ 22M¹
			25F² 24M² - 25G² 24G² 24G¹
			25G¹ 26Y³ 26G²
TURNING TRIX	--/ --	Sherwood S E	- 16G¹
TV PITCH	--/ 75	Lee D	- 16F¹ 16F³
TWIN OAKS	159/ --	Richards G W	26S¹ 28S¹ 32Y¹ 24S¹ 28S¹ -
			24G¹ 24G² 28Y³ 36Y⁵
TWO STEP RHYTHM	105/ --	McConnochie J	- 20G³ 20G¹ 20G¹
TYBURN LAD	--/ --	Collingridge H	16M¹ 16S² 16S⁴ 16S³ - 16Y³
			16Y¹
UNCLE ELI	--/ --	Hobbs P J	16S¹ - 16G¹
UNCLE OLIVER	--/ 63	Thompson V	- 22F² 24G³ 24S¹
UNEX-PLAINED	112/ --	Moore G M	16Y¹ 16S² 20Y³ 16S¹ 16S¹
			16S³ 16Y² 16S¹ 16M⁴ - 20Y⁴
			17S² 20G¹ 16S³ 16G²
UNINVITED	--/ 72	Glover J A	- 16Y¹
UNIQUE NEW YORK	93/ --	Woodman S	20W³ 16Y¹ - 18G² 26G² 20G¹
UP-A-POINT	--/ --	Hobbs P J	16G² 16Y¹ 17G² 17G² 16Y⁴
			16Y⁴ - 16M¹ 16M¹ 18G¹
URON V	--/ 86	Hammond M D	- 22M¹ 22G² 20S¹ 20Y³
VA LUTE	--/104	Nicholls P F	- 16M³ 16G⁴ 16G¹ 17M³ 16G¹
			16G¹ 16G¹ 16G³ 16S³ 16M²
			16F³
VA UTU	--/ 81	Channon M R	- 16G² 16Y² 16W² 16G² 19S³
			16Y² 19M³ 17G¹ 16M¹ 17F²
			16M²
VADO VIA	--/ 83	Wintle D J	- 16S¹ 16G² 20W² 18Y³ 18G²
			19S¹ 20G²
VAGOG	--/130	Pipe M C	22Y² 22G³ 24G¹ 24G³ - 24S²
			24G¹
VAIN PRINCE	--/117	Tinkler N	16F¹ 16F¹ 16G² 18F² 17G² -
			17F¹ 16M¹ 16M¹ 17F¹ 17F¹
			16M³ 16M²
VAL D'AUTHIE	--/ 99	Pipe M C	- 17M³ 16G¹ 22G¹
VALE OF SECRECY	92/ --	Fisher R F	24H³ 24H² - 20Y¹ 22G⁴ 24S⁴
VALFINET	--/110	Pipe M C	- 16Y¹ 16S⁴ 17G¹
VALIANT BOY	--/124	Kettlewell S E	16S² 20W¹ 20W² - 16M¹ 16Y¹
VALIANT DASH	--/104	Kettlewell S E	18G² 20S¹ 20Y¹ 24G² 20W¹
			22G³ - 17G² 20F¹ 24G¹ 20F¹
			20G⁴ 20W³ 24G² 20Y³ 20M³
VALRODIAN	--/ --	Robinson M H B	- 16G¹
VANTARD	75/ --	Jordan Mrs J	24Y³ 16G⁴ 21G⁴ - 22F² 17F²
			21S³ 16F⁴ 22F¹ 24M³ 20M⁴
			20M⁴ 20G⁴
VAYRUA	--/131	Hellens J A	- 16Y² 18S² 20G¹ 20Y³
VERY VERY ORDINARY	105/ --	Upson John R	- 20G⁴ 20G³ 20G¹ 20Y¹ 24S⁴
VICEROY GEM	--/ 83	Holder R J	- 17G¹ 16G² 16Y² 16S² 16G²
VICEROY JESTER	--/118	Balding G B	17M¹ 16M³ 16G¹ 16Y² 17G³ -
			17G³ 16Y⁴ 16G² 17G¹
VICOMPT DE VALMONT	--/109	Henderson N J	17G³ - 20Y¹ 21G¹

	CHS/HUR	TRAINER	FORM RANGE
VICTOR BRAVO	--/102	Gaselee N A	- 22Y² 22G¹ 24G² 22G¹
VICTORY ANTHEM	--/ 88	Henderson N J	- 16G¹ 16Y²
VICTORY TORCH	--/ 69	Whiting H A T	- 16M¹ 25M³
VIKING FLAGSHIP	--/127	Nicholson D	17S² 16S¹ 16W¹ 16Y¹ 16Y¹ - 16G⁴ 16M⁴ 17M¹ 16G⁴ 16G³ 16G³
VILLAGE REINDEER	--/101	Calver P	- 16Y² 16Y¹ 20S³ 20H¹
VINCANTO	93/ --	Gifford J T	19M² 19F¹ 19G² 20G² - 20Y³ 20G² 16G³ 20G² 18F¹
VIRIDIAN	--/103	King Mrs A L M	24G² 22S² 22G¹ 22Y¹ - 25M¹ 25M³ 25G¹
VISAGA	--/ --	Nicholson D	- 16M¹ 16Y³
VITAL WITNESS	--/ 93	Morgan K A	- 20Y¹
VOLCANIC DANCER	--/104	Mackie J	- 24M¹ 22G² 24M³ 25M³ 20G² 24M⁴ 22M²
VOYAGE SANS RETOUR	--/ --	O'Neill J J	- 20S¹ 24S¹
WAIT YOU THERE	100/ --	Alexander H	- 25M¹ 24F³ 20G² 20F² 20G³
WAKE UP	--/105	O'Leary R	16Y¹ 16S¹ 16G² 16S³ 20Y² 16G² 16F¹ 16M² - 16G¹ 16M¹ 16G³ 16G¹ 16G¹ 16G² 17M¹ 20G³ 16M³ 16G³
WALL GAME	--/ --	Delahooke J S	- 24G¹
WARNER FOR WINNERS	--/ 81	Hobbs P J	- 16S¹ 25G²
WARNER'S END	--/ --	Webber J	22G¹ - 21M⁴ 24M³ 21M² 18G³ 24M¹ 25Y³
WASHAKIE	--/ 87	Walton F T	- 18G² 25G³ 24M¹ 20F²
WATERLOO BOY	163/ --	Nicholson D	16S² 16G³ 16G¹ 16Y² 20S³ 20M² - 17G² 16G¹ 16Y¹ 16M¹ 17G¹ 16G³ 20Y²
WATERMEAD	--/ 82	Nicholson D	20M³ 21M¹ 16M³ - 16M² 20M³ 18F² 20M³
WATERTIGHT	85/ --	Reveley Mrs G	- 25G³ 24S² 24H² 24Y² 20M¹
WAY OF LIFE	98/ --	Mellor S	- 16G¹ 20G³ 20G² 16G²
WEBBS WONDER	87/ --	Hobbs P J	20G² - 16Y⁴ 18G¹
WEDDING FEAST	--/ --	McConnochie J	16W² 16W³ 16W¹ 18W² 16F³ - 16M² 18W³ 19G² 22S¹ 22M¹
WELKNOWN CHARACTER	--/ --	Barber R	- 21G² 21F¹ 26G³
WELL BRIEFED	--/102	Stephenson W A	- 26G³ 24M¹ 21M¹ 24M³
WELL WRAPPED	107/ --	Knight Miss H	- 20G³ 20Y¹ 20G²
WELLINGTON BROWN	--/ --	Trigg Mrs H	24G² 20M³ - 24M¹ 25G¹
WELLWOTDOUTHINK	--/ --	Reveley Mrs G	17G² - 17M¹ 16G¹ 16M¹
WELSH BARD	124/ --	Brooks C P E	16G¹ - 16M⁴ 20G⁴ 16M⁴ 16G¹ 17G² 16G⁴ 17M¹ 17S¹ 16S¹ 16Y³
WELSH COMMANDER	89/ --	Etherington T	16M² 16G² - 21M¹ 21G⁴ 24G² 20G⁴ 25G² 26G⁴
WELSH SIREN	--/105	Bailey K C	- 16M² 19M¹ 17F¹ 19G¹ 21G² 22G¹
WELSHMAN	--/127	Blanshard M	16M² 16G² 19G¹ 20S¹ 21G² - 18Y¹ 20M¹ 21G⁴ 20G²
WESSEX	90/ --	Tinkler N	24G² - 20M³ 24Y² 20G²
WEST WITH THE WIND	--/ 94	Moore G M	16Y³ 16G³ 16M² - 16M¹ 16G¹ 20M¹ 16Y²
WESTERN COUNTIES	104/ --	Holder R J	17Y² 16M¹ 16M¹ 21M¹ 16M² 16M³ - 22G⁴ 20G³ 20M³ 16Y² 16M³ 21S¹ 20G²
WESTWELL BOY	--/ 92	Beaumont P	20S² - 20G¹ 22M² 25M³ 22F²
WHAAT FETTLE	105/ --	Richards G W	- 24G¹ 24G¹ 20G³
WHASSAT	--/ 75	Muggeridge M P	- 19F² 18F³ 16M¹ 17G¹
WHAT IF	--/ 89	Brennan O	- 16M³ 17G¹ 20G³ 16S¹
WHATEVER YOU LIKE	122/ --	Henderson N J	16S⁴ 17G¹ 20G² 16Y² - 16G²

	CHS/HUR	TRAINER	FORM RANGE
			16G¹ 17G² 16G¹ 16G² 20G²
WHATS YOUR PROBLEM	103/ --	Knight Miss H	20G² 19G¹ 16S² 20G¹ 20Y² -
			20G² 20Y¹ 24G³ 20G²
WHEELIES NEWMEMBER	--/ --	Hamilton Mrs A	20G⁴ - 20P¹
WHIPPERS DELIGHT	--/ 72	Charles-Jones	- 16Y¹ 18Y² 16G¹ 16S¹ 16Y²
WHISPERING STEEL	--/ --	Richards G W	- 16G² 20S² 18S¹ 20G³ 16S¹
WHISTING TIGER	--/ 98	Burchell D	- 24S¹
WHISTLING GIPSY	--/ 96	Oliver Mrs S	- 20M¹ 18G³ 20M³
WHITEWEBB	--/ 87	Murray B W	16Y³ 16Y² - 16M¹
WHO'S IN CHARGE	76/ --	Coatsworth G M	- 20M³ 24M⁴ 24G² 16M² 16G⁴
			16G⁵ 20G⁴ 20G³
WHO'S NEXT	--/ --	Jenkins J R	- 16W¹
WHY RUN	--/ --	Smith D Murray	- 18S¹
WICK POUND	--/117	Old J A B	20W¹ 20W¹ 20W³ 24W² 20W²
			24W³ - 20W¹ 20W¹ 22W¹ 18W²
			20G¹
WICKET	--/ --	Wilkinson M J	17Y² 21M² 20M² 22M² - 18M¹
WIDE BOY	121/ --	Hobbs P J	16S³ 17S¹ 16Y¹ 16S¹ 16G⁴
			16Y⁴ 16G¹ 17Y³ - 16G³ 16G²
			18G¹ 16G² 17M² 17H¹ 16G³
			16G³ 20G⁴
WILL JAMES	--/ 85	Drewe C J	- 16M¹ 16M¹
WILLIE SPARKLE	--/ --	Bradburne Mrs	16G² - 16M¹
WILLOWSON	--/ --	White K	20G² 20G⁴ - 28M¹
WILTOSKI	--/ 90	Campbell I	- 20W¹ 22W² 16Y³ 16M¹ 16G²
WINABUCK	107/ --	Dickin R	24M¹ 27G² 24M² 21M³ 24S¹
			20M¹ - 24Y² 18Y² 24M¹ 24G³
WINDSOR PARK	--/ 86	Bridgwater K S	- 17F¹ 16M³ 16M¹ 16G³ 20F³
WINDWARD ARIOM	--/ 98	Bycroft N	16M¹ 16Y² 16S¹ 16S² 16G² -
			16G¹ 16G³ 16G⁴
WINGCOMMANDER EATS	--/ 86	Hobbs P J	- 17G¹
WINSLOW LAD	--/ --	Casey T	17M² 16G² 16M² 17M¹ - 17F¹
			18F²
WINTER SQUALL	--/ --	Pitman Mrs J	- 16S¹ 16M³
WOLVER GOLD	--/ 95	Roberts J D	17M² 17M² - 16M³ 16M¹ 17G²
			17G³ 17Y²
WONDER MAN	--/ --	Pitman Mrs J	- 16G¹
WOODGATE	125/ --	Forster Capt T	29Y² 28S² - 25G² 29G¹ 28G³
WOODLAND FLOWER	--/ 84	Sherwood O	- 22G¹ 25G³
WOODLAND MINSTREL	75/103	Pipe M C	22Y³ - 24G³ 21F⁴ 22M¹ 22S¹
WOODLANDS GENPOWER	--/ 82	Pritchard P A	- 24Y¹ 24Y¹
WOODURATHER	--/112	Pipe M C	- 16G¹ 17G¹ 17G¹ 18G¹ 20S³
			16Y³ 16Y²
WORKING SUCCESS	--/ --	Reveley Mrs J	21Y² - 24M¹
WORTHY KNIGHT	105/ --	Jenkins J R	20G⁴ 20G³ 20G¹ 20M⁴ 20G³
			20G² - 20M² 20G³ 20M¹ 19G²
			20G⁴ 20Y² 20M² 20M³
WREKIN HILL	109/ --	Stephenson W A	26G² 27S² 27G³ 24M² - 26Y¹
			22G¹ 20S¹ 24S³ 24S² 24Y³
			24Y² 24Y²
XHAI	--/100	Simpson R	16S⁴ 16Y³ - 16G³ 16M¹ 17G¹
			16M³
YACHT CLUB	--/ --	Eyre J L	24M² 20M² 25G¹ - 20F³ 24M¹
YAMANOUCHI	--/ --	Moffatt D	17F³ 20M³ 17G³ - 16M³ 17G¹
			16M³ 20F¹
YANKEE FLYER	--/ 69	Wilton Miss S	- 16Y¹
YELLOW SPRING	--/112	Grissell D M	18F¹ 22M¹ 21M² 20Y¹ - 20W³
			21G¹
YEOMAN CRICKETER	--/105	Gifford J T	- 20G¹ 22G² 20M²
YIRAGAN	119/ --	Barons D H	25H¹ 26M⁴ - 24G² 27Y¹ 30G²
			30G⁴ 29Y³ 28G¹ 24G¹ 26G³

	CHS/HUR	TRAINER	FORM RANGE
YORKSHIREMAN	103/ --	Glover J A	- 16M^1 19G^4 20G^4 16Y^2 19G^1 24G^2 19M^2
YOU ARE A STAR	--/ --	Tompkins M H	17M^2 16M^3 - 16M^1 16M^2 16F^1
YOUNG FACT	--/ 76	Baker J H	- 18W^1 16W^1
YOUNG HUSTLER	--/109	Twiston-Davies	- 19G^1 20Y^1 22G^1 21M^1 24G^4 20G^5
YOUNG POKEY	137/ --	Sherwood O	16M^2 16M^1 16G^2 16G^1 16S^3 - 16G^2 16M^1 16M^2 16M^1 16G^1
YOUNG SNUGFIT	153/ --	Sherwood O	17M^2 16G^1 16G^2 16Y^2 16Y^4 - 17G^5 16G^2 16M^2 16M^1
ZAM'S SLAVE	75/ --	Charlton J I A	24G^2 25F^1 - 16M^3 24M^2 16Y^2 24G^1 20M^3 22M^4 20G^4 16Y^4 20G^3
ZAMIL	--/109	Burke K R	- 16G^3 16G^1
ZANYMAN	--/ --	Edwards J A C	- 16G^1 16M^3 16G^4
ZEALOUS KITTEN	--/ 86	Price R J	- 20W^3 17M^2 16Y^1 16G^3
ZETA'S LAD	128/ --	Upson John R	- 25G^2 30Y^5 26G^1 24S^2 24G^2

22 . 1992/93 FIXTURES

+ = Evening Meeting
(R) = Replacement Fixture

* = Mixed meeting
(AW) = All Weather Track

OCTOBER		North	Midlands	South
19	Mon		FAKENHAM	
20	Tue			PLUMPTON
21	Wed	NEWCASTLE		ASCOT
22	Thu			WINCANTON
23	Fri		HEREFORD	EXETER
				NEWBURY
24	Sat	CATTERICK	HUNTINGDON	
			WORCESTER	
28	Wed	SEDGEFIELD		FONTWELL PARK
29	Thu		STRATFORD	KEMPTON PARK
30	Fri	WETHERBY	BANGOR	
31	Sat	WETHERBY	WARWICK	SANDOWN PARK

NOVEMBER

		North	Midlands	South
2	Mon		WOLVERHAMPTON	PLUMPTON
3	Tue		HEREFORD	EXETER
4	Wed	KELSO		NEWBURY
5	Thu		UTTOXETER	WINCANTON
6	Fri	HEXHAM	MARKET RASEN	
7	Sat			CHEPSTOW
				WINDSOR
9	Mon	CARLISLE	WOLVERHAMPTON	
10	Tue	SEDGEFIELD		
11	Wed	HAYDOCK PARK	WORCESTER	
12	Thu	KELSO	TOWCESTER	TAUNTON
13	Fri	AYR	CHELTENHAM	
			HUNTINGDON	
14	Sat	AYR	CHELTENHAM	
			NOTTINGHAM	
15	Sun		CHELTENHAM	
16	Mon		LEICESTER	WINDSOR
17	Tue	WETHERBY	WARWICK	NEWTON ABBOT
18	Wed	HAYDOCK PARK		KEMPTON PARK
19	Thu	HAYDOCK PARK	LUDLOW	WINCANTON
20	Fri	SEDGEFIELD	LEICESTER	ASCOT
21	Sat	CATTERICK	MARKET RASEN	ASCOT
		LIVERPOOL	TOWCESTER	

NOVEMBER		North	Midlands	South
23	Mon	CATTERICK	WOLVERHAMPTON	FOLKESTONE
24	Tue		HUNTINGDON	EXETER
			STRATFORD	
25	Wed	HEXHAM	HEREFORD	PLUMPTON
26	Thu	CARLISLE	NOTTINGHAM	TAUNTON
27	Fri		BANGOR	NEWBURY
28	Sat	NEWCASTLE	WARWICK	NEWBURY
30	Mon	KELSO	WORCESTER	

DECEMBER				
1	Tue	NEWCASTLE		FONTWELL PARK
2	Wed	CATTERICK	HUNTINGDON	
			LUDLOW	
3	Thu		UTTOXETER	WINDSOR
4	Fri		HEREFORD	EXETER
			NOTTINGHAM	SANDOWN PARK
5	Sat	WETHERBY	TOWCESTER	CHEPSTOW
				SANDOWN PARK
7	Mon	EDINBURGH	WARWICK	
8	Tue	SEDGEFIELD		PLUMPTON
9	Wed	HAYDOCK PARK	WORCESTER	
10	Thu	HAYDOCK PARK		TAUNTON
11	Fri	DONCASTER	CHELTENHAM	
		HEXHAM		
12	Sat	DONCASTER	CHELTENHAM	LINGFIELD PARK
		EDINBURGH		
14	Mon		LUDLOW	NEWTON ABBOT
15	Tue			FOLKESTONE
16	Wed		BANGOR	
17	Thu	KELSO	TOWCESTER	
18	Fri	CATTERICK	FAKENHAM	
			UTTOXETER	
19	Sat	NEWCASTLE	NOTTINGHAM	ASCOT
			UTTOXETER	
21	Mon	EDINBURGH		LINGFIELD PARK
22	Tue		HEREFORD	
26	Sat	SEDGEFIELD	HUNTINGDON	KEMPTON PARK
		WETHERBY	MARKET RASEN	NEWTON ABBOT
			WOLVERHAMPTON	WINCANTON
28	Mon	WETHERBY		CHEPSTOW
			WOLVERHAMPTON	KEMPTON PARK
29	Tue		STRATFORD	PLUMPTON
30	Wed	CARLISLE	WARWICK	FONTWELL PARK
				TAUNTON
31	Thu	CATTERICK	CHELTENHAM	FOLKESTONE
			LEICESTER	

JANUARY

1	Fri	CATTERICK	CHELTENHAM LEICESTER	EXETER WINDSOR
2	Sat	AYR	NOTTINGHAM	NEWBURY
4	Mon		WOLVERHAMPTON	NEWBURY
5	Tue			LINGFIELD (AW) NEWTON ABBOT
6	Wed	SEDGEFIELD	SOUTHWELL (AW)	LINGFIELD PARK
7	Thu		MARKET RASEN WORCESTER	
8	Fri	EDINBURGH	TOWCESTER	
9	Sat	HAYDOCK PARK	WARWICK	SANDOWN
11	Mon			LINGFIELD PARK
12	Tue		LEICESTER	CHEPSTOW LINGFIELD (AW)
13	Wed	KELSO	SOUTHWELL (AW)	PLUMPTON
14	Thu	WETHERBY		
15	Fri	EDINBURGH		ASCOT
16	Sat	NEWCASTLE	MARKET RASEN	ASCOT
18	Mon	CARLISLE		FONTWELL PARK
19	Tue			FOLKESTONE
20	Wed		LUDLOW SOUTHWELL (AW)	WINDSOR
21	Thu	AYR		LINGFIELD (AW)
22	Fri	CATTERICK		KEMPTON PARK
23	Sat	CATTERICK HAYDOCK PARK	WARWICK	KEMPTON PARK
25	Mon		LEICESTER	LINGFIELD PARK
26	Tue		NOTTINGHAM	CHEPSTOW LINGFIELD (AW)
27	Wed	SEDGEFIELD	SOUTHWELL (AW) WOLVERHAMPTON	
28	Thu		HUNTINGDON	NEWTON ABBOT
29	Fri	DONCASTER	UTTOXETER	WINCANTON
30	Sat	AYR DONCASTER	CHELTENHAM	

FEBRUARY

1	Mon			PLUMPTON
2	Tue	SEDGEFIELD	NOTTINGHAM	LINGFIELD (AW)
3	Wed		LEICESTER SOUTHWELL (AW)	WINDSOR
4	Thu	EDINBURGH	TOWCESTER	
5	Fri	KELSO		LINGFIELD PARK
6	Sat	WETHERBY	STRATFORD	CHEPSTOW SANDOWN
8	Mon		WOLVERHAMPTON	FONTWELL PARK
9	Tue	CARLISLE	WARWICK	LINGFIELD (AW)
10	Wed		LUDLOW SOUTHWELL (AW)	ASCOT

FEBRUARY		North	Midlands	South
11	Thu		HUNTINGDON	WINCANTON
12	Fri	AYR	BANGOR	NEWBURY
13	Sat	AYR	UTTOXETER	NEWBURY
		CATTERICK		
15	Mon		HEREFORD	PLUMPTON
16	Tue		TOWCESTER	LINGFIELD (AW)
				NEWTON ABBOT
17	Wed	SEDGEFIELD	SOUTHWELL (AW)	FOLKESTONE
			WORCESTER	
18	Thu		LEICESTER	SANDOWN
				TAUNTON
19	Fri	EDINBURGH	FAKENHAM	SANDOWN
20	Sat	NEWCASTLE	NOTTINGHAM	CHEPSTOW
				WINDSOR
22	Mon		WOLVERHAMPTON	FONTWELL PARK
23	Tue	SEDGEFIELD	HUNTINGDON	LINGFIELD (AW)
24	Wed	DONCASTER	SOUTHWELL (AW)	FOLKESTONE
			WARWICK	
25	Thu	CATTERICK		WINCANTON
26	Fri	HAYDOCK PARK		KEMPTON PARK
27	Sat	EDINBURGH	MARKET RASEN	KEMPTON PARK
		HAYDOCK PARK		

MARCH				
1	Mon		LEICESTER	PLUMPTON
2	Tue		NOTTINGHAM	LINGFIELD (AW)
3	Wed	WETHERBY	SOUTHWELL (AW)	
			WORCESTER	
4	Thu		LUDLOW	
			WARWICK	
5	Fri	KELSO		NEWBURY
6	Sat	DONCASTER	HEREFORD	NEWBURY
			STRATFORD	
8	Mon	DONCASTER	WOLVERHAMPTON	WINDSOR
9	Tue	SEDGEFIELD	LEICESTER	LINGFIELD (AW)
10	Wed	CATTERICK	BANGOR	FOLKESTONE
			SOUTHWELL (AW)	
11	Thu	CARLISLE	TOWCESTER	WINCANTON
12	Fri	AYR	MARKET RASEN	SANDOWN
13	Sat	AYR	SOUTHWELL	CHEPSTOW
				SANDOWN
15	Mon			PLUMPTON
				TAUNTON
16	Tue	SEDGEFIELD	CHELTENHAM	LINGFIELD (AW)
17	Wed		CHELTENHAM	NEWTON ABBOT
			HUNTINGDON	
18	Thu	HEXHAM	CHELTENHAM	

MARCH		North	Midlands	South
19	Fri		FAKENHAM WOLVERHAMPTON	LINGFIELD PARK
20	Sat	NEWCASTLE	UTTOXETER	CHEPSTOW LINGFIELD PARK
22	Mon	NEWCASTLE		PLUMPTON
23	Tue		NOTTINGHAM	FONTWELL PARK
24	Wed	KELSO	WORCESTER	EXETER
25	Thu		STRATFORD	WINCANTON
26	Fri		LUDLOW	NEWBURY
27	Sat	SEDGEFIELD	BANGOR	NEWBURY
29	Mon	HEXHAM		
30	Tue			SANDOWN
31	Wed		WORCESTER	ASCOT

APRIL				
1	Thu	LIVERPOOL		TAUNTON
2	Fri	LIVERPOOL		
3	Sat	LIVERPOOL	HEREFORD	
5	Mon	KELSO		
6	Tue	SEDGEFIELD		
7	Wed		LUDLOW	ASCOT
10	Sat	CARLISLE	TOWCESTER UTTOXETER	NEWTON ABBOT PLUMPTON
12	Mon	CARLISLE WETHERBY	FAKENHAM HEREFORD MARKET RASEN TOWCESTER UTTOXETER	CHEPSTOW NEWTON ABBOT PLUMPTON WINCANTON
13	Tue	WETHERBY		CHEPSTOW
14	Wed		WORCESTER	
15	Thu			FONTWELL PARK
16	Fri	AYR		TAUNTON✚
17	Sat	AYR	BANGOR STRATFORD	
19	Mon		HUNTINGDON	
20	Tue	SEDGEFIELD		NEWTON ABBOT
21	Wed	PERTH	CHELTENHAM	
22	Thu	PERTH	CHELTENHAM	
23	Fri	PERTH	LUDLOW✚	TAUNTON✚
24	Sat	HEXHAM	MARKET RASEN WORCESTER✚	SANDOWN✱
26	Mon	HEXHAM✚		
27	Tue			ASCOT✚
28	Wed	KELSO		EXETER
30	Fri		BANGOR✚	NEWTON ABBOT

MAY		North	Midlands	South
1	Sat	HEXHAM✚	HEREFORD UTTOXETER	
3	Mon	HAYDOCK PARK	LUDLOW SOUTHWELL TOWCESTER	EXETER FONTWELL PARK
4	Tue	SEDGEFIELD✚		NEWTON ABBOT
5	Wed	WETHERBY✚	CHELTENHAM✚	
6	Thu		UTTOXETER✚	
7	Fri			WINCANTON✚
8	Sat	NEWCASTLE✚	MARKET RASEN WARWICK✚	
11	Tue		TOWCESTER✚	CHEPSTOW FOLKESTONE
12	Wed	PERTH✚	HEREFORD SOUTHWELL	NEWTON ABBOT✚
13	Thu	PERTH	HUNTINGDON✚	
14	Fri	SEDGEFIELD	STRATFORD✚	
15	Sat		BANGOR	
19	Wed	PERTH✚	WORCESTER	
20	Thu		UTTOXETER✚	EXETER
21	Fri		STRATFORD✚	
22	Sat		SOUTHWELL✚ WARWICK✚	
26	Wed	CARTMEL		
27	Thu		HEREFORD	
28	Fri		TOWCESTER	
29	Sat	CARTMEL HEXHAM		
31	Mon	CARTMEL HEXHAM WETHERBY	FAKENHAM HEREFORD HUNTINGDON UTTOXETER	FONTWELL PARK
JUNE				
2	Wed		UTTOXETER	
4	Fri		STRATFORD✚	
5	Sat		MARKET RASEN✚ STRATFORD	

23 . BIG RACES 1992/93

These dates are provisional and subject to alteration

OCTOBER

| 31 | Charlie Hall Chase | Wetherby | 3m 100y |
| 31 | West Yorkshire Hurdle | Wetherby | 3m |

NOVEMBER

3	Plymouth Gin Haldon Gold Challenge Cup Chase	Exeter	2m 1f
7	Tote Silver Trophy Handicap Hurdle	Chepstow	2½m
11	Aga Worcester Novices' Chase	Worcester	3m
14	Whitbread White Label Handicap Hurdle	Cheltenham	2m
14	Mackeson Gold Cup	Cheltenham	2½m
18	Edward Hanmer Memorial Handicap Chase	Haydock	3m
20	Racecall Ascot Hurdle	Ascot	2½m
20	Hurst Park Novices' Chase	Ascot	2m
21	Forte H'cap Hurdle	Ascot	2m
21	H & T Walker Gold Cup	Ascot	2½m
28	Gerry Feilden Hurdle	Newbury	2m 100y
28	Hennessy Cognac Gold Cup	Newbury	3¼m 82y
28	Newbury Long Distance Hurdle	Newbury	3m 120y
28	Bellway Homes 'Fighting Fifth' Hurdle	Newcastle	2m (abt)

DECEMBER

2	Peterborough Chase	Huntingdon	2½m
5	Henry VIII Novices' Chase	Sandown	2m 18y
5	William Hill Handicap Hurdle	Sandown	2m
5	Mitsubishi Shogun Tingle Creek Handicap Chase	Sandown	2m 18y
5	Rehearsal Handicap Chase	Chepstow	3m
9	Tommy Whittle Chase	Haydock	3m
9	Waterloo Hurdle	Haydock	2½m

DECEMBER (cont.)

11	Food Brokers Fisherman's Friend H'cap Chase	Cheltenham	3m 1f
12	Charterhouse Mercantile Leisure Novices' Chase	Cheltenham	2½m
12	Bula Hurdle	Cheltenham	2m
12	A. F. Budge Gold Cup	Cheltenham	2½m
12	Mercury Communications Prince's Trust Hurdle	Cheltenham	2½m
12	Lowndes Lambert December Novices' Chase	Lingfield	3m
12	Summit Junior Hurdle	Lingfield	2m
19	H.S.S. Hire Shops Hurdle	Ascot	2m
19	Youngmans Long Walk Hurdle	Ascot	3¼m
19	SGB Handicap Chase	Ascot	3m
19	Northumberland Gold Cup Novices' Chase	Newcastle	2m
28	Coral Welsh National Handicap Chase	Chepstow	3m 6f
28	Finale Junior Hurdle	Chepstow	2m
26	King George VI Rank Chase	Kempton	3m
26	Butlin's Feltham Novices' Chase	Kempton	3m
28	Top Rank Christmas Hurdle	Kempton	2m
26	Rowland Meyrick Handicap Chase	Wetherby	3m 100y
28	Castleford Chase	Wetherby	2m 50y

JANUARY

2	Mandarin Handicap Chase	Newbury	3¼m 82y
2	Challow Novices Hurdle	Newbury	2½m 120y
9	Newton Chase	Haydock	2½m
9	A.Mildmay, P.Cazalet Mem. Handicap Chase	Sandown	3m 5f 18y
9	Baring Securities Tolworth Hurdle (Novices)	Sandown	2m
16	Victor Chandler Handicap Chase	Ascot	2m
23	Bic Razor Lanzarote Handicap Hurdle	Kempton	2m
23	F K Roofing Champion Hurdle Trial	Haydock	2m
23	Peter Marsh Handicap Chase	Haydock	3m
30	West of Scotland Pattern Novices' Chase	Ayr	2½m
30	William Hill Golden Spurs Handicap Chase	Doncaster	3m 122y
30	Bishops Cleeve Hurdle	Cheltenham	2m

FEBRUARY

6	Philip Cornes Saddle of Gold Hurdle Final (Nov)	Chepstow	2½m
6	John Hughes Grand National Trial (H'cap Chase)	Chepstow	3¾m
6	Scilly Isles Novices' Chase	Sandown	2½m 65y
6	Agfa Diamond Handicap Chase	Sandown	3m 118y
6	Tote Jackpot Handicap Hurdle	Sandown	2m 5f 75y

FEBRUARY (cont.)

10	Daily Telegraph Hurdle	Ascot	3m
10	Charterhouse Mercantile Handicap Chase	Ascot	3m
10	Reynoldstown Novices' Chase	Ascot	3m
13	Tote Gold Trophy Handicap Hurdle	Newbury	2m 100y
13	Byrne Brothers Compton Chase	Newbury	3m
13	Game Spirit Chase	Newbury	2m 160y
20	Persian War Premier Novices' Hurdle	Chepstow	2½m
20	Rising Stars Chase	Chepstow	2½m
20	Tote Eider Handicap Chase	Newcastle	4m 1f
25	Kingwell Hurdle	Wincanton	2m
25	Jim Ford Challenge Cup (Chase)	Wincanton	3m 1f
27	Tote Placepot Hurdle (4yo)	Kempton	2m
27	Racing Post Handicap Chase	Kempton	3m
27	Rendlesham Hurdle	Kempton	3m
27	Timeform Chase	Haydock	2½m
27	Greenalls Gold Cup Handicap Chase	Haydock	3½m
27	Victor Ludorum Hurdle (4yo)	Haydock	2m
27	Ladbroke Racing Handicap Hurdle	Haydock	2½m

MARCH

5	Geoffrey Gilbey Memorial Handicap Chase	Newbury	2½m
6	Berkshire Hurdle	Newbury	2½m
12	Horse & Hound G.Military Gold Cup Chase (Am)	Sandown	3m 118y
13	Sunderlands Imperial Cup Handicap Hurdle	Sandown	2m
16	Trafalgar House Supreme Novices' Hurdle	Cheltenham	2m
16	Waterford Castle Arkle Ch. Chase	Cheltenham	2m
16	Smurfit Champion Hurdle Chall. Trophy	Cheltenham	2m
16	Ritz Club National Hunt Handicap Chase	Cheltenham	3m 1f
16	F.Walwyn,K.Muir Mem. Handicap Chase (Am)	Cheltenham	3m
16	Hurdle Series Final	Cheltenham	3m 1f
17	Sun Alliance Novices' Hurdle	Cheltenham	2½m
17	Queen Mother Champion Chase	Cheltenham	2m1½m
17	The Coral Cup (Handicap Hurdle)	Cheltenham	2
17	Sun Alliance Novices' Chase	Cheltenham	3m
17	National Hunt Chall. Cup Nov Chase (Am)	Cheltenham	4m
17	Mildmay of Flete Challenge Cup H'cap Chase	Cheltenham	2½m
17	Tote Festival Bumper Race	Cheltenham	2m
18	Daily Express Triumph Hurdle (4yo)	Cheltenham	2m
18	Bonusprint Stayers Hurdle	Cheltenham	3m 1f
18	Tote Cheltenham Gold Cup Chase	Cheltenham	3¼m
18	Christies Foxhunters' Chal. Cup	Cheltenham	3¼m
18	Grand Annual Challenge Cup H'cap Chase	Cheltenham	2m
18	Cathcart Challenge Cup Chase	Cheltenham	2½m
18	County Handicap Hurdle	Cheltenham	2m

MARCH (cont.)

20	Lingfield Gold Cup Handicap Hurdle	Lingfield	2½m
20	Ansells National Handicap Chase	Uttoxeter	4m
31	Letherby & Christopher Long Distance Hurdle	Ascot	3m
31	Peregrine Handicap Chase	Ascot	2½m
31	Golden Eagle Novices' Chase	Ascot	2½m

APRIL

1	Seagram Top Novices' Hurdle	Liverpool	2m
1	Sandeman Maghull Novices' Chase	Liverpool	2m
1	Martell Cup Chase	Liverpool	3m 1f
1	John Hughes Memorial Trophy H'cap Chase	Liverpool	2 ¾m
1	Glenlivet Anniversary Hurdle (4yo)	Liverpool	2m
2	Perrier Jouet Handicap Chase	Liverpool	3m 1f
2	Mumm Melling Chase	Liverpool	2½m
2	Mumm Mildmay Novices' Chase	Liverpool	3m 1f
2	Martell Fox Hunters' Chase	Liverpool	2¾m
2	Oddbins Handicap Hurdle	Liverpool	2½m
3	Martell Aintree Handicap Chase	Liverpool	2m
3	Martell Aintree Hurdle	Liverpool	2½m
3	Martell Grand National Handicap Chase	Liverpool	4½m
3	Chivas Regal Nov. Handicap Chase (Am)	Liverpool	2½m
3	Janneau Mersey Novices' Hurdle	Liverpool	2½m
7	Fairview New Homes Novices' Chase	Ascot	3m
7	Bollinger Champagne Nov. Handicap Chase	Ascot	2½m
12	Welsh Champion Hurdle	Chepstow	2m
16	Scottish Champion Hurdle	Ayr	2m
17	Edin. Wool Mills Future Champions Nov Chase	Ayr	2m
17	Wm. Hill Scottish National Handicap Chase	Ayr	4m 120y
21	S. Wales Showers Silver Trophy Chase	Cheltenham	2½m
24	Whitbread Gold Cup Handicap Chase	Sandown	3m 5f 18y

MAY

3	Swinton Handicap Hurdle	Haydock	2m

FREE
LADBROKES
HORSES TO FOLLOW
COMPETITION

See page 108 for details